RIA's Complete Analysis of the Economic Stimulus Act of 2008,

and the AMT Patch, Mortgage Relief, Energy, Technical Corrections, and Other Late 2007 Tax Acts

With Code Sections as Amended and Committee Reports

Here's your copy of RIA's industry-leading
"Complete Analysis of the Economic Stimulus Act of 2008,
and the AMT Patch, Mortgage Relief, Energy, Technical Corrections,
and Other Late 2007 Tax Acts".
We appreciate your patronage.

Here's a list of handy reference numbers:

1-800-950-1216 — To place an order for this or other publications
1-800-431-9025 — If you have questions about a previously placed
order or a customer service issue
1-800-742-3348 — If you have a question about product content

THOMSON
TAX & ACCOUNTING

Copyright 2008
by
Thomson/RIA
395 Hudson Street
New York, N.Y. 10014

ria.thomson.com

RIA's Complete Analysis of the Economic Stimulus Act of 2008, and the AMT Patch, Mortgage Relief, Energy, Technical Corrections, and Other Late 2007 Tax Acts

Marie Rivera,
Supervisor

Melissa
Acquafredda

Sharon Alexander

Kathryn Grott

Esther Maclin

Eddie Rodriguez

Sue Ellen Sobel,
Supervisor

Alexis Brown

Adel Faltas

Amelia Massiah

Jennifer Stryshak

Data Analysts

Lisa Alcock

**Citator Data
Managers**

Janie Davis

Ivette Terry

Paralegals

Joann Casanova

Catherine Daleo

Monica Grier

Danny Wang

Indexing

David Thompson,
Manager

Janet Mazefsky,
Assistant Manager

Tom Adewolu

Oslin Busby

George Flynn

Linda Lao

Andrea Leal

Irene Richards

Arlene Verderber

**Legal Resource
Center**

Peter Durham,
Manager

Pierre Calixte

Sandra Crowder

Patricia Link

Edward Mack

Theresa Scherne

Bernadette Stanton

Michael Stanton

Holly Yue

Velma Goodwine-
McDermon,
Supervisor

Charyn Johnson

William Lesesne

**Product
Development**

Ruth F. Raftery
(J.D., C.P.A., NY,
NJ, PA Bar)
*Director, New
Product
Development, Tax
Products*

Nicole Gagnon
*Director, Customer
Insight*

Todd Gordon,
*Director, New
Product
Development*

Kim Chirls,
*Lead Project
Manager*

**End-User
Technical Services**

Jose Fiol,
Team Lead

Steven McGill,
Design Lead

Eric Bauer

Jay Loyola

Tanya McDonald

Joseph Oliveri

**Product
Technology**

Perry Townes,
Senior Director

Jay Liu,
Director

Tim Bills,
Manager

John Melazzo,
Manager

Laurie Mitchell,
Manager

Gene Wojna,
Manager

Eileen Wood,
*Information
Manager*

Daryl Alexander

Ron Bergeron

Mohan
Bhairavabhatia

Tom Bontrager

Geoff Braine

Isabel Cimitile

Resa Cirrincione

Tracey Cruz

Chris DiGanci

Andy Dreistadt

Tatyana Fersht

Janine Francesca

Sammy Francois

Peggy Frank

Terri Ganssley

Anthony Guglielmo

Michelle Harmon

Jay Kwon

Terry LaGoy

Cynthia Lewis

Jackie Lynott

Chris Macano

Alex Maskovyak

Garrett McAlistair

David McInerney

Ejelonu Onukogu

Pamela J. Otruba

Amish Parikh

Michelle Paulin

Genevie Peters

Dan Pirro

Steve Pitamber

Jason Rapaccuiolo

Patricia Reilly

Ruth Russell

Becky Sears

Alfred Sehayek

Jason Shen

Esme Smartt

Young Sone

Margaret Taylor
Volpe

Torrod Taylor

Victoria Tenny

Alana Trafford

Vivian Turner

Dmitriy Viner

Rhonda Waller

Jieping Wang

Dennis Wendell

Karen Wharton

Ava Williams

Steve Wisniewski

Hongtu Zhang

Teresa Zhang

Igor Zomin

**Content
Technology**

Brian McNamara,
Director

Gale Metz,
Director

Alanna Dixon,
Manager

David Levine,
Manager

Christopher Grillo,
Project Manager

Sergey Arutchev

David Bantel

Bob Bridier

Mary Jo Catlett

Karen de Luna

Louie Diaz

Nadine Graham

Steven Haber

Chris Jungheim

Stephen Karg

Julie Lu

Darren McNelis

Scott Murphy

William Peake

Tasso Quidera

Irina Resnikoff

Derek Sanders

Parin Shah

Ayca Tank

Linda Wiseman

**Manufacturing &
Fulfillment
Services**

Rick Bivona,
Director

Anthony Scribano,
*Scheduling and
Fulfillment
Manager*

Gail Gneiding,
*Manufacturing and
Outside
Composition
Manager*

Rachel Hassenbein,
*Associate
Fulfillment
Manager*

John Disposti,
*Senior
Manufacturing
Coordinator*

Greg Miller,
*Associate
Production
Manager*

Enid Skolnik,
*Associate
Fulfillment
Manager*

Bryan Gardner,
*Senior
Manufacturing
Coordinator*

Lourdes Barba

Linda Gottlieb

Chris Harrington

Jennifer Kalison

Table of Contents

¶ 1. Organization of the Book

Organization of RIA's Complete Analysis of the Economic Stimulus Act of 2008, and the AMT Patch, Mortgage Relief, Energy, Technical Corrections, and Other Late 2007 Tax Acts

This book contains RIA's Complete Analysis of the Economic Stimulus Act of 2008, and the AMT Patch, Mortgage Relief, Energy, Technical Corrections, and Other Late 2007 Tax Acts.

H.R. 5140, the Economic Stimulus Act of 2008 (generally referred to in the Analysis as the "2008 Economic Stimulus Act"), was passed by the House and Senate on Feb. 7, 2008, and signed into law by the President on Feb. 13, 2008. (PL 110-185, 2/13/2008.)

H.R. 3996, the Tax Increase Prevention Act of 2007 (i.e., the AMT Patch Act, which is generally referred to in the Analysis as the "2007 Tax Increase Prevention Act"), was signed into law by the President on Dec. 26, 2007. (PL 110-166, 12/26/2007).

H.R. 3648, the Mortgage Forgiveness Debt Relief Act of 2007, (i.e., the Mortgage Relief Act, which is generally referred to in the Analysis as the "2007 Mortgage Relief Act"), was signed into law by the President on Dec. 20, 2007. (PL 110-142, 12/20/2007).

H.R. 6, the Energy Independence and Security Act of 2007 (i.e., the Energy Act, which is generally referred to in the Analysis as the "2007 Energy Act"), was signed into law by the President on Dec. 19, 2007. (PL 110-140, 12/19/2007).

H.R. 4839, the Tax Technical Corrections Act of 2007 (i.e., the Technical Corrections Act, which is generally referred to in the Analysis as the "2007 Technical Corrections Act"), was signed into law by the President on Dec. 29, 2007. (PL 110-172, 12/29/2007).

Other Tax Acts include H.R. 4118, a bill to exclude from gross income payments from the Hokie Spirit Memorial Fund to the victims of the tragic event at Virginia Polytechnic Institute & State University, which is generally referred to in the Analysis as the "2007 Virginia Tech Victims Act". The 2007 Virginia Tech Victims Act was signed into law on Dec. 19, 2007 (PL 110-141, 12/19/2007). Also included are tax provisions in H.R. 2764, the Consolidated Appropriations Act, 2008, which is generally referred to in the Analysis as the "2008 Appropriations Act". It was signed into law by the President on Dec. 26, 2007. (PL 110-161, 12/26/2007).

The tax provisions of the 2008 Economic Stimulus Act (summarized in the Senate Finance Committee Summary of the Economic Stimulus Act of 2008, dated Feb. 7, 2008) include (1) recovery rebates for individuals, and (2) investment incentives in the form of enhanced expensing and depreciation provisions for businesses buying equipment and placing it into service in 2008.

- The 2008 Economic Stimulus Act provides for stimulus payments for most Americans, including seniors living only on Social Security and disabled veterans, and the survivors of disabled veterans, while providing safeguards to ensure that illegal immigrants do not obtain rebates or bonus payments for their children.

  The rebate has two components. The first is an amount based on filing status and the second is an increase in the child tax credit. Rebate checks will include a base amount determined by the greater of two options: (a) Income tax paid in 2007, with a maximum of $600 for a single taxpayer and $1,200 for married couples; or (b) $300 for an individual and $600 for a married couple. To be eligible for the rebate, the taxpayer must report $1 of tax liability or $3000 of qualifying income, defined as the sum of net self employment income, veterans' disability payments (including payments survivors of veterans), and social security benefits. If a taxpayer receives $1 of the income tax rebate and the taxpayer has children, the taxpayer will also receive $300 per qualifying child. This payment is refundable, meaning the recipient is entitled to the full child credit without regard to income tax liability. Individuals who do not qualify for a full rebate based on their 2007 income tax return may qualify for a credit based on their 2008 return.

  The amount of the credit (including both the basic credit and the qualifying child credit) is phased out at a rate of 5% of adjusted gross income beginning at $75,000 ($150,000 in the case of joint returns). Residents of the U.S. possessions will also receive the benefit, but the provision denies the basic credit and the qualifying child credit to individuals if the tax return does not include valid identification numbers for all persons listed on the return. A valid identification number is a Social Security Number issued by the Social Security Administration, and does not include a Taxpayer Identification Number issued by IRS.

- The 2008 Economic Stimulus Act includes enhanced expensing and depreciation provisions for businesses buying equipment and placing it into service in 2008. This tax relief will encourage businesses to make investments that will enable them to keep growing, and the requirement for investment in 2008 year will achieve the stimulus bill's goal of injecting money into the economy right away.

  Specifically, the 2008 Economic Stimulus Act (1) amends Code Sec. 179 by increasing the 2008 expensing limits from $128,00 to $250,000 and increasing the 2008 phase-out threshold from $510,000 to $800,000, and (2) amends Code Sec. 168(k) by allowing a trade or business to depreciate an additional 50 % of the cost of an asset acquired and placed into service during 2008. The types of property eligible for bonus depreciation will be the same as those included in the previous depreciation packages: (1) tangible property that had a recovery period not exceeding 20 years; (2) purchased computer software; (3) water utility property; and (4) qualified leasehold improvement property. The bonus depreciation will be allowed under the alternative minimum tax (AMT).

In the final days before it adjourned for 2007, Congress passed a long-awaited AMT patch for 2007. It also passed two other tax laws of wide interest. These laws provide mortgage debt forgiveness tax relief, other tax breaks and technical corrections, many of which are substantive. Tax changes also were enacted as part of the energy legislation and in a special measure to aid victims of the Virginia Tech shooting in 2007.

Key provisions in the various late 2007 Acts include:

• For tax year 2007 only, the 2007 Tax Increase Prevention Act boosts AMT exemption amounts for individuals, and provides that most personal, nonrefundable credits may offset AMT as well as regular tax.

• The 2007 Mortgage Relief Act provides for a new exclusion for up to $2 million of principal residence mortgage forgiveness debt, effective for debt discharged in 2007-2009. It also makes a number of other important changes, such as creating a new exclusion for certain state benefits and payments to members of qualified volunteer emergency response organizations, a three-year extension of the rule allowing mortgage insurance premiums to be treated as qualified residence interest, and a liberalized home-sale exclusion rule for surviving spouses.

• The 2007 Technical Corrections Act makes a number of substantive changes to legislation that was enacted in recent years. For example, it liberalizes the rules for claiming the refundable AMT credit (introduced by the Tax Relief and Health Care Act of 2006 (PL 109-432, 12/20/2006)), revises the rules for a shareholder basis reduction on account of contributions of appreciated property by S corporations (introduced by the Pension Protection Act of 2006 (PL 109-280, 8/17/2006), and revises several important tax rules dealing with the definition of active business income under Code Sec. 355 and computing the foreign earned income exclusion (introduced by the Tax Increase Prevention Act of 2005 (PL 109-222, 5/17/2006). Unless otherwise noted, changes made by the 2007 Technical Corrections Act are retroactively effective as if included in the legislation that enacted the provision being changed.

• The 2007 Energy Act includes two tax changes: a one-year extension of the FUTA surcharge, and for large oil companies a longer writeoff of geological and geophysical expenses.

• The 2007 Virginia Tech Victims Act exempts from income certain payments made from the Hokie Spirit Memorial Fund, and includes a $1 increase for 2008 in the per-partner penalty for failure to file a partnership return.

Contents.   A complete list of topics discussed, arranged by paragraph title and number begins at ¶ 2 . . . . p. v

Analysis of the Economic Stimulus Act of 2008, and the AMT Patch, Mortgage Relief, Energy, Technical Corrections, and Other Late 2007 Tax Acts.   This section includes the Analysis of the tax provisions of the Economic Stimulus Act of 2008, and the AMT Patch, Mortgage Relief, Energy, Technical Corrections, and Other Late 2007 Tax Acts arranged in topical order. Each analysis paragraph starts with a boldface title. That is followed by a list of the Code sections substantively affected by the change, the Economic Stimulus Act of 2008, the AMT Patch, Mortgage Relief, Energy, Technical Corrections, or Other Late 2007 Tax Act section that caused the change, and the generally effective date for the change. Each analysis paragraph discusses the background for the change, the new law change, and the effective date for that change. Analysis paragraphs may include (1) illustrations and observations providing practical insight into the effects of the change, (2) recommendations explaining how to take advantage of opportunities presented by the law change, (3) cautions explaining how to avoid pitfalls created by the law change, and (4) client letters highlighting important law changes. The Analysis of the Economic Stimulus Act of 2008, and the AMT Patch, Mortgage Relief, Energy, Technical Corrections, and Other Late 2007 Tax Acts is reproduced beginning at ¶ 50 *et seq.*
. . . . p. 1

Client Letters.   Client letters are included on the following topics:

• A letter highlighting the extension of relief from the AMT in the Tax Increase Prevention Act of 2007;

• A letter highlighting forgiven mortgage debt relief in the Mortgage Forgiveness Debt Relief Act of 2007;

• A letter highlighting the three-year extension of the mortgage insurance deduction in the Mortgage Forgiveness Debt Relief Act of 2007;

• A letter highlighting tax relief for volunteer responders in the Mortgage Forgiveness Debt Relief Act of 2007;

• A letter highlighting the business and corporate changes in the late-2007 tax laws;

• A letter highlighting payroll and penalty provisions in the late-2007 tax legislation;

• A letter explaining the cash rebate provisions in the 2008 Economic Stimulus Act; and

• A letter highlighting incentives for business investment in the 2008 Economic Stimulus Act.

Code as Amended. All Code sections that were amended, added, repealed, or redesignated by the tax provisions of the Economic Stimulus Act of 2008, the AMT Patch, Mortgage Relief, Energy, Technical Corrections, and Other Late 2007 Tax Acts, appear in Code section order as amended, added, repealed, or redesignated. New matter is shown in italics. Deleted material and effective dates are shown in footnotes. The Code as Amended is reproduced at ¶ 3001 *et seq.* . . . . p. 301

Act Sections Not Amending Code. This section reproduces in Act section order, all Economic Stimulus Act of 2008, the AMT Patch, Mortgage Relief, Energy, Technical Corrections, and Other Late 2007 Tax Acts Small Business Act sections, or portions thereof that are tax related but do not amend specific Code sections. The Act Sections Not Amending Code are reproduced at ¶ 4000 *et seq.* . . . . p. 501

Act sections not amending Code for P.L. 110-166, 12/26/2007, the Tax Increase Prevention Act of 2007 (i.e., the AMT Patch Act, which is generally referred to in the Analysis as the 2007 Tax Increase Prevention Act), are reproduced beginning at ¶ 4001 . . . . p. 501

Act sections not amending Code for P.L. 110-142, 12/20/2007, the Mortgage Forgiveness Debt Relief Act of 2007, (i.e., the Mortgage Relief Act, which is generally referred to in the Analysis as the 2007 Mortgage Relief Act), are reproduced beginning at ¶ 4011 . . . . p. 503

Act sections not amending Code for P.L. 110-140, 12/19/2007, the Energy Independence and Security Act of 2007 (i.e., the Energy Act, which is generally referred to in the Analysis as the 2007 Energy Act), are reproduced beginning at ¶ 4026 . . . . p. 505

Act sections not amending Code for P.L. 110-172, 12/29/2007, the Tax Technical Corrections Act of 2007 (i.e., the Technical Corrections Act, which is generally referred to in the Analysis as the 2007 Technical Corrections Act), are reproduced beginning at ¶ 4036 . . . . p. 507

Act sections not amending Code for P.L. 110-141, 12/19/2007, a bill to exclude from gross income payments from the Hokie Spirit Memorial Fund to the victims of the tragic event at Virginia Polytechnic Institute & State University, which is generally referred to in the Analysis as the 2007 Virginia Tech Victims Act, are reproduced beginning at ¶ 4051 . . . . p. 511

Act sections not amending Code for P.L. 110-161, 12/26/2007, the Consolidated Appropriations Act, 2008, which is generally referred to in the Analysis as the 2008 Appropriations Act, are reproduced beginning at ¶ 4056 . . . .
. . . . p. 513

Act sections not amending Code for P.L. 110-185, the Economic Stimulus Act of 2008 (generally referred to in the Analysis as the "2008 Economic Stimulus Act"), are reproduced beginning at ¶ 4060 .... p. 515

Committee Reports. This section reproduces all relevant parts of the Committee Reports or Joint Committee on Taxation explanatory language for the Economic Stimulus Act of 2008 (see JCX-16-08), and the AMT Patch (see H Rept No. 110-431), Mortgage Relief (see H Rept No. 110-356 and JCX-107-07), Energy (see JCX-111-07), Technical Corrections (see JCX-119-07), and Other Late 2007 Tax Acts (for the 2007 Virginia Tech Victims Act, see JCX-110-07). There are no relevant Committee Reports for the tax provisions in the 2008 Appropriations Act.

For H.R. 3648, the Mortgage Forgiveness Debt Relief Act of 2007, (i.e., the Mortgage Relief Act, which is generally referred to in the Analysis as the 2007 Mortgage Relief Act), the relevant Committee Reports are H Rept No. 110-356 and the relevant Joint Committee on Taxation Description is JCX-107-07.

The relevant portions of H Rept No. 110-356 and JCX-107-07 are reproduced at ¶ 5000 *et seq.* .... p. 601

For H.R. 6, the Energy Independence and Security Act of 2007 (i.e., the Energy Act, which is generally referred to in the Analysis as the 2007 Energy Act), the relevant Joint Committee on Taxation Technical Explanation is JCX-111-07.

The relevant portions of JCX-111-07 are reproduced at ¶ 5100 *et seq.* .... p. 607

For H.R. 3996, the Tax Increase Prevention Act of 2007 (i.e., the AMT Patch Act, which is generally referred to in the Analysis as the 2007 Tax Increase Prevention Act), the relevant Committee Reports are H Rept No. 110-431.

The relevant portions of H Rept No. 110-431 are reproduced at ¶ 5200 *et seq.* .... p. 609

For H.R. 4839, the Tax Technical Corrections Act of 2007 (i.e., the Technical Corrections Act, which is generally referred to in the Analysis as the 2007 Technical Corrections Act), the relevant Joint Committee on Taxation Description is JCX-119-07.

The relevant portions of JCX-119-07 are reproduced at ¶ 5300 *et seq.* .... p. 611

For H.R. 4118, a bill to exclude from gross income payments from the Hokie Spirit Memorial Fund to the victims of the tragic event at Virginia Polytechnic Institute & State University, which is generally referred to in the Analysis as the 2007 Virginia Tech Victims Act, the relevant Joint Committee on Taxation Technical Explanation is JCX-110-07.

The relevant portions of JCX-110-07 are reproduced at ¶ 5400 *et seq.* . . . .
. . . . p. 623

For P.L. 110-185, the Economic Stimulus Act of 2008 (generally referred to in the Analysis as the "2008 Economic Stimulus Act"), the relevant Joint Committee on Taxation Technical Explanation is JCX-16-08.

The relevant portions of JCX-16-08 are reproduced at ¶ 5500 . . . . . p. 625

Act Section Cross Reference Table. Arranged in Act section order, this table shows substantive Code section(s) amended, added, affected, repealed by or related to the Economic Stimulus Act of 2008, and the AMT Patch, Mortgage Relief, Energy, Technical Corrections, or Other Late 2007 Tax Act section, the topic involved, the generally effective date of the amendment, the relevant paragraph number for the Analysis and the paragraph where the relevant Committee Reports are reproduced. The table is reproduced at ¶ 6000 . . . . p. 701

Code Section Cross Reference Table. Arranged in Code section order, this table shows the Economic Stimulus Act of 2008, and the AMT Patch, Mortgage Relief, Energy, Technical Corrections, or Other Late 2007 Tax Act section(s) that amend, add, affect, repeal or relate to the Code Section, the topic involved, the generally effective date of the amendment, the relevant paragraph number for the Analysis and the paragraph where the relevant Committee Reports are reproduced. The table is reproduced at ¶ 6001 . . . . p. 719

Code Sections Amended by Acts. Arranged in Code section order, this table shows all changes to the Internal Revenue Code made by the tax provisions of the Economic Stimulus Act of 2008, and the AMT Patch, Mortgage Relief, Energy, Technical Corrections, and Other Late 2007 Tax Acts, including conforming amendments. The table is reproduced at ¶ 6002 . . . . p. 737

Act Sections Amending Code. Arranged in Act section order, this table shows all changes to the Internal Revenue Code made by the Economic Stimulus Act of 2007, and the AMT Patch, Mortgage Relief, Energy, Technical Corrections, and Other Late 2007 Tax Acts, including conforming amendments. The table is reproduced at ¶ 6003 . . . . p. 741

Federal Tax Coordinator 2d ¶ s Affected by Acts. Arranged in FTC 2d¶ order, this table shows the FTC 2d paragraphs that have been affected by the Economic Stimulus Act of 2008, and the AMT Patch, Mortgage Relief, Energy, Technical Corrections, and Other Late 2007 Tax Acts. The table is reproduced at ¶ 6004 . . . . p. 745

United States Tax Reporter ¶ s Affected by Acts. Arranged in USTR ¶ order, this table shows the USTR paragraphs that have been affected by the Economic Stimulus Act of 2008, and the AMT Patch, Mortgage Relief, Energy, Technical Corrections, and Other Late 2007 Tax Acts. The table is reproduced at ¶ 6005 . . . . p. 747

Tax Desk ¶ s Affected by Acts. Arranged in Tax Desk ¶ order, this table shows the Tax Desk paragraphs that have been affected by the Economic Stimulus Act of 2008, and the AMT Patch, Mortgage Relief, Energy, Technical Corrections, and Other Late 2007 Tax Acts. The table is reproduced at ¶ 6006 . . .

PCA ¶ s Affected by Acts. Arranged in Pension Analysis ¶ order, this table shows the Pension Analysis paragraphs that have been affected by the AMT Patch, Mortgage Relief, Energy, Technical Corrections, and Other Late 2007 Tax Acts. The table is reproduced at ¶ 6007

PE ¶ s Affected by Acts. Arranged in Pension and Profit Sharing 2d ¶ order, this table shows the Pension and Profit Sharing 2d paragraphs that have been affected by the AMT Patch, Mortgage Relief, Energy, Technical Corrections, and Other Late 2007 Tax Acts. The table is reproduced at ¶ 6008

EP ¶ s Affected by Acts. Arranged in Estate Planning Analysis ¶ order, this table shows the Estate Planning Analysis paragraphs that have been affected by the AMT Patch, Mortgage Relief, Energy, Technical Corrections, and Other Late 2007 Tax Acts. The table is reproduced at ¶ 6009

Index. A detailed index, which directs the reader to the appropriate Analysis paragraph, is reproduced immediately after the aforementioned Tables for the Complete Analysis

¶ 2. Contents

¶ 50. 2008 Economic Stimulus Act Provisions

Cash Rebates

¶ 51. IRS will issue cash rebates in 2008 to eligible individuals to stimulate the economy

Code Sec. 6428, as amended by 2008 Economic Stimulus Act § 101(a)
Code Sec. 6211(b)(4)(A), as amended by 2008 Economic Stimulus Act § 101(b)(1)
Code Sec. 6213(g)(2)(L), as amended by 2008 Economic Stimulus Act § 101(b)(2)
Code Sec. 6428, 2008 Economic Stimulus Act § 101(c)
Code Sec. 6428, 2008 Economic Stimulus Act § 101(d)
Code Sec. 1(i)(1), as amended by 2008 Economic Stimulus Act § 101(f)(2)
Generally effective: Tax years beginning after Dec. 31, 2007
Committee Reports, see ¶ 5501

Congress has provided cash rebates to taxpayers on several occasions. For example:

. . . The Tax Reduction Act of '75 provided a refund of 10% of an individual's tax liability, up to a $200 maximum ($100 minimum), that was phased out for adjusted gross income (AGI) from $20,000 to $30,000.

. . . The 2001 Economic Growth and Tax Relief Reconciliation Act (EGTRRA) provided a credit equivalent to the value of the rate reduction under the new 10% income tax rate bracket introduced by 2001 EGTRRA. Most taxpayers received the credit in the form of an advance payment check. See FTC 2d/FIN ¶ A-1105; USTR ¶ 64,284; TaxDesk ¶ 568,205.

. . . The 2003 Jobs and Growth Act provided for advance payment of the newly increased child credit amounts in a manner similar to the advance payment checks under 2001 EGTRRA. See FTC 2d/FIN ¶ A-4051.1; USTR ¶ 64,294.01; TaxDesk ¶ 569,101.1.

New Law. The 2008 Economic Stimulus Act provides a recovery rebate credit for 2008 that is refundable. The credit is phased out for taxpayers with AGI over $75,000 ($150,000 on a joint return).

FTC 2d References are to Federal Tax Coordinator 2d
FIN References are to RIA's Analysis of Federal Taxes: Income
USTR References are to United States Tax Reporter: Income, Estate & Gift, and Excise
PCA References are to Pension Analysis (print & electronic)
PE References are to Pension Explanations (print & electronic)
EP References are to Estate Planning Analysis (print & electronic)

The credit will generally be rebated to taxpayers as soon as possible during 2008 by check or direct deposit. IRS will use information from the taxpayer's 2007 return to compute the rebate.

When taxpayers file their 2008 returns, they will reconcile the amount of the credit with the rebate received. However, if the rebate was greater than the credit to which the taxpayer is entitled, the taxpayer won't have to repay the difference.

The rebates are intended to deliver an expedited fiscal stimulus to the economy. (Com Rept, see ¶ 5501)

Allowance of refundable credit. Eligible individuals are allowed an income tax credit for their first tax year beginning in 2008. (Code Sec. 6428(a) as amended by 2008 Economic Stimulus Act §101(a)) An "eligible individual" is any individual other than (Code Sec. 6428(e)(3)):

. . . a nonresident alien (NRA) (Code Sec. 6428(e)(3)(A)),

. . . a dependent (Com Rept, see ¶ 5501), i.e., an individual for whom a Code Sec. 151 deduction is allowable to another taxpayer for a tax year beginning in the calendar year in which the individual's tax year begins (Code Sec. 6428(e)(3)(B)), and

. . . an estate or trust. (Code Sec. 6428(e)(3)(C))

> *observation:* Students who are (or can be) claimed as dependents by their parents aren't eligible individuals, even if they have enough income to have to file a return. It makes no difference if the parent chooses not to claim the child as a dependent, because the dependency deduction is still "allowable" to the parent.

> *observation:* An individual who wasn't an eligible individual for 2007 may become one for 2008, e.g., where the individual was a dependent for 2007 but not for 2008. IRS won't send a rebate check to such an individual, because rebate checks are based on information on the 2007 return. However, the individual will be able to claim the credit when he files his 2008 return.

> In the opposite situation, where the taxpayer loses his status as an eligible individual in 2008, IRS will send a rebate check, and the rebate won't have to be refunded. See below under "Reconciliation of credit with amount of rebate received."

The credit consists of a basic credit and a qualifying child credit. (Com Rept, see ¶ 5501) The credit is refundable (Com Rept, see ¶ 5501), i.e., it is treated as allowed by subpart C (refundable credits) of part IV of subchapter A of chapter 1. (Code Sec. 6428(c))

Basic credit. Eligible individuals are allowed a basic credit equal to the greater of (Com Rept, see ¶ 5501):

• net income tax liability (as defined below) (Code Sec. 6428(a)(1)), not to exceed $600 ($1,200 for a joint return) (Code Sec. 6428(a)(2)), or

• $300 ($600 for a joint return) (Code Sec. 6428(b)(1)(A)), if the individual has:

(1) at least $3,000 of qualifying income (as defined below) (Code Sec. 6428(b)(2)(A)) or

(2) (a) net income tax liability that is greater than zero (Code Sec. 6428(b)(2)(B)(i)) and (b) gross income greater than the sum of the applicable basic standard deduction amount plus the exemption amount (twice the exemption amount for a joint return). (Code Sec. 6428(b)(2)(B)(ii)) The terms "basic standard deduction" and "exemption amount" have the same meanings as in Code Sec. 6012(a). (Code Sec. 6428(e)(5))

observation: Requirement (1) is referred to as the "qualifying income test." Requirement (2) is referred to as the "net tax liability test."

observation: The minimum basic credit for eligible individuals who meet the qualifying income test or the net tax liability test is $300 ($600 for a joint return). The maximum basic credit is $600 ($1,200 for a joint return).

The basic credit will fall between the minimum and maximum if the individual's net income tax liability is greater than $300 ($600 for a joint return) and less than $600 ($1,200 for a joint return). In that case, the basic credit will be equal to the individual's net income tax liability. See Illustration (4), below.

observation: The basic standard deduction for 2008 is $5,450 (unmarried taxpayers), $10,900 (joint returns), $5,450 (married taxpayers filing separately), $8,000 (heads of household). See FTC 2d/FIN ¶ A-2803; USTR ¶ 634; TaxDesk ¶ 562,002.

The exemption amount for 2008 is $3,500. See FTC 2d/FIN ¶ A-3500.1; USTR ¶ 1514; TaxDesk ¶ 562,201.

Thus, to qualify for the credit under part (b) of the net tax liability test, gross income would have to be greater than: $8,950 for an unmarried taxpayer ($5,450 basic standard deduction for 2008 + $3,500 ex-

---

FTC 2d References are to Federal Tax Coordinator 2d
FIN References are to RIA's Analysis of Federal Taxes: Income
USTR References are to United States Tax Reporter: Income, Estate & Gift, and Excise
PCA References are to Pension Analysis (print & electronic)
PE References are to Pension Explanations (print & electronic)
EP References are to Estate Planning Analysis (print & electronic)

emption amount); $17,900 for a married couple filing a joint return ($10,900 standard deduction for 2008 + $7,000 exemption amount); $8,950 for a married taxpayers filing separately ($5,450 standard deduction for 2008 + $3,500 exemption amount); and $11,500 for a head of household ($8,000 standard deduction for 2008 + $3,500 exemption amount).

"Net income tax liability" means the excess of (Code Sec. 6428(e)(2)):

... the sum of the individual's regular tax liability (within the meaning of Code Sec. 26(b)) and the alternative minimum tax (AMT) imposed by Code Sec. 55 for the tax year (Code Sec. 6428(e)(2)(A)), over

... the sum of all nonrefundable credits other than the child tax credit (Com Rept, see ¶ 5501), specifically the tax credits allowed by part IV, subchapter A, chapter 1 of the Code, other than the child tax credit and the refundable credits in subpart C of Part IV. (Code Sec. 6428(e)(2)(B))

Net income tax liability isn't reduced by the recovery rebate credit itself or by any refundable credit. (Com Rept, see ¶ 5501)

"Qualifying income" means (Code Sec. 6428(e)(1)):

... earned income (as defined below) (Code Sec. 6428(e)(1)(A));

... social security benefits (as defined in Code Sec. 86(d)) (Code Sec. 6428(e)(1)(B)); and

... any compensation or pension received under chapter 11 (compensation for service-connected disability or death), chapter 13 (dependency and indemnity compensation for service-connected deaths), or chapter 15 (pension for non-service-connected disability) of title 38, U.S. Code. (Code Sec. 6428(e)(1)(C))

observation: Thus, rebates will be provided to:

... taxpayers living only on social security (Finance Committee Staff Summary, Feb. 7, 2008);

... disabled veterans (Description of the Chairman's Modification of the Provisions of the "Economic Stimulus Act of 2008," JCX-11-08, Jan. 30, 2008)

... survivors of disabled veterans. (Finance Committee Staff Summary, Feb. 7, 2008)

IRS and the Secretary of Veterans Affairs (VA) are directed to work together to design and implement a mechanism under which the VA will deliver a rebate to individuals receiving veteran's disability payments. This mechanism will be designed to minimize fraud and inadvertent error and reduce administrative complexity in delivering the rebate to those individuals. (Description of the Chairman's Modification of the Provisions of the "Economic Stimulus Act of 2008," JCX-11-08, Jan. 30, 2008)

"Earned income" has the meaning set forth in Code Sec. 32(c)(2) for purposes of the earned income credit (EIC). (Code Sec. 6428(e)(4)) However, the taxpayer may elect to treat nontaxable combat pay as earned income for this purpose (although for EIC purposes that election isn't available for 2008). (Code Sec. 6428(e)(4)(A)) In addition, "earned income" for this purpose doesn't include net earnings from self-employment that aren't taken into account in computing taxable income. (Code Sec. 6428(e)(4)(B))

> *observation:* Earned income for EIC purposes includes wages, salaries, tips, and other employee compensation, but only if those amounts are includible in gross income, plus the taxpayer's net earnings from self-employment (within the meaning of Code Sec. 1402(a)) reduced by the Code Sec. 164(f) deduction for self-employment taxes. See FTC 2d/FIN ¶ A-4222; USTR ¶ 324.05; TaxDesk ¶ 569,023.

Qualifying child credit. An eligible individual who is entitled to any amount of the basic credit (Com Rept, see ¶ 5501), i.e., who meets the qualifying income test or the net tax liability test, is also allowed a credit equal to $300 for each qualifying child of the individual, in addition to the basic credit. "Qualifying child" has the same meaning for this purpose as it has under Code Sec. 24(c) for purposes of the child tax credit. (Code Sec. 6428(b)(1)(B))

> *observation:* For purposes of the child tax credit, the term "qualifying child" means a qualifying child of the taxpayer, as defined for purposes of the dependency exemption by Code Sec. 152(c), who hasn't attained age 17. This is generally the taxpayer's child, stepchild, adopted child, eligible foster child, sibling, stepsibling, or a descendant of any of those individuals, who lives with the taxpayer for more than half of the tax year (except for temporary absences) and doesn't provide more than half of his own support. See FTC 2d/FIN ¶ A-4053; USTR ¶ 244; TaxDesk ¶ 569,103.

> *observation:* Because the qualifying child credit is refundable, the recipient is entitled to the full credit without regard to income tax liability. (Finance Committee Staff Summary, Feb. 7, 2008)

FTC 2d References are to Federal Tax Coordinator 2d
FIN References are to RIA's Analysis of Federal Taxes: Income
USTR References are to United States Tax Reporter: Income, Estate & Gift, and Excise
PCA References are to Pension Analysis (print & electronic)
PE References are to Pension Explanations (print & electronic)
EP References are to Estate Planning Analysis (print & electronic)

observation: A child who will reach age 17 during 2008 won't be a qualifying child in 2008, even though he was a qualifying child in 2007.

observation: Parents of children who are born or adopted in 2008 won't get a rebate from IRS, because the child won't appear on the parent's 2007 return. However, they will be able to claim the recovery rebate credit when they file their 2008 return.

Illustration (1): Taxpayer A is a single taxpayer with $14,000 in social security income, no qualifying children, and no net tax liability before the application of refundable credits and the child tax credit.

Taxpayer A will receive a $300 rebate for meeting the qualifying income test. (Com Rept, see ¶ 5501)

Illustration (2): Taxpayer B is a head of household with $4,000 in earned income, one qualifying child, and no net tax liability before the application of refundable credits and the child tax credit.

Taxpayer B will receive a $600 rebate, consisting of $300 for meeting the qualifying income test and $300 per child. (Com Rept, see ¶ 5501)

Illustration (3): Taxpayer C is a married taxpayer filing jointly with $4,000 in earned income, one qualifying child, and no net tax liability before the application of refundable credits and the child tax credit.

Taxpayer C will receive a $900 rebate, consisting of $600 for meeting the qualifying income test and $300 per child. (Com Rept, see ¶ 5501)

Illustration (4): Taxpayer D is a married taxpayer filing jointly with $2,000 in earned income, one qualifying child, and $1,100 in net tax liability (resulting from unearned income) before the application of refundable credits and the child tax credit. (The taxpayer's actual liability after the child tax credit is $100.) The qualifying income test isn't met, but Taxpayer D has net tax liability for purposes of determining the rebate of $1,100.

Taxpayer D will receive a $1,400 rebate, consisting of $1,100 of net tax liability and $300 per child. (Com Rept, see ¶ 5501)

Illustration (5): Taxpayer E is a married taxpayer filing jointly with $40,000 in earned income, two qualifying children, and a net tax liability of $1,573 before the application of refundable credits and child tax credits. (The taxpayer's actual tax liability after the child tax credit is minus $427, i.e., a $427 credit.) Taxpayer E meets the qualifying income test and the net tax liability test.

Taxpayer E will receive an $1,800 rebate, consisting of $1,200 (greater of $600 or net tax liability not to exceed $1,200) and $300 per child. (Com Rept, see ¶ 5501)

Phaseout of credit based on AGI. The amount of the recovery rebate credit, i.e., the sum of the basic credit and qualifying child credit (Com Rept, see ¶ 5501), is reduced (but not below zero) by 5% of the taxpayer's AGI in excess of $75,000 ($150,000 for a joint return). (Code Sec. 6428(d))

Illustration (6): Taxpayer F is a married taxpayer filing jointly with $175,000 in earned income, two qualifying children, and a net tax liability of $31,189. (Taxpayer F's actual liability after the child tax credit also is $31,189, as their income is too high to qualify.) Taxpayer F meets the qualifying income test and the net tax liability test.

Taxpayer F would, in the absence of the rebate phaseout provision, receive an $1,800 rebate, consisting of $1,200 (greater of $600 or net tax liability not to exceed $1,200), and $300 per child.

The phaseout provision reduces the total rebate amount by 5% of the amount by which the taxpayer's AGI exceeds $150,000. Five percent of $25,000 ($175,000 minus $150,000) equals $1,250. Taxpayer F's rebate is thus $1,800 minus $1,250, or $550. (Com Rept, see ¶ 5501)

observation: IRS will base its rebate on the taxpayer's AGI for 2007, which may be more or less than the taxpayer's 2008 AGI. If the taxpayer's AGI is lower in 2008, he may be entitled to claim an additional amount of credit on his 2008 return. If the taxpayer's AGI is greater in 2008, he won't have to refund any difference between the rebate and the credit.

observation: There's no specific amount of AGI at which the credit is fully phased out. This depends on the amount of the recovery rebate credit to which the taxpayer would otherwise be entitled. Taxpayers lose $1 of credit for every $20 by which their AGI exceeds the applicable limit ($150,000 for joint filers, $75,000 for other taxpayers).

FTC 2d References are to Federal Tax Coordinator 2d
FIN References are to RIA's Analysis of Federal Taxes: Income
USTR References are to United States Tax Reporter: Income, Estate & Gift, and Excise
PCA References are to Pension Analysis (print & electronic)
PE References are to Pension Explanations (print & electronic)
EP References are to Estate Planning Analysis (print & electronic)

For joint filers with no children who would otherwise get the maximum $1,200 basic credit, the credit would be lost at AGI of $174,000 [5% × ($174,000 − $150,000) = $1,200].

For a single filer with no children who would otherwise get the maximum $600 basic credit, the credit would be lost at AGI of $87,000 [5% × ($87,000 − $75,000) = $600].

observation: Married couples should consider the impact of the rebate in deciding whether to file jointly or separately for 2007. Couples may benefit by filing separately if they: (a) are subject to the phaseout of the rebate when filing jointly but are less subject to the phaseout when filing separately (e.g., because one spouse isn't subject at all if he files separately) and (b) pay little more 2007 tax if they file separately than if they file jointly, e.g., because they don't take advantage of any tax benefits that are disallowed or are severely limited if separate filing is elected. The higher rebate won't be recaptured in 2008 if the couple files a joint return for that year. The effect of filing separate returns on state income tax must also be considered.

Advance refund of credit based on 2007 returns. Each individual who was an eligible individual for his first tax year beginning in 2007 is treated as having made a tax payment for that tax year in an amount equal to the "advance refund amount" for that tax year. (Code Sec. 6428(g)(1)) The "advance refund amount" is the amount that would have been allowed as a recovery rebate credit for that tax year if Code Sec. 6428 (other than Code Sec. 6428(f) and Code Sec. 6428(g)) applied to that year. (Code Sec. 6428(g)(2)) Thus, the amount of the payment will be computed in the same manner as the credit, except that it will be done on the basis of tax returns filed for 2007 (instead of 2008). (Com Rept, see ¶ 5501)

IRS will refund or credit any overpayment attributable to the recovery rebate credit as rapidly as possible, subject to any other Code provisions. (Code Sec. 6428(g)(3)) Most taxpayers will receive the credit through a rebate check mailed by IRS. To the extent practicable, IRS will expedite delivery of the amounts by using taxpayers' current direct deposit information in IRS's possession. (Com Rept, see ¶ 5501)

IRS will make every effort to issue payments as rapidly as possible to taxpayers who filed their 2007 tax returns on time. Taxpayers who file late or on extension will receive their payments later. (Com Rept, see ¶ 5501)

No refund or credit will be made or allowed under Code Sec. 6428(g) after Dec. 31, 2008. (Code Sec. 6428(g)(3)) Thus, no rebate checks be will issued after Dec. 31, 2008. This will prevent errors that would occur if taxpayers claimed the full amount of the credit on 2008 tax returns filed early in 2009 at the same time that IRS was mailing them a check. (Com Rept, see ¶ 5501)

The credit or rebate check is treated as a tax payment for all Code purposes. Any resulting overpayment is subject to the refund offset provisions, such as those applicable to past-due child support under Code Sec. 6402. (Com Rept, see ¶ 5501)

> 🟢 *observation:* In addition to past-due child support, offsets may be made under Code Sec. 6402 for back taxes and outstanding debts to federal agencies, such as student loans. See FTC 2d/FIN ¶ T-6001; USTR ¶ 64,024.23; TaxDesk ¶ 803,012.

No interest is allowed on any overpayment attributable to the recovery rebate credit. (Code Sec. 6428(g)(4))

Advance refund reduces credit allowed for 2008. The amount of the recovery rebate credit that would otherwise be allowable is reduced (but not below zero) by the aggregate refunds and credits made or allowed to the taxpayer under Code Sec. 6428(g). Any failure to reduce the credit is treated as arising out of a mathematical or clerical error that is assessed under Code Sec. 6213(b)(1). (Code Sec. 6428(f)(1)) For summary assessment and abatement procedures for mathematical or clerical errors, see FTC 2d/FIN ¶ T-3622; T-3902.1; USTR ¶ 62,134.02; TaxDesk ¶ 821,002; 836,019.

In the case of a refund or credit made or allowed under Code Sec. 6428(g) for a joint return, half of the refund or credit is treated as having been made or allowed to each individual filing the return. (Code Sec. 6428(f)(2))

> 🟢 *observation:* Thus, if taxpayers filed a joint return for 2007 and received an advance payment, but were divorced or filed separate returns for 2008, each individual will take into account half of the advance payment when reducing the credit allowed for 2008.

Reconciliation of credit with amount of rebate received. Taxpayers will reconcile the amount of the credit with the payment they received by (1) completing a worksheet calculating the amount of the credit based on their 2008 tax return and (2) subtracting from the credit the amount of the payment they received. (Com Rept, see ¶ 5501)

For many taxpayers, these two amounts will be the same. However:

. . . if the result is positive (because, for example, the taxpayer paid no tax in 2007 but is paying tax in 2008), the taxpayer may claim that amount as a credit against 2008 tax liability.

FTC 2d References are to Federal Tax Coordinator 2d
FIN References are to RIA's Analysis of Federal Taxes: Income
USTR References are to United States Tax Reporter: Income, Estate & Gift, and Excise
PCA References are to Pension Analysis (print & electronic)
PE References are to Pension Explanations (print & electronic)
EP References are to Estate Planning Analysis (print & electronic)

. . . if the result is negative (because, for example, the taxpayer paid tax in 2007 but owes no tax for 2008), the taxpayer isn't required to repay that amount to IRS. (Com Rept, see ¶ 5501)

Otherwise, the checks have no effect on tax returns filed in 2009. The amount isn't includible in gross income and it doesn't otherwise reduce the amount of withholding. (Com Rept, see ¶ 5501)

Identification number requirement. No recovery rebate credit is allowed to an eligible individual who doesn't include his valid identification number (defined below) on his tax return for the tax year. (Code Sec. 6428(h)(1)(A)) No credit is allowed on a joint return unless both spouses' valid identification numbers are included on the return. (Code Sec. 6428(h)(1)(B)) A qualifying child isn't taken into account in determining the amount of the credit unless a valid identification number for the child is included on the return. (Code Sec. 6428(h)(1)(C))

A "valid identification number" means a social security number issued to an individual by the Social Security Administration (SSA). The term doesn't include a taxpayer identification number (TIN) issued by IRS (Code Sec. 6428(h)(2)), e.g., an individual taxpayer identification number (ITIN). (Com Rept, see ¶ 5501)

> *observation:* This rule is intended to deny the basic credit and qualifying child credit to illegal immigrants. (JCX-11-08, Description of the Chairman's Modification of the Provisions of the "Economic Stimulus Act of 2008," Jan. 30, 2008)

> *observation:* ITINs are issued by IRS, on application, to alien individuals who aren't eligible for social security numbers. See FTC 2d/ FIN ¶ S-1508.1; USTR ¶ 61,094; TaxDesk ¶ 570,109. Although ITINs are valid for filing tax returns, they aren't valid for the recovery rebate credit.

If an individual fails to provide a correct identification number, the omission is treated as a mathematical or clerical error. IRS may summarily assess the additional tax due without sending the taxpayer a notice of deficiency and giving the taxpayer an opportunity to petition the Tax Court. Where IRS uses the summary assessment procedure for mathematical or clerical errors, the taxpayer must be given an explanation of the asserted error and given 60 days to request that IRS abate its assessment. (Com Rept, see ¶ 5501) See FTC 2d/FIN ¶ T-3622; T-3902.1; USTR ¶ 62,134.02; TaxDesk ¶ 821,002; 836,019.

The provisions for correcting mathematical or clerical errors also apply if the computation of the credit on a return reflects the treatment of an individual as being of an age different from the individual's age based on the identification number. (Code Sec. 6213(g)(2)(L) as amended by 2008 Economic Stimulus Act §101(b)(2))

> *observation:* Thus, it's a mathematical or clerical error if a qualifying child credit is claimed for a child, and the child's social security number reflects that the child is age 17 or older.

Rebates for residents of U.S. possessions. Rules are provided for U.S. possessions, including the Commonwealth of Puerto Rico and the Commonwealth of the Northern Mariana Islands (which are treated as U.S. possessions for this purpose). (2008 Economic Stimulus Act §101(c)(3)(A))

For U.S. possessions that have mirror code tax systems, i.e., the U.S. Virgin Islands, Guam, and the Northern Mariana Islands (Com Rept, see ¶ 5501), the U.S. Treasury will make a payment to that possession equal to the loss to that possession by reason of the recovery rebate credit. (2008 Economic Stimulus Act §101(c)(1)(A)) That amount is equal to the aggregate amount of recovery rebate credits allowable to that possession's residents against its income tax. (Com Rept, see ¶ 5501) Treasury will determine the amount of the payment based on information provided by the possession's government. (2008 Economic Stimulus Act §101(c)(1)(A)) A U.S. possession has a "mirror code tax system" if its residents' income tax liability is determined by reference to the U.S. income tax laws as if the possession were the U.S. (2008 Economic Stimulus Act §101(c)(3)(B))

For U.S. possessions that don't have mirror code tax systems, i.e., Puerto Rico and American Samoa (Com Rept, see ¶ 5501), the U.S. Treasury will make a payment to the possession in an amount estimated by Treasury as being equal to the aggregate credits that would have been allowed to that possession's residents if a mirror code tax system had been in effect in the possession. This payment won't be made to any U.S. possession unless it has a plan, approved by Treasury, under which it will promptly distribute the payment to its residents. (2008 Economic Stimulus Act §101(c)(1)(B))

> *observation:* Thus, residents of U.S. possessions will also receive the benefit of the credit. (Finance Committee Staff Summary, Feb. 7, 2008)
>
> Residents of a possession that has a mirror code tax system will receive the credit under a provision that mirrors Code Sec. 6428.
>
> Residents of a possession that doesn't have a mirror code tax system will receive the benefit of the credit if the possession enacts a plan as described under 2008 Economic Stimulus Act §101(c)(1)(B) (above).

FTC 2d References are to Federal Tax Coordinator 2d
FIN References are to RIA's Analysis of Federal Taxes: Income
USTR References are to United States Tax Reporter: Income, Estate & Gift, and Excise
PCA References are to Pension Analysis (print & electronic)
PE References are to Pension Explanations (print & electronic)
EP References are to Estate Planning Analysis (print & electronic)

No recovery rebate credit against U.S. income taxes will be allowed to any person (2008 Economic Stimulus Act §101(c)(2)):

. . . to whom a credit is allowed against possession income taxes as a result of Code Sec. 6428 (2008 Economic Stimulus Act §101(c)(2)(A)), e.g., under that possession's mirror income tax (Com Rept, see ¶ 5501), or

. . . who is eligible for a payment under a non-mirror code possession's plan for distributing to its residents the payment described above from the U.S. Treasury. (2008 Economic Stimulus Act §101(c)(2)(B))

Refunds disregarded for federal or federally-assisted programs. Any credit or refund of the recovery rebate credit, including a credit or refund to a resident of a U.S. possession (Com Rept, see ¶ 5501), isn't considered income and isn't taken into account as resources for the month of receipt and the following two months for purposes of determining the eligibility of the recipient or any other individual for benefits or assistance, or the amount or extent of benefits or assistance, under any federal program or any state or local program financed in whole or in part with federal funds. (2008 Economic Stimulus Act §101(d))

Credit treated as negative tax in deficiency computation. Any excess of the recovery rebate credit over the income tax is taken into account as a negative amount of tax in computing a taxpayer's tax deficiency. (Code Sec. 6211(b)(4)(A) as amended by 2008 Economic Stimulus Act §101(b)(1)) For how deficiencies are computed, see FTC 2d/FIN ¶ T-1501; USTR ¶ 62,114; TaxDesk ¶ 822,501.

2001 EGTRRA provisions eliminated. The provisions of Code Sec. 6428 relating to the recovery rebate credit replace the provisions relating to the 2001 EGTRRA 10% rate bracket credit, which were formerly in Code Sec. 6428. In addition, former Code Sec. 1(i)(i)(D), which provided that the 10% tax rate bracket didn't apply for any tax year to which the 10% rate bracket credit applied, has been eliminated. (Code Sec. 1(i)(1) as amended by 2008 Economic Stimulus Act §101(f)(2))

☐ **Effective:** Tax years beginning after Dec. 31, 2007. (Com Rept, see ¶ 5501)

Cost Recovery

¶ 52. Regular Code Sec. 179 expense deduction limit is increased to $250,000 and beginning of deduction phaseout is raised to $800,000 for tax years beginning in 2008

Code Sec. 179(b)(7), as amended by 2008 Economic Stimulus Act § 102(a)
Generally effective: Tax years beginning in 2008
Committee Reports, see ¶ 5502

Code Sec. 179 allows taxpayers to elect to treat the cost of section 179 property as an expense deduction for the tax year in which the section 179 property is placed in service, instead of having to capitalize the expense and recover the cost over several years. See FTC 2d/FIN ¶ L-9901; USTR ¶ 1794; TaxDesk ¶ 268,401. Generally, section 179 property is property which is acquired by purchase for use in the active conduct of a trade or business, and is either (i) tangible property (to which Code Sec. 168 accelerated cost recovery applies), or (ii) computer software (to which Code Sec. 167 depreciation applies) placed in service in tax years beginning after 2002 and before 2011. See FTC 2d/FIN ¶ L-9922; USTR ¶ 1794.02; TaxDesk ¶ 268,424.

    ⊘ *observation:* The Code Sec. 179 expense election is not available to estates and trusts (see FTC 2d/FIN ¶ L-9905; USTR ¶ 1794.01; TaxDesk ¶ 268,406), nor to certain non-corporate lessors (see FTC 2d/ FIN ¶ L-9905; TaxDesk ¶ 268,406).

    ⊘ *observation:* There is no alternative minimum tax adjustment with respect to property expensed under Code Sec. 179. See FTC 2d/FIN ¶ A-8222; TaxDesk ¶ 696,515.

    ⊘ *observation:* The amount of the allowable expense deduction does not depend on when in the tax year the qualifying property is placed in service. Thus, whether qualifying property is placed in service on the first day or the last day of the tax year does not affect the amount of the allowable deduction. See FTC 2d/FIN ¶ L-9902; TaxDesk ¶ 268,403.

FTC 2d References are to Federal Tax Coordinator 2d
FIN References are to RIA's Analysis of Federal Taxes: Income
USTR References are to United States Tax Reporter: Income, Estate & Gift, and Excise
PCA References are to Pension Analysis (print & electronic)
PE References are to Pension Explanations (print & electronic)
EP References are to Estate Planning Analysis (print & electronic)

observation: A full deduction is allowable even if the property is placed in service in a short tax year. See FTC 2d/FIN ¶ L-9902; TaxDesk ¶ 268,403.

Under pre-2008 Economic Stimulus Act law, for tax years beginning after 2006 and before 2011, the maximum regular Code Sec. 179 expense deduction is $125,000, and the expense deduction is phased-out (i.e., reduced, but not below zero) by the amount by which the cost of section 179 property placed in service during the tax year exceeds $500,000. (FTC 2d/FIN ¶ L-9907, ¶ L-9952; USTR ¶ 1794.01, ¶ 14,00L4.15; TaxDesk ¶ 268,411, ¶ 268,413, ¶ 268,502, ¶ 268,602) For tax years beginning after 2007 and before 2011, the $125,000 and $500,000 amounts, above, are each increased by a cost-of-living adjustment. (FTC 2d/FIN ¶ L-9907.1; USTR ¶ 1794.01; TaxDesk ¶ 268,411) For tax years beginning in 2008, the $125,000 and $500,000 amounts have been adjusted for inflation to $128,000 and $510,000, respectively. (FTC 2d/FIN ¶ L-9907.1; USTR ¶ 1794.01; TaxDesk ¶ 268,411)

observation: Therefore, under pre-2008 Economic Stimulus Act law, the maximum regular Code Sec. 179 expense deduction for tax years beginning in 2008 was $128,000, and this amount was reduced by the amount by which the cost of section 179 property placed in service during that tax year exceeds $510,000.

illustration: T, a calendar year taxpayer, places section 179 property costing $637,000 in service during 2008. Under pre-2008 Economic Stimulus Act law, if T elects Code Sec. 179 expensing, T is entitled to a Code Sec. 179 expense deduction of $1,000 ($128,000 – [$637,000 – $510,000]).

observation: In addition to the regular Code Sec. 179 maximum deductions and beginning-of-phaseout levels described above, enhanced Code Sec. 179 maximum deductions and beginning-of-phaseout levels are available for qualified property placed in service in an empowerment zone (FTC 2d/FIN ¶ L-9950 *et seq.*; USTR ¶ 1794.05; TaxDesk ¶s 268,402, 268,413), a renewal community (FTC 2d/FIN ¶s L-9986, L-9988.1; USTR ¶ 14,00J4; TaxDesk ¶s 268,701, 268,704), or the Gulf Opportunity Zone (FTC 2d/FIN ¶s L-9996, L-9996.1; USTR ¶ 14,00N4.025; TaxDesk ¶s 268,601, 268,602). For example, for an enterprise zone business, the maximum Code Sec. 179 expense deduction limit is increased (by up to $35,000) by the cost of qualified zone property placed in service during the tax year, and only 50% of the cost of qualified zone property is counted for purposes of determining the phaseout. (See FTC 2d/FIN ¶ L-9950 *et seq.*; USTR ¶ 1794.05; TaxDesk ¶s 268,402, 268,413.)

New Law. The 2008 Economic Stimulus Act provides that, for tax years beginning in 2008, the maximum regular Code Sec. 179 expense deduction is $250,000. (Code Sec. 179(b)(7)(A) as amended by 2008 Economic Stimulus Act §102(a)) The $250,000 limitation is reduced by the amount by which the cost of section 179 property placed in service during the tax year beginning in 2008 exceeds $800,000. (Code Sec. 179(b)(7)(B)) Thus, the 2008 Economic Stimulus Act increases the $128,000 and $510,000 amounts under Code Sec. 179 for 2008 to $250,000 and $800,000 respectively. (Com Rept, see ¶ 5502) However, neither the $250,000 nor the $800,000 amount described above is adjusted for inflation. (Code Sec. 179(b)(7)(C))

illustration: T, a calendar year taxpayer, places section 179 property costing $637,000 in service during 2008. T is entitled to a regular Code Sec. 179 expense deduction of $250,000 ($250,000 − $0).

observation: It is likely that many small businesses, and some moderately sized businesses with relatively modest capital equipment needs, would be able to obtain a full expense deduction for the cost of business machinery and equipment placed in service in tax years beginning in 2008, thereby reducing their effective cost for the assets.

observation: The enhanced Code Sec. 179 maximum deductions and beginning-of-phaseout levels available for qualified property placed in service in an empowerment zone (FTC 2d/FIN ¶ L-9950 *et seq.*; USTR ¶ 1794.05; TaxDesk ¶s 268,402, 268,413), a renewal community (FTC 2d/FIN ¶s L-9986, L-9988.1; USTR ¶ 14,00J4; TaxDesk ¶s 268,701, 268,704), or the Gulf Opportunity Zone (FTC 2d/FIN ¶s L-9996, L-9996.1; USTR ¶ 14,00N4.025; TaxDesk ¶s 268,601, 268,602) are available in addition to the increased regular Code Sec. 179 maximum expense deduction limit ($250,000) and the raised beginning-of-phaseout level ($800,000) for 2008 tax years.

illustration: X, an enterprise zone business taxpayer, places qualified zone property with a cost of $1,600,000 in its tax year beginning in 2008. X can elect to expense $285,000 in its 2008 tax year under Code Sec. 179. Under 2008 Economic Stimulus Act law, the maximum regular Code Sec. 179 expense deduction of $250,000 is increased by $35,000 for the cost of qualified zone property. Furthermore, when determining whether the beginning-of-phaseout level of $800,000 is exceeded, only 1/2 of the value of the cost of qualified zone property is

---

FTC 2d References are to Federal Tax Coordinator 2d
FIN References are to RIA's Analysis of Federal Taxes: Income
USTR References are to United States Tax Reporter: Income, Estate & Gift, and Excise
PCA References are to Pension Analysis (print & electronic)
PE References are to Pension Explanations (print & electronic)
EP References are to Estate Planning Analysis (print & electronic)

taken into account ($1,600,000 x 1/2 = $800,000). Since the beginning-of-phaseout level is not exceeded, the otherwise allowable expense deduction of $285,000 is not reduced.

☐ **Effective:** Tax years beginning after Dec. 31, 2007. (2008 Economic Stimulus Act §102(b))

> **🖝 observation:** Although the effective date in 2008 Economic Stimulus Act §102(b) of the Code Sec. 179 modifications described above could be read to mean that those modifications apply to tax years *beyond* those beginning in 2008 (as well as to tax years beginning *in* 2008), it is clear from Code Sec. 179(b)(7) that the increases in limitations apply only for tax years beginning in 2008.

¶ 53. 50% bonus depreciation and AMT depreciation relief are revived for most new tangible personal property and software and certain leasehold improvements acquired during 2008

Code Sec. 168(k), as amended by 2008 Economic Stimulus Act § 103(a)
Code Sec. 168(k)(1)(A), as amended by 2008 Economic Stimulus Act § 103(b)
Code Sec. 168(k)(2)(B)(i)(I), as amended by 2008 Economic Stimulus Act § 103(c)(1)
Code Sec. 168(k)(2)(B)(i)(IV), as amended by 2008 Economic Stimulus Act § 103(c)(2)
Code Sec. 168(k)(2)(C)(i), as amended by 2008 Economic Stimulus Act § 103(c)(3)
Code Sec. 168(k)(2)(D)(iii), as amended by 2008 Economic Stimulus Act § 103(c)(5)(B)
Code Sec. 168(k)(4), as amended by 2008 Economic Stimulus Act § 103(c)(5)(A)
Code Sec. 168(l)(4)(A), as amended by 2008 Economic Stimulus Act § 103(c)(6)
Code Sec. 1400N(d)(6)(E), as amended by 2008 Economic Stimulus Act § 103(c)(10)
Generally effective: Property acquired and placed in service during calendar year 2008
Committee Reports, see ¶ 5503

For most tangible property, the depreciation deduction under Code Sec. 167(a) is determined under the modified accelerated cost recovery system (MACRS) provided by Code Sec. 168, see FTC 2d/FIN ¶ L-8101; USTR ¶ 1684; TaxDesk ¶ 266,001.

Depreciable computer software—unless it is custom-made software acquired in the purchase of a business and, thus, amortized over 15 years under Code Sec. 197—is, generally, depreciated under Code Sec. 167(f)(1) using the straight-line method and a 36-month useful life, see FTC 2d/FIN ¶ L-7935; USTR ¶ 1674.033; TaxDesk ¶ 265,434.

Certain property depreciated on the 200% declining balance method for regular income tax purposes must be depreciated on the 150% declining balance method for alternative minimum tax purposes (the AMT depreciation adjustment), see FTC 2d/FIN ¶ A-8220; USTR ¶ 564.01; TaxDesk ¶ 696,513.

"Qualified property" is allowed additional depreciation (bonus depreciation) in the year that the property is placed in service (with corresponding reductions in basis for later years). (FTC 2d/FIN ¶ L-9311 *et seq.*, ¶ L-9321; USTR ¶ 1684.025 *et seq.*; TaxDesk ¶ 269,341 *et seq.*, ¶ 269,351 *et seq.*) Additionally, qualified property is exempt from the AMT depreciation adjustment. (FTC 2d/FIN ¶ A-8221; USTR ¶ 1684.029; TaxDesk ¶ 696,514) Also, qualified property is allowed an increase in the otherwise-applicable dollar limit on first-year depreciation for passenger cars (first-year passenger car depreciation limit increase). (FTC 2d/FIN ¶ L-10004.2, ¶ L-10004.3; USTR ¶ 1684.0281; TaxDesk ¶ 267,602.1, ¶ 267,602.2) The bonus depreciation for qualified property is subject to recapture under the special recapture rule, in Code Sec. 280F(b)(2), for listed property (the listed property depreciation recapture rule). (FTC 2d/FIN ¶ L-10032.1; USTR ¶ 1684.0282; TaxDesk ¶ 267,625.5)

The rules discussed above for qualified property don't apply to classes of property for which the taxpayer elects to not apply Code Sec. 168(k) (i.e., the taxpayer makes an "election-out"). (FTC 2d/FIN ¶ L-9318, ¶ L-9329; USTR ¶ 1684.0291; TaxDesk ¶ 269,348, ¶ 269,359)

Under pre-2008 Economic Stimulus Act law, there were two types of qualified property. One type was eligible for 30% bonus depreciation (pre-2008 30% bonus depreciation property). FTC 2d/FIN ¶ L-9321; USTR ¶ 1684.025; TaxDesk ¶ 269,351. The other type of "qualified property" was eligible for 50% bonus depreciation and was named "50-percent bonus depreciation property" (pre-2008 50% bonus depreciation property). FTC 2d/FIN ¶ L-9311; USTR ¶ 1684.025; TaxDesk ¶ 269,341. Apart from definitional differences (discussed immediately below), the only differences between pre-2008 30% bonus depreciation property and pre-2008 50% bonus depreciation property were that (1) for pre-2008 50% bonus depreciation property, in addition to being able to make an election-out (see above), a taxpayer could also elect to be allowed 30%

FTC 2d References are to Federal Tax Coordinator 2d
FIN References are to RIA's Analysis of Federal Taxes: Income
USTR References are to United States Tax Reporter: Income, Estate & Gift, and Excise
PCA References are to Pension Analysis (print & electronic)
PE References are to Pension Explanations (print & electronic)
EP References are to Estate Planning Analysis (print & electronic)

bonus depreciation (FTC 2d/FIN ¶ L-9317; USTR ¶ 1684.0292; TaxDesk ¶ 269,347) and (2) the amounts of the first-year passenger car depreciation limit increase were $4,650 for pre-2008 30% bonus depreciation property and $7,650 for pre-2008 50% bonus depreciation property. (FTC 2d/FIN ¶ L-10004.2, ¶ L-10004.3; USTR ¶ 1684.0281; TaxDesk ¶ 267,602.1, ¶ 267,602.2)

For both pre-2008 30% bonus depreciation property and pre-2008 50% bonus depreciation property, there were six requirements: a type of property requirement, an original use requirement, a timely acquisition requirement, a timely placement in service requirement, a requirement that the property not violate a disqualifying transactions rule and a requirement that the property not be ineligible property (i.e., property subject to the alternative depreciation system or "qualified New York Liberty Zone leasehold improvement property"). The requirements were the same for both pre-2008 30% bonus depreciation property and pre-2008 50% bonus depreciation property, except that the dates that define compliance with the original use requirement, the timely acquisition requirement and the requirement that the property not violate the disqualifying transactions rule were different for the two categories. (FTC 2d/FIN ¶ L-9312 *et seq.*, ¶ L-9322 *et seq.*; USTR ¶ 1684.026, ¶ 1684.028; TaxDesk ¶ 269,342 *et seq.*, ¶ 269,352 *et seq.*)

Under Code Sec. 168(l), 50% bonus depreciation and exemption from the AMT depreciation adjustment is available for "qualified cellulosic biomass ethanol plant property," see FTC 2d/FIN ¶s A-8221, L-9356, L-9357; USTR ¶s 1684.08, 1684.081; TaxDesk ¶s 267,801, 267,802, 696,514.

Under Code Sec. 1400N(d), 50% bonus depreciation and exemption from the AMT depreciation adjustment is also available for "qualified Gulf Opportunity Zone property" (qualified GO Zone property), i.e., certain property used in areas affected by Hurricane Katrina, see FTC 2d/FIN ¶s A-8221, L-9336, L-9337; USTR ¶s 14,00N4.02, 14,00N4.021; TaxDesk ¶s 269,331, 269,332, 696,514.

Under Code Sec. 1400L(b), 30% bonus depreciation and exemption from the AMT depreciation adjustment is available for "qualified New York Liberty Zone property," i.e., certain property used in a designated portion of lower Manhattan (in New York City) that includes the area damaged by the Sept. 11, 2001 terrorist attacks, see FTC 2d/FIN ¶s A-8221, L-9341, L-9342; USTR ¶s 14,00L4.05, 14,00L4.06; TaxDesk ¶s 267,701, 267,702, 696,514.

New Law. The 2008 Economic Stimulus Act replaces "30 percent" with "50 percent " in Code Sec. 168(k)(1)(A) (Code Sec. 168(k)(1)(A) as amended by 2008 Economic Stimulus Act §103(b)) and deletes Code Sec. 168(k)(4). (Code Sec. 168(k)(4) as amended by 2008 Economic Stimulus Act §103(c)(5)(A))

    observation: The effect of the substitution of "30 percent" for "50 percent" is that the bonus depreciation rules that applied to "pre-2008

30% bonus deprecation property" apply to "qualified property," except that the amount of bonus depreciation allowed is increased from 30% to 50%.

observation: The deletion of Code Sec. 168(k)(4), which provided the definition of "pre-2008 50% bonus depreciation property" (see above) and certain rules specific to "pre-2008 50% bonus depreciation property" means that under Code Sec. 168(k), as amended by the 2008 Economic Stimulus Act, there is only one type of qualified property, governed by one set of rules.

For "qualified property" (defined below) (Code Sec. 168(k)(1) as amended by 2008 Economic Stimulus Act §103(b))

. . . the depreciation deduction under Code Sec. 167(a) for the tax year in which the property is placed in service includes an allowance equal to 50% of the adjusted basis of the qualified property, and (Code Sec. 168(k)(1)(A))

. . . the adjusted basis of the qualified property is reduced by the amount of that deduction before computing the amount otherwise allowable as a depreciation deduction for the tax year and any later tax year. (Code Sec. 168(k)(1)(B)) Thus, the basis of the property and the depreciation allowances in the year of purchase and later years are appropriately adjusted to reflect the 50% bonus depreciation. (Com Rept, see ¶ 5503)

Illustration (1): In 2008, S buys new depreciable property and places it in service. The property's cost is $1,000 and the property is 5-year MACRS property, subject to the half-year convention (see illustration (2)). The amount of 50% bonus depreciation allowed is $500. The remaining $500 of the cost is deductible under the rules applicable to 5-year MACRS property (see illustration (2)). Thus, 20% (i.e. $100) is allowed as a depreciation deduction in 2008. Thus, the total depreciation deduction for the property for 2008 is $600. The remaining $400 of the property's cost is recovered under otherwise applicable rules for computing depreciation (see illustration (2)). (Com Rept, see ¶ 5503)

illustration (2): On Nov. 1, 2008, T, a calendar year taxpayer, acquires and places in service "qualified property" that is 5-year MACRS property (in this case, computers and other qualified technological equipment, see FTC 2d/FIN ¶ L-8205; USTR ¶ 1684.01; TaxDesk ¶ 266,205) that costs $1 million. Assume that T doesn't make an elec-

---

FTC 2d References are to Federal Tax Coordinator 2d
FIN References are to RIA's Analysis of Federal Taxes: Income
USTR References are to United States Tax Reporter: Income, Estate & Gift, and Excise
PCA References are to Pension Analysis (print & electronic)
PE References are to Pension Explanations (print & electronic)
EP References are to Estate Planning Analysis (print & electronic)

tion to forgo bonus depreciation (see "Election-out" below). T's bonus depreciation deduction for 2008 is $500,000 ($1,000,000 × 50%). Then, assuming that T applies the 200% declining balance method (switching to the straight-line method when that method yields larger deductions, see FTC 2d/FIN ¶ L-8909; USTR ¶ 1684.01; TaxDesk ¶ 267,013), the half-year convention, see FTC 2d/FIN ¶ L-8702; USTR ¶ 1684.01; TaxDesk ¶ 266,702, and the percentages provided by the optional depreciation tables, see FTC 2d/FIN ¶ L-8904; USTR ¶ 1684.01; TaxDesk ¶ 267,008, T's remaining depreciation deductions are as follows: for 2008, $100,000 (20% of $500,000); for 2009, $160,000 (32% of $500,000); for 2010, $96,000 (19.20% of $500,000); for 2011, $57,600 (11.52% of $500,000); for 2012, $57,600 (11.52% of $500,000); and for 2013, $28,800 (5.76% of $500,000), see FTC 2d/FIN ¶ L-9311; USTR ¶ 1684.025; TaxDesk ¶ 269,341.

observation: Illustration (1) indicates that the half-year, mid-quarter and mid-month depreciation conventions, see FTC 2d/FIN ¶ L-8701; USTR ¶s 1684.01, 1684.02; TaxDesk ¶ 266,701, don't apply to the bonus depreciation available for qualified property.

caution: Illustration (1) shows that the conventions do apply to the *other* first-year depreciation deductions allowed with respect to qualified property. Further, the placement of qualified property into service during the last quarter of a tax year may sometimes cause the taxpayer to be required to use a mid-quarter convention, rather than a half-year convention, for *all* of the taxpayer's MACRS property (other than buildings and railroad gradings or tunnel bores) placed into service during that tax year, see FTC 2d/FIN ¶ L-8707; USTR ¶ 1684.01; TaxDesk ¶ 266,707.

observation: Under pre-2008 Economic Stimulus Act law, amounts "expensed" under the election available under Code Sec. 179, see FTC 2d/FIN ¶ L-9901; USTR ¶ 1794; TaxDesk ¶ 268,401, reduced the basis of an asset that was qualified property before the bonus depreciation was calculated for the asset and before other depreciation was calculated for the asset, see FTC 2d/FIN ¶ L-9311; USTR ¶ 1684.025; TaxDesk ¶ 269,341 (pre-2008 50% bonus depreciation property) and FTC 2d/FIN ¶ L-9321; USTR ¶ 1684.025; TaxDesk ¶ 269,351 (pre-2008 30% bonus depreciation property). Presumably, a similar rule applies to qualified property under the 2008 Economic Stimulus Act.

Illustration (3): On Nov. 1, 2008, W, a calendar-year taxpayer, acquires and places in service qualified property that costs $350,000. Assume (1) that the property is section 179 property, (2) that after applying all the rules that can limit W's maximum allowable Code Sec. 179 expensing deduction for 2008, W can elect a Code Sec. 179 expensing deduction of up to $205,000, (3) that W does in fact make a $205,000 expensing election under Code Sec. 179 for the property, and (4) that W doesn't elect out of bonus depreciation (see above). For the qualified property, W is allowed, for 2008, a 50% bonus depreciation deduction of $72,500 (50% of $145,000, which is the $350,000 original cost minus $205,000). Then, assuming that W applies the 200% declining balance method (switching to the straight-line method when that method yields larger deductions), the half-year convention and the percentages provided by the optional depreciation tables (see illustration (2)), the other depreciation deductions allowed for the property are as follows: for 2008, $14,500 (20% of $72,500); for 2009, $23,200 (32% of $72,500); for 2010, $13,920 (19.20% of $72,500); for 2011, $8,352 (11.52% of $72,500); for 2012, $8,352 (11.52% of $72,500); and for 2013, $4,176 (5.76% of $72,500), see FTC 2d/FIN ¶ L-9311; USTR ¶ 1684.025; TaxDesk ¶ 269,341.

The amount of the 50% bonus depreciation deduction isn't affected by a short tax year. (Com Rept, see ¶ 5503)

observation: The rule concerning short tax years also applied to "pre-2008 30% bonus depreciation property" and "pre-2008 50% bonus depreciation property." (FTC 2d/FIN ¶ L-9311, ¶ L-9321; USTR ¶ 1684.025; TaxDesk ¶ 269,341, ¶ 269,351)

The 50% bonus depreciation deduction isn't allowed for purposes of computing earnings and profits. (Com Rept, see ¶ 5503)

observation: This rule, which concerns corporate earnings and profits, also applied to "pre-2008 30% bonus depreciation property" and "pre-2008 50% bonus depreciation property." (FTC 2d/FIN ¶ F-10303; USTR ¶ 3124.04)

The 50% bonus depreciation for qualified property is subject to the general rules regarding whether an item is deductible under Code Sec. 162 or subject to capitalization under Code Sec. 263 (the regular capitalization rules, see FTC 2d/FIN ¶ L-5601; USTR ¶ 2634; TaxDesk ¶ 256,201) or Code Sec. 263A (the uniform capitalization, or UNICAP, rules, see FTC 2d/FIN ¶ G-5450; USTR ¶ 263A4; TaxDesk ¶ 456,000). (Com Rept, see ¶ 5503)

FTC 2d References are to Federal Tax Coordinator 2d
FIN References are to RIA's Analysis of Federal Taxes: Income
USTR References are to United States Tax Reporter: Income, Estate & Gift, and Excise
PCA References are to Pension Analysis (print & electronic)
PE References are to Pension Explanations (print & electronic)
EP References are to Estate Planning Analysis (print & electronic)

☞ *observation:* The rule concerning the regular capitalization and uniform capitalization rules also applied to "pre-2008 30% bonus depreciation property" and "pre-2008 50% bonus depreciation property." (FTC 2d/FIN ¶ L-9311, ¶ L-9321; USTR ¶ 1684.025; TaxDesk ¶ 269,341, ¶ 269,351)

Changed dates regarding rules for qualification as "qualified property." The 2008 Economic Stimulus Act changes dates in Code Sec. 168(k) as follows:

. . . "Dec. 31, 2007" replaces "Sept. 10, 2001" wherever the latter date appears in Code Sec. 168(k). (Code Sec. 168(k) as amended by 2008 Economic Stimulus Act §103(a)(1))

. . . "Jan. 1, 2008" replaces "Sept. 11, 2001" wherever the latter date appears in Code Sec. 168(k). (Code Sec. 168(k) as amended by 2008 Economic Stimulus Act §103(a)(2))

. . . "Jan. 1, 2009" replaces "Jan. 1, 2005" wherever the latter date appears in Code Sec. 168(k). (Code Sec. 168(k) as amended by 2008 Economic Stimulus Act §103(a)(3))

. . . "Jan. 1, 2010" replaces "Jan. 1, 2006" wherever the latter date appears in Code Sec. 168(k). (Code Sec. 168(k) as amended by 2008 Economic Stimulus Act §103(a)(4))

☞ *observation:* Generally, under pre-2008 Economic Stimulus Act law, all of the time limits for complying with the various definitional requirements for being qualified property had expired. For example, under the pre-2008 Economic Stimulus Act version of the timely-placement-in-service requirement for qualified property, qualified property had to be placed in service before Jan. 1, 2005, with exceptions for (1) certain property with a longer production period and certain aircraft (which were allowed to be placed in service as late as Dec. 31, 2005) and (2) certain property placed in service in certain areas affected by the hurricanes of 2005 (which could be placed in service as late as Dec. 31, 2006). Thus, the time limits, discussed below, that are part of the definition of "qualified property" under the 2008 Economic Stimulus Act, in essence, "revive" 50% bonus depreciation for "qualified property." (FTC 2d/FIN ¶ L-9316 *et seq.*, ¶ L-9327 *et seq.*; USTR ¶ 1684.026, ¶ 1684.028; TaxDesk ¶ 269,342 *et seq.*, ¶ 269,352 *et seq.*)

☞ *observation:* The effect of the above date changes is that except for (1) changes in the relevant dates, (2) a change in the estimated-production-period requirement for "long-production-period property" (see "Timely placement into service requirement" below) and (3) two corrections of typographical errors (see "Timely placement into service requirement" below), the rules that determine what is "qualified property" are the same as the rules that, under pre-2008 Economic Stimulus Act law, determined what was "pre-2008 30% bonus depreciation property" (see above).

observation: None of the date changes affect the "type of property requirement" for "qualified property" from what that requirement was for "pre-2008 30% bonus depreciation property" (see above). Thus, most tangible personal property, most computer software and certain leasehold improvements ("qualified leasehold improvements") are the types of property that satisfy the requirement, see FTC 2d/FIN ¶ L-9324; USTR ¶ 1684.026; TaxDesk ¶ 269,354. Also, the rules that made property that is subject to the alternative depreciation system and "qualified New York Liberty Zone leasehold improvement property" ineligible to be "pre-2008 30% bonus depreciation property" (see above) are unaffected by the date changes. However, as discussed below, all of the other requirements were affected by the date changes.

Original use requirement. To be qualified property, the original use of the property must begin with the taxpayer after *Dec. 31, 2007.* (Code Sec. 168(k)(2)(A)(ii) as amended by 2008 Economic Stimulus Act §103(a)(1)) For purposes of this requirement, "original use" means the first use to which the property is put, whether or not that use corresponds to the use of the property by the taxpayer. (Com Rept, see ¶ 5503)

For purposes of the original use requirement (including the syndication rule discussed immediately below) (Code Sec. 168(k)(2)(E)(ii)), if property (1) is originally placed in service after *Dec. 31, 2007,* by a person, and (Code Sec. 168(k)(2)(E)(ii)(I)) (2) is sold and leased back by that person within three months after the date that property was originally placed in service (Code Sec. 168(k)(2)(E)(ii)(II)), the property is treated as originally placed in service not earlier than the date on which the property is used under the leaseback (the sale-leaseback rule). (Code Sec. 168(k)(2)(E)(ii)) Thus, in the case of any property that is originally placed in service by a person and that is sold to the taxpayer and leased back to that person by the taxpayer within three months after the date that the property was placed in service, the property is treated as originally placed in service by the taxpayer not earlier than the date that the property is used under the leaseback. (Com Rept, see ¶ 5503)

FTC 2d References are to Federal Tax Coordinator 2d
FIN References are to RIA's Analysis of Federal Taxes: Income
USTR References are to United States Tax Reporter: Income, Estate & Gift, and Excise
PCA References are to Pension Analysis (print & electronic)
PE References are to Pension Explanations (print & electronic)
EP References are to Estate Planning Analysis (print & electronic)

> **⦿** *observation:* As confirmed by the Committee Report's identification
> of "the taxpayer" as the buyer-lessor, the main effect of the sale-lease-
> back original use rule is to shift eligibility for 50% bonus depreciation
> from the seller-lessee to the buyer-lessor.

Also, for purposes of the original use requirement, property is treated as originally placed in service not earlier than the date of the last sale described at (3)
below if the following requirements are met: (Code Sec. 168(k)(2)(E)(iii))

(1) the property is originally placed in service after *Dec. 31, 2007* by the lessor of the property, (Code Sec. 168(k)(2)(E)(iii)(I))

(2) the property is sold by the lessor or any later purchaser within 3 months
after the date it is placed in service (or, in the case of multiple units of property
subject to the same lease, within 3 months after the date the final unit is placed
in service, so long as the period between the time the first unit is placed in service and the time the last unit is placed in service doesn't exceed 12 months),
and (Code Sec. 168(k)(2)(E)(iii)(II))

(3) the user of the property after the last sale during the 3-month period remains the same as when the property was originally placed in service (the syndication rule). (Code Sec. 168(k)(2)(E)(iii)(III))

If, in the normal course of its business, a taxpayer sells fractional interests in
property to unrelated third parties, the original use of that property begins with
the first user of the fractional interest (i.e., each fractional owner is considered
the original user of its proportionate share of the property). (Com Rept, see
¶ 5503)

> **⦿** *observation:* IRS issued regs, reflecting the above rules and others,
> that interpret the original use requirement for "pre-2008 30% bonus de-
> preciation property" and "pre-2008 50% bonus depreciation property."
> (FTC 2d/FIN ¶ L-9314 *et seq.,* ¶ L-9325 *et seq.;* USTR ¶ 1684.026,
> ¶ 1684.028; TaxDesk ¶ 269,344 *et seq.,* ¶ 269,355 *et seq.*) Presumably,
> the rules in these regs also apply to "qualified property."

Timely acquisition requirement. To be qualified property, property must be:
(Code Sec. 168(k)(2)(A)(iii))

(A) acquired by the taxpayer after *Dec. 31, 2007,* and before *Jan. 1, 2009,*
but only if no written binding contract for the acquisition was in effect before
Jan. 1, 2008, or (Code Sec. 168(k)(2)(A)(iii)(I) as amended by 2008 Economic
Stimulus Act §103(a)(1)) (Code Sec. 168(k)(2)(A)(iii)(I) as amended by 2008
Economic Stimulus Act §103(a)(2)) (Code Sec. 168(k)(2)(A)(iii)(I) as amended
by 2008 Economic Stimulus Act §103(a)(3))

(B) acquired by the taxpayer under a written binding contract which was entered into after *Dec. 31, 2007,* and before *Jan. 1, 2009.* (Code Sec.

168(k)(2)(A)(iii)(II) as amended by 2008 Economic Stimulus Act §103(a)(1)) (Code Sec. 168(k)(2)(A)(iii)(II) as amended by 2008 Economic Stimulus Act §103(a)(3))

For a taxpayer manufacturing, constructing or producing property for the taxpayer's own use, the requirements of Code Sec. 168(k)(2)(A)(iii) (immediately above) are treated as met if the taxpayer begins manufacturing, constructing, or producing the property after *Dec. 31, 2007* and before *Jan. 1, 2009.* (Code Sec. 168(k)(2)(E)(i) as amended by 2008 Economic Stimulus Act §103(a)(1))(Code Sec. 168(k)(2)(E)(i) as amended by 2008 Economic Stimulus Act §103(a)(3))

Property is considered manufactured, constructed or produced by the taxpayer if it is manufactured, constructed or produced for the taxpayer by another person under a contract that is entered into before the manufacture, construction or production of the property. (Com Rept, see ¶ 5503)

Property doesn't fail to qualify for the 50% bonus depreciation merely because a binding written contract to acquire a component of the property is in effect before Jan. 1, 2008. (Com Rept, see ¶ 5503)

> *observation:* IRS issued regs, reflecting the above rules and others, that interpret the timely acquisition requirement for "pre-2008 30% bonus depreciation property" and "pre-2008 50% bonus depreciation property." (FTC 2d/FIN ¶ L-9315 *et seq.,* ¶ L-9326 *et seq.*; USTR ¶ 1684.026, ¶ 1684.028; TaxDesk ¶ 269,345 *et seq.,* ¶ 269,356 *et seq.*) Presumably, the rules in these regs also apply to "qualified property."

Timely placement into service requirement. To be qualified property, the property must be placed in service by the taxpayer before *Jan. 1, 2009,* except that property which meets either of the two sets of requirements discussed immediately below is qualified property if it is placed in service before *Jan. 1, 2010.* (Code Sec. 168(k)(2)(A)(iv) as amended by 2008 Economic Stimulus Act §103(a)(3)) (Code Sec. 168(k)(2)(A)(iv) as amended by 2008 Economic Stimulus Act §103(a)(4))

"Qualified property" includes property ("long-production-period property") that (Code Sec. 168(k)(2)(B)(i))

(1) meets the requirements of Code Sec. 168(k)(2)(A)(i) (the type of property requirement, see above); Code Sec. 168(k)(2)(A)(ii) (the original use requirement, see above), Code Sec. 168(k)(2)(A)(iii) (the timely acquisition requirement, see above) and Code Sec. 168(k)(2)(A)(iv) (the timely placement in ser-

---

FTC 2d References are to Federal Tax Coordinator 2d
FIN References are to RIA's Analysis of Federal Taxes: Income
USTR References are to United States Tax Reporter: Income, Estate & Gift, and Excise
PCA References are to Pension Analysis (print & electronic)
PE References are to Pension Explanations (print & electronic)
EP References are to Estate Planning Analysis (print & electronic)

vice requirement, see above) (Code Sec. 168(k)(2)(B)(i)(I) as amended by 2008 Economic Stimulus Act §103(c)(1))

> 🅡🅐 *observation:*   Under pre-2008 Economic Stimulus Act law, Code Sec. 168(k)(2)(B)(i)(I) omitted the requirement that long-production-period property must satisfy Code Sec. 168(k)(2)(A)(iv). It appears, based on the wording of Code Sec. 168(k)(2)(A)(iv), which refers to "property described in subparagraph (B)," that the omission was a typographical error corrected by the 2008 Economic Stimulus Act.

(2) has a recovery period of at least 10 years or is "transportation property" (see below), (Code Sec. 168(k)(2)(B)(i)(II))

(3) is subject to Code Sec. 263A (i.e., the uniform capitalization rules (UNICAP), see above), and (Code Sec. 168(k)(2)(B)(i)(III))

(4) meets the requirements of Code Sec. 263A(f)(1)(B)(iii) (which requires that property have an estimated production period exceeding 1 year and a cost exceeding $1,000,000, see FTC 2d/FIN ¶ L-5920; USTR ¶ 263A4.11; TaxDesk ¶ 456,020) (the estimated-production-period requirement). (Code Sec. 168(k)(2)(B)(i)(IV) as amended by 2008 Economic Stimulus Act §103(c)(2)) Thus, to qualify for the extended placed in service date for long-production-period property, the property is required to have an estimated production period exceeding one year and a cost exceeding $1 million. (Com Rept, see ¶ 5503)

> 🅡🅐 *observation:*   Under pre-2008 Economic Stimulus Act law, property could also satisfy the estimated-production-period requirement if it met the requirements of Code Sec. 263A(f)(1)(B)(ii) (which requires that property have an estimated production period exceeding two years, see FTC 2d/FIN ¶ L-5920; USTR ¶ 263A4.11; TaxDesk ¶ 456,020).

Where property is "qualified property" solely because it qualifies under Code Sec. 168(k)(2)(B)(i) (immediately above), the property is eligible for 50% bonus depreciation only to the extent of the adjusted basis attributable to manufacture, construction, or production before *Jan. 1, 2009.* (Code Sec. 168(k)(2)(B)(ii) as amended by 2008 Economic Stimulus Act §103(a)(3)) Thus, for long-production period property, the costs eligible for 50% bonus depreciation are limited to the portion of the basis that is properly attributable to costs incurred before Jan. 1, 2009. To determine these "eligible progress expenditures," rules similar to the rules in Code Sec. 46(d)(3), before its repeal by the Tax Reform Act of '86 (PL 99-514), apply, see FTC 2d/FIN ¶ L-17126; USTR ¶ 464.10. (Com Rept, see ¶ 5503).

"Transportation property" means tangible personal property used in the trade or business of transporting persons or property. (Code Sec. 168(k)(2)(B)(iii))

The rules for long-production-period property don't apply to any property described under the rules for "qualifying aircraft" (discussed below). (Code Sec. 168(k)(2)(B)(iv))

observation: The exclusion of qualifying aircraft from treatment as long-production-period property seems generally taxpayer-favorable because long-production-period property is subject to the pre-2009 basis limitation discussed above, but qualifying aircraft don't appear to be subject to any basis limitation.

"Qualified property" includes property ("qualifying aircraft") that (Code Sec. 168(k)(2)(C))

(1) meets the requirements of Code Sec. 168(k)(2)(A)(ii) (the original use requirement, see above), Code Sec. 168(k)(2)(A)(iii) (the timely acquisition requirement, see above) and Code Sec. 168(k)(2)(A)(iv) (the timely placement in service requirement, see above), (Code Sec. 168(k)(2)(C)(i) as amended by 2008 Economic Stimulus Act §103(c)(3))

observation: Under pre-2008 Economic Stimulus Act law, Code Sec. 168(k)(2)(C)(i) omitted the requirement that qualifying aircraft must satisfy Code Sec. 168(k)(2)(A)(iv). It appears, based on the wording of Code Sec. 168(k)(2)(A)(iv), which refers to "property described in subparagraph...(C)," that the omission was a typographical error corrected by the 2008 Economic Stimulus Act.

(2) is an aircraft which isn't "transportation property" (as defined in Code Sec. 168(k)(2)(B)(iii), see above), other than for agricultural or firefighting purposes; (Code Sec. 168(k)(2)(C)(ii))

observation: Because the aircraft referred to in Code Sec. 168(k)(2)(C)(ii) are, generally, aircraft not used in the trade or business of transporting persons or property (because the aircraft can't be "transportation property," see above), aircraft used by freight or passenger airlines to serve the public aren't aircraft that benefit from the placed-in-service rule discussed above. On the other hand, aircraft used by non-airlines to provide complimentary, business-related transportation to employees and other business contacts may benefit from the rule.

(3) is purchased, and the purchaser, at the time of the contract for purchase, made a nonrefundable deposit of the lesser of (Code Sec. 168(k)(2)(C)(iii))

FTC 2d References are to Federal Tax Coordinator 2d
FIN References are to RIA's Analysis of Federal Taxes: Income
USTR References are to United States Tax Reporter: Income, Estate & Gift, and Excise
PCA References are to Pension Analysis (print & electronic)
PE References are to Pension Explanations (print & electronic)
EP References are to Estate Planning Analysis (print & electronic)

. . . 10% of the cost, or (Code Sec. 168(k)(2)(C)(iii)(I))

. . . $100,000; and (Code Sec. 168(k)(2)(C)(iii)(II))

(4) has (Code Sec. 168(k)(2)(C)(iv))

. . . an estimated production period exceeding 4 months, and (Code Sec. 168(k)(2)(C)(iv)(I))

. . . a cost exceeding $200,000. (Code Sec. 168(k)(2)(C)(iv)(II))

> **⊘ observation:** IRS issued regs, reflecting the above rules and others, that interpret the timely placement in service requirement for "pre-2008 30% bonus depreciation property" and "pre-2008 50% bonus depreciation property." (FTC 2d/FIN ¶ L-9316 *et seq.*, ¶ L-9327 *et seq.*; USTR ¶ 1684.026, ¶ 1684.028; TaxDesk ¶ 269,346 *et seq.*, ¶ 269,357 *et seq.*) Presumably, the rules in these regs also apply to "qualified property."

Disqualifying transactions rule. "Qualified property" doesn't include any property if: (Code Sec. 168(k)(2)(E)(iv))

(1) the user of the property (as of the date on which the property is originally placed in service) or a person which is related (within the meaning of Code Sec. 267(b), see FTC 2d/FIN ¶ G-2707; USTR ¶ 2674.03; TaxDesk ¶ 227,904 or Code Sec. 707(b), see FTC 2d/FIN ¶ B-2016; USTR ¶ 7074.03; TaxDesk ¶ 584,514) to the user or to the taxpayer has a written binding contract in effect for the acquisition of that property at any time before *Jan. 1, 2008,* or (Code Sec. 168(k)(2)(E)(iv)(I) as amended by 2008 Economic Stimulus Act §103(a)(2))

(2) in the case of property manufactured, constructed, or produced for the user's or person's own use, the manufacture, construction, or production of the property began at any time before *Jan. 1, 2008.* (Code Sec. 168(k)(2)(E)(iv)(II))

Thus, property doesn't qualify for the 50% bonus depreciation if the user of the property or a related party wouldn't have been eligible for the 50% bonus depreciation if the user or the related party were treated as the owner. (Com Rept, see ¶ 5503)

> *Illustration (4):* G sells to related party R property that was under construction before Jan. 1, 2008. The property doesn't qualify for 50% bonus depreciation. (Com Rept, see ¶ 5503)

> *Illustration (5):* H sells to related party R property that was subject to a binding written contract before Jan. 1, 2008. The property doesn't qualify for 50% bonus depreciation. (Com Rept, see ¶ 5503)

> *Illustration (5):* J sells property to K in a sale-leaseback in which J is the lessee and the property wouldn't have qualified for 50% bonus de-

preciation if it were owned by J. K, the lessor, isn't entitled to 50% bonus depreciation. (Com Rept, see ¶ 5503)

observation: IRS issued regs, reflecting the above rules and others, that interpret the disqualifying transaction rule for "pre-2008 30% bonus depreciation property" and "pre-2008 50% bonus depreciation property." (FTC 2d/FIN ¶ L-9315.2, ¶ L-9326.2; USTR ¶ 1684.026, ¶ 1684.028; TaxDesk ¶ 269,345.2, ¶ 269,356.2) Presumably, the rules in these regs also apply to "qualified property."

Denial of other bonus depreciation. Under the 2008 Economic Stimulus Act, "qualified cellulosic biomass ethanol plant property" doesn't include property to which Code Sec. 168(k) (discussed above) applies. (Code Sec. 168(l)(4)(A) as amended by 2008 Economic Stimulus Act §103(c)(6))

observation: Thus, property to which Code Sec. 168(k) applies is eligible for only the bonus depreciation available for "qualified property" (see above) under Code Sec. 168(k), and not *both* the bonus depreciation available for qualified property under Code Sec. 168(k) *and* the bonus depreciation available, as discussed above, for qualified cellulosic biomass ethanol plant property (FTC 2d/FIN ¶ L-9357; USTR ¶ 1684.081; TaxDesk ¶ 267,802) under Code Sec. 168(l).

Under the 2008 Economic Stimulus Act, "specified Gulf Opportunity Zone extension property" (specified GO Zone extension property) doesn't include property to which Code Sec. 168(k) applies. (Code Sec. 1400N(d)(6)(E) as amended by 2008 Economic Stimulus Act §103(c)(10))

observation: Thus, property to which Code Sec. 168(k) applies is eligible for only the bonus depreciation available for "qualified property" under Code Sec. 168(k), and not *both* the bonus depreciation available for qualified property under Code Sec. 168(k) *and* the bonus depreciation available for specified GO Zone extension property under Code Sec. 1400N(d).

Specified GO Zone extension property is a subcategory of "qualified GO Zone property" (see above). Specified GO Zone extension property is qualified GO Zone property that is placed in service in the portions of the GO Zone most damaged by Hurricane Katrina and meets certain other requirements. (FTC 2d/FIN ¶ L-9337.8; USTR ¶ 14,00N4.021; TaxDesk ¶ 269,332.1).

FTC 2d References are to Federal Tax Coordinator 2d
FIN References are to RIA's Analysis of Federal Taxes: Income
USTR References are to United States Tax Reporter: Income, Estate & Gift, and Excise
PCA References are to Pension Analysis (print & electronic)
PE References are to Pension Explanations (print & electronic)
EP References are to Estate Planning Analysis (print & electronic)

🔴 *observation:* In enacting a no-double-bonus-depreciation rule that is limited to qualified GO Zone property that is specified GO Zone extension property, Congress apparently assumed that "regular" qualified GO Zone property can't be "qualified property" because it must be either (1) placed in service before Jan. 1, 2008, see FTC 2d/FIN ¶ L-9337.7; USTR ¶ 14,00N4.021; TaxDesk ¶ 269,332—in which case it can't be "qualified property" within the meaning of Code Sec. 168(k) because it is used and acquired before Jan. 1, 2008 (see above)—or (2) placed in service before Jan. 1, 2009, see FTC 2d/FIN ¶ L-9337.7; USTR ¶ 14,00N4.021; TaxDesk ¶ 269,332—in which case it can't be "qualified property" within the meaning of Code Sec. 168(k) because it must be residential rental property or nonresidential real property, which are two types of property that Congress apparently assumed never satisfy the type of property requirement (see above) for "qualified property" within the meaning of Code Sec. 168(k). However, qualified leasehold improvements are a type of property that satisfies the type of property requirement for "qualified property" within the meaning of Code Sec. 168(k) and *are* also residential rental property or nonresidential real property. Thus, they are, arguably, eligible for the pre-Jan. 1, 2009 placed-in-service deadline. For discussion of this position, see FTC 2d/FIN ¶ L-9337.7; USTR ¶ 14,00N4.021. Thus, qualified leasehold improvements are, arguably, eligible for bonus depreciation as both "qualified property" and as "regular" "qualified GO Zone property." If that is so, the no-double-depreciation rule provided by Code Sec. 1400N(d)(6)(E) would fail to prevent double bonus depreciation for qualified leasehold improvements that are both "qualified property" and "regular" "qualified GO Zone property."

🔴 *observation:* Code Sec. 1400L(b)(2)(C)(i), which is unchanged by the 2008 Economic Stimulus Act, provides that "qualified New York Liberty Zone property" doesn't include property to which Code Sec. 168(k) applies, see FTC 2d/FIN ¶ L-9343; USTR ¶ 14,00L4.06; TaxDesk ¶ 267,703. Thus, consistent with the no-double-bonus-depreciation rules (above) provided by the 2008 Economic Stimulus Act for qualified cellulosic biomass ethanol plant property and specified GO Zone extension property, property to which Code Sec. 168(k) applies is eligible for only the bonus depreciation available under Code Sec. 168(k), and not *both* the bonus depreciation available under Code Sec. 168(k) *and* the bonus depreciation available, as discussed above, under Code Sec. 1400L(b), for qualified New York Liberty Zone property.

AMT computation and other rules that are revived but unchanged by the Act. There are no adjustments to the allowable amount of depreciation for purposes of computing a taxpayer's AMT with respect to property to which the provision (i.e., the bonus depreciation provision) applies. (Com Rept, see ¶ 5503)

> ♥ *observation:* The Committee Report statement reflects the fact that the rule that gives "qualified property" an exemption from the AMT depreciation adjustment is the same as the rule that exempted "pre-2008 30% bonus depreciation property" from the AMT depreciation adjustment.

> ♥ *observation:* Other rules that are the same for "qualified property" as for "pre-2008 30% bonus depreciation property" are (1) the listed property recapture rule (see above), (2) the rules for the "election-out" (except for the change discussed immediately below) and (3) the rules, discussed above, for computing the bonus depreciation and regular depreciation for qualified property (except for the change from 30% to 50%).

Clarification of "election-out" to reflect existence of only one category of qualified property. The 2008 Economic Stimulus Act deletes the last sentence of Code Sec. 168(k)(2)(D)(iii). That sentence read as follows: "The preceding sentence shall be applied separately with respect to property treated as qualified property by paragraph (4) and other qualified property." (Code Sec. 168(k)(2)(D)(iii) as amended by 2008 Economic Stimulus Act §103(c)(5)(B))

> ♥ *observation:* The "preceding sentence" referred to in the deleted sentence provides for, as discussed above, the "election out" of Code Sec. 168(k). "Paragraph (4)" is pre-2008 Economic Stimulus Act Code Sec. 168(k)(4), which, as discussed above, provided the category "pre-2008 50% bonus depreciation property" as a subcategory of "qualified property." Thus, the deletion of the last sentence of Code Sec. 168(k)(2)(D)(iii) conforms the "election-out" to the fact that, under the 2008 Economic Stimulus Act, there is only one, undivided category of qualified property. Because, under pre-2008 Economic Stimulus law, there was both "pre-2008 30% bonus depreciation property" and "pre-2008 50% bonus depreciation property," taxpayers had to separately make, for each type of property, the election-out of bonus depreciation, see FTC 2d/FIN ¶ L-9318, ¶ L-9329; USTR ¶ 1684.0291; TaxDesk ¶ 269,348, ¶ 269,359.

FTC 2d References are to Federal Tax Coordinator 2d
FIN References are to RIA's Analysis of Federal Taxes: Income
USTR References are to United States Tax Reporter: Income, Estate & Gift, and Excise
PCA References are to Pension Analysis (print & electronic)
PE References are to Pension Explanations (print & electronic)
EP References are to Estate Planning Analysis (print & electronic)

First-year passenger car depreciation. For the provision in the 2008 Economic Stimulus Act with respect to the first-year car depreciation limit increase for "qualified property," see ¶ 203.

Redesignations. Pre-2008 Economic Stimulus Act Code Sec. 168(l)(4)(A) and pre-2008 Economic Stimulus Act Code Sec. 168(l)(4)(B) (excluding certain property from being qualified cellulosic biomass ethanol plant property, see FTC 2d/FIN ¶ L-9357.1; USTR ¶ 1684.082; TaxDesk ¶ 267,803), and pre-2008 Economic Stimulus Act Code Sec. 168(l)(4)(C) (an "election-out" with respect to the tax benefits available for qualified cellulosic biomass ethanol plant property, see FTC 2d/FIN ¶ L-9358; USTR ¶ 1684.083; TaxDesk ¶ 267,809), have been redesignated as Code Sec. 168(l)(4)(B), Code Sec. 168(l)(4)(C) and Code Sec. 168(l)(4)(D) respectively. (2008 Economic Stimulus Act §103(c)(6))

☐ **Effective:** Property placed in service after Dec. 31, 2007, in tax years ending after Dec. 31, 2007 (2008 Economic Stimulus Act §103(d)), but only if, additionally, the property is (1) acquired by the taxpayer either (A) during calendar year 2008 (but only if no written binding contract for the acquisition was in effect before Jan. 1, 2008), or (B) under a written binding contract entered into during calendar year 2008 (Code Sec. 168(k)(2)(A)(iii)), and (2) placed in service before Jan. 1, 2009 (before Jan. 1, 2010 if the property is long-production period property (see above) or a qualifying aircraft (see above)). (Code Sec. 168(k)(2)(A)(iv))

¶ 54. First-year depreciation limit for passenger automobiles is increased by $8,000 if the passenger automobile is "qualified property"

Code Sec. 168(k)(2)(F)(i), as amended by 2008 Economic Stimulus Act § 103(c)(4)

Generally effective: Property acquired and placed in service during calendar year 2008

Committee Reports, see ¶ 5503

Code Sec. 280F(a) imposes dollar limits on the depreciation deductions (including deductions under the Code Sec. 179 expensing election) that can be claimed with respect to "passenger automobiles," as defined in Code Sec. 280F(d)(5), see FTC 2d/FIN ¶ L-10003; USTR ¶ 280F4; TaxDesk ¶ 267,603. Code Sec. 280F(a)(1)(A)(i) provides that the dollar limit for the first tax year in the automobile's recovery period is $2,560 and for the second tax year $4,100. Code Sec. 280F(d)(7) states that, in applying Code Sec. 280F(a), any dollar limits provided by Code Sec. 280F(a) must be adjusted annually to reflect changes in the automobile component of the Consumer Price Index (CPI), using Oct. '87 as the base period. Generally, for automobiles placed in service in 2007, the $2,560 limit for the first tax year in the automobile's recovery period, as adjusted to reflect the automobile component of the CPI, is $3,060, see FTC 2d/FIN ¶ L-10004; USTR ¶ 280F4; TaxDesk ¶ 267,601. For passenger automobiles built on a truck chassis ("qualifying trucks and vans") a different CPI component is used, and for 2007 the adjusted first-year limit is $3,260, see FTC 2d/FIN ¶ L-10004.4; USTR ¶ 280F4; TaxDesk ¶ 267,602.3. The limits are proportionally reduced to the extent that the automobile isn't exclusively used in business (the "non-business use rule"), see FTC 2d/FIN ¶ L-10004; USTR ¶ 280F4; TaxDesk ¶ 267,601.

Under pre-2008 Economic Stimulus Act law, for any passenger automobile that was "qualified property" that was "pre-2008 30% bonus depreciation property" (see ¶ 202), and, thus, eligible for 30% additional-first year depreciation ("30% bonus depreciation"), the above passenger automobile depreciation rules applied, except that Code Sec. 168(k)(2)(F) increased the otherwise applicable first-year limit by $4,600. The $4,600 increase wasn't indexed for inflation. The $4,600 increase didn't apply if the taxpayer elected not to apply Code Sec. 168(k) to the "class" of property eligible for 30% bonus depreciation to which the passenger automobile belonged. (FTC 2d/FIN ¶ L-10004.3; USTR ¶ 1684.0281; TaxDesk ¶ 267,602.1)

Under pre-2008 Economic Stimulus Act law, for any passenger automobile that was "qualified property" that was "pre-2008 50% bonus depreciation property" (see ¶ 202), and, thus, eligible for 50% additional-first year depreciation ("50% bonus depreciation"), the above passenger automobile depreciation rules applied, except that Code Sec. 168(k)(2)(F) increased the otherwise applicable first-year limit by $7,650. The $7,650 increase wasn't indexed for inflation. The $7,650 increase didn't apply if the taxpayer elected not to apply Code Sec. 168(k) to the "class" of property to which the passenger automobile belonged. (FTC 2d/FIN ¶ L-10004.2; USTR ¶ 1684.0281; TaxDesk ¶ 267,602.2)

New Law. The 2008 Economic Stimulus provides there is only one type of "qualified property," and that type is eligible for 50% bonus depreciation, see ¶ 202. The 2008 Economic Stimulus Act further provides that for "qualified property" the first-year limit on depreciation for passenger automobiles otherwise applicable under Code Sec. 280F(a)(1)(A)(i) is increased by $8,000 (Code Sec. 168(k)(2)(F)(i) as amended by 2008 Economic Stimulus Act §103(c)(4))

The $8,000 increase isn't indexed for inflation. (Com Rept, see ¶ 5503)

observation: For each calendar year, IRS calculates the CPI adjustments discussed above and, based on the calculation, announces the automobile depreciation limits that apply to cars placed in service in that

---

FTC 2d References are to Federal Tax Coordinator 2d
FIN References are to RIA's Analysis of Federal Taxes: Income
USTR References are to United States Tax Reporter: Income, Estate & Gift, and Excise
PCA References are to Pension Analysis (print & electronic)
PE References are to Pension Explanations (print & electronic)
EP References are to Estate Planning Analysis (print & electronic)

calendar year. IRS announced the limits for calendar year 2007 (see above), but has yet to do so for 2008. Thus, strictly for purposes of illustration, the illustrations below assume that the first-year depreciation limits for 2008 will be the same as for 2007.

🅡 illustration (1): On Oct. 15, 2008, T, a calendar year taxpayer, places a new car into service in his business. Assume that the car is "qualified property" (and an election-out doesn't apply to the car, see below). T is allowed first-year depreciation for 2008 of no more than $11,060 ($3,060 plus $8,000).

🅡 illustration (2): The facts are the same as in illustration (1) except that the vehicle that T places into service is a van that is a "qualifying truck or van" (see above). T is allowed first-year depreciation for 2008 of no more than $11,260 ($3,260 plus $8,000).

🅡 illustration (3): The facts are the same as in illustration (1), except that, in 2008, T uses the car 80% for business and 20% for personal activities. Because of the "non-business use rule" (above), T is allowed first-year depreciation for 2008 of no more than $8,848 (80% × $11,060).

🅡 observation: Property is "qualified property" if it satisfies the definitional requirements and isn't subject to certain ineligibility rules, see ¶ 202. As applied to passenger automobiles, the effect of these requirements and ineligibility rules is that in most, but not all, instances, a passenger automobile will be eligible for the $8,000 increase in the first-year depreciation limit, if (1) the automobile's original use begins with the taxpayer after Dec. 31, 2007, (2) the automobile is predominantly used by the taxpayer in his business, (3) the automobile is acquired by the taxpayer during calendar year 2008, and (4) the automobile is placed in service by the taxpayer during calendar year 2008, see ¶ 202. For the effect of an "election-out" on eligibility for the increase, see immediately below.

Effect of election-out.   Congress said that the $8,000 increase applies unless the taxpayer elects out of the increased deduction. (Com Rept, see ¶ 5503)

🅡 observation: The election referred to immediately above is the election, discussed above and at ¶ 202, to have Code Sec. 168(k) not apply to one or more "classes" of "qualified property." Thus, where that election is made with respect to the "qualified property" in the "class" of property (generally, 5-year MACRS property, see FTC 2d/FIN ¶ L-8205; USTR ¶ 1684.01; TaxDesk ¶ 266,205) to which a passenger automobile belongs, it is an election to not have any of the tax benefits available under Code Sec. 168(k) apply to that passenger automobile. These benefits include 50% bonus depreciation, exemption from the AMT depreciation adjustment (see ¶ 202) *and* the $8,000 increase in the first-year automobile depreciation limit.

☐ **Effective:** Property placed in service after Dec. 31, 2007 in tax years ending after Dec. 31, 2007 (2008 Economic Stimulus Act §103(d)) as long as the property is (1) acquired by the taxpayer during calendar year 2008 (but only if no written binding contract for the acquisition was in effect before Jan. 1, 2008, see ¶ 202), and (2) placed in service before Jan. 1, 2009 (see ¶ 202).

FTC 2d References are to Federal Tax Coordinator 2d
FIN References are to RIA's Analysis of Federal Taxes: Income
USTR References are to United States Tax Reporter: Income, Estate & Gift, and Excise
PCA References are to Pension Analysis (print & electronic)
PE References are to Pension Explanations (print & electronic)
EP References are to Estate Planning Analysis (print & electronic)

¶ 100. Alternative Minimum Tax

¶ 101. AMT exemption amounts for 2007 are increased to $44,350 for unmarrieds, to $66,250 for joint filers, and to $33,125 for marrieds filing separately

Code Sec. 55(d)(1)(A), as amended by 2007 Tax Increase Prevention Act § 2(a)(1)

Code Sec. 55(d)(1)(B), as amended by 2007 Tax Increase Prevention Act § 2(a)(2)

Generally effective: Tax years beginning in 2007

Committee Reports, see ¶ 5201

In computing the alternative minimum tax (AMT) for individuals, the AMT tax rate is applied against the taxpayer's alternative minimum taxable income (AMTI), as reduced by the taxpayer's exemption amount (which phases out for AMTI above certain threshold levels). Pre-2007 Tax Increase Prevention Act law provided the following AMT exemption amounts for tax years beginning in 2007:

. . . $33,750 for unmarried individuals who aren't surviving spouses;

. . . $45,000 for married couples filing jointly and surviving spouses; and

. . . $22,500 (technically, 50% of the joint return/surviving spouse amount) for married individuals filing separately.

For tax years beginning in 2006, the AMT exemption amounts were:

- $42,500 for unmarried individuals who weren't surviving spouses;

- $62,550 for married couples filing jointly and surviving spouses; and

- $31,275 for marrieds filing separately.

The higher amounts for 2006 reflected the temporary increases provided by 2005 Tax Increase Prevention Act § 301 (Sec. 301, PL 109-222, 5/17/2006) as part of an AMT "patch" to reduce the number of individuals who otherwise would be subject to the AMT. (Similar patches were enacted by 2001 Economic Growth and Tax Relief Reconciliation Act § 701 (Sec. 701, PL 107-16, 6/7/2001), as amended by 2003 Jobs and Growth Act § 106 (Sec. 106, PL 108-27, 5/28/2003) and 2004 Working Families Act § 103 (Sec. 103, PL 108-311, 10/4/2004).) Under pre-2007 Tax Increase Prevention Act law, the temporary in-

---

FTC 2d References are to Federal Tax Coordinator 2d

FIN References are to RIA's Analysis of Federal Taxes: Income

USTR References are to United States Tax Reporter: Income, Estate & Gift, and Excise

PCA References are to Pension Analysis (print & electronic)

PE References are to Pension Explanations (print & electronic)

EP References are to Estate Planning Analysis (print & electronic)

creases expired after 2006. (FTC 2d/FIN ¶ A-8162; USTR ¶ 554.01; TaxDesk ¶ 691,302)

New Law. For tax years beginning in 2007, the 2007 Tax Increase Prevention Act increases the AMT exemption amounts as follows (rather than allowing them to decrease to pre-"patch" levels):

. . . to $66,250 (up from $62,550 in 2006) for married couples filing a joint return and surviving spouses (Code Sec. 55(d)(1)(A) as amended by 2007 Tax Increase Prevention Act §2(a)(1));

. . . to $44,350 (up from $42,500 in 2006) for an individual who isn't married or a surviving spouse (Code Sec. 55(d)(1)(B) as amended by 2007 Tax Increase Prevention Act §2(a)(2));

. . . to $33,125 (up from $31,275 in 2006) for married individuals filing separate returns. (Com Rept, see ¶ 5201)

> *observation:* The 2007 Tax Increase Prevention Act doesn't change the rule that the AMT exemption amount for married individuals filing separately is 50% of the AMT exemption amount for joint filers and surviving spouses (see FTC 2d/FIN ¶ A-8162; USTR ¶ 554.01; TaxDesk ¶ 691,302). Thus, although the 2007 Tax Increase Prevention Act doesn't specifically provide an increased AMT exemption amount for married individuals filing separately in 2007, the exemption amount for those individuals is effectively increased for 2007, because the joint return/surviving spouse exemption amount is increased to $66,250. That is, the AMT exemption amount for married individuals filing separately is increased to $33,125 (50% × $66,250) for 2007. Under pre-2007 Tax Increase Prevention Act law, their AMT exemption amount would have dropped to $22,500 in 2007.

> *observation:* In addition to increasing the individual AMT exemption amounts for 2007, 2007 Tax Increase Prevention Act § 2 also has the effect of postponing for one year the reductions in those amounts that, under pre-2007 Tax Increase Prevention Act law, were scheduled to go into effect for tax years beginning after 2006. Thus, these reductions are now scheduled to go into effect for tax years beginning after 2007, i.e., for 2008 and later years.

> *observation:* In other words, 2007 Tax Increase Prevention Act § 2 provides a one-year "patch" for the individual AMT exemption amounts.

For the one-year extension of the rule allowing nonrefundable personal credits to offset AMT (as well as regular tax), see ¶ 102.

⚫) *observation:* Individuals may be entitled to further AMT-related tax relief under the AMT refundable credit rules. Those rules, enacted by the 2006 Tax Relief Act, allow individuals with unused minimum tax credits that are more than three years old to get a partial refund (see FTC 2d/FIN ¶ A-8808; USTR ¶ 534; TaxDesk ¶ 691,508). The 2007 Technical Corrections Act revised the AMT refundable credit rules to allow eligible taxpayers a credit for at least $5,000 a year for five years. For a discussion of the revised credit, see ¶ 103.

The impact of 2007 Tax Increase Prevention Act § 2 can be seen in the following table:

AMT Exemption Amount

	2007 Tax Increase Prevention Act			Pre-2007 Tax Increase Prevention Act		
	Unmarried	Joint	Married Filing Separate	Unmarried	Joint	Married Filing Separate
2006	$42,500	$62,550	$31,275	$42,500	$62,550	$31,275
2007	$44,350	$66,250	$33,125	$33,750	$45,000	$22,500
2008	$33,750	$45,000	$22,500	$33,750	$45,000	$22,500

⚫) *observation:* Congress's intent in enacting the "patch" is to minimize the "spread" of AMT liability to increasing numbers of taxpayers. However, given the enormous complexity of the AMT, the determination as to whether an individual has AMT liability still must be made on an individual basis.

Kiddie tax AMT exemption amount. For a child subject to the "kiddie tax" (i.e., a child under age 18 with unearned income over $1,700 for 2007, see FTC 2d/FIN ¶ A-1300 *et seq.*; USTR ¶ 14.09; TaxDesk ¶ 568,300 *et seq.*), the AMT exemption amount can't exceed the sum of the child's earned income plus $6,300 in 2007. In addition, the kiddie tax AMT exemption can't be more than the child's regular AMT exemption (the unmarried individual's exemption amount, discussed above). (FTC 2d/FIN ¶ A-8163; USTR ¶ 594; TaxDesk ¶ 691,303)

⚫) *observation:* The 2007 Small Business Act expanded the kiddie tax rules so that, in addition to children under age 18, they also apply to children age 18, and children age 19 to 23 who are full-time students,

---

FTC 2d References are to Federal Tax Coordinator 2d
FIN References are to RIA's Analysis of Federal Taxes: Income
USTR References are to United States Tax Reporter: Income, Estate & Gift, and Excise
PCA References are to Pension Analysis (print & electronic)
PE References are to Pension Explanations (print & electronic)
EP References are to Estate Planning Analysis (print & electronic)

whose earned income doesn't exceed one-half of the amount of their support. The expanded rules are effective for tax years beginning after May 25, 2007; thus, they don't apply in 2007. (See FTC 2d/FIN ¶ A-1301; USTR ¶ 14.09; TaxDesk ¶ 568,301) This means that for 2007, the year for which 2007 Tax Increase Prevention Act § 102 increases the AMT exemption amounts, the kiddie tax applies only to a child under age 18 with unearned income over $1,700.

☑ observation: As stated above, the unmarried individual's exemption amount is $44,350 for tax years beginning in 2007. Thus, the child's exemption amount for 2007 is $44,350. This means that in 2007, a child subject to the kiddie tax may have up to $38,050 of earned income (earned income + $6,300 = $44,350 or $44,350 − $6,300 = $38,050) without being subject to the AMT.

AMT exemption amount for estates and trusts.

☑ observation: The 2007 Tax Increase Prevention Act doesn't change the $22,500 exemption amount for an estate or trust (see FTC 2d/FIN ¶ A-8164; USTR ¶ 554.01; TaxDesk ¶ 691,304).

Phase-out of AMT exemption amount.

☑ observation: The 2007 Tax Increase Prevention Act doesn't change the phase-out rules for the AMT exemption amount. Under those rules, the AMT exemption amount is reduced by an amount equal to 25% of the amount by which the individual's AMTI (FTC 2d/FIN ¶ A-8101; USTR ¶ 554.01; TaxDesk ¶ 691,301) exceeds the following threshold amounts:

. . . $112,500 for unmarried individuals,

. . . $150,000 for married individuals filing a joint return and surviving spouses, and

. . . $75,000 for married individuals filing separate returns. (FTC 2d/FIN ¶ A-8162; USTR ¶ 554.01; TaxDesk ¶ 691,302)

Under these rules, the exemption is completely phased-out at an AMTI dollar amount equal to:

Applicable phase-out threshold + (4 × applicable exemption amount).

☑ observation: Thus, the AMT exemption for 2007 completely phases-out (i.e., the taxpayer is subject to AMT on *all* of his AMTI), at the following AMTI levels:

- $289,900 ($112,500 + $177,400 [4 × $44,350]) for an individual who isn't married and isn't a surviving spouse,

- $415,000 ($150,000 + $265,000 [4 × $66,250]) for married individuals filing jointly or for a surviving spouse, and

- $207,500 ($75,000 + $132,500 [4 × $33,125]) for a married individual filing separately.

Post-2007 AMT exemption amounts.

observation: Absent future legislation (e.g., an extension of the one-year AMT "patch"), the reduction in the AMT exemption amounts that, under pre-2007 Tax Increase Prevention Act law, was scheduled to apply to tax years beginning after 2006, will apply to tax years beginning after 2007. This means that in 2008, without further "patches," or broader changes to the AMT generally, the AMT exemption amounts will drop as follows:

. . . to $33,750 for unmarried individuals who aren't surviving spouses;

. . . to $45,000 for married couples filing jointly and surviving spouses; and

. . . to $22,500 for marrieds filing separately.

observation: The tax forms that IRS has already issued for 2007 don't reflect the AMT exemption amount increases provided by the 2007 Tax Increase Prevention Act. IRS announced in a News Release (IR-2007-209, 12/27/2007) that it has posted updated copies of all affected forms on its website (IRS.gov), and that it has created a special section on IRS.gov to provide taxpayers with additional information.

☐ **Effective:** Tax years beginning after 2006 (2007 Tax Increase Prevention Act §2(b)), but only tax years beginning in 2007. (Code Sec. 55(d)(1)) (Com Rept, see ¶ 5201)

observation: Although 2007 Tax Increase Prevention Act § 2(b) provides that the increased AMT exemption amounts apply for "tax years beginning after Dec. 31, 2006," Act § 2(a) amends Code Sec. 55(d)(1) so that the increased exemptions apply only for 2007. That is, the AMT exemption amounts the Act prescribes for 2007 don't apply in tax years beginning after 2007.

FTC 2d References are to Federal Tax Coordinator 2d
FIN References are to RIA's Analysis of Federal Taxes: Income
USTR References are to United States Tax Reporter: Income, Estate & Gift, and Excise
PCA References are to Pension Analysis (print & electronic)
PE References are to Pension Explanations (print & electronic)
EP References are to Estate Planning Analysis (print & electronic)

◐ *observation:* 2007 Tax Increase Prevention Act § 2 increases the AMT exemption amounts for 2007, and so applies retroactively to tax years beginning on or after Jan. 1, 2007.

¶ 102. Nonrefundable personal credits may offset AMT through 2007 (instead of 2006)

Code Sec. 26(a)(2), as amended by 2007 Tax Increase Prevention Act § 3(a)(1)
  Code Sec. 21, 2007 Tax Increase Prevention Act § 3(a)(1)
  Code Sec. 22, 2007 Tax Increase Prevention Act § 3(a)(1)
  Code Sec. 23, 2007 Tax Increase Prevention Act § 3(a)(1)
  Code Sec. 24, 2007 Tax Increase Prevention Act § 3(a)(1)
  Code Sec. 25, 2007 Tax Increase Prevention Act § 3(a)(1)
  Code Sec. 25A, 2007 Tax Increase Prevention Act § 3(a)(1)
  Code Sec. 25B, 2007 Tax Increase Prevention Act § 3(a)(1)
  Code Sec. 25C, 2007 Tax Increase Prevention Act § 3(a)(1)
  Code Sec. 25D, 2007 Tax Increase Prevention Act § 3(a)(1)
  Code Sec. 1400C, 2007 Tax Increase Prevention Act § 3(a)(1)
  Code Sec. 904(i), 2007 Tax Increase Prevention Act § 3(a)(1)
  Generally effective: Tax years beginning in 2007
  Committee Reports, see ¶ 5201

Individuals may qualify for a number of nonrefundable personal tax credits (e.g., the dependent care credit, the credit for the elderly and disabled, the adoption credit, the child tax credit, the credit for interest on certain home mortgages, the HOPE Scholarship and Lifetime Learning credits, and the D.C. homebuyer's credit). However, for tax years beginning in 2000–2006, the nonrefundable personal tax credits listed below are subject to a limitation based on tax liability. Under Code Sec. 26(a)(2), these credits are allowed only to the extent that the aggregate amount of the credits doesn't exceed the sum of:

. . . the taxpayer's regular tax liability (FTC 2d/FIN ¶ L-18103; USTR ¶ 264.01; TaxDesk ¶ 569,604) for the tax year, reduced by the foreign tax credit allowable under Code Sec. 27(a), and

. . . the alternative minimum tax (AMT) imposed by Code Sec. 55(a) for the tax year (i.e., the excess of the tentative minimum tax over the regular tax, see FTC 2d/FIN ¶ A-8801; USTR ¶ 554.01; TaxDesk ¶ 691,001).

◐ *observation:* A taxpayer is subject to the AMT if his "tentative minimum tax liability" for the tax year is greater than his regular tax liability for the tax year. The AMT equals the amount of that excess, if any (see FTC 2d/FIN ¶ A-8101; USTR ¶ 554.01; TaxDesk ¶ 691,001).

The Code Sec. 26(a)(2) AMT offset rule described above means that the specified nonrefundable personal credits may offset both the regular tax and the AMT. In other words, individual taxpayers may offset their entire regular tax liability and AMT tax liability by the nonrefundable personal credits. (Com Rept, see ¶ 5201)

The nonrefundable personal credits affected by the Code Sec. 26(a)(2) rule are:

(1) the Code Sec. 21 child and dependent care credit (see FTC 2d/FIN ¶ A-4300 *et seq.*; USTR ¶ 214; TaxDesk ¶ 569,300 *et seq.*);

(2) the Code Sec. 22 credit for the elderly and disabled (see FTC 2d/FIN ¶ A-4100 *et seq.*; USTR ¶ 224; TaxDesk ¶ 568,700 *et seq.*);

(3) the Code Sec. 23 adoption expense credit (see FTC 2d/FIN ¶ A-4400 *et seq.*; USTR ¶ 234; TaxDesk ¶ 569,500 *et seq.*);

(4) the Code Sec. 24 child tax credit (see FTC 2d/FIN ¶ A-4050 *et seq.*; USTR ¶ 244; TaxDesk ¶ 569,100 *et seq.*);

(5) the Code Sec. 25 credit for interest paid or accrued on certain home mortgages of low-income persons (the mortgage credit certificate (MCC) credit), see FTC 2d/FIN ¶ A-4008; USTR ¶ 254.01; TaxDesk ¶ 568,507);

(6) the Code Sec. 25A credit for higher education expenses (the Hope credit and the Lifetime Learning credit, see FTC 2d/FIN ¶ A-4500 *et seq.*; USTR ¶ 25A4; TaxDesk ¶ 568,900 *et seq.*);

(7) the Code Sec. 25B credit for elective deferrals and IRA contributions (the saver's credit, see FTC 2d/FIN ¶ A-4450 *et seq.*; USTR ¶ 25B4; TaxDesk ¶ 569,200 *et seq.*);

(8) the Code Sec. 25C nonbusiness energy property credit for energy-efficient improvements to a principal residence (see FTC 2d/FIN ¶ A-4750 *et seq.*; USTR ¶ 25C4; TaxDesk ¶ 569,550 *et seq.*);

(9) the Code Sec. 25D residential energy efficient property (REEP) credit for photovoltaic, solar hot water, and fuel cell property added to a residence (see FTC 2d/FIN ¶ A-4780 *et seq.*; USTR ¶ 25D4; TaxDesk ¶ 569,560 *et seq.*); and

(10) the Code Sec. 1400C first-time homebuyer credit for the District of Columbia (the "first-time D.C. homebuyer credit," see FTC 2d/FIN ¶ A-4250 *et seq.*; USTR ¶ 1400C4; TaxDesk ¶ 568,800 *et seq.*).

Under pre-2007 Tax Increase Prevention Act law, the Code Sec. 26(a)(2) AMT offset rule was scheduled to cease to apply for tax years beginning after 2006. Instead, for those tax years, the nonrefundable personal tax credits listed

---

FTC 2d References are to Federal Tax Coordinator 2d
FIN References are to RIA's Analysis of Federal Taxes: Income
USTR References are to United States Tax Reporter: Income, Estate & Gift, and Excise
PCA References are to Pension Analysis (print & electronic)
PE References are to Pension Explanations (print & electronic)
EP References are to Estate Planning Analysis (print & electronic)

above—except for the Code Sec. 23 adoption expense credit (item (3) above), the Code Sec. 24 child tax credit (item (4) above), and the Code Sec. 25B saver's credit (item (7) above)—were to be subject to a limitation prescribed by Code Sec. 26(a)(1). The credits subject to Code Sec. 26(a)(1)—collectively, the "Code Sec. 26(a)(1) limitation credits"—were to be allowed to the extent that the aggregate amount of those credits didn't exceed the excess of:

. . . the taxpayer's regular tax liability (FTC 2d/FIN ¶ L-18103; USTR ¶ 264.01; TaxDesk ¶ 569,604) for the tax year, over

. . . the taxpayer's tentative minimum tax for the tax year, determined under Code Sec. 55(b)(1) (FTC 2d/FIN ¶ A-8801; USTR ¶ 554.01; TaxDesk ¶ 691,001), but without regard to the AMT foreign tax credit (FTC 2d/FIN ¶ A-8181 *et seq.*; USTR ¶ 594; TaxDesk ¶ 691,401 *et seq.*).

> **RIA** *observation:* Under the post-2006 rule discussed above, the AMT could indirectly limit a taxpayer's nonrefundable personal tax credits even in situations where the taxpayer wasn't liable for the AMT. See FTC 2d/FIN ¶ A-8320; USTR ¶ 264.

Under pre-2007 Tax Increase Prevention Act law, for tax years beginning after 2006, the Code Sec. 23 adoption expense credit (item (3) above), the Code Sec. 24 child tax credit (item (4) above), and the Code Sec. 25B saver's credit (item (7) above) were to be subject to separate limitations that allowed those credits to offset both regular tax and AMT. (FTC 2d/FIN ¶ A-4405, ¶ A-4054, ¶ A-4455, ¶ A-8320; USTR ¶ 234, ¶ 244.01, ¶ 25B4; TaxDesk ¶ 569,505, ¶ 569,104, ¶ 569,205)

New Law. The 2007 Tax Increase Prevention Act extends the Code Sec. 26(a)(2) AMT offset rule to apply to tax years beginning in 2007. (Code Sec. 26(a)(2) as amended by 2007 Tax Increase Prevention Act §3(a)(1)) This means that for tax years beginning in 2007, the nonrefundable personal credits may offset AMT as well as regular tax. (Com Rept, see ¶ 5201)

Specifically, for tax years beginning in 2007 (as well as in 2000 through 2006), the aggregate amount of personal nonrefundable credits may not exceed the sum of:

. . . the taxpayer's regular tax liability (FTC 2d/FIN ¶ L-18103; USTR ¶ 264.01; TaxDesk ¶ 569,604) for the tax year, reduced by the foreign tax credit allowable under Code Sec. 27(a), and

. . . the tax imposed by Code Sec. 55(a) (Code Sec. 26(a)(2))—i.e., the AMT (see FTC 2d/FIN ¶ A-8101; USTR ¶ 554.01; TaxDesk ¶ 691,002).

> **RIA** *observation:* This means that in 2007 (as was the case in 2006), all of the otherwise allowable nonrefundable personal credits—i.e., not just the adoption credit, child tax credit, and saver's credit—may be used to

reduce AMT (as well as regular tax). This is because the maximum amount of total nonrefundable personal credits that a taxpayer may claim in 2007 can't exceed the sum of: (1) his regular tax liability (reduced by the foreign tax credit) for 2007, plus (2) his AMT liability for 2007. Under this rule, the taxpayer may claim up to the amount of that sum (i.e., regular tax plus AMT) as nonrefundable personal credits.

observation: 2007 Tax Increase Prevention Act § 3 thus provides a one-year extension for the rule allowing all the nonrefundable personal credits to be used to reduce AMT (as well as regular tax). This provision is part of the one-year "patch" that the 2007 Tax Increase Prevention Act provides for individual AMT relief. In addition, the 2007 Tax Increase Prevention Act also increases the AMT exemption amounts for 2007. For a discussion of the increased AMT exemptions for 2007, see ¶ 101.

observation: By extending the Code Sec. 26(a)(2) AMT offset rule for one year, 2007 Tax Increase Prevention Act § 3(a)(1) provides a one-year postponement of the effective date for the limitations that, under pre-2007 Tax Increase Prevention Act law, applied after 2006. Those postponed limitations will apply after 2007 (see "Tax liability limitations on nonrefundable personal credits after 2007," below).

observation: A taxpayer is subject to the AMT if his "tentative minimum tax liability" for the tax year is greater than his regular tax liability for the tax year. The AMT equals the amount of that excess, if any (see FTC 2d/FIN ¶ A-83; USTR ¶ 554.01; TaxDesk ¶ 691,002).

illustration (1): In 2007, the Greens' regular tax is $8,000, and their tentative minimum tax is $7,200. Thus, they pay only the regular tax of $8,000. The Greens can claim up to $8,000 of nonrefundable personal credits for 2007. Under pre-2007 Tax Increase Prevention Act law, the amount of nonrefundable personal credits the Greens could claim for 2007 would have been limited to $800—i.e., the excess of $8,000 regular tax over $7,200 tentative minimum tax.

illustration (2): In 2007, the Whites' regular tax is $5,000, and their tentative minimum tax is $5,500. Thus, they must pay a regular tax of $5,000, plus an AMT of $500 (excess of $5,500 tentative minimum tax over $5,000 regular tax). The Whites can claim up to $5,500 of

FTC 2d References are to Federal Tax Coordinator 2d
FIN References are to RIA's Analysis of Federal Taxes: Income
USTR References are to United States Tax Reporter: Income, Estate & Gift, and Excise
PCA References are to Pension Analysis (print & electronic)
PE References are to Pension Explanations (print & electronic)
EP References are to Estate Planning Analysis (print & electronic)

nonrefundable personal credits for 2007 (the sum of their $5,000 regular tax and $500 AMT). Under pre-2007 Tax Increase Prevention Act law, the Whites couldn't have claimed any nonrefundable personal credits for 2007, because their regular tax ($5,000) didn't exceed their tentative minimum tax ($5,500).

🅡 *observation:* The rule allowing the nonrefundable personal credits to reduce the AMT (as well as regular tax) benefits middle income individuals who:

. . . have low taxable income (and thus a low regular tax), e.g., because of a large number of personal exemptions;

. . . are subject to the AMT because personal exemptions (as well as the standard deduction and certain itemized deductions) are not allowed in computing the AMT (see FTC 2d/FIN ¶s A-8305, A-8315; USTR ¶ 564,02; TaxDesk ¶s 697,005, 697,015); and

. . . have substantial nonrefundable personal credits such as the child tax credit and Hope and Lifetime Learning credits.

How extension of Code Sec. 26(a)(2) through 2007 affects other credit limitations and carryover rules.

🅡 *observation:* The statutory rules that provide for the limitations on and carryover of certain unused personal credits and the foreign tax credit include two sets of rules: (1) rules for tax years in which the personal credits are allowed against the AMT—i.e., tax years when Code Sec. 26(a)(2) applies, and (2) rules for tax years in which the credits are not so allowed. Thus, the one-year extension of the period in which the Code Sec. 26(a)(2) AMT offset rule applies to include 2007 also affects the carryover rules for certain credits in 2007.

Adoption credit. The adoption credit is subject to the tax liability limitation prescribed by Code Sec. 23(b)(4) in tax years when Code Sec. 26(a)(2) doesn't apply (see FTC 2d/FIN ¶ A-4405; USTR ¶ 234; TaxDesk ¶ 569,505). The extension of Code Sec. 26(a)(2) so that it applies in 2007 means that the adoption credit is subject to that limitation in 2007. (Code Sec. 26(a)(2))

🅡 *observation:* As noted above, the separate tax liability limitation on the adoption credit lets taxpayers use the credit to offset AMT as well as regular tax. Thus, the one-year extension of the Code Sec. 26(a)(2) limitation (which lets *all* the nonrefundable personal credits offset AMT as well as regular tax) for an additional year doesn't affect the AMT offset allowance for the adoption credit in 2007. However, Code Sec. 23(b)(4) has specific ordering rules which may reduce the amount of the allowable adoption credit.

Child tax credit. The child tax credit is subject to the tax liability limitation prescribed by Code Sec. 24(b)(3) in tax years when Code Sec. 26(a)(2) doesn't apply (see FTC 2d/FIN ¶ A-4054; USTR ¶ 244.01; TaxDesk ¶ 569,104). The extension of Code Sec. 26(a)(2) so that it applies in 2007 means that the child tax credit is subject to that limitation in 2007. (Code Sec. 26(a)(2))

> *observation:* As noted above, the separate tax liability limitation on the child tax credit lets taxpayers use the credit to offset AMT as well as regular tax. Thus, the one-year extension of Code Sec. 26(a)(2) (which lets *all* the nonrefundable personal credits offset AMT as well as regular tax) for an additional year doesn't affect the AMT offset allowance for the child tax credit in 2006. However, Code Sec. 24(b)(3) has specific ordering rules which may reduce the amount of the allowable child tax credit.

Saver's credit. The saver's credit is subject to the tax liability limitation prescribed by Code Sec. 25B(g) in tax years when Code Sec. 26(a)(2) doesn't apply (see FTC 2d/FIN ¶ A-4455; USTR ¶ 25B4; TaxDesk ¶ 569,205). The extension of Code Sec. 26(a)(2) so that it applies in 2007 means that the saver's credit is subject to that limitation in 2007. (Code Sec. 26(a)(2))

> *observation:* As noted above, the separate tax liability limitation on the saver's credit lets taxpayers use the credit to offset AMT as well as regular tax. Thus, the one-year extension of the Code Sec. 26(a)(2) rule (which lets *all* the nonrefundable personal credits offset AMT as well as regular tax) for an additional year doesn't change the AMT offset allowance for the saver's credit in 2007. However, Code Sec. 25B(g) has specific ordering rules which may reduce the amount of the allowable saver's credit.

MCC credit. If the MCC credit for any tax year exceeds the limitation under Code Sec. 26(a)(2) (or under Code Sec. 26(a)(1), if Code Sec. 26(a)(2) doesn't apply) for the tax year, reduced by the sum of the nonrefundable personal credits (other than the MCC credit, adoption credit, REEP credit, and D.C. first-time homebuyer credit) for the year, the excess is carried over to each of the next three years. (FTC 2d/FIN ¶ A-4010; USTR ¶ 254.01; TaxDesk ¶ 380,502)

> *observation:* The extension of Code Sec. 26(a)(2) so that it applies in 2007 means that the Code Sec. 26(a)(2) limitation is the starting point for determining the MCC credit carryover for 2007.

FTC 2d References are to Federal Tax Coordinator 2d
FIN References are to RIA's Analysis of Federal Taxes: Income
USTR References are to United States Tax Reporter: Income, Estate & Gift, and Excise
PCA References are to Pension Analysis (print & electronic)
PE References are to Pension Explanations (print & electronic)
EP References are to Estate Planning Analysis (print & electronic)

Residential energy efficient property (REEP) credit. If the REEP credit exceeds the limitation under Code Sec. 26(a)(2) (or under Code Sec. 26(a)(1), if Code Sec. 26(a)(2) doesn't apply) for the tax year, reduced by the sum of the other nonrefundable personal credits, the excess is carried over to the next tax year and added to the REEP credit for that year. (FTC 2d/FIN ¶ A-4781; USTR ¶ 25D4; TaxDesk ¶ 569,561)

> **observation:** The extension of Code Sec. 26(a)(2) so that it applies in 2007 means that the Code Sec. 26(a)(2) limitation is the starting point for determining the REEP credit carryover for 2007.

D.C. first-time homebuyer credit. If the D.C. first-time homebuyer credit exceeds the limitation under Code Sec. 26(a)(2) (or under Code Sec. 26(a)(1), if Code Sec. 26(a)(2) doesn't apply) for the tax year, reduced by the nonrefundable personal credits (other than the D.C. first-time homebuyer credit and the REEP credit), the excess is carried over to the next tax year and added to the D.C. first-time homebuyer credit allowable for that year. (FTC 2d/FIN ¶ A-4255; USTR ¶ 14,00C4; TaxDesk ¶ 568,805)

> **observation:** The extension of Code Sec. 26(a)(2) so that it applies in 2007 means that the Code Sec. 26(a)(2) limitation is the starting point for determining the D.C. first-time homebuyer credit carryover for 2007.

Foreign tax credit. For tax years to which Code Sec. 26(a)(2) doesn't apply, the U.S. tax liability against which an individual's foreign tax credit is taken is reduced by the sum of the nonrefundable personal credits (other than the adoption credit, child tax credit, and saver's credit) allowable for the year. (FTC 2d/FIN ¶ O-4401; USTR ¶ 9044.01; TaxDesk ¶ 393,001)

> **observation:** The extension of Code Sec. 26(a)(2) so that it applies in 2007 means that the above-described reduction isn't made in computing the foreign tax credit for 2007. Thus, in computing the foreign tax credit for 2007, an individual doesn't reduce his U.S. tax liability by the allowable nonrefundable personal credits (other than the adoption credit, child tax credit, and saver's credit). This, in turn, results in a larger foreign tax credit for 2007.

> **observation:** The tax forms that IRS has already issued for 2007 don't reflect the one-year extension of the Code Sec. 26(a)(2) offset rule provided by the 2007 Tax Increase Prevention Act. IRS announced in a News Release (IR-2007-209, 12/27/2007) that it has posted updated copies of all affected forms on its web site (IRS.gov), and that it has created a special section on IRS.gov to provide taxpayers with additional information.

IRS also advised that the late enactment of the AMT patch will have only a limited impact on the 2007 filing season. IRS says that it has been able to reprogram its systems to begin processing returns in mid-January (including those that include Form 6251, Alternative Minimum Tax - Individuals) for the vast majority of taxpayers. However, taxpayers will have to wait to file returns that include the following five forms:

. . . Form 8863 (Education Credits),

. . . Form 5695 (Residential Energy Credits),

. . . Form 1040A's Schedule 2 (Child and Dependent Care Expenses for Form 1040A Filers),

. . . Form 8396 (MCC Credit), and

. . . Form 8859 (D.C. First-Time Homebuyer Credit).

IRS has targeted Feb. 11, 2008 as the potential starting date for taxpayers filing electronically or on paper to begin submitting returns including the above-listed forms.

AMT not offset by alternative motor vehicle credit or qualified alternative vehicle fuel refueling credit. The Code Sec. 26(a) limitations don't apply to the alternative motor vehicle (AMV) credit (see FTC 2d/FIN ¶ L-18020 *et seq.*; USTR ¶ 30B4; TaxDesk ¶ 397,100 *et seq.*) or the Code Sec. 30C qualified alternative vehicle fuel (QAVF) refueling property credit (see FTC 2d/FIN ¶ L-18040 *et seq.*; USTR ¶ 30C4; TaxDesk ¶ 397,200 *et seq.*). The separate tax liability limitations that apply to those credits don't permit the use of the nonbusiness portion of either credit (i.e., any portion that doesn't relate to depreciable property) as an offset against AMT in 2007 (see FTC 2d/FIN ¶ L-18022; L-18042; USTR ¶ 30B4; 30C4; TaxDesk ¶ 397,102; 397,202).

observation: The 2007 Tax Increase Prevention Act doesn't make any changes to the separate tax liability limitations that apply to the AMV credit (see FTC 2d/FIN ¶ L-18022; USTR ¶ 30B4; TaxDesk ¶ 397,102) or the QAVF refueling property credit (see FTC 2d/FIN ¶ L-18042; USTR ¶ 30C4; TaxDesk ¶ 397,202), or otherwise provide for those credits to be used to offset AMT in 2007 (e.g., by making them subject to the general Code Sec. 26(a) limitations). Thus, as under pre-2007 Tax Increase Prevention Act law, the nonbusiness portions of these credits can't be used to reduce AMT in 2007. However, the in-

FTC 2d References are to Federal Tax Coordinator 2d
FIN References are to RIA's Analysis of Federal Taxes: Income
USTR References are to United States Tax Reporter: Income, Estate & Gift, and Excise
PCA References are to Pension Analysis (print & electronic)
PE References are to Pension Explanations (print & electronic)
EP References are to Estate Planning Analysis (print & electronic)

creased AMT exemption amounts that 2007 Tax Increase Prevention Act § 3 provides for 2007 (see ¶ 101) will allow some previously ineligible taxpayers to claim a larger portion of these credits in 2007.

Tax liability limitations on the nonrefundable personal credits after 2007. As discussed above, 2007 Tax Increase Prevention Act § 3(a)(1) extends the Code Sec. 26(a)(2) AMT offset rule so that it applies through 2007 (instead of through 2006).

observation: Absent another extension, for tax years beginning after 2007, the *nonrefundable personal credits other than the adoption credit, the child tax credit, and the saver's credit* will be subject to the limitation under Code Sec. 26(a)(1). The aggregate amount of those credits— collectively, the "Code Sec. 26(a)(1) limitation credits"—can't exceed the excess of: (a) the individual's regular tax liability, over (b) the individual's tentative minimum tax, determined without regard to the AMT foreign tax credit (see FTC 2d/FIN ¶ L-18101; USTR ¶ 264; TaxDesk ¶ 569,600).

illustration (3): In 2008, the Greens' regular tax is $7,400, their tentative minimum tax is $6,500, and they have a $1,200 Code Sec. 26(a)(1) limitation credit. Although they don't owe AMT, they are able to claim only $900 of the credits ($7,400 regular tax liability minus $6,500 tentative minimum tax).

observation: Absent another extension, for tax years beginning after 2007, the *adoption credit, child tax credit,* and *saver's credit* will be limited as follows:

(1) The *adoption credit* can't exceed the excess of: (a) the sum of regular tax liability plus AMT liability, over (b) the sum of nonrefundable personal credits other than the adoption credit, plus the foreign tax credit (see FTC 2d/FIN ¶ A-4405; USTR ¶ 234; TaxDesk ¶ 569,505).

(2) The *child tax credit* can't exceed the excess of: (a) the sum of regular tax liability plus AMT liability, over (b) the sum of nonrefundable personal credits other than the child tax credit and the adoption credit, plus the foreign tax credit (see FTC 2d/FIN ¶ A-4054; USTR ¶ 244.01; TaxDesk ¶ 569,104).

(3) The *saver's credit* can't exceed the excess of: (a) the sum of nonrefundable personal credits other than the saver's credit and the adoption credit, plus the foreign tax credit (see FTC 2d/FIN ¶ A-4455; USTR ¶ 25B4; TaxDesk ¶ 569,205).

illustration (4): For 2008, H and W, married taxpayers, have a regular tax liability of $2,100 and no AMT liability. Without taking into account any credit limitations, they are entitled to a $1,200 child tax credit and a $1,000 Code Sec. 26(a)(1) limitation credit. The sum of their regular tax plus AMT exceeds the sum of their nonrefundable personal credits other than the child tax credit by $1,100 ($2,100 − $1,000). They are thus entitled to claim only $1,100 of the child tax credit. They may claim the full amount of the Code Sec. 26(a)(1) limitation credit.

observation: As a result of the 2007 Tax Increase Prevention Act, the adoption credit, child tax credit, and saver's credit are the only nonrefundable personal credits that may reduce AMT liability in tax years beginning after 2007.

illustration (5): In 2008, the Browns' regular tax is $4,000, and their tentative minimum tax is $4,500. They have a $1,000 Code Sec. 26(a)(1) limitation credit and a $1,000 child tax credit. Because their tentative minimum tax exceeds their regular tax liability, they can't claim any Code Sec. 26(a)(1) limitation credit for the year. However, they can use the full $1,000 child tax credit. Thus, their total tax after the child tax credit is $3,500 ($4,000 regular tax, plus $500 AMT, reduced by the $1,000 child tax credit).

observation: The Code Sec. 26(a)(1) limitation that will be in effect after 2007 may reduce a taxpayer's nonrefundable personal tax credits even if the taxpayer has no AMT liability.

observation: The specific limitations on the adoption credit, the child tax credit, and the saver's credit that will apply after 2007 are similar to the Code Sec. 26(a)(2) AMT offset rule that, as a result of the 2007 Tax Increase Prevention Act extension, applies through 2007. Each of the specific limitations allows individuals to use the specific credit to offset their AMT liability. However, the post-2007 limitations for each credit have specific ordering rules which may reduce the amount allowable for these credits.

☐ **Effective:** Tax years beginning after Dec. 31, 2006 (2007 Tax Increase Prevention Act §3(b)), but only tax years beginning in 2007. (Code Sec. 26(a)(2)) (Com Rept, see ¶ 5201)

FTC 2d References are to Federal Tax Coordinator 2d
FIN References are to RIA's Analysis of Federal Taxes: Income
USTR References are to United States Tax Reporter: Income, Estate & Gift, and Excise
PCA References are to Pension Analysis (print & electronic)
PE References are to Pension Explanations (print & electronic)
EP References are to Estate Planning Analysis (print & electronic)

¶ 103. AMT refundable credit for individuals is revised to allow at least $5,000 a year for five years

Code Sec. 53(e)(2)(A), as amended by 2007 Technical Corrections Act § 2(a)

Generally effective: Tax years beginning after Dec. 20, 2006 and before Jan. 1, 2013

Committee Reports, see ¶ 5301

Individuals are subject to the alternative minimum tax (AMT) for a tax year if AMT liability (i.e., "tentative minimum tax" liability) exceeds regular income tax liability. The AMT is imposed on alternative minimum taxable income (AMTI), which is taxable income as modified by certain "preferences" and "adjustments." The adjustments include "deferral adjustments"—i.e., the denial of the regular-tax income deferral allowed for certain items. An example of a deferral adjustment is the AMT adjustment for incentive stock options (ISOs), which requires an individual who exercises an ISO to include the value of the stock so acquired, minus what he paid for it, in AMTI for the exercise year (even though the "bargain element" isn't subject to regular tax) unless he sells the stock in the same tax year. (See FTC 2d/FIN ¶ A-8303; USTR ¶ 564.02; TaxDesk ¶ 697,002.)

AMT attributable to deferral adjustments generates a minimum tax credit ("MTC" or "AMT credit") that can be used to reduce regular tax in a later year. Generally, the AMT credit for a year is subject to a limitation imposed by Code Sec. 53(c), and is nonrefundable. That is, any amount in excess of the Code Sec. 53(c) limitation can't be refunded, although the excess can be carried forward (but not back) indefinitely. (See FTC 2d/FIN ¶ A-8801 *et seq.*; USTR ¶ 534; TaxDesk ¶ 691,501 *et seq.*)

The Code provides some immediate AMT relief, in the form of the AMT refundable credit, for individuals with "long-term unused minimum tax credits (MTCs)"—i.e., unused MTCs from before the third tax year immediately preceding the tax year (see FTC 2d/FIN ¶ A-8811; USTR ¶ 534; TaxDesk ¶ 691,511). The individual's AMT credit for a tax year beginning after 2006 and before 2013 can't be less than the "AMT refundable credit amount" (defined below), and is subject to a phaseout if the individual's adjusted gross income (AGI) exceeds an annually-adjusted threshold amount. If the refundable AMT credit amount is more than the individual's regular tax liability, he or she can get a refund for the excess, but only up to the amount of the "extra" credit allowed under this rule. (See FTC 2d/FIN ¶ A-8808; USTR ¶ 534.01; TaxDesk ¶ 691,508.)

The AMT refundable credit was enacted partly in response to the hardships that resulted from the AMT adjustment for ISOs. The AMT an individual pays on the ISO income in the exercise year generates an MTC that can be used to reduce tax in a later year, e.g., when the stock is sold. (Com Rept, see ¶ 5301) (See FTC 2d/FIN ¶ A-8303; USTR ¶ 564.02; TaxDesk ¶ 697,002.)

Under pre-2007 Technical Corrections Act law, the AMT refundable credit amount was, before the AGI-based phaseout, equal to the greater of:

(1) the lesser of:

(a) $5,000, or

(b) the amount of the long-term unused MTC for the tax year;

or

(2) 20% of the amount of the long-term unused MTC for the year.

Thus, long-term unused MTCs used in computing the AMT refundable credit amount for a tax year didn't enter into the AMT refundable credit amount for another year so as to increase that year's AMT credit. (FTC 2d/FIN ¶ A-8809; USTR ¶ 534.01; TaxDesk ¶ 691,509)

New Law. The 2007 Technical Corrections Act increases the AMT refundable credit amount used in computing the refundable portion of the MTC allowed to individuals who have long-term unused MTCs for a tax year beginning after 2006 and before 2013. As a result of the Act, an individual's AMT refundable credit amount for a tax year—before any reduction resulting from the AGI-based phaseout rules (Com Rept, see ¶ 5301)—is the amount (not in excess of the long-term unused MTC for the tax year, see below) equal to the greater of (Code Sec. 53(e)(2)(A) as amended by 2007 Technical Corrections Act §2(a)):

(1) $5,000 (Code Sec. 53(e)(2)(A)(i))—the "$5,000 amount,"

(2) 20% of the long-term unused MTC for the tax year (Code Sec. 53(e)(2)(A)(ii))—the "20% figure," or

(3) the amount (if any) of the AMT refundable credit amount determined under Code Sec. 53(e) for the taxpayer's preceding tax year, as determined before any reduction resulting from the AGI-based phaseout rules (Code Sec. 53(e)(2)(A)(iii))—the "preceding year's credit amount."

> *Illustration (1):* J, an individual, has a long-term unused MTC for 2007 of $100,000. J has no other AMT credits. J's AGI for all tax years is less than the phaseout threshold amount. J's AMT refundable credit amount is $20,000 in 2007 (20% of the $100,000 long-term unused MTC for 2007), the same as under pre-2007 Technical Corrections Act law. (Com Rept, see ¶ 5301)

FTC 2d References are to Federal Tax Coordinator 2d
FIN References are to RIA's Analysis of Federal Taxes: Income
USTR References are to United States Tax Reporter: Income, Estate & Gift, and Excise
PCA References are to Pension Analysis (print & electronic)
PE References are to Pension Explanations (print & electronic)
EP References are to Estate Planning Analysis (print & electronic)

observation: In *Illustration (1)*, J's item (1) amount (his "$5,000 amount") is $5,000; his item (2) amount (his "20% figure") is $20,000 (20% × J's $100,000 long-term unused MTC for the tax year; and his item (3) amount (his "preceding year's credit amount") is zero because the preceding year is 2006 and the credit provisions came into effect in 2007. J's AMT refundable credit amount for 2007 is the largest of these three amounts, $20,000. (J would have been entitled to the same amount under pre-2007 Technical Corrections Act law, see above.)

observation: By providing that an individual's AMT refundable credit amount for a tax year is the greatest of items (1), (2), and (3) listed above, the 2007 Technical Corrections Act gives the individual an AMT refundable credit amount of at least $5,000 for a tax year, provided the individual's long-term unused MTC is at least $5,000.

observation: If an individual's long-term unused MTCs are included in his AMT refundable credit amount for a tax year, they're no longer "unused" and so must be subtracted from long-term unused MTC for the next tax year. Thus, if an individual has an AMT refundable credit amount for a tax year (Year 1) equal to 20% of his long-term unused MTC for the year (the "20% figure" under item (2), above), the individual must reduce his long-term unused MTC for the next year (Year 2) by 20%. Unless the individual has additional long-term unused MTCs for Year 2, his long-term unused MTC for that year will be 80% of the long-term unused MTC for Year 1. As a result, the "20% figure" for Year 2 is reduced to 20% of *80%* of the long-term unused MTC for Year 1. The AMT refundable credit amount for Year 1 (which equals 20% of *100%* of long-term unused MTC for Year 1) is greater than the Year 2 "20% figure," so the individual uses that amount—the "preceding year's credit amount" under item (3), above—as his AMT refundable credit amount for Year 2.

Illustration (2): Assume the same facts as in *Illustration (1)*. J's AMT refundable credit amount in 2008 is $20,000—i.e., the greater of:

(a) $5,000,

(b) $16,000 (20% of J's $80,000 long-term unused MTC for 2008 [$100,000 long-term unused MTC from 2007 reduced by $20,000 AMT refundable credit amount for 2007]), or

(c) $20,000 (AMT refundable credit amount for 2007).

Under pre-2007 Technical Corrections Act law, J's AMT refundable credit amount in 2008 would have been $16,000—i.e., the greater of:

(a) $5,000—i.e., the lesser of:

(i) $5,000, or

(ii) $80,000 (long-term unused MTC for 2008); or

(b) $16,000 (20% of $80,000 long-term unused MTC for 2008). (Com Rept, see ¶ 5301)

⊘ observation: An individual who claims an AMT refundable credit for a tax year (Year 1) is entitled to that same Year 1 credit amount for each of the next four tax years, even if he has no additional long-term unused MTCs. As described above, the 20% of long-term unused MTCs (the "20% figure") that enters into the credit amount for a tax year is subtracted from the next year's long-term unused MTCs (the "20% reduction"), so that the AMT refundable credit amount for the next year will be the "preceding year's credit amount" (i.e., the Year 1 credit amount). This will require another 20% reduction, again resulting in a "preceding year's credit amount" that's greater than the "20% figure." But since the "preceding year's credit amount" (i.e., the Year 1 credit amount) was used for Year 2, the "preceding year's credit amount" used in the Year 3 credit computation is actually the Year 1 credit amount. In other words, the "preceding year's credit amount" is always the Year 1 credit amount. Thus, the Year 1 credit amount is used again in Year 2, Year 3, Year 4 and Year 5, requiring successive 20% reductions in long-term unused MTC. Under this rule, an individual's long-term unused MTC will be reduced to zero after five years. Thus, he won't be entitled to any AMT refundable credit amount in Year 6.

Illustration (3): Assume the same facts as in *Illustration (1)*. J's AMT refundable credit amounts for 2007 through 2012 are as follows:

. . . for 2007—$20,000 (20% × $100,000 long-term unused MTC for 2007), because it's more than $5,000, reducing J's long-term unused MTC to $80,000;

. . . for 2008—$20,000 (2007 AMT refundable credit amount—the "preceding year's credit amount), because that amount is more than $16,000 (20% × $80,000) or $5,000, reducing J's long-term unused MTC to $60,000;

. . . for 2009—$20,000 (the "preceding year's credit amount"—i.e., the 2007 AMT refundable credit amount), because it's more than $12,000

FTC 2d References are to Federal Tax Coordinator 2d
FIN References are to RIA's Analysis of Federal Taxes: Income
USTR References are to United States Tax Reporter: Income, Estate & Gift, and Excise
PCA References are to Pension Analysis (print & electronic)
PE References are to Pension Explanations (print & electronic)
EP References are to Estate Planning Analysis (print & electronic)

(20% × $60,000) or $5,000, reducing J's long-term unused MTC to $40,000;

... for 2010—$20,000 (the "preceding year's credit amount"—i.e., the 2007 credit amount) because that amount is more than $8,000 (20% × $40,000) or $5,000, reducing J's long-term unused MTC to $20,000;

... for 2011—$20,000 (the "preceding year's credit amount"—i.e., the 2007 credit amount) because that amount is more than $4,000 (20% × $20,000) or $5,000, reducing J's long-term unused MTC to zero;

... for 2012—zero, because J has no long-term unused MTCs for 2012. (Com Rept, see ¶ 5301)

The impact of 2007 Technical Corrections Act § 2(a) can be seen in the following table (Com Rept, see ¶ 5301):

AMT Refundable Credit Amount
($100,000 long-term unused MTC for 2007)

Year	2007 Technical Corrections Act	Pre-2007 Technical Corrections Act
2007	$20,000 (20% x $100,000)	$20,000 (20% x $100,000)
2008	$20,000 (2007 amount)	$16,000 (20% x $80,000)
2009	$20,000 (2008 amount)	$12,800 (20% x $64,000)
2010	$20,000 (2009 amount)	$10,240 (20% x $51,200)
2011	$20,000 (2010 amount)	$8,192 (20% x $40,960)
2012	0	$6,554 (20% x $32,768)

observation: As may be seen from the above table, the 2007 Technical Corrections Act increases the AMT refundable credit amounts that individuals may claim in Years 2 through 5 over what they could have claimed under pre-2007 Technical Corrections Act law. The Act also accelerates the exhaustion of the individual's long-term unused MTC. Under pre-2007 Technical Corrections Act law, the amount of the credit decreased over the years, because it was equal to 20% of decreasing amounts of long-term unused MTC. But the lower credit amounts for Years 2 through 5 also meant that the individual wouldn't have exhausted his long-term unused MTCs by the end of Year 5 (2011 in the above table), so he could have claimed a credit in Year 6 (2012, in the above table). Thus, under pre-2007 Technical Corrections Act law, the credit was available for potentially longer periods.

observation: As described above, the AMT refundable credit amount determined for a tax year may be used for each of the next four tax years. Under Code Sec. 53(e)(2)(A)(i), an individual's AMT refundable credit amount for a tax year is at least $5,000 (assuming at least $5,000 long-term unused MTCs). This entitles the individual to an AMT refundable credit amount of at least $5,000 for each of five consecutive tax years—i.e., the year of the initial AMT refundable credit amount determination and the next four tax years. The individual's AMT refundable credit amount for each year in the five-year sequence would be more than $5,000 if his AMT refundable credit amount for the first year is more than $5,000—i.e., long-term unused MTC is more than $25,000 so that the "20% figure" is more than $5,000.

(RIA) observation: An individual's AMT liability for the tax year in which he exercises an ISO that's attributable to the AMT ISO adjustment generates an MTC. If the MTC isn't used in the next three tax years, it becomes a long-term unused MTC (see below). As such, it's used in computing the AMT refundable credit amount and so can give rise to a refund. The 2007 Technical Corrections Act lets the individual use that same MTC five times, to compute his AMT refundable credit amount for each of five consecutive tax years. Thus, although the individual still has to pay AMT when he exercises the ISO, the 2007 Technical Corrections Act grants him additional relief later on.

(RIA) illustration (4): In 2003, Employee E exercises ISOs for 10,000 shares of stock. E is not subject to regular tax on the exercise, but the exercise does generate a $200,000 MTC that E can use to reduce regular tax in a later year, e.g., when he sells the stock at a gain. If E doesn't use the full $200,000 MTC during 2004, 2005, or 2006, any unused portion enters into his long-term unused MTC for 2007. Thus, E can use the MTC generated by the ISO exercise in 2003 to generate, or increase, his AMT refundable credit for 2007. Assume E's $200,000 MTC from the 2003 ISO exercise results in a $200,000 long-term unused MTC for 2007. E's AMT refundable credit amount for 2007 is $40,000 (20% × $200,000). E's long-term unused MTC is reduced to $160,000 ($200,000 − $40,000 AMT refundable credit amount for 2007) for 2008. As occurred in *Illustration (3)*, above, E's $40,000 AMT refundable credit amount determined for 2007 becomes his "preceding year's credit amount"—and his AMT refundable credit amount—for 2008, 2009, 2010, and 2011.

(RIA) observation: The changes that 2007 Technical Corrections Act § 2(a) makes to the rules for computing the AMT refundable credit amount don't include any changes to the phaseout rule for high income individuals (see FTC 2d/FIN ¶ A-8810; USTR ¶ 534; TaxDesk ¶ 691,510).

FTC 2d References are to Federal Tax Coordinator 2d
FIN References are to RIA's Analysis of Federal Taxes: Income
USTR References are to United States Tax Reporter: Income, Estate & Gift, and Excise
PCA References are to Pension Analysis (print & electronic)
PE References are to Pension Explanations (print & electronic)
EP References are to Estate Planning Analysis (print & electronic)

Long-term unused minimum tax credit. The long-term unused MTC amount for a tax year is the portion of the MTC attributable to the adjusted net minimum tax (ANMT—i.e., the AMT paid for the year reduced by the amount of AMT that would have arisen without the deferral adjustments, plus certain other amounts, see FTC 2d/FIN ¶ A-8802; USTR ¶ 534; TaxDesk ¶ 691,502) for tax years before the third tax year immediately preceding the tax year (assuming the credits are used on a first-in, first-out [FIFO] basis—the "FIFO requirement"). (See FTC 2d/FIN ¶ A-8811; USTR ¶ 534.01; TaxDesk ¶ 691,511.) (Com Rept, see ¶ 5301)

> *observation:* In other words, the long-term unused MTC—and, therefore, the AMT refundable credit amount—for a tax year doesn't take into account any MTC for the three immediately preceding tax years. The MTC amounts for those three years are allowable under the "regular" MTC rules. This means that any unused amounts are carried over to later tax years, rather than refunded.

> *observation:* The FIFO requirement precludes individuals from using their MTCs from the immediately preceding three tax years before any MTCs from earlier years, to increase the amount of unused credits that could qualify as long-term unused MTCs so as to increase their AMT refundable credit.

> *observation:* The 2007 Technical Corrections Act doesn't change the rules for determining the long-term unused MTC amount used in computing the AMT refundable credit amount. However, in allowing an individual to use the same AMT refundable credit amount for five tax years, the 2007 Technical Corrections Act increases the individual's overall AMT refundable credit amount. As a result, the individual uses up more long-term unused MTCs. This means that the individual has fewer MTCs to use against regular income tax in later years under the nonrefundable MTC provisions.

> *observation:* As stated above, the AMT refundable credit is available in tax years beginning after 2006 and before 2013. Thus, since most individuals use the calendar year as their tax year, it's generally available in 2007 through 2012. Because the long-term unused MTC (and, therefore, the AMT refundable credit amount) for a tax year includes only unused MTCs that are more than three years old, AMT refundable credit won't be available with respect to AMT deferral adjustments for tax years after 2008.

> *observation:* In addition to the above revisions to the AMT refundable credit rules under the 2007 Technical Corrections Act, AMT relief is also provided to individuals under the 2007 Tax Increase Prevention

Act, but only for 2007. This one-year AMT "patch" has two components:

(1) An increase in the AMT exemption amounts for 2007, see ¶ 101; and

(2) A one-year extension of the rule allowing all the nonrefundable personal credits to be used to reduce AMT (as well as regular tax), so that the rule applies through 2007, see ¶ 102.

☐ **Effective:** Tax years beginning after Dec. 20, 2006 and before Jan. 1, 2013. (2007 Technical Corrections Act §2(b))

observation: 2007 Technical Corrections Act § 2(b) provides that the above provision is effective as if included in the provision of the 2006 Tax Relief Act to which it relates. The above rule relates to 2006 Tax Relief Act § 402 (Sec. 402, PL 109-432, 12/20/2006) which, under 2006 Tax Relief Act §402(c) (Sec. 402(c), PL 109-432, 12/20/2006) and the accompanying Committee Reports, is effective for tax years beginning after Dec. 20, 2006 and before Jan. 1, 2013.

¶ 200. Mortgage Related Relief

¶ 201. Discharges of up to $2 million of acquisition debt on taxpayer's main home in 2007 through 2009 are excluded from income

Code Sec. 108(a)(1)(E), as amended by 2007 Mortgage Relief Act § 2(a)
Code Sec. 108(a)(2)(A), as amended by 2007 Mortgage Relief Act § 2(c)(1)
Code Sec. 108(a)(2)(C), as amended by 2007 Mortgage Relief Act § 2(c)(2)
Code Sec. 108(h), as amended by 2007 Mortgage Relief Act § 2(b)
Generally effective: Discharges of indebtedness after Dec. 31, 2006, and
* before Jan. 1, 2010*
Committee Reports, see ¶ 5001

For income tax purposes, a discharge of indebtedness—that is, a forgiveness of debt—is generally treated as giving rise to income that's includible in gross income. (FTC 2d/FIN ¶ J-7001; USTR ¶ 614.114; TaxDesk ¶ 186,001) The amount of income generally equals the difference between the debt's adjusted issue price—i.e., the outstanding amount of the debt just prior to the discharge—and any amount paid to satisfy the debt. (FTC 2d/FIN ¶ J-7201; USTR ¶ 1084.04; TaxDesk ¶ 186,002)

However, a discharge of indebtedness doesn't give rise to gross income if it: (1) occurs in a Title 11 bankruptcy case, (2) occurs when the taxpayer is insolvent, (3) is a discharge of "qualified farm indebtedness," or (4) is a discharge of "qualified real property business indebtedness." (FTC 2d/FIN ¶ J-7401; USTR ¶ 1084.01; TaxDesk ¶ 188,011) Where these exceptions apply, taxpayers generally reduce certain tax attributes, including basis in property, by the amount of the excluded income. (FTC 2d/FIN ¶ J-7404; USTR ¶ 1084.02; TaxDesk ¶ 188,016)

Under pre-2007 Mortgage Relief Act law, there were no special rules applicable to discharges of acquisition debt on the taxpayer's principal residence.

> *Illustration (1):* A taxpayer who isn't in bankruptcy and isn't insolvent owns a principal residence subject to a $200,000 mortgage debt for which the taxpayer has personal liability. The creditor forecloses and the home is sold for $180,000 in satisfaction of the debt.
>
> Under pre-2007 Mortgage Relief Act law, the debtor had $20,000 of debt discharge income. The result was the same if the creditor restruc-

tured the loan and reduced the principal amount to $180,000. (Com Rept, see ¶ 5001)

New Law. The 2007 Mortgage Relief Act excludes from a taxpayer's gross income any discharge of indebtedness income by reason of a discharge (in whole or in part) of qualified principal residence indebtedness before Jan. 1, 2010. (Code Sec. 108(a)(1)(E) as amended by 2007 Mortgage Relief Act §2(a)) The exclusion applies where taxpayers restructure their acquisition debt on a principal residence or lose their principal residence in a foreclosure. (Com Rept, see ¶ 5001)

> *illustration (2):* The facts are the same as in *Illustration (1),* except that the discharge occurs in 2008. Under the 2007 Mortgage Relief Act, the debtor has no debt discharge income when the creditor (1) restructures the loan and reduces the principal amount to $180,000 or (2) forecloses with the result that the $200,000 debt is satisfied for $180,000.

"Qualified principal residence indebtedness" defined. "Qualified principal residence indebtedness" means acquisition indebtedness, as defined by Code Sec. 163(h)(3)(B) for purposes of the interest deduction rules, with respect to the taxpayer's principal residence, but with a $2 million limit ($1 million for married individuals filing separately) on the aggregate amount of debt that may be treated as qualified principal residence indebtedness. (Code Sec. 108(h)(2) as amended by 2007 Mortgage Relief Act §2(b))

Acquisition indebtedness with respect to an individual's principal residence generally means indebtedness that is incurred to acquire, construct, or substantially improve, and is secured by, that residence. (Com Rept, see ¶ 5001)

> *observation:* Thus, "qualified principal residence indebtedness" generally has the same meaning as "acquisition indebtedness," with these important differences:
>
> . . . Qualified principal residence indebtedness is limited to $2 million, or $1 million on a separate return. Acquisition indebtedness is limited to half these amounts—$1 million of aggregate debt, or $500,000 on a separate return. See FTC 2d/FIN ¶ K-5485; USTR ¶ 1634.052; TaxDesk ¶ 314,516.
>
> . . . Qualified principal residence indebtedness must be incurred with respect to the taxpayer's principal residence only. Acquisition indebtedness can be incurred with respect to the taxpayer's principal residence and one other residence. See FTC 2d/FIN ¶ K-5484; USTR ¶ 1634.052; TaxDesk ¶ 314,515.

⚫️ observation: The exclusion rule described above doesn't apply to second homes, vacation homes, business property, or investment property, since these properties aren't the taxpayer's principal residence.

The exclusion rule also doesn't apply to discharges of second mortgages or home equity loans, unless the loan proceeds were used to acquire, construct, or substantially improve the taxpayer's principal residence.

⚫️ observation: In some foreclosures, the taxpayer will have gain or loss from the sale or exchange of the property instead of, or in addition to, income from discharge of indebtedness. For example, when a recourse debt is discharged or reduced on the debtor's transfer of property, the transfer is treated as a sale or exchange of the property to the extent of the transferred property's fair market value (FMV). Any gain on this deemed sale or exchange—i.e., any excess of the property's FMV over its adjusted basis—is treated as taxable gain, not as discharge of indebtedness income. The amount of discharged debt in excess of the property's FMV is treated as discharge of indebtedness income. FTC 2d/FIN ¶ J-7206; TaxDesk ¶ 186,005.

Illustration (3): As a result of nonpayment of a recourse mortgage, creditors foreclosed on taxpayers' home. At the time of the foreclosure, taxpayers' basis in the home was $170,000, the home's FMV was $200,000, and the outstanding amount of mortgage debt on the home was $220,000.

The foreclosure results in taxable gain of $30,000 and discharge of indebtedness income of $20,000, computed as follows:

Taxable gain from deemed sale or exchange. Taxpayers realizes $30,000 of gain from the deemed sale or exchange: $200,000 (home's FMV) − $170,000 (basis) = $30,000.

Discharge of indebtedness income. Taxpayers realizes $20,000 of discharge of indebtedness income: $220,000 (total outstanding indebtedness) − $200,000 (home's FMV) = $20,000. (IRS "Questions and Answers On Home Foreclosure and Debt Cancellation," IRS Fact Sheet HFDC, see FTC 2d/FIN ¶ I-2523.)

⚫️ observation: It's rare for a residential mortgage to be nonrecourse. If a homeowner whose home is foreclosed did have a nonrecourse mort-

---

FTC 2d References are to Federal Tax Coordinator 2d
FIN References are to RIA's Analysis of Federal Taxes: Income
USTR References are to United States Tax Reporter: Income, Estate & Gift, and Excise
PCA References are to Pension Analysis (print & electronic)
PE References are to Pension Explanations (print & electronic)
EP References are to Estate Planning Analysis (print & electronic)

gage, the transfer is treated as a sale or exchange of the property. The amount realized is the full amount of the debt, even if that is greater than the property's FMV. Because the discharged debt is treated as part of the amount realized, there's no discharge of indebtedness income. See FTC 2d/FIN ¶ J-7215; TaxDesk ¶ 186,029.

observation: To the extent that income on the foreclosure of a principal residence is treated as gain, it isn't eligible for the exclusion rule described above or for the bankruptcy or insolvency exclusions. However, all or part of the gain may be excludible from gross income under the Code Sec. 121 home-sale rules. See FTC 2d/FIN ¶ I-4521; USTR ¶ 1214; TaxDesk ¶ 225,701.

observation: A taxpayer who has had a debt discharge of $600 or more during the year should receive a Form 1099-C, Cancellation of Debt, from the lender by the following Feb. 28. The Form 1099-C is also filed with IRS. See FTC 2d/FIN ¶ S-4251; USTR ¶ 60,50P4; TaxDesk ¶ 816,008.

The form doesn't include enough information for the taxpayer to determine whether the discharge qualifies for the exclusion described above, e.g., whether the discharge relates to the taxpayer's principal residence. The taxpayer and the taxpayer's advisers must determine whether the exclusion applies.

Acquisition indebtedness also includes refinancing of an earlier acquisition indebtedness to the extent the refinancing doesn't exceed the refinanced indebtedness. (Com Rept, see ¶ 5001)

observation: The same rule applies to a refinancing of qualified principal residence indebtedness, i.e., it qualifies as qualified principal residence indebtedness to the extent it doesn't exceed the refinanced indebtedness.

"Principal residence" defined. For this purpose, "principal residence" has the same meaning as under the Code Sec. 121 home sale rules. (Code Sec. 108(h)(5))

observation: For Code Sec. 121 purposes, whether a property is the taxpayer's principal residence depends on the facts and circumstances. If a taxpayer alternates between two residences, the property that the taxpayer uses a majority of the time during the year is ordinarily the taxpayer's principal residence. (FTC 2d/FIN ¶ I-4522; USTR ¶ 1214; TaxDesk ¶ 225,702)

Portion of debt isn't qualified principal residence indebtedness. If only a portion of discharged indebtedness is qualified principal residence indebtedness immediately before the discharge, the exclusion rule discussed above applies only to so much of the amount discharged as exceeds the portion of the debt that isn't qualified principal residence indebtedness. (Code Sec. 108(h)(4))

observation: Under this rule, the portion of discharged indebtedness that *isn't* qualified principal residence indebtedness is treated as discharged first. The excludable amount is equal to the amount of discharged indebtedness minus the amount of indebtedness that isn't qualified principal residence indebtedness.

Illustration (4): A principal residence is subject to a recourse indebtedness of $1 million, of which $800,000 is qualified principal residence indebtedness. The residence is sold for $700,000 and $300,000 debt is discharged. Only $100,000 of the amount discharged is excludable from gross income under this provision. (Com Rept, see ¶ 5001)

observation: The $100,000 excludable amount in Illustration (4) is equal to the $300,000 of discharged debt minus the $200,000 portion of the original $1 million debt that wasn't qualified principal residence indebtedness.

Basis reduction required. The basis of the taxpayer's principal residence is reduced (but not below zero) by the amount excluded from income under the principal residence exclusion. (Code Sec. 108(h)(1))

observation: As a result of this basis reduction rule, the discharged indebtedness is—at least technically—not permanently excluded from income, but is subject to inclusion at a later time, when the taxpayer sells or exchanges the principal residence. However, in many cases the reduction won't result in any additional tax, because any gain on that sale or exchange will qualify for the Code Sec. 121 home-sale exclusion. See FTC 2d/FIN ¶ I-4521; USTR ¶ 1214; TaxDesk ¶ 225,701.

observation: It's unclear how, if at all, the basis reduction will be applied in case of a foreclosure, since the taxpayer no longer owns the foreclosed home. The Code doesn't specify the time at which the basis reduction is to be applied.

FTC 2d References are to Federal Tax Coordinator 2d
FIN References are to RIA's Analysis of Federal Taxes: Income
USTR References are to United States Tax Reporter: Income, Estate & Gift, and Excise
PCA References are to Pension Analysis (print & electronic)
PE References are to Pension Explanations (print & electronic)
EP References are to Estate Planning Analysis (print & electronic)

No exclusion where discharge was on account of services. The principal residence exclusion doesn't apply if the discharge of the loan was on account of services performed for the lender or any other factor not directly related to a decline in the residence's value or to the taxpayer's financial condition. (Code Sec. 108(h)(3))

> *illustration (5):* Where the debtor is employed by the lender, and the discharge of indebtedness relates to the employment services performed, the discharge won't qualify for the exclusion.

Coordination with bankruptcy and insolvency exceptions. The principal residence exclusion doesn't apply to a taxpayer in a Title 11 case. Instead, the Title 11 bankruptcy exclusion applies. (Code Sec. 108(a)(2)(A) as amended by 2007 Mortgage Relief Act §2(c)(1))

> *observation:* The basis-reduction rules for the bankruptcy exclusion are more extensive than those for the exclusion rule discussed above. In the case of bankruptcy, the debtor must reduce the following tax attributes: (1) net operating losses (NOLs) for and NOL carryovers to the discharge year; (2) carryovers of the general business credit; (3) minimum tax credit; (4) capital losses for and capital loss carryovers to the discharge year; (5) the basis of the debtor's depreciable and nondepreciable assets; (6) passive activity loss and credit carryovers; and (7) foreign tax credit carryovers. See FTC 2d/FIN ¶ J-7404; USTR ¶ 1084.02; TaxDesk ¶ 214,502.

The principal residence exclusion applies to an insolvent taxpayer not in a Title 11 case unless the taxpayer elects to have the insolvency exclusion apply instead. (Code Sec. 108(a)(2)(C) as amended by 2007 Mortgage Relief Act §2(c)(2))

> *observation:* Many taxpayers whose principal residences are foreclosed will be insolvent, but this isn't always the case. To be considered "insolvent," a taxpayer's liabilities must exceed the FMV of his assets, determined immediately before the discharge. See FTC 2d/FIN ¶ J-7403; USTR ¶ 1084.01; TaxDesk ¶ 188,014. Some taxpayers will have assets, such as retirement accounts, that are taken into account in determining insolvency but aren't accessible without a penalty.

> *observation:* The amount of discharge of indebtedness income that is excluded from income by reason of a debtor's insolvency is limited to the amount by which the debtor is insolvent. See FTC 2d/FIN ¶ J-7401; USTR ¶ 1084.01; TaxDesk ¶ 188,014. This limitation doesn't apply in the case of the principal residence exclusion.

☐ **Effective:** Discharges of indebtedness after Dec. 31, 2006 (2007 Mortgage Relief Act §2(d)), and before Jan. 1, 2010. (Code Sec. 108(a)(1)(E))

¶ 202. Interest deduction for mortgage insurance premiums is extended to amounts paid or incurred after 2007 and before 2011

Code Sec. 163(h)(3)(E)(iv)(I), as amended by 2007 Mortgage Relief Act § 3(a)
Generally effective: Amounts paid or accrued after Dec. 31, 2007
Committee Reports, None

Premiums paid or accrued during 2007 by a taxpayer for qualified mortgage insurance (as defined below) in connection with acquisition indebtedness with respect to a qualified residence of the taxpayer are treated as qualified residence interest and thus deductible (see FTC 2d/FIN ¶ K-5493.1; USTR ¶ 1634.052; TaxDesk ¶ 314,519.1), subject to phaseout rules affecting taxpayers with adjusted gross income (AGI) over $100,000 for the tax year (see FTC 2d/FIN ¶ K-5493.2; USTR ¶ 1634.052; TaxDesk ¶ 314,519.2).

"Qualified mortgage insurance" means:

(1) mortgage insurance provided by the Department of Veterans Affairs (formerly the Veterans Administration) (VA), the Federal Housing Administration (FHA), or the Rural Housing Administration (RHA), and

(2) private mortgage insurance (as defined by Sec. 2 of the Homeowners Protection Act of '98 (12 U.S.C. 4901), as in effect on Dec. 20, 2006). (FTC 2d/FIN ¶ K-5493.1; USTR ¶ 1634.052; TaxDesk ¶ 314,519.1)

Except for amounts paid for qualified mortgage insurance provided by the VA or the RHA, any amounts paid by the taxpayer for qualified mortgage insurance that is properly allocable to any mortgage the payment of which extends to periods that are after the close of the tax year in which that amount is paid are chargeable to capital account and must be treated as paid in those periods to which they are allocated. (FTC 2d/FIN ¶ K-5493.1; USTR ¶ 1634.052; TaxDesk ¶ 314,519.1)

The rules regarding the deduction of qualified mortgage insurance premiums don't apply with respect to any mortgage insurance contract issued before Jan. 1, 2007. In addition, under pre-2007 Mortgage Relief Act law, the rules regarding the deduction of qualified mortgage insurance premiums didn't apply to any

---

FTC 2d References are to Federal Tax Coordinator 2d
FIN References are to RIA's Analysis of Federal Taxes: Income
USTR References are to United States Tax Reporter: Income, Estate & Gift, and Excise
PCA References are to Pension Analysis (print & electronic)
PE References are to Pension Explanations (print & electronic)
EP References are to Estate Planning Analysis (print & electronic)

amount paid or accrued after Dec. 31, 2007, or properly allocable to any period after that date. (FTC 2d/FIN ¶ K-5493.1; USTR ¶ 1634.052; TaxDesk ¶ 314,519.1)

New Law. Under the 2007 Mortgage Relief Act, the rules regarding the deduction of qualified mortgage insurance premiums discussed above don't apply with respect to amounts paid or incurred after Dec. 31, 2010, or properly allocable to any period after that date. (Code Sec. 163(h)(3)(E)(iv)(I) as amended by 2007 Mortgage Relief Act §3(a))

> *observation:* Thus, the Act extends the deduction for private mortgage insurance to amounts paid or accrued after Dec. 31, 2007, and before Jan. 1, 2011.

IRS has issued a notice explaining how individuals may use a simplified method to allocate prepaid qualified mortgage insurance premiums to determine the amount that may be deducted in 2007. The simplified method allows prepaid premiums to be allocated ratably over 84 months or, if shorter, the term of the mortgage. Entities that report the amount actually received from the individual or the amount determined under the simplified allocation method will be treated as having met their information reporting requirements. (Notice 2008-15, 2008-4 IRB 313)

☐ **Effective:** Amounts paid or accrued after Dec. 31, 2007 (2007 Mortgage Relief Act §3(b)), and before Jan. 1, 2011. (Code Sec. 163(h)(3)(E)(iv)(I))

¶ 203. Returns and statements relating to certain mortgage insurance premiums are subject to information return and payee statement penalties

Code Sec. 6724(d)(1)(B), as amended by 2007 Technical Corrections Act § 11(b)(2)(A)
Code Sec. 6724(d)(2)(K), as amended by 2007 Technical Corrections Act § 11(b)(2)(B)
Generally effective: Amounts paid or accrued after Dec. 31, 2006
Committee Reports, None

Mortgage insurance premiums paid or accrued in connection with acquisition indebtedness are treated as qualified residence interest for purposes of the interest deduction. IRS may issue regs that require any person who in the course of a trade or business receives $600 or more of mortgage insurance premiums in a calendar year from an individual to file an information return for that individual. Every person required to file an information return under the above rules must furnish to each individual for whom a return is filed a written statement showing the information IRS requires. The written statement must be furnished on or before Jan. 31 of the year following the calendar year for which the return is filed. FTC 2d/FIN ¶ S-3923; USTR ¶ 60,50H4; TaxDesk ¶ 814,074.1

A person required to file an information return is subject to a penalty for any failure to file that return with IRS on or before the required filing date, and any failure to include all of the information required to be shown on that return or the inclusion of incorrect information. The penalty applies for each information return for which a failure occurs up to a prescribed maximum. FTC 2d/FIN ¶ V-1803; USTR ¶ 67,214; TaxDesk ¶ 861,053

For penalty purposes, an information return means any statement of the amount of payments to another person, or any return, required by certain designated Code sections, or any of certain documents on nonresident alien and foreign corporation withholding. Under pre-2007 Technical Corrections Act law, information returns required for mortgage insurance premiums were not included in the definition of information returns. Thus, failures to file those returns, etc., were not subject to the information return penalty. (FTC 2d/FIN ¶ V-1804; USTR ¶ 67,214; TaxDesk ¶ 861,054)

A person required to furnish a payee statement to another person is subject to a penalty for any failure to furnish that statement on or before the date prescribed, and any failure to include all of the information required to be shown on that statement or the inclusion of incorrect information on that payee statement. The penalty applies for each payee statement for which a failure occurs up to a prescribed maximum. FTC 2d/FIN ¶ V-1816; USTR ¶ 67,224; TaxDesk ¶ 861,033

For penalty purposes, a payee statement is defined as any statement required to be furnished to another person under certain listed Code sections. Under pre-2007 Technical Corrections Act law, written statements required to be furnished to individuals regarding mortgage insurance premiums were not included in the definition of payee statements. Thus, failures to furnish those statements, etc., were not subject to the payee statement penalty. (FTC 2d/FIN ¶ V-1815; USTR ¶ 67,224; TaxDesk ¶ 861,035)

New Law. The 2007 Technical Corrections Act adds information returns required for mortgage insurance premiums to the definition of information returns. (Code Sec. 6724(d)(1)(B) as amended by 2007 Technical Corrections Act §11(b)(2)(A))

observation: Thus, the Act makes clear that failures regarding the filing, etc., of mortgage insurance premium information returns, as re-

---

FTC 2d References are to Federal Tax Coordinator 2d
FIN References are to RIA's Analysis of Federal Taxes: Income
USTR References are to United States Tax Reporter: Income, Estate & Gift, and Excise
PCA References are to Pension Analysis (print & electronic)
PE References are to Pension Explanations (print & electronic)
EP References are to Estate Planning Analysis (print & electronic)

quired by Code Sec. 6050H(h)(1), will be subject to the Code Sec. 6721 information return penalty.

The 2007 Technical Corrections Act also adds written statements required to be furnished to individuals for mortgage insurance premiums to the definition of payee statements. (Code Sec. 6724(d)(2)(K) as amended by 2007 Technical Corrections Act §11(b)(2)(B))

> **☑ observation:** Thus, the Act makes clear that failures to provide written statements to individuals for mortgage insurance premiums, as required by Code Sec. 6050H(h)(2), will be subject to the Code Sec. 6722 payee statement penalty.

> **☑ observation:** The above changes were necessary because Congress failed to add all the appropriate cross references when it added Code Sec. 6050H(h) to the Code as part of the 2006 Tax Relief Act. Thus, the effective date of the above changes is the same as the effective date of the 2006 Tax Relief Act changes, as discussed below.

☐ **Effective:** Amounts paid or accrued after Dec. 31, 2006. (2007 Technical Corrections Act §11(b)(3))

2007 Technical Corrections Act §11(b)(3) provides that the amendments made by 2007 Technical Corrections Act §11(b) take effect as if included in the provision of the 2006 Tax Relief Act to which they relate. The above amendments relate to §419(c) of the 2006 Tax Relief Act (Sec. 419(c), PL 109-432, 12/20/2006). 2006 Tax Relief Act §419(d) provides that the amendments made by §419(c) take effect for amounts paid or accrued after Dec. 31, 2006.

¶ 300. Individual Income Exclusions

¶ 301. $500,000 exclusion applies to gain from certain sales or exchanges of a principal residence by a surviving spouse within two years of the death of the spouse

Code Sec. 121(b)(4), as amended by 2007 Mortgage Relief Act § 7(a)
Generally effective: Sales or exchanges after Dec. 31, 2007
Committee Reports, None

A taxpayer generally can exclude up to $250,000 ($500,000 for certain married couples filing joint returns) of gain realized on the sale or exchange of a principal residence. To be eligible for the exclusion, the taxpayer has to have owned the residence and used it as a principal residence for at least two years of the five-year period ending on the date of the sale or exchange. See FTC 2d/FIN ¶ I-4521; USTR ¶ 1214; TaxDesk ¶ 225,701.

The exclusion is generally limited to $250,000 for unmarried taxpayers, see FTC 2d/FIN ¶ I-4535; USTR ¶ 1214.02; TaxDesk ¶ 225,715. For a husband and wife who file a joint return for the tax year of the sale or exchange of the property, the $250,000 limitation that applies to the exclusion of gain from the sale or exchange of a principal residence is applied by substituting "$500,000" for "$250,000" if:

(1) either the surviving spouse or the deceased spouse met the two-year ownership requirements (described in Code Sec. 121(a), see FTC 2d/FIN ¶ I-4521; USTR ¶ 1214; TaxDesk ¶ 225,701) with respect to the property immediately before the spouse died;

(2) both spouses met the two-year use requirements (described in Code Sec. 121(a), see FTC 2d/FIN ¶ I-4521; USTR ¶ 1214; TaxDesk ¶ 225,701) with respect to the property immediately before the spouse died; and

(3) neither spouse was ineligible for the benefits of the exclusion with respect to the property by reason of the one sale every two years rule (contained in Code Sec. 121(b)(3), see FTC 2d/FIN ¶ I-4539; USTR ¶ 1214.04; TaxDesk ¶ 225,719). See FTC 2d/FIN ¶ I-4536; USTR ¶ 1214.02; TaxDesk ¶ 225,716.

For an unmarried individual whose spouse is deceased on the date of the sale or exchange of property, the period that unmarried individual owned and used the property includes the period the deceased spouse owned and used the prop-

---

FTC 2d References are to Federal Tax Coordinator 2d
FIN References are to RIA's Analysis of Federal Taxes: Income
USTR References are to United States Tax Reporter: Income, Estate & Gift, and Excise
PCA References are to Pension Analysis (print & electronic)
PE References are to Pension Explanations (print & electronic)
EP References are to Estate Planning Analysis (print & electronic)

erty before death. Under pre-2007 Mortgage Relief Act law, gain from a sale or exchange of a principal residence by a surviving spouse could only have qualified for an exclusion of up to $500,000 if: (a) the sale occurred in the year of the deceased spouse's death, (b) the surviving spouse and deceased spouse's executor (or personal representative) filed a joint return for the year of death, and (c) the three requirements listed above (items (1) through (3)) were satisfied. (FTC 2d/FIN ¶ I-4559; USTR ¶ 1214.10; TaxDesk ¶ 225,739)

> **observation:** If the residence was solely owned by the surviving spouse, pre-2007 Mortgage Relief Act law required quick action to preserve the full $500,000 exclusion where the spouse died late in a year and the survivor wanted to sell the family residence. However, there would have been no urgency to sell the residence where the deceased spouse owned the residence outright (due to a step-up in basis to the date of death or alternate valuation date value). If the couple owned the home as joint tenants, there would generally have been a step-up in basis to the date of death (or the alternate valuation date) value for the deceased spouse's interest in the residence (for estates of decedents dying before 2010, see FTC 2d/FIN ¶ P-4000; P-4060; USTR ¶ 10,144; 10,144.01; TaxDesk ¶ 215,500; 215,502). If there was a very large economic gain due to substantial appreciation in the value of the residence from the time it was purchased by the spouse or spouses, (e.g., over $1 million), selling in the year of death could have enabled the surviving spouse to combine the basis step-up for the deceased spouse's interest in the residence with the maximum $500,000 exclusion to minimize the amount of gain subject to tax.

New Law. In the case of a sale or exchange of property (i.e., the principal residence) by an unmarried individual whose spouse is deceased on the date of the sale, Code Sec. 121(b)(1) (rules limiting the amount of the exclusion to $250,000, see FTC 2d/FIN ¶ I-4535; USTR ¶ 1214.02; TaxDesk ¶ 225,715) is applied by substituting "$500,000" for "$250,000" if:

(1) the sale occurs not later than *two years* after the date of death of the spouse, and

(2) the requirements of Code Sec. 121(b)(2)(A) (rules permitting a maximum exclusion of $500,000 for certain married taxpayers filing a joint return, see FTC 2d/FIN ¶ I-4536; USTR ¶ 1214.02; TaxDesk ¶ 225,716) were met immediately before the date of death. (Code Sec. 121(b)(4) as amended by 2007 Mortgage Relief Act §7(a))

> **observation:** Thus, if a married couple would have qualified for a maximum exclusion of $500,000 immediately before the death of a spouse ("the deceased spouse"), gain up to $500,000 can be excluded on a sale of the residence by the unmarried surviving spouse within two

years of the deceased spouse's death. On that sale, the $250,000 limitation is applied by substituting "$500,000" for "$250,000" if the following three requirements (incorporated by reference from Code Sec. 121(b)(2)(A)) are satisfied:

(a) Either the surviving spouse or the deceased spouse met the two-year ownership requirements (described in Code Sec. 121(a), see FTC 2d/FIN ¶ I-4521; USTR ¶ 1214; TaxDesk ¶ 225,701) with respect to their principal residence immediately before the spouse died.

(b) Both spouses met the two-year use requirements (described in Code Sec. 121(a), see FTC 2d/FIN ¶ I-4521; USTR ¶ 1214; TaxDesk ¶ 225,701) with respect to the principal residence immediately before the spouse died.

(c) Neither spouse was ineligible for the benefits of the exclusion with respect to the principal residence by reason of the one sale every two years rule (contained in Code Sec. 121(b)(3), see FTC 2d/FIN ¶ I-4539; USTR ¶ 1214.04; TaxDesk ¶ 225,719).

If a sale meets the requirements described above, the gain realized on the sale is treated in the same manner as if the surviving spouse and/or the deceased spouse had sold the residence immediately before the deceased spouse's death.

illustration (1): Married taxpayers, H and W, have owned and used their principal residence since Jan. 1, Year 1. On Feb. 16, Year 4, H dies and W inherits H's interest in the residence. If W sells the residence not later than *two years* after H's date of death (i.e., before Feb. 16, Year 6), W would qualify for an exclusion of up to $500,000 on the gain from the sale.

observation: If the surviving spouse remarries before a sale or exchange of the residence within the two-year period, Code Sec. 121(b)(4) won't apply because the sale or exchange has to be by an "unmarried individual." If a surviving spouse is contemplating remarriage within the two-year period and is interested in selling the family home, the surviving spouse should consider selling the residence before the marriage if the gain realized on the sale of the residence would exceed $250,000 (the amount of gain that would be excluded if the sale doesn't meet the requirements provided in Code Sec. 121(b)(4)).

FTC 2d References are to Federal Tax Coordinator 2d
FIN References are to RIA's Analysis of Federal Taxes: Income
USTR References are to United States Tax Reporter: Income, Estate & Gift, and Excise
PCA References are to Pension Analysis (print & electronic)
PE References are to Pension Explanations (print & electronic)
EP References are to Estate Planning Analysis (print & electronic)

🅡🅐 *observation:* As a practical matter, Code Sec. 121(b)(4) will generally provide the greatest tax benefit on a sale of a principal residence owned solely by the surviving spouse before the death of the deceased spouse, and used by both the surviving spouse and the deceased spouse. In that case, the residence will not receive a step-up in basis to the fair market value at date of death (or alternate valuation date), see FTC 2d/FIN ¶ P-4000 *et seq.*; P-4060 *et seq.*; USTR ¶ 10,144; 10,144.01; TaxDesk ¶ 215,500; 215,502. Presumably, the surviving spouse would be entitled to a maximum exclusion up to $500,000 on the sale of exchange of the residence if the requirements provided in Code Sec. 121(b)(4) are satisfied.

🅡🅐 *illustration (2):* SS has solely owned the residence that SS and her spouse (DS) have used as their principal residence since Jan. 1, Year 1. On Jan. 1, Year 25, DS dies. SS and DS had not sold another residence within the two years before DS's death. SS sells the residence on Jan. 2, Year 26. Presumably, SS would be entitled to a maximum gain exclusion of up to $500,000 because:

. . . the sale occurred not later than *two years* after DS's date of death (i.e., before Jan. 1, Year 27);

. . . SS met the two-year ownership requirements with respect to the residence immediately before DS died;

. . . both DS and SS met the two-year use requirements with respect to the residence immediately before DS died; and

. . . neither DS nor SS was ineligible for the benefits of the exclusion with respect to the residence by reason of the one sale every two years rule.

🅡🅐 *observation:* Even if a person (or entity) other than the surviving spouse inherits the deceased spouse's interest in the residence, the surviving spouse is presumably entitled to a maximum exclusion of $500,000 for the gain attributable to the surviving spouse's interest in the residence if the requirements provided in Code Sec. 121(b)(4) are satisfied.

🅡🅐 *illustration (3):* The facts are the same as illustration (2), except that DS and SS had owned their residence as tenants in common since Jan. 1, Year 1. Under the terms of DS's will, DS's interest in the residence is left to a trust for the benefit of SS and DS's descendants (for example, a qualified terminable interest property trust or QTIP trust, see FTC 2d ¶ R-6403; USTR ¶ 20,564.08; TaxDesk ¶ 778,100). SS and the trustee of the trust sell the residence on Jan. 2, Year 26. Presumably, SS would be entitled to a maximum gain exclusion of up to $500,000 because:

. . . the sale occurred not later than *two years* after DS's date of death (i.e., before Jan. 1, Year 27);

. . . both DS and SS met the two-year ownership requirements with respect to the residence immediately before DS died;

. . . both DS and SS met the two-year use requirements with respect to the residence immediately before DS died; and

. . . neither DS nor SS was ineligible for the benefits of the exclusion with respect to the residence by reason of the one sale every two years rule.

observation: In illustration (3), there presumably would have been a step-up in basis to the date of death (or alternate valuation date) value for DS's interest in the residence (see FTC 2d/FIN ¶ P-4000 *et seq.*; P-4060 *et seq.*; USTR ¶ 10,144; 10,144.01; TaxDesk ¶ 215,500; 215,502). Thus, unless the residence had appreciated substantially during the year between DS's death and the sale, the trust would not have realized a substantial gain from the sale of its interest in the residence.

observation: The 2007 Mortgage Relief Act doesn't change the rule permitting a surviving spouse to qualify for a maximum gain exclusion of up to $500,000 by selling the principal residence in the year of the deceased spouse's death and filing a joint return with the executor (or personal representative), see FTC 2d/FIN ¶ I-4559; USTR ¶ 1214.10; TaxDesk ¶ 225,739. However, surviving spouses who can't meet those requirements can qualify for the up-to-$500,000 exclusion under Code Sec. 121(b)(4).

observation: For estates of decedents dying after Dec. 31, 2009, Code Sec. 121(d)(11) will permit certain sales of a decedent's principal residence by an estate, an heir, or a qualified revocable trust (QRT) to qualify for the exclusion based on the decedent's ownership and use of the residence, see FTC 2d/FIN ¶ I-4560; USTR ¶ 1214.14; TaxDesk ¶ 225,740. Under those rules, any sale of a decedent's principal residence (that he had owned and used as a principal residence for more than two years) within three years of his death will qualify for a

FTC 2d References are to Federal Tax Coordinator 2d
FIN References are to RIA's Analysis of Federal Taxes: Income
USTR References are to United States Tax Reporter: Income, Estate & Gift, and Excise
PCA References are to Pension Analysis (print & electronic)
PE References are to Pension Explanations (print & electronic)
EP References are to Estate Planning Analysis (print & electronic)

$250,000 exclusion even if the heir (including a surviving spouse) never used the residence as a principal residence.

☐ **Effective:** Sales or exchanges after Dec. 31, 2007. (2007 Mortgage Relief Act §7(b))

observation: Code Sec. 121(b)(4) can apply to sales or exchanges of principal residences by surviving spouses whose spouses died in either 2006 or 2007 as long as the sale or exchange occurs after Dec. 31, 2007, and the other requirements provided in Code Sec. 121(b)(4) are satisfied.

illustration (4): S and D have jointly owned and used their principal residence since Jan. 1, 2000. On Mar. 31, 2006, D dies and S inherits D's interest in the residence. S intended to sell the residence during the year of D's death (2006) so that S could have qualified for an exclusion of gain up to $500,000 by filing a joint return with the executor of D's estate. However, the buyer backed out of the sale and S had to put the house back on the market. If S sells the residence after Dec. 31, 2007 and before Mar. 31, 2008, S presumably would qualify for an exclusion of gain up to $500,000 because the sale occurs within two years of D's death, as long as the other requirements provided in Code Sec. 121(b)(4) are satisfied.

¶ 302. Tax relief and expense reimbursements provided by state and local governments to volunteer firefighters and emergency medical responders for services performed are tax-free for 2008–2010 tax years

Code Sec. 139B, as added by 2007 Mortgage Relief Act § 5(a)
Generally effective: Tax years beginning after Dec. 31, 2007 and before Jan. 1, 2011
Committee Reports, see ¶ 5003

All forms of compensation received for services are included in gross income, unless a specific exemption applies (e.g., for combat zone pay, see FTC 2d/FIN ¶ H-3106; USTR ¶ 1124.01; TaxDesk ¶ 138,005). In addition to amounts received in cash or property, compensation also includes other types of benefits, such as the foregone interest on a below-market interest rate loan provided as compensation. (See FTC 2d/FIN ¶ H-1001 *et seq.*; USTR ¶ 614.027; TaxDesk ¶ 130,500 *et seq.*)

Various states have programs that provide state and local tax relief to persons who volunteer their services as emergency responders. Under pre-2007 Mortgage Relief Act law, there was no statutory exemption for the tax relief provided under these programs. In Chief Counsel Advice 200302045, IRS took the position that reductions or rebates of property taxes by state or local governments on account of services performed by members of qualified volunteer emergency response organizations were in-kind payments for services, and so were taxable income to the volunteers. (FTC 2d/FIN ¶ H-1017.1; TaxDesk ¶ 130,511.5)

In determining regular tax liability, an itemized deduction is permitted for certain state and local taxes paid, including individual income taxes (unless the taxpayer elects to deduct sales taxes instead), real property taxes, and personal property taxes. (See FTC 2d/FIN ¶ K-4000 *et seq.*; USTR ¶ 1644 *et seq.*; TaxDesk ¶ 326,000 *et seq.*) Under pre-2007 Mortgage Relief Act law (specifically, Chief Counsel Advice 200302045), volunteer emergency responders who received state or local tax reductions on account of services performed didn't have to reduce the amount of their otherwise allowable itemized deduction for taxes by the amount of the tax relief (which was taxable). (FTC 2d/FIN ¶ K-4202; TaxDesk ¶ 329,002)

A deduction generally is allowed for contributions made to qualifying charitable donees, including Code Sec. 501(c)(3) organizations and federal, state or local governmental entities. (Com Rept, see ¶ 5003) Deductible amounts include out-of-pocket expenses incurred in connection with performing charitable services for a charity, to the extent the expenses aren't reimbursed. (See FTC 2d/ FIN ¶ K-3601; USTR ¶ 1704.37; TaxDesk ¶ 332,601.) Under the general rules for reimbursements received for expenses incurred, these reimbursements generally are taxable. However, specific statutory exclusions are provided where the reimbursement is for expenses incurred in performing volunteer services under certain government programs (e.g., the Foster Grandparent program). Under pre-2007 Mortgage Relief Act law, there was no specific statutory exclusion for reimbursements received by volunteer emergency medical responders. (FTC 2d/ FIN ¶ J-1484; USTR ¶ 614.006; TaxDesk ¶ 198,208)

New Law. The 2007 Mortgage Relief Act provides that, in the case of any member of a qualified volunteer emergency response organization (defined below), gross income does not include the following: (Code Sec. 139B(a) as added by 2007 Mortgage Relief Act §5(a))

(1) any qualified state and local tax benefit (Code Sec. 139B(a)(1)) as defined below, and

(2) any qualified payment (Code Sec. 139B(a)(2)) as defined below.

FTC 2d References are to Federal Tax Coordinator 2d
FIN References are to RIA's Analysis of Federal Taxes: Income
USTR References are to United States Tax Reporter: Income, Estate & Gift, and Excise
PCA References are to Pension Analysis (print & electronic)
PE References are to Pension Explanations (print & electronic)
EP References are to Estate Planning Analysis (print & electronic)

♦️observation: In JCX-107-07 relating to an amendment to HR 3997 which, in relevant part, contained identical language to that in 2007 Mortgage Relief Act § 5, Congress indicated it was providing new exclusions from gross income for individuals on account of services performed as a member of a qualified volunteer emergency response organization. (Com Rept, see ¶ 5003)

For purposes of the above rule (Code Sec. 139B(c)), a "qualified state and local tax benefit" is a reduction or rebate of certain specified taxes provided by a state or political division of a state on account of services performed as a member of a qualified volunteer emergency response organization (defined below). The specified taxes are the taxes described in:

. . . Code Sec. 164(a)(1), i.e., state and local real property taxes (see FTC 2d/FIN ¶ K-4504; USTR ¶ 1644.03; TaxDesk ¶ 326,012);

. . . Code Sec. 164(a)(2), i.e., state and local personal property taxes (see FTC 2d/FIN ¶ K-4502; USTR ¶ 1644.03; TaxDesk ¶ 326,014); or

. . . Code Sec. 164(a)(3), i.e., state and local income taxes (see FTC 2d/FIN ¶ K-4506; USTR ¶ 1644.03; TaxDesk ¶ 326,006).

(Code Sec. 139B(c)(1))

♦️observation: In JCX-107-07, Congress indicated that a qualified state or local tax benefit is any reduction or rebate of the above-listed taxes provided by state or local governments on account of services performed by individuals as members of a qualified volunteer emergency response organization. The exclusion is limited to rebates or refunds of state or local income taxes, state or local real property taxes, and state or local personal property taxes. (Com Rept, see ¶ 5003)

♦️observation: Code Sec. 164(a)(1) refers to state and local, and foreign, real property taxes (see FTC 2d/FIN ¶ K-4504; USTR ¶ 1644.03; TaxDesk ¶ 326,012). Code Sec. 164(a)(3) refers to state and local, and foreign, income taxes (see FTC 2d/FIN ¶ K-4506; USTR ¶ 1644.03; TaxDesk ¶ 326,006). However, new Code Sec. 139B(a)(1), which provides the new exclusions for the tax benefits provided to individuals on account of services performed as a member of a qualified volunteer emergency response organization, specifies "state and local" tax benefits. Because a qualified volunteer emergency response organization must be organized and operated to provide emergency response services in a state or a political subdivision of a state (see below), the members provide these services in a state or a political subdivision. Even if the member is subject to a foreign tax (e.g., as a foreign citizen), it's unlikely that a foreign taxing jurisdiction would provide tax relief for those services.

For purposes of the above rules, a "qualified payment" generally is any payment (whether reimbursement or otherwise) provided by a state or political division of a state on account of the performance of services as a member of a qualified volunteer emergency response organization. (Code Sec. 139B(c)(2)(A))

⦿ *observation:* In JCX-107-07, Congress indicated that the exclusion provided under the above rules is for payments provided as reimbursement for expenses incurred in connection with performing the volunteer emergency response services. Congress refers to these payments as "qualified reimbursement payments." (Com Rept, see ¶ 5003)

⦿ *illustration (1):* J, a member of a qualified volunteer emergency response organization in State X, performed volunteer firefighting services in August. State X reimburses J for the $20 in car expenses he incurred in connection with performing those services. The payment is a "qualified payment" that is excludible from J's income under new Code Sec. 139B(a).

⦿ *observation:* As described above, only payments made by a state or local government can be "qualified payments." Thus, a payment made by the qualified emergency response organization doesn't qualify. This means that if the organization reimburses its members for expenses incurred in connection with performing volunteer emergency response services, the members can't exclude the reimbursements. But if the state or local government provides the reimbursement, the exclusion applies. A reimbursement provided by the organization, out of funds provided to it by the state or local government, might be considered to be provided by the state or local government indirectly, so as to allow the exclusion. But neither the statute nor JCX-107-07 addresses this type of arrangement.

⦿ *observation:* The parenthetical "(whether reimbursement or otherwise)" in the Code Sec. 139B(c)(2)(B) definition of "qualified payment," above, means that the exclusion for "qualified payments" isn't limited to *reimbursements* for expenses incurred in connection with providing the volunteer services. Presumably, the exclusion also is available for allowances paid to the volunteers. The "or otherwise" language could mean the exclusion also applies to other types of taxable payments (e.g., length-of-service awards), that aren't meant as compensation, but that can't be treated as nontaxable gifts.

FTC 2d References are to Federal Tax Coordinator 2d
FIN References are to RIA's Analysis of Federal Taxes: Income
USTR References are to United States Tax Reporter: Income, Estate & Gift, and Excise
PCA References are to Pension Analysis (print & electronic)
PE References are to Pension Explanations (print & electronic)
EP References are to Estate Planning Analysis (print & electronic)

The amount determined as a qualified payment for any tax year cannot exceed $30 multiplied by the number of months during the year that the taxpayer performs the services. (Code Sec. 139B(c)(2)(B))

illustration (2): The facts are the same as in *Illustration (1)*, except that J's car expenses are $40, and J receives a $40 reimbursement from State X. J's exclusion is limited to $30 per month. J performed services only during the month of August, so only $30 of the reimbursement is excludible. J must include the $10 balance ($40 − $30) in income.

observation: Although Code Sec. 139B(c)(2)(B) limits the amount of the exclusion for qualified payments to $30 times the number of months during the year in which the individual performs the volunteer emergency response services, it doesn't provide a specific $30 limit for each month. For example, a volunteer emergency responder who performs services in more than one month may be able to exclude the full amount of the total reimbursement received during the year even if his expenses for one month were more than $30, if his total expenses for the year don't exceed $30 multiplied by the number of months in which he performed services.

illustration (3): K performs services as a volunteer emergency responder for County Q in July, August, and September. J incurs $90 of expenses in connection with these services: $40 in July, $20 in August, and $30 in September. County Q reimburses K for the full $90. The limit on K's exclusion is $90 (3 months × $30). Thus, K can exclude the full $90, even though K incurred more than $30 of expenses in July. If K had worked only in July, his exclusion would have been limited to $30 (as in *Illustration (2)*, above).

A "qualified volunteer emergency response organization" is any volunteer organization that meets the following requirements: (Code Sec. 139B(c)(3))

(i) it's required (by written agreement) by a state or political subdivision to furnish firefighting or emergency medical services in the state or political subdivision, and (Code Sec. 139B(c)(3)(B))

(ii) it's organized and operated to provide firefighting or emergency medical services for persons in the state or political subdivision, as the case may be. (Code Sec. 139B(c)(3)(A))

observation: Presumably, the statutory term "emergency medical services" refers to the types of medical personnel IRS referred to as "emergency responders" in Chief Counsel Advice 200302045 (i.e., emergency medical technicians (EMTs), paramedics, ambulance drivers, etc.). Thus, firefighters, EMTs, paramedics, and ambulance drivers who are members of an organization meeting the qualification requirements described above, and who receive state or local tax relief or qualified reimbursement payments on account of their services, won't be taxed on those benefits.

⚫️ observation: There is no requirement under Code Sec. 139B that the qualified volunteer emergency response organization be tax-exempt.

No double tax benefit. The 2007 Mortgage Relief Act provides that in the case of any member of a qualified volunteer emergency response organization, the deductions under Code Sec. 164 (taxes) and Code Sec. 170 (charitable contributions) are limited as described below. (Code Sec. 139B(b))

⚫️ observation: In JCX-107-07, Congress indicated that the exclusions provided under new Code Sec. 139B(a) can't give rise to a double tax benefit. (Com Rept, see ¶ 5003)

Deduction for taxes. The deduction under Code Sec. 164 is determined with regard to any qualified state and local tax benefit. (Code Sec. 139B(b)(1))

⚫️ observation: In JCX-107-07, Congress indicated that the amount of state or local taxes taken into account in determining the deduction for taxes is reduced by the amount of any qualified state or local tax benefit. (Com Rept, see ¶ 5003)

⚫️ observation: In other words, an individual whose state or local taxes are reduced or rebated on account of services performed as a volunteer emergency responder, and who is entitled to exclude the amount of the reduction or rebate from gross income by virtue of the rules discussed above—i.e., by virtue of new Code Sec. 139B—must decrease his deduction for the reduced or rebated taxes by the amount thus excluded. That is, he can't claim both an exclusion and a deduction for the same item.

⚫️ illustration (4): M volunteers as a paramedic for County B. M reduces M's local real property taxes for the year from $6,000 to $5,500, on account of M's volunteer services as a paramedic that year. Under rules discussed above, M's gross income doesn't include the $500 reduction in local real property taxes. M must reduce his other-

FTC 2d References are to Federal Tax Coordinator 2d
FIN References are to RIA's Analysis of Federal Taxes: Income
USTR References are to United States Tax Reporter: Income, Estate & Gift, and Excise
PCA References are to Pension Analysis (print & electronic)
PE References are to Pension Explanations (print & electronic)
EP References are to Estate Planning Analysis (print & electronic)

wise allowable deduction for state and local real property taxes by $500.

💬 *observation:* Taxpayers can elect to take an itemized deduction for state and local general sales taxes instead of state and local income taxes (see FTC 2d/FIN ¶ K-4510 *et seq.*; USTR ¶ 1644.03; TaxDesk ¶ 326,019.1 *et seq.*). However, the state or local tax benefits that are excludible under the rules described above are limited to state or local income taxes, personal property taxes, and real property taxes. Thus, any benefits with respect to sales tax that a state or local government provides to an individual on account of his volunteer emergency response services don't qualify for the new exclusion. And, an individual who elects to deduct state or local sales taxes instead of state or local income taxes doesn't have to reduce his deduction for taxes by the amount of any excluded state or local tax income tax benefit received. But since the excluded state or local income tax benefits do reduce the individual's deduction for state or local income taxes, taxpayers need to consider the new exclusion in determining whether to make the election to deduct state and local sales taxes instead of income taxes.

💬 *observation:* The provision allowing taxpayers to elect to deduct state and local general sales taxes instead of state and local income taxes is scheduled to expire after 2007. However, under proposed legislation, the provision would be extended for one year, so that it would apply through 2008.

Charitable deduction. As noted above, a charitable deduction is allowed for unreimbursed out-of-pocket expenses incurred by the taxpayer in performing services free for a charity, including a state or local government. (FTC 2d/FIN ¶ K-3601; USTR ¶ 1704.37; USTR Estate & Gift Taxes ¶ 20,554, ¶ 25,224; TaxDesk ¶ 332,601) The 2007 Mortgage Relief Act provides that expenses paid or incurred by the taxpayer in connection with the performance of services as a member of a qualified volunteer emergency response organization are taken into account under Code Sec. 170 only to the extent the expenses exceed the amount of any qualified payment excluded from gross income under Code Sec. 139B(a). (Code Sec. 139B(b)(2))

💬 *observation:* In JCX-107-07, Congress indicated that the expenses paid or incurred by a taxpayer in connection with the performance of services as a member of a qualified volunteer emergency response organization are taken into account for purposes of the charitable deduction only to the extent they exceed the amount of any qualified reimbursement payment excluded from income under the new provision. (Com Rept, see ¶ 5003)

observation: Presumably, an individual who performs services as a member of a state or local government's qualified volunteer emergency response organization is considered to be performing services for the state or local government, a qualified charitable donee. Thus, any unreimbursed expenses incurred by the individual in connection with performing those services are deductible as charitable contributions made to a state or local government. As noted above, a qualified volunteer emergency response organization doesn't have to be tax-exempt, and so might not be a qualified charitable donee.

illustration (5): R, a member of County W's volunteer firefighter department, performed volunteer firefighting services during March. R incurred $50 in expenses for clothing and transportation in connection with performing those services, and received a $30 reimbursement from County W. The $30 reimbursement is a "qualified payment" that's excludible from R's income under the rules discussed above. The charitable deduction that otherwise would be allowed to R for the out-of-pocket expenses incurred in performing services for County W must be reduced by $30, the amount of the qualified payment. R's charitable deduction for those expenses is limited to $20 ($50 expenses − $30 qualified payment).

Termination. The above rules won't apply for tax years beginning after Dec. 31, 2010. (Code Sec. 139B(d))

observation: In other words, as under pre-2007 Mortgage Relief Act law (specifically, Chief Counsel Advice 200302045), individuals whose property taxes for 2011 and later years are reduced or rebated by state or local governments on account of their volunteer emergency response services will be taxed on these benefits. But the individuals won't have to reduce their otherwise allowable deductions for taxes or for unreimbursed expenses incurred in performing services for charity.

☐ **Effective:** Tax years beginning after Dec. 31, 2007 (2007 Mortgage Relief Act §5(c)) and before Jan. 1, 2011. (Code Sec. 139B(d))

FTC 2d References are to Federal Tax Coordinator 2d
FIN References are to RIA's Analysis of Federal Taxes: Income
USTR References are to United States Tax Reporter: Income, Estate & Gift, and Excise
PCA References are to Pension Analysis (print & electronic)
PE References are to Pension Explanations (print & electronic)
EP References are to Estate Planning Analysis (print & electronic)

¶ 303. Certain payments received by surviving victims and survivors of slain victims of the Virginia Tech shootings are excluded from gross income

Code Sec. 61, 2007 Virginia Tech Victims Act § 1
Generally effective: Dec. 19, 2007
Committee Reports, see ¶ 5401

Gross income consists of all income, from whatever source derived—including gain from the sale of property—in whatever form realized, whether in money, property or services. However, certain items are specifically excluded from gross income—in some cases by the Code, in some cases by other federal statutes. (FTC 2d/FIN ¶ J-1000 *et seq.*; USTR ¶ 614 *et seq.*; TaxDesk ¶ 101,000 *et seq.*)

> **⊘** *observation:* On April 16, 2007, a student at Virginia Polytechnic Institute and State University, better known as Virginia Tech, shot and killed more than thirty students and faculty members, and wounded many more.

Following the shooting, a payment program for victims and survivors of the event was established. (Com Rept, see ¶ 5401)

> **⊘** *observation:* The program, known as the Hokie Spirit Memorial Fund (the Fund), was established by the Virginia Tech Foundation (the Foundation). The Foundation, a Code Sec. 501(c)(3) organization (see FTC 2d/FIN ¶ D-4101 *et seq.*; USTR ¶ 5014.05 *et seq.*; TaxDesk ¶ 670,601 *et seq.*), was established and organized in 1948 to receive, manage, and disburse private gifts in support of Virginia Tech programs. The Foundation established the Fund to receive and manage donations to those in need of aid as a result of the April 16, 2007 shootings. Some of those donations were intended to provide broad support to the university community and the families of those involved, in the aftermath of the shootings.

Under the program, surviving victims and survivors of the victims are eligible to receive cash payments from Virginia Tech. In lieu of receipt of a cash payment, claimants under the program may instead donate their payments to a Code Sec. 501(c)(3) charitable organization for the purpose of funding scholarships at Virginia Tech. (Com Rept, see ¶ 5401)

New Law. Under the 2007 Virginia Tech Victims Act, gross income does not include any amount received from Virginia Tech, out of amounts transferred from the Fund established by the Foundation, an organization organized and operated as described in Code Sec. 501(c)(3), if that amount is paid on account of the April 16, 2007 shootings at Virginia Tech. (2007 Virginia Tech Victims Act §1) In other words, if an individual receives amounts from Virginia Tech that are paid out of the Fund, on account of the April 16, 2007 shootings, those amounts are excluded from the individual's gross income. (Com Rept, see ¶ 5401)

☐ **Effective:** Dec. 19, 2007.

FTC 2d References are to Federal Tax Coordinator 2d
FIN References are to RIA's Analysis of Federal Taxes: Income
USTR References are to United States Tax Reporter: Income, Estate & Gift, and Excise
PCA References are to Pension Analysis (print & electronic)
PE References are to Pension Explanations (print & electronic)
EP References are to Estate Planning Analysis (print & electronic)

¶ 400. Energy Incentives

¶ 401. The low sulfur diesel fuel credit rules are amended retroactively to eliminate duplicate basis reduction and to permit election not to take credit

Code Sec. 45H(b)(1)(A), as amended by 2007 Technical Corrections Act § 7(a)(3)(A)

Code Sec. 45H(c)(2), as amended by 2007 Technical Corrections Act § 7(a)(3)(A)

Code Sec. 45H(d), as amended by 2007 Technical Corrections Act § 7(a)(1)(A)

Code Sec. 45H(e), as amended by 2007 Technical Corrections Act § 7(a)(3)(A)

Code Sec. 45H(g), as amended by 2007 Technical Corrections Act § 7(a)(2)(A)

Code Sec. 179B(a), as amended by 2007 Technical Corrections Act § 7(a)(3)(A)

Code Sec. 179B(a), as amended by 2007 Technical Corrections Act § 7(a)(3)(C)

Code Sec. 280C(d), as amended by 2007 Technical Corrections Act § 7(a)(1)(B)

Code Sec. 1016(a)(31), as amended by 2007 Technical Corrections Act § 7(a)(1)(C)

Code Sec. 6501(m), as amended by 2007 Technical Corrections Act § 7(a)(2)(B)

Generally effective: Expenses paid or incurred after Dec. 31, 2002

Committee Reports, see ¶ 5306

The amount of the low sulfur diesel fuel credit for any small business refiner is an amount equal to 5 cents for every gallon of low sulfur diesel fuel produced at a facility by the small business refiner during the tax year, see FTC 2d/FIN ¶ L-17551; USTR ¶ 45H4; TaxDesk ¶ 382,301.

The aggregate low sulfur diesel fuel credit for any tax year for any facility cannot exceed 25% of the "qualified capital costs" incurred by the small business refiner for the facility, reduced by the aggregate low sulfur diesel fuel credits for all earlier tax years for the facility. (FTC 2d/FIN ¶ L-17553; USTR ¶ 45H4; TaxDesk ¶ 382,303)

FTC 2d References are to Federal Tax Coordinator 2d
FIN References are to RIA's Analysis of Federal Taxes: Income
USTR References are to United States Tax Reporter: Income, Estate & Gift, and Excise
PCA References are to Pension Analysis (print & electronic)
PE References are to Pension Explanations (print & electronic)
EP References are to Estate Planning Analysis (print & electronic)

If a low sulfur diesel fuel production credit is determined for any expenditure for any property, the increase in the basis of that property which would otherwise result from the expenditure had to be reduced by the amount of the credit so determined under pre-2007 Technical Corrections Act law. Thus, the taxpayer's basis in the refinery property was reduced by the amount of production credit claimed. An adjustment to basis had to be made under Code Sec. 1016(a) to the extent provided above. (FTC 2d/FIN ¶ L-17557; USTR ¶ 45H4; TaxDesk ¶ 382,306)

Under pre-2007 Technical Corrections Act law, no deduction was allowed under Code Sec. 280C(d) for that portion of the expenses otherwise allowable as a deduction for the tax year that was equal to the amount of the low sulfur diesel fuel production credit determined for that tax year. (FTC 2d/FIN ¶ L-17557; USTR ¶ 280C4, ¶ 10,164; TaxDesk ¶ 382,306)

"Qualified capital costs" for purposes of the low sulfur diesel fuel production credit were those costs paid or incurred for a facility during the applicable period to comply with the applicable Environmental Protection Agency (EPA) regs for that facility, including expenditures for:

- constructing new process operation units or dismantling and reconstructing existing process units to be used in the production of low sulfur diesel fuel,
- associated adjacent or offsite equipment (including tankage, catalyst, and power supply),
- engineering,
- construction period interest, and
- sitework. (FTC 2d/FIN ¶ L-17554; USTR ¶ 45H4; TaxDesk ¶ 382,304)

In addition to the credit for qualified capital costs for low sulfur diesel fuel production, a small business refiner was allowed as a deduction an amount equal to 75% of qualified capital costs the taxpayer paid or incurred during the tax year in complying with EPA regs. For this purpose, qualified capital costs were defined the same as they were for the low sulfur diesel fuel production credit, as described above. (FTC 2d/FIN ¶ L-3164; USTR ¶ 179B4; TaxDesk ¶ 307,103)

The limitations period for IRS to assess a deficiency attributable to an election or revocation of an election to take the alcohol fuel credit, enhanced oil recovery credit, employer social security credit for taxes paid on employee tips, work opportunity credit, qualified electric vehicles credit, the alternative motor vehicle credit, the qualified alternative fuel vehicle refueling property credit, or the clinical drug testing (orphan drug) credit won't expire before the date one year after the date that IRS is notified of the election or revocation. (FTC 2d/FIN ¶ T-4014.1; USTR ¶ 65,014.28; TaxDesk ¶ 838,029)

New Law. The interaction of the basis reduction and deduction denial rules for the low sulfur diesel fuel credit added by the 2004 American Jobs Creation

Act (Sec. 339, PL 108-357, 10/22/2004) is unclear and may have an unintentionally duplicative effect. Thus, under the 2007 Technical Corrections Act, deductions are denied in an amount equal to the amount of the low sulfur diesel fuel credit and the pre-2007 Technical Corrections Act law rules reducing basis and denying a deduction are repealed. (Com Rept, see ¶ 5306)

In order to clarify the basis reduction and deduction denial rules, the following changes are made. First, the pre-2007 Technical Corrections Act provision requiring an adjustment to basis in refinery property to be made under Code Sec. 1016(a) for the amount of production credit claimed is retroactively repealed. (Code Sec. 1016(a)(31) as amended by 2007 Technical Corrections Act §7(a)(1)(C)) Second, the pre-2007 Technical Corrections Act reduction in basis requirement contained in former Code Sec. 45H(d) is also retroactively repealed. (Code Sec. 45H(d) as amended by 2007 Technical Corrections Act §7(a)(1)(A)) Third, the pre-2007 Technical Corrections Act provision stating that no deduction is allowed under Code Sec. 280C(d) for that portion of the expenses otherwise allowable as a deduction for the tax year that's equal to the amount of the low sulfur diesel fuel production credit determined for that tax year is amended to provide instead that deductions otherwise allowable for income tax purposes for the tax year must be reduced by the amount of the credit determined for the tax year under Code Sec. 45H(a). (Code Sec. 280C(d) as amended by 2007 Technical Corrections Act §7(a)(1)(B))

Election out. The 2007 Technical Corrections Act provides that no low sulfur fuel credit will be determined if a taxpayer elects not to have Code Sec. 45H(a) apply to the tax year. (Code Sec. 45H(g) as amended by 2007 Technical Corrections Act §7(a)(2)(A))

> **⊘** *observation:* The election out is probably intended to work together with the clarification of the interaction between the credit and otherwise allowable deductions. Taxpayers may find it advantageous to elect out of the credit when limitations on the credit prevent the taxpayer from making full use of it.

> **⊘** *observation:* IRS will need to issue guidance for making the election.

Qualified capital costs are now qualified costs. The 2007 Technical Corrections Act changes the name of the costs that qualify for the low sulfur diesel fuel credit and for the deduction for costs of complying with EPA regs from

---

FTC 2d References are to Federal Tax Coordinator 2d
FIN References are to RIA's Analysis of Federal Taxes: Income
USTR References are to United States Tax Reporter: Income, Estate & Gift, and Excise
PCA References are to Pension Analysis (print & electronic)
PE References are to Pension Explanations (print & electronic)
EP References are to Estate Planning Analysis (print & electronic)

89

"qualified capital costs" to "qualified costs." (Code Sec. 45H(b)(1)(A) as amended by 2007 Technical Corrections Act §7(a)(3)(A); Code Sec. 45H(c)(2) as amended by 2007 Technical Corrections Act §7(a)(3)(A); Code Sec. 45H(e)(1) as amended by 2007 Technical Corrections Act §7(a)(3)(A); Code Sec. 45H(e)(2) as amended by 2007 Technical Corrections Act §7(a)(3)(A))

> ⓇⒾⒶ *observation:* The change to the definition of qualified cost for purposes of the low sulfur diesel fuel credit is only to the nomenclature; there is no substantive change in the definition. Although Congress is silent on its reason, presumably the change simply clarifies the fact that the costs that qualify for the credit are not only capital costs.

The 2007 Technical Corrections Act also adds the following phrase to the definition of qualified costs for purposes of the deduction for costs of complying with EPA regs: "and which are properly chargeable to capital account." (Code Sec. 179B(a) as amended by 2007 Technical Corrections Act §7(a)(3)(A); Code Sec. 179B(a) as amended by 2007 Technical Corrections Act §7(a)(3)(C))

> ⓇⒾⒶ *observation:* For the definition of qualified costs for purposes of the deduction for EPA costs, the definition is changed somewhat by adding the modifying phrase that the costs are those that are properly chargeable to capital account.

Election out extends the limitation period. The 2007 Technical Corrections Act adds the election out of the low sulfur diesel fuel credit discussed above to the list of credits for which the limitations period in which IRS may assess a deficiency is extended so that it won't expire before the date one year after the date that IRS is notified of the election or revocation. (Code Sec. 6501(m) as amended by 2007 Technical Corrections Act §7(a)(2)(B))

> ⓇⒾⒶ *illustration:* Taxpayer files an amended return on Mar. 15, 2008 to elect out of the low sulfur diesel fuel credit for the 2004 tax year and take a deduction for the expenses instead. IRS has until Mar. 15, 2009 to assess any deficiency for 2004 for which the taxpayer might be liable that is attributable to the taxpayer's election out.

Redesignations. The 2007 Technical Corrections Act makes the following redesignations:

- Pre-2007 Technical Corrections Act Code Sec 45H(e) (special rule for determining refinery runs for defining small business refiners for the low sulfur diesel credit (FTC 2d/FIN ¶ L-17552; USTR ¶ 45H4; TaxDesk ¶ 382,302)), Code Sec. 45H(f) (EPA compliance certification requirement for the low sulfur diesel credit (FTC 2d/FIN ¶ L-17555; USTR ¶ 45H4; TaxDesk ¶ 382,305)), and Code Sec. 45H(g) (rules for cooperative organizations' use of the low sulfur diesel credit (FTC 2d/FIN ¶ L-17558; USTR ¶ 45H4; TaxDesk ¶ 382,307)) are redesignated as Code Sec. 45H(d), Code Sec. 45H(e), and Code Sec. 45H(f), respectively. (2007 Technical Corrections Act §7(a)(1)(A))

• Pre-2007 Technical Corrections Act Code Sec. 1016(a)(32) through Code Sec. 1016(a)(37), which are the following basis adjustment rules for various credits and deductions:

. . . Code Sec. 1016(a)(32), energy efficient commercial building property deduction (FTC 2d/FIN ¶ L-3176; USTR ¶ 10,164; TaxDesk ¶ 308,106)

. . . Code Sec. 1016(a)(33), energy efficient home credit (FTC 2d/FIN ¶ P-1710.01; USTR ¶ 10,164; TaxDesk ¶ 213,011.3)

. . . Code Sec. 1016(a)(34), nonbusiness energy credit (FTC 2d/FIN ¶ P-1710.4; USTR ¶ 10,164)

. . . Code Sec. 1016(a)(35), residential energy efficient property credit (FTC 2d/FIN ¶ P-1710.5; USTR ¶ 10,164)

. . . Code Sec. 1016(a)(36), alternative motor vehicle credit (USTR ¶ 10,164)

. . . Code Sec. 1016(a)(37), alternative fuel vehicle refueling property credit (FTC 2d/FIN ¶ L-18041; USTR ¶ 10,164; TaxDesk ¶ 397,201)

are redesignated as Code Sec. 1016(a)(31) through Code Sec. 1016(a)(36), respectively. (2007 Technical Corrections Act §7(a)(1)(C))

☐ **Effective:** Expenses paid or incurred after Dec. 31, 2002, in tax years ending after Dec. 31, 2002. (2007 Technical Corrections Act §7(e)(1))

> *observation:* 2007 Technical Corrections Act §7(e)(1) provides that the above provisions are effective as if included in the provisions of the 2004 American Jobs Creation Act to which they relate. The above rules relate to the effective date for Code Sec. 45H provided in Sec. 339(f), PL 108-357, 10/22/2004, which was effective for expenses paid or incurred after Dec. 31, 2002, in tax years ending after Dec. 31, 2002.

¶ 402. Dollar limits on credit for alternative fuel vehicle refueling property apply to all property placed in service at a location

Code Sec. 30C(b), as amended by 2007 Technical Corrections Act § 6(b)(1)
Generally effective: Property placed in service after Dec. 31, 2005 and
  before Jan. 1, 2010
Committee Reports, see ¶ 5305

A taxpayer is allowed a tax credit against his income tax for a tax year equal to 30% of the cost, subject to dollar limits, of any qualified alternative fuel vehicle (QAFV) refueling property placed in service by the taxpayer during the tax year, see FTC 2d/FIN ¶ L-18041; USTR ¶ 30C4; TaxDesk ¶ 397,201. However, the QAFV refueling property credit isn't allowed for any property if the taxpayer elects not to have it apply to that property, see FTC 2d/FIN ¶ L-18043.1; USTR ¶ 30C4; TaxDesk ¶ 397,204.

The QAFV refueling property credit terminates, effective for property placed in service after Dec. 31, 2009, except in the case of QAFV refueling property relating to hydrogen. For QAFV refueling property relating to hydrogen, the credit won't apply to property placed in service after Dec. 31, 2014, see FTC 2d/FIN ¶ L-18041; USTR ¶ 30C4; TaxDesk ¶ 397,201.

Under pre-2007 Technical Corrections Act law, Code Sec. 30C(b) stated that the credit with respect to any QAFV refueling property could not exceed: (1) $30,000 in the case of a property of a character subject to an allowance for depreciation, and (2) $1,000 in any other case. (FTC 2d/FIN ¶ L-18041; USTR ¶ 30C4; TaxDesk ¶ 397,201)

New Law. The 2007 Technical Corrections Act provides that the credit allowed for all QAFV refueling property placed in service by the taxpayer during the tax year at a location cannot exceed: (1) $30,000 in the case of a property of a character subject to an allowance for depreciation, and (2) $1,000 in any other case. (Code Sec. 30C(b) as amended by 2007 Technical Corrections Act §6(b)(1)) Thus, the 2007 Technical Corrections Act clarifies that the $30,000 and $1,000 limits apply to all QAFV refueling property placed in service by the taxpayer at a location. (Com Rept, see ¶ 5305)

observation: Thus, if a taxpayer installs depreciable QAFV refueling property at more than one location, up to $30,000 of the cost of that property is eligible for the credit at each location.

illustration (1): In 2008, T, a calendar-year taxpayer, installs several items of depreciable QAFV refueling property, with a total cost of $35,000, at one location and several items of QAFV refueling property, with a total cost of $25,000, at another location. T is allowed a $16,500 credit for the property (30% × [$30,000 + $25,000]) for 2008.

observation: The $30,000 and $1,000 limits are *annual,* not *lifetime.*

illustration (2): The facts are the same as in illustration (1), except that, in addition, T installs depreciable QAFV refueling property in 2009 in the same dollar amounts and at the same locations as he did in 2008. T is allowed a $16,500 credit for the property placed in service in 2009, as well as a $16,500 credit for 2008.

observation: The $1,000 limit for non-depreciable QAFV refueling property can apply to only one location. This is so because the only non-depreciable property eligible to be QAFV refueling property is property installed on property that is the taxpayer's principal residence, see FTC 2d/FIN ¶ L-18043; USTR ¶ 30C4.02; TaxDesk ¶ 397,203.

The above rule is consistent with similar deduction limits imposed under Code Sec. 179A(b)(2)(A) relating to the deduction for clean-fuel vehicles and certain refueling property. (Com Rept, see ¶ 5305)

observation: The Code Sec. 179A deduction for clean-fuel vehicles and certain refueling property doesn't apply to property placed in service after Dec. 31, 2005, see FTC 2d/FIN ¶ K-7001; USTR ¶ 179A4; TaxDesk ¶ 307,001.

For a modification of the definition of QAFV refueling property, see ¶ 403.

☐ **Effective:** Property placed in service after Dec. 31, 2005, in tax years ending after Dec. 31, 2005. (2007 Technical Corrections Act §6(e)(1))

2007 Technical Corrections Act §6(e)(1) provides that the amendment made by §6(b)(1) of the 2007 Technical Corrections Act takes effect as if included in the provisions of the 2005 Energy Tax Act to which the amendment relates. The amendment relates to 2005 Energy Tax Act §1342(a) (Sec. 1342(a), PL 109-58, 8/8/2005) which, under 2005 Energy Tax Act §1342(c) (Sec. 1342(c), PL 109-58, 8/8/2005), is effective for property placed in service after Dec. 31, 2005, in tax years ending after Dec. 31, 2005.

observation: As indicated above, the credit for QAFV refueling property only applies to property placed in service before Jan. 1, 2010

FTC 2d References are to Federal Tax Coordinator 2d
FIN References are to RIA's Analysis of Federal Taxes: Income
USTR References are to United States Tax Reporter: Income, Estate & Gift, and Excise
PCA References are to Pension Analysis (print & electronic)
PE References are to Pension Explanations (print & electronic)
EP References are to Estate Planning Analysis (print & electronic)

(or before Jan. 1, 2015, in the case of property relating to hydrogen) and, thus, these termination dates also apply to the above 2007 Technical Corrections Act amendment to the credit.

¶ 403. Definition of "qualified alternative fuel vehicle refueling property" is clarified

Code Sec. 30C(c), as amended by 2007 Technical Corrections Act § 6(b)(2)
Generally effective: Property placed in service after Dec. 31, 2005 and
    before Jan. 1, 2010
Committee Reports, see ¶ 5305

Code Sec. 30C allows a tax credit against income tax for a tax year equal to 30% of the cost, subject to dollar limits, of any qualified alternative fuel vehicle (QAFV) refueling property placed in service by the taxpayer during the tax year, see FTC 2d/FIN ¶ L-18041; USTR ¶ 30C4; TaxDesk ¶ 397,201. However, the QAFV refueling property credit isn't allowed for any property if the taxpayer elects not to have it apply to that property, see FTC 2d/FIN ¶ L-18043.1; USTR ¶ 30C4; TaxDesk ¶ 397,204.

The QAFV refueling property credit terminates, effective for property placed in service after Dec. 31, 2009, except in the case of QAFV refueling property relating to hydrogen. For QAFV refueling property relating to hydrogen, the credit won't apply to property placed in service after Dec. 31, 2014, see FTC 2d/FIN ¶ L-18041; USTR ¶ 30C4; TaxDesk ¶ 397,201.

For purposes of the QAFV refueling property credit, "qualified alternative fuel vehicle refueling property" is, with modifications, defined in Code Sec. 30C(c) by reference to a definition provided in Code Sec. 179A (which for property placed in service before Jan. 1, 2006 provided a deduction for qualified clean-fuel vehicle property and qualified clean-fuel vehicle refueling property, see FTC 2d/FIN ¶ K-7001; USTR ¶ 179A4; TaxDesk ¶ 307,001), see FTC 2d/FIN ¶ L-18043; USTR ¶ 30C4.02; TaxDesk ¶ 397,203.

Under pre-2007 Technical Corrections Act law, the reference made by the definition of "qualified alternative fuel vehicle refueling property" in Code Sec. 30C(c) was to "the meaning given to such term by section 179A(d)." (FTC 2d/FIN ¶ L-18043; USTR ¶ 30C4.02; TaxDesk ¶ 397,203) However, Code Sec. 179A(d) defines a different term. (Com Rept, see ¶ 5305)

The term defined in Code Sec. 179A(d) is "qualified clean-fuel vehicle refueling property" which is any property (not including a building and its structural components) if:

(1) the property is subject to depreciation,

(2) the original use of the property begins with the taxpayer, and

(3) the property is:

(A) for the storage or dispensing of a clean-burning fuel into the fuel tank of a motor vehicle propelled by that fuel, but only if the storage or dispensing of the fuel is at the point where the fuel is delivered into the fuel tank of the motor vehicle, or

(B) for the recharging of motor vehicles propelled by electricity, but only if the property is located at the point where the motor vehicles are recharged, see FTC 2d/FIN ¶ K-7017; USTR ¶ 179A4; TaxDesk ¶ 307,005.

New Law. The 2007 Technical Corrections Act modifies the language of Code Sec. 30C(c)(1) to refer to the correct term. (Com Rept, see ¶ 5305)

> **⊘** *observation:* As reflected below, the 2007 Technical Corrections Act modifies introductory language in Code Sec. 30C(c), and not, as stated in the Committee Report, in Code Sec. 30C(c)*(1)*, to replace the incorrect reference to the meaning of "qualified alternative fuel vehicle refueling property" in Code Sec. 179A(d) with a correct reference to the meaning of "qualified clean-fuel vehicle refueling property" in Code Sec. 179A(d).

> **⊘** *observation:* The 2007 Technical Corrections Act also makes other changes in the wording of Code Sec. 30C(c), which is reflected in its entirety below. However, unlike the change in the reference to Code Sec. 179A(d), the other changes don't appear to make any substantive change from Code Sec. 30C(c) as in effect under pre-2007 Technical Corrections Act law.

Thus, for purposes of Code Sec. 30C, the term "qualified alternative fuel vehicle refueling property" has the same meaning as the term "qualified clean-fuel vehicle refueling property" would have under Code Sec. 179A if— (Code Sec. 30C(c) as amended by 2007 Technical Corrections Act §6(b)(2))

(1) Code Sec. 179A(d)(1) (requiring that the property be depreciable, see FTC 2d/FIN ¶ K-7017; USTR ¶ 179A4; TaxDesk ¶ 307,005) did not apply to property installed on property which is used as the taxpayer's principal residence (within the meaning of Code Sec. 121, see FTC 2d/FIN ¶ I-4522; USTR ¶ 1214; TaxDesk ¶ 225,702), and (Code Sec. 30C(c)(1))

(2) only the following were treated as clean-burning fuels for purposes of Code Sec. 179A(d): (Code Sec. 30C(c)(2))

(A) any fuel at least 85 percent of the volume of which consists of one or more of the following: ethanol, natural gas, compressed natural gas, liquefied natural gas, liquefied petroleum gas, or hydrogen. (Code Sec. 30C(c)(2)(A))

(B) any mixture— (Code Sec. 30C(c)(2)(B))

(i) which consists of two or more of the following: biodiesel (as defined in Code Sec. 40A(d)(1), see FTC 2d/FIN ¶ L-17576; USTR ¶ 40A4; TaxDesk ¶ 382,405), diesel fuel (as defined in Code Sec. 4083(a)(3), see FTC 2d ¶ W-1515.1; USTR Excise Taxes ¶ 40,814), or kerosene, and (Code Sec. 30C(c)(2)(B)(i))

(ii) at least 20 percent of the volume of which consists of biodiesel (as defined above) determined without regard to any kerosene in the mixture. (Code Sec. 30C(c)(2)(B)(ii))

☐ **Effective:** Property placed in service after Dec. 31, 2005, in tax years ending after Dec. 31, 2005. (2007 Technical Corrections Act §6(e)(1))

2007 Technical Corrections Act §6(e)(1) provides that the amendment made by §6(b)(2) of the 2007 Technical Corrections Act takes effect as if included in the provisions of the 2005 Energy Tax Act to which the amendment relates. The amendment relates to 2005 Energy Tax Act §1342(a) (Sec. 1342(a), PL 109-58, 8/8/2005) which, under 2005 Energy Tax Act §1342(c) (Sec. 1342(c), PL 109-58, 8/8/2005), is effective for property placed in service after Dec. 31, 2005, in tax years ending after Dec. 31, 2005.

> **🅡🅘🅐** *observation:* As indicated above, the credit for QAFV refueling property only applies to property placed in service before Jan. 1, 2010 (or before Jan. 1, 2015, in the case of property relating to hydrogen) and, thus, these termination dates also apply to the above 2007 Technical Corrections Act amendment to the credit.

¶ 404. Energy research consortium amounts are included in allocation of the research credit among controlled group members and commonly controlled businesses

Code Sec. 41(f)(1)(A)(ii), as amended by 2007 Technical Corrections Act § 11(e)(2)
Code Sec. 41(f)(1)(B)(ii), as amended by 2007 Technical Corrections Act § 11(e)(2)
Generally effective: Amounts paid or incurred after Aug. 8, 2005
Committee Reports, None

The research credit has several components. The credit is (a) 20% of qualified research expenses in excess of a base amount, (b) 20% of basic research payments, and (c) 20% of certain amounts paid or incurred to an energy research consortium, see FTC 2d/FIN ¶ L-15302; USTR ¶ 414; TaxDesk ¶ 384,002.

An energy research consortium is defined as any organization:

(1) which is:

... described in Code Sec. 501(c)(3), exempt from tax under Code Sec. 501(a) and organized and operated primarily to conduct energy research, or

... organized and operated primarily to conduct energy research in the public interest (within the meaning of Code Sec. 501(c)(3));

> *observation:* The term "public interest" is not used in Code Sec. 501(c)(3). However, Reg §1.501(c)(3)-1(d)(1)(ii) says that an organization is not organized or operated exclusively for one or more of the exempt purposes specified in Code Sec. 501(c)(3) unless it serves a public interest rather than a private interest. For discussion of the difference between public and private interest for purposes of Reg §1.501(c)(3)-1(d)(1)(ii), see FTC 2d/FIN ¶ D-4126; USTR ¶ 5014.08; TaxDesk ¶ 670,609.

(2) which is not a private foundation;

(3) to which at least five unrelated persons paid or incurred, during the calendar year in which the tax year of the organization begins, amounts to that organization for energy research (including amounts paid or incurred as contributions); and

(4) to which no single person paid or incurred, during the calendar year, an amount (including any amount paid or incurred as a contribution) equal to more than 50% of the total amounts received by that organization during the calendar year for energy research, see FTC 2d/FIN ¶ L-15425.5; USTR ¶ 414.031; TaxDesk ¶ 384,014.1.

Under pre-2007 Technical Corrections Act law, the research credit allowable to each member of a controlled group or allowable under regs to each commonly controlled trade or business was its proportionate share of the qualified research expenses and basic research payments giving rise to the credit. (FTC 2d/FIN ¶ L-15317; USTR ¶ 414.03)

> *observation:* 2005 Energy Tax Act §1351(a)(1) (Sec. 1351(a)(1), PL 109-58, 8/8/2005) added the research credit for amounts paid or incurred to an energy research consortium, but the 2005 Energy Tax Act failed to add payments to an energy research consortium to the list of

research expenditures that must be allocated among members of a controlled group or among commonly controlled trades or businesses.

New Law. Under the 2007 Technical Corrections Act, the research credit allowable to each member of a controlled group or allowable under regs to each commonly controlled trade or business is its proportionate share of the qualified research expenses, basic research payments *and amounts paid or incurred to energy research consortiums* giving rise to the credit. (Code Sec. 41(f)(1)(A)(ii) as amended by 2007 Technical Corrections Act §11(e)(2)) (Code Sec. 41(f)(1)(B)(ii) as amended by 2007 Technical Corrections Act §11(e)(2))

For the requirement that amounts paid to an energy research consortium must be for energy research that is qualified research, see ¶ 405.

☐ **Effective:** Amounts paid or incurred after Aug. 8, 2005, in tax years ending after Aug. 8, 2005. (2007 Technical Corrections Act §11(e)(3))

> **✐ observation:** 2007 Technical Corrections Act §11(e)(3) provides that the provision discussed above takes effect as if included in the provision of the 2005 Energy Tax Act to which it relates. That provision is 2005 Energy Tax Act §1351 (Sec. 1351, PL 109-58, 8/8/2005). 2005 Energy Tax Act §1351(c) (Sec. 1351(c), PL 109-58, 8/8/2005) provides that the amendments made by §1351 apply to amounts paid or incurred after date of enactment of the 2005 Energy Tax Act, in tax years ending after date of enactment of the 2005 Energy Tax Act. The date of enactment of the 2005 Energy Tax Act was Aug. 8, 2005.

¶ 405. Research credit for research by an energy research consortium is clarified to require that the research be qualified energy research

Code Sec. 41(a)(3), as amended by 2007 Technical Corrections Act § 6(c)(1)
Code Sec. 41(f)(6)(E), as amended by 2007 Technical Corrections Act § 6(c)(2)
Generally effective: Amounts paid or incurred after Aug. 8, 2005
Committee Reports, see ¶ 5305

The research credit is the sum of three components— a qualified-research component, a basic-research component and an energy-research-consortium component, see FTC 2d/FIN ¶ L-15302; USTR ¶ 414; TaxDesk ¶ 384,002. The energy-research-consortium component is a credit equal to 20% of certain amounts (including contributed amounts) paid or incurred to an energy research consortium, see FTC 2d/FIN ¶ L-15425.4; USTR ¶ 414.031; TaxDesk ¶ 384,014.1.

An energy research consortium is defined as any organization:

(1) which is:

... described in Code Sec. 501(c)(3), exempt from tax under Code Sec. 501(a) and organized and operated primarily to conduct energy research, or

... organized and operated primarily to conduct energy research in the public interest (within the meaning of Code Sec. 501(c)(3));

> *observation:* The term "public interest" is not used in Code Sec. 501(c)(3). However, Reg §1.501(c)(3)-1(d)(1)(ii) says that an organization is not organized or operated exclusively for one or more of the exempt purposes specified in Code Sec. 501(c)(3) unless it serves a public interest rather than a private interest. For discussion of the difference between public and private interest for purposes of Reg §1.501(c)(3)-1(d)(1)(ii), see FTC 2d/FIN ¶ D-4126; USTR ¶ 5014.08; TaxDesk ¶ 670,609.

(2) which is not a private foundation;

(3) to which at least five unrelated persons paid or incurred, during the calendar year in which the tax year of the organization begins, amounts to that organization for energy research (including amounts paid or incurred as contributions); and

(4) to which no single person paid or incurred, during the calendar year, an amount (including any amount paid or incurred as a contribution) equal to more than 50% of the total amount received by that organization during the calendar year for energy research, see FTC 2d/FIN ¶ L-15425.5; USTR ¶ 414.031; TaxDesk ¶ 384,014.1.

Under pre-2007 Technical Corrections Act law, the only express credit-eligibility requirements in the Code that amounts paid or incurred to an energy-research consortium (see above) had to satisfy were that the amounts (1) had to be paid or incurred by a taxpayer in carrying on any trade or business of the taxpayer, and (2) weren't allowed to be paid or incurred for energy research conducted outside of the U.S., Puerto Rico or possessions of the U.S. (FTC 2d/FIN ¶ L-15425.4; USTR ¶ 414.031; TaxDesk ¶ 384,014.1)

> *observation:* However, the Joint Committee Staff's Description and Technical Explanation of the 2005 Energy Tax Act indicated that the energy-research-consortium portion of the research credit was to be available only for expenditures for *qualified energy research* undertaken

---

FTC 2d References are to Federal Tax Coordinator 2d
FIN References are to RIA's Analysis of Federal Taxes: Income
USTR References are to United States Tax Reporter: Income, Estate & Gift, and Excise
PCA References are to Pension Analysis (print & electronic)
PE References are to Pension Explanations (print & electronic)
EP References are to Estate Planning Analysis (print & electronic)

by an energy research consortium, see FTC 2d/FIN ¶ L-15425.4; USTR ¶ 414.031; TaxDesk ¶ 384,014.1.

New Law. Under the 2007 Technical Corrections Act, for amounts to be eligible for the energy-research-consortium portion of the research credit, the amounts must be for "energy research." (Code Sec. 41(a)(3) as amended by 2007 Technical Corrections Act §6(c)(1)) Energy research doesn't include any research which isn't qualified research. (Code Sec. 41(f)(6)(E) as amended by 2007 Technical Corrections Act §6(c)(2)) Thus, the 2007 Technical Corrections Act clarifies that the credit is available for amounts paid or incurred to an energy research consortium provided they are used for energy research that is qualified research. (Com Rept, see ¶ 5305)

> **⊘ observation:** For purposes of Code Sec. 41, which provides the research credit, Code Sec. 41(d)(1) defines "qualified research" as research (1) for which expenditures may be treated as expenses under Code Sec. 174, (2) which is undertaken for the purpose of discovering information that is technological in nature and the application of which is intended to be useful in the development of a new or improved business component of the taxpayer, (3) substantially all of the activities of which are elements of a process or experimentation for certain enumerated purposes and (4) that doesn't consist of certain excluded activities, see FTC 2d/FIN ¶ L-15406; USTR ¶ 414.01; TaxDesk ¶ 384,009.

For the allocation of the energy-research-consortium portion of the research credit among controlled group members and commonly controlled businesses, see ¶ 404.

☐ **Effective:** Amounts paid or incurred after Aug. 8, 2005, in tax years ending after Aug. 8, 2005. (2007 Technical Corrections Act §6(e)(1))

> **⊘ observation:** 2007 Technical Corrections Act §6(e)(1) provides that the provisions discussed above take effect as if included in the provision of the 2005 Energy Tax Act to which they relate. That provision is 2005 Energy Tax Act §1351 (Sec. 1351, PL 109-58, 8/8/2005). 2005 Energy Tax Act §1351(c) (Sec. 1351(c), PL 109-58, 8/8/2005) provides that the amendments made by §1351 apply to amounts paid or incurred after date of enactment of the 2005 Energy Tax Act, in tax years ending after date of enactment of the 2005 Energy Tax Act. The date of enactment of the 2005 Energy Tax Act was Aug. 8, 2005.

¶ 406. Clarification of proportionate limitation applicable to closed-loop biomass for purposes of the credit for electricity produced from renewable resources applies retroactively to electricity produced and sold after Oct. 22, 2004

Code Sec. 45(d)(2)(B)(ii), as amended by 2007 Technical Corrections Act § 7(b)(2)

Generally effective: Electricity produced and sold after Oct. 22, 2004

Committee Reports, see ¶ 5306

The credit under Code Sec. 45(a) for electricity produced from renewable resources (i.e., the electricity production credit) is 1.5 cents per kilowatt hour (KWH) of electricity produced by the taxpayer from qualified energy resources (including closed-loop biomass) at a qualified facility (see FTC 2d/FIN ¶ L-17770 *et seq.*; USTR ¶ 454.09 *et seq.*; TaxDesk ¶ 384,054) during a limited period (see FTC 2d/FIN ¶ L-17752; USTR ¶ 454.05; TaxDesk ¶ 384,055) and sold by the taxpayer (i.e., the producer of the electricity eligible for the credit) to an unrelated person during the tax year. See FTC 2d/FIN ¶ L-17751; USTR ¶ 454.01; TaxDesk ¶ 384,054.

Qualified facilities include closed-loop biomass facilities that are modified for co-firing (i.e., the burning of closed-loop biomass with coal, with other biomass, or with both). (FTC 2d/FIN ¶ L-17755, ¶ L-17771; USTR ¶ 454.09)

Code Sec. 45(d)(2)(B)(ii), under pre-2007 Technical Corrections Act law, provided that when closed-loop biomass was co-fired with coal, with other biomass, or with both, the amount of the credit determined under Code Sec. 45(a) for a facility was limited to the otherwise allowable credit multiplied by the ratio of: (1) the thermal content of the closed-loop biomass used in that facility to (2) the thermal content of all fuels used in that facility. (FTC 2d/FIN ¶ L-17771; USTR ¶ 454.09) This limitation duplicated a similar limitation in Code Sec. 45(a) (discussed above). The limitation under Code Sec. 45(a) had the effect of limiting the credit (or duration of the credit) to the appropriate portion of the fuel that constituted qualified energy resources, in the situations in which qualified energy resources are permitted to be co-fired with each other, or are permitted to be co-fired with other fuels. (Com Rept, see ¶ 5306)

New Law. The 2007 Technical Corrections Act strikes the clause that provided that when closed-loop biomass is co-fired with coal, with other biomass,

---

FTC 2d References are to Federal Tax Coordinator 2d
FIN References are to RIA's Analysis of Federal Taxes: Income
USTR References are to United States Tax Reporter: Income, Estate & Gift, and Excise
PCA References are to Pension Analysis (print & electronic)
PE References are to Pension Explanations (print & electronic)
EP References are to Estate Planning Analysis (print & electronic)

or with both, the amount of the credit determined under Code Sec. 45(a) for the facility is limited to the otherwise allowable credit multiplied by the ratio of the thermal content of the closed-loop biomass used in that facility to the thermal content of all fuel used in that facility. (Code Sec. 45(d)(2)(B)(ii) as amended by 2007 Technical Corrections Act §7(b)(2)) Thus, the 2007 Technical Corrections Act clarifies that the limitation applies only once, not twice, to closed-loop biomass co-fired with other fuels by striking the duplicate limitation. (Com Rept, see ¶ 5306)

Redesignation. Pre-2007 Technical Corrections Act Code Sec. 45(d)(2)(B)(iii) is redesignated by the 2007 Technical Corrections Act as Code Sec. 45(d)(2)(B)(ii). (2007 Technical Corrections Act §7(b)(2))

☐ **Effective:** Electricity produced and sold after Oct. 22, 2004, in tax years ending after that date. (2007 Technical Corrections Act §7(e)(1))

> **observation:** 2007 Technical Corrections Act §7(e)(1) provides that the amendment made by 2007 Technical Corrections Act §7(b)(2) takes effect as if included in 2004 Jobs Act §710 (Sec. 710, PL 108-357, 10/22/2004). 2004 Jobs Act §710(g)(1) (Sec. 710(g)(1), PL 108-357, 10/22/2004) provided that the provision applied to electricity produced and sold after Oct. 22, 2004, in tax years ending after that date.

¶ 407. Open-loop biomass segregation from other waste materials requirement is retroactively eliminated for purposes of the Code Sec. 45 electricity production credit

Code Sec. 45(c)(3)(A)(ii), as amended by 2007 Technical Corrections Act § 7(b)(1)
Generally effective: Electricity produced and sold after Oct. 22, 2004
Committee Reports, see ¶ 5306

The credit under Code Sec. 45(a) for electricity produced from renewable resources (i.e., the electricity production credit) is 1.5 cents per kilowatt hour (KWH) of electricity produced by the taxpayer from qualified energy resources (including open-loop biomass) at a qualified facility (see FTC 2d/FIN ¶ L-17770 *et seq.*; USTR ¶ 454.09 *et seq.*; TaxDesk ¶ 384,054) during a limited period (see FTC 2d/FIN ¶ L-17752; USTR ¶ 454.05; TaxDesk ¶ 384,055) and sold by the taxpayer (i.e., the producer of the electricity eligible for the credit) to an unrelated person during the tax year (see FTC 2d/FIN ¶ L-17751; USTR ¶ 454.01; TaxDesk ¶ 384,054).

Under pre-2007 Technical Corrections Act law, "open-loop biomass," one of the qualified energy resources for purposes of the credit for electricity produced from renewable resources ("the electricity production credit,") was defined in part as solid, nonhazardous, cellulosic waste material or any lignin material that was segregated from other waste materials. (FTC 2d/FIN ¶ L-17771.1; USTR ¶ 454.10)

New Law. Because both open-loop biomass and municipal solid waste can be treated as qualified energy resources (Com Rept, see ¶ 5306), the 2007 Technical Corrections Act eliminates the requirement that open-loop biomass must be segregated from other waste materials for purposes of the electricity production credit. (Code Sec. 45(c)(3)(A)(ii) as amended by 2007 Technical Corrections Act §7(b)(1))

> *observation:* If a taxpayer failed to claim the electricity production credit for electricity produced from open-loop biomass that was not segregated from other waste materials, and the electricity was sold after Oct. 22, 2004 (in tax years beginning after that date), those taxpayers may amend their returns to claim the credit.

☐ **Effective:** Electricity produced and sold after Oct. 22, 2004, in tax years ending after that date. (2007 Technical Corrections Act §7(e)(1)) For open-loop biomass facilities not using agricultural livestock waste nutrients and placed in service before Oct. 22, 2004, the above rules apply to electricity produced and sold after Dec. 31, 2004, in tax years ending after that date. (2007 Technical Corrections Act §7(e)(1))

> *observation:* The 2007 Technical Corrections Act §7(e)(1) provides that the amendment made by 2007 Technical Corrections Act §7(b)(1) takes effect as if included in 2004 Jobs Act §710 (Sec. 710, PL 108-357, 10/22/2004). 2004 Jobs Act §710(g)(1) (Sec. 710(g)(1), PL 108-357, 10/22/2004) provided that the provision applied to electricity produced at qualified open-loop biomass facilities and sold after Oct. 22, 2004, in tax years ending after that date. 2004 Jobs Act §710(g)(2) (Sec. 710(g)(2), PL 108-357, 10/22/2004) provided that for open-loop biomass facilities not using agricultural livestock waste nutrients and placed in service before Oct. 22, 2004, the provision applied to electricity produced and sold after Dec. 31, 2004, in tax years ending after Dec. 31, 2004.

FTC 2d References are to Federal Tax Coordinator 2d
FIN References are to RIA's Analysis of Federal Taxes: Income
USTR References are to United States Tax Reporter: Income, Estate & Gift, and Excise
PCA References are to Pension Analysis (print & electronic)
PE References are to Pension Explanations (print & electronic)
EP References are to Estate Planning Analysis (print & electronic)

¶ 408. Bonus depreciation and AMT exemption rules for qualified cellulosic biomass ethanol plant property are retroactively corrected to permit non-enzymatic hydrolysis

Code Sec. 168(l)(3), as amended by 2007 Technical Corrections Act § 11(b)(1)
Generally effective: Property purchased after Dec. 20, 2006 and placed in service before Jan. 1, 2013
Committee Reports, None

For most tangible property, the depreciation deduction under Code Sec. 167(a) is determined under the modified accelerated cost recovery system (MACRS) provided by Code Sec. 168, see FTC 2d/FIN ¶ L-8101; USTR ¶ 1684; TaxDesk ¶ 266,001.

Certain property depreciated on the 200% declining balance method for regular income tax purposes must be depreciated on the 150% declining balance method for alternative minimum tax purposes (the AMT depreciation adjustment), see FTC 2d/FIN ¶ A-8220; USTR ¶ 564.01; TaxDesk ¶ 696,513.

From time to time, for certain depreciable property, there has been allowed both 50% additional first-year depreciation (50% bonus depreciation) in the year that the property was placed in service (with corresponding reductions in basis), see FTC 2d/FIN ¶s L-9311, L-9336, L-9356; USTR ¶s 1684.025, 1684.08, 14,00N4.02; TaxDesk ¶s 269,331, 269,341, 267,801, and (2) exemption from the AMT depreciation adjustment (AMT exemption), see FTC 2d/FIN ¶ A-8221; USTR ¶s 1684.029, 1684.08, 14,00N4.02; TaxDesk ¶ 696,514.

One of the types of property for which both 50% bonus depreciation and AMT exemption is available is "qualified cellulosic biomass ethanol plant property" (QCBEPP), see FTC 2d/FIN ¶s A-8221, L-9356; USTR ¶ 1684.08; TaxDesk ¶s 267,801, 696,514.

Among the requirements for being QCBEPP are that the property be used solely to produce "cellulosic biomass ethanol," be acquired by the taxpayer by purchase after Dec, 20, 2006 (and not under a written binding contract for the acquisition in effect before Dec. 21, 2006) and be placed in service by the taxpayer before Jan. 1, 2013, see FTC 2d/FIN ¶ L-9357; USTR ¶ 1684.081; TaxDesk ¶ 267,802.

Under pre-2007 Technical Corrections Act law, "cellulosic biomass ethanol" was defined as "ethanol produced by *enzymatic* hydrolysis of any lignocellulosic or hemicellulosic matter that is available on a renewable or recurring basis." (FTC 2d/FIN ¶ L-9357; USTR ¶ 1684.081; TaxDesk ¶ 267,802)

New Law. The 2007 Technical Corrections Act removes the word "enzymatic" from the definition of "cellulosic biomass ethanol" discussed above. (Code Sec. 168(l)(3) as amended by 2007 Technical Corrections Act §11(b)(1))

> ⓡ*observation:* Thus, under the 2007 Technical Corrections Act, property that meets all of the other requirements for being QCBEPP will satisfy the definition, and thus qualify for 50% bonus depreciation and AMT exemption, if the product that the property is used to produce is "ethanol produced by hydrolysis of any lignocellulosic or hemicellulosic matter that is available on a renewable or recurring basis."

> Therefore, the form of hydrolysis used to "break down" lignocellulosic or hemicellulosic matter into ethanol (and some bi-products) can involve, but doesn't have to involve, cellulase enzymes. For example, the form of hydrolysis can be one in which the lignocellulosic or hemicellulosic matter is broken down using acids under high pressure and high heat ("chemical hydrolysis").

☐ **Effective:** Property placed in service after Dec. 20, 2006 in tax years ending after Dec. 20, 2006 (2007 Technical Corrections Act §11(b)(3)) but only if the property is (1) acquired by the taxpayer by purchase after Dec. 20, 2006 (and not under a written binding contract for the acquisition in effect before Dec. 21, 2006) (see above) and (2) placed in service by the taxpayer before Jan. 1, 2013 (see above).

> ⓡ*observation:* 2007 Technical Corrections Act §11(b)(3) provides that the provision discussed above is effective as if included in the provision of the 2006 Tax Relief Act to which it relates. That provision is 2006 Tax Relief Act §209(a) (Sec. 209(a), PL 109-432, 12/20/2006). 2006 Tax Relief Act §209(b) (Sec. 209(b), PL 109-432, 12/20/2006) provides that §209 took effect for property placed in service after Dec. 20, 2006 in tax years ending after Dec. 20, 2006.

¶ 409. IRS cannot allocate more than the national capacity limitation of 6,000 megawatts for purposes of advanced nuclear power facilities credit computation

Code Sec. 45J(b)(2), as amended by 2007 Technical Corrections Act § 6(a)
Generally effective: Production in tax years beginning after Aug. 8, 2005
Committee Reports, see ¶ 5305

FTC 2d References are to Federal Tax Coordinator 2d
FIN References are to RIA's Analysis of Federal Taxes: Income
USTR References are to United States Tax Reporter: Income, Estate & Gift, and Excise
PCA References are to Pension Analysis (print & electronic)
PE References are to Pension Explanations (print & electronic)
EP References are to Estate Planning Analysis (print & electronic)

A credit is available under Code Sec. 45J equal to 1.8¢ for each kilowatt hour of electricity produced by a taxpayer at an advanced nuclear power facility during the 8-year period beginning on the date the facility was originally placed in service and sold by the taxpayer to an unrelated person during the tax year. See FTC 2d/FIN ¶ L-17691; USTR ¶ 45J4; TaxDesk ¶ 384,061. However, the amount of credit which would otherwise be allowed is limited to an amount which bears the same ratio to the amount of credit which would otherwise be allowed as (A) the national megawatt capacity limitation allocated to the facility by IRS, bears to (B) the total megawatt nameplate capacity of the facility. See FTC 2d/FIN ¶ L-17695; USTR ¶ 45J4; TaxDesk ¶ 384,061. Under pre-2007 Technical Corrections Act law, the national megawatt capacity limitation is 6,000 megawatts. (FTC 2d/FIN ¶ L-17696; USTR ¶ 45J4)

New Law. The 2007 Technical Corrections Act provides that the aggregate amount of national megawatt capacity limitation allocated by IRS under Code Sec. 45J(b)(3) cannot exceed 6,000 megawatts. (Code Sec. 45J(b)(2) as amended by 2007 Technical Corrections Act §6(a)) Thus, the 2007 Technical Corrections Act clarifies that the national capacity limitation of 6,000 megawatts represents the total number of megawatts that IRS has authority to allocate under Code Sec. 45J. (Com Rept, see ¶ 5305)

☐ **Effective:** Production in tax years beginning after Aug. 8, 2005. (2007 Technical Corrections Act §6(e)(1))

> **⊘** *observation:* The 2007 Technical Corrections Act §6(e)(1) provides that the amendment made by 2007 Technical Corrections Act §6(a) takes effect as if included in the provision of the 2005 Energy Tax Act to which the rule relates. The above rule relates to 2005 Energy Tax Act § 1306 (Sec. 1306, PL 109-58, 8/8/2005), which under 2005 Energy Tax Act § 1306(d) (Sec. 1306(d), PL 109-58, 8/8/2005) is effective for production in tax years beginning after Aug. 8, 2005.

¶ 410. Credit for electricity produced at qualified wind facilities originally placed in service before July 1, '99 and sold to utilities under certain pre-'87 contracts is not disallowed due to a change in ownership

Code Sec. 45(e)(7)(A)(i), as amended by 2007 Technical Corrections Act § 9(a)
Generally effective: Dec. 17, '99
Committee Reports, see ¶ 5308

Under pre-2007 Technical Corrections Act law, the Code Sec. 45 credit for electricity produced from renewable resources ("electricity production credit," see FTC 2d/FIN ¶ L-17750 *et seq.*; USTR ¶ 454 *et seq.*; TaxDesk ¶ 384,054 *et seq.*) didn't apply to electricity sold to utilities under certain pre-'87 contracts (see FTC 2d/FIN ¶ L-17764.1; USTR ¶ 454.04), where the electricity was produced at a qualified wind facility (see FTC 2d/FIN ¶ L-17771.5; USTR ¶ 454.14) that was *placed in service by the taxpayer* after June 30, '99. (FTC 2d/FIN ¶ L-17764.1; USTR ¶ 454.04)

> 🅡🄸🄰 *observation:* Thus, under pre-2007 Technical Corrections Act law, if another person placed a qualified wind facility in service *before* July 1, '99, and then sold or otherwise transferred the facility to the taxpayer after June 30, '99, the taxpayer couldn't take the credit for electricity sold to utilities under certain pre-'87 contracts because the taxpayer had placed the facility (producing the electricity) in service *after* June 30, '99.

> 🅡🄸🄰 *observation:* The rule discussed above (that disallowed the credit when electricity was sold to utilities under certain pre-'87 contracts under pre-2007 Technical Corrections Act law) applied only to electricity produced at qualified *wind* facilities that were placed in service by the taxpayer after June 30, '99. The credit is not disallowed when electricity produced at other types of qualified facilities (such as closed-loop biomass, open-loop biomass, geothermal energy, solar energy, small irrigation power, municipal solid waste or hydropower) is sold to utilities.

New Law. Under the 2007 Technical Corrections Act, the electricity production credit doesn't apply to electricity sold to utilities under certain pre-'87 contracts if the electricity is produced at a qualified wind facility *originally* placed in service after June 30, '99. (Code Sec. 45(e)(7)(A)(i) as amended by 2007 Technical Corrections Act §9(a)) Thus, facilities placed in service before June 30, '99 that sell electricity under applicable pre-'87 contracts are not denied the electricity production credit solely by reason of a change in ownership after June 30, '99. (Com Rept, see ¶ 5308)

> 🅡🄸🄰 *observation:* Thus, the limitation on the electricity production credit provided in Code Sec. 45(e)(7)(A) doesn't apply to electricity sold to utilities under certain pre-'87 contracts if the electricity was produced by a qualified wind facility even if a person or entity other than the taxpayer originally placed a facility in service before July 1, '99 and later sold or otherwise transferred the qualified wind facility to the taxpayer. As long as the facility was originally placed in service before

---

FTC 2d References are to Federal Tax Coordinator 2d
FIN References are to RIA's Analysis of Federal Taxes: Income
USTR References are to United States Tax Reporter: Income, Estate & Gift, and Excise
PCA References are to Pension Analysis (print & electronic)
PE References are to Pension Explanations (print & electronic)
EP References are to Estate Planning Analysis (print & electronic)

July 1, '99 and otherwise meets the requirements provided in Code Sec. 45(e)(7)(A), the fact that the taxpayer placed the facility in service after June 30, '99 doesn't disqualify the taxpayer from claiming the electricity production credit.

☐ **Effective:** Dec. 17, '99. (2007 Technical Corrections Act §9(c))

    🅡 *observation:* 2007 Technical Corrections Act §9(c) provides that the amendment made by 2007 Technical Corrections Act §9(a) takes effect as if included in '99 Tax Relief Extension Act provision to which it relates. This amendment relates to '99 Tax Relief Extension Act §507 (Sec. 507, PL 106-170, 12/17/1999). '99 Tax Relief Extension Act §507(d) (Sec. 507(d), PL 106-170, 12/17/1999) provides that the amendments in §507 take effect on the date of enactment of the '99 Tax Relief Extension Act, i.e., Dec. 17, '99.

    🅡 *observation:* Although the effective date of 2007 Technical Corrections Act §9(a) is retroactive to Dec. 17 '99, the practical effect of the change is that the limitation on the electricity production credit provided in Code Sec. 47(e)(7)(A) doesn't apply to electricity produced at a qualified wind facility that was originally placed in service before June 30, '99 and sold to utilities under certain pre-'87 contracts.

    🅡 *recommendation:* As a result of the change made by 2007 Technical Corrections Act §9(a) (discussed above), some taxpayers who didn't claim the electricity production credit (due to the limitation in Code Sec. 47(e)(7)(A) under pre-2007 Technical Corrections Act law) on production from qualified facilities that were originally placed in service before July 1, '99 may be eligible to claim the credit for that production. Those taxpayers should consider claiming a refund (based on the credit) on an amended return for all tax years that aren't barred by the limitations period.

    🅡 *observation:* Generally, a refund claim has to be filed (1) within three years of the time the return was filed, except, if the return was filed before it was due, it must be filed within three years of the return's due date, or (2) within two years from the time the tax was paid (if later). (FTC 2d/FIN ¶ T-7501; USTR ¶ 65,114.01; TaxDesk ¶ 806,001). Thus, even though the change made by the 2007 Technical Corrections Act is retroactive to Dec. 17, '99, several tax years (e.g., '99 through 2003) may be barred for purposes of refunds or credits to many taxpayers.

¶ 411. Clarification that the definitions of qualified fuel cell property and qualified microturbine property apply for all purposes of the Code Sec. 48 energy credit

Code Sec. 48(c), as amended by 2007 Technical Corrections Act § 11(a)(8)
Generally effective: Dec. 29, 2007
Committee Reports, None

Qualified fuel cell property is a fuel cell power plant which has a nameplate capacity of at least 0.5 kilowatt of electricity using an electrochemical process, and has an electricity-only generation efficiency greater than 30%, see FTC 2d/FIN ¶ L-16436.1; USTR ¶ 484; TaxDesk ¶ 381,602.

Qualified microturbine property means a "stationary microturbine power plant" that has (1) a nameplate capacity of less than 2,000 kilowatts and (2) an electricity-only generation efficiency of not less than 26% at International Standard Organization conditions, see FTC 2d/FIN ¶ L-16437.1; USTR ¶ 484; TaxDesk ¶ 381,602.

The energy percentage is 30% in the case of:

(1) qualified fuel cell property;

(2) energy property described in Code Sec. 48(a)(3)(A)(i) (equipment using solar energy to generate electricity, to heat or cool (or provide hot water for use in) a structure, or to provide solar process heat, excepting property used to generate energy for the purpose of heating a swimming pool), but only for periods ending before Jan. 1, 2009; and

(3) energy property described in Code Sec. 48(a)(3)(A)(ii) (equipment that uses solar energy to illuminate the inside of a structure using fiber-optic distributed sunlight, but only for periods before Jan. 1, 2009. See FTC 2d/FIN ¶ L-16401; USTR ¶ 484.

The credit is 10% for any energy property not listed at (1) through (3), above. See FTC 2d/FIN ¶ L-16401; USTR ¶ 484.

> **♥️ observation:** Energy property not listed at (1) through (3) refers to geothermal property, qualified microturbine property, and solar energy property.

FTC 2d References are to Federal Tax Coordinator 2d
FIN References are to RIA's Analysis of Federal Taxes: Income
USTR References are to United States Tax Reporter: Income, Estate & Gift, and Excise
PCA References are to Pension Analysis (print & electronic)
PE References are to Pension Explanations (print & electronic)
EP References are to Estate Planning Analysis (print & electronic)

Energy property for which the business energy credit is allowed includes qualified fuel cell property or qualified microturbine property. See FTC 2d/FIN ¶ L-16401; USTR ¶ 484.

Under 2005 Energy Tax Act §1336(b) (Sec. 1336(b), PL 109-58, 8/8/2005), Code Sec. 48(c) provided that qualified fuel cell property and qualified microturbine property, as defined under Code Sec. 48(c), applied for purposes of this "subsection," i.e., Code Sec. 48(c), rather than for all of Code Sec. 48. (FTC 2d/FIN ¶ L-16401; USTR ¶ 484; TaxDesk ¶ 381,602)

New Law. The 2007 Technical Corrections Act clarifies that the definitions of qualified fuel cell property and qualified microturbine property (and the other provisions relating to qualified fuel cell property and qualified microturbine property contained in Code Sec. 48(c)) apply to *all* of Code Sec. 48, including the provision under Code Sec. 48(a)(2)(A)(i)(I) at (1) above that the energy percentage is 30% for qualified fuel cell property and the definition of energy property under Code Sec. 48(a)(3)(A)(iv) above as including qualified fuel cell property and qualified microturbine property. (Code Sec. 48(c) as amended by 2007 Technical Corrections Act §11(a)(8))

☐ **Effective:** Dec. 29, 2007.

¶ 412. Amortization period of geological and geophysical (G&G) expenditures for certain major integrated oil companies is extended from 5 years to 7 years

Code Sec. 167(h)(5)(A), as amended by 2007 Energy Act § 1502(a)
Generally effective: Amounts paid or incurred after Dec. 19, 2007
Committee Reports, see ¶ 5102

Under pre-2007 Energy Act law, the amortization period for geological and geophysical (G&G) costs is five years for certain "major integrated oil companies" (defined at FTC 2d/FIN ¶ N-3201; USTR ¶ 1674.126; TaxDesk ¶ 271,701). Code Sec. 167(h)(1) (allowing any G&G expenses paid or incurred in connection with the exploration for, or development of, oil and gas to be deducted ratably over a 24-month period) and Code Sec. 167(h)(4) (treatment of amortization expenses on abandonment during the 24-month period) were applied by substituting "five-year" period for "24-month" period in the case of a major integrated oil company. That meant that the amortization period for G&G costs was extended to five years for certain integrated oil companies. (FTC 2d/FIN ¶ N-3201; USTR ¶ 1674.126; TaxDesk ¶ 271,701)

> *observation:* Thus, major integrated oil companies had to amortize any G&G expenditures paid or incurred after May 17, 2006 over the five-year period beginning on the date that the expenses are paid or incurred. Also, if a major integrated oil company retired or abandoned

any property with respect to which G&G expenditures were paid or incurred during that five-year amortization period, it couldn't take a deduction at the time of the retirement or abandonment. Instead, the amortization over five years continued with respect to the payment. Thus, in the case of abandoned property, remaining basis wasn't recovered in the year of abandonment of the property, since all basis was recovered over the five-year period.

🖉 *observation:* Except for the five-year amortization that was allowed to major integrated oil companies for post-May 17, 2006 G&G expenditures under pre-2007 Energy Act law, no depreciation or amortization deduction was allowed for those payments.

🖉 *observation:* Since Code Sec. 263A(c)(3) provides that the UNICAP rules don't apply to any cost allowable as a deduction under Code Sec. 167(h) (see FTC 2d/FIN ¶ G-5518; USTR ¶ 263A4.05; TaxDesk ¶ 456,013), the UNICAP rules do not apply to major integrated oil companies' post-May 17, 2006 G&G costs for which five-year amortization was allowable.

New Law. The 2007 Energy Act extends from five years to seven years the amortization period for G&G costs for major integrated oil companies. (Com Rept, see ¶ 5102) Specifically, for major integrated oil companies, Code Sec. 167(h)(1) (allowing any G&G expenses paid or incurred in connection with the exploration for, or development of, oil and gas to be deducted ratably over a 24-month period) and Code Sec. 167(h)(4) (providing that if any property is retired or abandoned during the 24-month period, no deduction is allowed on account of the retirement or abandonment and the amortization deduction continues) are applied by substituting "seven-year period" for "24-month period." (Code Sec. 167(h)(5)(A) as amended by 2007 Energy Act §1502(a))

🖉 *observation:* Under the 2007 Energy Act, certain major integrated oil companies must amortize G&G costs over seven years, whereas other taxpayers (for example, oil companies that aren't major integrated oil companies) can amortize these costs over 24 months. The seven-year period has the effect of reducing the annual expense deduction for G&G costs that major integrated oil companies could have taken in a tax year under the five-year rule under pre-2007 Energy Act law.

FTC 2d References are to Federal Tax Coordinator 2d
FIN References are to RIA's Analysis of Federal Taxes: Income
USTR References are to United States Tax Reporter: Income, Estate & Gift, and Excise
PCA References are to Pension Analysis (print & electronic)
PE References are to Pension Explanations (print & electronic)
EP References are to Estate Planning Analysis (print & electronic)

☐ **Effective:** Amounts paid or incurred after Dec. 19, 2007. (2007 Energy Act §1502(b))

¶ 500. Exempt Organizations

¶ 501. Code Sec. 501(c)(3) organizations must make available for public inspection copies of Form 990-T relating to UBIT for three years

Code Sec. 6104(d)(1)(A)(ii), as amended by 2007 Technical Corrections Act § 3(g)(2)

Code Sec. 6104(d)(2), as amended by 2007 Technical Corrections Act § 3(g)(3)

Generally effective: Returns filed after Aug. 17, 2006

Committee Reports, see ¶ 5302

Code Sec. 501(c)(3) organizations (see FTC 2d/FIN ¶ D-4101 *et seq.*; USTR ¶ 5014.05; TaxDesk ¶ 670,501) must allow public inspection of their annual returns (see FTC 2d/FIN ¶ S-6601; USTR ¶ 61,044). Under this rule, tax-exempt organizations must make their annual information returns available for public inspection. For this purpose, the term "annual information return" means an exact copy of any return filed by a tax-exempt organization under Code Sec. 6033, or any amended return the organization filed with IRS after the date the original return was filed. Returns filed under Code Sec. 6033 include Form 990, Return of Organization Exempt From Income Tax, Form 990-PF, Return of Private Foundation, and Form 1065 (U.S. partnership return). (FTC 2d/FIN ¶ S-6603; USTR ¶ 61,044)

Under pre-2007 Technical Corrections Act law, annual returns filed under Code Sec. 6033 (i.e., Form 990) had to be made available for inspection only during the three-year period beginning on the due date (including extensions) for filing the return. (FTC 2d/FIN ¶ S-6644; USTR ¶ 61,044)

In the 2006 Pension Protection Act (Sec. 1225(a), PL 109-280, 8/17/2006), Congress amended Code Sec. 6101(d)(1)(A)(ii) to require that Code Sec. 501(c)(3) organizations make publicly available their unrelated business income tax (UBIT) returns. However, as drafted, the requirement that, with respect to a Form 990, an organization had to make publicly available only the last three years of returns under Code Sec. 6104(d)(2) did not apply to disclosure of Form 990-T because Form 990-T was required under Code Sec. 6011, not Code Sec. 6033. (Com Rept, see ¶ 5302)

FTC 2d References are to Federal Tax Coordinator 2d
FIN References are to RIA's Analysis of Federal Taxes: Income
USTR References are to United States Tax Reporter: Income, Estate & Gift, and Excise
PCA References are to Pension Analysis (print & electronic)
PE References are to Pension Explanations (print & electronic)
EP References are to Estate Planning Analysis (print & electronic)

New Law. The 2007 Technical Corrections Act provides that the public inspection of returns under Code Sec. 6104(d)(1) applies to annual returns filed under Code Sec. 6011 during the three-year period beginning on the last day prescribed for filing those returns (determined with regard to any filing extensions). (Code Sec. 6104(d)(2) as amended by 2007 Technical Corrections Act §3(g)(3)) Thus, the 2007 Technical Corrections Act clarifies that the three-year limitation on making returns publicly available applies to Form 990-T. (Com Rept, see ¶ 5302)

> **◆ *observation:*** Thus, the 2007 Technical Corrections Act law provides that Forms 990-T have to be publicly available for inspection at the organization's principal office or at a regional or district office for three years after the due date of the return in the same manner as annual returns filed under Code Sec. 6033 were available under pre-2007 Technical Corrections Act law.

The 2007 Technical Corrections Act provides that the public inspection of returns applies to:

. . . any annual return which is filed under Code Sec. 6011 by an organization described in Code Sec. 501(c)(3) and

. . . which relates to any tax imposed by Code Sec. 511(relating to imposition of tax on unrelated business income of charitable, etc., organizations.

(Code Sec. 6104(d)(1)(A)(ii) as amended by 2007 Technical Corrections Act §3(g)(2))

> **◆ *observation:*** Although Congress rewrote Code Sec. 6104(d)(1)(A)(ii), there is presumably no substantive change to the definition.

For discussion of the requirement that IRS allow public inspection of UBIT returns of tax-exempt organizations filed under Code Sec. 6011, see ¶ 502.

☐ **Effective:** Returns filed after Aug. 17, 2006. (2007 Technical Corrections Act §3(j))

> **◆ *observation:*** The 2007 Technical Corrections Act §3(j) provides that the amendments made by 2007 Technical Corrections Act §3(g)(2) and §3(g)(3) apply as if included in 2006 Pension Protection Act §1225(a). (Sec. 1225(a), PL 109-280, 8/17/2006). 2006 Pension Protection Act §1225(b) (Sec. 1225(b), PL 109-280, 8/17/2006) provided that the amendments made by 2006 Pension Protection Act §1225(a) apply to returns filed after Aug. 17, 2006.

¶ 502. IRS must allow public inspection of unrelated business income tax (UBIT) returns of tax-exempt organizations, such as Form 990-T, filed under Code Sec. 6011

Code Sec. 6104(b), as amended by 2007 Technical Corrections Act § 3(g)(1)(B)
Generally effective: Returns filed after Aug. 17, 2006
Committee Reports, see ¶ 5302

Under pre-2007 Technical Corrections Act law, IRS was required to allow public inspection for the following information:

(1) information required under Code Sec. 6033 from exempt organizations such as Form 990 (Return of Organization Exempt From Income Tax) and Form 990-PF (Return of Private Foundation) (FTC 2d/FIN ¶ S-2800 :; USTR ¶ 60,334; TaxDesk ¶ 688,001)

(2) information required from certain charitable trusts under Code Sec. 6034, see FTC 2d/FIN ¶ S-2806; USTR ¶ 60,344; TaxDesk ¶ 688,009; and

(3) information required in connection with certain deferred compensation plans under Code Sec. 6058, see FTC 2d/FIN ¶ S-3351; USTR ¶ 60,584; TaxDesk ¶ 813,001.

Information such as names, addresses, and amounts of contributions or bequests to organizations other than private foundations are redacted and aren't available for public inspection under the above rules.

Under item (1) above, public inspection of Form 990-T (Exempt Organization Business Income Tax Return used for reporting unrelated business income tax or UBIT) was not available under pre-2007 Technical Corrections Act law, because Form 990-T is required under Code Sec. 6011, not under Code Sec. 6033. (Com Rept, see ¶ 5302)

New Law. The 2007 Technical Corrections Act provides that any annual return filed under Code Sec. 6011 by a Code Sec. 501(c)(3) charitable organization and that relates to any UBIT tax imposed by Code Sec. 511 is treated in the same manner as if furnished under Code Sec. 6033 for purposes of the rules requiring IRS to make information publicly available. (Code Sec. 6104(b) as amended by 2007 Technical Corrections Act §3(g)(1)(B)) Thus, the 2007 Technical Corrections Act clarifies that IRS is required to make Form 990-T publicly

---

FTC 2d References are to Federal Tax Coordinator 2d
FIN References are to RIA's Analysis of Federal Taxes: Income
USTR References are to United States Tax Reporter: Income, Estate & Gift, and Excise
PCA References are to Pension Analysis (print & electronic)
PE References are to Pension Explanations (print & electronic)
EP References are to Estate Planning Analysis (print & electronic)

available, subject to redaction procedures applicable to Form 990 under Code Sec. 6104(b). (Com Rept, see ¶ 5302)

> **⊘** *observation:* The redaction procedures relating to annual returns relating to UBIT by Code Sec. 501(c)(3) charitable organizations should be similar to the procedures provided in Reg §301.6104(b)-1 for disclosure relating to returns of exempt organizations and private foundations (i.e., returns filed under Code Sec. 6033, see FTC 2d/FIN ¶ S-2800 *et seq.*; USTR ¶ 60,334; TaxDesk ¶ 688,001), and certain non-exempt charitable trusts (i.e., returns filed under Code Sec. 6034, see FTC 2d/FIN ¶ S-2806; USTR ¶ 60,344; TaxDesk ¶ 688,009.

For the requirement that tax-exempt organizations make copies of Form 990-T relating to UBIT available for public inspection for three years, see ¶ 501.

☐ **Effective:** Returns filed after Aug. 17, 2006. (2007 Technical Corrections Act §3(j))

> **⊘** *observation:* 2007 Technical Corrections Act §3(j) provides that the amendments made by 2007 Technical Corrections Act §3(g)(1)(B) take effect as if included in 2006 Pension Protection Act §1225(a) (Sec. 1225(a), PL 109-280, 8/17/2006). 2006 Pension Protection Act §1225(b) (Sec. 1225(b), PL 109-280, 8/17/2006) provided that the amendments made by 2006 Pension Protection Act §1225(a) apply to returns filed after Aug. 17, 2006.

¶ 503. Donor advised fund excise taxes added to list of "qualified first tier taxes" for abatement purposes

Code Sec. 4962(b), as amended by 2007 Technical Corrections Act § 3(h)
Generally effective: Tax years beginning after Aug. 17, 2006
Committee Reports, see ¶ 5302

The 2006 Pension Protection Act (PPA) added two new excise taxes to circumscribe the activities of donor advised funds. (Sec. 1231, PL 109-280, 8/17/2006) Code Sec. 4966 levies a 20% tax on the sponsoring organization that makes a "taxable distribution," and a 5% tax on a fund manager who agrees to the "taxable distribution." Subject to exceptions, a "taxable distribution" is:

(1) a distribution to a natural person; or

(2) a distribution to any other person (a) that is not for a charitable purpose, or (b) for which the sponsor doesn't exercise expenditure responsibility.

Exceptions include distributions to a public charity, unless it is a disqualified supporting organization, or to the sponsoring organization. (FTC 2d/FIN ¶ D-8152; USTR ¶ 49,664; TaxDesk ¶ 685,519)

Code Sec. 4967 imposes an excise tax on prohibited benefits. This tax applies if a donor or donor designee advises that the fund make a distribution that results in the donor, the designee or a "related" individual or entity (collectively, a Subsection (d) person) receiving a more than an incidental benefit from the distribution. The tax is equal to 125% of the amount of the benefit. The Subsection (d) person who advised that the distribution be made and the Subsection (d) person who receives the benefit are jointly liable for the tax. In addition, a 10% tax (subject to a $10,000 ceiling) is imposed on the agreement of a fund manager to the making of a distribution knowing that it would confer the benefit. The 10% tax is paid by the fund manager. (FTC 2d/FIN ¶ D-8160; USTR ¶ 49,674; TaxDesk ¶ 685,519)

PPA also added these Code Sec. 4966 and Code Sec. 4967 taxes to the list of first tier taxes in Code Sec. 4963(a), and the acts giving rise to those taxes to the list of taxable events in Code Sec. 4963(c). (Sec. 1231(b), PL 109-280, 8/17/2006) These definitions relate to the abatement of first tier tax in Code Sec. 4962(a). Under Code Sec. 4962(a) a "qualified first tier tax" can be abated if (a) the taxable event was due to reasonable cause and not to willful neglect, and (b) the event is corrected during the correction period for the event. (FTC 2d/FIN ¶ D-8161, ¶ D-8201; USTR ¶ 49,624; TaxDesk ¶ 685,516)

> ⚡ *observation:* Congress clearly intended that the taxes imposed by Code Sec. 4966 and Code Sec. 4967 be subject to abatement. However, Congress failed to accomplish this objective, because, although PPA made these taxes first tier taxes, and made the events giving rise to the taxes taxable events, Congress neglected to include these taxes among the "qualified first tier taxes." Under Code Sec. 4962(a), only qualified first tier taxes can be abated. For these purposes, under pre-2007 Technical Corrections Act law, a "qualified first tier tax" was defined in Code Sec. 4962(b) as any first tier tax imposed under subchapter A, C or D. Since PPA had included Code Sec. 4966 and Code Sec. 4967 in a new subchapter G, a technical amendment became necessary to add these taxes, imposed by Subchapter G, to the list of qualified first tier taxes.

New Law. The 2007 Technical Corrections Act adds subchapter G to the list of qualified first tier taxes. (Code Sec. 4962(b) as amended by 2007 Technical Corrections Act §3(h))

> ⚡ *observation:* Thus, the Code Sec. 4966 and the Code Sec. 4967 excise taxes are qualified first tier taxes eligible for tax abatement.

FTC 2d References are to Federal Tax Coordinator 2d
FIN References are to RIA's Analysis of Federal Taxes: Income
USTR References are to United States Tax Reporter: Income, Estate & Gift, and Excise
PCA References are to Pension Analysis (print & electronic)
PE References are to Pension Explanations (print & electronic)
EP References are to Estate Planning Analysis (print & electronic)

☐ **Effective:** For tax years beginning after Aug. 17, 2006. (2007 Technical Corrections Act §3(j))

2007 Technical Corrections Act §3(j) provides that the above amendment takes effect as if included in the PPA provision to which it relates. The above amendment relates to PPA §1231(b) (Sec. 1231(b), PL 109-280, 8/17/2006), which, under PPA §1231(c) (Sec. 1231(c), PL 109-280, 8/17/2006), was effective for tax years beginning after the PPA date of enactment. The PPA date of enactment was Aug. 17, 2006.

¶ 504. Excise tax on private foundation's net investment income applies to capital gains from appreciation, including gains on assets used for exempt purposes

Code Sec. 4940(c)(4)(A), as amended by 2007 Technical Corrections Act § 3(f)
Generally effective: Tax years beginning after Aug. 17, 2006
Committee Reports, see ¶ 5302

Tax-exempt private foundations are subject to a 2% excise tax on their net investment income. The rate is reduced to 1% if the foundation makes certain distributions for charitable purposes. FTC 2d/FIN ¶ D-7501; USTR ¶ 49,404; TaxDesk ¶ 684,001

Taxable private foundations are subject to an excise tax equal to the amount by which (1) the sum of (a) the excise tax on net investment income that would have been imposed if the foundation were tax-exempt, and (b) the unrelated business income tax (UBIT) that would have been imposed if the foundation were tax-exempt, exceeds (2) the income tax actually imposed on the foundation. FTC 2d/FIN ¶ D-7506; USTR ¶ 49,404

For purposes of the excise taxes on both tax-exempt and taxable private foundations, "net investment income" is the amount by which the sum of gross investment income and capital gain net income exceeds the deductions relating to the production of gross investment income. FTC 2d/FIN ¶ D-7507; USTR ¶ 49,404; TaxDesk ¶ 684,002

Under pre-2006 Pension Protection Act law, Code Sec. 4940(c)(4) provided that "capital gain net income" took into account only gains and losses from the sale or other disposition of:

(1) property used for the production of interest, dividends, rents, and royalties, and

(2) property used for the production of income included in computing the UBIT (except to the extent that the gain or loss was taken into account for purposes of the UBIT).

The 2006 Pension Protection Act amended the definition of "capital gain net income," effective for tax years beginning after Aug. 17, 2006, by deleting the phrase "used for the production of interest, dividends, rents, and royalties" and inserting, in its place, the phrase "used for the production of gross investment income" (as defined in Code Sec. 4940(c)(2)). The committee reports for the 2006 Pension Protection Act said that, as a result of this change, capital gains and losses subject to the excise tax on net investment income include capital gains from appreciation, including capital gains and losses from the sale or other disposition of assets used to further an exempt purpose. (FTC 2d/FIN ¶ D-7509; USTR ¶ 49,404; TaxDesk ¶ 684,004)

New Law. The 2007 Technical Corrections Act conforms the statutory language to the committee reports for the 2006 Pension Protection Act. Thus, the 2007 Technical Corrections Act clarifies that capital gains from appreciation are included in the base of the tax on a private foundation's net investment income. (Com Rept, see ¶ 5302)

Specifically, the 2007 Technical Corrections Act provides that, for purposes of the definition of "net investment income," gain or loss from the sale or other disposition of property is not taken into account to the extent that the gain or loss is taken into account for purposes of computing the UBIT. (Code Sec. 4940(c)(4)(A) as amended by 2007 Technical Corrections Act §3(f))

☐ **Effective:** Tax years beginning after Aug. 17, 2006. (2007 Technical Corrections Act §3(j))

2007 Technical Corrections Act §3(j) provides that the amendments made by 2007 Technical Corrections Act §3 take effect as if included in the provisions of the 2006 Pension Protection Act to which they relate. The above rules relate to 2006 Pension Protection Act §1221 (Sec. 1221, PL 109-280, 8/17/2006), which, under 2006 Pension Protection Act §1221(c) (Sec. 1221(c), PL 109-280, 8/17/2006), is effective for tax years beginning after Aug. 17, 2006.

FTC 2d References are to Federal Tax Coordinator 2d
FIN References are to RIA's Analysis of Federal Taxes: Income
USTR References are to United States Tax Reporter: Income, Estate & Gift, and Excise
PCA References are to Pension Analysis (print & electronic)
PE References are to Pension Explanations (print & electronic)
EP References are to Estate Planning Analysis (print & electronic)

¶ 505. Excess benefit transactions rules don't apply to transactions between supporting organizations and Code Sec. 501(c)(4), Code Sec. 501(c)(5), or Code Sec. 501(c)(6) supported organizations

Code Sec. 4958(c)(3)(A)(i)(II), as amended by 2007 Technical Corrections Act § 3(i)(1)

Code Sec. 4958(c)(3)(C)(ii), as amended by 2007 Technical Corrections Act § 3(i)(2)

Generally effective: For transactions occurring after July 25, 2006.

Committee Reports, see ¶ 5302

Excise taxes are imposed on disqualified persons who improperly benefit from "excess benefit transactions" involving public charities and social welfare organizations. An "excess benefit transaction" is any transaction in which an economic benefit is provided by an "applicable tax-exempt organization" directly or indirectly to or for the use of any "disqualified person," if the value of the economic benefit provided exceeds the value of the consideration, including the performance of services, that the organization received for providing the benefit. (FTC 2d/FIN ¶ D-6650; USTR ¶ 49,584; TaxDesk ¶ 676,505)

"Excess benefit transactions" include:

(1) any grants, loans, compensation or other similar payments provided by a supporting organization to, among others, a substantial contributor; and

(2) any loan provided by a supporting organization to a disqualified person (other than an organization described in the private foundation rules at Code Sec. 509(a)(1), Code Sec. 509(a)(2) or Code Sec. 509(a)(4)). (FTC 2d/FIN ¶ D-6654.1; USTR ¶ 49,584; TaxDesk ¶ 676,502.2)

> **⊘ observation:** Thus, an exception to the excess benefit transaction excise tax applies to loans from a supporting organization to a Code Sec. 509(a)(1), Code Sec. 509(a)(2) or Code Sec. 509(a)(4) organization. The organizations described at Code Sec. 509(a)(1) (e.g., churches, schools, hospitals, states and subdivisions, and government supported charities), Code Sec. 509(a)(2) (broadly supported organizations) or Code Sec. 509(a)(4) (entities organized and operated exclusively for testing for public safety purposes) are public charities that are not supporting organizations.

A *supporting* organization is one that is:

• organized and operated exclusively for the benefit of, to perform the functions of, or to carry out the purposes of, certain tax-exempt organizations (called "supported organizations," see below),

- operated, supervised or controlled by or in connection with one or more supported organizations, and
- not controlled directly or indirectly by disqualified persons.

An organization meeting these requirements is a supporting organization that is excluded from private foundation status. (FTC 2d/FIN ¶ D-7211; USTR ¶ 5074)

A *supported* organization is a public charity typically described in Code Sec. 509(a)(1) or Code Sec. 509(a)(2):

(i) for whose benefit the supporting organization is organized and operated, or

(ii) for which the supporting organization performs the functions of, or carries out the purposes of. (FTC 2d/FIN ¶ D-7213.2; USTR ¶ 5074; TaxDesk ¶ 683,508)

However, organizations that are exempt from tax under Code Sec. 501(c)(4), Code Sec. 501(c)(5), and Code Sec. 501(c)(6) (such as a social welfare organizations, labor or agricultural organizations, business leagues, or real estate boards) can also be supported organizations, if their supporting organizations otherwise meet the requirements for supporting organizations under Code Sec. 509(a)(3). Additionally, the Code Sec. 501(c)(4), Code Sec. 501(c)(5), or Code Sec. 501(c)(6) supported organization must meet the public support requirement of Code Sec. 509(a)(2).

> *illustration:* The Smithville Civic League (a Code Sec. 501(c)(4) social welfare organization) forms and controls a scholarship organization that provides financial aid for college-bound students in Smithville. If the civic league meets the public support requirements of Code Sec. 509(a)(2), and the scholarship organization otherwise meets the supporting organization requirements of Code Sec. 509(a)(3), the civic league is a "supported organization" and the scholarship organization is a "supporting organization."

If a supporting organization makes a grant, loan, payment of compensation, or other similar payment to a substantial contributor (or person related to the substantial contributor) of the supporting organization, for purposes of the excess benefit transaction rules, the substantial contributor is treated as a disqualified person and the payment is treated automatically as an excess benefit transaction with the entire amount of the payment treated as the excess benefit.

FTC 2d References are to Federal Tax Coordinator 2d
FIN References are to RIA's Analysis of Federal Taxes: Income
USTR References are to United States Tax Reporter: Income, Estate & Gift, and Excise
PCA References are to Pension Analysis (print & electronic)
PE References are to Pension Explanations (print & electronic)
EP References are to Estate Planning Analysis (print & electronic)

Under pre-2007 Technical Corrections Act law, the term "substantial contributor" did not include organizations that were public charities. (FTC 2d/FIN ¶ D-6654.1; USTR ¶ 49,584; TaxDesk ¶ 676,502.2)

New Law. The 2007 Technical Corrections Act expands the exception to the definition of "substantial contributor" to provide that the term does not include Code Sec. 501(c)(4), Code Sec. 501(c)(5), or Code Sec. 501(c)(6) supported organizations. (Code Sec. 4958(c)(3)(C)(ii)(II) as amended by 2007 Technical Corrections Act §3(i)(2))

Since Code Sec. 501(c)(4), Code Sec. 501(c)(5), and Code Sec. 501(c)(6) supported organizations are not considered "substantial contributors" for purposes of the excess benefit transaction rules, the tax on excess benefit transactions does not apply to transactions between these supported organizations and their supporting organizations. (Com Rept, see ¶ 5302)

The Act also expands the exception to the "excess benefit transaction" rules for loans made to public charities by including Code Sec. 501(c)(4), Code Sec. 501(c)(5), and Code Sec. 501(c)(6) supported organizations in the list of organizations that are eligible for this exception. (Code Sec. 4958(c)(3)(A)(i)(II) as amended by 2007 Technical Corrections Act §3(i)(1))

☐ **Effective:** For transactions occurring after 7/25/2006. (2007 Technical Corrections Act §3(j))

2007 Technical Corrections Act §3(j) provides that the above provision is effective as if included in the provision of the 2006 Pension Protection Act to which it relates. The above rules relate to 2006 Pension Protection Act §1242 (Sec. 1242, PL 109-280, 8/17/2006) which, under 2006 Pension Protection Act §1242(b) (Sec. 1242(b), PL 109-280, 8/17/2006), is effective for transactions occurring after July 25, 2006.

¶ 600. Charitable Contributions

¶ 601. Limits on estate and gift tax charitable deductions for series of fractional contributions of tangible personal property are retroactively repealed

Code Sec. 2055(g), as amended by 2007 Technical Corrections Act § 3(d)(1)
Code Sec. 2522(e), as amended by 2007 Technical Corrections Act § 3(d)(2)
Generally effective: Bequests and gifts made after Aug. 17, 2006
Committee Reports, see ¶ 5302

A taxpayer may contribute property to a charity by making a series of gifts of fractional interests in the property. The 2006 Pension Protection Act imposed limits on the income, gift, and estate tax charitable deductions allowed for contributions, gifts, or bequests of fractional interests in *tangible personal* property, where the taxpayer had previously made a contribution or gift of a fractional interest in the same property.

The 2006 Pension Protection Act (PPA) included a rule which provided that, if a taxpayer made a lifetime gift of an undivided portion of his entire interest in any tangible personal property, for which an income tax charitable deduction was allowed (an "initial fractional contribution"), and then, on his death, the taxpayer made an additional bequest, legacy, devise, or transfer of an interest in the same property (an "additional contribution"), there was a limit on the amount of the *estate tax* charitable deduction allowable for the additional contribution. For estate tax charitable deduction purposes, the fair market value of the additional contribution was determined by using the lesser of—

... the fair market value of the property at the time of the initial fractional contribution, or

... the fair market value of the property at the time of the additional contribution. (FTC 2d ¶ R-5789.1; USTR Estate & Gift Taxes ¶ 20,554.21; TaxDesk ¶ 777,002.1; EP ¶ 44,390.1)

> ⓇⒾⒶ *observation:* Thus, under PPA, any post-gift appreciation in the value of the tangible personal property was not taken into account in determining the amount of the estate tax charitable deduction. If, however, the property declined in value after the date of the lifetime gift, the reduction in value *was* taken into account for purposes of determining the estate tax charitable deduction.

FTC 2d References are to Federal Tax Coordinator 2d
FIN References are to RIA's Analysis of Federal Taxes: Income
USTR References are to United States Tax Reporter: Income, Estate & Gift, and Excise
PCA References are to Pension Analysis (print & electronic)
PE References are to Pension Explanations (print & electronic)
EP References are to Estate Planning Analysis (print & electronic)

illustration (1): The decedent owns a painting. In Year 1, the decedent gives an undivided ¼ interest in the painting to a museum. (Under such an arrangement, the museum would be entitled to possession of the painting for ¼ of the year, or three months, and the donor would be entitled to possession of the painting for the remaining ¾ of the year, or nine months.) On the date of the gift, the fair market value of the painting is $20 million. The taxpayer is entitled to an income tax charitable deduction of $5 million ($20 million × ¼) for the gift (assuming the percentage ceilings on income tax charitable deductions don't apply).

In Year 5, the decedent dies. In his will, the decedent bequeaths his remaining interest in the painting to the museum. On the date of the decedent's death, the fair market value of the painting is $24 million. Under PPA, the fair market value of the interest bequeathed to the museum was determined by using the $20 million date-of-gift value of the painting, since that is less than the $24 million date-of-death value. Thus, the allowable estate tax charitable deduction for the bequest of the decedent's remaining ¾ interest in the painting was $15 million ($20 million × ¾).

observation: In Illustration (1), the ¾ interest in the painting which the decedent owned at his death was included in his gross estate at its full date-of-death fair market value of $18 million (the painting's date-of-death value of $24 million × ¾), even though Code Sec. 2055(g) limited the charitable deduction to $15 million. Some commentators on the 2006 Pension Protection Act referred to this result as a "valuation whipsaw."

The 2006 Pension Protection Act also provided a similar rule for *gift tax* charitable deduction purposes. Under this rule, if a donor made a gift of an undivided portion of his entire interest in any tangible personal property, for which a gift tax charitable deduction was allowed (an "initial fractional contribution"), there was a limit on the amount of the gift tax charitable deduction allowable for any later gift of an interest in property with respect to which the donor had previously made an initial fractional contribution (an "additional contribution"). For gift tax charitable contribution purposes, the value of an additional contribution was determined by using the lesser of—

. . . the fair market value of the property at the time of the initial fractional contribution, or

. . . the fair market value of the property at the time of the additional contribution. (FTC 2d ¶ Q-6002.2; USTR Estate & Gift Taxes ¶ 25,224; TaxDesk ¶ 733,002.1; EP ¶ 48,304.2)

observation: Thus, if the tangible personal property appreciated in value after the date of the initial fractional contribution, the appreciation was not taken into account in determining the amount of the gift tax charitable deduction allowed for additional contributions. If, however, the property declined in value after the date of the initial fractional contribution, the reduction in value was taken into account for purposes of determining the gift tax charitable deduction for additional contributions.

illustration (2): The donor owns a painting. In Year 1, the donor gives an undivided ¼ interest in the painting to a museum. On the date of the gift, the fair market value of the painting is $20 million. The donor is entitled to an income tax charitable deduction of $5 million ($20 million × ¼) for the gift (assuming the percentage ceilings on income tax charitable deductions don't apply).

In Year 3, when the fair market value of the painting has increased to $24 million, the donor makes an additional contribution of another undivided ¼ interest in the painting to the museum. Under PPA, the fair market value of the Year 3 gift was determined by using the value of the painting at the time of the Year 1 gift ($20 million), since that is less than the value of the painting at the time of the Year 3 gift ($24 million). Thus, the allowable gift tax charitable deduction for the Year 3 gift was $5 million ($20 million × ¼).

observation: In Illustration (2), the ¼ interest in the painting which the donor contributed to the museum in Year 3 was included in his Year 3 taxable gifts at its full fair market value of $6 million (the painting's value, on the date of the Year 3 gift, of $24 million × ¼), even though the charitable deduction was limited to $5 million. Thus, PPA created a gift tax "valuation whipsaw" that was similar to the estate tax "valuation whipsaw" discussed above.

The 2006 Pension Protection Act also imposes similar limits on the *income tax* charitable deduction allowable for "additional contributions" of fractional interests in tangible personal property. FTC 2d/FIN ¶ K-3174.1; USTR ¶ 1704.41; TaxDesk ¶ 331,614.1; EP ¶ 41,425.1

observation: The limits on the income tax charitable deduction for additional contributions of fractional interests in tangible personal prop-

---

FTC 2d References are to Federal Tax Coordinator 2d
FIN References are to RIA's Analysis of Federal Taxes: Income
USTR References are to United States Tax Reporter: Income, Estate & Gift, and Excise
PCA References are to Pension Analysis (print & electronic)
PE References are to Pension Explanations (print & electronic)
EP References are to Estate Planning Analysis (print & electronic)

erty do not result in the kind of "valuation whipsaw" that was caused by the limits on the estate and gift tax charitable deductions.

New Law. Congress realized that the limits imposed by the 2006 Pension Protection Act on the estate and gift tax charitable deductions allowable for "additional contributions" of tangible personal property had unintended consequences (i.e., the valuation whipsaws described above). (Com Rept, see ¶ 5302) Thus, the 2007 Technical Corrections Act repeals these rules, effective retroactively to PPA's date of enactment. (Code Sec. 2055(g) as amended by 2007 Technical Corrections Act §3(d)(1)) (Code Sec. 2522(e)(2) as amended by 2007 Technical Corrections Act §3(d)(2)(A))

observation: Thus, the 2007 Technical Corrections Act eliminates the valuation whipsaws that would have resulted from the limits imposed by the 2006 Pension Protection Act on the estate and gift tax charitable deductions allowable for "additional contributions" of fractional interests in tangible personal property.

illustration (3): The facts are the same as in Illustration (1). Under the 2007 Technical Corrections Act, the estate tax charitable deduction allowable for the interest in the painting bequeathed to the museum (i.e., a ¾ undivided interest in a painting having a fair market value of $24 million) is $18 million ($24 million × ¾), not the $15 million to which the deduction would have been limited under PPA.

illustration (4): The facts are the same as in Illustration (2). Under the 2007 Technical Corrections Act, the gift tax charitable deduction allowable for the Year 3 gift (i.e, a gift of an undivided ¼ interest in a painting having a fair market value of $24 million) is $6 million ($24 million × ¼), not the $5 million to which the deduction would have been limited under PPA.

observation: The 2007 Technical Corrections Act does *not* repeal Code Sec. 170(o)(2), which imposes limits on the *income tax* charitable deduction allowable for "additional contributions" of fractional interests in tangible personal property. As mentioned above, those limits do not result in the kind of "valuation whipsaw" that would have been caused by the repealed limits on the estate and gift tax charitable deductions. However, the limits on the income tax charitable deduction still provide a disincentive to making charitable contributions of fractional interests in tangible personal property because, even if the property appreciates in value after the initial fractional contribution, the income tax charitable deduction must nevertheless be based on the value of the property at the time of the initial fractional contribution.

The 2007 Technical Corrections Act also eliminates the definitions of "additional contribution" and "initial fractional contribution" for gift tax charitable deduction purposes (2007 Technical Corrections Act §3(d)(2)(A)), but retains the definition of "initial fractional contribution." (Code Sec. 2522(e)(2)(C))

> **☙ observation:** IRS still must provide for the recapture of any gift tax charitable deduction allowed for the contribution of an undivided portion of a taxpayer's entire interest in tangible personal property, if certain conditions are not met within ten years of the initial fractional contribution or the donor's death, if earlier. (FTC 2d ¶ Q-6081; USTR ¶ 25,224; TaxDesk ¶ 733,006.2; EP ¶ 48,383) That recapture requirement (now contained in Code Sec. 2522(e)(2)) is *not* affected by the 2007 Technical Corrections Act. Thus, a definition of the term "initial fractional contribution" is still needed for purposes of the recapture rules, even though such a definition is no longer needed for purposes of the repealed limits on the gift tax charitable deduction for additional contributions.

☐ **Effective:** Gifts and bequests made after Aug. 17, 2006. (2007 Technical Corrections Act §3(j))

2007 Technical Corrections Act §3(j) provides that the amendments made by 2007 Technical Corrections Act §3 take effect as if included in the provisions of the 2006 Pension Protection Act to which they relate. The above rules relate to the estate and gift tax provisions of 2006 Pension Protection Act §1218 (Sec. 1218, PL 109-280, 8/17/2006), which, under 2006 Pension Protection Act §1218(d) (Sec. 1218(d), PL 109-280, 8/17/2006), are effective for gifts and bequests made after Aug. 17, 2006.

¶ 602. Rule clarified for determining what portion of an IRA distribution that includes nondeductible contributions is tax-free under the IRA qualified charitable distribution rules

Code Sec. 408(d)(8)(D), as amended by 2007 Technical Corrections Act § 3(a)
Generally effective: For IRA distributions made during 2006 and 2007
Committee Reports, see ¶ 5302

FTC 2d References are to Federal Tax Coordinator 2d
FIN References are to RIA's Analysis of Federal Taxes: Income
USTR References are to United States Tax Reporter: Income, Estate & Gift, and Excise
PCA References are to Pension Analysis (print & electronic)
PE References are to Pension Explanations (print & electronic)
EP References are to Estate Planning Analysis (print & electronic)

The Pension Protection Act of 2006 (PPA 2006, Sec. 1201, PL 109-280, 8/17/2006) created a new exclusion from gross income for otherwise taxable IRA distributions, where the distributions are donated to charity in 2006 and 2007. Under the IRA qualified charitable distribution rules, amounts up to $100,000 each year may be distributed tax-free, as long as (1) the distribution is made directly by the IRA trustee to a qualified charitable organization, and (2) the IRA owner has attained age 70-1/2. (FTC 2d/FIN ¶ H-12253.2; USTR ¶ 4084.03; TaxDesk ¶ 143,003.2; PCA ¶ 35,154.2; PE ¶ 408-4.03)

If the IRA (which may be either a traditional or a Roth IRA) includes nondeductible contributions (i.e., contributions for which a deduction is not allowed), a special rule applies in determining the portion of the distribution that would otherwise be includible in gross income (but for the IRA qualified charitable distribution rules), and that is thus eligible for qualified charitable distribution treatment.

Specifically, notwithstanding the Code Sec. 72 annuity rules (see below), in determining the extent to which a distribution is a qualified charitable distribution, the entire amount of the distribution must be treated as includible in gross income (without regard to the IRA qualified charitable distribution exclusion). This treatment applies to the extent that the distributed amount does not exceed the aggregate amount which would have been includible in income if, under the pre-2007 Technical Corrections Act version of Code Sec. 408(d)(8)(D), all amounts distributed from all of the IRAs were treated as one contract under the Code Sec. 72 annuity rules (via Code Sec. 408(d)(2)(A)) that determine whether and to what extent the distribution is includible in income. (FTC 2d/FIN ¶ H-12253.3; USTR ¶ 4084.03; TaxDesk ¶ 143,003.2; PCA ¶ 35,154.3; PE ¶ 408-4.03)

Under the Code Sec. 72 annuity rules, distributions from a traditional IRA are includible in income when withdrawn (except to the extent the withdrawal represents a return of nondeductible contributions). If an individual has made nondeductible contributions to a traditional IRA, a portion of each distribution from an IRA is nontaxable, until the total amount of nondeductible contributions has been received. In general, the amount of a distribution that is nontaxable is determined by multiplying the amount of the distribution by the ratio of the remaining nondeductible contributions to the account balance. (FTC 2d/FIN ¶ H-12253; USTR ¶ 4084.03; TaxDesk ¶ 143,001; PCA ¶ 35,154; PE ¶ 408-4.03)

Distributions from a Roth IRA are not includible in gross income if the distribution is a "qualified distribution." A qualified distribution from a Roth IRA is a distribution that is made after the five-year period beginning with the first tax year in which the individual or the individual's spouse made a contribution to the Roth IRA, and which is made:

. . . on or after the individual attains age 59-1/2;

. . . after the death of the individual;

... on account of the individual becoming disabled; or

... for a "qualified special purpose distribution" (e.g., a distribution for first-time home buyer expenses). (FTC 2d/FIN ¶ H-12290.28; USTR ¶ 408A4; TaxDesk ¶ 283,336; PCA ¶ 35,229; PE ¶ 408A-4)

Distributions from a Roth IRA that are not qualified distributions are includible in gross income to the extent attributable to earnings. In determining the portion of the distribution attributable to earnings, contributions and distributions are deemed to be distributed in the following order: (1) regular Roth IRA contributions; (2) taxable conversion contributions (i.e., conversions of amounts in a traditional IRA to a Roth IRA); (3) nontaxable conversion contributions; and (4) earnings. (FTC 2d/FIN ¶ H-12290.35; USTR ¶ 408A4; TaxDesk ¶ 283,343; PCA ¶ 35,236; PE ¶ 408A-4)

New Law. As under pre-Act law, in determining the extent to which a distribution is a qualified charitable distribution, the entire amount of the distribution must be treated as includible in gross income (without regard to the IRA qualified charitable distribution exclusion). The Act amends Code Sec. 408(d)(8)(D) to provide that this treatment applies to the extent that the distributed amount does not exceed the aggregate amount which would be includible in income if all amounts in all of the individual's IRAs were distributed during the tax year, and all of the IRAs were treated as one contract for purposes of determining the aggregate amount which would have been includible under Code Sec. 72. (Code Sec. 408(d)(8)(D) as amended by 2007 Technical Corrections Act §3(a))

In other words, when determining the portion of a distribution that would otherwise be includible in income, the otherwise includible amount is determined as if all amounts were distributed from all of the individual's IRAs. (Com Rept, see ¶ 5302)

> *observation:* The Act's amendment of Code Sec. 408(d)(8)(D) does not make a substantive change. The Act merely clarifies that the rule under Code Sec. 408(d)(8)(D) is applied as if all IRAs *of the individual* making the qualified charitable distribution were distributed *in the same tax year* during which the qualified charitable distribution is made.

> *observation:* As under pre-Act law, the tax-free treatment of IRA distributions donated to charity only applies to donations made in 2006 and 2007.

FTC 2d References are to Federal Tax Coordinator 2d
FIN References are to RIA's Analysis of Federal Taxes: Income
USTR References are to United States Tax Reporter: Income, Estate & Gift, and Excise
PCA References are to Pension Analysis (print & electronic)
PE References are to Pension Explanations (print & electronic)
EP References are to Estate Planning Analysis (print & electronic)

☐ **Effective:** For IRA distributions made in tax years beginning after Dec. 31, 2005 (2007 Technical Corrections Act §3(j)), and before Jan. 1, 2008 (Code Sec. 408(d)(8)(F)).

> ✒ *observation:* 2007 Technical Corrections Act §3(j) provides that the amendments made by §3 of the Technical Corrections Act take effect as if included in 2006 Pension Protection Act §1201 (Sec. 1201, PL 109-280, 8/17/2006). 2006 Pension Protection Act §1201(c)(1) provides that the amendments made by §1201 take effect for IRA distributions made in tax years beginning after Dec. 31, 2005, and Code Sec. 408(d)(8)(F) itself provides that the IRA qualified charitable distribution rules do not apply to distributions made in tax years beginning after Dec. 31, 2007.

¶ 603. Charitable deduction allowed where S corporation's charitable contribution of property reduces shareholder's basis only by contributed property's basis

Code Sec. 1366(d)(4), as amended by 2007 Technical Corrections Act § 3(b)
Generally effective: Contributions made in tax years beginning after Dec. 31, 2005
Committee Reports, see ¶ 5302

The 2006 Pension Protection Act amended the S corporation rules so that the decrease in a shareholder's basis in his S corporation stock by reason of a charitable contribution made by the S corporation equals the shareholder's pro rata share of the adjusted basis of the contributed property. This is referred to below as the "basis adjustment rule." The basis adjustment rule is effective for contributions made in tax years beginning after Dec. 31, 2005, but does not apply for contributions in tax years beginning after Dec. 31, 2007. (FTC 2d/FIN ¶ D-1865; USTR ¶ 13,664; TaxDesk ¶ 617,001) Where this rule applied there was no special provision that would allow a deduction for a contribution in excess of the shareholder's basis in the S corporation. (FTC 2d/FIN ¶ D-1775; USTR ¶ 13,664; TaxDesk ¶ 614,716)

> ✒ *observation:* Under the pre-2006 Pension Protection Act rules, when an S corporation made a charitable contribution of appreciated property, the shareholder's basis was reduced by the fair market value of the property. When the shareholder sold his stock, the basis reduction caused him to recognize more gain. This result differed from that of a direct charitable contribution of appreciated property, which didn't result in any gain recognition by the contributor.

New Law. The 2007 Technical Corrections Act provides that where the above rule applies to limit the decrease in the basis resulting from the charitable contribution, the rule that limits the aggregate amount of losses and deductions that may be taken by the S corporation shareholder to his basis in the S corporation's stock and debt does not apply to the extent of the excess (if any) of:

- the shareholder's pro rata share of the charitable contribution (Code Sec. 1366(d)(4)(A) as amended by 2007 Technical Corrections Act §3(b)), over

- the shareholder's pro rata share of the adjusted basis of such property. (Code Sec. 1366(d)(4)(B))

> *Illustration:* A 100% shareholder in an S corporation has a $300 basis in his S corporation stock. The S corporation contributes property in 2007 with a basis of $200 and a fair market value of $500 to a charity. Under pre-2007 Technical Corrections Act law, the shareholder could only take a $300 deduction for the contribution, since his basis in the stock was $300. The 2007 Technical Corrections Act allows the shareholder to take a full $500 deduction. The shareholder reduces his basis in his S corporation stock from $300 to $100. (Com Rept, see ¶ 5302)

> *observation:* This rule allows deductions only to the extent of the sum of the shareholder's basis in the S corporation plus the difference between the basis of the property and the fair market value. Thus, if the shareholder in the Illustration had a zero basis in his S corporation stock, he would be allowed only a $300 deduction.

This provision does not apply to contributions made in tax years starting after Dec. 31, 2007. (Com Rept, see ¶ 5302)

> *observation:* That's because the basis adjustment rule doesn't apply for contributions in tax years beginning after Dec. 31, 2007. Thus, unless the basis adjustment rule is extended, this technical correction will not apply for tax years beginning after 2007.

☐ **Effective:** The above technical correction is effective as if included in the provision of the 2006 Pension Protection Act to which it relates. (2007 Technical Corrections Act §3(j)) The technical correction provision relates to 2006 Pension Protection Act §1203 (Sec. 1203, PL 109-280, 8/17/2006) which, under 2006 Pension Protection Act §1203(b) (Sec. 1203(b), PL 109-280, 8/17/2006) is effective for contributions made in tax years beginning after Dec. 31, 2005.

FTC 2d References are to Federal Tax Coordinator 2d
FIN References are to RIA's Analysis of Federal Taxes: Income
USTR References are to United States Tax Reporter: Income, Estate & Gift, and Excise
PCA References are to Pension Analysis (print & electronic)
PE References are to Pension Explanations (print & electronic)
EP References are to Estate Planning Analysis (print & electronic)

¶ 604. Definition of "applicable property" for purposes of reduced deduction for contribution is clarified

Code Sec. 170(e)(1)(B)(i), as amended by 2007 Technical Corrections Act § 11(a)(15)
Generally effective: Dec. 29, 2007
Committee Reports, None

Generally, the deduction allowed for a charitable contribution of property is equal to the fair market value (FMV) of the donated property. (See FTC 2d/FIN ¶ K-3150 *et seq.*; USTR ¶ 1704.40 *et seq.*; TaxDesk ¶ 331,600 *et seq.*) However, in cases of contributions of "applicable property" where the donee disposes of the property within specified time periods following the contribution, the donor's deduction is subject to reduction (if the disposition occurs in the contribution year) or recapture (if the disposition occurs with specified time periods following the contribution year). See FTC 2d/FIN ¶ K-3167 *et seq.*; USTR ¶ 1704.42; TaxDesk ¶ 331,613 *et seq.*

Under pre-2007 Technical Corrections Act Law, "applicable property" for purposes of the contribution year reduction rule had the definition given by Code Sec. 170(e)(7)(C) for the recapture rule. Under Code Sec. 170(e)(7)(C), "applicable property" for purposes of the recapture rule is charitable deduction property as defined in Code Sec. 6050L(a)(2)(A) (generally, property other than publicly-traded securities that's been contributed to an eligible charitable donee, for which the taxpayer has claimed a charitable deduction of more than $5,000, see FTC 2d/FIN ¶ S-2876; USTR ¶ 60,50L4; TaxDesk ¶ 688,034):

(1) that is tangible personal property whose use is identified by the donee as related to the purpose or function that is the basis of the donee's tax-exemption, and

(2) for which a deduction in excess of the donor's basis is allowed.

(FTC 2d/FIN ¶ K-3167.2; USTR ¶ 1704.42; TaxDesk ¶ 331,613.2)

New Law. Under the 2007 Technical Corrections Act, the definition of "applicable property" for purposes of the reduction required in the amount of the taxpayer's deduction for a contribution of "applicable property" if the donee disposes of the property before the end of the contribution year no longer includes the requirement described at (2), above. (Code Sec. 170(e)(1)(B)(i) as amended by 2007 Technical Corrections Act §11(a)(15))

The 2007 Technical Corrections Act also changes the requirements for the certification by the donee that avoids the reduction and/or recapture of the donor's deduction, see ¶ 605.

☐ **Effective:** Dec. 29, 2007.

¶ 605. Donee's use of donated "applicable property" for its exempt purpose or function must be substantial for taxpayer to avoid reduction or recapture of deduction for contribution

Code Sec. 170(e)(7)(D)(i)(I), as amended by 2007 Technical Corrections Act § 3(c)
Generally effective: Contributions after Sept. 1, 2006
Committee Reports, see ¶ 5302

Generally, if a taxpayer makes a contribution of property, rather than money, to an eligible charitable organization or governmental body, the taxpayer is entitled to a deduction equal to the fair market value (FMV) of the donated property. (See FTC 2d/FIN ¶ K-3150 *et seq.*; USTR ¶ 1704.40 *et seq.*; TaxDesk ¶ 331,600 *et seq.*) However, in cases of contributions of "applicable property" where the donee disposes of the property within specified time periods following the contribution, the donor's deduction is subject to reduction (if the disposition occurs in the same year as the contribution) or recapture (if the disposition occurs with specified time periods following the year of the contribution). (See FTC 2d/FIN ¶ K-3167 *et seq.*; USTR ¶ 1704.42; TaxDesk ¶ 331,613 *et seq.*)

The reduction and/or recapture consequences can be avoided if the donee provides a certification. This certification consists of a written statement that satisfies one of two sets of requirements. Under the pre-2007 Technical Corrections Act law version of one of these sets of requirements, the written statement:

(1) had to be signed under penalty of perjury by an officer of the donee organization;

(2) had to certify that the donee's use of the property was related to the purpose or function that was the basis for its tax-exemption; and

(3) had to describe how the property was used and how that use furthered that purpose or function.

⚡️ *observation:* Under the second set of requirements—unchanged by the 2007 Technical Corrections Act—the written statement must state the intended use of the property by the donee at the time of the contri-

---

FTC 2d References are to Federal Tax Coordinator 2d
FIN References are to RIA's Analysis of Federal Taxes: Income
USTR References are to United States Tax Reporter: Income, Estate & Gift, and Excise
PCA References are to Pension Analysis (print & electronic)
PE References are to Pension Explanations (print & electronic)
EP References are to Estate Planning Analysis (print & electronic)

bution, and must certify that the intended use has become impossible or infeasible to implement.

(FTC 2d/FIN ¶ K-3167.1; USTR ¶ 1704.42; TaxDesk ¶ 331,613.1)

New Law. Under the 2007 Technical Corrections Act, the written statement satisfies the requirement at (2) above only if, in addition to certifying that its use of the donated property was related to its exempt use or function, the donee organization certifies that its use of the donated property was substantial. (Code Sec. 170(e)(7)(D)(i)(I) as amended by 2007 Technical Corrections Act §3(c)) That is, the officer of the donee organization must certify that the donee's use of the property was substantial. (Com Rept, see ¶ 5302)

> *observation:* In other words, the donee must certify not only that its use of the donated property was related to its exempt purpose or function, but also that its use of the property was substantial.

> *observation:* The 2007 Technical Corrections Act doesn't provide a definition of "substantial" for this purpose.

Thus, the 2007 Technical Corrections Act protects a donation from the reduction and/or recapture rules if an officer of the donee organization certifies upon disposition of the donated property that the donee's use of the property was related to the purpose or function constituting the basis of the donee's tax-exempt status and that use of the property by the donee was substantial. (Com Rept, see ¶ 5302)

> *observation:* Where the reduction or recapture rules don't apply, the donor is generally entitled to a charitable deduction equal to the FMV of the donated property (see FTC 2d/FIN ¶ K-3150 *et seq.*; USTR ¶ 1704.40 *et seq.*; TaxDesk ¶ 331,600 *et seq.*).

The 2007 Technical Corrections Act also changes the definition of "applicable property," see ¶ 604.

☐ **Effective:** Contributions after Sept. 1, 2006. (2007 Technical Corrections Act §3(j))

> *observation:* 2007 Technical Corrections Act § 3(j) provides that the above provision is effective as if included in the provision of the 2006 Pension Protection Act to which it relates. The above provision relate to 2006 Pension Protection Act § 1215 (Sec. 1215, PL 109-280, 8/17/2006) which, under 2006 Pension Protection Act § 1215(d)(1) (Sec. 1215(d)(1), PL 109-280, 8/17/2006) is effective for contributions after Sept. 1, 2006.

¶ 700. Foreign Provisions

¶ 701. Computation of regular tax and AMT modified where foreign earned income or housing exclusion is claimed

Code Sec. 911(f), as amended by 2007 Technical Corrections Act § 4(c)
Generally effective: Tax years beginning after Dec. 31, 2006
Committee Reports, see ¶ 5303

An individual's regular tax liability is calculated by using graduated rates. However, for regular tax purposes, net capital gain is subject to a maximum 15% rate, net capital gain consisting of unrecaptured Code Sec. 1250 gain is subject to a maximum 25% rate and certain collectibles gain is subject to a maximum 28% rate. (FTC 2d/FIN ¶ I-5110; USTR ¶ 14.08; TaxDesk ¶ 223,309)

In addition to regular tax, both individuals and corporations are subject to the alternative minimum tax (AMT). The AMT is based on alternative minimum taxable income (AMTI) which generally equals regular taxable income for the tax year increased by certain tax preference items and adjusted to reflect the recomputation of certain other tax items taken in account in computing regular tax. The taxpayer subtracts the exemption amount from the AMTI to get the "taxable excess." The AMT equals the tentative minimum tax less the regular tax for the year. For individuals and noncorporate taxpayers the tentative minimum tax is 26% of the taxable excess up to $175,000, plus 28% of the taxable excess above $175,000 reduced by any AMT foreign tax credit for the year. However, for a noncorporate taxpayer with net capital gain the same rates that apply for regular tax purposes (discussed above) apply for AMT purposes. (FTC 2d/FIN ¶ A-8101; A-8102; USTR ¶ 554.01; TaxDesk ¶s 691,001, 691,002)

Under pre-2007 Technical Corrections Act law, where a taxpayer claimed a foreign earned income or foreign housing cost exclusion ("excluded amounts") the regular tax was calculated under a stacking rule. Thus, the regular tax was equal to the excess (if any) of:

• the regular tax that would be imposed for the tax year if the taxpayer's taxable income were increased by the amount of these exclusions for the tax year, over

---

FTC 2d References are to Federal Tax Coordinator 2d
FIN References are to RIA's Analysis of Federal Taxes: Income
USTR References are to United States Tax Reporter: Income, Estate & Gift, and Excise
PCA References are to Pension Analysis (print & electronic)
PE References are to Pension Explanations (print & electronic)
EP References are to Estate Planning Analysis (print & electronic)

- the tax which would be imposed for the tax year if the taxpayer's taxable income were equal to the amount of these exclusions for the tax year.

Similarly, his tentative minimum tax for the tax year was equal to the excess (if any) of:

- the amount that would be the tentative minimum tax for the tax year (calculated after reduction for any AMT foreign tax credits) if the taxpayer's taxable excess were increased by the amount of these exclusions for the tax year, over

- the amount that would be the tentative minimum tax for the tax year (calculated after reduction for any AMT foreign tax credits) if the taxpayer's taxable excess were equal to the amount of these exclusions for the tax year. (FTC 2d/FIN ¶ O-1101.1; USTR ¶ 9114; TaxDesk ¶ 191,001.1)

New Law. The 2007 Technical Corrections Act amends the regular tax computation and the AMT computation when an individual taxpayer has excluded amounts (i.e., foreign earned income or foreign housing cost exclusions).

Regular tax computation. The 2007 Technical Corrections Act amends the regular tax computation to provide that where a taxpayer has excluded amounts and has taxable income for the tax year, the regular tax is equal to the excess (if any) of:

(A) the regular tax that would be imposed for the tax year if the taxpayer's taxable income were increased by the amount of these exclusions for the tax year (Code Sec. 911(f)(1)(A)(i) as amended by 2007 Technical Corrections Act §4(c)); over

(B) the tax which would be imposed for the tax year if the taxpayer's taxable income were equal to the amount of these exclusions for the tax year. (Code Sec. 911(f)(1)(A)(ii))

However, if the taxpayer's net capital gain exceeds his taxable income for a tax year (i.e., there is a "capital gain excess"):

(1) the taxpayer's net capital gain (determined without including any qualified dividend income in net capital gain) is reduced (but not below zero) by the capital gain excess (Code Sec. 911(f)(2)(A)(i));

(2) the taxpayer's qualified dividend income is reduced by the portion of the capital gain excess that exceeds the taxpayer's net capital gain (determined without including any qualified dividend income in net capital gain) and the reduction under item (1), above (Code Sec. 911(f)(2)(A)(ii));

(3) adjusted net capital gain, unrecaptured section 1250 gain, and 28% rate gain are each determined after increasing the Code Sec. 1(h)(4)(B) amount that is treated as capital loss for purposes of calculating 28% rate gain and unrecaptured section 1250 gain (see FTC 2d/FIN ¶s I-5010.8, I-5010.11; USTR

¶ 14.08; TaxDesk ¶s 223,318, 223,321) by the capital gain excess. (Code Sec. 911(f)(2)(A)(iii)) Thus, the amount of the excess is treated in the same manner as an increase in the long-term capital loss carried to the tax year. (Com Rept, see ¶ 5303)

> *Illustration (1):* In 2007, an unmarried individual has $80,000 of excluded income, a $30,000 gain from the sale of a long-term capital asset, and $20,000 deductions. The taxpayer's taxable income is $10,000. The taxpayer's tax is the excess of the amount of tax computed on taxable income of $90,000 ($10,000 taxable income plus $80,000 excluded income) of which $30,000 is adjusted net capital gain, over the tax computed on the $80,000. In determining the tax on the $90,000, the net capital gain and the adjusted net capital gain are each $10,000. This results in a tax of $1,500 (15% of $10,000 of adjusted net capital gain). (Com Rept, see ¶ 5303)

> *observation:* Before this provision became effective, the tax on the $90,000 was calculated as if $30,000 were capital gain, while the tax on the $80,000 was presumably calculated at ordinary income rates, with the result that no tax was imposed as a result of the stacking rule.

> *Illustration (2):* In 2007, an unmarried individual has $90,000 of excluded income, a $5,000 gain on the sale of a capital asset held for more than a year, $25,000 unrecaptured section 1250 gain, and $20,000 deductions. The taxpayer's taxable income is $10,000. The taxpayer's tax is the excess of the amount of tax computed on taxable income of $100,000 ($10,000 taxable income plus $90,000 excluded income) over the amount of tax computed on taxable income of $90,000 (excluded income). In determining the tax on the $100,000, the net capital gain is $10,000, of which $5,000 is adjusted net capital gain and $5,000 is unrecaptured section 1250 gain. This results in a tax of $2,000 (15% of $5,000 adjusted net capital gain plus 25% of $5,000 unrecaptured section 1250 gain. (Com Rept, see ¶ 5303)

Alternative minimum tax computation: The 2007 Technical Corrections Act amends the alternative minimum tax computation to provide that where a taxpayer has excluded amounts and has a taxable excess, his tentative minimum tax *before reduction by the AMT foreign tax credit* is equal to the excess (if any) of:

FTC 2d References are to Federal Tax Coordinator 2d
FIN References are to RIA's Analysis of Federal Taxes: Income
USTR References are to United States Tax Reporter: Income, Estate & Gift, and Excise
PCA References are to Pension Analysis (print & electronic)
PE References are to Pension Explanations (print & electronic)
EP References are to Estate Planning Analysis (print & electronic)

(a) the amount that would be the tentative minimum tax (taking into account the special capital gains rates) for the tax year *before reduction by the AMT foreign tax credit* if the taxpayer's taxable excess (generally, the AMTI minus the exemption amount) were increased by the amount of these exclusions for the tax year (Code Sec. 911(f)(1)(B)(i)); over

(b) the amount that would be the tentative minimum tax (taking into account the special capital gains rates) for the tax year *before reduction by the AMT foreign tax credit* if the taxpayer's taxable excess were equal to the amount of these exclusions for the tax year. (Code Sec. 911(f)(1)(B)(ii))

Thus, in computing the tentative minimum tax on the remaining income, the tax computation is made before the reduction for the AMT foreign tax credit. This conforms the AMT computation to the regular tax computation, which is also made before the application of the foreign tax credit. (Com Rept, see ¶ 5303)

In applying the Code Sec. 55(b)(3) alternative minimum tax capital gains calculation where, without regard to this rule, a taxpayer's net capital gain exceeds his taxable excess for a tax year:

- the regular tax rules described above in items (1), (2), and (3) under the "Regular tax computation" apply, except the term taxable excess is substituted for the term taxable income (Code Sec. 911(f)(2)(B)(i)), and

- the reference in the alternative minimum tax capital gains calculation to the net capital gain that is subject to a 5% rate under Code Sec. 1(h)(1)(B) is treated as a reference to that amount determined by applying the regular tax rules described in items (1), (2), and (3). (Code Sec. 911(f)(2)(B)(ii))

For this purpose, terms in the above rules that are also used in the Code Sec. 1(h) capital gains rules have the meanings used in the capital gains rules, except that in applying the above rules for minimum tax purposes, the minimum tax rules are taken into account. (Code Sec. 911(f)(2)(C))

☐ **Effective:** Tax years beginning after Dec. 31, 2006. (2007 Technical Corrections Act §4(d)(3))

> 🅡🅘🅐 *observation:* Thus this provision is not effective retroactively to the date the stacking rule became effective for taxpayers with foreign exclusions.

¶ 702. TIPRA look-through rule doesn't apply to interest, rent or royalty payments between related CFCs that create or increase a deficit that reduces subpart F income

Code Sec. 954(c)(6)(B), as amended and redesignated by 2007 Technical Corrections Act § 4(a)

Generally effective: Tax years of foreign corporations beginning after Dec. 31, 2005 and before Jan. 1, 2009, and tax years of U.S. shareholders with or within which such tax years of foreign corporations end

Committee Reports, see ¶ 5303

Under subpart F, U.S. persons who are 10% shareholders of a controlled foreign corporation (CFC) are required to include in income their pro rata share of the CFC's subpart F income whether or not this income is distributed to the shareholders. Subpart F income includes foreign base company income (FBCI), which in turn includes foreign personal holding company income (FPHCI). For subpart F purposes, FPHCI includes dividends, interest, income equivalent to interest, rents and royalties. (FTC 2d/FIN ¶s O-2400, O-2424.1, O-2432; USTR ¶s 9524, 9544, 9544.02)

The 2005 Tax Increase Prevention Act (2005 TIPRA) look-through rule provided that FPHCI does not include dividends, interest, rent, and royalties received or accrued from a CFC which is a related person to the extent attributable or properly allocable to income of the related person which is neither subpart F income nor income effectively connected to a trade or business (ECI). (Hereafter the TIPRA look-through rule.) Whether dividends, interest, rents or royalties are allocable to particular income is determined under look-through rules similar to those used for the foreign tax credit limitation. The TIPRA look-through rule is applicable for tax years of foreign corporations beginning after Dec. 31, 2005 and before Jan. 1, 2009, and tax years of U.S. shareholders with or within which such tax years of foreign corporations end. (FTC 2d/FIN ¶ O-2447.2 *et seq.*; USTR ¶ 9544.02)

In Notice 2007-9, IRS issued guidance regarding the TIPRA look-though rule. Under the guidance, the look-through rule applied to interest, rents and royalties that were allocated and apportioned to non-subpart F income even if interest, rent and royalty deductions exceeded the gross income of the related

---

FTC 2d References are to Federal Tax Coordinator 2d
FIN References are to RIA's Analysis of Federal Taxes: Income
USTR References are to United States Tax Reporter: Income, Estate & Gift, and Excise
PCA References are to Pension Analysis (print & electronic)
PE References are to Pension Explanations (print & electronic)
EP References are to Estate Planning Analysis (print & electronic)

CFC payor in the year paid or accrued. However, the look-through rule did not apply to interest, rent or royalties if deductions for those amounts created (or increased) a deficit which reduced the subpart F income of the related CFC payor or another CFC. (FTC 2d/FIN ¶ O-2447.5, ¶ O-2447.6; USTR ¶ 9544.02)

New Law. Under the Technical Corrections Act of 2007, the TIPRA look-through rule does not apply to any interest, rent, or royalty to the extent the interest, rent, or royalty creates (or increases) a deficit which under Code Sec. 952(c) (see FTC 2d/FIN ¶ O-2558; USTR ¶ 9524.01) may reduce the subpart F income of the payor or another controlled foreign corporation. (Code Sec. 954(c)(6) as amended by 2007 Technical Corrections Act §4(a))

> *observation:* Thus, the technical correction conforms the Code to the IRS guidance in Notice 2007-9.

The provision parallels the rule applicable to interest, rents, or royalties that would otherwise qualify for exclusion from FPHCI under the "same country" exception of Code Sec. 954(c)(3)(B) (see FTC 2d/FIN ¶s O-2439, O-2445; USTR ¶ 9544.02). Thus interest, rents, and royalties will be treated as subpart F income, notwithstanding the general TIPRA look-through rule, if the payment creates or increases a deficit of the payor corporation and that deficit is from an activity that could reduce the payor's subpart F income under the Code Sec. 952(c)(1)(B) accumulated deficit rule (see FTC 2d/FIN ¶ O-2558.5; USTR ¶ 9524.01) or could reduce the income of a qualified chain member under the Code Sec. 952(c)(1)(C) chain deficit rule (see FTC 2d/FIN ¶ O-2562; USTR ¶ 9524.01). For example, under the provision, items that do not qualify for the "same country" exception will also not qualify under the TIPRA look-through rule. (Com Rept, see ¶ 5303)

☐ **Effective:** Tax years of foreign corporations beginning after Dec. 31, 2005 and before Jan. 1, 2009, and tax years of U.S. shareholders with or within which such tax years for foreign corporations end. (2007 Technical Corrections Act §(4)(d)(1))

The 2006 Technical Corrections Act provides that the above provision is effective as if included in the provision of 2005 TIPRA to which the above rules relate. The above rules relate to 2005 TIPRA §103(b)(1), (Sec. 103(b)(1), PL 109-222, 05/17/2006) which, under 2005 TIPRA §103(b)(2) (Sec. 103(b)(2), PL 109-222, 05/17/2006) is effective for tax years of foreign corporations beginning after Dec. 31, 2005 and before Jan. 1, 2009, and tax years of U.S. shareholders with or within which such tax years for foreign corporations end.

¶ 800. Loss Limits

¶ 801. Identification of offsetting positions in identified straddles is required

Code Sec. 1092(a)(2)(B), as amended by 2007 Technical Corrections Act § 7(d)(2)(A)
Generally effective: Straddles acquired after Dec. 29, 2007
Committee Reports, see ¶ 5306

Under the straddle loss deferral rule, a loss realized on a position in a straddle must be deferred to the extent that the taxpayer has unrecognized gain in offsetting positions in the straddle. (FTC 2d/FIN ¶ I-7523; USTR ¶ 10,924; TaxDesk ¶ 228,403)

However, the straddle loss deferral rule doesn't apply to identified positions in an identified straddle. One requirement for an identified straddle is that the straddle must be clearly identified on the taxpayer's records as an identified straddle before the earlier of (a) the close of the day on which the straddle is acquired or (b) the time prescribed by IRS regs. (FTC 2d/FIN ¶ I-7527; USTR ¶ 10,924; TaxDesk ¶ 228,416)

> **⟪RIA⟫ observation:** Under pre-2007 Technical Corrections Act law, taxpayers weren't required to identify the positions in an identified straddle that were offsetting to one another.

New Law. The 2007 Technical Corrections Act provides that a straddle isn't "clearly identified" unless the positions in the straddle that are offsetting to other positions in the straddle are identified. (Code Sec. 1092(a)(2)(B) as amended by 2007 Technical Corrections Act §7(d)(2)(A)) Thus, taxpayers must identify not only the positions that make up an identified straddle but also which positions in that identified straddle are offsetting to one another. (Com Rept, see ¶ 5306)

> **⟪RIA⟫ observation:** This type of identification is sometimes called "microidentification."

For basis adjustments to positions in identified straddles, see ¶ 802.

☐ **Effective:** Straddles acquired after Dec. 29, 2007. (2007 Technical Corrections Act §7(e)(2))

FTC 2d References are to Federal Tax Coordinator 2d
FIN References are to RIA's Analysis of Federal Taxes: Income
USTR References are to United States Tax Reporter: Income, Estate & Gift, and Excise
PCA References are to Pension Analysis (print & electronic)
PE References are to Pension Explanations (print & electronic)
EP References are to Estate Planning Analysis (print & electronic)

¶ 802. Loss in identified straddle where there is no offsetting gain position or where an offsetting position is a liability results in basis increase to offsetting positions under reasonable, consistent method

Code Sec. 1092(a)(2)(A), as amended by 2007 Technical Corrections Act § 7(d)(2)(B)

Code Sec. 1092(a)(2)(A)(iii), as amended by 2007 Technical Corrections Act § 7(d)(1)

Code Sec. 1092(a)(2)(C), as amended and redesignated by 2007 Technical Corrections Act § 7(d)(3)

Code Sec. 1092(a)(2)(D), as amended by 2007 Technical Corrections Act § 7(d)(4)

Code Sec. 1092(a)(3)(B), as amended by 2007 Technical Corrections Act § 7(d)(2)(C)

Generally effective: Positions established after Oct. 21, 2004

Committee Reports, see ¶ 5306

The term "straddle" means offsetting positions in actively traded personal property. (FTC 2d/FIN ¶ I-7503; USTR ¶ 10,924; TaxDesk ¶ 228,406) Under the straddle loss deferral rule, a loss realized on a position in a straddle must be deferred to the extent that the taxpayer has unrecognized gain in offsetting positions in the straddle. (FTC 2d/FIN ¶ I-7523; USTR ¶ 10,924; TaxDesk ¶ 228,403)

However, under pre-2007 Technical Corrections Act law, the straddle loss deferral rule didn't apply to identified positions in an identified straddle. To qualify as an identified straddle:

. . . the straddle must be clearly identified on the taxpayer's records as an identified straddle before the earlier of (a) the close of the day on which the straddle is acquired or (b) the time prescribed by regs;

. . . to the extent that IRS provides in regs, the value of each position of the straddle (in the hands of the taxpayer immediately before the creation of the straddle) may not be less than the basis of that position in the hands of the taxpayer at the time the straddle was created; and

. . . the straddle may not be part of a larger straddle. (FTC 2d/FIN ¶ I-7527; USTR ¶ 10,924; TaxDesk ¶ 228,416)

Under pre-2007 Technical Corrections Act law, Code Sec. 1092(a)(2)(A)(ii) provided that a loss on an identified position in an identified straddle increased the basis of each of the identified offsetting positions in the identified straddle by an amount equal to the product of the amount of the loss multiplied by the ratio of the amount of unrecognized straddle-period gain in that offsetting position to the aggregate amount of unrecognized straddle-period gain in all offsetting positions. The loss wasn't otherwise taken into account for federal tax purposes. (FTC 2d/FIN ¶ I-7526; USTR ¶ 10,924; TaxDesk ¶ 228,415)

Under pre-2007 Technical Corrections Act law, unrecognized gain in any identified offsetting position was the excess of the fair market value of the position at the time of the determination over its fair market value at the time the taxpayer identified it as a position in an identified straddle. (FTC 2d/FIN ¶ P-5021.1; USTR ¶ 10,924; TaxDesk ¶ 216,029)

Under pre-2007 Technical Corrections Act law, the treatment of a loss on a position in an identified straddle was unclear in at least two circumstances:

(1) when there are no offsetting positions in the identified straddle with unrecognized straddle-period gain. (Com Rept, see ¶ 5306)

> *observation:* An example is a straddle involving shares and options on those shares, because both sides of the straddle may move in the same direction. The taxpayer may have a loss on both positions in the straddle or a loss on one position and no gain on the other position.

(2) when an offsetting position in the identified straddle is or has been a liability to the taxpayer. (Com Rept, see ¶ 5306)

> *observation:* An example is a call option written on a long position in shares. The treatment was unclear because the taxpayer has no basis in the written call.

> *observation:* Under pre-2007 Technical Corrections Act law, the statute could have been read as either permanently disallowing or currently recognizing losses on straddle positions where there were no offsetting positions in the identified straddle with unrecognized straddle-period gain.

> This ambiguity resulted in a situation in which conservative taxpayers avoided identifying straddles, out of concern that their losses could be permanently disallowed. Aggressive taxpayers would identify their straddles. Then, if both positions in an identified straddle showed a loss, they would close out one position and claim a loss in the year of sale, taking the position that the losses should be currently recognized.

New Law. The 2007 Technical Corrections Act addresses the treatment of losses in the two circumstances described above. It generally reaffirms that a

---

FTC 2d References are to Federal Tax Coordinator 2d
FIN References are to RIA's Analysis of Federal Taxes: Income
USTR References are to United States Tax Reporter: Income, Estate & Gift, and Excise
PCA References are to Pension Analysis (print & electronic)
PE References are to Pension Explanations (print & electronic)
EP References are to Estate Planning Analysis (print & electronic)

loss on a position in an identified straddle is neither currently recognized nor permanently disallowed. (Com Rept, see ¶ 5306)

Under the 2007 Technical Corrections Act, if the application of Code Sec. 1092(a)(2)(A)(ii) doesn't result in a basis increase in any offsetting position in the identified straddle (because there is no unrecognized straddle-period gain in any offsetting position (Com Rept, see ¶ 5306)), the basis of each offsetting position in the identified straddle must be increased in a manner that (Code Sec. 1092(a)(2)(A)(iii) as amended by 2007 Technical Corrections Act §7(d)(1)):

. . . is reasonable,

. . . is consistent with the purposes of the identified straddle rules,

. . . is consistently applied by the taxpayer (Code Sec. 1092(a)(2)(A)(iii)(I)), and

. . . allocates the full amount of the loss (but no more than that amount (Com Rept, see ¶ 5306)) to offsetting positions. (Code Sec. 1092(a)(2)(A)(iii)(II))

Taxpayers are expected to describe their method of allocating the basis increase in their books and records at the time the method is adopted. (Com Rept, see ¶ 5306)

Similar basis-increase rules apply (unless IRS provides otherwise) when there is a loss on a position in an identified straddle and an offsetting position in the identified straddle is or has been a liability or an obligation (Code Sec. 1092(a)(2)(C) as amended by 2007 Technical Corrections Act §7(d)(3)), such as a debt obligation issued by the taxpayer, a written option, or a notional principal contract entered into by the taxpayer. (Com Rept, see ¶ 5306)

> **⊘ observation:** Notional principal contracts include interest rate swaps, currency swaps, basis swaps, interest rate caps and floors, commodity swaps, equity swaps, equity index swaps, and similar agreements. See FTC 2d/FIN ¶ G-2554; USTR ¶ 4464.90; TaxDesk ¶ 447,001.

> **Illustration:** A taxpayer receives $1 to enter into a five-year short forward contract. The next day, $100 of loss is allocated to that position. Under the above rule, the resulting basis of the contract is $99. (Com Rept, see ¶ 5306)

> **⊘ observation:** A forward contract is an agreement to buy or sell an asset at a designated future time. The party that agrees to sell the asset has the short forward contract. Thus, the taxpayer in the above illustration has received $1 in return for agreeing to sell an asset in five years.

> When the taxpayer's basis in the forward contract is increased by $100 because of loss allocated to that position, the $100 increase is offset by the $1 that the taxpayer received, leaving the taxpayer with a $99 basis in the position.

For identification of offsetting positions in identified straddles, see ¶ 801.

IRS regulatory authority expanded. The regs or other guidance that IRS prescribes for carrying out the purposes of the identified straddle rules may include:

... methods of loss allocation, i.e., safe-harbor basis-allocation methods (Com Rept, see ¶ 5306), that satisfy the Code Sec. 1092(a)(2)(A)(iii) requirements for allocating basis (as described above);

... rules for applying Code Sec. 1092 to a position that is or has been a liability or an obligation. (Code Sec. 1092(a)(2)(D) as amended by 2007 Technical Corrections Act §7(d)(4))

Terms "identified positions" and "identified offsetting positions" eliminated. Under the 2007 Technical Corrections Act:

... the straddle loss deferral rule doesn't apply to *positions* in an identified straddle. (Code Sec. 1092(a)(2)(A)(i) as amended by 2007 Technical Corrections Act §7(d)(2)(B)(i))

> *observation:* Under pre-2007 Technical Corrections Act law, the straddle loss deferral rule didn't apply to "identified positions" in an identified straddle. See above. For further discussion, see *RIA observations* below.

... a loss on a *position* in an identified straddle increases the basis of each of the *offsetting positions* in the identified straddle by an amount equal to the product of the amount of the loss multiplied by the ratio of the amount of unrecognized gain in that offsetting position to the aggregate amount of unrecognized gain in all offsetting positions. (Code Sec. 1092(a)(2)(A)(ii) as amended by 2007 Technical Corrections Act §7(d)(2)(B)(ii); Code Sec. 1092(a)(2)(A)(ii) as amended by 2007 Technical Corrections Act §7(d)(2)(B)(iii))

> *observation:* Under pre-2007 Technical Corrections Act law, a loss on an "identified position" in an identified straddle increased the basis of each of the "identified offsetting positions" in the identified straddle by an amount equal to the product of the amount of the loss multiplied by the ratio of the amount of unrecognized gain in that offsetting position to the aggregate amount of unrecognized gain in all offsetting positions. See above. For further discussion, see *RIA observations* below.

FTC 2d References are to Federal Tax Coordinator 2d
FIN References are to RIA's Analysis of Federal Taxes: Income
USTR References are to United States Tax Reporter: Income, Estate & Gift, and Excise
PCA References are to Pension Analysis (print & electronic)
PE References are to Pension Explanations (print & electronic)
EP References are to Estate Planning Analysis (print & electronic)

. . . Unrecognized gain in any *offsetting position* is the excess of the fair market value of the position at the time of the determination over its fair market value at the time the taxpayer identified it as a position in an identified straddle. (Code Sec. 1092(a)(3)(B) as amended by 2007 Technical Corrections Act §7(d)(2)(C))

> **☑ observation:**   Under pre-2007 Technical Corrections Act law, unrecognized gain in any "identified offsetting position" was the excess of the fair market value of the position at the time of the determination over its fair market value at the time the taxpayer identified it as a position in an identified straddle. See above. For further discussion, see *RIA observations* below.

> **☑ observation:** In the above straddle rules, the 2007 Technical Corrections Act thus substitutes the term "positions" for "identified positions," and "offsetting positions" for "identified offsetting positions." The reasons for these substitutions are not entirely clear. Under pre-2007 Technical Corrections Act law, the Code's straddle rules didn't define or otherwise refer to "identified positions" or "identified offsetting positions," except that Code Sec. 1092(a)(2)(C) gave IRS authority to issue regulations which could specify, among other things, the proper methods for clearly identifying the positions comprising an identified straddle—authority unchanged by the 2007 Technical Corrections Act. See FTC 2d/FIN ¶ I-7527; TaxDesk ¶ 228,416. It is therefore possible that the intention behind the Act's substitutions was simply to eliminate superfluous terminology. (For 2007 Technical Corrections Act requirement that taxpayers identify offsetting positions in an identified straddle, see ¶ 801.)

☐ **Effective:** Positions established after Oct. 21, 2004. (2007 Technical Corrections Act §7(e)(1))

The 2007 Technical Corrections Act §7(e)(1) provides that the above provisions are effective as if included in the provision of the 2004 Jobs Act to which they relate. Those provisions relate to 2004 Jobs Act §888 (Sec. 888, PL 108-357, 10/22/2004) which, under 2004 Jobs Act §888(e) (Sec. 888(e), PL 108-357, 10/22/2004), is effective for positions established after Oct. 21, 2004.

¶ 803. Ownership by certain pass-thru entities making nonqualified allocations is no longer a reason for property to be subject to the "tax-exempt use loss" rules

Code Sec. 470(c)(2)(B), as amended by 2007 Technical Corrections Act § 7(c)(1)

Generally effective: Property acquired after Mar. 12, 2004

Committee Reports, see ¶ 5306

Code Sec. 470 provides that a "tax-exempt use loss" for any tax year is not allowed, see FTC 2d/FIN ¶ L-6901; USTR ¶ 4704; TaxDesk ¶ 261,201. A "tax-exempt use loss" is the amount, if any, by which:

. . . the aggregate deductions (other than interest) directly allocable to "tax-exempt use property" plus the aggregate deductions for interest properly allocable to the property exceed

. . . the aggregate income from the property, see FTC 2d/FIN ¶ L-6901; USTR ¶ 4704; TaxDesk ¶ 261,201.

Generally, losses not allowed under the above limitation can be carried forward and applied against future net income from the property and are, in any event, deductible when the property is disposed of, see FTC 2d/FIN ¶ L-6902 *et seq.*; USTR ¶ 4704; TaxDesk ¶ 261,202 *et seq.*

Under Code Sec. 470(c)(1), "tax-exempt-use property," for purposes of the tax-exempt use loss rules, includes, with certain modifications, "tax-exempt use property" as defined in Code Sec. 168(h) (which defines tax-exempt use property for purposes of certain depreciation rules). Thus, tax-exempt use property, for purposes of the tax-exempt use loss rules, includes most property leased to tax-exempt organizations, governmental units, or certain foreign individuals or entities ("leased property"), see FTC 2d/FIN ¶s L-6905, L-9606 *et seq.*, L-9625 *et seq.*; USTR ¶s 1684.06, 4704; TaxDesk ¶ 261,205. Certain qualifying leases are excepted from the tax-exempt use loss rules, see FTC 2d/FIN ¶ L-6906 *et seq.*; USTR ¶ 4704.01; TaxDesk ¶ 261,206 *et seq.*

Under pre 2007 Technical Corrections Act law, tax-exempt use property, for purposes of the tax-exempt use loss rules, included property described in Code Sec. 168(h)(6). Thus, tax-exempt use property, for purposes of the tax-exempt use loss rules, included most property held by a partnership or other pass-thru

FTC 2d References are to Federal Tax Coordinator 2d
FIN References are to RIA's Analysis of Federal Taxes: Income
USTR References are to United States Tax Reporter: Income, Estate & Gift, and Excise
PCA References are to Pension Analysis (print & electronic)
PE References are to Pension Explanations (print & electronic)
EP References are to Estate Planning Analysis (print & electronic)

entity (including a group of tiered partnerships or entities) that (a) had both tax-exempt and taxable partners (or other interest holders) and (b) made nonqualified allocations (i.e., certain disproportionate allocations) of income, deduction or other tax items among its partners (or other interest holders) ("pass-thru property"), see FTC 2d/FIN ¶s L-6905, L-9606 *et seq.*, L-9620 *et seq.*; USTR ¶s 1684.06, 4704; TaxDesk ¶ 261,205. However, property that would have been tax-exempt use property solely because it was pass-thru property was excepted from being tax-exempt use property if any credit was allowable for the property under Code Sec. 42 (the low-income housing credit, see FTC 2d/FIN ¶ L-15701; USTR ¶ 424; TaxDesk ¶ 383,001) or Code Sec. 47 (the rehabilitation credit, see FTC 2d/FIN ¶ L-16101; USTR ¶ 474; TaxDesk ¶ 381,501). (FTC 2d/FIN ¶ L-6905; USTR ¶ 4704; TaxDesk ¶ 261,205)

New Law. Under the 2007 Technical Corrections Act, any property that would have been tax-exempt use property, for purposes of the tax-exempt use loss rules, solely by reason of Code Sec. 168(h)(6) is excepted from being tax-exempt use property for purposes of the tax-exempt use loss rules. (Code Sec. 470(c)(2)(B) as amended by 2007 Technical Corrections Act §7(c)(1))

> **observation:** Thus, under the 2007 Technical Corrections Act, property that would have been subject to the tax-exempt use loss rules solely because it is pass-thru property isn't subject to the tax-exempt-use loss rules, whether or not any low-income housing credit or rehabilitation credit is allowable for the property.

For clarification of the application of the tax-exempt use loss rules to partnerships that are, in substance, leases, see ¶ 805.

For a modification of the rules that except certain qualifying leases from the tax-exempt use loss rules, see ¶ 804.

☐ **Effective:** Property acquired after Mar. 12, 2004. (2007 Technical Corrections Act §7(e)(1)).

> **observation:** 2007 Technical Corrections Act §7(e)(1) (above) provides that the change concerning pass-thru property discussed above is effective as if included in the provisions of the 2004 Jobs Act to which it relates. Under 2004 Jobs Act §849(a) (Sec. 849(a), PL 108-357, 10/22/2004), as amended by 2005 Gulf Opportunity Zone Act §403(ff) (Sec. 403(ff), PL 109-135, 12/21/2005), the tax-exempt-use-loss rules, which were provided by 2004 Jobs Act §848 (Sec. 848, PL 108-357, 10/22/2004), are, for property treated as tax-exempt use property other than by reason of a lease, effective for property acquired after Mar. 12, 2004.

Congress didn't intend that the effective date discussed above supersede the rules set forth in Notice 2005-29, 2005-13 IRB 796, Notice 2006-2, 2006-2 IRB

278 and Notice 2007-4, 2007-1 IRB 260 with respect to the application of Code Sec. 470 (which provides the tax-exempt use loss rules, see above) in the case of partnerships for tax years beginning in 2004, 2005 and 2006. These notices state that IRS won't apply Code Sec. 470 to disallow losses associated with property that is treated as tax-exempt use property solely because it is pass-thru property, but that abusive transactions involving partnerships and other pass-thru entities remain subject to challenge by IRS under other provisions of the tax law, see FTC 2d/FIN ¶ L-6905; USTR ¶ 4704; TaxDesk ¶ 261,215. Accordingly for partnership tax years beginning in 2004, 2005 and 2006, IRS may apply Code Sec. 470 to a partnership that would be treated as a lease under Code Sec. 7701(e)(2), see FTC 2d/FIN ¶ L-9635; USTR ¶ 77014.54. (Com Rept, see ¶ 5306).

¶ 804. The "limited-available-funds" requirement for excepting certain leases from the "tax-exempt use loss" rules must be satisfied for the full lease term

Code Sec. 470(d)(1)(A), as amended by 2007 Technical Corrections Act § 7(c)(2)
Generally effective: Leases entered into after Mar. 12, 2004
Committee Reports, see ¶ 5306

Code Sec. 470 provides that a "tax-exempt use loss" for any tax year is not allowed, see FTC 2d/FIN ¶ L-6901; USTR ¶ 4704; TaxDesk ¶ 261,201. A "tax-exempt use loss" is the amount, if any, by which:

... the aggregate deductions (other than interest) directly allocable to "tax-exempt use property" plus the aggregate deductions for interest properly allocable to the property exceed

... the aggregate income from the property, see FTC 2d/FIN ¶ L-6901; USTR ¶ 4704; TaxDesk ¶ 261,201.

Generally, losses not allowed under the above limitation can be carried forward and applied against future net income from the property and are, in any event, deductible when the property is disposed of, see FTC 2d/FIN ¶ L-6902 *et seq.*; USTR ¶ 4704; TaxDesk ¶ 261,202 *et seq.*

Under Code Sec. 470(c)(1), "tax-exempt-use property," for purposes of the tax-exempt use loss rules, includes, with certain modifications, "tax-exempt use property" as defined in Code Sec. 168(h) (which defines tax-exempt use prop-

---

FTC 2d References are to Federal Tax Coordinator 2d
FIN References are to RIA's Analysis of Federal Taxes: Income
USTR References are to United States Tax Reporter: Income, Estate & Gift, and Excise
PCA References are to Pension Analysis (print & electronic)
PE References are to Pension Explanations (print & electronic)
EP References are to Estate Planning Analysis (print & electronic)

erty for purposes of certain depreciation rules). Thus, tax-exempt use property, for purposes of the tax-exempt use loss rules, includes most property leased to tax-exempt organizations, governmental units, or certain foreign individuals or entities, see FTC 2d/FIN ¶s L-6905, L-9606 *et seq.*, L-9625 *et seq.*; USTR ¶s 1684.06, 4704; TaxDesk ¶ 261,205. For the elimination, by the 2007 Techni-cal Corrections Act, of ownership by certain pass-thru entities as an independent basis for treating property as tax-exempt use property for purposes of the tax-exempt use loss rules, see ¶ 803.

Certain qualifying leases are excepted from the tax-exempt use loss rules, see FTC 2d/FIN ¶ L-6906 *et seq.*; USTR ¶ 4704.01; TaxDesk ¶ 261,206 *et seq.*

One of the requirements for being an excepted lease is a limited-available-funds requirement. Under this requirement, not more than an allowable amount (as further specified in the Code) of funds are:

. . . subject to any arrangement to or for the benefit of the lessor or any lender, or to or for the benefit of the lessee to satisfy the lessee's obligations or options under the lease, or

. . . set aside or expected to be set aside to or for the benefit of the lessor or any lender, or to or for the benefit of the lessee to satisfy the lessee's obligations or options under the lease, see FTC 2d/FIN ¶ L-6907; USTR ¶ 4704.01; TaxDesk ¶ 261,207.

Under pre-2007 Technical Corrections Act law, Code Sec. 470(d)(1)(A) stated that the limited-available-funds requirement had to be satisfied at *any time* during the lease term. (FTC 2d/FIN ¶ L-6907; USTR ¶ 4704.01; TaxDesk ¶ 261,207)

New Law. The 2007 Technical Corrections Act requires that the limited-available funds requirement be satisfied at *all times* during the lease term. (Code Sec. 470(d)(1)(A) as amended by 2007 Technical Corrections Act §7(c)(2))

For the treatment of partnerships that are, in substance, leases as leases for purposes of the tax-exempt use loss rules, see ¶ 805.

☐ **Effective:** Leases entered into after Mar. 12, 2004, but not "qualified trans-portation property" (i.e., domestic property subject to a lease for which a formal application that (1) was submitted for approval to the Federal Transit Adminis-tration (an agency of the Department of Transportation) after June 30, 2003, and before Mar. 13, 2004, (2) was approved by the Federal Transit Administration before Jan. 1, 2006, and (3) included a description of the property and the value of the property). (2007 Technical Corrections Act §7(e)(1)).

> **⊘** *observation:* 2007 Technical Corrections Act §7(e)(1) (above) pro-vides that the change concerning excepted leases discussed above is ef-fective as if included in the provisions of the 2004 Jobs Act to which it

relates. Under 2004 Jobs Act §849 (Sec. 849, PL 108-357, 10/22/2004), the tax-exempt-use-loss rules, which were provided by 2004 Jobs Act §848 (Sec. 848, PL 108-357, 10/22/2004), are, for leases, effective, as described above, for leases entered into after Mar. 12, 2004, subject to an exception for qualified transportation property.

¶ 805. Rules treating partnerships as leases are made expressly applicable to the "tax-exempt use loss" rules

Code Sec. 470(c)(2)(C), as amended by 2007 Technical Corrections Act § 7(c)(1)
Generally effective: Leases entered into after Mar. 12, 2004
Committee Reports, see ¶ 5306

Code Sec. 470 provides that a "tax-exempt use loss" for any tax year is not allowed, see FTC 2d/FIN ¶ L-6901; USTR ¶ 4704; TaxDesk ¶ 261,201. A "tax-exempt use loss" is the amount, if any, by which:

. . . the aggregate deductions (other than interest) directly allocable to "tax-exempt use property" plus the aggregate deductions for interest properly allocable to the property exceed

. . . the aggregate income from the property, see FTC 2d/FIN ¶ L-6901; USTR ¶ 4704; TaxDesk ¶ 261,201.

Generally, losses not allowed under the above limitation can be carried forward and applied against future net income from the property and are, in any event, deductible when the property is disposed of, see FTC 2d/FIN ¶ L-6902 *et seq.*; USTR ¶ 4704; TaxDesk ¶ 261,202 *et seq.*

Under Code Sec. 470(c)(1), "tax-exempt-use property," for purposes of the tax-exempt use loss rules, includes, with certain modifications, "tax-exempt use property" as defined in Code Sec. 168(h) (which defines tax-exempt use property for purposes of certain depreciation rules). Thus, tax-exempt use property, for purposes of the tax-exempt use loss rules, includes most property leased to tax-exempt organizations, governmental units, or certain foreign individuals or entities, see FTC 2d/FIN ¶s L-6905, L-9606 *et seq.*, L-9625 *et seq.*; USTR ¶s 1684.06, 4704; TaxDesk ¶ 261,205. Certain qualifying leases are excepted from the tax-exempt use loss rules, see FTC 2d/FIN ¶ L-6906 *et seq.*; USTR ¶ 4704.01; TaxDesk ¶ 261,206 *et seq.* For the elimination, by the 2007 Techni-

---

cal Corrections Act, of ownership by certain pass-thru entities as an independent basis for treating property as tax-exempt use property for purposes of the tax-exempt use loss rules, see ¶ 803.

Under Code Sec. 7701(e)(2), for purposes of Chapter 1 of Subtitle A of the Code (the income tax rules, except for certain withholding and consolidated return rules), an arrangement, including a partnership or other pass-thru entity, is treated as a lease if the arrangement is properly treated as a lease, taking into account factors similar to those that, under Code Sec. 7701(e)(1), are used to determine whether a service contract is a lease, see FTC 2d/FIN ¶s L-9933, L-9934, L-9935; USTR ¶ 77,014.54. Under pre-2007 Technical Corrections Act law, there was no Code provision that expressly referred to Code Sec. 7701(e) in determining whether a partnership was a lease for purposes of the tax-exempt use loss rules. (FTC 2d/FIN ¶ L-6905; USTR ¶ 4704; TaxDesk ¶ 261,205)

New Law. Congress believed that under pre-2007 Technical Corrections Act law the manner of applying Code Sec. 470 (which provides the tax-exempt use loss rules, see above) in the case of property owned by a partnership with a tax-exempt partner was unclear. (Com Rept, see ¶ 5306).

Thus, the 2007 Technical Corrections Act includes in Code Sec. 470 a cross reference that reads as follows: "For treatment of partnerships as leases to which section 168(h) applies, see section 7701(e)." (Code Sec. 470(c)(2)(C) as amended by 2007 Technical Corrections Act §7(c)(1))

Accordingly, if a partnership is recharacterized as a lease under Code Sec. 7701(e) (see above), and a provision of Code Sec. 168(h) (see above), other than Code Sec. 168(h)(6) (see the second observation below), applies to cause the property characterized as leased to be treated as tax-exempt use property, the loss deferral rules of Code Sec. 470 apply. (Com Rept, see ¶ 5306)

> **⊘** *observation:* In other words, it appears that Congress provided the cross reference discussed above to remove any doubt that, to the extent that being leased is one of the elements of being tax-exempt use property for purposes of the tax-exempt use loss rules (see above), that element is present where an arrangement is in the form of a partnership, but is, in substance, a lease.

> **⊘** *observation:* As discussed at ¶ 803, the 2007 Technical Correction Act eliminated, as an independent basis for classifying property as tax-exempt use property for purposes of the tax-exempt use loss rules, the fact that the property is described in Code Sec. 168(h)(6) (i.e., is owned by certain pass-thru entities).

For property of a partnership in which a tax-exempt entity is a partner, factors similar to those in Code Sec. 7701(e)(1) (and in the legislative history of Code Sec. 7701(e)(1), see the first observation below) that are relevant in determining whether a partnership is properly treated as a lease of property held by the partnership include the following:

... whether a tax-exempt partner maintains physical possession or control or holds the benefits and burdens of ownership with respect to the property;

... whether there is insignificant equity investment by any taxable partner;

... whether the transfer of the property to the partnership doesn't result in a change in use of the property;

... whether the property is necessary for the provision of government services;

... whether a disproportionately large portion of the deductions for depreciation with respect to the property are allocated to one or more taxable partners relative to the partner's risk of loss with respect to the property or to the partner's allocation of other partnership items; and

... whether amounts payable on behalf of the tax-exempt partner relating to the property are defeased or funded by set-asides or expected set-asides. (Com Rept, see ¶ 5306)

> **ⓡ⁄observation:** Presumably, the legislative history of Code Sec. 7701(e)(1) referred to above includes Conference Report No. 98-861 (PL 98-369), p. 138 and Senate Print No. 98-169, Vol I (PL 98-369), pp. 137 *et seq.*, see FTC 2d/FIN ¶s L-9633, L-9634.

It is intended that regs or other IRS guidance provide additional factors that can be taken into account in determining whether a partnership with taxable and tax-exempt partners is an arrangement that resembles a lease of property under which Code Sec. 470 defers the allowance of losses. (Com Rept, see ¶ 5306)

For a modification of the rules that except certain qualifying leases from the tax-exempt use loss rules, see ¶ 804.

☐ **Effective:** Leases entered into after Mar. 12, 2004, but not "qualified transportation property" (i.e., domestic property subject to a lease for which a formal application that (1) was submitted for approval to the Federal Transit Administration (an agency of the Department of Transportation) after June 30, 2003, and before Mar. 13, 2004, (2) was approved by the Federal Transit Administration before Jan. 1, 2006, and (3) included a description of the property and the value of the property). (2007 Technical Corrections Act §7(e)(1)).

> **ⓡ⁄observation:** 2007 Technical Corrections Act §7(e)(1) (above) provides that the change concerning partnerships treated as leases dis-

---

FTC 2d References are to Federal Tax Coordinator 2d
FIN References are to RIA's Analysis of Federal Taxes: Income
USTR References are to United States Tax Reporter: Income, Estate & Gift, and Excise
PCA References are to Pension Analysis (print & electronic)
PE References are to Pension Explanations (print & electronic)
EP References are to Estate Planning Analysis (print & electronic)

cussed above is effective as if included in the provisions of the 2004 Jobs Act to which it relates. Under 2004 Jobs Act §849 (Sec. 849, PL 108-357, 10/22/2004), the tax-exempt-use-loss rules, which were provided by 2004 Jobs Act §848 (Sec. 848, PL 108-357, 10/22/2004), are, for leases, effective, as described above, for leases entered into after Mar. 12, 2004, subject to an exception for qualified transportation property.

¶ 900. Tax Credits

¶ 901. Errors in refundable child tax credit rules are corrected

Code Sec. 24(d)(1)(B), as amended by 2007 Technical Corrections Act § 11(c)(1)(A)

Code Sec. 24(d)(1)(B)(ii)(II), as amended by 2007 Technical Corrections Act § 11(c)(1)(B)

Generally effective: Tax years beginning after Dec. 31, 2005

Committee Reports, None

Before 2010, individuals may claim a child tax credit of up to $1,000 for each qualifying child under age 17 at the close of the calendar year. The credit is reduced (not below zero) by $50 for each $1,000 (or fraction thereof) of modified adjusted gross income (AGI)—AGI increased by excluded foreign, possessions, and Puerto Rico income—above $110,000 for joint filers, $75,000 for unmarried individuals, and $55,000 for marrieds filing separately. (FTC 2d/ FIN ¶ A-4050; USTR ¶ 244; TaxDesk ¶ 569,101)

Under Code Sec. 24(d)(1)(B), the child tax credit is refundable to the extent of the *excess (if any)* of:

(1) 15% of earned income above $10,000, as adjusted for inflation ($11,750 for 2007); or

(2) for a taxpayer with three or more qualifying children, the excess of social security taxes for the tax year over the credit allowed under an unidentified *"section"* for the tax year.

The two italicized phrases above were introduced when the rules for the refundable child tax credit (also called the "additional child tax credit") were amended by the Sec. 402(i)(3)(B)(ii) of the 2005 Gulf Opportunity Zone Act (Sec. 402(i)(3)(B)(ii), PL 109-135, 12/21/2005). Prior to that amendment, Code Sec. 24(d)(1)(B) provided that child tax credit was refundable to the extent of the greater of:

. . . 15% of earned income above $10,000, as adjusted for inflation; or

. . . for a taxpayer with three or more qualifying children, the excess of social security taxes for the tax year over the credit allowed under Code Sec. 32, i.e.,

---

FTC 2d References are to Federal Tax Coordinator 2d
FIN References are to RIA's Analysis of Federal Taxes: Income
USTR References are to United States Tax Reporter: Income, Estate & Gift, and Excise
PCA References are to Pension Analysis (print & electronic)
PE References are to Pension Explanations (print & electronic)
EP References are to Estate Planning Analysis (print & electronic)

the earned income credit (see FTC 2d/FIN ¶ A-4201 *et seq.*; USTR ¶ 324 *et seq.*; TaxDesk ¶ 569,001 *et seq.*), for the tax year.

> **⊘** *observation:* The two italicized phrases are apparently erroneous. In the case of the first phrase, the meaning of "the excess of" item (1) "or" item (2) is unclear, at the very least. In the case of the second phrase, the intended credit is simply not identified.

(FTC 2d/FIN ¶ A-4055; USTR ¶ 244; TaxDesk ¶ 569,105)

New Law. The 2007 Technical Corrections Act corrects the above two errors. Thus, under the Act, the child tax credit is refundable to the extent of "the greater of" (rather than "the excess (if any) of") the amounts listed at (1) and (2) above. (Code Sec. 24(d)(1)(B) as amended by 2007 Technical Corrections Act §11(c)(1)(A))

In addition, item (2), above, is amended so that it refers to the credit allowed under Code Sec. 32—the earned income credit—rather than to a credit under an unidentified "section." (Code Sec. 24(d)(1)(B)(ii)(II) as amended by 2007 Technical Corrections Act §11(c)(1)(B))

> **⊘** *observation:* The IRS form for figuring the refundable child tax credit (Form 8812) applies the rules as if the technical corrections described above had already been made.

☐ **Effective:** Tax years beginning after Dec. 31, 2005. (2007 Technical Corrections Act §11(c)(2))

The 2007 Technical Corrections Act §11(c)(2) provides that the above provision is effective as if included in the provision of the 2005 Gulf Opportunity Zone Act to which it relates. The above provision relates to 2005 Gulf Opportunity Zone Act §402(i)(3)(B)(ii) (Sec. 402(i)(3)(B)(ii), PL 109-135, 12/21/2005) which, under 2005 Gulf Opportunity Zone Act §402(m)(3) (Sec. 402(m)(3), PL 109-135, 12/21/2005), is effective for tax years beginning after Dec. 31, 2005.

¶ 902. Rule that prevents full-time students from disqualifying housing units from the low-income housing credit is clarified

Code Sec. 42(i)(3)(D)(ii)(I), as amended by 2007 Mortgage Relief Act § 6(a)
Generally effective: Housing credit amounts, whenever allocated, and certain
*   tax-exempt-financed buildings, whenever placed in service*
Committee Reports, None

The low-income housing credit is a business tax credit equal to a percentage of the qualified basis of qualified low-income buildings, see FTC 2d/FIN ¶ L-

15701; USTR ¶ 424; TaxDesk ¶ 383,001. Generally, the qualified basis increases by the extent to which a building consists of "low-income units," see FTC 2d/FIN ¶ L-15901; USTR ¶ 424.30; TaxDesk ¶ 383,007.

Units don't fail to qualify as low-income units merely because they are occupied by full-time students if the full-time students (1) are married and file a joint return (the joint return test) or (2) are single parents and their children, as further described in the Code (the single-parents-and-children test), see FTC 2d/ FIN ¶ L-15811; USTR ¶ 424.60; TaxDesk ¶ 383,007.

Under pre-2007 Mortgage Relief Act law, the single-parents-and-children test described the eligible single parents and their children as single parents and children of those parents that aren't dependents of another individual. (FTC 2d/ FIN ¶ L-15811; USTR ¶ 424.60; TaxDesk ¶ 383,007) For this purpose, dependents are defined in Code Sec. 152, except that the following rules aren't taken into account: the rule that prohibits dependents from claiming others as dependents; the rule that prohibits a married joint filer from being treated as a dependent; and the rule that sets a gross income limit for qualifying relatives (the modified-dependency test), see FTC 2d/FIN ¶ A-3601 *et seq.*; USTR ¶ 1524 *et seq.*; TaxDesk ¶ 562,401 *et seq.*

New Law. Under the 2007 Mortgage Relief Act, the single-parents-and-children test describes the eligible single parents and their children as (A) single parents that aren't dependents of another individual (defining dependents as that term is defined under the modified-dependency test) and (B) children of those parents that aren't dependents of another individual other than a parent of those children (defining dependents as that term is defined under the modified-dependency test). (Code Sec. 42(i)(3)(D)(ii)(I) as amended by 2007 Mortgage Relief Act §6(a))

> *observation:* The change made by the 2007 Mortgage Relief Act relates to the description in (B) immediately above. The description in (A) immediately above remains unchanged from pre-2007 Mortgage Relief Act law.

> *observation:* The intent of the 2007 Mortgage Relief Act's amendment of Code Sec. 42(i)(3)(D)(ii)(I) is, presumably, to clarify that the status of a child (or children) as a dependent (or as dependents) of the *single parent* won't disqualify the single parent and child (or children) from passing the single-parents-and-children test.

FTC 2d References are to Federal Tax Coordinator 2d
FIN References are to RIA's Analysis of Federal Taxes: Income
USTR References are to United States Tax Reporter: Income, Estate & Gift, and Excise
PCA References are to Pension Analysis (print & electronic)
PE References are to Pension Explanations (print & electronic)
EP References are to Estate Planning Analysis (print & electronic)

☐ **Effective:** Housing credit amounts allocated before, on or after Dec. 20, 2007, and (2007 Mortgage Relief Act §6(b)(1)) buildings placed in service before, on, or after Dec. 20, 2007 to the extent that Code Sec. 42(h)(1) doesn't apply to any building by reason of Code Sec. 42(h)(4). (2007 Mortgage Relief Act §6(b)(2))

> **⊘** *observation:* Generally, under Code Sec. 42(h)(1), low-income housing credits are allowable with respect to a building only to the extent that a housing credit dollar amount is allocated to the building by a housing credit agency, see FTC 2d/FIN ¶ L-16001; USTR ¶ 424.70. However, under Code Sec. 42(h)(4), buildings financed with certain tax-exempt obligations aren't subject to the allocation requirement, see FTC 2d/FIN ¶ L-16014; USTR ¶ 424.70.

¶ 903. List of taxes excluded from "regular tax liability" is expanded to include the 10% penalty taxes imposed for failures to maintain HDHP coverage or for recapture of charitable deduction claimed for a fractional interest contribution

Code Sec. 26(b)(2)(S), as amended by 2007 Technical Corrections Act § 11(a)(3)

Code Sec. 26(b)(2)(T), as amended by 2007 Technical Corrections Act § 11(a)(3)

Generally effective: Dec. 29, 2007

Committee Reports, None

"Regular tax liability" is used to compute the limitations on the amount of credits (personal and business) that can be claimed in a tax year (see FTC 2d/FIN ¶ L-18101; USTR ¶ 264.01; TaxDesk ¶ 569,601 (personal credits) and FTC 2d/FIN ¶ L-15202; USTR ¶ 384.02; TaxDesk ¶ 380,502 (business credits)). "Regular tax liability" is also important for alternative minimum tax (AMT) purposes. A taxpayer is subject to the AMT in a tax year if his "tentative minimum tax" exceeds his "regular tax liability" for the year (see FTC 2d/FIN ¶ A-8101; USTR ¶ 554.01; TaxDesk ¶ 691,001). Code Sec. 26(b)(2) defines "regular tax liability" as the tax imposed by Chapter 1 of the Code (i.e., Code Sec. 1 through Code Sec. 1400T) for the tax year, other than certain specifically enumerated taxes. (FTC 2d/FIN ¶ L-18103; USTR ¶ 264.01; TaxDesk ¶ 569,604)

New Law. The Code Sec. 26(b)(2) list of taxes that are specifically excluded from the taxpayer's "regular tax liability" is expanded to include the taxes imposed under the following Code sections:

(1) Code Sec. 106(e)(3)(A)(ii), Code Sec. 223(b)(8)(B)(i)(II), and Code Sec. 408(d)(9)(D)(i)(II) (Code Sec. 26(b)(2)(S) as amended by 2007 Technical

Corrections Act §11(a)(3))—i.e., the 10% penalty taxes enacted under the 2006 Tax Relief Act that relate to failures to maintain high deductible health plan (HDHP) coverage, including:

. . . the Code Sec. 106(e)(3)(A)(ii) tax with respect to rollovers from flexible spending accounts and health reimbursement accounts into health savings accounts (HSAs) (see FTC 2d/FIN ¶ H-1101.11; USTR ¶ 1064; TaxDesk ¶ 289,108.8),

. . . the Code Sec. 223(b)(8)(B)(i)(II) tax with respect to contributions made to HSAs (see FTC 2d/FIN ¶ H-1350.7A; USTR ¶ 2234.035; TaxDesk ¶ 289,107.1), and

. . . the Code Sec. 408(d)(9)(D)(i)(II) tax with respect to rollovers from IRAs to HSAs (see FTC 2d/FIN ¶ H-12253.1B; USTR ¶ 4084.03; TaxDesk ¶ 143,003.1B);

(2) Code Sec. 170(o)(3)(B) (Code Sec. 26(b)(2)(T) as amended by 2007 Technical Corrections Act §11(a)(3))—i.e., the 10% recapture tax imposed on a taxpayer who is required, under the rules for fractional interest contributions enacted under the 2006 Pension Protection Act, to recapture the charitable deduction he claimed for a gift of a fractional interest in tangible personal property (see FTC 2d/FIN ¶ K-3472.4; USTR ¶ 1704.45; TaxDesk ¶ 331,621.3).

☐ **Effective:** Dec. 29, 2007.

FTC 2d References are to Federal Tax Coordinator 2d
FIN References are to RIA's Analysis of Federal Taxes: Income
USTR References are to United States Tax Reporter: Income, Estate & Gift, and Excise
PCA References are to Pension Analysis (print & electronic)
PE References are to Pension Explanations (print & electronic)
EP References are to Estate Planning Analysis (print & electronic)

¶ 1000. Excise Taxes

¶ 1001. Airport and airway trust fund excise taxes are extended through Feb. 29, 2008

Code Sec. 4081(d)(2)(B), as amended by 2008 Appropriations Act § 116(a)(Div. K, Title I)
Code Sec. 4261(j)(1)(A)(ii), as amended by 2008 Appropriations Act § 116(b)(1)(Div. K, Title I)
Code Sec. 4271(d)(1)(A)(ii), as amended by 2008 Appropriations Act § 116(b)(2)(Div. K, Title I)
Generally effective: Oct. 1, 2007
Committee Reports, None

Under pre-2008 Appropriations Act law, the following excise taxes that fund the Federal Airport and Airway Trust Fund program expired after 2007 (the Code provides for termination of the taxes after Sept. 30, 2007, but Congress has by several temporary measures extended them through the end of 2007):

(1) The 7.5% tax on amounts paid for domestic air passenger tickets. (FTC 2d ¶ W-5101; USTR Excise Taxes ¶ 42,614.01)

(2) The $3.00 tax ($3.40 for 2007 as indexed for inflation) imposed on each domestic segment of taxable air transportation (the "domestic segment tax"). (FTC 2d ¶ W-5101; USTR Excise Taxes ¶ 42,614.01)

(3) The $12 per person tax ($15.10 for 2007 as indexed for inflation) on international departures and arrivals by air (the "international air transportation tax"); $6 ($7.50 for 2007 as indexed for inflation) for departures that begin or end in Alaska or Hawaii. (FTC 2d ¶ W-5103, ¶ W-5126; USTR Excise Taxes ¶ 42,614.01)

(4) The 6.25% tax on domestic air transportation of property. (FTC 2d ¶ W-5201; USTR Excise Taxes ¶ 42,714)

(5) 17.5¢ per gallon of the 21.8¢ per gallon tax imposed on kerosene removed from a terminal or refinery directly into the fuel tank of an aircraft for use in noncommercial aviation (allowing the rate to drop to 4.3¢ per gallon). (FTC 2d ¶ W-1501.1; USTR Excise Taxes ¶ 40,814)

(6) 15¢ per gallon of the 19.3¢ per gallon tax imposed on aviation gasoline upon its removal from the terminal (allowing the rate to drop to 4.3¢ per gallon). (FTC 2d ¶ W-1501; USTR Excise Taxes ¶ 40,814)

FTC 2d References are to Federal Tax Coordinator 2d
FIN References are to RIA's Analysis of Federal Taxes: Income
USTR References are to United States Tax Reporter: Income, Estate & Gift, and Excise
PCA References are to Pension Analysis (print & electronic)
PE References are to Pension Explanations (print & electronic)
EP References are to Estate Planning Analysis (print & electronic)

New Law. The 2008 Appropriations Act modifies the Code to provide that the Airport and Airway Trust Fund excise taxes apply through Feb. 29, 2008 (instead of through Sept. 30, 2007). (Code Sec. 4081(d)(2)(B) as amended by 2008 Appropriations Act §H116(a)(Div. K, Title I)) (Code Sec. 4261(j)(1)(A)(ii) as amended by 2008 Appropriations Act §H116(b)(1)(Div. K, Title I)) (Code Sec. 4271(d)(1)(A)(ii) as amended by 2008 Appropriations Act §H116(b)(2)(Div. K, Tiltle I))

> **observation:** As described above, Congress had already by temporary measures extended these taxes through the end of 2007. Thus, the effect of the 2008 Appropriations Act amendment above is to continue the taxes in effect from Jan. 1, 2008 through Feb. 29, 2008.

> **observation:** As noted above, the statutorily prescribed rates for the domestic segment tax (item (2) above) and international air transportation tax (item (3) above) are indexed annually for inflation. However, because under pre-2008 Appropriations Act law these taxes were scheduled to expire after 2007, IRS hadn't released the 2008 inflation adjusted amounts. Immediately following enactment of the 2008 Appropriations Act extension, IRS released IR-2007-208, 12/27/2007, providing the 2008 inflation adjusted amounts. For 2008, the domestic segment tax is $3.50, and the international air transportation tax is $15.40 ($7.70 for departures that begin or end in Alaska or Hawaii).

> **observation:** Code Sec. 4261(j)(1) and Code Sec. 4271(d)(1) provide with respect to each of the above-described air transportation taxes (i.e., the taxes listed at items (1) - (4) above), that the taxes apply to transportation beginning during the period the taxes are in effect under the Code—i.e., after the 2008 Appropriations Act extension, through Feb. 29, 2008—*and to amounts paid during that period for transportation beginning after that period.* This means that amounts paid on or before Feb. 29, 2008 for taxable transportation are subject to the applicable air transportation taxes even if the trip itself will take place after Feb. 29, 2008.

> **observation:** Because the 0.1¢ per gallon Leaking Underground Storage Tank trust fund financing rate ("LUST tax") is also imposed on kerosene and aviation gasoline (see FTC 2d ¶s W-1501, W-1501.1, USTR Excise ¶ 40,814), after the 2008 Appropriations Act extension, the total tax actually imposed on removal at the terminal through Feb. 29, 2008 is:

... 21.9¢ per gallon for kerosene used in noncommercial aviation; and

... 19.4¢ per gallon for aviation gasoline.

After Feb. 29, 2008, if there's no additional extension of (or increase in) the Federal Airport and Airway Trust Fund portion of the removal-at-terminal excise tax, the total tax imposed on kerosene used in non-commercial aviation and aviation gasoline will drop to 4.4¢ per gallon (i.e., the 0.1¢ per gallon LUST tax, and a 4.3¢ per gallon removal-at-terminal tax).

☐ **Effective:** Oct. 1, 2007 (2008 Appropriations Act §116(d)(Div. K, Title I)) through Feb. 29, 2008, as described above.

¶ 1002. Fuel used in vessels or aircraft in foreign trade or trade between U.S. and its possessions is exempted from the LUST tax retroactively, for fuel entered, removed, or sold after Sept. 30, 2005

Code Sec. 4041(d)(5), as amended by 2007 Technical Corrections Act § 6(d)(2)(A)

Code Sec. 4082(e), as amended by 2007 Technical Corrections Act § 6(d)(2)(C)

Code Sec. 4082(f), as amended by 2007 Technical Corrections Act § 6(d)(2)(B)

Code Sec. 6430, as amended by 2007 Technical Corrections Act § 6(d)(2)(D)

Generally effective: Fuel entered, removed, or sold after Sept. 30, 2005

Committee Reports, see ¶ 5305

Fuel supplied in the U.S. for use in aircraft engaged in foreign trade is exempt from U.S. customs duties and internal revenue taxes. (Com Rept, see ¶ 5305) (See FTC 2d ¶s W-1515.2C, W-1729, W-2218 *et seq.*; USTR Excise Taxes ¶s 40,414.04, 40,824, 42,214.) However, for aircraft registered in a foreign state, this rule applies only if the state of registry provides substantially reciprocal privileges for U.S.-registered aircraft (see FTC 2d ¶ W-2225; USTR Excise Taxes ¶ 42,214).

Effective for fuel entered, removed, or sold after Sept. 30, 2005, § 1362(b) of the 2005 Energy Act (Sec. 1362(b), PL 109-58, 8/8/2005) provided that, other than in cases of export, various exemptions from the Code Sec. 4081 removal-at-terminal and the Code Sec. 4041 retail fuels excise taxes didn't apply with respect to the Leaking Underground Storage Tank Trust Fund financing rate

---

FTC 2d References are to Federal Tax Coordinator 2d
FIN References are to RIA's Analysis of Federal Taxes: Income
USTR References are to United States Tax Reporter: Income, Estate & Gift, and Excise
PCA References are to Pension Analysis (print & electronic)
PE References are to Pension Explanations (print & electronic)
EP References are to Estate Planning Analysis (print & electronic)

(i.e., the "LUST tax" rate) (see FTC 2d ¶ W-1515.2C, ¶ W-1729, ¶ W-2218; USTR Excise Taxes ¶ 40,414.04, ¶ 40,824, ¶ 40,824).

In addition, 2005 Energy Act § 1362(b) added Code Sec. 6430, which provided that where the LUST tax was imposed on fuel, other than in cases of export, a refund, credit, or payment couldn't be obtained for that tax under subchapter B of chapter 65 of the Code (i.e., under Code Sec. 6411 through Code Sec. 6430) (see FTC 2d ¶ W-1542; USTR Excise Taxes ¶ 64,304).

As a result of these rules, under pre-2007 Technical Corrections Act law, the Code provided that fuel used in aviation was no longer exempt from the LUST tax. However, according to the State Department, almost all of the U.S.'s bilateral air services agreements contain provisions exempting from taxation all fuel supplied in the territory of one party for use in the aircraft of the other party, and the U.S. has interpreted these provisions to prohibit the taxation, in any form, of aviation fuel supplied in the U.S. to the aircraft of airlines of the foreign countries that are parties to these air service agreements. (Com Rept, see ¶ 5305)

New Law. The 2007 Technical Corrections Act provides that fuel for use in vessels (including civil aircraft) employed in foreign trade, or trade between the U.S. and any of its possessions, is exempted from the LUST tax rate. (Com Rept, see ¶ 5305) This provision is effective retroactively for fuel entered, removed, or sold after Sept. 30, 2005 (see the effective date rules below).

Specifically, the 2007 Technical Corrections Act accomplishes this by modifying the following:

(A) Code Sec. 4041(d)—which, other than in cases of export, generally imposed the "additional" retail fuel tax (i.e., the LUST tax) on fuel that was also taxed at retail under Code Sec. 4041(a) (i.e., diesel fuel, kerosene, and alternative fuels) or Code Sec. 4041(c) (liquid fuels, other than gasoline, used as aircraft fuel), see FTC 2d ¶ W-1720; USTR Excise Taxes ¶ 40,414. This rule is changed to provide that the additional retail fuels tax doesn't apply to a sale or use described in Code Sec. 4041(g)(3) (i.e., a sale for export) *or* so much of Code Sec. 4041(g)(1) (i.e., generally, the exemption for sale for use, or use, as supplies for vessels or aircraft), as relates to vessels (within the meaning of Code Sec. 4221(d)(3)) employed in foreign trade or trade between the U.S. and any of its possessions. (Code Sec. 4041(d)(5) as amended by 2007 Technical Corrections Act §6(d)(2)(A)) (For another change to Code Sec. 4041(d)(5) relating to imposition of the additional retail fuels tax where fuel is used for an off-highway business use, see ¶ 1003.)

> *observation:* Thus, in addition to sales for export, under the rule above, the Code Sec. 4041(d) additional retail fuels tax (the LUST tax rate) won't be imposed on fuel sold for use, or used, as supplies for "vessels" employed in foreign trade or trade between the U.S. and any

of its possessions. "Vessels" for this purpose are vessels within the meaning of Code Sec. 4221(d)(3), which include:

(i) every watercraft or other facility used, or capable of being used, as a means of transportation on water;

(ii) civil aircraft registered in the U.S. and employed in foreign trade or in trade between the U.S. and any of its possessions; and

(iii) civil aircraft registered in a foreign country and employed in foreign trade or in trade between the U.S. and any of its possessions. See FTC 2d ¶ W-2220; USTR Excise Taxes ¶ 42,214.

For the exemption to apply to vessels described in (iii) above, as noted above, the U.S. Commerce Secretary must inform the Treasury Secretary that the foreign country allows, or will allow, substantially reciprocal privileges to aircraft registered in the U.S., see USTR Excise Taxes ¶ 42,214.

(B) Code Sec. 4082—which, other than in cases of export, generally, provided that the exemption from the Code Sec. 4081 removal-at-terminal tax for dyed diesel fuel or dyed kerosene used for certain "nontaxable purposes" didn't apply to tax imposed at the LUST tax rate, see FTC 2d ¶ W-1515.2; USTR Excise Taxes ¶ 40,824. This rule is changed to provide that while the exemption, generally, doesn't apply to tax imposed at the LUST tax rate (Code Sec. 4082(f)(1) as amended by 2007 Technical Corrections Act §6(d)(2)(B)), it may apply to the LUST tax rate if IRS determines that the fuel is destined for export *or* for use by the purchaser as supplies for vessels (within the meaning of Code Sec. 4221(d)(3)) employed in foreign trade or trade between the U.S. and any of its possessions (see the exemption described at (A) above and the *RIA observation* above). (Code Sec. 4082(f)(2))

(C) Code Sec. 4082(e)—which provided that, where kerosene that's exempt from tax under the Code Sec. 4041(c) retail fuel tax rules (other than by reason of a prior imposition of tax) is removed from a refinery or terminal directly into the fuel tank of an aircraft, the (regular) removal-at-terminal tax rate imposed under Code Sec. 4081(a)(2)(A)(iii) was zero, see FTC 2d ¶ W-1515.2C; USTR Excise Taxes ¶ 40,824. This rule is changed to provide that, in the described cases, if the aircraft is employed in foreign trade or trade between the U.S. and any of its possessions, in addition to the regular removal-at-terminal tax rate being zero (Code Sec. 4082(e)(1) as amended by 2007 Technical Corrections Act §6(d)(2)(C)), the rate increase imposed under Code Sec. 4081(a)(2)(B) (i.e., the

---

FTC 2d References are to Federal Tax Coordinator 2d
FIN References are to RIA's Analysis of Federal Taxes: Income
USTR References are to United States Tax Reporter: Income, Estate & Gift, and Excise
PCA References are to Pension Analysis (print & electronic)
PE References are to Pension Explanations (print & electronic)
EP References are to Estate Planning Analysis (print & electronic)

LUST tax rate that's imposed in addition to the regular removal-at-terminal tax) is also zero (Code Sec. 4082(e)(2)).

(D) Code Sec. 6430—which, other than in cases of fuel destined for export, barred any refund, credit, or payments of the LUST tax rate under the rules of subchapter B of Chapter 65 of the Code (i.e., under Code Sec. 6411 through Code Sec. 6430), see FTC 2d ¶ W-1542; USTR Excise Taxes ¶ 64,304. This rule is changed to provide that the bar to refund, credit, or payment doesn't apply in the case of fuels:

. . . which are exempt from removal-at-terminal tax by reason of Code Sec. 4081(f)(2) (i.e., under the rules at (A) above);

. . . which are exempt from the additional retail fuel tax by reason of the last sentence of Code Sec. 4041(d)(5) (i.e., under the rules at (B) above); or

. . . with respect to which the LUST tax rate under the removal-at-terminal tax rules is zero by reason of Code Sec. 4082(e)(2) (i.e., under the rules at (C) above). (Code Sec. 6430 as amended by 2007 Technical Corrections Act §6(d)(2)(D))

> **🅁🅃🄰** *observation:* That is, if the LUST tax was imposed on a fuel, but that fuel is one described under any of the exemptions described at (A) through (C) above, Code Sec. 6430 won't bar the later claim for refund, credit, or payment of that LUST tax.

☐ **Effective:** For fuel entered, removed, or sold after Sept. 30, 2005. (2007 Technical Corrections Act §6(e)(1))

2007 Technical Corrections Act § 6(e)(1) provides that the above provision is effective as if included in the provision of the 2005 Energy Act to which the above rules relate. The above rules relate to 2005 Energy Act § 1362(b) (Sec. 1362(b), PL 109-58, 8/8/2005) which, under 2005 Energy Act § 1362(d)(2) (Sec. 1362(d)(2), PL 109-58, 8/8/2005), is effective for fuel entered, removed, or sold after Sept. 30, 2005.

¶ 1003. Fuel sold for use, or used, for an off-highway business use isn't excepted from the LUST tax rate imposed under the retail fuel tax rules

Code Sec. 4041(d)(5), as amended by 2007 Technical Corrections Act § 6(d)(3)
Generally effective: Fuel sold for use or used after Dec. 29, 2007
Committee Reports, see ¶ 5305

The Congressional intent behind § 1362(b) of the 2005 Energy Act (Sec. 1362(b), PL 109-58, 8/8/2005), effective for fuel entered, removed, or sold after

Sept. 30, 2005, was to make the various exemptions from the Code Sec. 4081 removal-at-terminal and the Code Sec. 4041 retail fuels excise taxes—other than the exemptions for export—inapplicable with respect to the Leaking Underground Storage Tank Trust Fund financing rate (i.e., the "LUST tax" rate) (see FTC 2d ¶ W-1515.2C, ¶ W-1729, ¶ W-2218; USTR Excise Taxes ¶ 40,414.04, ¶ 40,824, ¶ 40,824). However, in modifying Code Sec. 4041(d)(5) to provide that the "additional" retail excise tax (i.e., the LUST tax rate) imposed on the retail sale or use of specified fuels would apply without regard to the exemptions from the Code Sec. 4041 retail excise tax (other than for export), Congress failed to include in the list of inapplicable exemptions (i.e., exemptions to be disregarded), the Code Sec. 4041(b)(1)(A) exemption (see FTC 2d ¶ W-1724, USTR Excise Taxes ¶ 40,414.10) for diesel fuel, kerosene, alternative fuel, or compressed natural gas used for an off-highway business use (see FTC 2d ¶ W-1720; USTR Excise Taxes ¶ 40,414).

New Law. The 2007 Technical Corrections Act adds the Code Sec. 4041(b)(1)(A) exemption from the retail fuel taxes for off-highway business use of fuel (described above) to the list of exemptions under Code Sec. 4041(d)(5) that are to be disregarded in imposing the additional retail excise tax (i.e., the LUST tax rate imposed on retail sale or use of specified fuels). (Code Sec. 4041(d)(5) as amended by 2007 Technical Corrections Act §6(d)(3))

> *observation:* Thus, off-highway business use of fuel within the meaning of Code Sec. 4041(b)(1)(A) won't bar imposition of the LUST tax rate on the retail sale or use of the fuel.

Congress describes the change above as clarifying that off-highway business use is not exempt from the LUST tax rate. But Congress says that for administrative reasons associated with collecting the tax, the off-highway business use clarification is being made effective for fuel sold for use or used after Dec. 29, 2007 (Com Rept, see ¶ 5305) (see the effective date rules below).

> *observation:* Thus, although described as a clarification, based on the effective date of the change to the Code and Congress' statement above, it appears that Congress does not intend for IRS to attempt to collect LUST tax from taxpayers who didn't pay it on a retail sale or use after Sept. 30, 2005 and before Dec. 29, 2007 based on their off-highway business use of the fuel.

The 2007 Technical Corrections Act also makes the LUST tax rate imposed under Code Sec. 4081 or Code Sec. 4041 inapplicable to fuel used in vessels or

FTC 2d References are to Federal Tax Coordinator 2d
FIN References are to RIA's Analysis of Federal Taxes: Income
USTR References are to United States Tax Reporter: Income, Estate & Gift, and Excise
PCA References are to Pension Analysis (print & electronic)
PE References are to Pension Explanations (print & electronic)
EP References are to Estate Planning Analysis (print & electronic)

aircraft engaged in foreign trade or trade between the U.S. and its possessions, retroactive for fuel entered, removed, or sold after Sept. 30, 2005, see ¶ 1002.

☐ **Effective:** For fuel sold for use or used after Dec. 29, 2007. (2007 Technical Corrections Act §6(e)(2))

¶ 1004. Double LUST tax on certain dyed diesel fuel and kerosene and fuels used on inland waterways is eliminated retroactively, for fuel entered, removed, or sold after Sept. 30, 2005

Code Sec. 4041(d)(1), as amended by 2007 Technical Corrections Act § 6(d)(1)(A)
Code Sec. 4042(b)(3), as amended by 2007 Technical Corrections Act § 6(d)(1)(B)
Generally effective: Fuel entered, removed, or sold after Sept. 30, 2005
Committee Reports, see ¶ 5305

Effective for fuel entered, removed, or sold after Sept. 30, 2005, § 1362(b) of the 2005 Energy Act (Sec. 1362(b), PL 109-58, 8/8/2005) provided that, other than in cases of export, various exemptions from imposition of the Code Sec. 4081 removal-at-terminal excise tax (including the exemption for dyed diesel fuel or kerosene sold for certain "nontaxable uses"), and the Code Sec. 4041 retail fuels excise tax, do not apply with respect to tax imposed at the Leaking Underground Storage Tank Trust Fund financing rate (i.e., the "LUST tax rate") (see FTC 2d ¶ W-1515.2C, ¶ W-1729, ¶ W-2218; USTR Excise Taxes ¶ 40,414.04, ¶ 40,824, ¶ 40,824).

In addition, 2005 Energy Act § 1362(b) provided under Code Sec. 6430 that where the LUST tax was imposed on fuel, other than in cases of export, that a refund, credit, or payment couldn't be obtained for that tax under subchapter B of chapter 65 of the Code (i.e., under Code Sec. 6411 through Code Sec. 6430) (see FTC 2d ¶ W-1542; USTR Excise Taxes ¶ 64,304).

As a result of these rules, under pre-2007 Technical Corrections Act law, the Code inadvertently imposed a second tax at the LUST tax rate on the later retail sale or use of certain fuels that were previously taxed at the LUST tax rate under the Code Sec. 4081 removal-at-terminal tax rules. Specifically, a second LUST tax was imposed under:

... Code Sec. 4041 (the retail fuel excise tax rules, see FTC 2d ¶ W-1720; USTR Excise Taxes ¶ 40,414) on the later sale for use, or use of, dyed diesel fuel or dyed kerosene in a diesel-powered highway vehicle or train, or

... Code Sec. 4042 (the retail excise tax on inland waterways fuels, see FTC 2d ¶ W-3201; USTR Excise Taxes ¶ 40,424) on the later use of a liquid fuel in commercial transportation on inland waterways. (Com Rept, see ¶ 5305)

New Law. The 2007 Technical Corrections Act eliminates imposition of the LUST tax rate a second time (under Code Sec. 4041 or Code Sec. 4042) where the LUST tax rate was previously imposed under the Code Sec. 4081 removal-at-terminal excise tax rules. (Com Rept, see ¶ 5305) This provision is effective for fuel entered, removed, or sold after Sept. 30, 2005 (see the effective date rules below, which also discuss refund of any second LUST tax imposed under these provisions before enactment of the 2007 Technical Corrections Act).

Specifically, the 2007 Technical Corrections Act modifies:

(1) Code Sec. 4041(d)(1)—which, generally, imposes the LUST tax rate (as an "additional" retail excise tax) on the retail sale or use of diesel fuel, kerosene, various alternative fuels, and kerosene used in aviation. This rule is changed to provide that the additional retail tax (i.e., the LUST tax rate) won't apply to the sale or use of any liquid if tax was already imposed on that liquid under the Code Sec. 4081 removal-at-terminal tax rules at the LUST tax rate (Code Sec. 4041(d)(1) as amended by 2007 Technical Corrections Act §6(d)(1)(A)); and

(2) Code Sec. 4042(b)(3)—which provides that the LUST tax rate generally applicable to the use of liquid fuels in commercial waterway transportation doesn't apply to fuel that was already taxed at the LUST tax rate under Code Sec. 4041(d). This rule is changed to provide that the LUST tax rate won't apply to the use of liquid fuels in commercial waterway transportation where the fuel was already taxed at the LUST tax rate under Code Sec. 4041(d) *or* Code Sec. 4081. (Code Sec. 4042(b)(3) as amended by 2007 Technical Corrections Act §6(d)(1)(B))

☐ **Effective:** For fuel entered, removed, or sold after Sept. 30, 2005. (2007 Technical Corrections Act §6(e)(1))

2007 Technical Corrections Act § 6(e)(1) provides that the above provision is effective as if included in the provision of the 2005 Energy Act to which the above rules relate. The above rules relate to 2005 Energy Act § 1362(b) (Sec. 1362(b), PL 109-58, 8/8/2005) which, under 2005 Energy Act § 1362(d)(2) (Sec. 1362(d)(2), PL 109-58, 8/8/2005), is effective for fuel entered, removed, or sold after Sept. 30, 2005.

Under the 2007 Technical Corrections Act, a refund (credit or payment, as applicable) is permitted in the amount of the LUST tax if that tax was imposed a second time under Code Sec. 4041(d)(1) or Code Sec. 4042 from Oct. 1, 2005 through Dec. 29, 2007. (Com Rept, see ¶ 5305) Specifically, the 2007 Technical

---

FTC 2d References are to Federal Tax Coordinator 2d
FIN References are to RIA's Analysis of Federal Taxes: Income
USTR References are to United States Tax Reporter: Income, Estate & Gift, and Excise
PCA References are to Pension Analysis (print & electronic)
PE References are to Pension Explanations (print & electronic)
EP References are to Estate Planning Analysis (print & electronic)

Corrections Act provides that notwithstanding Code Sec. 6430—which, other than in cases of export or (based on another 2007 Technical Corrections Act change, see ¶ 1002) for fuel used in vessels or aircraft in foreign trade or trade between the U.S. and its possessions, bars refund, credit, or payment of any LUST tax imposed on fuels—a refund, credit, or payment may be made under subchapter B of chapter 65 of the Code (i.e., under Code Sec. 6411 through Code Sec. 6430) for taxes imposed with respect to any liquid after Sept. 30, 2005, and before Dec. 29, 2007 under Code Sec. 4041(d)(1) or Code Sec. 4042 at the LUST tax rate, to the extent that the LUST tax was imposed with respect to that liquid under Code Sec. 4081. (2007 Technical Corrections Act §6(d)(1)(C))

¶ 1005. Fuel eligible for alternative fuel excise tax credit is expanded retroactively

Code Sec. 6426(d)(2)(F), as amended by 2007 Technical Corrections Act § 5(a)(2)
Code Sec. 6426(h), as amended by 2007 Technical Corrections Act § 5(a)(3)
Generally effective: Any sale or use for any period after Sept. 30, 2006
Committee Reports, see ¶ 5304

A 50-cent per gallon (or, gasoline gallon equivalent [GGE] for non-liquid fuel) excise tax credit is allowed against:

. . . Code Sec. 4041 retail fuel excise tax liability for alternative fuel (defined below) sold for use, or used, by the taxpayer as a fuel in a motor vehicle or motorboat (the "alternative fuel excise tax credit"); and (FTC 2d ¶ W-1737.1, USTR Excise ¶ 64,264)

. . . Code Sec. 4081 removal-at-terminal excise tax liability for alternative fuel used by a taxpayer to produce an alternative fuel mixture (i.e., alternative fuel and at-least-0.1% by volume of gasoline, diesel fuel, or kerosene) for sale or use in the taxpayer's trade or business (the "alternative fuel mixture excise tax credit"). (FTC 2d ¶ W-1518; USTR Excise ¶ 64,264)

In addition, to the extent the taxpayer's alternative fuel excise tax credit, or alternative fuel mixture excise tax credit, exceeds the taxpayer's Code Sec. 4041 or Code Sec. 4081 excise tax liability, respectively, the taxpayer may be able to claim an excise tax refund (or, in some cases, an income tax credit) equal to the amount of that credit. (See FTC 2d ¶s W-1519, W-1737.2, USTR Excise ¶ 64,274, and ¶ 1008.)

Under pre-2007 Technical Corrections Act law, the alternative fuels qualifying for the above-described incentives included:

(a) liquefied petroleum gas;

(b) P Series Fuels (as defined by the Secretary of Energy under 42 USC § 13211);

(c) compressed or liquefied natural gas (i.e., CNG or LNG);

(d) liquefied hydrogen;

(e) any liquid fuel derived from coal (including peat) through the Fisher-Tropsch process; and

(f) "liquid hydrocarbons derived from biomass (as defined in Code Sec. 45K(c)(3)," i.e., any organic material other than oil, natural gas or coal (including lignite), or any products of such organic material. (FTC 2d ¶ W-1737.1; USTR Excise Taxes ¶ 64,264)

With respect to fuels described at (f) above, the Code doesn't define "liquid hydrocarbons." (Com Rept, see ¶ 5304) However, the Code does provide that fuel that is ethanol, methanol, biodiesel or renewable diesel doesn't qualify as an alternative fuel. (FTC 2d ¶ W-1737.1, ¶ W-1737.2; USTR Excise Taxes ¶ 64,264) Congress says that it is aware questions have arisen as to whether a "liquid hydrocarbon from biomass" for purposes of these rules may contain oxygen, or must consist exclusively of hydrogen and carbon. (Com Rept, see ¶ 5304)

New Law. Congress says that it intended for biomass fuels such as fish oil, which is not exclusively made of hydrogen and carbon, to qualify for the above-described credit. (Com Rept, see ¶ 5304) Consequently, the 2007 Technical Corrections Act modifies the definition of alternative fuels to replace the term "hydrocarbon" with the term "fuel." (Code Sec. 6426(d)(2)(F) as amended by 2007 Technical Corrections Act §5(a)(2))

> ⚡ *observation:* That is, alternative fuel is defined under the 2007 Technical Corrections Act to include a "liquid fuel derived from biomass (as defined in Code Sec. 45K(c)(3))," instead of "liquid hydrocarbons derived from biomass (as defined in Code Sec. 45K(c)(3))."

> ⚡ *observation:* Thus, it is now clear that liquid hydrocarbons derived from biomass that qualify for the alternative fuel tax incentives may include liquid fuels that contain oxygen, as well as hydrogen and carbon. Examples of such fuels would include fish oils, and liquids derived from other rendered fats.

The 2007 Technical Corrections Act also adds a rule providing that a credit can't be determined under Code Sec. 6426(d) (the alternative fuel excise tax

FTC 2d References are to Federal Tax Coordinator 2d
FIN References are to RIA's Analysis of Federal Taxes: Income
USTR References are to United States Tax Reporter: Income, Estate & Gift, and Excise
PCA References are to Pension Analysis (print & electronic)
PE References are to Pension Explanations (print & electronic)
EP References are to Estate Planning Analysis (print & electronic)

credit) or Code Sec. 6426(e) (the alternative fuel mixture credit) with respect to any fuel to which a credit may be determined under:

... Code Sec. 6426(b) (i.e., the alcohol fuel mixture excise tax credit, see FTC 2d ¶s W-1518, W-1518.1), USTR Excise ¶ 64,264;

... Code Sec. 6426(c) (i.e., the biodiesel mixture excise tax credit, see FTC 2d ¶s W-1518, W-1518.3), USTR Excise ¶ 64,264;

... Code Sec. 40 (i.e., the alcohol fuel income tax credit, see FTC 2d/FIN ¶ L-17501 *et seq.*; USTR ¶ 404 *et seq.*; TaxDesk ¶ 382,201 *et seq.*); or

... Code Sec. 40A (i.e., the biodiesel and renewable diesel fuel income tax credit, see FTC 2d/FIN ¶s L-17571 *et seq.*, L-17585.1; USTR ¶s 404A4, 40A4.05; TaxDesk ¶ 382,401 *et seq.*). (Code Sec. 6426(h) as amended by 2007 Technical Corrections Act §5(a)(3))

> **observation:** As noted above, the Code already provides that fuel that is ethanol, methanol, biodiesel or renewable diesel doesn't qualify as an alternative fuel. The provision above further clarifies that any fuel qualifying for an alcohol, biodiesel, or renewable diesel fuel credit or refund won't qualify for the alternative fuel or alternative fuel mixture credit or refund.

> **observation:** Recently issued IRS guidance (Notice 2007-97, 2007-49 IRB, see FTC 2d ¶ W-1737.1) summarizes both the issues relating to the pre-2007 Technical Corrections Act definition of "liquid hydrocarbons derived from biomass," and the technical corrections discussed above (which were in proposed form at the time the guidance was published). IRS notes that although ethanol and methanol, which are defined as types of alcohol under Code Sec. 40(d)(1), were already excluded from the definition of alternative fuel under pre-2007 Technical Corrections Act law, the addition of Code Sec. 6426(h) above has the effect of making any other type of alcohol fuel ineligible for the alternative fuel or alternative fuel mixture credit.
>
> In addition, IRS concluded that if this technical correction were made retroactively (as, in fact, it has been, see the effective date discussion below), that any taxpayer allowed an alternative fuel credit or refund with respect to any alcohol fuel before enactment of the technical correction, will be required to repay the amount of that credit or refund with interest.

☐ **Effective:** Any sale or use for any period after Sept. 30, 2006. (2007 Technical Corrections Act §5(b))

2007 Technical Corrections Act § 5(b) provides that the above provisions are effective as if included in 2005 Transportation Act section to which the above rules relate. The above rules relate to 2005 Transportation Act § 11113 (Sec. 11113, PL 109-59, 8/10/2005). 2005 Transportation Act § 11113(d) provides that the amendments made by § 11113 apply for any sale or use for any period after Sept. 30, 2006.

¶ 1006. Rules relating to registered credit card issuer's electronic excise tax refund claims for sales of gasoline to certain exempt entities, are clarified for sales after Dec. 31, 2005

Code Sec. 6416(a)(4)(C), as amended by 2007 Technical Corrections Act § 11(d)(1)
Generally effective: Sales after Dec. 31, 2005
Committee Reports, None

Generally, if a registered ultimate vendor buys gasoline on which the Code Sec. 4081 removal-at-terminal excise tax has been paid and then sells that gasoline to a state or local government or a nonprofit educational organization for its exclusive use, and specified conditions are met, the registered ultimate vendor is the only person permitted to claim a refund or credit of that excise tax. However, effective for sales after Dec. 31, 2005, § 11163(b) of the 2005 Transportation Act (Sec. 11163(b), PL 109-59, 8/10/2005) provided that, if specified conditions are met, a registered credit card issuer, and not the registered ultimate vendor, is treated as the only person permitted to claim the credit or refund where the state, local government, or nonprofit educational organization purchases the tax-paid gasoline from an ultimate vendor using a credit card issued by that credit card issuer. In making this change, Congress intended to make all of the refund amount and timing rules applicable to registered ultimate vendors also apply to refunds claimed by registered credit card issuers. However, in modifying Code Sec. 6416(a)(4)(C)—which provides a special rule for determining if IRS is required to pay interest in the case of an electronically filed registered ultimate vendor refund claim—Congress didn't clearly direct that the phrase "credit card issuer" be reflected each place it had to appear in the provision to make it clear how to apply the rule where the registered credit card issuer filed an electronic refund claim. (FTC 2d ¶ W-1563; USTR Excise Taxes ¶ 64,164)

New Law. Under the 2007 Technical Corrections Act, Code Sec. 6416(a)(4)(C) is modified, retroactive for sales after Dec. 31, 2005 (see ef-

---

FTC 2d References are to Federal Tax Coordinator 2d
FIN References are to RIA's Analysis of Federal Taxes: Income
USTR References are to United States Tax Reporter: Income, Estate & Gift, and Excise
PCA References are to Pension Analysis (print & electronic)
PE References are to Pension Explanations (print & electronic)
EP References are to Estate Planning Analysis (print & electronic)

fective date rules below), to provide that as to a claim made under Code Sec. 6416(a)(4)(A) or Code Sec. 6416(a)(4)(B) (i.e., a registered ultimate vendor or registered credit card issuer refund claim for gasoline sold to a state or local government or a nonprofit educational organization for its exclusive use) that's filed electronically, the general rule for electronically filed registered ultimate vendor refund claims—i.e., that IRS must pay interest on the claim if it fails to pay the refund within 20 days of the claim's filing (see FTC 2d ¶ W-1563; USTR Excise Taxes ¶ 64,164)—won't apply unless the ultimate vendor *or the credit card issuer* has certified to IRS for the most recent quarter of the tax year that all ultimate purchasers of the vendor *or credit card issuer* are certified and entitled to the refund as a state or local government, or a nonprofit educational organization. (Code Sec. 6416(a)(4)(C) as amended by 2007 Technical Corrections Act §11(d)(1))

> **🅡 *observation:*** Thus, the effect of the change above is to make the same refund rules (i.e., for determining refund amount and the timing claims) apply to registered credit card issuers as apply to registered ultimate vendors.

☐ **Effective:** For sales after Dec. 31, 2005. (2007 Technical Corrections Act §11(d)(2))

2007 Technical Corrections Act § 11(d)(2) provides that the above provision is effective as if included in the provision of the 2005 Transportation Act to which the above rules relate. The above rules relate to 2005 Transportation Act § 11163(b) (Sec. 11163(b), PL 109-59, 8/10/2005) which, under 2005 Transportation Act § 11163(e) (Sec. 11163(e), PL 109-59, 8/10/2005), is effective for sales after Dec. 31, 2005.

¶ 1007. Termination dates for excise tax refund/income tax credit rules for biodiesel mixtures, alternative fuel mixtures, and alternative fuels are corrected

Code Sec. 6427(e)(5), as redesignated by 2007 Technical Corrections Act § 11(a)(37)
Code Sec. 6427(e)(5)(B), as amended by 2007 Technical Corrections Act § 11(e)(1)
Generally effective: Aug. 8, 2005
Committee Reports, None

Excise tax credits are allowed under Code Sec. 6426:

(1) against Code Sec. 4081 removal-at-terminal excise tax liability in an amount equal to the alcohol fuel mixture credit, the biodiesel mixture credit, and alternative fuel mixture credit (see FTC 2d ¶ W-1518; USTR Excise Taxes ¶ 64,264); and

(2) against Code Sec. 4041 retail fuels excise tax liability for sale or use of an alternative fuel, see FTC 2d ¶ W-1737.1; USTR Excise Taxes ¶ 64,264.

In addition, under Code Sec. 6427(e), provided certain conditions are met, if either of the above credits exceed a taxpayer's liability for removal-at-terminal tax or retail fuels tax, respectively, the taxpayer may file a claim for payment (i.e., for an excise tax refund or income tax credit) for an amount equal to that unclaimed alternative fuel mixture credit (under Code Sec. 6427(e)(1), see FTC 2d ¶ W-1519; USTR Excise Taxes ¶ 64,267) or alternative fuel credit (under Code Sec. 6427(e)(2), see FTC 2d ¶ W-1737.2; USTR Excise Taxes ¶ 64,267). Expedited refunds may be claimed for any period:

(a) for which $200 or more is payable (less if the claimant files electronically), and

(b) that isn't less than one week (see FTC 2d ¶ W-1519.1; USTR Excise Taxes ¶ 64,274.01 and ¶ 1008).

The Code Sec. 6427(e) excise tax refund claim rules above terminate for any alcohol fuel mixture sold or used after Dec. 31, 2010, see FTC 2d ¶ W-1519; USTR Excise Taxes ¶ 64,274.

> **⚫ᴿᴵᴬ** *caution:* Under pre-2007 Technical Corrections Act law, Congress intended, but technically failed, to enact the termination rules described below. The technical errors are described in the *observation* below.

Congress intended to provide that the Code Sec. 6427(e) excise tax refund rules for biodiesel, alternative fuels and alternative fuel mixtures terminate for:

. . . any biodiesel mixture sold or used after Dec. 31, 2008;

. . . any alternative fuel or alternative fuel mixture (other than one involving liquefied hydrogen) sold or used after Sept. 30, 2009; or

. . . any alternative fuel or alternative fuel mixture involving liquefied hydrogen sold or used after Sept. 30, 2014. (FTC 2d ¶ W-1519; USTR Excise Taxes ¶ 64,274)

> **⚫ᴿᴵᴬ** *observation:* However, Congress technically failed to enact the termination provisions listed above due to the following errors it made in amending Code Sec. 6427(e) in the 2005 Energy Act (PL 109-58, 8/8/2005) and the 2005 Transportation Act (PL 109-59, 8/10/2005):

FTC 2d References are to Federal Tax Coordinator 2d
FIN References are to RIA's Analysis of Federal Taxes: Income
USTR References are to United States Tax Reporter: Income, Estate & Gift, and Excise
PCA References are to Pension Analysis (print & electronic)
PE References are to Pension Explanations (print & electronic)
EP References are to Estate Planning Analysis (print & electronic)

... In § 1344(a) of the 2005 Energy Act (Sec. 1344(a), PL 109-58, 8/8/2005), Congress intended to extend application of the Code Sec. 6427(e) refund provisions for biodiesel mixtures from Dec. 31, 2006, through Dec. 31, 2008. However, Congress mistakenly modified (then nonexistent) Code Sec. 6427(e)(4)(B), instead of Code Sec. 6427(e)(3)(B), to change "2006" to "2008." Thus, a technical correction was required to actually extend application of the rules permitting biodiesel mixture claims through 2008.

... In § 11113(b)(3)(C)(ii) of the 2005 Transportation Act (Sec. 11113(b)(3)(C)(ii), PL 109-59, 8/10/2005), Congress intended to redesignate the Code Sec. 6427(e)(3) termination rules as Code Sec. 6427(e)(5), and then add to that re-designated Code Sec. 6427(e)(5) the termination rules for alternative fuel and alternative fuel mixture claims. However, Congress mistakenly redesignated (then nonexistent) Code Sec. 6427(e)(4) (instead of Code Sec. 6427(e)(3)), as new Code Sec. 6427(e)(5). Thus, a technical correction was required to actually add the alternative fuel and alternative fuel mixture claim termination rules to the Code.

New Law. The 2007 Technical Corrections Act retroactively (see below) corrects the errors in the termination provisions of the excise tax refund rules for biodiesel mixtures, alternative fuel mixtures, and alternative fuels described above. The Act does so by:

(1) redesignating Code Sec. 6427(e)(3) (as added by the 2005 Transportation Act Sec. 11113, PL 109-59, 8/10/2005) as Code Sec. 6427(e)(5) (Code Sec. 6427(e)(5) as redesignated by 2007 Technical Corrections Act §11(a)(37)); and

(2) amending the redesignated Code Sec. 6427(e)(5)(B) (the termination provision for biodiesel mixture claims), by striking "2006" and inserting "2008." (Code Sec. 6427(e)(5)(B) as amended by 2007 Technical Corrections Act §11(e)(1))

observation: Thus, after these corrections the applicable Code Sec. 6427(e) excise tax refund rules terminate for:

... any biodiesel mixture sold or used after Dec. 31, 2008;

... any alternative fuel or alternative fuel mixture (other than one involving liquefied hydrogen) sold or used after Sept. 30, 2009; or

... any alternative fuel or alternative fuel mixture involving liquefied hydrogen sold or used after Sept. 30, 2014.

☐ **Effective:** Aug. 8, 2005 (2007 Technical Corrections Act §11(e)(3)) for the change described at (2) above; for redesignation described at (1), see above.

The 2007 Technical Corrections Act § 11(e)(3) above provides that the amendments made by 2007 Technical Corrections Act § 11(e) are effective as if included in the provision of the 2005 Energy Tax Act to which they relate. The above provision relates to 2005 Energy Tax Act § 1344(a) (Sec. 1344(a), PL 109-58, 8/8/2005) which, under 2005 Energy Tax Act § 1344(b) (Sec. 1344(b), PL 109-58, 8/8/2005), was effective on Aug. 8, 2005 (the date of enactment of the 2005 Energy Tax Act).

¶ 1008. Expedited excise tax refund claims permitted for alternative fuels, for any sale or use for any period after Sept. 30, 2006

Code Sec. 6427(i)(3)(A), as amended by 2007 Technical Corrections Act § 5(a)(1)(A)

Code Sec. 6427(i)(3)(A)(i), as amended by 2007 Technical Corrections Act § 5(a)(1)(B)

Code Sec. 6427(i)(3)(B), as amended by 2007 Technical Corrections Act § 5(a)(1)(B)

Generally effective: Sale or use for any period after Sept. 30, 2006
Committee Reports, see ¶ 5304

Effective for any sale or use for any period after Sept. 30, 2006, § 11113 of the 2005 Transportation Act (Sec. 11113, PL 109-59, 8/10/2005) added two new excise tax credit provisions to the Code (under Code Sec. 6426) that permit taxpayers to claim an excise tax credit against:

(1) Code Sec. 4081 removal-at-terminal excise tax liability for the sale or use of an alternative fuel mixture ("the alternative fuel mixture credit"), see FTC 2d ¶ W-1518; USTR Excise Taxes ¶ 64,264; or

(2) Code Sec. 4041 retail fuels excise tax liability for the sale or use of an alternative fuel (the "alternative fuel credit"), see FTC 2d ¶ W-1737.1; USTR Excise Taxes ¶ 64,264.

For definitions of alternative fuel and alternative fuel mixtures, see ¶ 1005.

In addition, if certain conditions are met, to the extent that either of the above-described credits exceeds a taxpayer's liability for removal-at-terminal tax or retail fuels tax, respectively, the credit is refundable. That is, a taxpayer may file an excise tax refund claim for an amount equal to that unclaimed alternative fuel mixture credit (under Code Sec. 6427(e)(1), see FTC 2d ¶ W-1519; USTR

FTC 2d References are to Federal Tax Coordinator 2d
FIN References are to RIA's Analysis of Federal Taxes: Income
USTR References are to United States Tax Reporter: Income, Estate & Gift, and Excise
PCA References are to Pension Analysis (print & electronic)
PE References are to Pension Explanations (print & electronic)
EP References are to Estate Planning Analysis (print & electronic)

Excise Taxes ¶ 64,267) or alternative fuel credit (under Code Sec. 6427(e)(2), see FTC 2d ¶ W-1737.2; USTR Excise Taxes ¶ 64,267). However, claims made under Code Sec. 6427(e) are subject to the general limitations of Code Sec. 6427(k), which provide that, unless a specified exception under Code Sec. 6427(i) applies, the only persons permitted to make an excise tax refund claim under various Code Sec. 6427 provisions are:

(i) the U.S.,

(ii) a state, political subdivision of a state, or the District of Columbia (DC), and

(iii) exempt organizations.

Other taxpayers must, instead, claim a credit against income tax on their annual income tax returns.

Under pre-2007 Technical Corrections Act law, an exception to the general Code Sec. 6427(k) limitations—namely Code Sec. 6427(i)(3), which permits an expedited (weekly) excise tax refund to be claimed—applied for claims made under Code Sec. 6427(e)(1) for alternative fuel mixtures, but not for claims made under Code Sec. 6427(e)(2) for alternative fuels. Thus, all taxpayers could make an expedited excise tax refund claim for sales or use of an alternative fuel mixture, but could not make the expedited claim for sales or use of alternative fuels. (FTC 2d ¶ W-1519.1, ¶ W-1737.2; USTR Excise Taxes ¶ 64,274.01)

New Law. The 2007 Technical Corrections Act clarifies the expedited excise tax refund rules under Code Sec. 6427(i)(3)—retroactive for any sale or use for any period after Sept. 30, 2006 (see effective date rules below)—to provide that the same rules apply for filing refund claims for alternative fuel mixtures and alternative fuels. (Com Rept, see ¶ 5304)

Specifically, the Code Sec. 6427(i)(3) expedited excise tax refund rules are modified to provide that, for any sale or use for any period after Sept. 30, 2006, taxpayers may file a claim for refund:

(a) under Code Sec. 6427(e)(1) with respect to an alternative fuel mixture (as described under the Code Sec. 6426 excise tax credit rules), or

(b) under Code Sec. 6427(e)(2) with respect to an alternative fuel (as defined in Code Sec. 6426(d)(2)) for any period (Code Sec. 6427(i)(3)(A) as amended by 2007 Technical Corrections Act §5(a)(1)(A))—

(i) for which $200 or more is payable (or, if filed electronically, for any amount) under Code Sec. 6427(e)(1) or Code Sec. 6427(e)(2) (Code Sec. 6427(i)(3)(A)(i) as amended by 2007 Technical Corrections Act §5(a)(1)(B)); and

(ii) that isn't less than a week (Code Sec. 6427(i)(3)(A)(ii)).

In addition, notwithstanding the rules of Code Sec. 6427(e)(1) or Code Sec. 6427(e)(2) which provide that refunds under those provisions are to be made without interest (see FTC 2d ¶s W-1519, W-1737.2; USTR Excise Taxes ¶ 64,267), if IRS hasn't paid a claim under the above-described expedited excise tax refund rules within 45 days of the date the refund claim was filed (or within 20 days, if the claim was electronic), IRS will pay the claim with interest from that date, determined using the underpayment rate and method under Code Sec. 6621 (see FTC 2d/FIN ¶ V-1101; USTR ¶ 66,214; TaxDesk ¶ 851,001). (Code Sec. 6427(i)(3)(B) as amended by 2007 Technical Corrections Act §5(a)(1)(B))

> **⊘** *observation:* The expedited refund claim is made on Form 8849. The claim must be filed on or before the last day of the first quarter following the earliest quarter of the claimant's income tax year included in the refund claim (see FTC 2d ¶ W-1519.1; USTR Excise Taxes ¶ 64,274.01). Thus, for example a calendar year claimant's claim for alternative fuel sold or used during Dec. 2007 and Jan. 2008, would have to be filed by Mar. 31, 2008.

> **⊘** *observation:* If a taxpayer doesn't meet the above requirements for making an expedited refund claim, the taxpayer can still file an annual income tax credit claim for the sale or use on Form 4136, which is filed with the taxpayer's income tax return. (The U.S., a state, political subdivision of a state, DC, or an exempt organization, would still have the option of filing an excise tax refund claim on Form 8849, although not under the expedited rules above.)

☐ **Effective:** For any sale or use for any period after Sept. 30, 2006. (2007 Technical Corrections Act §5(b))

2007 Technical Corrections Act § 5(b) provides that the above provision is effective as if included in the provision of the 2005 Transportation Act to which the above rules relate. The above rules relate to 2005 Transportation Act § 11113(b) (Sec. 11113(b), PL 109-59, 8/10/2005) which, under 2005 Transportation Act § 11113(d) (Sec. 11113(d), PL 109-59, 8/10/2005), is effective for any sale or use for any period after Sept. 30, 2006.

FTC 2d References are to Federal Tax Coordinator 2d
FIN References are to RIA's Analysis of Federal Taxes: Income
USTR References are to United States Tax Reporter: Income, Estate & Gift, and Excise
PCA References are to Pension Analysis (print & electronic)
PE References are to Pension Explanations (print & electronic)
EP References are to Estate Planning Analysis (print & electronic)

¶ 1100. Penalties

¶ 1101. Penalty for valuation misstatements attributable to incorrect appraisals applies to substantial estate or gift tax valuation understatements and is subject to 3-year limitation period

Code Sec. 6695A(a)(2), as amended by 2007 Technical Corrections Act § 3(e)(1)

Code Sec. 6696(d)(1), as amended by 2007 Technical Corrections Act § 3(e)(2)

Generally effective: Appraisals prepared for returns or submissions filed after Aug. 17, 2006

Committee Reports, see ¶ 5302

Under pre-2007 Technical Corrections Act law, a penalty was imposed on any person who:

(A) prepared a property appraisal and knew, or reasonably should have known, that the appraisal would be used in connection with a return or a refund claim, and

(B) the claimed property value on the return or refund claim that was based on the appraisal resulted in a substantial valuation misstatement under Code Sec. 6662(e) or a gross valuation misstatement under Code Sec. 6662(h) for the property. (FTC 2d/FIN ¶ V-2691; USTR ¶ 66,95A4; TaxDesk ¶ 867,201)

The penalty equalled the lesser of:

(1) the greater of: (a) 10% of the underpayment (as defined in Code Sec. 6664(a) (see FTC 2d/FIN ¶ V-2052; USTR ¶ 66,644; TaxDesk ¶ 863,003) attributable to the misstatement described in (B) above, or (b) $1,000, or

(2) 125% of the gross income for preparing the appraisal received by the person who prepared it. FTC 2d/FIN ¶ V-2692; USTR ¶ 66,95A4; TaxDesk ¶ 867,202

Under pre-2007 Technical Corrections Act law, the above penalty did not apply to substantial estate or gift tax valuation understatements. (FTC 2d/FIN ¶ V-2691; USTR ¶ 66,95A4; TaxDesk ¶ 867,201) A substantial estate or gift tax valuation understatement occurs when the value of any property claimed on an

---

FTC 2d References are to Federal Tax Coordinator 2d

FIN References are to RIA's Analysis of Federal Taxes: Income

USTR References are to United States Tax Reporter: Income, Estate & Gift, and Excise

PCA References are to Pension Analysis (print & electronic)

PE References are to Pension Explanations (print & electronic)

EP References are to Estate Planning Analysis (print & electronic)

estate or gift tax return is 65% or less of the amount determined to be correct. FTC 2d/FIN ¶ V-2251; USTR ¶ 66,624.10; TaxDesk ¶ 863,013 However, in Chief Counsel Memorandum AM 2007-0017 (Oct 31, 2007), IRS stated that the above penalty did apply to gross estate or gift tax valuation misstatements attributable to incorrect appraisals prepared after May 25, 2007. A gross estate or gift tax valuation misstatement occurs when the value of any property claimed on an estate or gift tax return is 40% or less of the amount determined to be correct. FTC 2d/FIN ¶ V-2252; USTR ¶ 66,624.10; TaxDesk ¶ 863,013

Under pre-2007 Technical Corrections Act law, the period of limitations for the assessment of Code Sec. 6694(a) penalties (preparer penalties for understatements of taxpayer liability due to an unreasonable position) and Code Sec. 6695 penalties (certain other preparer penalties) was three years from the date that the return or refund claim for which the penalty was assessed, was filed. No limitations period, however, applied to the penalty on substantial and gross valuation misstatements attributable to incorrect appraisals. (FTC 2d/FIN ¶ T-4029; USTR ¶ 66,964; TaxDesk ¶ 838,027)

New Law. The 2007 Technical Corrections Act provides that the valuation misstatement penalty for incorrect appraisals described above will also apply to any person who prepares an appraisal upon which a Code Sec. 6662(g) substantial estate or gift tax valuation understatement is based. (Code Sec. 6695A(a)(2) as amended by 2007 Technical Corrections Act §3(e)(1))

> *observation:* Thus, in addition to persons who are currently subject to the penalty for valuation misstatements attributable to incorrect appraisals, that penalty will also apply to any person who:
>
> (A) prepares a property appraisal and knows, or reasonably should have known, that the appraisal would be used in connection with a return or a refund claim, and
>
> (B) the claimed property value on the return or refund claim that is based on the appraisal results in a substantial estate or gift tax valuation understatement under Code Sec. 6662(g).
>
> *observation:* As stated above, Code Sec. 6662(g)(1) provides that a substantial estate or gift tax valuation understatement occurs when the value of any property claimed on an estate or gift tax return is 65% or less of the amount determined to be correct. Nevertheless, Code Sec. 6662(g)(2) states that the 20% Code Sec. 6662 accuracy related penalty won't apply to a substantial estate or gift tax valuation understatement unless the portion of the underpayment attributable to that substantial valuation understatement exceeds $5,000. However, the above changes to Code Sec. 6695A made by the 2007 Technical Corrections Act don't limit assessment of the Code Sec. 6695A valuation

misstatement penalty to amounts in excess of $5,000. Thus, it's doubtful that IRS will apply the limitation to the Code Sec. 6695A penalty.

The 2007 Technical Corrections Act also provides that the Code Sec. 6695A penalty for valuation misstatements attributable to incorrect appraisals is subject to a 3-year limitations period. (Code Sec. 6696(d)(1) as amended by 2007 Technical Corrections Act §3(e)(2))

> **observation:** Thus, the period of limitations for the assessment of a Code Sec. 6695A penalty is three years from the date that the return or refund claim for which the penalty is assessed, is filed.

> **observation:** The above changes relate to the addition of Code Sec. 6695A to the Code as part of the 2006 Pension Protection Act. Thus, the effective date of the above changes is the same as the effective date of the 2006 Pension Protection Act changes, as discussed below.

☐ **Effective:** Appraisals prepared for returns or submissions filed after Aug. 17, 2006. However, in the case of a contribution of a qualified real property interest that is a restriction regarding the exterior of a building described in Code Sec. 170(h)(4)(C)(ii) and any property appraisal for that contribution, the above changes apply to returns filed after July 25, 2006. (2007 Technical Corrections Act §3(j))

2007 Technical Corrections Act §3(j) provides that the amendments made by §3(e) of the Technical Corrections Act take effect as if included in the provision of the 2006 Pension Protection Act to which they relate. The above amendments relate to §1219(b) of the 2006 Pension Protection Act (Sec. 1219(b), PL 109-280, 8/17/2006). 2006 Pension Protection Act §1219(e) provides that the amendments made by §1219(b) take effect for appraisals prepared for returns or submissions filed after Aug. 17, 2006, except that in the case of a contribution of a qualified real property interest that is a restriction regarding the exterior of a building described in Code Sec. 170(h)(4)(C)(ii) and any property appraisal for that contribution, Code Sec. 6695A and the changes to Code Sec. 6696 that relate to it apply to returns filed after July 25, 2006.

> **observation:** Code Sec. 170(h)(4)(C)(ii) describes a building which is located in a registered historic district and certified by the Secretary of the Interior to IRS as being of historic significance to the district, see FTC 2d/FIN ¶ K-3517.

FTC 2d References are to Federal Tax Coordinator 2d
FIN References are to RIA's Analysis of Federal Taxes: Income
USTR References are to United States Tax Reporter: Income, Estate & Gift, and Excise
PCA References are to Pension Analysis (print & electronic)
PE References are to Pension Explanations (print & electronic)
EP References are to Estate Planning Analysis (print & electronic)

¶ 1102. Monthly failure to file partnership return penalty is increased; inspection of returns by persons having a material interest is restricted

Code Sec. 6698(a), as amended by 2007 Mortgage Relief Act § 8(a)
Code Sec. 6698(b)(1), as amended by 2007 Mortgage Relief Act § 8(b)
Code Sec. 6103(e)(10), as amended by 2007 Mortgage Relief Act § 8(c)
Code Sec. 6698(b)(1), 2007 Virginia Tech Victims Act § 2
Generally effective: Returns required to be filed after Dec. 20, 2007
Committee Reports, see ¶ 5402

Income earned by a partnership, whether distributed or not, is taxed to the partners. A partnership is required to file a tax return for each tax year, regardless of whether its income is distributed. The partnership's return must include the names and addresses of the partners who would be entitled to share in the taxable income and the amount of the distributive share for each partner.

Under pre-2007 Mortgage Relief Act law, the civil penalty for the failure to timely file a partnership return was $50 per partner for each month (or fraction of a month) that the failure continued, up to a maximum of five months. (FTC 2d/FIN ¶ V-1762; USTR ¶ 66,984; TaxDesk ¶ 861,041)

A partnership must also provide to its partners by its return filing date specified information that will enable them to complete their returns. A $50 penalty applies for each failure to furnish a required statement to a partner. FTC 2d/FIN ¶s S-2706, V-1814, V-1816; USTR ¶ 67,224; TaxDesk ¶ 861,036

Persons having a material interest in a partnership, S corporation, estate, or trust may, upon written request, have the return of that partnership, S corporation, estate, or trust opened to inspection or disclosure. For those entities, a person having an material interest includes:

(1) Partnership: any person who was a member of the partnership for any part of the period covered by the return.

(2) S corporation: anyone who was a shareholder for any part of the period covered by the return during which the S election was in effect.

(3) Estate: the administrator, executor or trustee of the estate, and any heir, next of kin, or beneficiary under the decedent's will, but only if IRS is satisfied that the person has a material interest which will be affected by information contained in the return.

(4) Trust: the trust's trustees, jointly or separately, and any beneficiary of the trust but only if IRS is satisfied that the beneficiary has a material interest which will be affected by information contained in the return. (FTC 2d/FIN ¶ S-6305, ¶ S-6306, ¶ S-6307, ¶ S-6308; USTR ¶ 61,034.08)

New Law. The 2007 Mortgage Relief Act increases the penalty per partner, for failure to file a partnership return from $50 to $85 for each month, or part thereof, that the failure continues. (Code Sec. 6698(b) as amended by 2007 Mortgage Relief Act §8(b)) The Act also extends the maximum period for which the penalty may be imposed from 5 months to 12 months. (Code Sec. 6698(a))

However, under the 2007 Virginia Tech Victims Act, the penalty amount is increased by $1, i.e., to $86, for partnership returns for tax years starting in 2008. (2007 Virginia Tech Victims Act §2)

> **⊘ observation:** Thus, for tax years starting in 2008, the maximum penalty that may be imposed on a 2-person partnership is increased from $500 to $2,064. For tax years starting after 2008, the maximum penalty that may be imposed on a 2-person partnership is $2,040.

In addition, the 2007 Mortgage Relief Act limits the inspection or disclosure of partnership, S corporation, estate and trust returns. Specifically, the information inspected or disclosed regarding partnership, S corporation, trust, or estate returns cannot include any supporting schedule, attachment, or list which includes the taxpayer identity information of a person other than the entity making the return or the person conducting the inspection or to whom the disclosure is made. (Code Sec. 6103(e)(10) as amended by 2007 Mortgage Relief Act §8(c)(1))

> **⊘ observation:** This means that while partners are entitled to see partnership items on a return they are not permitted to see taxpayer identity information concerning other partners.

☐ **Effective:** The penalty increase applies to returns required to be filed after Dec. 20, 2007. (2007 Mortgage Relief Act §8(d)) The disclosure limitation applies on Dec. 20, 2007. (2007 Mortgage Relief Act §8(c)(2))

The $1 increase applies to partnership returns for tax years starting in 2008. (2007 Virginia Tech Victims Act §2)

FTC 2d References are to Federal Tax Coordinator 2d
FIN References are to RIA's Analysis of Federal Taxes: Income
USTR References are to United States Tax Reporter: Income, Estate & Gift, and Excise
PCA References are to Pension Analysis (print & electronic)
PE References are to Pension Explanations (print & electronic)
EP References are to Estate Planning Analysis (print & electronic)

¶ 1103. Penalty imposed for failure to file timely S corporation return

Code Sec. 6699, as added by 2007 Mortgage Relief Act § 9(a)
Generally effective: Returns required to be filed after Dec. 20, 2007
Committee Reports, None

An S corporation passes through items of income and deduction to its shareholders. An S corporation that has always been an S corporation (and is not the transferee of C corporation assets) is not subject to Federal income tax on its income. If an S corporation was originally a C corporation (or is a transferee of C corporation assets), a corporate level tax may apply to certain income items. FTC 2d/FIN ¶s D-1761, D-1641, D-1650, D-1691, D-1580; USTR ¶ 13,634; TaxDesk ¶s 615,002, 615,021.

An S corporation is required to file an annual Federal income tax return on Form 1120S reporting:

• its income and deductions,

• the names and addresses of all persons owning stock in the corporation at any time during the tax year,

• the number of shares of stock owned by each shareholder at all times during the tax year,

• the amount of money and other property distributed by the corporation during the tax year to each shareholder and the date of each distribution,

• each shareholder's pro rata share of each item of the corporation for the tax year, and

• any other information IRS requires by forms or regs. FTC 2d/FIN ¶ S-1905; USTR ¶ 60,374; TaxDesk ¶s 628,001, 628,002

An S corporation is required to provide to its shareholders by its return filing date specified information which will enable them to complete their returns. A $50 penalty applies to each failure to furnish a required statement to a shareholder. FTC 2d/FIN ¶s S-1906, V-1814, V-1816; USTR ¶ 67,224; TaxDesk ¶ 861,036

Under pre-2007 Mortgage Relief Act law, the civil penalty for the late filing of an income tax return ordinarily did not apply to an S corporation. That's because an S corporation normally doesn't owe Federal income tax, and the penalty is based on the amount of tax due multiplied by the number of months the return was not timely filed. (FTC 2d/FIN ¶ V-1751, ¶ V-1768; USTR ¶ 66,514.01; TaxDesk ¶ 861,001, ¶ 861,002)

New Law. The 2007 Mortgage Relief Act adds a new provision that imposes a penalty on S corporations that fail to file timely S corporation returns.

(Code Sec. 6699 as added by 2007 Mortgage Relief Act §9(a)) Under that provision:

(I) if an S corporation that is required to file an income tax return for any tax year:

(A) fails to file a timely return (taking into account any filing extension), (Code Sec. 6699(a)(1)) or

(B) files a return which fails to show the required information, (Code Sec. 6699(a)(2))

(II) it is liable for a penalty (late filing penalty) for each month (or fraction thereof), not to exceed 12 months, during which the failure continues, unless the failure is due to reasonable cause. (Code Sec. 6699(a))

The monthly penalty amount equals:

(1) $85, multiplied by (Code Sec. 6699(b)(1))

(2) the number of persons who were shareholders in the S corporation during any part of the tax year. (Code Sec. 6699(b)(2))

> *observation:* Item (2) (above) includes any person who was a shareholder during the year to which the return applies. Thus, if A sells her shares to B, A and B are both counted. If C is the only other shareholder during Year 1, the late filing penalty for each month there is a failure equals $255.

> *observation:* Since an S corporation is limited to 100 shareholders (at any time), the penalty will generally be limited to $8,500 a month (assuming no share transfers). But the amount could be higher, since husbands and wives and family members don't count separately toward the 100-shareholder limit, but would presumably be counted separately for the penalty. Also, where a partnership of S corporations is used to avoid the 100-shareholder limit, the penalty on late-filed partnership returns would presumably also apply, see ¶ 1102. FTC 2d/FIN ¶ D-1441; USTR ¶ 13,614.02; TaxDesk ¶s 611,003, 611,003.1.

The late filing penalty is assessed against the S corporation. (Code Sec. 6699(c))

FTC 2d References are to Federal Tax Coordinator 2d
FIN References are to RIA's Analysis of Federal Taxes: Income
USTR References are to United States Tax Reporter: Income, Estate & Gift, and Excise
PCA References are to Pension Analysis (print & electronic)
PE References are to Pension Explanations (print & electronic)
EP References are to Estate Planning Analysis (print & electronic)

observation: Even though the late filing penalty is computed by reference to the number of shareholders, they are not (directly) liable for the penalty.

The deficiency procedures of Code Sec. 6211 through Code Sec. 6216 don't apply to the assessment or collection of the late filing penalty. (Code Sec. 6699(d))

observation: Thus, IRS won't have to issue a 90 day letter, the S corporation can't contest the penalty in Tax Court, and IRS is not barred from immediately assessing the late filing penalty.

Finally, the late filing penalty applies in addition to the criminal penalty under Code Sec. 7203 for willful failure to file a return, supply information or pay a tax. (Code Sec. 6699(a))

For the 2007 Mortgage Relief Act limitations on the disclosure of S corporation return information, see ¶ 1102.

☐ **Effective:** Tax returns required to be filed after Dec. 20, 2007. (2007 Mortgage Relief Act §9(c))

observation: It is not entirely clear if "required to be filed" in the effective date provision takes extensions into account, so that an S corporation that filed for an extension and then fails to file a return by the extended due date could subject itself to a late filing penalty that it could have avoided by not obtaining the extension. However, based on the 2007 Mortgage Relief Act effective date, and the fact that S corporations generally use the calendar year, this is unlikely to make a practical difference.

¶ 1104. Estimated tax payment amounts due from corporations with assets of $1 billion or more are increased for installments due in July, Aug., or Sept. of 2012

Code Sec. 6655, 2007 Mortgage Relief Act § 10
Generally effective: Dec. 20, 2007
Committee Reports, see ¶ 5004

In general, corporations are required to make quarterly estimated tax payments of their income tax liability. For a corporation whose tax year is a calendar year, these estimated tax payments must be made by Apr. 15, June 15, Sept. 15, and Dec. 15 (assuming that the 15th of the month is not a Saturday, Sunday, or legal holiday, see FTC 2d/FIN ¶ T-10796; USTR ¶ 75,034; TaxDesk ¶ 570,240). Fiscal year (non-calendar-year) taxpayers make quarterly payments on "corresponding" dates (i.e., for corporations with fiscal years, there is substituted, for the months listed above, the months that "correspond" to them; that is, the due dates for installment payments are 3½, 5½, 8½ and 11½ months, respectively, after the fiscal year beginning date). See FTC 2d/FIN ¶ S-5353; USTR ¶ 66,554; TaxDesk ¶ 609,201.

> *illustration:* If a corporation uses a fiscal year beginning on Apr. 1, Year 1, the due dates for its installments are: July 15, Sept. 15, and Dec. 15, of Year 1, and Mar. 15 of Year 2.

> *observation:* Congress has, on occasion, accelerated or delayed the due date of all or part of an installment payment. It has also increased or decreased the percentage of the required annual payment for particular payments.

2005 Tax Increase Prevention Act (TIPRA) §401(1) (Sec. 401(1), PL 109-222, 5/17/2006) provided that, in the case of a corporation with assets of at least $1,000,000,000 (determined as of the end of the preceding tax year):

(A) the amount of any required installment of corporate estimated tax which is otherwise due in July, Aug., or Sept. of 2006 is 105% of that amount,

(B) the amount of any required installment of corporate estimated tax which is otherwise due in July, Aug., or Sept. of 2012 is 106.25% of that amount,

(C) the amount of any required installment of corporate estimated tax which is otherwise due in July, Aug., or Sept. of 2013 is 100.75% of that amount, and

(D) the amount of the next required installment after an installment referred to in (A), (B), or (C) is appropriately reduced to reflect the amount of the increase required by (A), (B), or (C), respectively. (FTC 2d/FIN ¶ S-5353; USTR ¶ 66,554; TaxDesk ¶ 609,201)

2005 TIPRA §401(1)(B) (see (B), above) has been amended several times to incrementally change the amount of any required installment of corporate estimated tax that is otherwise due in July, Aug., or Sept. of 2012, from 106.25% to 114.25% (Sec. 8248, PL 110-28, 5/25/2007); from 114.25% to 114.50% (Sec. 4, PL 110-42, 6/30/2007); from 114.50% to 114.75% (Sec. 3, PL 110-52, 8/1/2007); and from 114.75% to 115.00% (Sec. 2(a), PL 110-89, 9/28/2007). (FTC 2d/FIN ¶ S-5353; USTR ¶ 66,554; TaxDesk ¶ 609,201)

New Law. The 2007 Mortgage Relief Act provides that the percentage under 2005 TIPRA §401(1)(B) in effect on Dec. 20, 2007 is increased by 1.50

FTC 2d References are to Federal Tax Coordinator 2d
FIN References are to RIA's Analysis of Federal Taxes: Income
USTR References are to United States Tax Reporter: Income, Estate & Gift, and Excise
PCA References are to Pension Analysis (print & electronic)
PE References are to Pension Explanations (print & electronic)
EP References are to Estate Planning Analysis (print & electronic)

percentage points. (2005 TIPRA §401(1)(B) (Sec. 401(1)(B), PL 109-222, 5/17/2006) as amended by 2007 Mortgage Relief Act §10)

observation: Thus, 2007 Mortgage Relief Act §10 increases the otherwise applicable percentage for payments due in July, Aug., and Sept., 2012, 115.00%, by 1½ percentage points.

observation: Accordingly, 2007 Mortgage Relief Act §10 increases the corporate estimated tax payment due in July, Aug., or Sept. 2012 from 115.00% to 116.50% of the payment otherwise due.

observation: The U.S.-Peru Trade Promotion Agreement Implementation Act (PL 110-138), which was signed by the President on Dec. 14, 2007, provides, in Sec. 602, for an increase in the 115.00% amount discussed above to 115.75%. However, this Act does not take effect until the date on which the Trade Agreement enters into force, and that cannot occur until the President determines that Peru has taken measures necessary to comply with the provisions of the Agreement. At that time, the President is authorized to exchange notes with Peru providing for the entry into force, but no earlier than Jan. 1, 2008. Therefore, the starting point for the 1.50% increase mandated by 2007 Mortgage Relief Act §10 is 115.00%, rather than 115.75%.

observation: 2007 Mortgage Relief Act §10 further accelerates government revenue for one estimated tax installment in the government's 2012 fiscal year (Oct. 1, 2011 through Sept. 30, 2012), but the next required installment payment is reduced in the same amount as the amount of the accelerated payment. However, the reduced payment applies for the government's 2013 fiscal year (Oct. 1, 2012 through Sept. 30, 2013). The result of this is to shift additional revenue from the government's fiscal year ending Sept. 30, 2013 into the government's fiscal year ending Sept. 30, 2012.

illustration: Corp X, a calendar year taxpayer, calculates its estimated tax payment otherwise due in Sept. of 2012 to be $100,000. Instead, X must make a payment of $116,500 ($100,000 x 116.50%) on the due date in Sept. of 2012. X calculates its estimated tax payment otherwise due in Dec. of 2012 to be the same amount as the Sept. 2012 payment, that is, $100,000. This time, X reduces the estimated tax payment otherwise due in Dec. of 2012 by $16,500 ($116,500 - $100,000). Therefore, X must make a payment of $83,500 ($100,000 - $16,500) on the due date in Dec. of 2012. The accelerated payment is due during the government's 2012 fiscal year (Oct. 1, 2011 through Sept. 30, 2012), and the reduced payment is due during the government's 2013 fiscal year (Oct. 1, 2012 through Sept. 30, 2013).

observation: It would appear that corporations with a fiscal year that begins July 1, 2012 will not be affected by these rules because they will not have any estimated tax payments due in July, Aug., or Sept. of 2012.

illustration: Corp Z has a fiscal year beginning on July 1 and ending on June 30. The final installment of Z's estimated tax for Z's 2011-2012 fiscal year will be due on June 15, 2012. The first installment of Z's 2012-2013 fiscal year estimated tax will not be due until Oct. 15, 2012.

☐ **Effective:** Dec. 20, 2007. (Com Rept, see ¶ 5004)

observation: Often, a modification of an earlier Act provision is effective as if the modification was part of the earlier Act, so that the modification is retroactive. But here, the modification that is related to 2012 is prospective.

FTC 2d References are to Federal Tax Coordinator 2d
FIN References are to RIA's Analysis of Federal Taxes: Income
USTR References are to United States Tax Reporter: Income, Estate & Gift, and Excise
PCA References are to Pension Analysis (print & electronic)
PE References are to Pension Explanations (print & electronic)
EP References are to Estate Planning Analysis (print & electronic)

¶ 1200. Payroll Taxes

¶ 1201. Additional 0.2% FUTA surtax is extended to apply through 2008

Code Sec. 3301, as amended by 2007 Energy Act § 1501(a)
Generally effective: Wages paid in 2008
Committee Reports, see ¶ 5101

Employers must pay the Federal Unemployment Tax Act ("FUTA") tax for wages paid to their employees with respect to employment (see FTC 2d/FIN ¶ H-4726; USTR ¶ 33,014; TaxDesk ¶ 550,501). The maximum amount of wages subject to FUTA tax is $7,000 of wages for each employee during a calendar year (see FTC 2d/FIN ¶ H-4801; USTR ¶ 35,014.07; TaxDesk ¶ 550,502).

Under pre-2007 Energy Act law, the FUTA tax was imposed at a rate of 6.2% through 2007 (the total of the permanent 6% tax rate, and a temporary 0.2% surtax rate (Com Rept, see ¶ 5101)), and 6.0% for calendar year 2008 and later years. (FTC 2d ¶ H-4801; USTR ¶ 35,014.07; TaxDesk ¶ 550,502)

New Law. The 2007 Energy Act provides that the 6.2% FUTA tax rate continues to apply through 2008, and the 6.0% rate applies for calendar year 2009 and later years. (Code Sec. 3301 as amended by 2007 Energy Act §1501(a)) That is, the temporary 0.2% surtax is extended through Dec. 31, 2008. (Com Rept, see ¶ 5101)

> **💡** *observation:* As noted above, the FUTA tax applies to the first $7,000 of an employee's wages. Thus, the 2007 Energy Act's extension of the 6.2% rate to 2008 results in a maximum increase in the amount of FUTA tax paid for 2008 of $14 per employee (i.e., .002 × $7,000 = $14).

> **💡** *observation:* Employers who pay state unemployment tax on a timely basis receive an offset credit of up to 5.4% of FUTA tax (see FTC 2d/FIN ¶ H-4802 *et seq.*; USTR ¶ 35,014.07; TaxDesk ¶ 550,503 *et seq.*). Therefore, generally, the net FUTA tax rate for employers is actually 0.8% (6.2% − 5.4%), for a maximum FUTA tax of $56.00 per employee, per year (.008 × $7,000. = $56.00).

FTC 2d References are to Federal Tax Coordinator 2d
FIN References are to RIA's Analysis of Federal Taxes: Income
USTR References are to United States Tax Reporter: Income, Estate & Gift, and Excise
PCA References are to Pension Analysis (print & electronic)
PE References are to Pension Explanations (print & electronic)
EP References are to Estate Planning Analysis (print & electronic)

⊘ observation: Employers are generally subject to FUTA tax during a calendar year if during the prior or current calendar year they paid wages of $1,500 or more in any calendar quarter, or had one or more employees at any time in each of 20 calendar weeks. But special rules apply for employers of domestic workers (see the *RIA caution* below) and agricultural workers, and to state or local government employers. (See FTC 2d/FIN ¶s H-4731 *et seq.*, H-4764; TaxDesk ¶s 550,507 *et seq.*, 551,010.)

⊘ caution: Employers of domestic employees are required to pay FUTA taxes if they pay a total of $1,000 or more in cash wages to a household worker in any calendar quarter of the current year or last year (see FTC 2d/FIN ¶ H-4771; TaxDesk ¶ 550,507). Domestic workers for these purposes include babysitters, caretakers, cleaning people, drivers, nannies, health aides, yard workers, and private nurses.

⊘ observation: Employers report FUTA taxes on Form 940, Employer's Annual Federal Unemployment (FUTA) Tax Return.

If the amount of FUTA tax due exceeds $500 for the calendar year, the employer must deposit at least one quarterly payment. FUTA tax may be deposited electronically using the Electronic Federal Tax Payment System (EFTPS), or by depositing the tax with an authorized financial institution (e.g., a commercial bank that's qualified to accept federal tax deposits) with a Form 8109, Federal Tax Coupon. In some cases, employers may be required to deposit FUTA tax using EFTPS. For example, employers must use EFTPS in 2008 if (a) total payments of employment tax, excise tax, and corporate income tax were more than $200,000 for 2006, or (b) the employer was required to use EFTPS in 2007. (See the Instructions to Form 940 (2007), pp. 3–4, and FTC 2d/FIN ¶ S-5571 *et seq.*; USTR ¶ 63,014; TaxDesk ¶ 558,006).

☐ **Effective:** For wages paid after Dec. 31, 2007 (2007 Energy Act §1501(b)), and before 2009 (Code Sec. 3301).

¶ 1202. Application of cumulative limit on designated Roth contributions corrected; elective deferrals designated as Roth contributions are FICA "wages"

Code Sec. 402(g)(7)(A)(ii)(II), as amended by 2007 Technical Corrections Act § 8(a)(1)
Code Sec. 3121(v)(1)(A), as amended and redesignated by 2007 Technical Corrections Act § 8(a)(2)
Generally effective: Tax years beginning after Dec. 31, 2005
Committee Reports, see ¶ 5307

In general, a "designated Roth contribution" is an elective deferral that is designated irrevocably by the employee at the time of the election as a Roth contribution, and treated as includible in the employee's gross income. FTC 2d/ FIN ¶ H-12295.4; USTR ¶ 4014.1745; PCA ¶ 35,251.5; PE ¶ 401-4.175

A special rule enables certain employees to make additional elective deferrals to a Code Sec. 403(b) annuity contract. Specifically, for elective deferrals under a Code Sec. 403(b) annuity contract, the applicable limit is adjusted by increasing the otherwise adjusted limit by whichever of the following amounts is smallest—

(1) $3,000,

(2) $15,000 reduced by the sum of:

(a) the amounts not included in gross income for prior tax years by reason of this rule, plus

(b) the aggregate amount of designated Roth contributions, for prior tax years, or

(3) the excess of (i) $5,000 multiplied by the employee's number of years of service with the qualified organization, over (ii) the employer contributions made to the employee's tax-sheltered annuity contract on his behalf by the organization for a prior tax year in the manner prescribed by IRS. (FTC 2d/FIN ¶ H-9157; USTR ¶ 402A4; PCA ¶ 28,408; PE ¶ 402A-4)

Pre-2007 Technical Corrections Act law provided the rule, in item 2(b), above, to coordinate the cumulative limit with the ability to make designated Roth contributions, but inadvertently reduced the $15,000 amount by all designated Roth contributions made in prior years. (Com Rept, see ¶ 5307)

Although elective deferrals are included in wages for purposes of social security and Medicare taxes (FICA), pre-2007 Technical Corrections Act law did not provide FICA tax treatment for elective deferrals that are designated as Roth contributions.

New Law. The 2007 Technical Corrections Act provides that the $15,000 cumulative limit (item 2(b), above) is reduced only by additional designated Roth contributions made under the special rule. (Code Sec. 402(g)(7)(A)(ii)(II) as amended and redesignated by 2007 Technical Corrections Act §8(a)(1))

observation: Thus, for elective deferrals under a Code Sec. 403(b) annuity contract, the special rule provides that the applicable limit is

---

FTC 2d References are to Federal Tax Coordinator 2d
FIN References are to RIA's Analysis of Federal Taxes: Income
USTR References are to United States Tax Reporter: Income, Estate & Gift, and Excise
PCA References are to Pension Analysis (print & electronic)
PE References are to Pension Explanations (print & electronic)
EP References are to Estate Planning Analysis (print & electronic)

adjusted by increasing the otherwise adjusted limit by whichever of the following amounts is smallest—

(1) $3,000,

(2) $15,000 reduced by the sum of:

(a) the amounts not included in gross income for earlier tax years by reason of this rule, plus

(b) the aggregate amount of designated Roth contributions *permitted* for prior tax years by reason of this special rule, or

(3) the excess of (i) $5,000 multiplied by the number of years of service of the employee with the qualified organization, over (ii) the employer contributions made to the employee's tax-sheltered annuity contract on his behalf by the organization for a prior tax year in the manner prescribed by IRS.

⟐ observation: Only item (2)(b) of the special rule (above) has been changed. Under the 2007 Technical Corrections Act, any designated Roth contributions outside of the special rule are no longer counted when making the $15,000 reduction computation.

⟐ illustration: E, a Code Sec. 403(b) annuity contract plan participant, is eligible to make designated Roth contributions under the special rule. In 2007, E's designated Roth contribution under the special rule is $600. E's other designated Roth contribution is $1,000. Thus, under pre-2007 Technical Corrections Act law, E's cumulative limit was reduced to $13,400 ($15,000 − $600 − $1,000). After the 2007 Technical Corrections Act, E's cumulative limit is reduced to $14,400 ($15,000 − $600, E's 2007 designated Roth contributions under the special rule).

In 2008, E's designated Roth contribution under the special rule is $400. E makes no other designated Roth contributions. Thus, under pre-2007 Technical Corrections Act law, E's cumulative limit would have been reduced to $13,000 ($13,400 − $400). After the 2007 Technical Corrections Act, E's cumulative limit is reduced to $14,000 ($14,400 − $400, E's 2008 designated Roth contributions under the special rule).

⟐ observation: In light of the 2007 Technical Corrections Act changes, taxpayers, such as E in the illustration above, who reduced their cumulative limit by designated Roth contributions outside of the special rule, should consider filing an amended return if a refund opportunity exists.

FICA Change. The 2007 Technical Corrections Act provides that elective deferrals that are designated as Roth IRA contributions are treated as wages for

FICA tax purposes. (Code Sec. Code Sec. 3121(v)(1)(A) as amended by 2007 Technical Corrections Act §8(a)(2))

☐ **Effective:** Tax years beginning after Dec. 31, 2005. (2007 Technical Corrections Act §8(b))

2007 Technical Corrections Act §8(b) provides that amendments made by §8(a) take effect as if included in the 2001 Economic Growth and Tax Relief Reconciliation Act (EGTRRA) provision to which it relates. The above provision relates to EGTRRA §617 (Sec. 617, PL 107-16, 6/7/2001). EGTRRA §617(f) provided that the amendments made by §617 were effective for tax years beginning after Dec. 31, 2005.

FTC 2d References are to Federal Tax Coordinator 2d
FIN References are to RIA's Analysis of Federal Taxes: Income
USTR References are to United States Tax Reporter: Income, Estate & Gift, and Excise
PCA References are to Pension Analysis (print & electronic)
PE References are to Pension Explanations (print & electronic)
EP References are to Estate Planning Analysis (print & electronic)

¶ 1300. Miscellaneous

¶ 1301. Modification of active business definition under Code Sec. 355.

Code Sec. 355(b)(2), as amended by 2007 Technical Corrections Act § 4(b)(1)

Code Sec. 355(b)(3)(C), as amended by 2007 Technical Corrections Act § 4(b)(2)

Code Sec. 355(b)(3)(D), as amended by 2007 Technical Corrections Act § 4(b)(2)

Generally effective: Distributions made after May 17, 2006

Committee Reports, see ¶ 5303

One of the requirements for a tax-free Code Sec. 355 corporate division (e.g., a spin-off) in which a distributing corporation (D) distributes a controlling interest in its subsidiary (C) to one or more D shareholders is that immediately after the distribution D and C must each be engaged in the active conduct of a trade or business. This requires D and C to satisfy the Code Sec. 355(b)(2) business test. Under pre-2005 Tax Increase Prevention Act (2005 TIPRA) law, a corporation could only satisfy this test if it first met the following requirements:

(1) it was engaged in the active conduct of a trade or business, or

(2) substantially all of its assets consisted of stock and securities of a corporation (or corporations) it controlled immediately after the distribution and the controlled corporation(s) were engaged in the active conduct of a trade or business. (This list is referred to below as the Sec. 355(b)(2)(A) active business test).

Under pre-2005 TIPRA law, the Sec. 355(b)(2)(A) active business test resulted in applying a more stringent test where D held stock of corporations that were engaged in the active conduct of a trade or business, but was not directly engaged in the active conduct of a trade or business itself, than the test that applied where D directly conducted an active business. Thus, a corporate group often had to undergo elaborate restructuring to satisfy the Sec. 355(b)(2)(A) active business test (see Illustration (1) below). To address this problem 2005 TIPRA added a new rule under Code Sec. 355(b)(3) that stated that for distributions made after the date of enactment (i.e., May 17, 2006), a corporation is only treated as satisfying the Sec. 355(b)(2)(A) active business test if, and only

FTC 2d References are to Federal Tax Coordinator 2d
FIN References are to RIA's Analysis of Federal Taxes: Income
USTR References are to United States Tax Reporter: Income, Estate & Gift, and Excise
PCA References are to Pension Analysis (print & electronic)
PE References are to Pension Explanations (print & electronic)
EP References are to Estate Planning Analysis (print & electronic)

if, it is engaged in the active conduct of a trade or business. In applying this requirement, all members of the corporation's "separate affiliated group" are treated as one corporation. Thus, the active business test is applied on a group basis to each separate affiliated group. As a practical matter this replaced the item (2) Sec. 355(b)(2)(A) active business test.

A corporation's separate affiliated group is the affiliated group that would have existed under Code Sec. 1504(a) (generally requiring ownership of stock with 80% of the voting power and 80% of the value) if the corporation were the common parent and the Code Sec. 1504(b) exclusions (e.g., for insurance companies and foreign corporations) did not apply. All corporations that satisfied this mechanical test were included in the separate affiliated group. (FTC 2d/FIN ¶ F-4803; USTR ¶ 3554.02; TaxDesk ¶ 237,426.1) (FTC 2d/FIN ¶ E-7601; FTC 2d/FIN ¶ E-7606; FTC 2d/FIN ¶ E-7618; USTR ¶ 15,024.17; TaxDesk ¶ 603,300; TaxDesk ¶ 603,301; TaxDesk ¶ 603,303)

> **⦿ illustration (1):** D owns 100% of the stock of C1 and C2, each of which is engaged in the active conduct of a trade or business, and 100% of the stock of C3, which holds the group's investments. D performs headquarters functions for its subsidiaries and is not directly engaged in the active conduct of a trade or business. C3's investments represent more than 25% of D's assets. In Oct. 2006, D decides to spin-off C1. D is engaged in the active conduct of a trade or business, because this requirement is tested for D by treating D, C2 and C3 as one corporation. Under pre-2005 TIPRA law, D would have had to assume that it didn't satisfy the active trade or business requirement (without restructuring) because it wasn't directly engaged in the active conduct of a trade or business and C2 didn't represent substantially all of its assets. Thus is would have had to merge C2 with C3 or liquidate C2.

Special rule for pre-2005 TIPRA distributions. 2005 TIPRA added a special transition rule for determining the continued qualification under the Sec. 355(b)(2) business test of a pre-2005 TIPRA effective date (i.e., pre-May 18, 2006) distribution where there was a post-effective date acquisition, disposition or other restructuring. Under Code Sec. 355(b)(3)(D), this distribution was treated as made on the date of the post-effective date acquisition, disposition or restructuring in applying the 2005 TIPRA amendment that added the separate affiliated group rule. Thus, if before May 18, 2006, D distributed controlled C1 in a distribution that satisfied the Sec. 355(b)(2)(A) active business test of pre-2005 TIPRA law, D was not treated as violating any requirement that it continue that same qualified structure after the distribution solely because of a restructuring that occurred after May 17, 2006 if the new structure satisfied the Sec 355(b)(2)(A) active business test under the separate affiliated group rule. FTC 2d/FIN ¶ F-4803; USTR ¶ 3554.02; TaxDesk ¶ 237,426.1

☞illustration (2): Same facts as illustration (1), except that D distributed C1 in 2005 and before the distribution merged C2 and C3 to satisfy the Sec. 355(b)(2)(A) active business test under pre-2005 TIPRA law. After May 17, 2006, C3 is again organized as a separate corporation to protect its assets from C2 liabilities. The special rule for pre-2005 TIPRA distributions bars IRS from contending that the merger of C2 and C3 was a transitory step that should be ignored so that D didn't satisfy pre-2005 TIPRA law when it distributed C1.

Before the 2006 Tax Relief Act, the Code Sec. 355(b)(3) separate affiliated group rule was scheduled to sunset for post-Dec. 31, 2010 distributions. Therefore, although the item (2) Sec. 355(b)(2)(A) active business test had been effectively replaced by the affiliated group rule for pre-2011 distributions, item (2) was retained in the Code, so that the post-Dec. 31, 2010 rules would be in place after Code Sec. 355(b)(3) sunset. The 2006 Tax Relief Act made Code Sec. 355(b)(3) permanent, thereby rendering item (2) irrelevant. Nevertheless, it remained in the Code.

In addition to satisfying the Sec. 355(b)(2)(A) active business test (applying the Code Sec. 355(b)(3) affiliated group rule), the following additional requirements must be met to satisfy the Sec. 355(b)(2) business test:

(1) the trade or business relied on must have been actively conducted for the five-year period ending on the date of the distribution (the five-year period); (FTC 2d/FIN ¶ F-4819; USTR ¶ 3554.02; TaxDesk ¶ 237,403)

(2) the trade or business must not have been acquired within the five-year period in a transaction in which gain or loss was recognized; (FTC 2d/FIN ¶ F-4826; USTR ¶ 3554.02; TaxDesk ¶ 237,409) and

(3) control of a corporation, which at the time of the acquisition of control was conducting the trade or business, must not have been acquired directly or indirectly within the five-year period, unless control was acquired only by reason of transactions in which no gain or loss was recognized. For this purpose, all distributee corporations satisfying a separate affiliated group test (see above) are treated as one corporation. (This list is referred to as the Sec. 355(b)(2) five-year list.) (FTC 2d/FIN ¶ F-4828; FTC 2d/FIN ¶ F-4830; USTR ¶ 3554.02; TaxDesk ¶ 237,410; TaxDesk ¶ 237,412)

Under an exception to item (2) of the Sec. 355(b)(2) five-year list (immediately above) if a purchased trade or business represents an expansion of a business conducted by the separate affiliated group, the expansion trumps the taxa-

FTC 2d References are to Federal Tax Coordinator 2d
FIN References are to RIA's Analysis of Federal Taxes: Income
USTR References are to United States Tax Reporter: Income, Estate & Gift, and Excise
PCA References are to Pension Analysis (print & electronic)
PE References are to Pension Explanations (print & electronic)
EP References are to Estate Planning Analysis (print & electronic)

ble purchase and the purchased business immediately qualifies as a good active business. FTC 2d/FIN ¶ F-4822; USTR ¶ 3554.02; TaxDesk ¶ 237,409. However, under pre-2007 Technical Corrections Act Law the expansion exception could only apply to an item (2) asset acquisition. If the acquisition was a stock acquisition, the expansion rule could not apply and the item (3) prohibition against the acquisition of a corporation conducting the trade or business in a transaction in which gain or loss was recognized in whole or in part prevented the target's trade or business from being relied on to satisfy the business test during the five-year post-acquisition period. (FTC 2d/FIN ¶ F-4803.5, ¶ F-4828.1; USTR ¶ 3554.021)

New Law. Under the 2007 Technical Corrections Act, if a corporation becomes a member of a separate affiliated group by reason of one or more transactions in which gain or loss was recognized in whole or in part any trade or business conducted by the corporation when it became a member is treated as acquired in a transaction in which gain or loss was recognized in whole or in part in a transaction to which item (2) of the Sec. 355(b)(2) five-year list applies. (Code Sec. 355(b)(3)(C) as amended by 2007 Technical Corrections Act §4(b)(2))

This technical amendment makes a stock acquisition subject to Code Sec. 355(b)(2)(C) (i.e., item (2) of the Sec. 355(b)(2) five-year list), and therefore the trade or business conducted by the corporation may qualify as an expansion of an existing active trade or business conducted by the distributing corporation or the controlled corporation, as the case may be. (Com Rept, see ¶ 5303)

> *observation:* This provision only applies where there is a violation of item (3) of the Sec. 355(b)(2) five-year list, because C's stock was acquired in a transaction in which gain or loss was recognized in whole or part. If the expansion exception doesn't apply there is a five year wait until the business can qualify as a good active business. If C is acquired in a tax-free reorganization in which there is no boot, an otherwise qualifying good five year business can immediately be relied on without regard to the expansion exception.

> *observation:* Since any amount of boot in a reorganization disqualifies a reorganization under item (3) of the Sec. 355(b)(2) five-year list, under pre-2007 Technical Corrections Act law an acquisition had to be an asset acquisition if the targets's business was to be relied on under the expansion exception. Now the affiliated group is free to let business considerations (and other tax considerations) determine whether to make an asset acquisition or a stock acquisition.

> *caution:* Under Code Sec. 355(a)(3)(B), stock acquired in a taxable transaction is treated as boot if it is distributed within five years. In ad-

dition, the distributing corporation then recognizes gain on the distribution under Code Sec. 355(c)(2). The 2007 Technical Corrections Act gives IRS specific regulatory authority to solve this problem (see "Regulatory authority" (below)). However, pending the issuance of regs or an official IRS announcement, an abundance of caution suggests not relying on the expansion exception to distribute stock of a corporation acquired in a taxable transaction within the five years preceding the distribution. See illustrations (3) and (4) below.

illustration (3): Corporation D purchases all of C's stock. C is engaged in the same active business as members of the D separate affiliated group and its business represents an expansion of that business. Under Code Sec. 355(b)(3)(C), the stock purchase qualifies as an asset purchase for purposes of applying item (2) (and not item (3)) of the Sec. 355(b)(2) five-year list so the expansion exception applies. Thus, C's business immediately represents a good active business. Within five years of the purchase D spins off C to its shareholders. The distribution violates Code Sec. 355(a)(3)(B) and, unless regs have provided relief (see below), D and its shareholders recognize income and gain.

illustration (4): Same facts as illustration (3) except that D retains its C stock and instead spins off a controlled subsidiary that was engaged in the same line of business as C. Code Sec. 355(a)(3)(B) doesn't apply since C was not distributed, and C's business can satisfy the Sec. 355(b)(2)(A) active business test for the remaining members of D's separate affiliated group. Thus, unlike the distribution in illustration (3) this distribution can proceed without regs or an equivalent IRS announcement.

observation: The above 2007 Technical Corrections Act amendment has the potential to create a trap for the unwary by providing that the acquisition of C stock in a taxable transaction can qualify for the business expansion exception even though the distribution of C within five years of the acquisition generates income and gain under clear Code language. IRS was acutely aware of this problem because a recently proposed reg (Prop. Reg. 1.355-3 (May 8, 2007)), generally treats D's taxable acquisition of C's stock as an asset purchase, and thus created the same potential trap. (FTC 2d/FIN ¶ F-4828.1; USTR ¶ 3554.021) IRS was in a quandary as to what to do since a solution requires re-

FTC 2d References are to Federal Tax Coordinator 2d
FIN References are to RIA's Analysis of Federal Taxes: Income
USTR References are to United States Tax Reporter: Income, Estate & Gift, and Excise
PCA References are to Pension Analysis (print & electronic)
PE References are to Pension Explanations (print & electronic)
EP References are to Estate Planning Analysis (print & electronic)

stricting clear Code language. However, the 2007 Technical Corrections Act gives IRS specific regulatory authority (see below) to solve this problem.

Regulatory authority. IRS is to issue regs that are necessary or appropriate to carry out the purposes of the above amendments including regs which:

(1) provide for the proper application of the Sec. 355(b)(2) five-year list, and

(2) modify the application of Code Sec. 355(a)(3)(B) in connection with the application of the above amendments. (Code Sec. 355(b)(3)(D))

> *observation:* Item (2) gives IRS the authority to issue regs providing that Code Sec. 355(a)(3)(B) will not apply to a distribution of stock of a controlled corporation acquired in a taxable transaction if the purchase was treated as an asset purchase under item (2) of the Sec. 355(b)(2) five-year list and satisfied the Sec. 355(b)(2)(A) active business test under the expansion exception. Presumably IRS will use this authority and any regs will be retroactive to the date of enactment.

Dead wood provisions removed. The 2007 Technical Corrections Act removes the item (2) Sec. 355(b)(2)(A) active business test from the Code. (Code Sec. 355(b)(2)(A) as amended by 2007 Technical Corrections Act §4(b)(1))

> *observation:* This provision was only relevant following the scheduled sunset of the affiliated group rule. Once the 2006 Tax Relief Act made that rule permanent, the item (2) Sec. 355(b)(2)(A) active business test became "dead wood" and it is now removed.

The 2007 Technical Corrections Act also removes dead-wood language from Code Sec. 355(b)(3)(A) which introduced the affiliated group rule and provided that it applied to distributions after the date of enactment. This was a residue of language that originally incorporated the above sunset rule. This subparagraph is also reworded (see "Provisions moved or reworded (below)). (Code Sec. 355(b)(3)(A))

Provisions moved or reworded. The 2007 Technical Corrections Act rewords Code Sec. 355(b)(3)(A) to provide that in determining if a corporation meets the Sec. 355(b)(2)(A) active business test all members of the corporation's separate affiliated group are treated as one corporation. (Code Sec. 355(b)(3)(A))

> *observation:* This separates the separate affiliated group rule from the definition of a separate affiliated group. Thus, Code Sec. 355(b)(3)(A) (immediately above) now states the separate affiliated group rule and Code Sec. 355(b)(3)(B) retains the definition of a sepa-

rate affiliated group. Before the 2007 Technical Corrections Act, both the rule and the definition were included in Code Sec. 355(b)(3)(B). Code Sec. 355(b)(3)(A) then stated that a corporation met the requirements of the Sec. 355(b)(2)(A) active business test only if it was "engaged in the active conduct of a trade or business." This language was at best redundant and was subject to possible confusion as to whether it may have created a special active business rule, and it is now removed.

Provisions removed from the Code but retained. The Code is to be applied and administered as if the amendments made by Sec. 202 of 2005 TIPRA and Sec. 410(a) of the 2006 Tax Relief Act had never been enacted. (2007 Technical Corrections Act §4(b)(3))

> **observation:** The rules removed from the Code are (i) the Code Sec. 355(b)(3)(C) effective date rules for the separate affiliated group rule applicable to binding contracts, ruling requests, and public announcements or filings with the Securities and Exchange Commission and (ii) the special rule for pre-enactment distributions, see "Special rule for pre-2005 TIPRA distributions" (above).

However, these rules remain in effect under the effective date rules of the Technical Corrections Act (see below). (2007 Technical Corrections Act §4(d)(2))

☐ **Effective:** Distributions made after May 17, 2006, except as provided by the below transition rules. (2007 Technical Corrections Act §4(d)(2)(A))

Transition rules. The above amendments do not apply to any distribution pursuant to a transaction which is:

(1) made under an agreement which was binding on May 17, 2006, and at all times thereafter, (2007 Technical Corrections Act §4(d)(2)(B)(i))

(2) described in a ruling request submitted to IRS on or before that date, (2007 Technical Corrections Act §4(d)(2)(B)(ii)) or

(3) described on or before that date in a public announcement or in a filing with the Securities and Exchange Commission. (2007 Technical Corrections Act §4(d)(2)(B)(iii))

The rules of the immediately preceding list do not apply if the distributing corporation elects not to have them apply to its distributions. Any election, once made, is irrevocable. (2007 Technical Corrections Act §4(d)(2)(C))

FTC 2d References are to Federal Tax Coordinator 2d
FIN References are to RIA's Analysis of Federal Taxes: Income
USTR References are to United States Tax Reporter: Income, Estate & Gift, and Excise
PCA References are to Pension Analysis (print & electronic)
PE References are to Pension Explanations (print & electronic)
EP References are to Estate Planning Analysis (print & electronic)

For purposes of determining the continued qualification under the Sec. 355(b)(2)(A) active business test of distributions made on or before May 17, 2006, as a result of an acquisition, disposition, or other restructuring after that date, the distribution is treated as made on the date of the acquisition, disposition, or restructuring for purposes of applying the above effective date, transition, and election out rules. The preceding sentence only applies to the corporation that undertakes the acquisition, disposition, or other restructuring, and only if its application results in continued qualification under the Sec. 355(b)(2)(A) active business test. (2007 Technical Corrections Act §4(d)(2)(D))

> *observation:* All of the above transition rules with the exception of the last sentence were included in the pre-2007 Technical Corrections Act version of Code Sec. 355(b)(3)(C) and Code Sec. 355(b)(3)(D). The last sentence could apply where, e.g., a distribution made on the date of a restructuring couldn't qualify as a tax-free corporate division because of a change in circumstances since the actual distribution.

¶ 1302. Cooperatives can use alternative tests based on square footage or expenditures in lieu of the 80/20 gross income test to qualify as a cooperative housing corporation

Code Sec. 216(b)(1)(D), as amended by 2007 Mortgage Relief Act § 4(a)
Generally effective: Tax years ending after Dec. 20, 2007
Committee Reports, see ¶ 5002

A tenant-stockholder in a cooperative housing corporation can deduct amounts paid or accrued to the cooperative to the extent those amounts represent the tenant-stockholder's (see FTC 2d/FIN ¶ E-1078; USTR ¶ 2164.01; TaxDesk ¶ 265,020) proportionate share of:

. . . real estate taxes allowable as a deduction to the cooperative which are paid or incurred by the cooperative on the cooperative's land or buildings and (see FTC 2d/FIN ¶ K-5140; K-5900; USTR ¶ 2164.01; TaxDesk ¶ 326,012)

. . . interest allowable as a deduction to the cooperative that is paid or incurred by the cooperative on its indebtedness contracted in the acquisition of the cooperative's land or in the acquisition, construction, alteration, rehabilitation, or maintenance of the cooperative's buildings. (see FTC 2d/FIN ¶ K-4103; USTR ¶ 2164.01; TaxDesk ¶ 314,511)

Under pre-2007 Mortgage Relief Act law, a cooperative housing corporation generally was a corporation:

(1) that has one class of stock (see FTC 2d/FIN ¶ E-1060; USTR ¶ 2164.02),

(2) each of the stockholders of which can, solely by reason of ownership of stock in the corporation, occupy a dwelling owned or leased by the cooperative (see FTC 2d/FIN ¶ E-1064; USTR ¶ 2164.02),

(3) no stockholder of which can receive any distribution not out of the cooperative's earnings and profits, except on complete or partial liquidation of the cooperative, and (see FTC 2d/FIN ¶ E-1063; USTR ¶ 2164.02)

(4) 80% or more of the gross income of which for the tax year in which the taxes and interest are paid or incurred is derived from tenant-stockholders. (FTC 2d/FIN ¶ E-1073; E-1074; USTR ¶ 2164.02)

> *observation:* The requirement described in item (4) above is commonly known as the "80/20" test. Gross income that is "derived from tenant-stockholders" is generally referred to as "good 80/20 income" and other income (not derived from tenant-stockholders) is generally referred to as "bad 80/20 income." Bad 80/20 income includes income received from third parties such as rent from commercial tenants as well as investment returns on funds held as reserves or funds being accumulated for an anticipated major expenditure. For the effect of rental value of commercial space on the 80/20 test, see FTC 2d/FIN ¶ E-1075; USTR ¶ 2165.02(30).

> *illustration (1):* ABC, a cooperative, meets the requirements described in items (1) through (3) above for qualification as a cooperative housing corporation. ABC had gross income of $10,000,000 consisting of $8,000,000 of "good 80/20 income" and $2,000,000 of "bad 80/20 income" during its tax year. Since ABC's good 80/20 income is exactly 80% of its gross income, ABC satisfied the 80/20 test (item (4) above) for purposes of determining whether ABC qualifies as a cooperative housing corporation during the tax year under pre-2007 Mortgage Relief Act law.

> *illustration (2):* The facts are the same as in illustration (1) except that ABC had $7,995,000 of "good 80/20 income" and $2,005,000 of "bad 80/20 income" during its tax year. Since ABC's good 80/20 income is less than 80% of its gross income (i.e., 79.95% of ABC's gross income), ABC didn't satisfy the 80/20 test for purposes of determining whether ABC qualifies as a cooperative housing corporation during the tax year under pre-2007 Mortgage Relief Act law.

FTC 2d References are to Federal Tax Coordinator 2d
FIN References are to RIA's Analysis of Federal Taxes: Income
USTR References are to United States Tax Reporter: Income, Estate & Gift, and Excise
PCA References are to Pension Analysis (print & electronic)
PE References are to Pension Explanations (print & electronic)
EP References are to Estate Planning Analysis (print & electronic)

observation: If a cooperative didn't satisfy each of the four requirements for qualification as a cooperative housing corporation, the tenant-stockholders couldn't deduct their proportionate share of the corporation's tax deductions for interest and real estate taxes, see FTC 2d/FIN ¶s E-1050, K-5901; USTR ¶ 2164; TaxDesk ¶ 265,019. Also, a sale or exchange of a cooperative apartment doesn't qualify for the up to $250,000 ($500,000 for certain joint filers) exclusion that applies to the sale or exchange of a principal residence if the cooperative doesn't qualify as a cooperative housing corporation, see FTC 2d/FIN ¶ I-4564; USTR ¶ 1214.14; TaxDesk ¶ 225,744.

To satisfy the 80/20 test under pre-2007 Mortgage Relief Act law, Congress believed that some cooperative housing corporations had been making rentals to commercial tenants at below-market rates. (Com Rept, see ¶ 5002)

observation: Cooperatives have used various methods to control the amount of gross income received from commercial tenants (i.e., bad 80/20 income) to prevent violations of the 80/20 test under pre-2007 Mortgage Relief Act law. For example, some cooperatives included provisions in commercial leases that expressly limited the amount of rent to the maximum amount that could be received by the cooperative without violating the 80% gross income requirement. Some cooperatives also require commercial tenants to pay for incidental services (for example, utilities and cleaning services) rather than including those amounts in the rent.

Alternatively, a cooperative can increase the good 80/20 income by increasing the maintenance or other amounts (such as amounts paid for parking spaces used by tenants or the tenant's utilities) paid by tenants.

New Law. The 2007 Mortgage Relief Act provides two non-income-based alternatives to the 80% requirement (the 80/20 test described in item (4) above) in the definition of a cooperative housing corporation. Specifically, the 2007 Mortgage Relief Act amends requirement (4) above to provide that the requirement is satisfied if (Com Rept, see ¶ 5002) a corporation meets one or more of the following requirements for the tax year in which the taxes and interest described in Code Sec. 216(a) are paid or incurred: (Code Sec. 216(b)(1)(D) as amended by 2007 Mortgage Relief Act §4(a))

(a) 80% or more of the corporation's gross income for the tax year is derived from tenant-stockholders. (Code Sec. 216(b)(1)(D)(i))

observation: The test described in (a) above is the same test (i.e., the 80/20 test) that applied under pre-2007 Mortgage Relief Act law (see item (4) above).

(b) At all times during the tax year, 80% or more of the total square footage of the corporation's property is used or available for use by the tenant-stock-holders for residential purposes or purposes ancillary to the residential use. (Code Sec. 216(b)(1)(D)(ii))

> *observation:* Presumably, "purposes ancillary to the residential use" would include square footage of the corporation's property used for facilities that the tenant-stockholders could use such as a laundry room, an exercise room, storage lockers, parking spaces, a swimming pool, a tennis court, or a playground.

> *illustration (3):* The facts are the same as in illustration (2) above. Also, the total square footage of ABC's property is 200,000 square feet. If, at all times during the tax year, at least 160,000 (80% × 200,000) square feet of ABC's property is used or available for use by the ten-ant-stockholders for residential purposes or purposes ancillary to the residential use, ABC qualifies as a cooperative housing corporation.

(c) 90% or more of the expenditures of the corporation paid or incurred during the tax year are paid or incurred for the acquisition, construction, management, maintenance, or care of the corporation's property for the benefit of the tenant-stockholders. (Code Sec. 216(b)(1)(D)(iii))

> *illustration (4):* The facts are the same as in illustration (3) above except that only 150,000 square feet (75% of the square footage of ABC's property) of ABC's property is used or available for use by the tenant-stockholders for residential purposes or purposes ancillary to the residential use at all times during the tax year. Thus, ABC doesn't meet the square footage test provided in Code Sec. 216(b)(1)(D)(ii) (see item (b) above). Also, ABC's expenditures paid or incurred during the tax year amounted to $8,000,000. Since ABC doesn't meet either the 80/20 test or the square footage test, ABC's expenditures paid or incurred for the acquisition, construction, management, maintenance, or care of its property for the benefit of the tenant-stockholders have to be at least $7,200,000 (90% × $8,000,000) in order for ABC to qualify as a cooperative housing corporation during the tax year.

> *observation:* A cooperative can qualify as a cooperative housing corporation so long as any one of the three alternative tests is satisfied (in addition to the tests described in items (1), (2), and (3) above) during

---

FTC 2d References are to Federal Tax Coordinator 2d
FIN References are to RIA's Analysis of Federal Taxes: Income
USTR References are to United States Tax Reporter: Income, Estate & Gift, and Excise
PCA References are to Pension Analysis (print & electronic)
PE References are to Pension Explanations (print & electronic)
EP References are to Estate Planning Analysis (print & electronic)

the tax year. Since a cooperative's qualification as a cooperative housing corporation is determined for each tax year (i.e., on an annual basis) under Code Sec. 216(b)(1)(D) (see above), a cooperative could presumably qualify under a different test (i.e., the 80/20 test, the square footage test, or the expenditures test) in each tax year.

Congress believes that the tax rules (such as the 80/20 test described in item (a) or item (4) above) should not create an incentive for a cooperative housing corporation to charge below-market-rate rents. (Com Rept, see ¶ 5002)

☐ **Effective:** Tax years ending after Dec. 20, 2007. (2007 Mortgage Relief Act §4(b))

¶ 1303. Hotels and motels are lodging facilities for qualified REIT subsidiaries purposes regardless of whether rentals are transient

Code Sec. 856(d)(9)(D)(ii), as amended by 2007 Technical Corrections Act § 9(b)
Generally effective: For tax years beginning after Dec. 31, 2007
Committee Reports, see ¶ 5308

A corporation qualifies as a REIT only if, in addition to other tests, it satisfies a two-fold income test under which it must derive at least 95% of its income from real property rents and securities and 75% of its income from real property rents and other real property related items. Rents from (i) corporations in which a REIT owned 10% or more of the total combined voting power of all classes of stock, or 10% or more of the total number of shares of all classes of stock or (ii) other entities in which the REIT owned a 10% or greater interest in the assets or net profits are excluded from rents from real property. However, an exception applies for rents paid by a taxable REIT subsidiary:

• where at least 90% of the leased space of the property is rented to persons other than taxable REIT subsidiaries of the REIT and other 10%-owned persons to the extent that the amounts paid to the REIT as rents from real property are substantially comparable to rents paid by the other tenants of the REIT's property for comparable space; or

• relating to an interest in real property that is a qualified lodging facility leased by the REIT to a taxable REIT subsidiary of the REIT, if the property is operated on behalf of the subsidiary by an eligible independent contractor. (FTC 2d/FIN ¶ E-6527.1; USTR ¶ 8564.045)

Under pre-2007 Technical Corrections Act law, a qualified lodging facility was any lodging facility unless wagering activities were conducted at or in connection with the facility by any person who was engaged in the business of accepting wagers and was legally authorized to engage in that business at or in connection with such facility. A lodging facility was a hotel, motel, or other establishment in which more than one-half of the dwelling units were used on a transient basis.

The requirement that more than one-half of the dwelling units were used on a transient basis raised concerns in situations where people dislodged from their homes because of disasters and people providing disaster relief were housed in hotels and motels for more than a brief period. IRS issued Notice 2005-89 and Notice 2006-58 which provided that temporary lodging provided to certain persons (e.g., survivors and relief workers) in certain situations relating to Hurricane Katrina or Hurricane Rita would not cause a facility to fail to be a lodging facility. (FTC 2d/FIN ¶ E-6527.3; USTR ¶ 8564.045)

New Law. The 2007 Technical Corrections Act provides that a lodging facility is a

(1) hotel (Code Sec. 856(d)(9)(D)(ii)(I) as amended by 2007 Technical Corrections Act §9(b));

(2) motel (Code Sec. 856(d)(9)(D)(ii)(II)); or

(3) other establishment in which more than one-half of the dwelling units are used on a transient basis. (Code Sec. 856(d)(9)(D)(ii)(III)).

Thus, the requirement that more than one-half of the dwelling units are used on a transient basis does not apply to hotels and motels. (Com Rept, see ¶ 5308)

☐ **Effective:** For tax years beginning after December 31, 2000. (2007 Technical Corrections Act §9(c))

The 2007 Technical Corrections Act (§9(c) provides that the above provision is effective as if included in the provision of the Tax Relief Extension Act of 1999 to which it relates. The technical correction provision relates to Tax Relief Extension Act of 1999 §542 (Sec. 542, PL 106-170, 12/17/1999) which, under Tax Relief Extension Act of 1999 §546(a) (Sec. 546(a), PL 106-170, 12/17/1999) is effective for tax years beginning after Dec. 31, 2000.

FTC 2d References are to Federal Tax Coordinator 2d
FIN References are to RIA's Analysis of Federal Taxes: Income
USTR References are to United States Tax Reporter: Income, Estate & Gift, and Excise
PCA References are to Pension Analysis (print & electronic)
PE References are to Pension Explanations (print & electronic)
EP References are to Estate Planning Analysis (print & electronic)

¶ 1304. Permitted redactions to Chief Counsel Advice otherwise open to public inspection include redactions to background file documents related to Chief Counsel Advice issued after Oct. 20, '98

Code Sec. 6110(i)(3), as amended by 2007 Technical Corrections Act § 10(a)

Generally effective: Chief Counsel Advice issued after Oct. 20, '98

Committee Reports, see ¶ 5309

Chief Counsel Advice is subject to public disclosure in a manner similar to technical advice memoranda or other written determinations (see FTC 2d/FIN ¶ T-10401; USTR ¶ 61,104). "Chief Counsel Advice" (CCA) is defined as advice or instruction, under whatever name or designation, prepared by any national office component of the Office of Chief Counsel, which is issued to field or service center employees of IRS or regional or district employees of the Office of Chief Counsel; and conveys any legal interpretation of a revenue provision; any IRS or Office of Chief Counsel position or policy concerning a revenue provision, or any legal interpretation of state, foreign, or other federal law relating to the assessment or collection of any liability under a revenue provision. (FTC 2d/FIN ¶ T-10423; USTR ¶ 61,104.07)

CCA includes field service advice, technical assistance to the field, service center advice, litigation guideline memoranda, tax litigation bulletins, general litigation bulletins, and criminal tax bulletins. The definition applies not only to the case-specific field service advice issued from the offices of the Associate Chief Counsel (International), Associate Chief Counsel (Employee Benefits and Exempt Organizations), and the Assistant Chief Counsel (Field Service), but also to any case-specific or noncase-specific written advice or instructions issued by the National Office of Chief Counsel to field personnel of either the IRS or the Office of Chief Counsel. CCA includes any documents created after July 22, '98 that satisfy the general statutory definition, regardless of their name or designation. CCA also includes this advice or instruction even if the organizations currently issuing them are reorganized or reconstituted as part of IRS restructuring. The definition of CCA, however, is not meant to include advice written with respect to nontax matters, including but not limited to employment law, conflicts of interest, or procurement matters. See FTC 2d ¶ T-10420; USTR ¶ 61,104.

For CCA that is open to public inspection, the deletions from disclosure listed in Code Sec. 6110(c)(2) through Code Sec. 6110(c)(7) (see FTC 2d/FIN ¶ T-10404; USTR ¶ 61,104) do not apply. IRS may instead make the following deletions of material under the Freedom of Information Act (FOIA): types of matters that are not subject to disclosure under FOIA, such as procedures related to internal personnel practices (see 5 USC §552(b)); and records or information compiled for law enforcement purposes that are excluded from disclosure requirements when there is an ongoing investigation involving a possible violation of criminal law (see 5 USC §552(c)). See FTC 2d/FIN ¶ T-10423; USTR ¶ 61,104.07.

> ♥ *observation:* The deletions from disclosure listed in Code Sec. 6110(c)(2) through Code Sec. 6110(c)(7) (i.e., the deletions from disclosure that don't apply to CCAs) are classified national security secrets, information exempt from disclosure under any statute applicable to IRS, trade secrets and confidential business information, information that would invade personal privacy if disclosed, information in reports prepared by an agency responsible for supervising financial institutions, and geological and geophysical information about wells, see FTC 2d/FIN ¶ T-10404; USTR ¶ 61,104. However, Code Sec. 6110(c)(1), which exempts from disclosure names, addresses, or any other identifying details of the person the written determination is about, continues to apply to CCAs and to background file documents, see FTC 2d/FIN ¶ T-10404; USTR ¶ 61,104.

Pre-2007 Technical Corrections Act law did not expressly address redactions to the "background file documents" of CCA. (Com Rept, see ¶ 5309)

New Law. The 2007 Technical Corrections Act clarifies that the CCA background file documents are governed by the same redactions as CCAs. (Com Rept, see ¶ 5309) The 2007 Technical Corrections Act adds the phrase "and related background file documents" to the permitted deletions from CCA. Thus, in the case of CCA *and related background file documents* open to public inspection under Code Sec. 6110 (Code Sec. 6110(i)(3) as amended by 2007 Technical Corrections Act §10(a)), the deletions from disclosure listed in Code Sec. 6110(c)(2) through Code Sec. 6110(c)(7) (described above) do not apply (Code Sec. 6110(i)(3)(A)), and IRS may make the deletions of material under FOIA noted above. (Code Sec. 6110(i)(3)(B))

> ♥ *observation:* Presumably, since CCAs include field service advice, technical assistance memorandum, service center advice, litigation guideline memoranda, tax litigation bulletins, general litigation bulletins, and criminal tax bulletins, this background file rule also applies to IRS background files for those documents.

☐ **Effective:** Chief Counsel Advice issued after Oct. 20, '98. (2007 Technical Corrections Act §10(b))

FTC 2d References are to Federal Tax Coordinator 2d
FIN References are to RIA's Analysis of Federal Taxes: Income
USTR References are to United States Tax Reporter: Income, Estate & Gift, and Excise
PCA References are to Pension Analysis (print & electronic)
PE References are to Pension Explanations (print & electronic)
EP References are to Estate Planning Analysis (print & electronic)

⊘observation: The 2007 Technical Corrections Act provides that the amendment made by 2007 Technical Corrections Act §10(a) takes effect as if it were included in '98 IRS Restructuring and Reform Act §3509(b) (Sec. 3509(b), PL 105-206, 7/22/1998). '98 IRS Restructuring and Reform Act §3509(d)(1) (Sec. 3509(d)(1), PL 105-206, 7/22/1998) provided that the provision applies to any CCA issued 90 days after the date of enactment. The enactment date was July 22, '98. '98 IRS Restructuring and Reform Act §3509(d)(2) (Sec. 3509(d)(2), PL 105-206, 7/22/1998) also contains the transitional rules for the effective date of the disclosure rules for older IRS documents, see FTC 2d/FIN ¶ T-10429; USTR ¶ 61,104.

¶ 1400. Client Letters

¶ 1401. Extension of relief from the AMT in the Tax Increase Prevention Act of 2007

> **To the practitioner:** You can use the following letter to inform clients of these important provisions in the Tax Increase Prevention Act of 2007. For analysis of the AMT exemption amount changes for 2007, see ¶ 101. For analysis of the change allowing nonrefundable personal credits to offset AMT through 2007, see ¶ 102. For analysis of the liberalization of the AMT refundable credit amount, see ¶ 103.

Dear Client,

I am writing to provide details regarding two key provisions in the recently enacted Tax Increase Prevention Act of 2007 which extend partial relief to individual taxpayers from the alternative minimum tax, or AMT. Earlier temporary measures to deal with the AMT expired at the end of 2006, meaning that more than 20 million additional taxpayers would have faced paying the tax on their 2007 returns without the new relief.

Brief overview of the AMT.

The AMT is a parallel tax system which does not permit several of the deductions permissible under the regular tax system, such as state, local and property taxes. Taxpayers who may be subject to the AMT must calculate their tax liability under the regular federal tax system and under the AMT system taking into account certain "preferences" and "adjustments." If their liability is found to be greater under the AMT system, that's what they owe the federal government. Originally enacted to make sure that wealthy Americans did not escape paying taxes, the AMT has started to apply to more middle-income taxpayers, due in part to the fact that the AMT parameters are not indexed for inflation.

In recent years, Congress has provided a measure of relief from the AMT by raising the AMT "exemption amounts"—allowances that reduce the amount of alternative minimum taxable income (AMTI), reducing or eliminating AMT liability. (However, these exemption amounts are phased out for taxpayers whose AMTI exceeds specified amounts.) For 2006, the AMT exemption amounts were $62,550 for married couples filing jointly and surviving spouses; $42,500 for single taxpayers; and $31,275 for mar-

---

FTC 2d References are to Federal Tax Coordinator 2d
FIN References are to RIA's Analysis of Federal Taxes: Income
USTR References are to United States Tax Reporter: Income, Estate & Gift, and Excise
PCA References are to Pension Analysis (print & electronic)
PE References are to Pension Explanations (print & electronic)
EP References are to Estate Planning Analysis (print & electronic)

ried filing separately. However, for 2007, those amounts were scheduled to fall back to the amounts that applied in 2000: $45,000, $33,750, and $22,500, respectively. This would have brought millions of additional middle-income Americans under the AMT system, resulting in higher federal tax bills for many of them, along with higher compliance costs associated with filling out and filing the complicated AMT tax form.

New law provides one-year stopgap fix.

To prevent the unintended result of having millions of middle-income taxpayers fall prey to the AMT, Congress has once again relied on a temporary "patch" to the problem, this time a one-year extension of the 2006 AMT exemption amounts, increased slightly. Under the new law, for tax years beginning in 2007, the AMT exemption amounts are increased to: (1) $66,250 in the case of married individuals filing a joint return and surviving spouses; (2) $44,350 in the case of unmarried individuals other than surviving spouses; and (3) $33,125 in the case of married individuals filing a separate return.

Personal credits may be used to offset AMT through 2007.

Another provision in the new law provides AMT relief for taxpayers claiming personal tax credits. The tax liability limitation rules generally provide that certain nonrefundable personal credits (including the dependent care credit, the elderly and disabled credit, and the Hope Scholarship and Lifetime Learning credits) are allowed only to the extent that a taxpayer has regular income tax liability in excess of the tentative minimum tax, which has the effect of disallowing these credits against AMT. Temporary provisions had been enacted which permitted these credits to offset the entire regular and AMT liability through the end of 2006. The new law extends this temporary provision to tax years beginning in 2007.

AMT refundable credit amount liberalized.

I should also note that in a technical correction, the AMT refundable credit amount was liberalized. To understand this change, you need to go back to 2006, when, in an effort to help taxpayers who were stung by the AMT as a result of exercising incentive stock options (ISOs), legislation was enacted that increased the amount of the minimum tax credit ("MTC" or "AMT credit") and made it partially refundable. For tax years starting in 2007 and before 2013, individuals with unused MTCs that are long-term (i.e., more than three years old) are entitled to an AMT refundable credit, subject to a phase-out based on adjusted gross income (AGI). As originally enacted, the AMT refundable credit for a tax year could be as much as 20% of the taxpayer's long-term unused MTC for the year. The taxpayer's long-term unused MTC is reduced by the amount of the AMT refundable credit.

Before the technical correction, if the taxpayer had no additional long-term unused MTCs, his credit would decrease in later years.

Under the technical correction, the taxpayer's AMT refundable credit for a tax year is the amount (not exceeding long-term unused MTC for the year) equal to the greater of:

(1) $5,000;

(2) 20% of the long-term unused MTC; or

(3) the AMT refundable credit amount (if any) for the prior tax year— the preceding year's credit amount (before any AGI-based reduction).

Thus, a taxpayer who doesn't have additional unused long-term MTCs uses the preceding year's credit amount (or $5,000, if greater) as his AMT refundable credit, provided he has sufficient long-term unused MTC. This allows taxpayers to claim the full 20% amount they claimed in the first year (e.g., 2007) per year for five years, provided their AGI does not reach the phase-out range.

I hope this information is helpful. If you would like more details about these changes, or any other aspects of the new law, please do not hesitate to call.

Very truly yours,

¶ 1402. Forgiven mortgage debt relief in the Mortgage Forgiveness Debt Relief Act of 2007

To the practitioner: You can use the following letter to inform clients of this important provision in the 2007 Mortgage Relief Act. For analysis of this exclusion of discharges of up to $2 million of acquisition debt on a taxpayer's main home in 2007 through 2009, see ¶ 201.

Dear Client,

Addressing the subprime lending crisis, Congress recently passed and the President signed into law a new measure giving tax breaks to homeowners who have mortgage debt forgiven. Under preexisting law, the debt forgiven by a lender, such as for short sales and refinances, was generally taxable to the borrower as debt discharge income. With the passage of the Mortgage Forgiveness Debt Relief Act of 2007, a taxpayer does not have to pay federal income tax on up to $2 million of debt forgiven for a loan secured by a qualified principal residence. The change in the tax law applies to debts discharged from January 1, 2007 to December 31, 2009. Here are the details.

Discharge of indebtedness income: background.

For income tax purposes, a discharge of indebtedness—that is, a forgiveness of debt—is generally treated as giving rise to income that's includible in gross income. However, a discharge of indebtedness doesn't give rise to gross income if it: (1) occurs in a Title 11 bankruptcy case, (2) occurs when the taxpayer is insolvent, (3) is a discharge of qualified farm indebtedness, or (4) is a discharge of qualified real property business indebtedness.

Under pre-2007 Mortgage Relief Act law, there were no special rules applicable to discharges of acquisition debt on the taxpayer's principal residence. For example, assume a taxpayer who isn't in bankruptcy and isn't insolvent owns a principal residence subject to a $200,000 mortgage debt for which the taxpayer has personal liability. The creditor forecloses and the home is sold for $180,000 in satisfaction of the debt. Under pre-2007 Mortgage Relief Act law, the debtor had $20,000 of debt discharge income. The result was the same if the creditor restructured the loan and reduced the principal amount to $180,000.

New law relief provision.

FTC 2d References are to Federal Tax Coordinator 2d
FIN References are to RIA's Analysis of Federal Taxes: Income
USTR References are to United States Tax Reporter: Income, Estate & Gift, and Excise
PCA References are to Pension Analysis (print & electronic)
PE References are to Pension Explanations (print & electronic)
EP References are to Estate Planning Analysis (print & electronic)

The 2007 Mortgage Relief Act excludes from a taxpayer's gross income any discharge of indebtedness income by reason of a discharge (in whole or in part) of qualified principal residence indebtedness before Jan. 1, 2010. The exclusion applies where taxpayers restructure their acquisition debt on a principal residence or lose their principal residence in a foreclosure. For example, assume the same facts as in the example above except that the discharge occurs in 2008. Under the 2007 Mortgage Relief Act, the debtor has no debt discharge income when the creditor (1) restructures the loan and reduces the principal amount to $180,000 or (2) forecloses with the result that the $200,000 debt is satisfied for $180,000.

Here is some of the critical fine print in this new relief provision:

• The tax relief applies to the original purchase price, plus improvements, of the taxpayer's principal residence. It doesn't apply to discharges of second mortgages or home equity loans, unless the loan proceeds were used to acquire, construct, or substantially improve the taxpayer's principal residence. Refinanced indebtedness qualifies to the extent it doesn't exceed the amount of indebtedness being refinanced. (Cash out from refinancing doesn't qualify for the exclusion.)

• The indebtedness must be incurred with respect to the taxpayer's principal residence only. The exclusion rule doesn't apply to second homes, vacation homes, business property, or investment property, since these properties aren't the taxpayer's principal residence.

• The relief provision is not a permanent fixture of the tax code. It only applies to forgiveness during 2007, 2008, or 2009.

• Nontaxable forgiven mortgage debt is capped at $2 million ($1 million for married individuals filing separately).

• When the relief provision applies, the basis of the individual's principal residence is reduced by the amount excluded from income. As a result of this basis reduction rule, the discharged indebtedness is, at least technically, subject to taxation at a later time, when the taxpayer sells or exchanges the principal residence. However, in many cases the reduction won't result in any additional tax, because any gain on that sale or exchange will qualify for the $250,000 ($500,000 for married couples filing jointly) home-sale exclusion.

Please keep in mind that this is only a summary of this important tax relief provision. If you would like more details about this change, or any other aspect of the new law, please do not hesitate to call.

Very truly yours,

¶ 1403. Mortgage insurance deduction extended for three years in the Mortgage Forgiveness Debt Relief Act of 2007

> **To the practitioner:** You can use the following letter to inform clients of this important provision in the 2007 Mortgage Relief Act. For analysis of this extension of the interest deduction for mortgage insurance premiums to amounts paid or incurred after 2007 and before 2011, see ¶ 202.

Dear Client,

Mortgage insurance will continue to be deductible after 2007, thanks to a key provision in the recently enacted Mortgage Forgiveness Debt Relief Act of 2007. The new law extends the mortgage interest deduction, which was set to expire at the end of 2007, for three years (through 2010). Here is a brief overview of this potentially valuable deduction.

Financing a home with a small down payment.

When you buy a house, lenders consider you a riskier borrower if you make a down payment of less than 20%. There are two main ways to make you pay for that risk: mortgage insurance and piggyback loans. Mortgage insurance is insurance that is paid for by the borrower, but the lender is the beneficiary. If the borrower falls behind on the loan payments and the lender has to foreclose, the mortgage insurance policy reimburses the lender for legal costs and lost income. The premiums depend on the size of the loan, the percentage of the down payment, the borrower's credit score and the type of mortgage insurance the borrower gets.

Alternatively, a borrower with less than the 20% down payment needed to avoid a mortgage insurance requirement might be able to make use of a second mortgage (sometimes referred to as a piggy-back loan) to make up the difference. One advantage of using a piggy-back arrangement was that under prior (pre-2007) law, mortgage interest payments were deductible on the borrower's income taxes, whereas mortgage insurance premiums were not.

How the mortgage interest deduction works.

Under the deduction that was originated in 2007 and has now been extended for three years (through 2010), taxpayers can treat amounts paid dur-

---

FTC 2d References are to Federal Tax Coordinator 2d
FIN References are to RIA's Analysis of Federal Taxes: Income
USTR References are to United States Tax Reporter: Income, Estate & Gift, and Excise
PCA References are to Pension Analysis (print & electronic)
PE References are to Pension Explanations (print & electronic)
EP References are to Estate Planning Analysis (print & electronic)

ing the year for qualified mortgage insurance as home mortgage interest and thus deductible. The insurance must be in connection with home acquisition debt, the insurance contract must have been issued after 2006, and the taxpayer must have paid the premiums for coverage in effect during the year. Qualified mortgage insurance is mortgage insurance provided by the Department of Veterans Affairs, the Federal Housing Administration, or the Rural Housing Service, and private mortgage insurance (as defined in section 2 of the Homeowners Protection Act of 1998 as in effect on December 20, 2006).

Mortgage insurance provided by the Department of Veterans Affairs is commonly known as a funding fee. If provided by the Rural Housing Service, it is commonly known as a guarantee fee. The funding fee and guarantee fee can either be included in the amount of the loan or paid in full at the time of closing. These fees can be deducted fully in the year the mortgage insurance contract was issued.

Premiums for qualified mortgage insurance that are properly allocable to periods after the close of the tax year are treated as paid in the period to which they are allocated. No deduction is allowed for the unamortized balance if the mortgage is satisfied before its term (except in the case of qualified mortgage insurance provided by the Department of Veterans Affairs or Rural Housing Service).

There are income limits on the deduction. You can get the full deduction if your adjusted gross income is $100,000 or less ($50,000 if your filing status is married filing separately). The amount you can deduct phases out rapidly after that, and no mortgage insurance deduction is available if you make more than $109,000 ($54,500 if married filing separately).

I hope this information is helpful. If you would like more details about these changes or any other aspects of the new law, please do not hesitate to call.

Very truly yours,

¶ 1404. Tax relief for volunteer responders in the Mortgage Forgiveness Debt Relief Act of 2007

> **To the practitioner:** You can use the following client letter to inform clients of this important change in the 2007 Mortgage Relief Act. For analysis of this change in treatment of state and local tax relief and expense reimbursements to volunteer firefighters and emergency medical responders for the 2008 through 2010 tax years, see ¶ 302.

Dear Client,

Tax relief is on the way for volunteer firefighters and emergency medical responders, thanks to a little publicized provision in the recently enacted Mortgage Forgiveness Debt Relief Act of 2007. The new law creates an income tax exclusion for qualified state or local tax benefits (such as reduction or rebate of state or local income or property tax) and qualified reimbursement payments (up to $360 a year) granted to members of qualified volunteer emergency response organizations (e.g., state or local organizations whose members provide volunteer firefighting or emergency medical services (EMS)). The new exclusion will apply for the 2008 through 2010 tax years. Following is a brief overview of this new provision.

Reasons for tax relief.

Many cities and towns in our country depend for their safety on volunteer firefighters and emergency first responders. To help recruit and retain volunteers, some localities offer incentives like property tax abatements to volunteer firefighters, search-and-rescue teams, emergency medical technicians, paramedics and ambulance drivers.

In 2002, volunteer benefits took a hit when the IRS ruled that reductions or rebates of taxes by state or local governments on account of services performed by members of qualified volunteer emergency response organizations are taxable income to the taxpayers receiving these reductions or rebates of taxes. Taxing these benefits reduced their value as an incentive and created a significant administrative burden on small municipalities and townships.

Specifics on the new law.

Under the new legislation, these benefits are tax free. In technical jargon, the new law provides that any qualified state or local tax benefit provided to members of qualified voluntary emergency response organiza-

FTC 2d References are to Federal Tax Coordinator 2d
FIN References are to RIA's Analysis of Federal Taxes: Income
USTR References are to United States Tax Reporter: Income, Estate & Gift, and Excise
PCA References are to Pension Analysis (print & electronic)
PE References are to Pension Explanations (print & electronic)
EP References are to Estate Planning Analysis (print & electronic)

tions (e.g., volunteer firefighters and EMS personnel) on account of their volunteer services is excluded from the member's gross income. This exclusion covers any rebate or reduction of state or local income taxes, real property taxes, or personal property taxes. In addition, the new law allows volunteer firefighters and EMS personnel to exclude from income any qualified payments provided by a state or local government as reimbursement for expenses incurred in connection with their performance of voluntary emergency response services. The amount determined as a qualified payment for any tax year cannot exceed $30 multiplied by the number of months during the year that the taxpayer performs the services. The Act carries provisions to deny double tax benefits for excluded amounts.

The hope is that with these new incentives, volunteer numbers will rise nationwide. The new provisions take effect beginning in 2008 and are scheduled to expire at the end of 2010.

I hope this information is helpful. If you would like more details about this provision or any other aspect of the new law, please do not hesitate to call.

Very truly yours,

¶ 1405. Business and corporate changes in the late-2007 tax laws

> **To the practitioner:** You can use the following letter to provide clients with an overview of the business and corporate changes in the AMT patch, mortgage debt relief, technical corrections and other late-2007 tax laws. For analysis of the increase in the penalty for failure to file a partnership return, see ¶ 1102. For analysis of the new penalty for failure to file an S corporation return, see ¶ 1103. For analysis of the extension of the FUTA surtax through 2008, see ¶ 1201. For analysis of the lengthened amortization period for certain expenses of large integrated oil companies, see ¶ 412. For analysis of the change made to expand housing options for college students with children, see ¶ 902. For analysis of the change helping co-op tenant/owners deduct real estate taxes and mortgage insurance, see ¶ 1302. For analysis of the clarification of the look-through rule for related CFCs, see ¶ 702. For analysis of the revision in the rules for a shareholder basis reduction on account of contributions of appreciated property by S corporations, see ¶ 603. For analysis of the change modifying the Code Sec. 355 active business definition, see ¶ 1301. For analysis of the change clarifying the rules regarding partnerships treated as leases and the tax-exempt loss rules, see ¶ 805.

Dear Client,

In the final days before it adjourned for 2007, Congress passed a long-awaited AMT "patch" for 2007. It also passed two other tax laws of wide interest. These laws provide mortgage debt forgiveness tax relief, other tax breaks and technical corrections, many of which are substantive. Tax changes also were enacted as part of the energy legislation and in a special measure to aid victims of the Virginia Tech shooting in 2007. Some of the changes in the late-2007 legislation directly affect business and corporations. The key changes in this area include:

. . . *Partnership failure to file penalty increased.* Under pre-Mortgage Relief Act law, any partnership required to file a return for any year, which failed to file on time (including extensions) or whose return failed to show the information required, was liable for a monthly penalty equal to $50 times the number of persons who were partners during any part of the tax year, for each month or fraction of a month for which the failure continued. However, the total penalty could not be imposed for more than five months. The Mortgage Relief Act extends the period for calculating the monthly failure-to-file-penalty for partnership returns from 5 to 12 months and increases the per-partner penalty amount from $50 to $85 per partner, effective for returns required to be filed after Dec. 20, 2007. Note also that under the Virginia Tech Victim's Relief Act, for tax years beginning in 2008 only, the dollar

---

FTC 2d References are to Federal Tax Coordinator 2d
FIN References are to RIA's Analysis of Federal Taxes: Income
USTR References are to United States Tax Reporter: Income, Estate & Gift, and Excise
PCA References are to Pension Analysis (print & electronic)
PE References are to Pension Explanations (print & electronic)
EP References are to Estate Planning Analysis (print & electronic)

amount per partner is increased by $1. Thus, for tax years beginning in 2008, the per-partner penalty for failure to file a partnership return is $86.

... *New failure to file penalty for S corporation returns.* Under pre-Mortgage Relief Act law, there was no penalty for failure to file an S corporation return. The Mortgage Relief Act imposes a monthly penalty for any failure to timely file an S corporation return or any failure to provide the information required to be shown on such a return, effective for returns required to be filed after Dec. 20, 2007. The penalty, assessed against the S corporation, is $85 times the number of shareholders in the S corporation during any part of the tax year for which the return was required, for each month (or a fraction of a month) during which the failure continues, up to a maximum of 12 months.

FUTA surtax extended through 2008. The Federal Unemployment Tax Act (FUTA) imposes a 6.2% gross tax rate on the first $7,000 paid annually by covered employers to each employee, consisting of a permanent tax rate of 6%, and a temporary surtax rate of 0.2%. Under pre-Energy Independence and Security Act of 2007 law, the temporary surtax only applied through the end of 2007. Under the Energy Act, the temporary surtax rate (which amounts to $14 per worker) is extended through Dec. 31, 2008. Thus, the FUTA rate remains at 6.2% through the end of 2008.

... *Lengthened amortization period for certain expenses of large integrated oil companies.* Under pre-Energy Act law, major integrated oil companies (certain companies with gross receipts of more than $1 billion for their last tax year ending in 2005) were required to amortize their geological and geophysical expenditures (G&G costs) over five years (instead of the 24 month period that applies for other taxpayers). Effective for amounts paid or incurred after Dec. 19, 2007, major integrated oil companies must amortize their geological and geophysical expenditures over seven years.

... *Help to expand housing options for college students with children.* A change in the Mortgage Forgiveness Debt Relief Act of 2007 clarifies that certain full-time students who are single parents and their children are permitted to live in housing units eligible for the low-income housing tax credit if their children are not dependents of another individual *other than* a parent of such children. In general, this change applies to housing credit amounts allocated before, on or after Dec. 20, 2007, and to buildings placed in service before, on or after Dec. 20, 2007.

... *Flexibility to help co-op tenant/owners deduct real estate taxes and mortgage insurance.* The Mortgage Forgiveness Debt Relief Act of 2007 modifies the requirements for qualifying for the special rules available to cooperative housing corporations. Under pre-Act law, a cooperative housing corporation was required to meet several requirements, including a requirement that 80% or more of the cooperative housing corporation's income be earned from the corporation's tenant-stockholders. The Act provides two alternatives to this 80% rule (i.e., one based on square footage and another based on cooperative expenditures). These two alternatives, which take effect for tax years ending after Dec. 20, 2007, will make it easier to qualify as a cooperative housing corporation.

In addition, other business and corporate changes in the late-'07 tax legislation:

- Clarify the look-through rule for related CFCs.
- Revise the rules for a shareholder basis reduction on account of contributions of appreciated property by S corporations.
- Modify the Code Sec. 355 active business definition.
- Clarify the tax-exempt use loss rules.

Please keep in mind that this is only a summary of these new provisions. If you would like more details about these or any other aspect of the new law, please do not hesitate to call.

Very truly yours,

FTC 2d References are to Federal Tax Coordinator 2d
FIN References are to RIA's Analysis of Federal Taxes: Income
USTR References are to United States Tax Reporter: Income, Estate & Gift, and Excise
PCA References are to Pension Analysis (print & electronic)
PE References are to Pension Explanations (print & electronic)
EP References are to Estate Planning Analysis (print & electronic)

¶ 1406. Payroll and penalty provisions in the late-2007 tax legislation

> **To the practitioner:** You can use the following client letter to inform clients of these important changes in the late-2007 tax legislation. For analysis of the increase in the penalty for failure to file a partnership return, see ¶ 1102. For analysis of the new penalty for failure to file an S corporation return, see ¶ 1103. For analysis of the changes in the penalty for valuation misstatements attributable to incorrect appraisals, see ¶ 1101. For analysis of the extension of the FUTA surtax through 2008, see ¶ 1201. For analysis of the rule providing that designated Roth contributions are subject to FICA, see ¶ 1202.

Dear Client,

Contained in the flurry of legislation passed by Congress at the end of 2007—including the Mortgage Forgiveness Debt Relief Act of 2007, the Tax Technical Corrections Act of 2007, the Energy Independence and Security Act of 2007 and the Virginia Tech Victim's Relief Act—were measures that included new or revised payroll and tax penalty provisions. Here is a quick overview of the payroll and penalty provisions in the new law.

Partnership failure to file penalty increased.

Under pre-Mortgage Relief Act law, any partnership required to file a return for any year, which failed to file on time (including extensions) or whose return failed to show the information required, was liable for a monthly penalty equal to $50 times the number of persons who were partners during any part of the tax year, for each month or fraction of a month for which the failure continued. However, the total penalty could not be imposed for more than five months. The Mortgage Relief Act extends the period for calculating the monthly failure-to-file-penalty for partnership returns from 5 to 12 months and increases the per-partner penalty amount from $50 to $85 per partner, effective for returns required to be filed after Dec. 20, 2007. Note also that under the Virginia Tech Victim's Relief Act, for tax years beginning in 2008 only, the dollar amount per partner is increased by $1. Thus, for tax years beginning in 2008, the per-partner penalty for failure to file a partnership return is $86.

New failure to file penalty for S corporation returns.

Under pre-Mortgage Relief Act law, there was no penalty for failure to file an S corporation return. The Mortgage Relief Act imposes a monthly

---

FTC 2d References are to Federal Tax Coordinator 2d
FIN References are to RIA's Analysis of Federal Taxes: Income
USTR References are to United States Tax Reporter: Income, Estate & Gift, and Excise
PCA References are to Pension Analysis (print & electronic)
PE References are to Pension Explanations (print & electronic)
EP References are to Estate Planning Analysis (print & electronic)

penalty for any failure to timely file an S corporation return or any failure to provide the information required to be shown on such a return, effective for returns required to be filed after Dec. 20, 2007. The penalty, assessed against the S corporation, is $85 times the number of shareholders in the S corporation during any part of the tax year for which the return was required, for each month (or a fraction of a month) during which the failure continues, up to a maximum of 12 months.

Penalty for substantial and gross valuation misstatements attributable to incorrect appraisals.

In the 2006 Pension Protection Act, a penalty was added for substantial and gross valuation misstatements attributable to incorrect appraisals. That legislation omitted to apply the penalty with respect to substantial valuation understatements for estate and gift tax purposes. The Tax Technical Corrections Act of 2007 clarifies that the penalty applies for such purposes. The 2006 Pension Protection Act made another omission in the cross references for the penalty where the language relating to the time period for assessment of the penalty was not properly described. The new legislation corrects that error by providing that the penalty for valuation misstatements attributable to incorrect appraisals is subject to a 3-year limitation period.

FUTA surtax extended through 2008.

The Federal Unemployment Tax Act (FUTA) imposes a 6.2% gross tax rate on the first $7,000 paid annually by covered employers to each employee, consisting of a permanent tax rate of 6%, and a temporary surtax rate of 0.2%. Under pre-Energy Act law, the temporary surtax only applied through the end of 2007. Under the Energy Act, the temporary surtax rate (which amounts to $14 per worker) is extended through Dec. 31, 2008. Thus, the FUTA rate remains at 6.2% through the end of 2008.

Designated Roth contributions are subject to FICA.

Beginning in 2006, plan sponsors have been able to offer their employees the ability to make after-tax 401(k) contributions where earnings are not usually taxed on distribution. These contributions are called "Roth contributions." The Tax Technical Corrections Act of 2007 clarifies that Roth contributions are subject to FICA taxes (i.e., Social Security and Medicare) at the time they are made.

I hope this information is helpful. If you would like more details about these provisions or any other aspect of the new laws, please do not hesitate to call.

Very truly yours,

¶ 1407. Cash rebate provisions in the Economic Stimulus Act of 2008

> **To the practitioner:** You can use the following client letter to inform clients of the rebate provisions in the Economic Stimulus Act of 2008. For analysis of the cash rebate provisions, see ¶ 101.

Dear Client,

By now, you've probably heard about the recently-passed economic stimulus package (the Economic Stimulus Act of 2008), the centerpiece of which is the government's issuance of rebate checks to most Americans. In brief, the measure will bring tax rebates of $600 for individuals and $1,200 for couples to most taxpayers and $300 checks to low-income people, including disabled veterans and the elderly. Here are the key details of the rebate provisions in the stimulus package.

Amount of rebate. Eligible individuals will receive a rebate for 2008 equal to the greater of:

(1) the taxpayer's net income tax liability, up to a maximum of $600 ($1,200 for a joint return); or

(2) $300 ($600 for a joint return) if either (a) the taxpayer's qualifying income is at least $3,000; or (b) his net income tax liability is at least $1 and gross income is greater than the sum of the applicable basic standard deduction amount and one personal exemption (two personal exemptions for a joint return). Qualifying income is earned income generally, social security benefits, and veterans' disability payments (including payments to survivors of disabled veterans).

There is an additional $300 credit for each qualifying child for whom the child tax credit can be claimed. This is generally a dependent child who is under age 17 at the end of the year.

The amount of the rebate credit (both the basic and qualifying child amounts) will phase out at a rate of 5% of adjusted gross income (AGI) above $75,000 ($150,000 for joint returns). For joint filers with no children who would otherwise get the maximum $1,200 basic credit, the credit will be entirely lost at AGI of $174,000. A single filer with no children who

---

FTC 2d References are to Federal Tax Coordinator 2d
FIN References are to RIA's Analysis of Federal Taxes: Income
USTR References are to United States Tax Reporter: Income, Estate & Gift, and Excise
PCA References are to Pension Analysis (print & electronic)
PE References are to Pension Explanations (print & electronic)
EP References are to Estate Planning Analysis (print & electronic)

would otherwise get the maximum $600 basic credit will lose the entire credit at AGI of $87,000.

The amount of the rebate is not includible in gross income and does not otherwise reduce the amount of withholding. The rebates will be subject to offsets for items like past-due child support and debts owed to the federal government.

Eligible individuals. An eligible individual is any individual other than a nonresident alien, a dependent, or an estate or trust. Residents of the U.S. possessions will also receive the benefit. However, in an effort to bar illegal immigrants from receiving rebates, the rebate will not be available if an individual's tax return does not include social security numbers of the taxpayer, spouse, and any qualifying children. Taxpayer identification numbers (ITINs) that the Internal Revenue Service issues to aliens who are ineligible for social security numbers are not valid for this purpose.

Delivery of rebate checks. Most taxpayers will receive the credit in the form of a check issued by the Treasury. The amount of that check will be computed on the basis of tax returns filed for 2007 (instead of 2008).

Treasury will make every effort to issue payments as rapidly as possible to taxpayers who filed their 2007 tax returns on time. Taxpayers who file late or on extension will receive their payments later. No rebate checks will be issued after Dec. 31, 2008.

When taxpayers file their 2008 returns early in 2009, they will reconcile the amount of the credit with the rebate they received in the following manner. They will complete a worksheet calculating the amount of the credit based on their 2008 tax return. They will then subtract from the credit the amount of the rebate they received.

For many taxpayers, these two amounts will be the same. However, if the result is a positive number (because, for example, the taxpayer paid no tax in 2007 but is paying tax in 2008), the taxpayer will be able to claim that amount as a credit against 2008 tax liability. If the result is negative (because, for example, the taxpayer paid tax in 2007 but owes no tax for 2008), the taxpayer will not be required to repay the rebate amount to the Treasury.

I hope this information is helpful. If you would like more details about this or any other aspect of the new law, please do not hesitate to call.

Very truly yours,

¶ 1408. Business incentives in the Economic Stimulus Act of 2008

To the practitioner: You can use the following client letter to inform clients of these important business incentive provisions in the Economic Stimulus Act of 2008. For analysis of expanded expensing for 2008, see ¶ 201. For analysis of bonus depreciation for 2008, see ¶ 202. For analysis of the increased first-year depreciation limit for passenger automobiles, see ¶ 203.

Dear Client,

As you probably know, Congress recently passed an economic stimulus package (the Economic Stimulus Act of 2008) which is intended to jump-start our economy, in part through tax incentives aimed at encouraging businesses to increase their investments in new equipment by the end of 2008. Under the Act, small businesses will be able to write off up to $250,000 of qualifying expenses in 2008. In addition, businesses will be able to deduct an additional 50% of the cost of certain investments in 2008. Here are the details.

Boosted section 179 expensing. Under pre-Act law, taxpayers can expense (i.e., deduct currently, as opposed to taking depreciation deductions over a period of years) up to $128,000 for 2008. This annual expensing limit is reduced (but not below zero) by the amount by which the cost of qualifying property placed in service during 2008 exceeds $510,000. The expensing rules are eased for qualifying empowerment zone property, renewal property, and GO Zone property. The amount of the expensing deduction is limited to the amount of taxable income from any of the taxpayer's active trades or businesses.

Under the Act, for tax years beginning in 2008, the $128,000 expensing limit is increased to $250,000, and the overall investment limit is increased from $510,000 to $800,000.

As a result of this incentive, most small businesses, and even some moderate-sized businesses with moderate capital equipment needs, will be able to obtain a full deduction for the cost of business machinery and equipment purchased in 2008, thereby reducing their effective cost for those assets. What's more, there is no alternative minimum tax (AMT) adjustment with respect to property expensed under Code Sec. 179.

FTC 2d References are to Federal Tax Coordinator 2d
FIN References are to RIA's Analysis of Federal Taxes: Income
USTR References are to United States Tax Reporter: Income, Estate & Gift, and Excise
PCA References are to Pension Analysis (print & electronic)
PE References are to Pension Explanations (print & electronic)
EP References are to Estate Planning Analysis (print & electronic)

Bonus depreciation makes a comeback. Bonus first year depreciation was first allowed following the terrorist attacks of 2001 but generally isn't available for property acquired after 2004. (There are some exceptions, such as for qualified GO Zone property generally placed in service before 2008.)

The Act provides for bonus (accelerated) depreciation by allowing a bonus first-year depreciation deduction of 50% of the adjusted basis of qualified property placed in service after Dec. 31, 2007, and, generally, before Jan. 1, 2009. The basis of the property and the depreciation allowances in the year the property is placed in service and later years are appropriately adjusted to reflect the additional first-year depreciation deduction. The amount of the additional first-year depreciation deduction is not affected by a short taxable year. The taxpayer may elect out of additional first-year depreciation for any class of property for any taxable year.

The interaction of the additional first-year depreciation allowance with the otherwise applicable depreciation allowance may be illustrated as follows. Assume that in 2008 a taxpayer purchases new depreciable property and places it in service. The property's cost is $1,000 and it is 5-year property subject to the half-year convention. The amount of additional first-year depreciation allowed under the provision is $500. The remaining $500 of the cost of the property is deductible under the rules applicable to 5-year property. Thus, 20 percent, or $100, is also allowed as a depreciation deduction in 2008. Accordingly, the total depreciation deduction with respect to the property for 2008 is $600. The remaining $400 cost of the property is recovered under otherwise applicable rules for computing depreciation.

Bonus depreciation is allowed for AMT purposes as well as for regular tax purposes. Additionally, bonus depreciation is permitted only for: (1) property to which MACRS applies that has an applicable recovery period of 20 years or less, (2) water utility property, (3) non-custom-made computer software, and (4) qualified leasehold improvement property. Original use of the property must begin with the taxpayer after Dec. 31, 2007. Additionally, the placed-in-service cutoff date is extended for an additional year (i.e., before Jan. 1, 2010) for certain property with a recovery period of ten years or longer and certain transportation and aircraft property.

The otherwise applicable "luxury auto" cap on first-year depreciation is increased by $8,000 for vehicles that qualify.

I hope this information is helpful. If you would like more details about these aspects or any other aspect of the new law, please do not hesitate to call.

Very truly yours,

[¶ 3000]   **Code as Amended**

This section reproduces Code as Amended, by the Tax Increase Prevention Act of 2007, P.L. 110-166, 12/26/2007, the Mortgage Forgiveness Debt Relief Act of 2007, P.L. 110-142, 12/20/2007, the Energy Independence and Security Act of 2007, P.L. 110-140, 12/19/2007, the Tax Technical Corrections Act of 2007, PL 110-172, 12/29/2007, the 2007 Virginia Tech Victims Act, PL 110-141, 12/19/2007, the Consolidated Appropriations Act, 2008, PL 110-161, 12/26/2007, and the Economic Stimulus Act of 2008, P.L. 110-185, Code sections appear in order, as amended, added or repealed. New matter is shown in *italics*. All changes and effective dates are shown in the endnotes.

[¶ 3001]   **Code Sec. 1.**   **Tax imposed.**

* * * * * * * * * * * *

(i)   **Rate reductions after 2000.**

    (1)   **10-percent rate bracket.**

       (A) In general. In the case of taxable years beginning after December 31, 2000—

         (i) the rate of tax under subsections (a), (b), (c), and (d) on taxable income not over the initial bracket amount shall be 10 percent, and

         (ii) the 15 percent rate of tax shall apply only to taxable income over the initial bracket amount but not over the maximum dollar amount for the 15-percent rate bracket.

       (B) Initial bracket amount. For purposes of this paragraph, the initial bracket amount is—

         (i) $14,000 in the case of subsection (a),

         (ii) $10,000 in the case of subsection (b), and

         (iii) ½ the amount applicable under clause (i) (after adjustment, if any, under subparagraph (C)) in the case of subsections (c) and (d).

       (C) Inflation adjustment. In prescribing the tables under subsection (f) which apply with respect to taxable years beginning in calendar years after 2003—

         (i) the cost-of-living adjustment shall be determined under subsection (f)(3) by substituting "2002" for "1992" in subparagraph (B) thereof, and

         (ii) the adjustments under clause (i) shall not apply to the amount referred to in subparagraph (B)(iii).

       If any amount after adjustment under the preceding sentence is not a multiple of $50, such amount shall be rounded to the next lowest multiple of $50.

       [1]*(D) Repealed.*

       [For Analysis, see ¶ 51. For Committee Reports, see ¶ 5501.]

[Endnote Code Sec. 1]

    Matter in *italics* in Code Sec. 1(i)(1)(D) was added by Sec. 101(f)(2) of the Economic Stimulus Act of 2008, P.L. 110-185, 2/13/2008, which struck out:

1. "(D) Coordination with acceleration of 10 percent rate bracket benefit for 2001. This paragraph shall not apply to any taxable year to which section 6428 applies."

Effective Date Enacted 2/13/2008

[¶ 3002]   **Code Sec. 21.**   **Expenses for household and dependent care services necessary for gainful employment.**

* * * * * * * * * * * *

    (e)   **Special rules.** For purposes of this section—

* * * * * * * * * * * *

(5)　Special dependency test in case of divorced parents, etc. If—

(A)　section 152(e) applies to any child with respect to any calendar year, and

(B)　such child is under the age of 13 or is physically or mentally incapable of caring for himself,

in the case of any taxable year beginning in such calendar year, such child shall be treated as a qualifying individual described in subparagraph (A) or (B) of subsection (b)(1) (whichever is appropriate) with respect to the custodial parent (as defined in [1]*section 152(e)(4)(A)*), and shall not be treated as a qualifying individual with respect to the noncustodial parent.

* * * * * * * * * * * *

[For Analysis, see ¶ 102. For Committee Reports, see ¶ 5201.]

[Endnote Code Sec. 21]

Matter in *italics* in Code Sec. 21(e)(5) was added by Sec. 11(a)(1) of the Tax Technical Corrections Act of 2007, P.L. 110-172, 12/29/2007, which struck out:

1. "section 152(e)(3)(A)"

Effective Date (P.L. 110-172, 12/29/2007) enacted 12/29/2007.

[¶ 3003]　　Code Sec. 24.　　Child tax credit.

* * * * * * * * * * * *

(d)　Portion of credit refundable.

(1)　In general. The aggregate credits allowed to a taxpayer under subpart C shall be increased by the lesser of—

(A)　the credit which would be allowed under this section without regard to this subsection and the limitation under section 26(a)(2) or subsection (b)(3), as the case may be, or

(B)　the amount by which the aggregate amount of credits allowed by this subpart (determined without regard to this subsection) would increase if the limitation imposed by section 26(a)(2) or subsection (b)(3), as the case may be, were increased by [1]*the greater of*—

(i)　15 percent of so much of the taxpayer's earned income (within the meaning of section 32) which is taken into account in computing taxable income for the taxable year as exceeds $10,000, or

(ii)　in the case of a taxpayer with 3 or more qualifying children, the excess (if any) of—

(I)　the taxpayer's social security taxes for the taxable year, over

(II)　the credit allowed under [2]*section 32* for the taxable year.

The amount of the credit allowed under this subsection shall not be treated as a credit allowed under this subpart and shall reduce the amount of credit otherwise allowable under subsection (a) without regard to section 26(a)(2) or subsection (b)(3), as the case may be. For purposes of subparagraph (B), any amount excluded from gross income by reason of section 112 shall be treated as earned income which is taken into account in computing taxable income for the taxable year.

* * * * * * * * * * * *

[For Analysis, see ¶ 102 and ¶ 901. For Committee Reports, see ¶ 5201.]

[Endnote Code Sec. 24]

Matter in *italics* in Code Sec. 24(d)(1)(B) was added by Sec. 11(c)(1)(A) and (B) of the Tax Technical Corrections Act of 2007, P.L. 110-172, 12/29/2007, which struck out:

1. "the excess (if any) of"
2. "section"

Effective Date (Sec. 11(c)(2), P.L. 110-172) effective for tax. yrs. begin. after 12/31/2005.

[¶ 3004]   Code Sec. 25C.   Nonbusiness energy property.

* * * * * * * * * * * *

(c) Qualified energy efficiency improvements. For purposes of this section—

* * * * * * * * * * * *

(3) Manufactured homes included. The term "dwelling unit" includes a manufactured home which conforms to Federal Manufactured Home Construction and Safety Standards (¹*part 3280* of title 24, Code of Federal Regulations).

[For Analysis, see ¶ 102. For Committee Reports, see ¶ 5201.]

[Endnote Code Sec. 25C]
   Matter in *italics* in Code Sec. 25C(c)(3) was added by Sec. 11(a)(2) of the Tax Technical Corrections Act of 2007, P.L. 110-172, 12/29/2007, which struck out:
   1. "section 3280"
Effective Date Enacted 12/29/2007.

[¶ 3005]   Code Sec. 26.   Limitation based on tax liability; definition of tax liability.

(a) Limitation based on amount of tax.

(1) In general. The aggregate amount of credits allowed by this subpart (other than sections 23, 24, and 25B) for the taxable year shall not exceed the excess (if any) of—

(A) the taxpayer's regular tax liability for the taxable year, over

(B) the tentative minimum tax for the taxable year (determined without regard to the alternative minimum tax foreign tax credit).

For purposes of subparagraph (B), the taxpayer's tentative minimum tax for any taxable year beginning during 1999 shall be treated as being zero.

(2) Special rule for taxable years 2000 through ¹*2007.* For purposes of any taxable year beginning during 2000, 2001, 2002, 2003, 2004, 2005, ²*2006, or 2007*, the aggregate amount of credits allowed by this subpart for the taxable year shall not exceed the sum of—

(A) the taxpayer's regular tax liability for the taxable year reduced by the foreign tax credit allowable under section 27(a), and

(B) the tax imposed by section 55(a) for the taxable year.

(b) Regular tax liability. For purposes of this part—

(1) In general. The term "regular tax liability" means the tax imposed by this chapter for the taxable year.

(2) Exception for certain taxes. For purposes of paragraph (1), any tax imposed by any of the following provisions shall not be treated as tax imposed by this chapter:

* * * * * * * * * * * *

³*(S) sections 106(e)(3)(A)(ii), 223(b)(8)(B)(i)(II), and 408(d)(9)(D)(i)(II) (relating to certain failures to maintain high deductible health plan coverage),*

⁴*(T) section 170(o)(3)(B) (relating to recapture of certain deductions for fractional gifts),*

⁵*(U) section 223(f)(4) (relating to additional tax on health savings account distributions not used for qualified medical expenses), and*

⁶*(V) subsections (a)(1)(B)(i) and (b)(4)(A) of section 409A (relating to interest and additional tax with respect to certain deferred compensation).*

* * * * * * * * * * * *

[For Analysis, see ¶ 102 and ¶ 903. For Committee Reports, see ¶ 5201.]

[Endnote Code Sec. 26]

Matter in *italics* in Code Sec. 26(a)(2) heading and Code Sec. 26(a)(2) was added by Sec. 3(a)(1) and (2) of the Tax Increase Prevention Act of 2007, P.L. 110-166, 12/16/2007, which struck out:

1. "2006"
2. "or 2006"

Effective Date (Sec. 3(b), P.L. 110-166, 12/16/2007) effective for tax. yrs. begin. after 12/31/2006.

Matter in *italics* in Code Sec. 26(b)(2)(S), Code Sec. 26(b)(2)(T), Code Sec. 26(b)(2)(U) and Code Sec. 26(b)(2)(V) was added by Sec. 11(a)(3) of the Tax Technical Corrections Act of 2007, P.L. 110-172, 12/29/2007 which struck out:

3. added subpara. (b)(2)(S)
4. added subpara. (b)(2)(T)
5. "(S)"
6. "(T)"

Effective Date Enacted 12/29/2007.

[¶ 3006]   Code Sec. 30C.   Alternative fuel vehicle refueling property credit.

* * * * * * * * * * * *

[1]*(b)   Limitation. The credit allowed under subsection (a) with respect to all qualified alternative fuel vehicle refueling property placed in service by the taxpayer during the taxable year at a location shall not exceed—*

(1) $30,000 in the case of a property of a character subject to an allowance for depreciation, and

(2) $1,000 in any other case.

[2]*(c)   Qualified alternative fuel vehicle refueling property. For purposes of this section, the term "qualified alternative fuel vehicle refueling property" has the same meaning as the term "qualified clean-fuel vehicle refueling property" would have under section 179A if—*

(1) *paragraph (1) of section 179A(d) did not apply to property installed on property which is used as the principal residence (within the meaning of section 121) of the taxpayer, and*

(2) *only the following were treated as clean-burning fuels for purposes of section 179A(d):*

(A) Any fuel at least 85 percent of the volume of which consists of one or more of the following: ethanol, natural gas, compressed natural gas, liquefied natural gas, liquefied petroleum gas, or hydrogen.

(B) Any mixture—

(i) which consists of two or more of the following: biodiesel (as defined in section 40A(d)(1)), diesel fuel (as defined in section 4083(a)(3)), or kerosene, and

(ii) at least 20 percent of the volume of which consists of biodiesel (as so defined) determined without regard to any kerosene in such mixture.

* * * * * * * * * * * *

[For Analysis, see ¶ 402 and ¶ 403. For Committee Reports, see ¶ 5305.]

[Endnote Code Sec. 30C]

Matter in *italics* in Code Sec. 30C(b) and Code Sec. 30C(c) was added by Sec. 6(b)(1)-(2) of the Tax Technical Corrections Act of 2007, P.L. 110-172, 12/29/2007, which struck out:

1. "(b) Limitation. The credit allowed under subsection (a) with respect to any alternative fuel vehicle refueling property shall not exceed—"

2. "(c) Qualified alternative fuel vehicle refueling property.

"(1) In general. Except as provided in paragraph (2), the term 'qualified alternative fuel vehicle refueling property' has the meaning given to such term by section 179A(d), but only with respect to any fuel—

"(A) at least 85 percent of the volume of which consists of 1 or more of the following: ethanol, natural gas, compressed natural gas, liquefied natural gas, liquefied petroleum gas, or hydrogen, or

"(B) any mixture of biodiesel (as defined in section 40A(d)(1)) and diesel fuel (as defined in section 4083(a)(3)), determined without regard to any use of kerosene and containing at least 20 percent biodiesel.

"(2) Residential property. In the case of any property installed on property which is used as the principal residence (within the meaning of section 121) of the taxpayer, paragraph (1) of section 179A(d) shall not apply."

Effective Date (Sec. 6(e)(1), P.L. 110-172, 12/29/2007) effective for property placed in service after 12/31/2005, in tax. yrs. end. after 12/31/2005.

[¶ 3007]   Code Sec. 34.   Certain uses of gasoline and special fuels.

(a) **General rule.** There shall be allowed as a credit against the tax imposed by this subtitle for the taxable year an amount equal to the sum of the amounts payable to the taxpayer—

(1) under section 6420[1] (determined without regard to section 6420(g)),

(2) under section 6421[2] (determined without regard to section 6421(i)), and

(3) under section 6427[3] (determined without regard to section 6427(k)).

* * * * * * * * * * *

[Endnote Code Sec. 34]

Matter in Code Sec. 34(a)(1), Code Sec. 34(a)(2) and Code Sec. 34(a)(3) was deleted by Sec. 11(a)(4)(A), (B) and (C) of the Tax Technical Corrections Act of 2007, P.L. 110-172, 12/29/2007, which struck out:

1."with respect to gasoline used during the taxable year on a farm for farming purposes"

2."with respect to gasoline used during the taxable year (A) otherwise than as a fuel in a highway vehicle or (B) in vehicles while engaged in furnishing certain public passenger land transportation service"

3."with respect to fuels used for nontaxable purposes or resold during the taxable year"

Effective Date Enacted 12/29/2007.

[¶ 3008]   Code Sec. 35.   Health insurance costs of eligible individuals.

* * * * * * * * * * *

(d) **Qualifying family member.** For purposes of this section—

(1) **In general.** The term "qualifying family member" means—

(A) the taxpayer's spouse, and

(B) any dependent of the taxpayer with respect to whom the taxpayer is entitled to a deduction under section 151(c).

Such term does not include any individual who has other specified coverage.

(2) **Special dependency test in case of divorced parents, etc.** If[1] of section 152(e) applies to any child with respect to any calendar year, in the case of any taxable year beginning in such calendar year, such child shall be treated as described in paragraph (1)(B) with respect to the custodial parent [2]*(as defined in section 152(e)(4)(A))* and not with respect to the noncustodial parent.

* * * * * * * * * * *

[Endnote Code Sec. 35]

Matter in Code Sec. 35(d)(2) in *italics*, was added by Sec. 11(a)(5)(A) and (B) of the Tax Technical Corrections Act of 2007, P.L. 110-172, 12/29/2007, which struck out:

1. "paragraph (2) or (4) of"

2. "(within the meaning of section 152(e)(1))"

Effective Date Enacted 12/29/2007.

[¶ 3009]   Code Sec. 41.   Credit for increasing research activities.

(a) **General rule.** For purposes of section 38, the research credit determined under this section for the taxable year shall be an amount equal to the sum of—

(1) 20 percent of the excess (if any) of—

(A) the qualified research expenses for the taxable year, over

(B) the base amount,

(2) 20 percent of the basic research payments determined under subsection (e)(1)(A), and

(3) 20 percent of the amounts paid or incurred by the taxpayer in carrying on any trade or business of the taxpayer during the taxable year (including as contributions) to an energy research consortium [1]*for energy research.*

* * * * * * * * * * * *

(f) Special rules. For purposes of this section—

(1) Aggregation of expenditures.

(A) Controlled group of corporations. In determining the amount of the credit under this section—

(i) all members of the same controlled group of corporations shall be treated as a single taxpayer, and

(ii) the credit (if any) allowable by this section to each such member shall be its proportionate shares of the [2]*qualified research expenses, basic research payments, and amounts paid or incurred to energy research consortiums,* giving rise to the credit.

(B) Common control. Under regulations prescribed by the Secretary, in determining the amount of the credit under this section—

(i) all trades or businesses (whether or not incorporated) which are under common control shall be treated as a single taxpayer, and

(ii) the credit (if any) allowable by this section to each such person shall be its proportionate shares of the [3]*qualified research expenses, basic research payments, and amounts paid or incurred to energy research consortiums,* giving rise to the credit.

The regulations prescribed under this subparagraph shall be based on principles similar to the principles which apply in the case of subparagraph (A).

* * * * * * * * * * * *

(6) Energy research consortium.

(A) In general. The term "energy research consortium" means any organization—

(i) which is—

(I) described in section 501(c)(3) and is exempt from tax under section 501(a) and is organized and operated primarily to conduct energy research, or

(II) organized and operated primarily to conduct energy research in the public interest (within the meaning of section 501(c)(3)),

(ii) which is not a private foundation,

(iii) to which at least 5 unrelated persons paid or incurred during the calendar year in which the taxable year of the organization begins amounts (including as contributions) to such organization for energy research, and

(iv) to which no single person paid or incurred (including as contributions) during such calendar year an amount equal to more than 50 percent of the total amounts received by such organization during such calendar year for energy research.

(B) Treatment of persons. All persons treated as a single employer under subsection (a) or (b) of section 52 shall be treated as related persons for purposes of subparagraph (A)(iii) and as a single person for purposes of subparagraph (A)(iv).

(C) Foreign research. For purposes of subsection (a)(3), amounts paid or incurred for any energy research conducted outside the United States, the Commonwealth of Puerto Rico, or any possession of the United States shall not be taken into account.

(D) Denial of double benefit. Any amount taken into account under subsection (a)(3) shall not be taken into account under paragraph (1) or (2) of subsection (a).

[4]*(E) Energy research. The term "energy research" does not include any research which is not qualified research.*

* * * * * * * * * * * *

[For Analysis, see ¶ 404 and ¶ 405. For Committee Reports, see ¶ 5305.]

[Endnote Code Sec. 41]

Matter in *italics* in Code Sec. 41(a)(3) was added by Sec. 6(c)(1) of the Tax Technical Corrections Act of 2007, P.L. 110-172, 12/29/2007.

1. added matter in para. (a)(3)

Effective Date (Sec. 6(e)(1), P.L. 110-172, 12/29/2007) effective for amounts paid or incurred after 8/8/2005 in tax. yrs. end. after 8/8/2005.

Matter in *italics* in Code Sec. 41(f)(1)(A)(ii) and Code Sec. 41(f)(1)(B)(ii) was added by Sec. 11(e)(2), P.L. 110-172, 12/29/2007, which struck out:

2. "qualified research expenses and basic research payments"

3. "qualified research expenses and basic research payments"

Effective Date (Sec. 11(e)(3), P.L. 110-172, 12/29/2007) effective for amounts paid or incurred after 8/8/2005 in tax. yrs. end. after 8/8/2005.

Code Sec. 41(f)(6)(E) in *italics* was added by Sec. 6(c)(2), P.L. 110-172, 12/29/2007.

4. added subpara. (f)(6)(E)

Effective Date (Sec. 6(e)(1), P.L. 110-172, 12/29/2007) effective for amounts paid or incurred after 8/8/2005 in tax. yrs. end. after 8/8/2005.

[¶ 3010]   Code Sec. 42.   Low-income housing credit.

* * * * * * * * * * * *

(i) Definitions and special rules. For purposes of this section—

* * * * * * * * * * * *

(3) Low-income unit.

(A) In general. The term "low-income unit" means any unit in a building if—

(i) such unit is rent-restricted (as defined in subsection (g)(2)), and

(ii) the individuals occupying such unit meet the income limitation applicable under subsection (g)(1) to the project of which such building is a part.

(B) Exceptions.

(i) In general. A unit shall not be treated as a low-income unit unless the unit is suitable for occupancy and used other than on a transient basis.

(ii) Suitability for occupancy. For purposes of clause (i), the suitability of a unit for occupancy shall be determined under regulations prescribed by the Secretary taking into account local health, safety, and building codes.

(iii) Transitional housing for homeless. For purposes of clause (i), a unit shall be considered to be used other than on a transient basis if the unit contains sleeping accommodations and kitchen and bathroom facilities and is located in a building—

(I) which is used exclusively to facilitate the transition of homeless individuals (within the meaning of section 103 of the Stewart B. McKinney Homeless Assistance Act (42 U.S.C. 11302), as in effect on the date of the enactment of this clause) to independent living within 24 months, and

(II) in which a governmental entity or qualified nonprofit organization (as defined in subsection (h)(5)) provides such individuals with temporary housing and supportive services designed to assist such individuals in locating and retaining permanent housing.

(iv) Single-room occupancy units. For purposes of clause (i), a single-room occupancy unit shall not be treated as used on a transient basis merely because it is rented on a month-by-month basis.

(C) Special rule for buildings having 4 or fewer units. In the case of any building which has 4 or fewer residential rental units, no unit in such building shall be treated as a low-income unit if the units in such building are owned by—

(i) any individual who occupies a residential unit in such building, or

(ii) any person who is related (as defined in subsection (d)(2)(D)(iii)) to such individual.

(D) Certain students not to disqualify unit. A unit shall not fail to be treated as a low-income unit merely because it is occupied—

(i) by an individual who is—

(I) a student and receiving assistance under title IV of the Social Security Act, or

(II) enrolled in a job training program receiving assistance under the Job Training Partnership Act or under other similar Federal, State, or local laws, or

(ii) entirely by full-time students if such students are—

[1]*(I) single parents and their children and such parents are not dependents (as defined in section 152, determined without regard to subsections (b)(1), (b)(2), and (d)(1)(B) thereof) of another individual and such children are not dependents (as so defined) of another individual other than a parent of such children, or. [sic ,]*

(II) married and file a joint return.

(E) Owner-occupied buildings having 4 or fewer units eligible for credit where development plan.

(i) In general. Subparagraph (C) shall not apply to the acquisition or rehabilitation of a building pursuant to a development plan of action sponsored by a State or local government or a qualified nonprofit organization (as defined in subsection (h)(5)(C)).

(ii) Limitation on credit. In the case of a building to which clause (i) applies, the applicable fraction shall not exceed 80 percent of the unit fraction.

(iii) Certain unrented units treated as owner-occupied. In the case of a building to which clause (i) applies, any unit which is not rented for 90 days or more shall be treated as occupied by the owner of the building as of the 1st day it is not rented.

* * * * * * * * * * * *

[For Analysis, see ¶ 902.]

[Endnote Code Sec. 42]

Code Sec. 42(i)(3)(D)(ii)(I), in *italics*, was added by Sec. 6(a) of the Mortgage Forgiveness Debt Relief Act of 2007, P.L. 110-142, 12/20/2007, which struck out:

1. "(I) single parents and their children and such parents and children are not dependents (as defined in section 152, determined without regard to subsections (b)(1), (b)(2), and (d)(1)(B) thereof) of another individual, or"

Effective Date (Sec. 6(b), P.L. 110-142, 12/20/2007) effective for housing credit amounts allocated before, on, or after 12/20/2007, and buildings placed in service before, on, or after 12/20/2007 to the extent paragraph (1) of section 42(h) of the Internal Revenue Code of 1986 does not apply to any building by reason of paragraph (4) thereof.

[¶ 3011]   Code Sec. 45.   Electricity produced from certain renewable resources, etc.

* * * * * * * * * * * *

(c) Resources. For purposes of this section—

(1) In general. The term "qualified energy resources" means—

(A) wind,

(B) closed-loop biomass,

(C) open-loop biomass,

(D) geothermal energy,

(E) solar energy,

(F) small irrigation power,

(G) municipal solid waste, and

(H) qualified hydropower production.

(2) Closed-loop biomass. The term "closed-loop biomass" means any organic material from a plant which is planted exclusively for purposes of being used at a qualified facility to produce electricity.

(3) Open-loop biomass.

(A) In general. The term "open-loop biomass" means—

(i) any agricultural livestock waste nutrients, or

(ii) any solid, nonhazardous, cellulosic waste material or any lignin material[1] which is derived from—

(I) any of the following forest-related resources: mill and harvesting residues, precommercial thinnings, slash, and brush,

(II) solid wood waste materials, including waste pallets, crates, dunnage, manufacturing and construction wood wastes (other than pressure-treated, chemically-treated, or painted wood wastes), and landscape or right-of-way tree trimmings, but not including municipal solid waste, gas derived from the biodegradation of solid waste, or paper which is commonly recycled, or

(III) agriculture sources, including orchard tree crops, vineyard, grain, legumes, sugar, and other crop by-products or residues.

Such term shall not include closed-loop biomass or biomass burned in conjunction with fossil fuel (cofiring) beyond such fossil fuel required for startup and flame stabilization.

(B) Agricultural livestock waste nutrients.

(i) In general. The term "agricultural livestock waste nutrients" means agricultural livestock manure and litter, including wood shavings, straw, rice hulls, and other bedding material for the disposition of manure.

(ii) Agricultural livestock. The term "agricultural livestock" includes bovine, swine, poultry, and sheep.

* * * * * * * * * * * *

(d) Qualified facilities. For purposes of this section—

* * * * * * * * * * * *

(2) Closed-loop biomass facility.

(A) In general. In the case of a facility using closed-loop biomass to produce electricity, the term "qualified facility" means any facility—

(i) owned by the taxpayer which is originally placed in service after December 31, 1992, and before January 1, 2009 , or

(ii) owned by the taxpayer which before January 1, 2009, is originally placed in service and modified to use closed-loop biomass to co-fire with coal, with other biomass, or with both, but only if the modification is approved under the Biomass Power for Rural Development Programs or is part of a pilot project of the Commodity Credit Corporation as described in 65 Fed. Reg. 63052.

(B) Special rules. In the case of a qualified facility described in subparagraph (A)(ii)—

(i) the 10-year period referred to in subsection (a) shall be treated as beginning no earlier than the date of the enactment of this clause, [2]*and*

[3]*(ii)* if the owner of such facility is not the producer of the electricity, the person eligible for the credit allowable under subsection (a) shall be the lessee or the operator of such facility.

* * * * * * * * * * * *

(e) Definitions and special rules. For purposes of this section—

* * * * * * * * * * * *

(7) Credit not to apply to electricity sold to utilities under certain contracts.

(A) In general. The credit determined under subsection (a) shall not apply to electricity—

(i) produced at a qualified facility described in subsection (d)(1) which is [4]*originally placed in service* after June 30, 1999, and

(ii) sold to a utility pursuant to a contract originally entered into before January 1, 1987 (whether or not amended or restated after that date).

(B) Exception. Subparagraph (A) shall not apply if—

(i) the prices for energy and capacity from such facility are established pursuant to an amendment to the contract referred to in subparagraph (A)(ii),

(ii) such amendment provides that the prices set forth in the contract which exceed avoided cost prices determined at the time of delivery shall apply only to annual quantities of electricity (prorated for partial years) which do not exceed the greater of—

(I) the average annual quantity of electricity sold to the utility under the contract during calendar years 1994, 1995, 1996, 1997, and 1998, or

(II) the estimate of the annual electricity production set forth in the contract, or, if there is no such estimate, the greatest annual quantity of electricity sold to the utility under the contract in any of the calendar years 1996, 1997, or 1998, and

(iii) such amendment provides that energy and capacity in excess of the limitation in clause (ii) may be—

(I) sold to the utility only at prices that do not exceed avoided cost prices determined at the time of delivery, or

(II) sold to a third party subject to a mutually agreed upon advance notice to the utility.

For purposes of this subparagraph, avoided cost prices shall be determined as provided for in 18 CFR 292.304(d)(1) or any successor regulation.

* * * * * * * * * * * *

[For Analysis, see ¶406, ¶407 and ¶410. For Committee Reports, see ¶5306 and ¶5308.]

[Endnote Code Sec. 45]

Matter in *italics* in Code Sec. 45(c)(3)(A)(ii), Code Sec. 45(d)(2)(B)(i) and Code Sec. 45(d)(2)(B)(ii) was added by Sec. 7(b)(1)-(2) of the Tax Technical Corrections Act of 2007, P.L. 110-172, 12/29/2007, which struck out:

1. "which is segregated from other waste materials"

2. added matter in clause (d)(2)(B)(i)

3. "(ii) the amount of the credit determined under subsection (a) with respect to the facility shall be an amount equal to the amount determined without regard to this clause multiplied by the ratio of the thermal content of the closed-loop biomass used in such facility to the thermal content of all fuels used in such facility, and

"(iii)"

Effective Date (Sec. 7(e)(1), P.L. 110-172, 12/29/2007) effective for electricity produced and sold after 10/22/2004, in tax. yrs. end. after 10/22/2004. Sec. 710(g)(4) of the American Jobs Creation Act of 2004, P.L. 108-357, 10/22/2004, provides:

"(4) Nonapplication of amendments to preeffective date poultry waste facilities. The amendments made by this section shall not apply with respect to any poultry waste facility (within the meaning of section 45(c)(3)(C), as in effect on the day before the date of the enactment of this Act) placed in service before January 1, 2005."

Matter in *italics* in Code Sec. 45(e)(7)(A)(i) was added by Sec. 9(a), P.L. 110-172, 12/29/2007, which struck out:

4. "placed in service by the taxpayer"

Effective Date (Sec. 9(c), P.L. 110-172, 12/29/2007) effective 12/17/99.

[¶3012]　　Code Sec. 45H.　　Credit for production of low sulfur diesel fuel.

* * * * * * * * * * * *

(b)　Maximum credit.

(1)　In general. The aggregate credit determined under subsection (a) for any taxable year with respect to any facility shall not exceed—

(A) 25 percent of the ¹*qualified costs* incurred by the small business refiner with respect to such facility, reduced by

(B) the aggregate credits determined under this section for all prior taxable years with respect to such facility.

(2)　Reduced percentage. In the case of a small business refiner with average daily domestic refinery runs for the 1-year period ending on December 31, 2002, in excess of 155,000 barrels, the number of percentage points described in paragraph (1) shall be reduced (not below zero) by the product of such number (before the application of this paragraph) and the ratio of such excess to 50,000 barrels.

(c) Definitions and special rule. For purposes of this section—

(1) Small business refiner. The term "small business refiner" means, with respect to any taxable year, a refiner of crude oil—

(A) with respect to which not more than 1,500 individuals are engaged in the refinery operations of the business on any day during such taxable year, and

(B) the average daily domestic refinery run or average retained production of which for all facilities of the taxpayer for the 1-year period ending on December 31, 2002, did not exceed 205,000 barrels.

(2) Qualified[2] costs. The term "[3]*qualified costs*" means, with respect to any facility, those costs paid or incurred during the applicable period for compliance with the applicable EPA regulations with respect to such facility, including expenditures for the construction of new process operation units or the dismantling and reconstruction of existing process units to be used in the production of low sulfur diesel fuel, associated adjacent or offsite equipment (including tankage, catalyst, and power supply), engineering, construction period interest, and sitework.

(3) Applicable EPA regulations. The term "applicable EPA regulations" means the Highway Diesel Fuel Sulfur Control Requirements of the Environmental Protection Agency.

(4) Applicable period. The term "applicable period" means, with respect to any facility, the period beginning on January 1, 2003, and ending on the earlier of the date which is 1 year after the date on which the taxpayer must comply with the applicable EPA regulations with respect to such facility or December 31, 2009.

(5) Low sulfur diesel fuel. The term "low sulfur diesel fuel" means diesel fuel with a sulfur content of 15 parts per million or less.

[4]**(d) Special rule for determination of refinery runs.** For purposes this section and section 179B(b), in the calculation of average daily domestic refinery run or retained production, only refineries which on April 1, 2003, were refineries of the refiner or a related person (within the meaning of section 613A(d)(3)), shall be taken into account.

[5]**(e) Certification.**

(1) Required. No credit shall be allowed unless, not later than the date which is 30 months after the first day of the first taxable year in which the low sulfur diesel fuel production credit is determined with respect to a facility, the small business refiner obtains certification from the Secretary, after consultation with the Administrator of the Environmental Protection Agency, that the taxpayer's [6]*qualified costs* with respect to such facility will result in compliance with the applicable EPA regulations.

(2) Contents of application. An application for certification shall include relevant information regarding unit capacities and operating characteristics sufficient for the Secretary, after consultation with the Administrator of the Environmental Protection Agency, to determine that such [7]*qualified costs* are necessary for compliance with the applicable EPA regulations.

(3) Review period. Any application shall be reviewed and notice of certification, if applicable, shall be made within 60 days of receipt of such application. In the event the Secretary does not notify the taxpayer of the results of such certification within such period, the taxpayer may presume the certification to be issued until so notified.

(4) Statute of limitations. With respect to the credit allowed under this section—

(A) the statutory period for the assessment of any deficiency attributable to such credit shall not expire before the end of the 3-year period ending on the date that the review period described in paragraph (3) ends with respect to the taxpayer, and

(B) such deficiency may be assessed before the expiration of such 3-year period notwithstanding the provisions of any other law or rule of law which would otherwise prevent such assessment.

[8](f)　**Cooperative organizations.**

(1)　**Apportionment of credit.**

(A) In general. In the case of a cooperative organization described in section 1381(a), any portion of the credit determined under subsection (a) for the taxable year may, at the election of the organization, be apportioned among patrons eligible to share in patronage dividends on the basis of the quantity or value of business done with or for such patrons for the taxable year.

(B) Form and effect of election. An election under subparagraph (A) for any taxable year shall be made on a timely filed return for such year. Such election, once made, shall be irrevocable for such taxable year.

(2)　**Treatment of organizations and patrons.**

(A) Organizations. The amount of the credit not apportioned to patrons pursuant to paragraph (1) shall be included in the amount determined under subsection (a) for the taxable year of the organization.

(B) Patrons. The amount of the credit apportioned to patrons pursuant to paragraph (1) shall be included in the amount determined under subsection (a) for the first taxable year of each patron ending on or after the last day of the payment period (as defined in section 1382(d)) for the taxable year of the organization or, if earlier, for the taxable year of each patron ending on or after the date on which the patron receives notice from the cooperative of the apportionment.

(3)　**Special rule.** If the amount of a credit which has been apportioned to any patron under this subsection is decreased for any reason—

(A) such amount shall not increase the tax imposed on such patron, and

(B) the tax imposed by this chapter on such organization shall be increased by such amount.

The increase under subparagraph (B) shall not be treated as tax imposed by this chapter for purposes of determining the amount of any credit under this chapter or for purposes of section 55.

[9](g)　*Election not to take credit. No credit shall be determined under subsection (a) for the taxable year if the taxpayer elects not to have subsection (a) apply to such taxable year.* [For Analysis, see ¶ 401. For Committee Reports, see ¶ 5306.]

[Endnote Code Sec. 45H]

Matter in *italics* in Code Sec. 45H(b)(1)(A), Code Sec. 45H(c)(2), Code Sec. 45H(d), Code Sec. 45H(e), Code Sec. 45H(f) and Code Sec. 45H(g) was added by Sec. 7(a)(1)(A), (a)(2)(A), and (a)(3)(A)-(B) of the Tax Technical Corrections Act of 2007, P.L. 110-172, 12/29/2007, which struck out:

1. "qualified capital costs"
2. "capital"
3. "qualified capital costs"
4. "(d) Reduction in basis. For purposes of this subtitle, if a credit is determined under this section for any expenditure with respect to any property, the increase in basis of such property which would (but for this subsection) result from such expenditure shall be reduced by the amount of the credit so determined.
"(e)" "
5. "(f)"
6. "qualified capital costs"
7. "qualified capital costs"
8. "(g)"
9. added subsec. (g)

Effective Date (Sec. 7(e)(1), P.L. 110-172, 12/29/2007) effective for expenses paid or incurred after 12/31/2002, in tax. yrs. end. after 12/31/2002.

[¶ 3013]　　**Code Sec. 45J.**　　**Credit for production from advanced nuclear power facilities.**

* * * * * * * * * * * *

(b) National limitation.

(1) In general. The amount of credit which would (but for this subsection and subsection (c)) be allowed with respect to any facility for any taxable year shall not exceed the amount which bears the same ratio to such amount of credit as—

(A) the national megawatt capacity limitation allocated to the facility, bears to

(B) the total megawatt nameplate capacity of such facility.

¹**(2) Amount of national limitation.** *The aggregate amount of national megawatt capacity limitation allocated by the Secretary under paragraph (3) shall not exceed 6,000 megawatts.*

* * * * * * * * * * * *

[For Analysis, see ¶ 409. For Committee Reports, see ¶ 5305.]

[Endnote Code Sec. 45J]

Matter in *italics* in Code Sec. 45J(b)(2) was added by Sec. 6(a) of the Tax Technical Corrections Act of 2007, P.L. 110-172, 12/29/2007, which struck out:

1. "(2) Amount of national limitation. The national megawatt capacity limitation shall be 6,000 megawatts."

Effective Date (Sec. 6(e)(1), P.L. 110-172, 12/29/2007) effective for production in tax. yrs. begin. after 8/8/2005.

[¶ 3014]   Code Sec. 45L.   New energy efficient home credit.

* * * * * * * * * * * *

(c) Energy saving requirements. A dwelling unit meets the energy saving requirements of this subsection if such unit is—

(1) certified—

(A) to have a level of annual heating and cooling energy consumption which is at least 50 percent below the annual level of heating and cooling energy consumption of a comparable dwelling unit—

(i) which is constructed in accordance with the standards of chapter 4 of the 2003 International Energy Conservation Code, as such Code (including supplements) is in effect on the date of the enactment of this section, and

(ii) for which the heating and cooling equipment efficiencies correspond to the minimum allowed under the regulations established by the Department of Energy pursuant to the National Appliance Energy Conservation Act of 1987 and in effect at the time of completion of construction, and

(B) to have building envelope component improvements account for at least 1/5 of such 50 percent,

(2) a manufactured home which conforms to Federal Manufactured Home Construction and Safety Standards (¹*part 3280* of title 24, Code of Federal Regulations) and which meets the requirements of paragraph (1), or

(3) a manufactured home which conforms to Federal Manufactured Home Construction and Safety Standards (²*part 3280* of title 24, Code of Federal Regulations) and which—

(A) meets the requirements of paragraph (1) applied by substituting "30 percent" for "50 percent" both places it appears therein and by substituting "1/3" for "1/5" in subparagraph (B) thereof, or

(B) meets the requirements established by the Administrator of the Environmental Protection Agency under the Energy Star Labeled Homes program.

* * * * * * * * * * * *

[Endnote Code Sec. 45L]

Matter in *italics* in Code Sec. 45L(c)(2) and Code Sec. 45L(c)(3) was added by Sec. 11(a)(7) of the Tax Technical Corrections Act of 2007, P.L. 110-172, 12/29/2007, which struck out:

1. "section 3280"
2. "section 3280"

Effective Date Enacted 12/29/2007.

[¶ 3015]   Code Sec. 48.   Energy credit.

* * * * * * * * * * * *

(c)   Qualified fuel cell property; qualified microturbine property. For purposes of this ¹*section*—

(1)   Qualified fuel cell property.

(A) In general. The term "qualified fuel cell property" means a fuel cell power plant which—

(i) has a nameplate capacity of at least 0.5 kilowatt of electricity using an electro-chemical process, and

(ii) has an electricity-only generation efficiency greater than 30 percent.

(B) Limitation. In the case of qualified fuel cell property placed in service during the taxable year, the credit otherwise determined under ²*subsection (a)* for such year with respect to such property shall not exceed an amount equal to $500 for each 0.5 kilowatt of capacity of such property.

(C) Fuel cell power plant. The term "fuel cell power plant" means an integrated system comprised of a fuel cell stack assembly and associated balance of plant components which converts a fuel into electricity using electrochemical means.

(D) Special rule. The first sentence of the matter in subsection (a)(3) which follows subparagraph (D) thereof shall not apply to qualified fuel cell property which is used predominantly in the trade or business of the furnishing or sale of telephone service, telegraph service by means of domestic telegraph operations, or other telegraph services (other than international telegraph services).

(E) Termination. The term "qualified fuel cell property" shall not include any property for any period after December 31, 2008.

(2)   Qualified microturbine property.

(A) In general. The term "qualified microturbine property" means a stationary microturbine power plant which—

(i) has a nameplate capacity of less than 2,000 kilowatts, and

(ii) has an electricity-only generation efficiency of not less than 26 percent at International Standard Organization conditions.

(B) Limitation. In the case of qualified microturbine property placed in service during the taxable year, the credit otherwise determined under ³*subsection (a)* for such year with respect to such property shall not exceed an amount equal $200 for each kilowatt of capacity of such property.

(C) Stationary microturbine power plant. The term "stationary microturbine power plant" means an integrated system comprised of a gas turbine engine, a combustor, a recuperator or regenerator, a generator or alternator, and associated balance of plant components which converts a fuel into electricity and thermal energy. Such term also includes all secondary components located between the existing infrastructure for fuel delivery and the existing infrastructure for power distribution, including equipment and controls for meeting relevant power standards, such as voltage, frequency, and power factors.

(D) Special rule. The first sentence of the matter in subsection (a)(3) which follows subparagraph (D) thereof shall not apply to qualified microturbine property which is used predominantly in the trade or business of the furnishing or sale of telephone service, telegraph service by means of domestic telegraph operations, or other telegraph services (other than international telegraph services).

(E) Termination. The term "qualified microturbine property" shall not include any property for any period after December 31, 2008.

[For Analysis, see ¶ 411.]

[Endnote Code Sec. 48]

Matter in *italics* in Code Sec. 48(c), Code Sec. 48(c)(1)(B), and Code Sec. 48(c)(2)(B) was added by Sec. 11(a)(8) and (9) of the Tax Technical Corrections Act of 2007, P.L. 110-172, 12/29/2007 which struck out:

1. "subsection"
2. "paragraph (1)"
3. "paragraph (1)"

Effective Date Enacted 12/29/2007.

[¶ 3016]   **Code Sec. 48A.**   **Qualifying advanced coal project credit.**

* * * * * * * * * * *

(d) Qualifying advanced coal project program.

* * * * * * * * * * *

(4) Review and redistribution.

(A) Review. Not later than 6 years after the date of enactment of this section, the Secretary shall review the credits allocated under this section as of the date which is 6 years after the date of enactment of this section.

(B) Redistribution. The Secretary may reallocate credits available under clauses (i) and (ii) of paragraph (3)(B) if the Secretary determines that—

(i) there is an insufficient quantity of qualifying applications for certification pending at the time of the review, or

(ii) any certification made pursuant to[1] paragraph (2) has been revoked pursuant to[2] paragraph (2)(D) because the project subject to the certification has been delayed as a result of third party opposition or litigation to the proposed project.

(C) Reallocation. If the Secretary determines that credits under clause (i) or (ii) of paragraph (3)(B) are available for reallocation pursuant to the requirements set forth in paragraph (2), the Secretary is authorized to conduct an additional program for applications for certification.

* * * * * * * * * * *

[Endnote Code Sec. 48A]

In Code Sec. 48A(d)(4)(B)(ii), Sec. 11(a) of the Tax Technical Corrections Act of 2007, P.L. 110-172, 12/29/2007 struck out;

1."subsection"
2."subsection"

Effective Date Enacted 12/29/2007.

[¶ 3017]   **Code Sec. 53.**   **Credit for prior year minimum tax liability.**

* * * * * * * * * * *

(e) Special rule for individuals with long-term unused credits.

(1) In general. If an individual has a long-term unused minimum tax credit for any taxable year beginning before January 1, 2013, the amount determined under subsection (c) for such taxable year shall not be less than the AMT refundable credit amount for such taxable year.

(2) AMT refundable credit amount. For purposes of paragraph (1)—

[1]*(A) In general. The term "AMT refundable credit amount" means, with respect to any taxable year, the amount (not in excess of the long-term unused minimum tax credit for such taxable year) equal to the greater of—*

(i) $5,000,

(ii) 20 percent of the long-term unused minimum tax credit for such taxable year, or

(iii) the amount (if any) of the AMT refundable credit amount determined under this paragraph for the taxpayer's preceding taxable year (as determined before any reduction under subparagraph (B)).

(B) Phaseout of AMT refundable credit amount.

(i) In general. In the case of an individual whose adjusted gross income for any taxable year exceeds the threshold amount (within the meaning of section 151(d)(3)(C)), the AMT refundable credit amount determined under subparagraph (A) for such taxable year shall be reduced by the applicable percentage (within the meaning of section 151(d)(3)(B)).

(ii) Adjusted gross income. For purposes of clause (i), adjusted gross income shall be determined without regard to sections 911, 931, and 933.

(3) Long-term unused minimum tax credit.

(A) In general. For purposes of this subsection, the term "long-term" unused minimum tax credit' means, with respect to any taxable year, the portion of the minimum tax credit determined under subsection (b) attributable to the adjusted net minimum tax for taxable years before the 3rd taxable year immediately preceding such taxable year.

(B) First-in, first-out ordering rule. For purposes of subparagraph (A), credits shall be treated as allowed under subsection (a) on a first-in, first-out basis.

(4) Credit refundable. For purposes of this title (other than this section), the credit allowed by reason of this subsection shall be treated as if it were allowed under subpart C.

[For Analysis, see ¶ 103. For Committee Reports, see ¶ 5301.]

[Endnote Code Sec. 53]

Matter in *italics* in Code Sec. 53(e)(2)(A) was added by Sec. 2(a) of the Tax Technical Corrections Act of 2007, P.L. 110-172, 12/29/2007, which struck out:

1. "(A) In general. The term 'AMT refundable credit amount' means, with respect to any taxable year, the amount equal to the greater of—

"(i) the lesser of—

"(I) $5,000, or

"(II) the amount of long-term unused minimum tax credit for such taxable year, or

"(ii) 20 percent of the amount of such credit."

Effective Date (Sec. 2(b), P.L. 110-172, 12/29/2007) effective for tax. yrs. begin. after 12/20/2006.

[¶ 3018]   Code Sec. 55.   Alternative minimum tax imposed.

* * * * * * * * * * * *

(d) Exemption amount. For purposes of this section—

(1) Exemption amount for taxpayers other than corporations. In the case of a taxpayer other than a corporation, the term "exemption amount" means—

(A) $45,000 [1]*($66,250 in the case of taxable years beginning in 2007)* in the case of—

(i) a joint return, or

(ii) a surviving spouse,

(B) $33,750 [2]*($44,350 in the case of taxable years beginning in 2007)* in the case of an individual who—

(i) is not a married individual, and

(ii) is not a surviving spouse,

(C) 50 percent of the dollar amount applicable under paragraph (1)(A) in the case of a married individual who files a separate return, and

(D) $22,500 in the case of an estate or trust.

For purposes of this paragraph, the term "surviving spouse" has the meaning given to such term by section 2(a), and marital status shall be determined under section 7703.

(2) Corporations. In the case of a corporation, the term "exemption amount" means $40,000.

(3) Phase-out of exemption amount. The exemption amount of any taxpayer shall be reduced (but not below zero) by an amount equal to 25 percent of the amount by which the alternative minimum taxable income of the taxpayer exceeds—

(A) $150,000 in the case of a taxpayer described in paragraph (1)(A) or (2),

(B) $112,500 in the case of a taxpayer described in paragraph (1)(B), and

(C) $75,000 in the case of a taxpayer described in subparagraph (C) or (D) of paragraph (1).

In the case of a taxpayer described in paragraph (1)(C), alternative minimum taxable income shall be increased by the lesser of (i) 25 percent of the excess of alternative minimum taxable income (determined without regard to this sentence) over the minimum amount of such income (as so determined) for which the exemption amount under paragraph (1)(C) is zero, or (ii) such exemption amount (determined without regard to this paragraph).

* * * * * * * * * * * *

[For Analysis, see ¶ 101. For Committee Reports, see ¶ 5201.]

[Endnote Code Sec. 55]

Matter in *italics* in Code Sec. 55(d)(1)(A) and Code Sec. 55(d)(1)(B) was added by Sec. 2(a)(1) and (2) of the Tax Increase Prevention Act of 2007, P.L. 110-166, 12/16/2007, which struck out:

1. "($62,550 in the case of taxable years beginning in 2006)"

2. "($42,500 in the case of taxable years beginning in 2006)"

Effective Date (Sec. 2(b), P.L. 110-166, 12/16/2007) effective for tax. yrs. begin. after 12/31/2006.

[¶ 3019]   Code Sec. 56.   Adjustments in computing alternative minimum taxable income.

* * * * * * * * * * * *

(g) Adjustments based on adjusted current earnings.

(1) In general. The alternative minimum taxable income of any corporation for any taxable year shall be increased by 75 percent of the excess (if any) of—

(A) the adjusted current earnings of the corporation, over

(B) the alternative minimum taxable income (determined without regard to this subsection and the alternative tax net operating loss deduction).

(2) Allowance of negative adjustments.

(A) In general. The alternative minimum taxable income for any corporation of any taxable year, shall be reduced by 75 percent of the excess (if any) of—

(i) the amount referred to in subparagraph (B) of paragraph (1), over

(ii) the amount referred to in subparagraph (A) of paragraph (1).

(B) Limitation. The reduction under subparagraph (A) for any taxable year shall not exceed the excess (if any) of—

(i) the aggregate increases in alternative minimum taxable income under paragraph (1) for prior taxable years, over

(ii) the aggregate reductions under subparagraph (A) of this paragraph for prior taxable years.

(3) Adjusted current earnings. For purposes of this subsection, the term "adjusted current earnings" means the alternative minimum taxable income for the taxable year—

(A) determined with the adjustments provided in paragraph (4), and

(B) determined without regard to this subsection and the alternative tax net operating loss deduction.

(4) Adjustments. In determining adjusted current earnings, the following adjustments shall apply:

(A) Depreciation.

(i) Property placed in service after 1989. The depreciation deduction with respect to any property placed in service in a taxable year beginning after 1989 shall be determined under the alternative system of section 168(g). The preceding sentence shall not apply to any property placed in service after December 31, 1993, and the depreciation deduction with respect to such property shall be determined under the rules of subsection (a)(1)(A).

(ii) Property to which new ACRS system applies. In the case of any property to which the amendments made by section 201 of the Tax Reform Act of 1986 apply and which is placed in service in a taxable year beginning before 1990, the depreciation deduction shall be determined—

(I) by taking into account the adjusted basis of such property (as determined for purposes of computing alternative minimum taxable income) as of the close of the last taxable year beginning before January 1, 1990, and

(II) by using the straight-line method over the remainder of the recovery period applicable to such property under the alternative system of section 168(g).

(iii) Property to which original ACRS system applies. In the case of any property to which section 168 (as in effect on the day before the date of the enactment [10/22/86] of the Tax Reform Act of 1986 and without regard to subsection (d)(1)(A)(ii) thereof) applies and which is placed in service in a taxable year beginning before 1990, the depreciation deduction shall be determined—

(I) by taking into account the adjusted basis of such property (as determined for purposes of computing the regular tax) as of the close of the last taxable year beginning before January 1, 1990, and

(II) by using the straight line method over the remainder of the recovery period which would apply to such property under the alternative system of section 168(g).

(iv) Property placed in service before 1981. In the case of any property not described in clause (i), (ii), or (iii), the amount allowable as depreciation or amortization with respect to such property shall be determined in the same manner as for purposes of computing taxable income.

(v) Special rule for certain property. In the case of any property described in paragraph (1), (2), (3), or (4) of section 168(f), the amount of depreciation allowable for purposes of the regular tax shall be treated as the amount allowable under the alternative system of section 168(g).

(B) Inclusion of items included for purposes of computing earnings and profits.

(i) In general. In the case of any amount which is excluded from gross income for purposes of computing alternative minimum taxable income but is taken into account in determining the amount of earnings and profits—

(I) such amount shall be included in income in the same manner as if such amount were includible in gross income for purposes of computing alternative minimum taxable income, and

(II) the amount of such income shall be reduced by any deduction which would have been allowable in computing alternative minimum taxable income if such amount were includible in gross income.

The preceding sentence shall not apply in the case of any amount excluded from gross income under section 108 (or the corresponding provisions of prior law) or under section 139A or 1357. In the case of any insurance company taxable under section 831(b), this clause shall not apply to any amount not described in section 834(b).

(ii) Inclusion of buildup in life insurance contracts. In the case of any life insurance contract—

(I) the income on such contract (as determined under section 7702(g)) for any taxable year shall be treated as includible in gross income for such year, and

(II) there shall be allowed as a deduction that portion of any premium which is attributable to insurance coverage.

(C) Disallowance of items not deductible in computing earnings and profits.

(i) In general. A deduction shall not be allowed for any item if such item would not be deductible for any taxable year for purposes of computing earnings and profits.

(ii) Special rule for certain dividends.

(I) In general. Clause (i) shall not apply to any deduction allowable under section 243 or 245 for any dividend which is a 100-percent dividend or which is received from a 20-percent owned corporation (as defined in section 243(c)(2)), but only to the extent such dividend is attributable to income of the paying corporation which is subject to tax under this chapter (determined after the application of sections 30A, 936 (including subsections (a)(4), (i), and (j) thereof) and [1]921 *(as in effect before its repeal by the FSC Repeal and Extraterritorial Income Exclusion Act of 2000)).*

(II) 100-percent dividend. For purposes of subclause (I), the term "100 percent dividend" means any dividend if the percentage used for purposes of determining the amount allowable as a deduction under section 243 or 245 with respect to such dividend is 100 percent.

(iii) Treatment of taxes on dividends from 936 corporations.

(I) In general. For purposes of determining the alternative minimum foreign tax credit, 75 percent of any withholding or income tax paid to a possession of the United States with respect to dividends received from a corporation eligible for the credit provided by section 936 shall be treated as a tax paid to a foreign country by the corporation receiving the dividend.

(II) Limitation. If the aggregate amount of the dividends referred to in subclause (I) for any taxable year exceeds the excess referred to in paragraph (1), the amount treated as tax paid to a foreign country under subclause (I) shall not exceed the amount which would be so treated without regard to this subclause multiplied by a fraction the numerator of which is the excess referred to in paragraph (1) and the denominator of which is the aggregate amount of such dividends.

(III) Treatment of taxes imposed on 936 corporation. For purposes of this clause, taxes paid by any corporation eligible for the credit provided by section 936 to a possession of the United States shall be treated as a withholding tax paid with respect to any dividend paid by such corporation to the extent such taxes would be treated as paid by the corporation receiving the dividend under rules similar to the rules of section 902 (and the amount of any such dividend shall be increased by the amount so treated).

(IV) Separate application of foreign tax credit limitations. In determining the alternative minimum foreign tax credit, section 904(d) shall be applied as if dividends from a corporation eligible for the credit provided by section 936 were a separate category of income referred to in a subparagraph of section 904(d)(1).

(V) Coordination with limitation on 936 credit. Any reference in this clause to a dividend received from a corporation eligible for the credit provided by section 936 shall be treated as a reference to the portion of any such dividend for which the dividends received deduction is disallowed under clause (i) after the application of clause (ii)(I).

(VI) Application to section 30A corporations. References in this clause to section 936 shall be treated as including references to section 30A.

(iv) Special rule for certain dividends received by certain cooperatives. In the case of [2]*[Sec. 11(g)(2), P.L. 110-172, 12/29/2007, directs that Code Sec. 54(g)(4)(C)(iv) be amended. It appears as if the amendment should be made to Code Sec. 56(g)(4)(C)(iv) and is in place here. See notes following this Code Sec.]* an organization to which part I of subchapter T (relating to tax treatment of cooperatives) applies which is engaged in the marketing of agricultural or horticultural products, clause (i) shall not apply to any amount allowable as a deduction under section 245(c).

(v) Deduction for domestic production. Clause (i) shall not apply to any amount allowable as a deduction under section 199.

(vi) Special rule for certain distributions from controlled foreign corporations. Clause (i) shall not apply to any deduction allowable under section 965.

(D) Certain other earnings and profits adjustments.

(i) Intangible drilling costs. The adjustments provided in section 312(n)(2)(A) shall apply in the case of amounts paid or incurred in taxable years beginning after December 31, 1989. In the case of a taxpayer other than an integrated oil company (as defined in section 291(b)(4)), in the case of any oil or gas well, this clause shall not apply in the case of amounts paid or incurred in taxable years beginning after December 31, 1992.

(ii) Certain amortization provisions not to apply. Sections 173 and 248 shall not apply to expenditures paid or incurred in taxable years beginning after December 31, 1989.

(iii) LIFO inventory adjustments. The adjustments provided in section 312(n)(4) shall apply, but only with respect to taxable years beginning after December 31, 1989.

(iv) Installment sales. In the case of any installment sale in a taxable year beginning after December 31, 1989, adjusted current earnings shall be computed as if the corporation did not use the installment method. The preceding sentence shall not apply to the applicable percentage (as determined under section 453A) of the gain from any installment sale with respect to which section 453A(a)(1) applies.

(E) Disallowance of loss on exchange of debt pools. No loss shall be recognized on the exchange of any pool of debt obligations for another pool of debt obligations having substantially the same effective interest rates and maturities.

(F) Depletion.

(i) In general. The allowance for depletion with respect to any property placed in service in a taxable year beginning after December 31, 1989, shall be cost depletion determined under section 611.

(ii) Exception for independent oil and gas producers and royalty owners. In the case of any taxable year beginning after December 31, 1992, clause (i) (and subparagraph (C)(i)) shall not apply to any deduction for depletion computed in accordance with section 613A(c).

(G) Treatment of certain ownership changes. If—

(i) there is an ownership change (within the meaning of section 382) in a taxable year beginning after 1989 with respect to any corporation, and

(ii) there is a net unrealized built-in loss (within the meaning of section 382(h)) with respect to such corporation,
 then the adjusted basis of each asset of such corporation (immediately after the ownership change) shall be its proportionate share (determined on the basis of respective fair market values) of the fair market value of the assets of such corporation (determined under section 382(h)) immediately before the ownership change.

(H) Adjusted basis. The adjusted basis of any property with respect to which an adjustment under this paragraph applies shall be determined by applying the treatment prescribed in this paragraph.

(J) Treatment of charitable contributions. Notwithstanding subparagraphs (B) and (C), no adjustment related to the earnings and profits effects of any charitable contribution shall be made in computing adjusted current earnings.

* * * * * * * * * * * *

[Endnote Code Sec. 56]

Matter in *italics* in Code Sec. 56(g)(4)(C)(ii)(I) and Code Sec. 56(g)(4)(C)(iv) was added by Sec. 11(g)(1)-(2) of the Tax Technical Corrections Act of 2007, P.L. 110-172, 12/29/2007, which struck out:

1. "921"

2. "a cooperative described in section 927(a)(4)"

Effective Date Enacted 12/29/2007.

[¶ 3020]   **Code Sec. 108.**   **Income from discharge of indebtedness.**

(a)   Exclusion from gross income.

(1)   In general. Gross income does not include any amount which (but for this subsection) would be includible in gross income by reason of the discharge (in whole or in part) of indebtedness of the taxpayer if—

(A) the discharge occurs in a title 11 case,

(B) the discharge occurs when the taxpayer is insolvent,

(C) the indebtedness discharged is qualified farm indebtedness, [1]

(D) in the case of a taxpayer other than a C corporation, the indebtedness discharged is qualified real property business indebtedness[2], *or*

[3]*(E) the indebtedness discharged is qualified principal residence indebtedness which is discharged before January 1, 2010.*

(2)   Coordination of exclusions.

(A) Title 11 exclusion takes precedence. Subparagraphs (B), (C), [4]*(D), and (E)* of paragraph (1) shall not apply to a discharge which occurs in a title 11 case.

(B) Insolvency exclusion takes precedence over qualified farm exclusion and qualified real property business exclusion. Subparagraphs (C) and (D) of paragraph (1) shall not apply to a discharge to the extent the taxpayer is insolvent.

[5]*(C) Principal residence exclusion takes precedence over insolvency exclusion unless elected otherwise. Paragraph (1)(B) shall not apply to a discharge to which paragraph (1)(E) applies unless the taxpayer elects to apply paragraph (1)(B) in lieu of paragraph (1)(E).*

(3)   Insolvency exclusion limited to amount of insolvency. In the case of a discharge to which paragraph (1)(B) applies, the amount excluded under paragraph (1)(B) shall not exceed the amount by which the taxpayer is insolvent.

* * * * * * * * * * * *

[6]*(h)   Special rules relating to qualified principal residence indebtedness.*

(1)   Basis reduction. The amount excluded from gross income by reason of subsection (a)(1)(E) shall be applied to reduce (but not below zero) the basis of the principal residence of the taxpayer.

(2)   Qualified principal residence indebtedness. For purposes of this section, the term "qualified principal residence indebtedness" means acquisition indebtedness (within the meaning of section 163(h)(3)(B), applied by substituting "$2,000,000 ($1,000,000" for "$1,000,000 ($500,000" in clause (ii) thereof) with respect to the principal residence of the taxpayer.

(3)   Exception for certain discharges not related to taxpayer's financial conditions. Subsection (a)(1)(E) shall not apply to the discharge of a loan if the discharge is on account of services performed for the lender or any other factor not directly related to a decline in the value of the residence or to the financial condition of the taxpayer.

(4)   Ordering rules. If any loan is discharged, in whole or in part, and only a portion of such loan is qualified principal residence indebtedness, subsection (a)(1)(E) shall apply only to so much of the amount discharged as exceeds the amount of the loan (as determined immediately before such discharge) which is not qualified principal residence indebtedness.

(5)   Principal residences. For purposes of this subsection, the term "principal residence" has the same meaning as when used in section 121.

[For Analysis, see ¶ 201. For Committee Reports, see ¶ 5501.]

[Endnote Code Sec. 108]

Matter in *italics* in Code Sec. 108(a)(1)(C), Code Sec. 108(a)(1)(D), Code Sec. 108(a)(1)(E), Code Sec. 108(a)(2)(A), Code Sec. 108(a)(2)(C) and Code Sec. 108(h) was added by Secs. 2(a), (b), (c)(1) and (2) of the Mortgage Forgiveness Debt Relief Act of 2007, P.L. 110-142, 12/20/2007, which struck out:

1. "or"

2. "."

3. added new subpara. (a)(1)(E)

4. "and (D)"
5. added new subpara. (a)(2)(C)
6. added new subsec. (h)
Effective Date (Sec. 2(d), P.L. 110-142, 12/20/2007) effective for discharges of indebtedness on or after 1/1/2007.

[¶ 3021]   Code Sec. 121.   Exclusion of gain from sale of principal residence.

(a) **Exclusion.** Gross income shall not include gain from the sale or exchange of property if, during the 5-year period ending on the date of the sale or exchange, such property has been owned and used by the taxpayer as the taxpayer's principal residence for periods aggregating 2 years or more.

(b) **Limitations.**

(1) **In general.** The amount of gain excluded from gross income under subsection (a) with respect to any sale or exchange shall not exceed $250,000.

* * * * * * * * * * * *

¹*(4) Special rule for certain sales by surviving spouses. In the case of a sale or exchange of property by an unmarried individual whose spouse is deceased on the date of such sale, paragraph (1) shall be applied by substituting "$500,000" for "$250,000" if such sale occurs not later than 2 years after the date of death of such spouse and the requirements of paragraph (2)(A) were met immediately before such date of death.*

* * * * * * * * * * * *

(d) **Special rules.**

* * * * * * * * * * * *

(9) **Uniformed services, foreign service, and intelligence community.**

(A) In general. At the election of an individual with respect to a property, the running of the 5-year period described in subsections (a) and (c)(1)(B) and paragraph (7) of this subsection with respect to such property shall be suspended during any period that such individual or such individual's spouse is serving on qualified official extended duty—

(i) as a member of the uniformed services,

(ii) as a member of the Foreign Service of the United States, or

(iii) as an employee of the intelligence community.

(B) Maximum period of suspension. The 5-year period described in subsection (a) shall not be extended more than 10 years by reason of subparagraph (A).

(C) Qualified official extended duty. For purposes of this paragraph—

(i) In general. The term "qualified official extended duty" means any extended duty while serving at a duty station which is at least 50 miles from such property or while residing under Government orders in Government quarters.

(ii) Uniformed services. The term "uniformed services" has the meaning given such term by section 101(a)(5) of title 10, United States Code, as in effect on the date of the enactment of this paragraph.

(iii) Foreign Service of the United States. The term "member of the Foreign Service of the United States" has the meaning given the term "member of the Service" by paragraph (1), (2), (3), (4), or (5) of section 103 of the Foreign Service Act of 1980, as in effect on the date of the enactment of this paragraph.

(iv) Employee of intelligence community. The term "employee of the intelligence community" means an employee (as defined by section 2105 of title 5, United States Code) of—

(I) the Office of the Director of National Intelligence,

(II) the Central Intelligence Agency,

(III) the National Security Agency,

(IV) the Defense Intelligence Agency,

(V) the National Geospatial-Intelligence Agency,

(VI) the National Reconnaissance Office,

(VII) any other office within the Department of Defense for the collection of specialized national intelligence through reconnaissance programs,

(VIII) any of the intelligence elements of the Army, the Navy, the Air Force, the Marine Corps, the Federal Bureau of Investigation, the Department of Treasury, the Department of Energy, and the Coast Guard,

(IX) the Bureau of Intelligence and Research of the Department of State, or

(X) any of the elements of the Department of Homeland Security concerned with the analyses of foreign intelligence information.

(v) Extended duty. The term "extended duty" means any period of active duty pursuant to a call or order to such duty for a period in excess of 90 days or for an indefinite period.

(vi) Special rule relating to intelligence community. An employee of the intelligence community shall not be treated as serving on qualified extended duty unless such duty is at a duty station located outside the United States.

(D) Special rules relating to election.

(i) Election limited to 1 property at a time. An election under subparagraph (A) with respect to any property may not be made if such an election is in effect with respect to any other property.

(ii) Revocation of election. An election under subparagraph (A) may be revoked at any time.

²(E) **Termination with respect to employees of intelligence community.** *Clause (iii) of subparagraph (A) shall not apply with respect to any sale or exchange after December 31, 2010.*

* * * * * * * * * * * *

[For Analysis, see ¶ 301.]

[Endnote Code Sec. 121]

Code Sec. 121(b)(4), in *italics*, was added by Sec. 7(a) of the Mortgage Forgiveness Debt Relief Act of 2007, P.L. 110-142, 12/20/2007.

1. added new para. (b)(4)

Effective Date (Sec. 7(b), P.L. 110-142, 12/20/2007) effective for sales or exchanges after 12/31/2007.

Code Sec. 121(d)(9)(E), in *italics*, was added by Sec. 11(a)(11)(A) of the Tax Technical Corrections Act of 2007, P.L. 110-172, 12/29/2007.

2. added subpara. (d)(9)(E)

Effective Date Enacted 12/29/2007.

[¶ 3022]   Code Sec. 125.   Cafeteria plans.

* * * * * * * * * * * *

(b)   Exception for highly compensated participants and key employees.

(1)   Highly compensated participants. In the case of a highly compensated participant, subsection (a) shall not apply to any benefit attributable to a plan year for which the plan discriminates in favor of—

(A) highly compensated individuals as to eligibility to participate, or

(B) highly compensated participants as to contributions and benefits.

(2)   Key employees. In the case of a key employee (within the meaning of section 416(i)(1)), subsection (a) shall not apply to any benefit attributable to a plan for which the statutory nontaxable benefits provided to key employees exceed 25 percent of the aggregate of such benefits provided for all employees under the plan. For purposes of the preceding sentence, statutory nontaxable benefits shall be determined without regard to the ¹*second sentence* of subsection (f).

(3) **Year of inclusion.** For purposes of determining the taxable year of inclusion, any benefit described in paragraph (1) or (2) shall be treated as received or accrued in the taxable year of the participant or key employee in which the plan year ends.

* * * * * * * * * * * *

[Endnote Code Sec. 125]

Matter in *italics* in Code Sec. 125(b)(2) was added by Sec. 11(a)(12) of the Tax Technical Corrections Act of 2007, P.L. 110-172, 12/29/2007, which struck out:

1. "last sentence"

Effective Date Enacted 12/29/2007.

[¶ 3023]   *Code Sec.[1] 139B.*   *Benefits provided to volunteer firefighters and emergency medical responders.*

(a)   *In general.* *In the case of any member of a qualified volunteer emergency response organization, gross income shall not include—*

    (1) any qualified State and local tax benefit, and

    (2) any qualified payment.

(b)   *Denial of double benefits.* *In the case of any member of a qualified volunteer emergency response organization—*

    (1) the deduction under 164 shall be determined with regard to any qualified State and local tax benefit, and

    (2) expenses paid or incurred by the taxpayer in connection with the performance of services as such a member shall be taken into account under section 170 only to the extent such expenses exceed the amount of any qualified payment excluded from gross income under subsection (a).

(c)   *Definitions.* *For purposes of this section—*

    (1)   *Qualified State and local tax benefit.* *The term "qualified state and local tax benefit" means any reduction or rebate of a tax described in paragraph (1), (2), or (3) of section 164(a) provided by a State or political division thereof on account of services performed as a member of a qualified volunteer emergency response organization.*

    (2)   *Qualified payment.*

      (A) In general. The term "qualified payment" means any payment (whether reimbursement or otherwise) provided by a State or political division thereof on account of the performance of services as a member of a qualified volunteer emergency response organization.

      (B) Applicable dollar limitation. The amount determined under subparagraph (A) for any taxable year shall not exceed $30 multiplied by the number of months during such year that the taxpayer performs such services.

    (3)   *Qualified volunteer emergency response organization. The term "qualified volunteer emergency response organization' means any volunteer organization—*

      (A) which is organized and operated to provide firefighting or emergency medical services for persons in the State or political subdivision, as the case may be, and

      (B) which is required (by written agreement) by the State or political subdivision to furnish firefighting or emergency medical services in such State or political subdivision.

(d)   *Termination.* *This section shall not apply with respect to taxable years beginning after December 31, 2010.*

[For Analysis, see ¶ 302. For Committee Reports, see ¶ 5503.]

[Endnote Code Sec. 139B]

Code Sec. 139B, in *italics*, was added by Sec. 5(a) of the Mortgage Forgiveness Debt Relief Act of 2007, P.L. 110-142, 12/20/2007.

1. added new Code Sec. 139B

Effective Date (Sec. 5(c), P.L. 110-142, 12/20/2007) effective for tax. yrs. begin. after 12/31/2007.

[¶ 3024]   Code Sec. 163.   Interest.

* * * * * * * * * * * *

(h)   Disallowance of deduction for personal interest.

   (1)   In general. In the case of a taxpayer other than a corporation, no deduction shall be allowed under this chapter for personal interest paid or accrued during the taxable year.

* * * * * * * * * * * *

   (3)   Qualified residence interest. For purposes of this subsection—

   (A) In general. The term "qualified residence interest" means any interest which is paid or accrued during the taxable year on—

      (i) acquisition indebtedness with respect to any qualified residence of the taxpayer, or

      (ii) home equity indebtedness with respect to any qualified residence of the taxpayer.

   For purposes of the preceding sentence, the determination of whether any property is a qualified residence of the taxpayer shall be made as of the time the interest is accrued.

   (B) Acquisition indebtedness.

      (i) In general. The term "acquisition indebtedness" means any indebtedness which—

         (I) is incurred in acquiring, constructing, or substantially improving any qualified residence of the taxpayer, and

         (II) is secured by such residence.

      Such term also includes any indebtedness secured by such residence resulting from the refinancing of indebtedness meeting the requirements of the preceding sentence (or this sentence); but only to the extent the amount of the indebtedness resulting from such refinancing does not exceed the amount of the refinanced indebtedness.

      (ii) $1,000,000 Limitation. The aggregate amount treated as acquisition indebtedness for any period shall not exceed $1,000,000 ($500,000 in the case of a married individual filing a separate return).

   (C) Home equity indebtedness.

      (i) In general. The term "home equity indebtedness" means any indebtedness (other than acquisition indebtedness) secured by a qualified residence to the extent the aggregate amount of such indebtedness does not exceed—

         (I) the fair market value of such qualified residence, reduced by

         (II) the amount of acquisition indebtedness with respect to such residence.

      (ii) Limitation. The aggregate amount treated as home equity indebtedness for any period shall not exceed $100,000 ($50,000 in the case of a separate return by a married individual).

   (D) Treatment of indebtedness incurred on or before October 13, 1987.

      (i) In general. In the case of any pre-October 13, 1987, indebtedness—

         (I) such indebtedness shall be treated as acquisition indebtedness, and

         (II) the limitation of subparagraph (B)(ii) shall not apply.

      (ii) Reduction in $1,000,000 limitation. The limitation of subparagraph (B)(ii) shall be reduced (but not below zero) by the aggregate amount of outstanding pre-October 13, 1987, indebtedness.

      (iii) Pre-October 13, 1987, indebtedness. The term "pre-October 13, 1987, indebtedness" means—

         (I) any indebtedness which was incurred on or before October 13, 1987, and which was secured by a qualified residence on October 13, 1987, and at all times thereafter before the interest is paid or accrued, or

(II) any indebtedness which is secured by the qualified residence and was incurred after October 13, 1987, to refinance indebtedness described in subclause (I) (or refinanced indebtedness meeting the requirements of this subclause) to the extent (immediately after the refinancing) the principal amount of the indebtedness resulting from the refinancing does not exceed the principal amount of the refinanced indebtedness (immediately before the refinancing).

(iv) Limitation on period of refinancing. Subclause (II) of clause (iii) shall not apply to any indebtedness after—

(I) the expiration of the term of the indebtedness described in clause (iii)(I), or

(II) if the principal of the indebtedness described in clause (iii)(I) is not amortized over its term, the expiration of the term of the 1st refinancing of such indebtedness (or if earlier, the date which is 30 years after the date of such 1st refinancing).

(E) Mortgage insurance premiums treated as interest.

(i) In general. Premiums paid or accrued for qualified mortgage insurance by a taxpayer during the taxable year in connection with acquisition indebtedness with respect to a qualified residence of the taxpayer shall be treated for purposes of this section as interest which is qualified residence interest.

(ii) Phaseout. The amount otherwise treated as interest under clause (i) shall be reduced (but not below zero) by 10 percent of such amount for each $1,000 ($500 in the case of a married individual filing a separate return) (or fraction thereof) that the taxpayer's adjusted gross income for the taxable year exceeds $100,000 ($50,000 in the case of a married individual filing a separate return).

(iii) Limitation. Clause (i) shall not apply with respect to any mortgage insurance contracts issued before January 1, 2007.

(iv) Termination. Clause (i) shall not apply to amounts—

(I) paid or accrued after [1]December 31, 2010, or

(II) properly allocable to any period after such date.

* * * * * * * * * * * *

[For Analysis, see ¶ 202.]

[Endnote Code Sec. 163]

Matter in *italics* in Code Sec. 163(h)(3)(E)(iv)(I) was added by Sec. 3(a) of the Mortgage Forgiveness Debt Relief Act of 2007, P.L. 110-142, 12/20/2007, which struck out:

1. "December 31, 2007"

Effective Date (Sec. 3(b), P.L. 110-142, 12/20/2007) effective for amounts paid or accrued after 12/31/2007.

[¶ 3025]   Code Sec. 167.   Depreciation.

* * * * * * * * * * * *

(g) Depreciation under income forecast method.

(1) In general. If the depreciation deduction allowable under this section to any taxpayer with respect to any property is determined under the income forecast method or any similar method—

(A) the income from the property to be taken into account in determining the depreciation deduction under such method shall be equal to the amount of income earned in connection with the property before the close of the 10th taxable year following the taxable year in which the property was placed in service,

(B) the adjusted basis of the property shall only include amounts with respect to which the requirements of section 461(h) are satisfied,

(C) the depreciation deduction under such method for the 10th taxable year beginning after the taxable year in which the property was placed in service shall be equal to the adjusted basis of such property as of the beginning of such 10th taxable year, and

(D) such taxpayer shall pay (or be entitled to receive) interest computed under the look-back method of paragraph (2) for any recomputation year.

* * * * * * * * * * * *

(8) Special rules for certain musical works and copyrights.

(A) In general. If an election is in effect under this paragraph for any taxable year, then, notwithstanding paragraph (1), any expense which—

(i) is paid or incurred by the taxpayer in creating or acquiring any applicable musical property placed in service during the taxable year, and

(ii) is otherwise properly chargeable to capital account,

shall be amortized ratably over the 5-year period beginning with the month in which the property was placed in service. The preceding sentence shall not apply to any expense which, without regard to this paragraph, would not be allowable as a deduction.

(B) Exclusive method. Except as provided in this paragraph, no depreciation or amortization deduction shall be allowed with respect to any expense to which subparagraph (A) applies.

(C) Applicable musical property. For purposes of this paragraph—

(i) In general. The term "applicable musical property" means any musical composition (including any accompanying words), or any copyright with respect to a musical composition, which is property to which this subsection applies without regard to this paragraph.

(ii) Exceptions. Such term shall not include any property—

(I) with respect to which expenses are treated as qualified creative expenses to which section 263A(h) applies,

(II) to which a simplified procedure established under ¹*section 263A(i)(2)* applies, or

(III) which is an amortizable section 197 intangible (as defined in section 197(c)).

(D) Election. An election under this paragraph shall be made at such time and in such form as the Secretary may prescribe and shall apply to all applicable musical property placed in service during the taxable year for which the election applies.

(E) Termination. An election may not be made under this paragraph for any taxable year beginning after December 31, 2010.

(h) Amortization of geological and geophysical expenditures.

(1) In general. Any geological and geophysical expenses paid or incurred in connection with the exploration for, or development of, oil or gas within the United States (as defined in section 638) shall be allowed as a deduction ratably over the 24-month period beginning on the date that such expense was paid or incurred.

* * * * * * * * * * * *

(5) Special rule for major integrated oil companies.

(A) In general. In the case of a major integrated oil company, paragraphs (1) and (4) shall be applied by substituting ²*"7-year"* for "24 month".

(B) Major integrated oil company. For purposes of this paragraph, the term "major integrated oil company" means, with respect to any taxable year, a producer of crude oil—

(i) which has an average daily worldwide production of crude oil of at least 500,000 barrels for the taxable year,

(ii) which had gross receipts in excess of $1,000,000,000 for its last taxable year ending during calendar year 2005, and

(iii) to which subsection (c) of section 613A does not apply by reason of paragraph (4) of section 613A(d), determined—

(I) by substituting "15 percent" for "5 percent" each place it occurs in paragraph (3) of section 613A(d), and

(II) without regard to whether subsection (c) of section 613A does not apply by reason of paragraph (2) of section 613A(d).

For purposes of clauses (i) and (ii), all persons treated as a single employer under subsections (a) and (b) of section 52 shall be treated as 1 person and, in case of a short taxable year, the rule under section 448(c)(3)(B) shall apply.

* * * * * * * * * * * *

[For Analysis, see ¶ 412. For Committee Reports, see ¶ 5102.]

[Endnote Code Sec. 167]

Matter in *italics*, in Code Sec. 167(g)(8)(C)(ii)(II) was added by Sec. 11(a)(13) of the Tax Technical Corrections Act of 2007, P.L. 110-172, 12/29/2007, which struck out:

1. "section 263A(j)(2)"

Effective Date enacted 12/29/2007.

Matter in *italics*, in Code Sec. 167(h)(5)(A) was added by Sec. 1502(a) of the Energy Independence and Security Act of 2007, P.L. 110-140, 12/19/2007, which struck out:

2. "5-year"

Effective Date (Sec. 1502(b), P.L. 110-140, 12/19/2007) effective for amounts paid or incurred after 12/19/2007.

[¶ 3026]   Code Sec. 168.   Accelerated cost recovery system.

* * * * * * * * * * * *

(k) Special allowance for certain property acquired after [1]*December 31, 2007*, **and before** [2]*January 1, 2009*.

(1) Additional allowance. In the case of any qualified property—

(A) the depreciation deduction provided by section 167(a) for the taxable year in which such property is placed in service shall include an allowance equal to [3]*50 percent* of the adjusted basis of the qualified property, and

(B) the adjusted basis of the qualified property shall be reduced by the amount of such deduction before computing the amount otherwise allowable as a depreciation deduction under this chapter for such taxable year and any subsequent taxable year.

(2) Qualified property. For purposes of this subsection—

(A) In general. The term "qualified property" means property—

(i) (I) to which this section applies which has a recovery period of 20 years or less,

(II) which is computer software (as defined in section 167(f)(1)(B)) for which a deduction is allowable under section 167(a) without regard to this subsection,

(III) which is water utility property, or

(IV) which is qualified leasehold improvement property,

(ii) the original use of which commences with the taxpayer after [4]*December 31, 2007*,

(iii) which is—

(I) acquired by the taxpayer after [5]*December 31, 2007*, and before [6]*January 1, 2009*, but only if no written binding contract for the acquisition was in effect before [7]*January 1, 2008*, or

(II) acquired by the taxpayer pursuant to a written binding contract which was entered into after [8]*December 31, 2007*, and before [9]*January 1, 2009*, and

(iv) which is placed in service by the taxpayer before [10]*January 1, 2009*, or, in the case of property described in subparagraph (B) or (C), before [11]*January 1, 2010*.

(B) Certain property having longer production periods treated as qualified property.

(i) In general. The term "qualified property" includes any property if such property—

(I) meets the requirements of clauses (i), (ii), [12]*(iii), and (iv)* of subparagraph (A),

(II) has a recovery period of at least 10 years or is transportation property,

(III) is subject to section 263A, and

(IV) meets the requirements of [13]*clause (iii)* of section 263A(f)(1)(B) (determined as if such clauses also apply to property which has a long useful life (within the meaning of section 263A(f))).

(ii) Only [14]*pre-January 1, 2009,* basis eligible for additional allowance. In the case of property which is qualified property solely by reason of clause (i), paragraph (1) shall apply only to the extent of the adjusted basis thereof attributable to manufacture, construction, or production before [15]*January 1, 2009.*

(iii) Transportation property. For purposes of this subparagraph, the term "transportation property" means tangible personal property used in the trade or business of transporting persons or property.

(iv) Application of subparagraph. This subparagraph shall not apply to any property which is described in subparagraph (C).

(C) Certain aircraft. The term "qualified property" includes property—

(i) which meets the requirements of clauses (ii) [16], *(iii)*, and (iv) of subparagraph (A),

(ii) which is an aircraft which is not a transportation property (as defined in subparagraph (B)(iii)) other than for agricultural or firefighting purposes,

(iii) which is purchased and on which such purchaser, at the time of the contract for purchase, has made a nonrefundable deposit of the lesser of—

(I) 10 percent of the cost, or

(II) $100,000, and

(iv) which has—

(I) an estimated production period exceeding 4 months, and

(II) a cost exceeding $200,000.

(D) Exceptions.

(i) Alternative depreciation property. The term "qualified property" shall not include any property to which the alternative depreciation system under subsection (g) applies, determined—

(I) without regard to paragraph (7) of subsection (g) (relating to election to have system apply), and

(II) after application of section 280F(b) (relating to listed property with limited business use).

(ii) Qualified New York Liberty Zone leasehold improvement property. The term "qualified property" shall not include any qualified New York Liberty Zone leasehold improvement property (as defined in section 1400L(c)(2)).

(iii) Election out. If a taxpayer makes an election under this clause with respect to any class of property for any taxable year, this subsection shall not apply to all property in such class placed in service during such taxable year. [17]

(E) Special rules.

(i) Self-constructed property. In the case of a taxpayer manufacturing, constructing, or producing property for the taxpayer's own use, the requirements of clause (iii) of subparagraph (A) shall be treated as met if the taxpayer begins manufacturing, constructing, or producing the property after [18]*December 31, 2007,* and before [19]*January 1, 2009.*

(ii) Sale-leasebacks. For purposes of clause (iii) and subparagraph (A)(ii), if property is—

(I) originally placed in service after [20]*December 31, 2007,* by a person, and

(II) sold and leased back by such person within 3 months after the date such property was originally placed in service,

such property shall be treated as originally placed in service not earlier than the date on which such property is used under the leaseback referred to in subclause (II).

(iii) Syndication. For purposes of subparagraph (A)(ii), if—

(I) property is originally placed in service after [21]*December 31, 2007,* by the lessor of such property,

329

(II) such property is sold by such lessor or any subsequent purchaser within 3 months after the date such property was originally placed in service (or, in the case of multiple units of property subject to the same lease, within 3 months after the date the final unit is placed in service, so long as the period between the time the first unit is placed in service and the time the last unit is placed in service does not exceed 12 months), and

(III) the user of such property after the last sale during such 3-month period remains the same as when such property was originally placed in service, such property shall be treated as originally placed in service not earlier than the date of such last sale.

(iv) Limitations related to users and related parties. The term "qualified property" shall not include any property if—

(I) the user of such property (as of the date on which such property is originally placed in service) or a person which is related (within the meaning of section 267(b) or 707(b)) to such user or to the taxpayer had a written binding contract in effect for the acquisition of such property at any time on or before [22]December 31, 2007, or

(II) in the case of property manufactured, constructed, or produced for such user's or person's own use, the manufacture, construction, or production of such property began at any time on or before [23]December 31, 2007.

(F) Coordination with section 280F. For purposes of section 280F—

(i) Automobiles. In the case of a passenger automobile (as defined in section 280F(d)(5)) which is qualified property, the Secretary shall increase the limitation under section 280F(a)(1)(A)(i) by [24]$8,000.

(ii) Listed property. The deduction allowable under paragraph (1) shall be taken into account in computing any recapture amount under section 280F(b)(2).

(G) Deduction allowed in computing minimum tax. For purposes of determining alternative minimum taxable income under section 55, the deduction under subsection (a) for qualified property shall be determined under this section without regard to any adjustment under section 56.

(3) **Qualified leasehold improvement property.** For purposes of this subsection—

(A) In general. The term "qualified leasehold improvement property" means any improvement to an interior portion of a building which is nonresidential real property if—

(i) such improvement is made under or pursuant to a lease (as defined in subsection (h)(7))—

(I) by the lessee (or any sublessee) of such portion, or

(II) by the lessor of such portion,

(ii) such portion is to be occupied exclusively by the lessee (or any sublessee) of such portion, and

(iii) such improvement is placed in service more than 3 years after the date the building was first placed in service.

(B) Certain improvements not included. Such term shall not include any improvement for which the expenditure is attributable to—

(i) the enlargement of the building,

(ii) any elevator or escalator,

(iii) any structural component benefiting a common area, and

(iv) the internal structural framework of the building.

(C) Definitions and special rules. For purposes of this paragraph—

(i) Commitment to lease treated as lease. A commitment to enter into a lease shall be treated as a lease, and the parties to such commitment shall be treated as lessor and lessee, respectively.

(ii) Related persons. A lease between related persons shall not be considered a lease. For purposes of the preceding sentence, the term "related persons" means—

(I) members of an affiliated group (as defined in section 1504), and

(II) persons having a relationship described in subsection (b) of section 267; except that, for purposes of this clause, the phrase "80 percent or more" shall be substituted for the phrase "more than 50 percent" each place it appears in such subsection.

²⁵*(4)* **Repealed.**

(l) Special allowance for cellulosic biomass ethanol plant property.

(1) Additional allowance. In the case of any qualified cellulosic biomass ethanol plant property—

(A) the depreciation deduction provided by section 167(a) for the taxable year in which such property is placed in service shall include an allowance equal to 50 percent of the adjusted basis of such property, and

(B) the adjusted basis of such property shall be reduced by the amount of such deduction before computing the amount otherwise allowable as a depreciation deduction under this chapter for such taxable year and any subsequent taxable year.

(2) Qualified cellulosic biomass ethanol plant property. The term "qualified cellulosic biomass ethanol plant property" means property of a character subject to the allowance for depreciation—

(A) which is used in the United States solely to produce cellulosic biomass ethanol,

(B) the original use of which commences with the taxpayer after the date of the enactment of this subsection,

(C) which is acquired by the taxpayer by purchase (as defined in section 179(d)) after the date of the enactment of this subsection, but only if no written binding contract for the acquisition was in effect on or before the date of the enactment of this subsection, and

(D) which is placed in service by the taxpayer before January 1, 2013.

(3) Cellulosic biomass ethanol. For purposes of this subsection, the term "cellulosic biomass ethanol" means ethanol produced by ²⁵ᴬhydrolysis of any lignocellulosic or hemicellulosic matter that is available on a renewable or recurring basis.

(4) Exceptions.

²⁶*(A) Bonus depreciation property under subsection (k). Such term shall not include any property to which section 168(k) applies.*

²⁷*(B)* Alternative depreciation property. Such term shall not include any property described in section 168(k)(2)(D)(i).

²⁸*(C)* Tax-exempt bond-financed property. Such term shall not include any property any portion of which is financed with the proceeds of any obligation the interest on which is exempt from tax under section 103.

²⁹*(D)* Election out. If a taxpayer makes an election under this subparagraph with respect to any class of property for any taxable year, this subsection shall not apply to all property in such class placed in service during such taxable year.

(5) Special rules. For purposes of this subsection, rules similar to the rules of subparagraph (E) of section 168(k)(2) shall apply, except that such subparagraph shall be applied—

(A) by substituting "the date of the enactment of subsection (l)" for ³⁰*"December 31, 2007"* each place it appears therein,

(B) by substituting "January 1, 2013" for ³¹*"January 1, 2009"* in clause (i) thereof, and

(C) by substituting "qualified cellulosic biomass ethanol plant property" for "qualified property" in clause (iv) thereof.

(6) Allowance against alternative minimum tax. For purposes of this subsection, rules similar to the rules of section 168(k)(2)(G) shall apply.

(7) Recapture. For purposes of this subsection, rules similar to the rules under section 179(d)(10) shall apply with respect to any qualified cellulosic biomass ethanol plant property which ceases to be qualified cellulosic biomass ethanol plant property.

(8) Denial of double benefit. Paragraph (1) shall not apply to any qualified cellulosic biomass ethanol plant property with respect to which an election has been made under section 179C (relating to election to expense certain refineries).

[For Analysis, see ¶ 53, ¶ 54 and ¶ 408. For Committee Reports, see ¶ 5503.]

[Endnote Code Sec. 168]

Matter in *italics* in Code Sec. 168(k) was added by Sec. 103(a)(1)-(3), (b), (c)(1)-(5) and (c)(11)-(12) of the Economic Stimulus Act of 2008, P.L. 110-185, 2/13/2008, which struck out:

1. "September 10, 2001"
2. "January 1, 2005"
3. "30 percent"
4. "September 10, 2001"
5. "September 10, 2001"
6. "January 1, 2005"
7. "September 11, 2001"
8. "September 10, 2001"
9. "January 1, 2005"
10. "January 1, 2005"
11. "January 1, 2006"
12. "and (iii)"
13. "clauses (ii) and (iii)"
14. "Pre-January 1, 2005"
15. "January 1, 2005"
16. "and (iii)"
17. "The preceding sentence shall be applied separately with respect to property treated as qualified property by paragraph (4) and other qualified property."
18. "September 10, 2001"
19. "January 1, 2005"
20. "September 10, 2001"
21. "September 10, 2001"
22. "September 10, 2001"
23. "September 10, 2001"
24. "$4,600"
25. "(4) 50-percent bonus depreciation for certain property.

"(A) In general. In the case of 50-percent bonus depreciation property—

"(i) paragraph (1)(A) shall be applied by substituting '50 percent' for '30 percent', and

"(ii) except as provided in paragraph (2)(D), such property shall be treated as qualified property for purposes of this subsection.

"(B) 50-percent bonus depreciation property. For purposes of this subsection, the term '50-percent bonus depreciation property' means property described in paragraph (2)(A)(i)—

"(i) the original use of which commences with the taxpayer after May 5, 2003,

"(ii) which is—

"(I) acquired by the taxpayer after May 5, 2003, and before January 1, 2005, but only if no written binding contract for the acquisition was in effect before May 6, 2003, or

"(II) acquired by the taxpayer pursuant to a written binding contract which was entered into after May 5, 2003, and before January 1, 2005, and

"(iii) which is placed in service by the taxpayer before January 1, 2005, or, in the case of property described in paragraph (2)(B) (as modified by subparagraph (C) of this paragraph) or paragraph (2)(C) (as so modified), before January 1, 2006.

"(C) Special rules. Rules similar to the rules of subparagraphs (B), (C), and (E) of paragraph (2) shall apply for purposes of this paragraph; except that references to September 10, 2001, shall be treated as references to May 5, 2003.

"(D) Automobiles. Paragraph (2)(F) shall be applied by substituting '$7,650' for '$4,600' in the case of 50-percent bonus depreciation property.

"(E) Election of 30-percent bonus. If a taxpayer makes an election under this subparagraph with respect to any class of property for any taxable year, subparagraph (A)(i) shall not apply to all property in such class placed in service during such taxable year."

Effective Date (Sec. 103(d), P.L. 110-185, 2/13/2008) effective for property placed in service after 12/31/2007, in tax. yrs. end. after 12/31/2007.

[Endnote Code Sec. 168]

In Code Sec. 168(l)(3), Sec. 11(b)(1) of the Tax Technical Corrections Act of 2007, P.L. 110-172, 12/29/2007, struck out:

25A. "enzymatic"

Effective Date (Sec. 11(b)(3), P.L. 110-172, 12/29/2007) Effective for property placed in service after 12/20/2006 in tax. yrs. end. after 12/20/2006.

Matter in *italics* in Code Sec. 168(l)(4) and Code Sec. 168(l)(5) was added by Sec. 103(c)(6) and (7) of the Economic Stimulus Act of 2008, P.L. 110-185, 2/13/2008, which struck out:
26. added new subpara. (l)(4)(A)
27. "(B)"
28. "(C)"
29. "(D)"
30. "September 10, 2001"
31. "January 1, 2005"
Effective Date (Sec. 103(d), P.L. 110-185, 2/13/2008) effective for property placed in service after 12/31/2007, in tax. yrs. end. after 12/31/2007.

[¶ 3027]   Code Sec. 170.   Charitable, etc., contributions and gifts.

* * * * * * * * * * * *

(b) Percentage limitations.

   (1) Individuals. In the case of an individual, the deduction provided in subsection (a) shall be limited as provided in the succeeding subparagraphs.

      (A) General rule. Any charitable contribution to—

         (i) a church or a convention or association of churches,

         (ii) an educational organization which normally maintains a regular faculty and curriculum and normally has a regularly enrolled body of pupils or students in attendance at the place where its educational activities are regularly carried on,

         (iii) an organization the principal purpose or functions of which are the providing of medical or hospital care or medical education or medical research, if the organization is a hospital, or if the organization is a medical research organization directly engaged in the continuous active conduct of medical research in conjunction with a hospital, and during the calendar year in which the contribution is made such organization is committed to spend such contributions for such research before January 1 of the fifth calendar year which begins after the date such contribution is made,

         (iv) an organization which normally receives a substantial part of its support (exclusive of income received in the exercise or performance by such organization of its charitable, educational, or other purpose or function constituting the basis for its exemption under section 501(a)) from the United States or any State or political subdivision thereof or from direct or indirect contributions from the general public, and which is organized and operated exclusively to receive, hold, invest, and administer property and to make expenditures to or for the benefit of a college or university which is an organization referred to in clause (ii) of this subparagraph and which is an agency or instrumentality of a State or political subdivision thereof, or which is owned or operated by a State or political subdivision thereof or by an agency or instrumentality of one or more States or political subdivisions,

         (v) a governmental unit referred to in subsection (c)(1),

         (vi) an organization referred to in subsection (c)(2) which normally receives a substantial part of its support (exclusive of income received in the exercise or performance by such organization of its charitable, educational, or other purpose or function constituting the basis for its exemption under section 501(a)) from a governmental unit referred to in subsection (c)(1) or from direct or indirect contributions from the general public,

         (vii) a private foundation described in [1]*subparagraph (F)*, or

         (viii) an organization described in section 509(a)(2) or (3),

      shall be allowed to the extent that the aggregate of such contributions does not exceed 50 percent of the taxpayer's contribution base for the taxable year.

* * * * * * * * * * * *

(e) Certain contributions of ordinary income and capital gain property.

   (1) General rule. The amount of any charitable contribution of property otherwise taken into account under this section shall be reduced by the sum of—

(A) the amount of gain which would not have been long-term capital gain (determined without regard to section 1221(b)(3)) if the property contributed had been sold by the taxpayer at its fair market value (determined at the time of such contribution), and

(B) in the case of a charitable contribution—

(i) of tangible personal property—

(I) if the use by the donee is unrelated to the purpose or function constituting the basis for its exemption under section 501 (or, in the case of a governmental unit, to any purpose or function described in subsection (c)), or

(II) which is applicable property (as defined in paragraph (7)(C)², *but without regard to clause (ii) thereof*) which is sold, exchanged, or otherwise disposed of by the donee before the last day of the taxable year in which the contribution was made and with respect to which the donee has not made a certification in accordance with paragraph (7)(D),

(ii) to or for the use of a private foundation (as defined in section 509(a)), other than a private foundation described in ³*subsection (b)(1)(F)*,

(iii) of any patent, copyright (other than a copyright described in section 1221(a)(3) or 1231(b)(1)(C)), trademark, trade name, trade secret, know-how, software (other than software described in section 197(e)(3)(A)(i)), or similar property, or applications or registrations of such property, or

(iv) of any taxidermy property which is contributed by the person who prepared, stuffed, or mounted the property or by any person who paid or incurred the cost of such preparation, stuffing, or mounting,

the amount of gain which would have been long-term capital gain if the property contributed had been sold by the taxpayer at its fair market value (determined at the time of such contribution).

> • ***Caution:*** The following flush material for para. (e)(1), following, is effective for estates of decedents dying before 1/1/2010. For the flush material for para. (e)(1) effective for estates of decedents dying after 12/31/2009, see below.

For purposes of applying this paragraph (other than in the case of gain to which section 617(d)(1), 1245(a), 1250(a), 1252(a), or 1254(a) applies), property which is property used in the trade or business (as defined in section 1231(b)) shall be treated as a capital asset. For purposes of applying this paragraph in the case of a charitable contribution of stock in an S corporation, rules similar to the rules of section 751 shall apply in determining whether gain on such stock would have been long-term capital gain if such stock were sold by the taxpayer.

> • ***Caution:*** The following flush material for para. (e)(1) is effective for estates of decedents dying after 12/31/2009. For the flush material for para. (e)(1) effective before 1/1/2010, see above.

For purposes of applying this paragraph (other than in the case of gain to which section 617(d)(1), 1245(a), 1250(a), 1252(a), or 1254(a) applies), property which is property used in the trade or business (as defined in section 1231(b)) shall be treated as a capital asset. For purposes of applying this paragraph in the case of a charitable contribution of stock in an S corporation, rules similar to the rules of section 751 shall apply in determining whether gain on such stock would have been long-term capital gain if such stock were sold by the taxpayer. For purposes of this paragraph, the determination of whether property is a capital asset shall be made without regard to the exception contained in section 1221(a)(3)(C) for basis determined under section 1022.

* * * * * * * * * * * *

(7)   Recapture of deduction on certain dispositions of exempt use property.

(A) In general. In the case of an applicable disposition of applicable property, there shall be included in the income of the donor of such property for the taxable year of such donor in which the applicable disposition occurs an amount equal to the excess (if any) of—

(i) the amount of the deduction allowed to the donor under this section with respect to such property, over

(ii) the donor's basis in such property at the time such property was contributed.

(B) Applicable disposition. For purposes of this paragraph, the term "applicable disposition" means any sale, exchange, or other disposition by the donee of applicable property—

(i) after the last day of the taxable year of the donor in which such property was contributed, and

(ii) before the last day of the 3-year period beginning on the date of the contribution of such property,

unless the donee makes a certification in accordance with subparagraph (D).

(C) Applicable property. For purposes of this paragraph, the term "applicable property" means charitable deduction property (as defined in section 6050L(a)(2)(A))—

(i) which is tangible personal property the use of which is identified by the donee as related to the purpose or function constituting the basis of the donee's exemption under section 501, and

(ii) for which a deduction in excess of the donor's basis is allowed.

(D) Certification. A certification meets the requirements of this subparagraph if it is a written statement which is signed under penalty of perjury by an officer of the donee organization and—

(i) which—

(I) certifies that the use of the property by the donee was [4]*substantial and related* to the purpose or function constituting the basis for the donee's exemption under section 501, and

(II) describes how the property was used and how such use furthered such purpose or function, or

(ii) which—

(I) states the intended use of the property by the donee at the time of the contribution, and

(II) certifies that such intended use has become impossible or infeasible to implement.

* * * * * * * * * * * *

(o)   Special rules for fractional gifts.

(1)   Denial of deduction in certain cases.

(A) In general. No deduction shall be allowed for a contribution of an undivided portion of a taxpayer's entire interest in tangible personal property unless [5]*all interests in the property are* held immediately before such contribution by—

(i) the taxpayer, or

(ii) the taxpayer and the donee.

(B) Exceptions. The Secretary may, by regulation, provide for exceptions to subparagraph (A) in cases where all persons who hold an interest in the property make proportional contributions of an undivided portion of the entire interest held by such persons.

(2)   Valuation of subsequent gifts. In the case of any additional contribution, the fair market value of such contribution shall be determined by using the lesser of—

(A) the fair market value of the property at the time of the initial fractional contribution, or

(B) the fair market value of the property at the time of the additional contribution.

(3) Recapture of deduction in certain cases; addition to tax.

(A) Recapture. The Secretary shall provide for the recapture of the amount of any deduction allowed under this section (plus interest) with respect to any contribution of an undivided portion of a taxpayer's entire interest in tangible personal property—

(i) in any case in which the donor does not contribute all of the remaining [6]*interests* in such property to the donee (or, if such donee is no longer in existence, to any person described in section 170(c)) [7]*on or before* the earlier of—

(I) the date that is 10 years after the date of the initial fractional contribution, or

(II) the date of the death of the donor, and

(ii) in any case in which the donee has not, during the period beginning on the date of the initial fractional contribution and ending on the date described in clause (i)—

(I) had substantial physical possession of the property, and

(II) used the property in a use which is related to a purpose or function constituting the basis for the organizations' exemption under section 501.

(B) Addition to tax. The tax imposed under this chapter for any taxable year for which there is a recapture under subparagraph (A) shall be increased by 10 percent of the amount so recaptured.

(4) Definitions. For purposes of this subsection—

(A) Additional contribution. The term "additional contribution" means any charitable contribution by the taxpayer of any interest in property with respect to which the taxpayer has previously made an initial fractional contribution.

(B) Initial fractional contribution. The term "initial fractional contribution" means, with respect to any taxpayer, the first charitable contribution of an undivided portion of the taxpayer's entire interest in any tangible personal property.

* * * * * * * * * * * *

[For Analysis, see ¶604 and ¶605. For Committee Reports, see ¶5302.]

[Endnote Code Sec. 170]

Matter in *italics* in Code Sec. 170(b)(1)(A)(vii), Code Sec. 170(e)(1)(B)(i)(II) and Code Sec. 170(e)(1)(B)(ii) was added by Sec. 11(a)(14)(A), 11(a)(14)(B) and (a)(15) of the Tax Technical Corrections Act of 2007, P.L. 110-172, which struck out:

1. "subparagraph (E)"
2. added matter in subclause (e)(1)(B)(i)(II)
3. "subsection (b)(1)(E)"

Effective Date enacted 12/29/2007.

_____

Matter in *italics* in Code Sec. 170(e)(7)(D)(i)(I) was added by Sec. 3(c), P.L. 110-172, 12/29/2007, which struck out:

4. "related"

Effective Date (Sec. 3(j), P.L. 110-172, 12/29/2007) effective for contributions after 9/1/2006.

_____

Matter in *italics* in Code Sec. 170(o)(1)(A), and Code Sec. 170(o)(3)(A)(i) was added by Sec. 11(a)(16)(A), and (a)(16)(B)(i)-(ii), P.L. 110-172, 12/29/2007, which struck out:

5. "all interest in the property is"
6. "interest"
7. "before"

Effective Date enacted 12/29/2007.

_____

[¶3028]   Code Sec. 179.   Election to expense certain depreciable business assets.

* * * * * * * * * * * *

(b) Limitations.

[1]*(7) Increase in limitations for 2008. In the case of any taxable year beginning in 2008—*

(A) the dollar limitation under paragraph (1) shall be $250,000,

(B) the dollar limitation under paragraph (2) shall be $800,000, and

(C) the amounts described in subparagraphs (A) and (B) shall not be adjusted under paragraph (5).

[For Analysis, see ¶ 52. For Committee Reports, see ¶ 5502.]

[Endnote Code Sec. 179]

Code Sec. 179(b)(7) in *italics* was added by Sec. 102(a) of the Economic Stimulus Act of 2008, P.L. 110-185, 2/13/2008.

1. added para. (b)(7)

Effective Date (Sec. 102(b), P.L. 110-185, 2/13/2008) effective for tax. yrs. begin. after 12/31/2007.

[¶ 3029]   Code Sec. 179B.   Deduction for capital costs incurred in complying with Environmental Protection Agency sulfur regulations.

(a)   Allowance of deduction. In the case of a small business refiner (as defined in section 45H(c)(1)) which elects the application of this section, there shall be allowed as a deduction an amount equal to 75 percent of ^{1}*qualified costs* (as defined in section 45H(c)(2)) which are paid or incurred by the taxpayer during the taxable year ^{2}*and which are properly chargeable to capital account.*

* * * * * * * * * * * *

[For Analysis, see ¶ 401. For Committee Reports, see ¶ 5306.]

[Endnote Code Sec. 179B]

Matter in *italics* in Code Sec. 179B(a) was added by Sec. 7(a)(3)(A) and (C) of the Tax Technical Corrections Act of 2007, P.L. 110-172, 12/29/2007.

1. "qualified capital costs"

2. added matter in subsec. (a)

Effective Date (Sec. 7(e)(1), P.L. 110-172, 12/29/2007) effective for expenses paid or incurred after 12/31/2002, in tax. yrs. end. after such date.

[¶ 3030]   Code Sec. 216.   Deduction of taxes, interest, and business depreciation by cooperative housing corporation tenant-stockholder.

* * * * * * * * * * * *

(b)   Definitions. For purposes of this section —

(1)   Cooperative housing corporation. The term "cooperative housing corporation" means a corporation —

(A) having one and only one class of stock outstanding,

(B) each of the stockholders of which is entitled, solely by reason of his ownership of stock in the corporation, to occupy for dwelling purposes a house, or an apartment in a building, owned or leased by such corporation,

(C) no stockholder of which is entitled (either conditionally or unconditionally) to receive any distribution not out of earnings and profits of the corporation except on a complete or partial liquidation of the corporation, and

^{1}*(D) meeting 1 or more of the following requirements for the taxable year in which the taxes and interest described in subsection (a) are paid or incurred:*

(i) 80 percent or more of the corporation's gross income for such taxable year is derived from tenant-stockholders.

(ii) At all times during such taxable year, 80 percent or more of the total square footage of the corporation's property is used or available for use by the tenant-stockholders for residential purposes or purposes ancillary to such residential use.

(iii) 90 percent or more of the expenditures of the corporation paid or incurred during such taxable year are paid or incurred for the acquisition, construction, management, maintenance, or care of the corporation's property for the benefit of the tenant-stockholders.

* * * * * * * * * * * *

[For Analysis, see ¶ 1302. For Committee Reports, see ¶ 5502.]

[Endnote Code Sec. 216]

　　Matter in *italics* in Code Sec. 216(b)(1)(D) was added by Sec. 4(a) of the Mortgage Forgiveness Debt Relief Act of 2007, P.L. 110-142, 12/20/2007, which struck out:

　　1. "(D) 80 percent or more of the gross income of which for the taxable year in which the taxes and interest described in subsection (a) are paid or incurred is derived from tenant-stockholders."

Effective Date (Sec. 4(b), P.L. 110-142, 12/20/2007) effective for tax. yrs. end. after 12/20/2007.

[¶ 3031]　　　**Code Sec. 245.**　　　**Dividends received from certain foreign corporations.**

* * * * * * * * * * * *

(c)　Certain dividends received from FSC.

　　(1)　In general. In the case of a domestic corporation, there shall be allowed as a deduction an amount equal to—

　　　　(A) 100 percent of any dividend received from another corporation which is distributed out of earnings and profits attributable to foreign trade income for a period during which such other corporation was a FSC, and

　　　　(B) 70 percent (80 percent in the case of dividends from a 20-percent owned corporation as defined in section 243(c)(2)) of any dividend received from another corporation which is distributed out of earnings and profits attributable to effectively connected income received or accrued by such other corporation while such other corporation was a FSC.

　　(2)　Exception for certain dividends. Paragraph (1) shall not apply to any dividend which is distributed out of earnings and profits attributable to foreign trade income which—

　　　　(A) is section 923(a)(2) nonexempt income (within the meaning of section 927(d)(6)), or

　　　　(B) would not, but for section 923(a)(4), be treated as exempt foreign trade income.

　　(3)　No deduction under subsection (a) or (b). No deduction shall be allowable under subsection (a) or (b) with respect to any dividend which is distributed out of earnings and profits of a corporation accumulated while such corporation was a FSC.

　　(4)　Definitions. For purposes of this subsection—

　　　　(A) Foreign trade income; exempt foreign trade income. The terms "foreign trade income" and "exempt foreign trade income" have the respective meanings given such terms by section 923.

　　　　(B) Effectively connected income. The term "effectively connected income" means any income which is effectively connected (or treated as effectively connected) with the conduct of a trade or business in the United States and is subject to tax under this chapter. Such term shall not include any foreign trade income.

　　　　[1]*(C) FSC. The term "FSC" has the meaning given such term by section 922.*

　　[2]*(5)　References to prior law. Any reference in this subsection to section 922, 923, or 927 shall be treated as a reference to such section as in effect before its repeal by the FSC Repeal and Extraterritorial Income Exclusion Act of 2000.*

[Endnote Code Sec. 245]

　　Code Sec. 245(c)(4)(C) and Code Sec. 245(c)(5) in *italics* were added by Sec. 11(g)(3) and (4) of the Tax Technical Corrections Act of 2007, P.L. 110-172, 12/29/2007.

　　1. added subpara. (c)(4)(C).

　　2. added para. (c)(5).

Effective Date (P.L. 110-172, 12/29/2007) enacted 12/29/2007

[¶ 3032] Code Sec. 275. Certain taxes.

(a) General rule. No deduction shall be allowed for the following taxes:

(1) Federal income taxes, including—

(A) the tax imposed by section 3101 (relating to the tax on employees under the Federal Insurance Contributions Act);

(B) the taxes imposed by sections 3201 and 3211 (relating to the taxes on railroad employees and railroad employee representatives); and

(C) the tax withheld at source on wages under section 3402.

(2) Federal war profits and excess profits taxes.

(3) Estate, inheritance, legacy, succession, and gift taxes.

(4) Income, war profits, and excess profits taxes imposed by the authority of any foreign country or possession of the United States [1]*if the taxpayer chooses to take to any extent the benefits of section 901.*

(5) Taxes on real property, to the extent that section 164(d) requires such taxes to be treated as imposed on another taxpayer.

(6) Taxes imposed by chapters 41, 42, 43, 44, 45, 46, and 54.

Paragraph (1) shall not apply to any taxes to the extent such taxes are allowable as a deduction under section 164(f). Paragraph (1) shall not apply to the tax imposed by section 59A.

* * * * * * * * * * * *

(b) Cross reference. For disallowance of certain other taxes, see section 164(c).

[Endnote Code Sec. 275]

Matter in *italics* in Code Sec. 275(a)(4) was added by Sec. 11(g)(5) of the Tax Technical Corrections Act of 2007, P.L. 110-172, 12/29/2007, which struck out:

1. "if—

"(A) the taxpayer chooses to take to any extent the benefits of section 901, or

"(B) such taxes are paid or accrued with respect to foreign trade income (within the meaning of section 923(b)) of a FSC."

Effective Date (P.L. 110-172 12/29/2007) enacted 12/29/2007.

[¶ 3033] Code Sec. 280C. Certain expenses for which credits are allowable.

* * * * * * * * * * * *

[1]*(d) Credit for low sulfur diesel fuel production.* The deductions otherwise allowed under this chapter for the taxable year shall be reduced by the amount of the credit determined for the taxable year under section 45H(a).

* * * * * * * * * * * *

(e) Mine rescue team training credit. No deduction shall be allowed for that portion of the expenses otherwise allowable as a deduction for the taxable year which is equal to the amount of the credit determined for the taxable year under section 45N(a).

[For Analysis, see ¶ 401. For Committee Reports, see ¶ 5306.]

[Endnote Code Sec. 280C]

Code Sec. 280C(d), in *italics*, was added by Sec. 7(a)(1)(B) of the Tax Technical Corrections Act of 2007, P.L. 110-172, 12/29/2007, which struck out:

1. "(d) Low sulfur diesel fuel production credit. No deduction shall be allowed for that portion of the expenses otherwise allowable as a deduction for the taxable year which is equal to the amount of the credit determined for the taxable year under section 45H(a)."

Effective Date (Sec. 7(e)(1), P.L. 110-172, 12/29/2007) effective for expenses paid or incurred after 12/31/2002, in tax. yrs. end. after 12/31/2002.

[¶ 3034]   Code Sec. 291.   Special rules relating to corporate preference items.

(a) **Reduction in certain preference items, etc.** For purposes of this subtitle, in the case of a corporation—

(1) **Section 1250 capital gain treatment.** in the case of section 1250 property which is disposed of during the taxable year, 20 percent of the excess (if any) of—

(A) the amount which would be treated as ordinary income if such property was section 1245 property, over

(B) the amount treated as ordinary income under section 1250 (determined without regard to this paragraph),

shall be treated as gain which is ordinary income under section 1250 and shall be recognized notwithstanding any other provision of this title. Under regulations prescribed by the Secretary, the provisions of this paragraph shall not apply to the disposition of any property to the extent section 1250(a) does not apply to such disposition by reason of section 1250(d).

(2) **Reduction in percentage depletion.** In the case of iron ore and coal (including lignite), the amount allowable as a deduction under section 613 with respect to any property (as defined in section 614) shall be reduced by 20 percent of the amount of the excess (if any) of —

(A) the amount of the deduction allowable under section 613 for the taxable year (determined without regard to this paragraph), over

(B) the adjusted basis of the property at the close of the taxable year (determined without regard to the depletion deduction for the taxable year).

(3) **Certain financial institution preference items.** The amount allowable as a deduction under this chapter (determined without regard to this section) with respect to any financial institution preference item shall be reduced by 20 percent.

[1](4) **Amortization of pollution control facilities.** If an election is made under section 169 with respect to any certified pollution control facility, the amortizable basis of such facility for purposes of such section shall be reduced by 20 percent.

* * * * * * * * * * * *

(c) **Special rules relating to pollution control facilities.** For purposes of this subtitle—

(1) **Accelerated cost recovery deduction.** Section 168 shall apply with respect to that portion of the basis of any property not taken into account under section 169 by reason of [2]*subsection (a)(4).*

(2) **1250 recapture.** Subsection (a)(1) shall not apply to any section 1250 property which is part of a certified pollution control facility (within the meaning of section 169(d)(1)) with respect to which an election under section 169 was made.

* * * * * * * * * * * *

[Endnote Code Sec. 291]

Matter in *italics* in Code Sec. 291(a)(4) was added by Sec. 11(g)(6)(A) of Tax Technical Corrections Act of 2007, P.L. 110-172, 12/29/2007, which struck out:

1.

"(4) Certain FSC income.

"In the case of taxable years beginning after December 31, 1984, section 923(a) shall be applied with respect to any FSC by substituting—

"(A) '30 percent' for '32 percent' in paragraph (2), and

"(B) '15⁄23' for '16⁄23' in paragraph (3).

"If all of the stock in the FSC is not held by 1 or more C corporations throughout the taxable year, under regulations, proper adjustments shall be made in the application of the preceding sentence to take into account stock held by persons other than C corporations."

"(5)"

Matter in *italics* in Code Sec. 291(c)(1) was added by Sec. 11(g)(6)(B), P.L. 110-172, 12/29/2007, which struck out:

2. "subsection (a)(5)"

Effective Date (P.L. 110-172 12/29/2007) enacted 12/29/2007.

[¶ 3035]   Code Sec. 355.   Distribution of stock and securities of a controlled corporation.

* * * * * * * * * * *

(b)   Requirements as to active business.

(1)   In general. Subsection (a) shall apply only if either—

(A) the distributing corporation, and the controlled corporation (or, if stock of more than one controlled corporation is distributed, each of such corporations), is engaged immediately after the distribution in the active conduct of a trade or business, or

(B) immediately before the distribution, the distributing corporation had no assets other than stock or securities in the controlled corporations and each of the controlled corporations is engaged immediately after the distribution in the active conduct of a trade or business.

(2)   Definition. For purposes of paragraph (1), a corporation shall be treated as engaged in the active conduct of a trade or business if and only if—

¹*(A) it is engaged in the active conduct of a trade or business,*

(B) such trade or business has been actively conducted throughout the 5-year period ending on the date of the distribution,

(C) such trade or business was not acquired within the period described in subparagraph (B) in a transaction in which gain or loss was recognized in whole or in part, and

(D) control of a corporation which (at the time of acquisition of control) was conducting such trade or business—

(i) was not acquired by any distributee corporation directly (or through 1 or more corporations, whether through the distributing corporation or otherwise) within the period described in subparagraph (B) and was not acquired by the distributing corporation directly (or through 1 or more corporations) within such period, or

(ii) was so acquired by any such corporation within such period, but, in each case in which such control was so acquired, it was so acquired, only by reason of transactions in which gain or loss was not recognized in whole or in part, or only by reason of such transactions combined with acquisitions before the beginning of such period.

For purposes of subparagraph (D), all distributee corporations which are members of the same affiliated group (as defined in section 1504(a) without regard to section 1504(b)) shall be treated as 1 distributee corporation.

²*(3)   Special rules for determining active conduct in the case of affiliated groups.*

(A) In general. For purposes of determining whether a corporation meets the requirements of paragraph (2)(A), all members of such corporation's separate affiliated group shall be treated as one corporation.

(B) Separate affiliated group. For purposes of this paragraph, the term "separate affiliated group" means, with respect to any corporation, the affiliated group which would be determined under section 1504(a) if such corporation were the common parent and section 1504(b) did not apply.

(C) Treatment of trade or business conducted by acquired member. If a corporation became a member of a separate affiliated group as a result of one or more transactions in which gain or loss was recognized in whole or in part, any trade or business conducted by such corporation (at the time that such corporation became such a member) shall be treated for purposes of paragraph (2) as acquired in a transaction in which gain or loss was recognized in whole or in part.

(D) Regulations. The Secretary shall prescribe such regulations as are necessary or appropriate to carry out the purposes of this paragraph, including regulations which provide for the proper application of subparagraphs (B), (C), and (D) of paragraph (2), and modify the application of subsection (a)(3)(B), in connection with the application of this paragraph.

* * * * * * * * * * *

341

[For Analysis, see ¶1301. For Committee Reports, see ¶5303.]

[Endnote Code Sec. 355]

Matter in *italics* in Code Sec. 355(b)(2)(A) and Code Sec. 355(b)(3) was added by Sec. 4(b)(1)-(2) of the Tax Technical Corrections Act of 2007, P.L. 110-172, 12/29/2007, which struck out:

1. "(A) it is engaged in the active conduct of a trade or business, or substantially all of its assets consist of stock and securities of a corporation controlled by it (immediately after the distribution) which is so engaged,"

2. "(3) Special rule relating to active business requirement.

"(A) In general. In the case of any distribution made after the date of the enactment of this paragraph and on or before December 31, 2010, a corporation shall be treated as meeting the requirement of paragraph (2)(A) if and only if such corporation is engaged in the active conduct of a trade or business.

"(B) Affiliated group rule. For purposes of subparagraph (A), all members of such corporation's separate affiliated group shall be treated as one corporation. For purposes of the preceding sentence, a corporation's separate affiliated group is the affiliated group which would be determined under section 1504(a) if such corporation were the common parent and section 1504(b) did not apply.

"(C) Transition rule. Subparagraph (A) shall not apply to any distribution pursuant to a transaction which is—

"(i) made pursuant to an agreement which was binding on the date of the enactment of this paragraph and at all times thereafter,

"(ii) described in a ruling request submitted to the Internal Revenue Service on or before such date, or

"(iii) described on or before such date in a public announcement or in a filing with the Securities and Exchange Commission.

The preceding sentence shall not apply if the distributing corporation elects not to have such sentence apply to distributions of such corporation. Any such election, once made, shall be irrevocable.

"(D) Special rule for certain pre-enactment distributions. For purposes of determining the continued qualification under paragraph (2)(A) of distributions made on or before the date of the enactment of this paragraph and on or before December 31, 2010 as a result of an acquisition, disposition, or other restructuring after such date, such distribution shall be treated as made on the date of such acquisition, disposition, or restructuring for purposes of applying subparagraphs (A) through (C) of this paragraph."

Effective Date (Sec. 4(d)(2), P.L. 110-172, 12/29/2007) effective for distributions made after 5/17/2006, except as provided in Sec. 4(d)(2)(B)-(D) of this Act, which reads as follows:

"(B) Transition rule. The amendments made by subsection (b) shall not apply to any distribution pursuant to a transaction which is--

"(i) made pursuant to an agreement which was binding on May 17, 2006, and at all times thereafter,

"(ii) described in a ruling request submitted to the Internal Revenue Service on or before such date, or

"(iii) described on or before such date in a public announcement or in a filing with the Securities and Exchange Commission.

"(C) Election out of transition rule. Subparagraph (B) shall not apply if the distributing corporation elects not to have such subparagraph apply to distributions of such corporation. Any such election, once made, shall be irrevocable.

"(D) Special rule for certain pre-enactment distributions. For purposes of determining the continued qualification under section 355(b)(2)(A) of the Internal Revenue Code of 1986 of distributions made on or before May 17, 2006, as a result of an acquisition, disposition, or other restructuring after such date, such distribution shall be treated as made on the date of such acquisition, disposition, or restructuring for purposes of applying subparagraphs (A) through (C) of this paragraph. The preceding sentence shall only apply with respect to the corporation that undertakes such acquisition, disposition, or other restructuring, and only if such application results in continued qualification under section 355(b)(2)(A) of such Code."

[¶3036]　　Code Sec. 402.　　Taxability of beneficiary of employees' trust.

* * * * * * * * * * * *

(g) Limitation on exclusion for elective deferrals.

* * * * * * * * * * * *

(7) Special rule for certain organizations.

(A) In general. In the case of a qualified employee of a qualified organization, with respect to employer contributions described in paragraph (3)(C) made by such organization, the limitation of paragraph (1) for any taxable year shall be increased by whichever of the following is the least:

(i) $3,000,

(ii) $15,000 reduced by the sum of—

(I) the amounts not included in gross income for prior taxable years by reason of this paragraph, plus

(II) the aggregate amount of designated Roth contributions (as defined in section 402A(c)) [1]*permitted for prior taxable years by reason of this paragraph, or*

(iii) the excess of $5,000 multiplied by the number of years of service of the employee with the qualified organization over the employer contributions described in paragraph (3) made by the organization on behalf of such employee for prior taxable years (determined in the manner prescribed by the Secretary).

(B) Qualified organization. For purposes of this paragraph, the term "qualified organization" means any educational organization, hospital, home health service agency, health and welfare service agency, church, or convention or association of churches. Such term includes any organization described in section 414(e)(3)(B)(ii). Terms used in this subparagraph shall have the same meaning as when used in section 415(c)(4) (as in effect before the enactment of the Economic Growth and Tax Relief Reconciliation Act of 2001).

(C) Qualified employee. For purposes of this paragraph, the term "qualified employee" means any employee who has completed 15 years of service with the qualified organization.

(D) Years of service. For purposes of this paragraph, the term "years of service" has the meaning given such term by section 403(b).

* * * * * * * * * * * *

[For Analysis, see ¶ 1202. For Committee Reports, see ¶ 5307.]

[Endnote Code Sec. 402]

Matter in *italics* in Code Sec. 402(g)(7)(A)(ii)(II) was added by Sec. 8(a)(1) of the Tax Technical Corrections Act of 2007, P.L. 110-172, 12/29/2007, which struck out:

1. "for prior taxable years"

Effective Date (Sec. 8(b), P.L. 110-172, 12/29/2007) effective for tax. yrs. begin. after 12/31/2005.

[¶ 3037]   Code Sec. 408.   Individual retirement accounts.

* * * * * * * * * * * *

(d)   Tax treatment of distributions.

(1)   In general. Except as otherwise provided in this subsection, any amount paid or distributed out of an individual retirement plan shall be included in gross income by the payee or distributee, as the case may be, in the manner provided under section 72.

* * * * * * * * * * * *

(8)   Distributions for charitable purposes.

(A) In general. So much of the aggregate amount of qualified charitable distributions with respect to a taxpayer made during any taxable year which does not exceed $100,000 shall not be includible in gross income of such taxpayer for such taxable year.

(B) Qualified charitable distribution. For purposes of this paragraph, the term "qualified charitable distribution" means any distribution from an individual retirement plan (other than a plan described in subsection (k) or (p))—

(i) which is made directly by the trustee to an organization described in section 170(b)(1)(A) (other than any organization described in section 509(a)(3) or any fund or account described in section 4966(d)(2)), and

(ii) which is made on or after the date that the individual for whose benefit the plan is maintained has attained age 70 ½.

A distribution shall be treated as a qualified charitable distribution only to the extent that the distribution would be includible in gross income without regard to subparagraph (A).

(C) Contributions must be otherwise deductible. For purposes of this paragraph, a distribution to an organization described in subparagraph (B)(i) shall be treated as a qualified charitable distribution only if a deduction for the entire distribution would be allowable under section 170 (determined without regard to subsection (b) thereof and this paragraph).

(D) Application of section 72. Notwithstanding section 72, in determining the extent to which a distribution is a qualified charitable distribution, the entire amount of the distribution shall be treated as includible in gross income without regard to subparagraph (A) to the extent that such amount does not exceed the aggregate amount which would have been so includible if [1]*all amounts in all individual retirement plans of the individual were distributed during such taxable year and all such plans were treated as 1 contract for purposes of determining under section 72 the aggregate amount which would have been so includible.* Proper adjustments shall be made in applying section 72 to other distributions in such taxable year and subsequent taxable years.

(E) Denial of deduction. Qualified charitable distributions which are not includible in gross income pursuant to subparagraph (A) shall not be taken into account in determining the deduction under section 170.

(F) Termination. This paragraph shall not apply to distributions made in taxable years beginning after December 31, 2007.

* * * * * * * * * * * *

[For Analysis, see ¶ 602. For Committee Reports, see ¶ 5302.]

[Endnote Code Sec. 408]

Matter in *italics*, in Code Sec. 408(d)(8)(D) was added by Sec. 3(a) of the Tax Technical Corrections Act of 2007, P.L. 110-172, 12/29/2007, which struck out:

1. "all amounts distributed from all individual retirement plans were treated as contract under paragraph (2)(A) for purposes of determining the inclusion of such distribution under section 72"

Effective Date (Sec. 3(j), P.L. 110-172, 12/29/2007) effective for distributions made in tax. yrs. begin. after 12/31/2005.

[¶ 3038]   Code Sec. 441.   Period for computation of taxable income.

* * * * * * * * * * * *

(b) Taxable year. For purposes of this subtitle, the term "taxable year" means—

(1) the taxpayer's annual accounting period, if it is a calendar year or a fiscal year;

(2) the calendar year, if subsection (g) applies;

(3) the period for which the return is made, if a return is made for a period of less than 12 months; or

(4) in the case of a [1]DISC filing a return for a period of at least 12 months, the period determined under subsection (h).

* * * * * * * * * * * *

(h) Taxable year of [2]DISC's.

(1) In general. For purposes of this subtitle, the taxable year of any [3]DISC shall be the taxable year of that shareholder (or group of shareholders with the same 12-month taxable year) who has the highest percentage of voting power.

(2) Special rule where more than one shareholder (or group) has highest percentage. If 2 or more shareholders (or groups) have the highest percentage of voting power under paragraph (1), the taxable year of the [4]DISC shall be the same 12-month period as that of any such shareholder (or group).

(3) Subsequent changes of ownership. The Secretary shall prescribe regulations under which paragraphs (1) and (2) shall apply to a change of ownership of a corporation after the taxable year of the corporation has been determined under paragraph (1) or (2) only if such change is a substantial change of ownership.

(4) Voting power determined. For purposes of this subsection, voting power shall be determined on the basis of total combined voting power of all classes of stock of the corporation entitled to vote.

* * * * * * * * * * * *

[Endnote Code Sec. 441]
   In Code Sec. 441(b)(4), Code Sec. 441(h) heading, Code Sec. 441(h)(1) and Code Sec. 441(h)(2) Sec. 11(g)(7)(A),
(B)(i)-(ii) of the Tax Technical Corrections Act of 2007, P.L. 110-172, 12/29/2007, struck out:
   1. "FSC or"
   2. "FSC's and"
   3. "FSC or"
   4. "FSC or"
Effective Date Enacted 12/29/2007.

[¶ 3039]   Code Sec. 470.   Limitation on deductions allocable to property used by governments or other tax-exempt entities.

* * * * * * * * * * * *

(c)   **Definitions.** For purposes of this section—

   (1)   **Tax-exempt use loss.** The term "tax-exempt use loss" means, with respect to any taxable year, the amount (if any) by which—

      (A) the sum of—

         (i) the aggregate deductions (other than interest) directly allocable to a tax-exempt use property, plus

         (ii) the aggregate deductions for interest properly allocable to such property, exceed

      (B) the aggregate income from such property.

   ¹(2)   *Tax-exempt use property.*

      (A) In general. The term "tax-exempt use property" has the meaning given to such term by section 168(h), except that such section shall be applied—

         (i) without regard to paragraphs (1)(C) and (3) thereof, and

         (ii) as if section 197 intangible property (as defined in section 197), and property described in paragraph (1)(B) or (2) of section 167(f), were tangible property.

      (B) Exception for partnerships. Such term shall not include any property which would (but for this subparagraph) be tax-exempt use property solely by reason of section 168(h)(6).

      (C) Cross reference. For treatment of partnerships as leases to which section 168(h) applies, see section 7701(e).

   (d)   **Exception for certain leases.** This section shall not apply to any lease of property which meets the requirements of all of the following paragraphs:

   (1)   **Availability of funds.**

      (A) In general. A lease of property meets the requirements of this paragraph if ²*(at all times during the lease term)* not more than an allowable amount of funds are—

         (i) subject to any arrangement referred to in subparagraph (B), or

         (ii) set aside or expected to be set aside,

      to or for the benefit of the lessor or any lender, or to or for the benefit of the lessee to satisfy the lessee's obligations or options under the lease. For purposes of clause (ii), funds shall be treated as set aside or expected to be set aside only if a reasonable person would conclude, based on the facts and circumstances, that such funds are set aside or expected to be set aside.

      (B) Arrangements. The arrangements referred to in this subparagraph include a defeasance arrangement, a loan by the lessee to the lessor or any lender, a deposit arrangement, a letter of credit collateralized with cash or cash equivalents, a payment undertaking agreement, prepaid rent (within the meaning of the regulations under section 467), a sinking fund arrangement, a guaranteed investment contract, financial guaranty insurance, and any similar arrangement (whether or not such arrangement provides credit support).

      (C) Allowable amount.

(i) In general. Except as otherwise provided in this subparagraph, the term "allowable amount" means an amount equal to 20 percent of the lessor's adjusted basis in the property at the time the lease is entered into.

(ii) Higher amount permitted in certain cases. To the extent provided in regulations, a higher percentage shall be permitted under clause (i) where necessary because of the credit-worthiness of the lessee. In no event may such regulations permit a percentage of more than 50 percent.

(iii) Option to purchase. If under the lease the lessee has the option to purchase the property for a fixed price or for other than the fair market value of the property (determined at the time of exercise), the allowable amount at the time such option may be exercised may not exceed 50 percent of the price at which such option may be exercised.

(iv) No allowable amount for certain arrangements. The allowable amount shall be zero with respect to any arrangement which involves—

(I) a loan from the lessee to the lessor or a lender,

(II) any deposit received, letter of credit issued, or payment undertaking agreement entered into by a lender otherwise involved in the transaction, or

(III) in the case of a transaction which involves a lender, any credit support made available to the lessor in which any such lender does not have a claim that is senior to the lessor.

For purposes of subclause (I), the term "loan" shall not include any amount treated as a loan under section 467 with respect to a section 467 rental agreement.

* * * * * * * * * * * *

[For Analysis, see ¶ 803, ¶ 804, and ¶ 805. For Committee Reports, see ¶ 5306.]

[Endnote Code Sec. 470]

Matter in *italics* in Code Sec. 470(c)(2), and Code Sec. 470(d)(1)(A) was added by Sec. 7(c)(1) and (2) of the Tax Technical Corrections Act of 2007, P.L. 110-172, 12/29/2007, which struck out:

1. "(2) Tax-exempt use property. The term 'tax-exempt use property' has the meaning given to such term by section 168(h), except that such section shall be applied—

"(A) without regard to paragraphs (1)(C) and (3) thereof, and

"(B) as if property described in—

"(i) section 167(f)(1)(B),

"(ii) section 167(f)(2), and

"(iii) section 197 intangible,

were tangible property.

"Such term shall not include property which would (but for this sentence) be tax-exempt use property solely by reason of section 168(h)(6) if any credit is allowable under section 42 or 47 with respect to such property."

2. "(at any time during the lease term)"

Effective Date Effective as if included in the provisions of Sec. 849(a)-(b), P.L. 108-357, 10/22/2004 [as amended by Sec. 403(ff) of the Gulf Opportunity Zone Act of 2005, P.L. 109-135, 12/21/2005]), which reads as follows:

"(a) In general. Except as provided in this section, the amendments made by this part shall apply to leases entered into after March 12, 2004, and in the case of property treated as tax-exempt use property other than by reason of a lease, to property acquired after March 12, 2004.

"(b) Exception.

"(1) In general. The amendments made by this part shall not apply to qualified transportation property.

"(2) Qualified transportation property. For purposes of paragraph (1), the term 'qualified transportation property' means domestic property subject to a lease with respect to which a formal application—

"(A) was submitted for approval to the Federal Transit Administration (an agency of the Department of Transportation) after June 30, 2003, and before March 13, 2004,

"(B) is approved by the Federal Transit Administration before January 1, 2006, and

"(C) includes a description of such property and the value of such property.

"(3) Exchanges and conversion of tax-exempt use property. Section 470(e)(4) of the Internal Revenue Code of 1986, as added by section 848, shall apply to property exchanged or converted after the date of the enactment of this Act.

"(4) Intangibles and Indian Tribal governments. The amendments made subsections (b)(2), (b)(3), and (e) of section 847, and the treatment of property described in clauses (ii) and (iii) of section 470(c)(2)(B) of the Internal Revenue Code of 1986 (as added by section 848) as tangible property, shall apply to leases entered into after October 3, 2004."

[¶ 3040]   Code Sec. 852.   Taxation of regulated investment companies and their shareholders.

* * * * * * * * * * *

(b)   Method of taxation of companies and shareholders.

* * * * * * * * * * *

(4)   Loss on sale or exchange of stock held 6 months or less.

(A) Loss attributable to capital gain dividend. If—

(i) subparagraph (B) or (D) of paragraph (3) provides that any amount with respect to any share is to be treated as long-term capital gain, and

(ii) such share is held by the taxpayer for 6 months or less,

then any loss (to the extent not disallowed under subparagraph (B)) on the sale or exchange of such share shall, to the extent of the amount described in clause (i), be treated as a long-term capital loss.

(B) Loss attributable to exempt-interest dividend. If—

(i) a shareholder of a regulated investment company receives an exempt-interest dividend with respect to any share, and

(ii) such share is held by the taxpayer for 6 months or less.

then any loss on the sale or exchange of such share shall, to the extent of the amount of such exempt-interest dividend, be disallowed.

[1]*(C) Determination of holding periods. For purposes of this paragraph, in determining the period for which the taxpayer has held any share of stock—*

(i) the rules of paragraphs (3) and (4) of section 246(c) shall apply, and

(ii) there shall not be taken into account any day which is more than 6 months after the date on which such share becomes ex-dividend.

(D) Losses incurred under a periodic liquidation plan. To the extent provided in regulations, subparagraphs (A) and (B) shall not apply to losses incurred on the sale or exchange of shares of stock in a regulated investment company pursuant to a plan which provides for the periodic liquidation of such shares.

(E) Authority to shorten required holding period. In the case of a regulated investment company which regularly distributes at least 90 percent of its net tax-exempt interest, the Secretary may by regulations prescribe that subparagraph (B) (and subparagraph (C) to the extent it relates to subparagraph (B)) shall be applied on the basis of a holding period requirement shorter than 6 months; except that such shorter holding period requirement shall not be shorter than the greater of 31 days or the period between regular distributions of exempt-interest dividends.

* * * * * * * * * * *

[Endnote Code Sec. 852]

Matter in *italics* in Code Sec. 852(b)(4)(C) was added by Sec. 11(a)(17)(A) of the Tax Technical Corrections Act of 2007, P.L. 110-172, 12/29/2007, which struck out:

1. "(C) Determination of holding periods. For purposes of this paragraph, the rules of paragraphs (3) and (4) of section 246(c) shall apply in determining the period for which the taxpayer has held any share of stock; except that "6 months" shall be substituted for each number of days specified in subparagraph (B) of section 246(c)(3)."

Effective Date enacted 12/29/2007.

[¶ 3041]   Code Sec. 856.   Definition of real estate investment trust.

* * * * * * * * * * *

(d)   Rents from real property defined.

* * * * * * * * * * *

(9)   Eligible independent contractor. For purposes of paragraph (8)(B)—

(A) In general. The term "eligible independent contractor" means, with respect to any qualified lodging facility, any independent contractor if, at the time such contractor enters into a management agreement or other similar service contract with the taxable REIT subsidiary to operate the facility, such contractor (or any related person) is actively engaged in the trade or business of operating qualified lodging facilities for any person who is not a related person with respect to the real estate investment trust or the taxable REIT subsidiary.

(B) Special rules. Solely for purposes of this paragraph and paragraph (8)(B), a person shall not fail to be treated as an independent contractor with respect to any qualified lodging facility by reason of any of the following:

(i) The taxable REIT subsidiary bears the expenses for the operation of the facility pursuant to the management agreement or other similar service contract.

(ii) The taxable REIT subsidiary receives the revenues from the operation of such facility, net of expenses for such operation and fees payable to the operator pursuant to such agreement or contract.

(iii) The real estate investment trust receives income from such person with respect to another property that is attributable to a lease of such other property to such person that was in effect as of the later of—

(I) January 1, 1999, or

(II) the earliest date that any taxable REIT subsidiary of such trust entered into a management agreement or other similar service contract with such person with respect to such qualified lodging facility.

(C) Renewals, etc., of existing leases. For purposes of subparagraph (B)(iii)—

(i) a lease shall be treated as in effect on January 1, 1999, without regard to its renewal after such date, so long as such renewal is pursuant to the terms of such lease as in effect on whichever of the dates under subparagraph (B)(iii) is the latest, and

(ii) a lease of a property entered into after whichever of the dates under subparagraph (B)(iii) is the latest shall be treated as in effect on such date if—

(I) on such date, a lease of such property from the trust was in effect, and

(II) under the terms of the new lease, such trust receives a substantially similar or lesser benefit in comparison to the lease referred to in subclause (I).

(D) Qualified lodging facility. For purposes of this paragraph—

(i) In general. The term "qualified lodging facility" means any lodging facility unless wagering activities are conducted at or in connection with such facility by any person who is engaged in the business of accepting wagers and who is legally authorized to engage in such business at or in connection with such facility.

[1]*(ii) Lodging facility. The term "lodging facility" means a—*

(I) hotel,

(II) motel, or

(III) other establishment more than one-half of the dwelling units in which are used on a transient basis.

(iii) Customary amenities and facilities. The term "lodging facility" includes customary amenities and facilities operated as part of, or associated with, the lodging facility so long as such amenities and facilities are customary for other properties of a comparable size and class owned by other owners unrelated to such real estate investment trust.

(E) Operate includes manage. References in this paragraph to operating a property shall be treated as including a reference to managing the property.

(F) Related person. Persons shall be treated as related to each other if such persons are treated as a single employer under subsection (a) or (b) of section 52.

* * * * * * * * * * * *

(l) **Taxable REIT subsidiary.** For purposes of this part—

* * * * * * * * * * * *

(2) **35 percent ownership in another taxable REIT subsidiary.** The term "taxable REIT subsidiary" includes, with respect to any real estate investment trust, any corporation

(other than a real estate investment trust) with respect to which a taxable REIT subsidiary of such trust owns directly or indirectly—

(A) securities possessing more than 35 percent of the total voting power of the outstanding securities of such corporation, or

(B) securities having a value of more than 35 percent of the total value of the outstanding securities of such corporation.

[2]*For purposes of subparagraph (B), securities described in subsection (m)(2)(A) shall not be taken into account.*

* * * * * * * * * * * *

[For Analysis, see ¶1303. For Committee Reports, see ¶5308.]

[Endnote Code Sec. 856]

Code Sec. 856(d)(9)(D)(ii) in *italics* was added by Sec. 9(b), the Tax Technical Corrections Act of 2007, P.L. 110-172, 12/29/2007, which struck out:

1. "(ii) Lodging facility. The term 'lodging facility' means a hotel, motel, or other establishment more than one-half of the dwelling units in which are used on a transient basis."

Effective Date (Sec. 9(c), P.L. 110-172, 12/29/2007) effective (as if included in PL 106-170, Sec. 542) for tax. yrs. begin. after 12/30/2000.

Matter in *italics* in Code Sec. 856(l)(2) was added by Sec. 11(a)(18), which struck out:

2. "The preceding sentence shall not apply to a qualified REIT subsidiary (as defined in subsection (i)(2)). The rule of section 856(c)(7) shall apply for purposes of subparagraph (B)."

Effective Date Enacted 12/29/2007

[¶3042]   Code Sec. 857.   Taxation of real estate investment trusts and their beneficiaries.

* * * * * * * * * * * *

(b)   Method of taxation of real estate investment trusts and holders of shares or certificates of beneficial interest.

* * * * * * * * * * * *

(8)   Loss on sale or exchange of stock held 6 months or less.

(A) In general. If—

(i) subparagraph (B) or (D) of paragraph (3) provides that any amount with respect to any share or beneficial interest is to be treated as a long-term capital gain, and

(ii) the taxpayer has held such share or interest for 6 months or less,

then any loss on the sale or exchange of such share or interest shall, to the extent of the amount described in clause (i), be treated as a long-term capital loss.

[1]*(B) Determination of holding period. For purposes of this paragraph, in determining the period for which the taxpayer has held any share of stock or beneficial interest—*

(i) the rules of paragraphs (3) and (4) of section 246(c) shall apply, and

(ii) there shall not be taken into account any day which is more than 6 months after the date on which such share or interest becomes ex-dividend.

(C) Exception for losses incurred under periodic liquidation plans. To the extent provided in regulations, subparagraph (A) shall not apply to any loss incurred on the sale or exchange of shares of stock of, or beneficial interest in, a real estate investment trust pursuant to a plan which provides for the periodic liquidation of such shares or interests.

* * * * * * * * * * * *

[Endnote Code Sec. 857]

Matter in *italics* in Code Sec. 857(b)(8)(B) was added by Sec. 11(a)(17)(B) of the Tax Technical Corrections Act of 2007, P.L. 110-172, 12/29/2007, which struck out:

1. "(B) Determination of holding period. For purposes of this paragraph, the rules of paragraphs (3) and (4) of section 246(c) shall apply in determining the period for which the taxpayer has held any share of stock or beneficial interest; except that "6 months" shall be substituted for the number of days specified in subparagraph (B) of section 246(c)(3)."

Effective Date enacted 12/29/2007.

[¶ 3043]   Code Sec. 884.   Branch profits tax.

* * * * * * * * * * * *

(d) Effectively connected earnings and profits. For purposes of this section—

(1) In general. The term "effectively connected earnings and profits" means earnings and profits (without diminution by reason of any distributions made during the taxable year) which are attributable to income which is effectively connected (or treated as effectively connected) with the conduct of a trade or business within the United States.

(2) Exception for certain income. The term "effectively connected earnings and profits" shall not include any earnings and profits attributable to—

(A) income not includible in gross income under paragraph (1) or (2) of section 883(a),

(B) income treated as effectively connected with the conduct of a trade or business within the United States under section 921(d) or 926(b) [1]*(as in effect before their repeal by the FSC Repeal and Extraterritorial Income Exclusion Act of 2000).*

(C) gain on the disposition of a United States real property interest described in section 897(c)(1)(A)(ii),

(D) income treated as effectively connected with the conduct of a trade or business within the United States under section 953(c)(3)(C), or

(E) income treated as effectively connected with the conduct of a trade or business within the United States under section 882(e).

Property and liabilities of the foreign corporation treated as connected with such income under regulations prescribed by the Secretary shall not be taken into account in determining the U.S. assets or U.S. liabilities of the foreign corporation.

* * * * * * * * * * * *

[Endnote Code Sec. 884]

Matter in *italics* in Code Sec. 884(d)(2)(B) was added by Sec. 11(g)(8), the Tax Technical Corrections Act of 2007, P.L. 110-172, 12/29/2007.

1. added matter in subpara. (d)(2)(B)

Effective Date Enacted 12/29/2007.

[¶ 3044]   Code Sec. 901.   Taxes of foreign countries and of possessions of United States.

* * * * * * * * * * * *

[1]**(h) Repeal.**

* * * * * * * * * * * *

[Endnote Code Sec. 901]

Sec. 11(g)(9), the Tax Technical Corrections Act of 2007, P.L. 110-172, 12/29/2007, deleted Code Sec. 901(h).

1. "(h) Taxes paid with respect to foreign trade income.

"No credit shall be allowed under this section for any income, war profits, and excess profits taxes paid or accrued with respect to the foreign trade income (within the meaning of section 923(b)) of a FSC, other than section 923(a)(2) non-exempt income (within the meaning of section 927(d)(6))."

Effective Date (P.L. 110-172, 12/29/2007) enacted 12/29/2007.

[¶ 3045]   Code Sec. 904.   Limitation on credit.

* * * * * * * * * * * *

(d)   Separate application of section with respect to certain categories of income.

(1)   In general. The provisions of subsections (a), (b), and (c) and sections 902, 907, and 960 shall be applied separately with respect to—

(A) passive category income, and

(B) general category income.

(2)   Definitions and special rules. For purposes of this subsection—

(A) Categories.

(i) Passive category income. The term "passive category income" means passive income and specified passive category income.

(ii) General category income. The term "general category income" means income other than passive category income.

(B) Passive income.

(i) In general. Except as otherwise provided in this subparagraph, the term "passive income" means any income received or accrued by any person which is of a kind which would be foreign personal holding company income (as defined in section 954(c)).

(ii) Certain amounts included. Except as provided in clause (iii), the term "passive income" includes any amount includible in gross income under section 551 or, except as provided in subparagraph (E)(iii) or paragraph (3)(I), section 1293 (relating to certain passive foreign investment companies).

(iii) Exceptions. The term "passive income" shall not include—

(I) any export financing interest, and

(II) any high-taxed income.

(iv) Clarification of application of section 864(d)(6). In determining whether any income is of a kind which would be foreign personal holding company income, the rules of section 864(d)(6) shall apply only in the case of income of a controlled foreign corporation.

(v) Specified passive category income. The term "specified passive category income" means—

(I) dividends from a DISC or former DISC (as defined in section 992(a)) to the extent such dividends are treated as income from sources without the United States, [1]and

[2](II) distributions from [3]a former FSC (as defined in section 922) out of earnings and profits attributable to foreign trade income (within the meaning of section 923(b)) or interest or carrying charges (as defined in section 927(d)(1)) derived from a transaction which results in foreign trade income (as defined in section 923(b)).

[4]Any reference in subclause II to section 922, 923, pr 927 shall be treated as a reference to such section as in effect before its repeal by the FSC Repeal and Extraterritorial Income Exclusion Act of 2000.

* * * * * * * * * * * *

(f)   Recapture of overall foreign loss.

(1)   General rule. For purposes of this subpart and section 936, in the case of any taxpayer who sustains an overall foreign loss for any taxable year, that portion of the taxpayer's taxable income from sources without the United States for each succeeding taxable year which is equal to the lesser of—

(A) the amount of such loss (to the extent not used under this paragraph in prior taxable years), or

(B) 50 percent (or such larger percent as the taxpayer may choose) of the taxpayer's taxable income from sources without the United States for such succeeding taxable year, shall be treated as income from sources within the United States (and not as income from sources without the United States).

* * * * * * * * * * * *

(3) Dispositions.

(A) In general. For purposes of this chapter, if property which has been used predominantly without the United States in a trade or business is disposed of during any taxable year—

(i) the taxpayer, notwithstanding any other provision of this chapter (other than paragraph (1)), shall be deemed to have received and recognized taxable income from sources without the United States in the taxable year of the disposition, by reason of such disposition, in an amount equal to the lesser of the excess of the fair market value of such property over the taxpayer's adjusted basis in such property or the remaining amount of the overall foreign losses which were not used under paragraph (1) for such taxable year or any prior taxable year, and

(ii) paragraph (1) shall be applied with respect to such income by substituting "100 percent" for "50 percent".

In determining for purposes of this subparagraph whether the predominant use of any property has been without the United States, there shall be taken into account use during the 3-year period ending on the date of the disposition (or, if shorter, the period during which the property has been used in the trade or business).

(B) Disposition defined and special rules.

(i) For purposes of this subsection, the term "disposition" includes a sale, exchange, distribution, or gift of property whether or not gain or loss is recognized on the transfer.

(ii) Any taxable income recognized solely by reason of subparagraph (A) shall have the same characterization it would have had if the taxpayer had sold or exchanged the property.

(iii) The Secretary shall prescribe such regulations as he may deem necessary to provide for adjustments to the basis of property to reflect taxable income recognized solely by reason of subparagraph (A).

(C) Exceptions. Notwithstanding subparagraph (B), the term "disposition" does not include—

(i) a disposition of property which is not a material factor in the realization of income by the taxpayer, or

(ii) a disposition of property to a domestic corporation in a distribution or transfer described in section 381(a).

(D) Application to certain dispositions of stock in controlled foreign corporation.

(i) In general. This paragraph shall apply to an applicable disposition in the same manner as if it were a disposition of property described in subparagraph (A), except that the exception contained in subparagraph (C)(i) shall not apply.

(ii) Applicable disposition. For purposes of clause (i), the term "applicable disposition" means any disposition of any share of stock in a controlled foreign corporation in a transaction or series of transactions if, immediately before such transaction or series of transactions, the taxpayer owned more than 50 percent (by vote or value) of the stock of the controlled foreign corporation. Such term shall not include a disposition described in clause (iii) or (iv), except that clause (i) shall apply to any gain recognized on any such disposition.

(iii) Exception for certain exchanges where ownership percentage retained. A disposition shall not be treated as an applicable disposition under clause (ii) if it is part of a transaction or series of transactions—

(I) to which section 351 or 721 applies, or under which the transferor receives stock in a foreign corporation in exchange for the stock in the controlled foreign corporation and the stock received is exchanged basis property (as defined in section 7701(a)(44)), and

(II) immediately after which, the transferor owns (by vote or value) at least the same percentage of stock in the controlled foreign corporation (or, if the controlled foreign corporation is not in existence after such transaction or series of transactions, in another foreign corporation stock in which was received by the transferor in exchange for stock in the controlled foreign corporation) as the percentage of stock in the controlled foreign corporation which the taxpayer owned immediately before such transaction or series of transactions.

(iv) Exception for certain asset acquisitions. A disposition shall not be treated as an applicable disposition under clause (ii) if it is part of a transaction or series of transactions in which the taxpayer (or any member of [5]*an affiliated group* of corporations filing a consolidated return under section 1501 which includes the taxpayer) acquires the assets of a controlled foreign corporation in exchange for the shares of the controlled foreign corporation in a liquidation described in section 332 or a reorganization described in section 368(a)(1).

(v) Controlled foreign corporation. For purposes of this subparagraph, the term "controlled foreign corporation" has the meaning given such term by section 957.

(vi) Stock ownership. For purposes of this subparagraph, ownership of stock shall be determined under the rules of subsections (a) and (b) of section 958.

* * * * * * * * * * *

[Endnote Code Sec. 904]

Matter in *italics* in Code Sec. 904(d)(2)(B)(v) was added by Sec. 11(g)(10)(A)-(C) of the Tax Technical Correction Act of 2007, P.L. 110-172, 12/29/2007, which struck out:

1. added matter in subcl. (d)(2)(B)(v)(I) subpara. (d)(2)(D)

2. "(II) taxable income attributable to foreign trade income (within the meaning of section 923(b)), and "(III)"

3. "a FSC (or a former FSC)"

4. added matter in clause (d)(2)(B)(v)

Effective Date Effective for transactions after 9/30/2000.

Matter in *italics* in Code Sec. 904(f)(3)(D)(iv) was added by Sec. 11(f)(3), P.L. 110-172, 12/29/2007, which struck out:

5. "a controlled group"

Effective Date (Sec. 11(f)(4), P.L. 110-172, 12/29/2007) effective for dispositions after 10/22/2004.

[¶ 3046]   **Code Sec. 906.**   **Nonresident alien individuals and foreign corporations.**

* * * * * * * * * * *

(b)   **Special rules.**

* * * * * * * * * * *

[1]*(5)* For purposes of section 902, any income, war profits, and excess profits taxes paid or accrued (or deemed paid or accrued) to any foreign country or possession of the United States with respect to income effectively connected with the conduct of a trade or business within the United States shall not be taken into account, and any accumulated profits attributable to such income shall not be taken into account.

[2]*(6)* No credit shall be allowed under this section against the tax imposed by section 884.

[Endnote Code Sec. 906]

Matter in *italics* in Code Sec. 906(b)(5) and Code Sec. 906(b)(6) was added by Sec. 11(g)(11), the Tax Technical Corrections Act of 2007, P.L. 110-172, 12/29/2007, which struck out:

1. "(5) No credit shall be allowed under this section for any income, war profits, and excess profits taxes paid or accrued with respect to the foreign trade income (within the meaning of section 923(b)) of a FSC. "(6)"

2. "(7)"

Effective Date (P.L. 110-172, 12/29/2007) enacted 12/29/2007

[¶ 3047]   Code Sec. 911.   Citizens or residents of the United States living abroad.

* * * * * * * * * * * *

[1]*(f)* **Determination of tax liability.**

(1) **In general.** *If, for any taxable year, any amount is excluded from gross income of a taxpayer under subsection (a), then, notwithstanding sections 1 and 55—*

(A) if such taxpayer has taxable income for such taxable year, the tax imposed by section 1 for such taxable year shall be equal to the excess (if any) of—

(i) the tax which would be imposed by section 1 for such taxable year if the taxpayer's taxable income were increased by the amount excluded under subsection (a) for such taxable year, over

(ii) the tax which would be imposed by section 1 for such taxable year if the taxpayer's taxable income were equal to the amount excluded under subsection (a) for such taxable year, and

(B) if such taxpayer has a taxable excess (as defined in section 55(b)(1)(A)(ii)) for such taxable year, the amount determined under the first sentence of section 55(b)(1)(A)(i) for such taxable year shall be equal to the excess (if any) of—

(i) the amount which would be determined under such sentence for such taxable year (subject to the limitation of section 55(b)(3)) if the taxpayer's taxable excess (as so defined) were increased by the amount excluded under subsection (a) for such taxable year, over

(ii) the amount which would be determined under such sentence for such taxable year if the taxpayer's taxable excess (as so defined) were equal to the amount excluded under subsection (a) for such taxable year.

(2) **Special rules.**

(A) Regular tax. In applying section 1(h) for purposes of determining the tax under paragraph (1)(A)(i) for any taxable year in which, without regard to this subsection, the taxpayer's net capital gain exceeds taxable income (hereafter in this subparagraph referred to as the capital gain excess)—

(i) the taxpayer's net capital gain (determined without regard to section 1(h)(11)) shall be reduced (but not below zero) by such capital gain excess,

(ii) the taxpayer's qualified dividend income shall be reduced by so much of such capital gain excess as exceeds the taxpayer's net capital gain (determined without regard to section 1(h)(11) and the reduction under clause (i)), and

(iii) adjusted net capital gain, unrecaptured section 1250 gain, and 28-percent rate gain shall each be determined after increasing the amount described in section 1(h)(4)(B) by such capital gain excess.

(B) Alternative minimum tax. In applying section 55(b)(3) for purposes of determining the tax under paragraph (1)(B)(i) for any taxable year in which, without regard to this subsection, the taxpayer's net capital gain exceeds the taxable excess (as defined in section 55(b)(1)(A)(ii))—

(i) the rules of subparagraph (A) shall apply, except that such subparagraph shall be applied by substituting "the taxable excess (as defined in section 55(b)(1)(A)(ii))" for "taxable income", and

(ii) the reference in section 55(b)(3)(B) to the excess described in section 1(h)(1)(B) shall be treated as a reference to such excess as determined under the rules of subparagraph (A) for purposes of determining the tax under paragraph (1)(A)(i).

(C) Definitions. Terms used in this paragraph which are also used in section 1(h) shall have the respective meanings given such terms by section 1(h), except that in applying subparagraph (B) the adjustments under part VI of subchapter A shall be taken into account.

* * * * * * * * * * * *

[For Analysis, see ¶ 701. For Committee Reports, see ¶ 5303.]

[Endnote Code Sec. 911]

Matter in *italics* in Code Sec. 911(f) was added by Sec. 4(c), the Tax Technical Corrections Act of 2007, P.L. 110-172, 12/29/2007, which struck out:

1. "(f) Determination of tax liability on nonexcluded amounts. For purposes of this chapter, if any amount is excluded from the gross income of a taxpayer under subsection (a) for any taxable year, then, notwithstanding section 1 or 55—

"(1) the tax imposed by section 1 on the taxpayer for such taxable year shall be equal to the excess (if any) of—

"(A) the tax which would be imposed by section 1 for the taxable year if the taxpayer's taxable income were increased by the amount excluded under subsection (a) for the taxable year, over

"(B) the tax which would be imposed by section 1 for the taxable year if the taxpayer's taxable income were equal to the amount excluded under subsection (a) for the taxable year, and

"(2) the tentative minimum tax under section 55 for such taxable year shall be equal to the excess (if any) of—

"(A) the amount which would be such tentative minimum tax for the taxable year if the taxpayer's taxable excess were increased by the amount excluded under subsection (a) for the taxable year, over

"(B) the amount which would be such tentative minimum tax for the taxable year if the taxpayer's taxable excess were equal to the amount excluded under subsection (a) for the taxable year.

For purposes of this subsection, the amount excluded under subsection (a) shall be reduced by the aggregate amount of any deductions or exclusions disallowed under subsection (d)(6) with respect to such excluded amount."

Effective Date (Sec. 4(d)(3), P.L. 110-172, 12/29/2007) effective for tax. yrs. begin. after 12/31/2006.

[¶ 3048] Code Sec. 936. Puerto Rico and possession tax credit.

* * * * * * * * * * * *

(f) Limitation on credit for DISC's and FSC's. No credit shall be allowed under this section to a corporation for any taxable year—

(1) for which it is a DISC or former DISC, or

(2) in which it owns at any time stock in a—

(A) DISC or former DISC, or

(B) ¹former FSC.

* * * * * * * * * * * *

[Endnote Code Sec. 936]

In Code Sec. 936(f)(2)(B) Sec. 11(g)(12) of the Tax Technical Corrections Act of 2007, P.L. 110-172, 12/29/2007, struck out:

1. "FSC or"

Effective Date Enacted 12/29/2007.

[¶ 3049] Code Sec. 951. Amounts included in gross income of United States shareholders.

* * * * * * * * * * * *

¹**(c) Coordination with passive foreign investment company provisions.** If, but for this subsection, an amount would be included in the gross income of a United States shareholder for any taxable year both under subsection (a)(1)(A)(i) and under section 1293 (relating to current taxation of income from certain passive foreign investment companies), such amount shall be included in the gross income of such shareholder only under subsection (a)(1)(A).

¹**(d)** [Repealed.]

[Endnote Code Sec. 951]

Matter in *italics* in Code Sec. 951(c) was added and Code Sec. 951(d) was deleted by Sec. 11(g)(13) of the Tax Technical Corrections Act of 2007, P.L. 110-172, 12/29/2007, which struck out:

1. "(c) Foreign trade income not taken into account.

"(1) In general. The foreign trade income of a FSC and any deductions which are apportioned or allocated to such income shall not be taken into account under this subpart.

"(2) Foreign trade income. For purposes of this subsection, the term 'foreign trade income' has the meaning given such term by section 923(b), but does not include section 923(a)(2) non-exempt income (within the meaning of section 927(d)(6))."

"(d)"

Effective Date Enacted 12/29/2007.

[¶ 3050]   Code Sec. 952.   Subpart F income defined.

* * * * * * * * * * * *

(b)   Exclusion of United States income. In the case of a controlled foreign corporation, subpart F income does not include any item of income from sources within the United States which is effectively connected with the conduct by such corporation of a trade or business within the United States unless such item is exempt from taxation (or is subject to a reduced rate of tax) pursuant to a treaty obligation of the United States. [1]For purposes of this subsection, any exemption (or reduction) with respect to the tax imposed by section 884 shall not be taken into account.

* * * * * * * * * * * *

[Endnote Code Sec. 952]

In Code Sec. 952(b) Sec. 11(g)(14) of the Tax Technical Corrections Act of 2007, P.L. 110-172, 12/29/2007, struck out:

1. "For purposes of the preceding sentence, income described in paragraph (2) or (3) of section 921(d) shall be treated as derived from sources within the United States. "

Effective Date enacted 12/29/2007.

[¶ 3051]   Code Sec. 954.   Foreign base company income.

* * * * * * * * * * * *

(c)   Foreign personal holding company income.

   (1)   In general. For purposes of subsection (a)(1), the term "foreign personal holding company income" means the portion of the gross income which consists of:

   (A) Dividends, etc. Dividends, interest, royalties, rents, and annuities.

   (B) Certain property transactions. The excess of gains over losses from the sale or exchange of property—

      (i) which gives rise to income described in subparagraph (A) (after application of paragraph (2)(A)) other than property which gives rise to income not treated as foreign personal holding company income by reason of subsection (h) or (i) for the taxable year,

      (ii) which is an interest in a trust, partnership, or REMIC, or

      (iii) which does not give rise to any income.

   Gains and losses from the sale or exchange of any property which, in the hands of the controlled foreign corporation, is property described in section 1221(a)(1) shall not be taken into account under this subparagraph.

   (C) Commodities transactions. The excess of gains over losses from transactions (including futures, forward, and similar transactions) in any commodities. This subparagraph shall not apply to gains or losses which—

      (i) arise out of commodity hedging transactions (as defined in paragraph (5)(A)),

      (ii) are active business gains or losses from the sale of commodities, but only if substantially all of the controlled foreign corporation's commodities are property described in paragraph (1), (2), or (8) of section 1221(a), or

      (iii) are foreign currency gains or losses (as defined in section 988(b)) attributable to any section 988 transactions.

(D) Foreign currency gains. The excess of foreign currency gains over foreign currency losses (as defined in section 988(b)) attributable to any section 988 transactions. This subparagraph shall not apply in the case of any transaction directly related to the business needs of the controlled foreign corporation.

(E) Income equivalent to interest. Any income equivalent to interest, including income from commitment fees (or similar amounts) for loans actually made.

[1]*(F) Income from notional principal contracts.*

(i) In general. Net income from notional principal contracts.

(ii) Coordination with other categories of foreign personal holding company income. —Any item of income, gain, deduction, or loss from a notional principal contract entered into for purposes of hedging any item described in any preceding subparagraph shall not be taken into account for purposes of this subparagraph but shall be taken into account under such other subparagraph.

(G) Payments in lieu of dividends. Payments in lieu of dividends which are made pursuant to an agreement to which section 1058 applies.

[2]*(H) Personal service contracts.*

(i) Amounts received under a contract under which the corporation is to furnish personal services if—

(I) some person other than the corporation has the right to designate (by name or by description) the individual who is to perform the services, or

(II) the individual who is to perform the services is designated (by name or by description) in the contract, and

(ii) amounts received from the sale or other disposition of such a contract.

This subparagraph shall apply with respect to amounts received for services under a particular contract only if at some time during the taxable year 25 percent or more in value of the outstanding stock of the corporation is owned, directly or indirectly, by or for the individual who has performed, is to perform, or may be designated (by name or by description) as the one to perform, such services.

* * * * * * * * * * * *

(6)   Look-thru rule for related controlled foreign corporations.

(A) In general. For purposes of this subsection, dividends, interest, rents, and royalties received or accrued from a controlled foreign corporation which is a related person shall not be treated as foreign personal holding company income to the extent attributable or properly allocable (determined under rules similar to the rules of subparagraphs (C) and (D) of section 904(d)(3)) to income of the related person which is neither subpart F income nor income treated as effectively connected with the conduct of a trade or business in the United States. For purposes of this subparagraph, interest shall include factoring income which is treated as income equivalent to interest for purposes of paragraph (1)(E). The Secretary shall prescribe such regulations as may be necessary or appropriate to carry out this paragraph, including such regulations as may be necessary or appropriate to prevent the abuse of the purposes of this paragraph.

[4]*(B) Exception. Subparagraph (A) shall not apply in the case of any interest, rent, or royalty to the extent such interest, rent, or royalty creates (or increases) a deficit which under section 952(c) may reduce the subpart F income of the payor or another controlled foreign corporation.*

[5]*(C) Application. Subparagraph (A) shall apply to taxable years of foreign corporations beginning after December 31, 2005, and before January 1, 2009, and to taxable years of United States shareholders with or within which such taxable years of foreign corporations end.*

* * * * * * * * * * * *

[For Analysis, see ¶ 702. For Committee Reports, see ¶ 5303.]

[Endnote Code Sec. 954]

Code Sec. 954(c)(1)(F), in *italics*, was added by Sec. 11(a)(19) of the Tax Technical Corrections Act of 2007, P.L. 110-172, 12/29/2007, which struck out:

1. "(F) Income from notional principal contracts. Any item of income, gain, deduction, or loss from a notional principal contract entered into for purposes of hedging any item described in any preceding subparagraph shall not be taken into account for purposes of this subparagraph but shall be taken into account under such other subparagraph."

Code Sec. 954(c)(1)(H) in *italics*, was added by Sec. 11(a)(20), P.L. 110-172, 12/29/2007.

2. redesignated subpara. (c)(1)(I) as subpara. (c)(1)(H)

Matter in *italics* in Code Sec. 954(c)(2)(C)(ii) was added by Sec. 11(g)(15)(B) of the Tax Technical Corrections Act of 2007, P.L. 110-172, 12/29/2007, which struck out:

3. "section 956(c)(2)(J)"

Effective Date enacted 12/29/2007.

Code Sec. 954(c)(6)(B) and Code Sec. 954(c)(6)(C), in *italics*, was added by Sec. 4(a), P.L. 110-172, 12/29/2007.

4. added subpara. (c)(6)(A)

5. redesignated subpara. (c)(6)(B) as subpara. (c)(6)(C)

Effective Date (Sec. 4(d)(1), P.L. 110-172, 12/29/2007) effective for tax. yrs. of foreign corporations begin. after 12/31/2005, and for tax. yrs. of United States shareholders with or within which such tax. yrs. of foreign corporations end.

[¶ 3052]   Code Sec. 956.   Investment of earnings in United States property.

* * * * * * * * * * * *

(c) United States property defined.

  (1) In general. For purposes of subsection (a), the term "United States property" means any property acquired after December 31, 1962, which is—

  (A) tangible property located in the United States;

  (B) stock of a domestic corporation;

  (C) an obligation of a United States person; or

  (D) any right to the use in the United States of—

    (i) a patent or copyright,

    (ii) an invention, model, or design (whether or not patented),

    (iii) a secret formula or process, or

    (iv) any other similar property right,

  which is acquired or developed by the controlled foreign corporation for use in the United States.

  (2) Exceptions. For purposes of subsection (a), the term "United States property" does not include—

* * * * * * * * * * * *

  [1](*I*) deposits of cash or securities made or received on commercial terms in the ordinary course of a United States or foreign person's business as a dealer in securities or in commodities, but only to the extent such deposits are made or received as collateral or margin for (i) a securities loan, notional principal contract, options contract, forward contract, or futures contract, or (ii) any other financial transaction in which the Secretary determines that it is customary to post collateral or margin;

  [2](*J*) an obligation of a United States person to the extent the principal amount of the obligation does not exceed the fair market value of readily marketable securities sold or purchased pursuant to a sale and repurchase agreement or otherwise posted or received as collateral for the obligation in the ordinary course of its business by a United States or foreign person which is a dealer in securities or commodities;

  [3](*K*) securities acquired and held by a controlled foreign corporation in the ordinary course of its business as a dealer in securities if—

    (i) the dealer accounts for the securities as securities held primarily for sale to customers in the ordinary course of business, and

    (ii) the dealer disposes of the securities (or such securities mature while held by the dealer) within a period consistent with the holding of securities for sale to customers in the ordinary course of business; and

  (M) an obligation of a United States person which—

    (i) is not a domestic corporation, and

(ii) is not—

(I) a United States shareholder (as defined in section 951(b)) of the controlled foreign corporation, or

(II) a partnership, estate, or trust in which the controlled foreign corporation, or any related person (as defined in section 954(d)(3)), is a partner, beneficiary, or trustee immediately after the acquisition of any obligation of such partnership, estate, or trust by the controlled foreign corporation.

For purposes of [4]*subparagraphs (I), (J), and (K)* the term "dealer in securities" has the meaning given such term by section 475(c)(1), and the term "dealer in commodities" has the meaning given such term by section 475(e), except that such term shall include a futures commission merchant.

* * * * * * * * * * * *

[Endnote Code Sec. 956]

Matter in *italics* in Code Sec. 956(c)(2), Code Sec. 956(c)(2)(I) through Code Sec. 956(c)(2)(L)

"(I) to the extent provided in regulations prescribed by the Secretary, property which is otherwise United States property which is held by a FSC and which is related to the export activities of such FSC;"

2. "(I)"

3. "(J)"

4. "subparagraphs (J), (K), and (L)"

Effective Date (P.L. 110-172, 12/29/2007) enacted 12/29/2007.

[¶ 3053]   Code Sec. 992.   Requirements of a domestic international sales corporation.

(a)   Definition of "DISC" and "Former DISC".

(1)   DISC. For purposes of this title, the term "DISC" means, with respect to any taxable year, a corporation which is incorporated under the laws of any State and satisfies the following conditions for the taxable year:

(A) 95 percent or more of the gross receipts (as defined in section 993(f)) of such corporation consist of qualified export receipts (as defined in section 993(a)),

(B) the adjusted basis of the qualified export assets (as defined in section 993(b)) of the corporation at the close of the taxable year equals or exceeds 95 percent of the sum of the adjusted basis of all assets of the corporation at the close of the taxable year,

(C) such corporation does not have more than one class of stock and the par or stated value of its outstanding stock is at least $2,500 on each day of the taxable year, [1]*and*

(D) the corporation has made an election pursuant to subsection (b) to be treated as a DISC and such election is in effect for the taxable year[2].

[3]*(E) [Repealed.]*

(2)   Status as DISC after having filed a return as a DISC. The Secretary shall prescribe regulations setting forth the conditions under and the extent to which a corporation which has filed a return as a DISC for a taxable year shall be treated as a DISC for such taxable year for all purposes of this title, notwithstanding the fact that the corporation has failed to satisfy the conditions of paragraph (1).

(3)   "Former DISC". For purposes of this title, the term "former DISC" means, with respect to any taxable year, a corporation which is not a DISC for such year but was a DISC in a preceding taxable year and at the beginning of the taxable year has undistributed previously taxed income or accumulated DISC income.

* * * * * * * * * * * *

[Endnote Code Sec. 992]

Matter in *italics* in Code Sec. 992(a)(1)(C), Code Sec. 992(a)(1)(D), and Code Sec. 992(a)(1)(E) was added by Sec. 11(g)(16) of the Tax Technical Corrections Act of 2007, P.L. 110-172, 12/29/2007, which struck out:

1. added matter in subpara. (a)(1)(C)

2. ", and"

3. "(E) such corporation is not a member of any controlled group of which a FSC is a member."

Effective Date enacted 12/29/2007.

[¶ 3054]   Code Sec. 1016.   Adjustments to basis.

(a)   General rule. Proper adjustment in respect of the property shall in all cases be made—

(1) for expenditures, receipts, losses, or other items, properly chargeable to capital account, but no such adjustment shall be made—

(A) for taxes or other carrying charges described in section 266, or

(B) for expenditures described in section 173 (relating to circulation expenditures), for which deductions have been taken by the taxpayer in determining taxable income for the taxable year or prior taxable years;

* * * * * * * * * * * *

[1]*(31)* to the extent provided in section 179D(e),

[2]*(32)* to the extent provided in section 45L(e), in the case of amounts with respect to which a credit has been allowed under section 45L,

[3]*(33)* to the extent provided in [4]*section 25C(f)*, in the case of amounts with respect to which a credit has been allowed under section 25C,

[5]*(34)* to the extent provided in section 25D(f), in the case of amounts with respect to which a credit has been allowed under section 25D,

[6]*(35)* to the extent provided in section 30B(h)(4), and

[7]*(36)* to the extent provided in [8]*section 30C(e)(1)*.

* * * * * * * * * * * *

[For Analysis, see ¶ 401. For Committee Reports, see ¶ 5306.]

[Endnote Code Sec. 1016]

Matter in *italics* in Code Sec. 1016(a)(31), Code Sec. 1016(a)(32), and Code Sec. 1016(a)(33) was added by Sec. 7(a)(1)(C) of the Tax Technical Corrections Act of 2007, P.L. 110-172, 12/29/2007, which struck out:

1. "(31) in the case of a facility with respect to which a credit was allowed under section 45H, to the extent provided in section 45H(d),"

"(32)"

2. "(33)"

3. "(34)"

Effective Date Effective for expenses paid or incurred after 12/31/2002, in tax. yrs. end. after 12/31/2002.

Matter in *italics* in Code Sec. 1016(a)(33) [as redes. by Sec. 7(a)(1)(C) of this act], was added by Sec. 11(a)(21), P.L. 110-172, 12/29/2007, which struck out:

4. "section 25C(e)"

Effective Date enacted 12/29/2007.

Matter in *italics* in Code Sec. 1016(a)(34), Code Sec. 1016(a)(35), and Code Sec. 1016(a)(36), was added by Sec. 7(a)(1)(C) of the Tax Technical Corrections Act of 2007, P.L. 110-172, 12/29/2007, which struck out:

5. "(35)"

6. "(36)"

7. "(37)"

Effective Date (Sec. 7(e)(1), P.L. 110-172, 12/29/2007) Effective for expenses paid or incurred after 12/31/2002, in tax. yrs. end. after 12/31/2002.

Matter in *italics* in Code Sec. 1016(a)(36) [as redes. by Sec. 7(a)(1)(C) of this act], was added by Sec. 11(a)(22), P.L. 110-172, 12/29/2007, which struck out:

8. "section 30C(f)"

Effective Date enacted 12/29/2007.

[¶ 3055]   Code Sec. 1092.   Straddles.
  (a)   Recognition of loss in case of straddles, etc.
    (1)   Limitation on recognition of loss.
      (A) In general. Any loss with respect to 1 or more positions shall be taken into account for any taxable year only to the extent that the amount of such loss exceeds the unrecognized gain (if any) with respect to 1 or more positions which were offsetting positions with respect to 1 or more positions from which the loss arose.
      (B) Carryover of loss. Any loss which may not be taken into account under subparagraph (A) for any taxable year shall, subject to the limitations under subparagraph (A), be treated as sustained in the succeeding taxable year.
    (2)   Special rule for identified straddles.
      (A) In general. In the case of any straddle which is an identified straddle—
        (i) paragraph (1) shall not apply with respect to [1]*positions* comprising the identified straddle,
        (ii) if there is any loss with respect to any [2]*position* of the identified straddle, the basis of each of the [3]*offsetting positions* in the identified straddle shall be increased by an amount which bears the same ratio to the loss as the unrecognized gain with respect to such offsetting position bears to the aggregate unrecognized gain with respect to all such offsetting positions,[4]
        [5]*(iii) if the application of clause (ii) does not result in an increase in the basis of any offsetting position in the identified straddle, the basis of each of the offsetting positions in the identified straddle shall be increased in a manner which—*
          (I) is reasonable, consistent with the purposes of this paragraph, and consistently applied by the taxpayer, and
          (II) results in an aggregate increase in the basis of such offsetting positions which is equal to the loss described in clause (ii), and
        [6]*(iv) any loss described in clause (ii) shall not otherwise be taken into account for purposes of this title.*
      (B) Identified straddle. The term "identified straddle" means any straddle—
        (i) which is clearly identified on the taxpayer's records as an identified straddle before the earlier of—
          (I) the close of the day on which the straddle is acquired, or
          (II) such time as the Secretary may prescribe by regulations.
        (ii) to the extent provided by regulations, the value of each position of which (in the hands of the taxpayer immediately before the creation of the straddle) is not less than the basis of such position in the hands of the taxpayer at the time the straddle is created, and
        (iii) which is not part of a larger straddle.
      [7]*A straddle shall be treated as clearly identified for purposes of clause (i) only if such identification includes an identification of the positions in the straddle which are offsetting with respect other positions in the straddle.*
      [8]*(C) Application to liabilities and obligations. Except as otherwise provided by the Secretary, rules similar to the rules of clauses (ii) and (iii) of subparagraph (A) shall apply for purposes of this paragraph with respect to any position which is, or has been, a liability or obligation.*
      [9]*(D)* Regulations. The Secretary shall prescribe such regulations or other guidance as may be necessary or appropriate to carry out the purposes of this paragraph. Such regulations or other guidance may specify the proper methods for clearly identifying a straddle as an identified straddle (and for identifying the positions comprising such straddle), the rules for the application of this section to a taxpayer which fails to comply with those identification requirements, [10]*the rules for the application of this section to a position which is or has been a liability or obligation, methods of loss allocation which satisfy the requirements of subparagraph (A)(iii),* and the ordering rules in cases where a taxpayer disposes (or otherwise ceases to be the holder) of any part of any position which is part of an identified straddle.

(3) Unrecognized gain. For purposes of this subsection—

(A) In general. The term "unrecognized gain" means—

(i) in the case of any position held by the taxpayer as of the close of the taxable year, the amount of gain which would be taken into account with respect to such position if such position were sold on the last business day of such taxable year at its fair market value, and

(ii) in the case of any position with respect to which, as of the close of the taxable year, gain has been realized but not recognized, the amount of gain so realized.

(B) Special rule for identified straddles. For purposes of paragraph (2)(A)(ii), the unrecognized gain with respect to any [11]*offsetting position* shall be the excess of the fair market value of the position at the time of the determination over the fair market value of the position at the time the taxpayer identified the position as a position in an identified straddle.

(C) Reporting of gain.

(i) In general. Each taxpayer shall disclose to the Secretary, at such time and in such manner and form as the Secretary may prescribe by regulations—

(I) each position (whether or not part of a straddle) with respect to which, as of the close of the taxable year, there is unrecognized gain, and

(II) the amount of such unrecognized gain.

(ii) Reports not required in certain cases. Clause (i) shall not apply—

(I) to any position which is part of an identified straddle,

(II) to any position which, with respect to the taxpayer, is property described in paragraph (1) or (2) of section 1221(a) or to any position which is part of a hedging transaction (as defined in section 1256(e)), or

(III) with respect to any taxable year if no loss on a position (including a regulated futures contract) has been sustained during such taxable year or if the only loss sustained on such position is a loss described in subclause (II).

* * * * * * * * * * * *

[For Analysis, see ¶ 801 and ¶ 802. For Committee Reports, see ¶ 5306.]

[Endnote Code Sec. 1092]

Matter in *italics* in Code Sec. 1092(a)(2)(A)(i), Code Sec. 1092(a)(2)(A)(ii), Code Sec. 1092(a)(2)(A)(iii) and Code Sec. 1092(a)(2)(A)(iv) was added by Sec. 7(d)(1) and (d)(2)(B)(i)-(iii) of the Tax Technical Corrections Act of 2007, P.L. 110-172, 12/29/2007, which struck out:

1. "identified positions"
2. "identified position"
3. "identified offsetting positions"
4. "and"
5. added clause (d)(2)(A)(iii)
6. "(iii)"

Effective Date (Sec. 7(e)(1), P.L. 110-172, 12/29/2007) effective for positions established on or after 10/22/2004.

Matter in *italics* in Code Sec. 1092(a)(2)(B) was added by Sec. 7(d)(2)(A), P.L. 110-172, 12/29/2007.

7. added matter in subpara. (a)(2)(B)

Effective Date (Sec. 7(e)(2), P.L. 110-172, 12/29/2007) effective for straddles acquired after 12/29/2007.

Matter in *italics* in Code Sec. 1092(a)(2)(C), Code Sec. 1092(a)(2)(D) and Code Sec. 1092(a)(3)(B) was added by Sec. 7(d)(2)(C) and (d)(3)-(4), P.L. 110-172, 12/29/2007, which struck out:

8. added subpara. (a)(2)(C)
9. "(C)"
10. added matter in subpara. (a)(2)(D)
11. "identified offsetting position"

Effective Date (Sec. 7(e)(1), P.L. 110-172, 12/29/2007) effective for positions established on or after 10/22/2004.

[¶ 3056]   Code Sec. 1248.   Gain from certain sales or exchanges of stock in certain foreign corporations.

* * * * * * * * * * * *

(d) Exclusions from earnings and profits. For purposes of this section, the following amounts shall be excluded, with respect to any United States person, from the earnings and profits of a foreign corporation:

* * * * * * * * * * * *

(5) Foreign trade income. Earnings and profits of the foreign corporation attributable to foreign trade income of a FSC [1]*(as defined in section 922)* other than foreign trade income which—

(A) is section 923(a)(2) non-exempt income (within the meaning of section 927(d)(6)), or

(B) would not (but for section 923(a)(4)) be treated as exempt foreign trade income.

For purposes of the preceding sentence, the terms "foreign trade income" and "exempt foreign trade income" have the respective meanings given such terms by section 923. [2]*Any reference in this paragraph to section 922, 923, or 927 shall be treated as a reference to such section as in effect before its repeal by the FSC Repeal and Extraterritorial Income Exclusion Act of 2000.*

* * * * * * * * * * * *

[Endnote Code Sec. 1248]

Matter in *italics* in Code Sec. 1248(d)(5) was added by Sec. 11(g)(17)(A)-(B) of the Tax Technical Corrections Act of 2007, P.L. 110-172, 12/29/2007

1. added matter in para. (d)(5)

2. added matter in para. (d)(5)

Effective Date Effective for transactions after 9/30/2000.

[¶ 3057]   Code Sec. 1260.   Gains from constructive ownership transactions.

* * * * * * * * * * * *

(c) Financial asset. For purposes of this section—

(1) In general. The term "financial asset" means—

(A) any equity interest in any pass-thru entity, and

(B) to the extent provided in regulations—

(i) any debt instrument, and

(ii) any stock in a corporation which is not a pass-thru entity.

(2) Pass-thru entity. For purposes of paragraph (1), the term "pass-thru entity" means—

(A) a regulated investment company,

(B) a real estate investment trust,

(C) an S corporation,

(D) a partnership,

(E) a trust,

(F) a common trust fund,

(G) a passive foreign investment company (as defined in section 1297 without regard to [1]*subsection (d)* thereof), [2]*and*

(H) a REMIC.

* * * * * * * * * * * *

[Endnote Code Sec. 1260]

Matter in *italics* in Code Sec. 1260(c)(2)(G) was added by Sec. 11(a)(24)(B) of the Tax Technical Corrections Act of 2007, P.L. 110-172, 12/29/2007, which struck out:

1. "subsection (e)"

2. added matter in subpara. (c)(2)(G)

Effective Date enacted 12/29/2007.

[¶ 3058]   Code Sec. 1297.   Passive foreign investment company.

* * * * * * * * * * * *

(b)   Passive income. For purposes of this section—

(1)   In general. Except as provided in paragraph (2), the term "passive income" means any income which is of a kind which would be foreign personal holding company income as defined in section 954(c).

(2)   Exceptions. Except as provided in regulations, the term "passive income" does not include any income—

(A) derived in the active conduct of a banking business by an institution licensed to do business as a bank in the United States (or, to the extent provided in regulations, by any other corporation),

(B) derived in the active conduct of an insurance business by a corporation which is predominantly engaged in an insurance business and which would be subject to tax under subchapter L if it were a domestic corporation,

(C) which is interest, a dividend, or a rent or royalty, which is received or accrued from a related person (within the meaning of section 954(d)(3)) to the extent such amount is properly allocable (under regulations prescribed by the Secretary) to income of such related person which is not passive income, or

(D) which is [1] export trade income of an export trade corporation (as defined in section 971).

For purposes of subparagraph (C), the term "related person" has the meaning given such term by section 954(d)(3) determined by substituting "foreign corporation" for "controlled foreign corporation" each place it appears in section 954(d)(3).

* * * * * * * * * * * *

[2](d)   Exception for United States shareholders of controlled foreign corporations.

(1)   In general. For purposes of this part, a corporation shall not be treated with respect to a shareholder as a passive foreign investment company during the qualified portion of such shareholder's holding period with respect to stock in such corporation.

(2)   Qualified portion. For purposes of this subsection, the term "qualified portion" means the portion of the shareholder's holding period—

(A) which is after December 31, 1997, and

(B) during which the shareholder is a United States shareholder (as defined in section 951(b)) of the corporation and the corporation is a controlled foreign corporation.

(3)   New holding period if qualified portion ends.

(A) In general. Except as provided in subparagraph (B), if the qualified portion of a shareholder's holding period with respect to any stock ends after December 31, 1997, solely for purposes of this part, the shareholder's holding period with respect to such stock shall be treated as beginning as of the first day following such period.

(B) Exception. Subparagraph (A) shall not apply if such stock was, with respect to such shareholder, stock in a passive foreign investment company at any time before the qualified portion of the shareholder's holding period with respect to such stock and no election under section 1298(b)(1) is made.

(4)   Treatment of holders of options. Paragraph (1) shall not apply to stock treated as owned by a person by reason of section 1298(a)(4) (relating to the treatment of a person that has an option to acquire stock as owning such stock) unless such person establishes that such stock is owned (within the meaning of section 958(a)) by a United States shareholder (as defined in section 951(b)) who is not exempt from tax under this chapter.

³*(e)* **Methods for measuring assets.**

(1) Determination using value. The determination under subsection (a)(2) shall be made on the basis of the value of the assets of a foreign corporation if—

(A) such corporation is a publicly traded corporation for the taxable year, or

(B) paragraph (2) does not apply to such corporation for the taxable year.

(2) Determination using adjusted bases. The determination under subsection (a)(2) shall be based on the adjusted bases (as determined for the purposes of computing earnings and profits) of the assets of a foreign corporation if such corporation is not described in paragraph (1)(A) and such corporation—

(A) is a controlled foreign corporation, or

(B) elects the application of this paragraph.

An election under subparagraph (B), once made, may be revoked only with the consent of the Secretary.

(3) Publicly traded corporation. For purposes of this subsection, a foreign corporation shall be treated as a publicly traded corporation if the stock in the corporation is regularly traded on—

(A) a national securities exchange which is registered with the Securities and Exchange Commission or the national market system established pursuant to section 11A of the Securities and Exchange Act of 1934, or

(B) any exchange or other market which the Secretary determines has rules adequate to carry out the purposes of this subsection.

[Endnote Code Sec. 1297]

Matter in Code Sec. 1297(b)(2)(D), Code Sec. 1297(d), and Code Sec. 1297(e) was added by Sec. 11(g)(18) and Sec. 11(a)(24)(A) of the Tax Technical Corrections Act of 2007, P.L. 110-172, 12/29/2007, which struck out:

1. "foreign trade income of a FSC or"

2. "(d) Section 1247 corporations. For purposes of this part, the term "passive foreign investment company" does not include any foreign investment company to which section 1247 applies."

"(d)"

3. "(e)"

Effective Date enacted 12/29/2007.

[¶ 3059]   Code Sec. 1298.   Special rules.

(a) Attribution of ownership. For purposes of this part—

(1) Attribution to United States persons. This subsection—

(A) shall apply to the extent that the effect is to treat stock of a passive foreign investment company as owned by a United States person, and

(B) except to the extent provided in regulations, shall not apply to treat stock owned (or treated as owned under this subsection) by a United States person as owned by any other person.

(2) Corporations.

(A) In general. If 50 percent or more in value of the stock of a corporation is owned, directly or indirectly, by or for any person, such person shall be considered as owning the stock owned directly or indirectly by or for such corporation in that proportion which the value of the stock which such person so owns bears to the value of all stock in the corporation.

(B) 50-percent limitation not to apply to PFIC. For purposes of determining whether a shareholder of a passive foreign investment company is treated as owning stock owned directly or indirectly by or for such company, subparagraph (A) shall be applied without regard to the 50-percent limitation contained therein. ¹*Section 1297(d)* shall not apply in determining whether a corporation is a passive foreign investment company for purposes of this subparagraph.

* * * * * * * * * * * *

(b) Other special rules. For purposes of this part—

* * * * * * * * * * * *

[2]**(7) Treatment of certain foreign corporations owning stock in 25-percent owned domestic corporation.**

(A) In general. If—

(i) a foreign corporation is subject to the tax imposed by section 531 (or waives any benefit under any treaty which would otherwise prevent the imposition of such tax), and

(ii) such foreign corporation owns at least 25 percent (by value) of the stock of a domestic corporation,

for purposes of determining whether such foreign corporation is a passive foreign investment company, any qualified stock held by such domestic corporation shall be treated as an asset which does not produce passive income (and is not held for the production of passive income) and any amount included in gross income with respect to such stock shall not be treated as passive income.

(B) Qualified stock. For purposes of subparagraph (A), the term "qualified stock" means any stock in a C corporation which is a domestic corporation and which is not a regulated investment company or real estate investment trust.

[3]**(8) Treatment of certain subpart F inclusions.** Any amount included in gross income under section 951(a)(1)(B) shall be treated as a distribution received with respect to the stock.

* * * * * * * * * * * *

[Endnote Code Sec. 1298]

Matter in *italics* in Code Sec. 1298(a)(2)(B) was added by Sec. 11(a)(24)(C) of the Tax Technical Corrections Act of 2007, P.L. 110-172, 12/29/2007, which struck out:

1. "Section 1297(e)"

Effective Date enacted 12/29/2007.

Matter in *italics* in Code Sec. 1298(b)(7) and Code Sec. 1298(b)(8) was added by Sec. 11(f)(2), P.L. 110-172, 12/29/2007, which struck out:

2. "(7) Coordination with section 1246. Section 1246 shall not apply to earnings and profits of any company for any taxable year beginning after December 31, 1986, if such company is a passive foreign investment company for such taxable year.

"(8)"

3. "(9)"

Effective Date (Sec. 11(f)(4), P.L. 110-172, 12/29/2007) effective for tax. yrs. of foreign corporations begin. after 12/31/2004, and for tax. yrs. of U.S. shareholders with or within which such tax. yrs. of foreign corporations end.

[¶ 3060]   Code Sec. 1362.   Election; revocation; termination.

* * * * * * * * * * * *

(f) Inadvertent invalid elections or terminations. If—

(1) an election under subsection (a) [1]*or section 1361(b)(3)(B)(ii)* by any corporation—

(A) was not effective for the taxable year for which made (determined without regard to subsection (b)(2)) by reason of a failure to meet the requirements of section 1361(b) or to obtain shareholder consents, or

(B) was terminated under paragraph (2) or (3) of subsection (d) or [2]*section 1361(b)(3)(C),*

(2) the Secretary determines that the circumstances resulting in such ineffectiveness or termination were inadvertent,

(3) no later than a reasonable period of time after discovery of the circumstances resulting in such ineffectiveness or termination, steps were taken—

(A) so that the corporation for which the election was made or the termination occurred is a small business corporation or a qualified subchapter S subsidiary, as the case may be, or

(B) to acquire the required shareholder consents, and

(4) the corporation for which the election was made or the termination occurred, and each person who was a shareholder in such corporation at any time during the period specified pursuant to this subsection, agrees to make such adjustments (consistent with the treatment of such corporation as an S corporation or a qualified subchapter S subsidiary, as the case may be) as may be required by the Secretary with respect to such period,

then, notwithstanding the circumstances resulting in such ineffectiveness or termination, such corporation shall be treated as an S corporation or a qualified subchapter S subsidiary, as the case may be during the period specified by the Secretary.

* * * * * * * * * * * *

[Endnote Code Sec. 1362]
Matter in *italics* in Code Sec. 1362(f)(1) and Code Sec. 1362(f)(1)(B) was added by Sec. 11(a)(25)(A)-(B) of the Tax Technical Corrections Act of 2007, P.L. 110-172, 12/29/2007, which struck out:
1. ", section 1361(b)(3)(B)(ii), or section 1361(c)(1)(A)(ii)"
2. ", section 1361(b)(3)(C), or section 1361(c)(1)(D)(iii)"
Effective Date enacted 12/29/2007.

[¶ 3061]   Code Sec. 1366.   Pass-thru of items to shareholders.

* * * * * * * * * * * *

(d) Special rules for losses and deductions.

* * * * * * * * * * * *

[1](4) *Application of limitation on charitable contributions.* In *the case of any charitable contribution of property to which the second sentence of section 1367(a)(2) applies, paragraph (1) shall not apply to the extent of the excess (if any) of—*

(A) *the shareholder's pro rata share of such contribution, over*

(B) *the shareholder's pro rata share of the adjusted basis of such property.*

* * * * * * * * * * * *

[For Analysis, see ¶ 603. For Committee Reports, see ¶ 5302.]

[Endnote Code Sec. 1366]
Code Sec. 1366(d)(4), in *italics*, was added by 3(b) of the Tax Technical Corrections Act of 2007, P.L. 110-172, 12/29/2007.
1. added para. (d)(4)
Effective Date (Sec. 3(j), P.L. 110-172, 12/29/2007) effective for contributions made in tax. yrs. begin. after 12/31/2005.

[¶ 3062]   Code Sec. 1400L.   Tax benefits for New York Liberty Zone.

* * * * * * * * * * * *

(b) Special allowance for certain property acquired after September 10, 2001.

* * * * * * * * * * * *

(2) Qualified New York Liberty Zone property.

(D) Special rules. For purposes of this subsection, rules similar to the rules of section 168(k)(2)(E) shall apply, except that clause (i) thereof shall be applied without regard to "and before ¹*January 1, 2010*", and clause (iv) thereof shall be applied by substituting "qualified New York Liberty Zone property" for "qualified property".

[Endnote Code Sec. 1400L]

Matter in *italics* in Code Sec. 1400L(b)(2)(D) was added by Sec. 103(c)(8) of the Economic Stimulus Act of 2008, P.L. 110-185, 2/13/2008, which struck out:

1. "January 1, 2005"

Effective Date (Sec. 103(d), P.L. 110-185, 2/13/2008) effective for property placed in service after December 31, 2007, in tax. yrs. end. after 2/13/2008.

[¶ 3063]   Code Sec. 1400N.   Tax benefits for Gulf Opportunity Zone.

* * * * * * * * * * * *

(d)   Special allowance for certain property acquired on or after August 28, 2005.

* * * * * * * * * * * *

(3) Special rules. For purposes of this subsection, rules similar to the rules of subparagraph (E) of section 168(k)(2) shall apply, except that such subparagraph shall be applied—

(A) by substituting "August 27, 2005" for "¹*December 31, 2007*" each place it appears therein,

(B) by substituting "January 1, 2008" for "²*January 1, 2009*" in clause (i) thereof, and

(C) by substituting "qualified Gulf Opportunity Zone property" for "qualified property" in clause (iv) thereof.

* * * * * * * * * * * *

(6) Extension for certain property.

(A) In general. In the case of any specified Gulf Opportunity Zone extension property, paragraph (2)(A) shall be applied without regard to clause (v) thereof.

(B) Specified Gulf Opportunity Zone extension property. For purposes of this paragraph, the term "specified Gulf Opportunity Zone extension property" means property—

(i) substantially all of the use of which is in one or more specified portions of the GO Zone, and

(ii) which is—

(I) nonresidential real property or residential rental property which is placed in service by the taxpayer on or before December 31, 2010, or

(II) in the case of a taxpayer who places a building described in subclause (I) in service on or before December 31, 2010, property described in section 168(k)(2)(A)(i) if substantially all of the use of such property is in such building and such property is placed in service by the taxpayer not later than 90 days after such building is placed in service.

(C) Specified portions of the GO Zone. For purposes of this paragraph, the term "specified portions of the GO Zone" means those portions of the GO Zone which are in any county or parish which is identified by the Secretary as being a county or parish in which hurricanes occurring during 2005 damaged (in the aggregate) more than 60 percent of the housing units in such county or parish which were occupied (determined according to the 2000 Census).

(D) Only pre-January 1, 2010, basis of real property eligible for additional allowance. In the case of property which is qualified Gulf Opportunity Zone property solely by reason of subparagraph (B)(ii)(I), paragraph (1) shall apply only to the extent of the adjusted basis thereof attributable to manufacture, construction, or production before January 1, 2010.

³*(E) Exception for bonus depreciation property under section 168(k). The term "specified Gulf Opportunity Zone extension property" shall not include any property to which section 168(k) applies.*

[For Analysis, see ¶ 53. For Committee Reports, see ¶ 5503.]

[Endnote Code Sec. 1400N]

Matter in *italics* in Code Sec. 1400N(d)(3)(A), Code Sec. 1400N(d)(3)(B) and Code Sec. 1400N(d)(6)(E) of the Economic Stimulus Act of 2008, P.L. 110-185, 2/13/2008, which struck out:

1. "September 10, 2001"
2. "January 1, 2005"
3. added subpara. (d)(6)(E)

Effective Date (Sec. 103(d), P.L. 110-185, 2/13/2008) effective for property placed in service after December 31, 2007, in tax. yrs. end. after 2/13/2008.

[¶ 3064]   Code Sec. 1400O.   Education tax benefits.

In the case of an individual who attends an eligible educational institution (as defined in section 25A(f)(2)) located in the Gulf Opportunity Zone for any taxable year beginning during 2005 or 2006—

(1) in applying section 25A, the term "qualified tuition and related expenses" shall include any costs which are qualified higher education expenses (as defined in section 529(e)(3)),

(2) each of the dollar amounts in effect ¹*under* subparagraphs (A) and (B) of section 25A(b)(1) shall be twice the amount otherwise in effect before the application of this subsection, and

(3) section 25A(c)(1) shall be applied by substituting "40 percent" for "20 percent".

[Endnote Code Sec. 1400O]

Matter in Code Sec. 1400O(2), in *italics*, was added by Sec. 11(a)(26) of the Tax Technical Corrections Act of 2007, P.L. 110-172, 12/29/2007 which struck out:

1. "under of"

Effective Date enacted 12/29/2007.

[¶ 3065]   Code Sec. 1400S.   Additional tax relief provisions.

(a)   Temporary suspension of limitations on charitable contributions.

(1)   **In general.** Except as otherwise provided in paragraph (2), section 170(b) shall not apply to qualified contributions and such contributions shall not be taken into account for purposes of applying subsections (b) and (d) of section 170 to other contributions.

(2)   **Treatment of excess contributions.** For purposes of section 170—

(A) Individuals. In the case of an individual—

(i) Limitation. Any qualified contribution shall be allowed only to the extent that the aggregate of such contributions does not exceed the excess of the taxpayer's contribution base (as defined in ¹*subparagraph (G) of section 170(b)(1))* over the amount of all other charitable contributions allowed under section 170(b)(1).

(ii) Carryover. If the aggregate amount of qualified contributions made in the contribution year (within the meaning of section 170(d)(1)) exceeds the limitation of clause (i), such excess shall be added to the excess described in the portion of subparagraph (A) of such section which precedes clause (i) thereof for purposes of applying such section.

(B) Corporations. In the case of a corporation—

(i) Limitation. Any qualified contribution shall be allowed only to the extent that the aggregate of such contributions does not exceed the excess of the taxpayer's taxable income (as determined under paragraph (2) of section 170(b)) over the amount of all other charitable contributions allowed under such paragraph.

(ii) Carryover. Rules similar to the rules of subparagraph (A)(ii) shall apply for purposes of this subparagraph.

* * * * * * * * * * * *

[Endnote Code Sec. 1400S]

Matter in *italics* in Code Sec. 1400S(a)(2)(A)(i) was added by Sec. 11(a)(14)(C) of the Tax Technical Corrections Act of 2007, P.L.110-172, 12/29/2007, which struck out:

1. "subparagraph (F)"

Effective Date enacted 12/29/2007.

[¶ 3066]   Code Sec. 2055.   Transfers for public, charitable, and religious uses.

* * * * * * * * * * * *

[1](g) **Cross references.**

(1) For option as to time for valuation for purpose of deduction under this section, see section 2032.

(2) For treatment of certain organizations providing child care, see section 501(k).

(3) For exemption of gifts and bequests to or for the benefit of Library of Congress, see section 5 of the Act of March 3, 1925, as amended (2 U.S.C. 161).

(4) For treatment of gifts and bequests for the benefit of the Naval Historical Center as gifts or bequests to or for the use of the United States, see section 7222 of title 10, United States Code.

(5) For treatment of gifts and bequests to or for the benefit of National Park Foundation as gifts or bequests to or for the use of the United States, see section 8 of the Act of December 18, 1967 (16 U.S.C. 191).

(6) For treatment of gifts, devises, or bequests accepted by the Secretary of State, the Director of the International Communication Agency, or the Director of the United States International Development Cooperation Agency as gifts, devises, or bequests to or for the use of the United States, see section 25 of the State Department Basic Authorities Act of 1956.

(7) For treatment of gifts or bequests of money accepted by the Attorney General for credit to "Commissary Funds, Federal Prisons," as gifts or bequests to or for the use of the United States, see section 4043 of title 18, United States Code.

(8) For payment of tax on gifts and bequests of United States obligations to the United States, see section 3113(e) of title 31, United States Code.

(9) For treatment of gifts and bequests for benefit of the Naval Academy as gifts or bequests to or for the use of the United States, see section 6973 of title 10, United States Code.

(10) For treatment of gifts and bequests for benefit of the Naval Academy Museum as gifts or bequests to or for the use of the United States, see section 6974 of title 10, United States Code.

(11) For exemption of gifts and bequests received by National Archives Trust Fund Board, see section 2308 of title 44, United States Code.

(12) For treatment of gifts and bequests to or for the use of Indian tribal governments (or their subdivisions), see section 7871.

[For Analysis, see ¶ 601. For Committee Reports, see ¶ 5302.]

[Endnote Code Sec. 2055]

Matter in *italics* in Code Sec. 2055(g) was added by Sec. 3(d)(1) of the Tax Technical Corrections Act of 2007, P.L. 110-172, 12/29/2007, which struck out:

1. "(g) Valuation of subsequent gifts.

"(1) In general. In the case of any additional contribution, the fair market value of such contribution shall be determined by using the lesser of—

"(A) the fair market value of the property at the time of the initial fractional contribution, or

"(B) the fair market value of the property at the time of the additional contribution.

"(2) Definitions. For purposes of this paragraph—

"(A) Additional contribution. The term 'additional contribution' means a bequest, legacy, devise, or transfer described in subsection (a) of any interest in a property with respect to which the decedent had previously made an initial fractional contribution.

"(B) Initial fractional contribution. The term 'initial fractional contribution' means, with respect to any decedent, any charitable contribution of an undivided portion of the decedent's entire interest in any tangible personal property for which a deduction was allowed under section 170.

"(h)"

Effective Date (Sec. 3(j), P.L. 110-172, 12/29/2007) effective for contributions, bequests, and gifts made after 8/17/2006.

[¶ 3067]   **Code Sec. 2522.**   **Charitable and similar gifts.**

* * * * * * * * * * *

(e)   **Special rules for fractional gifts.**

   (1)   **Denial of deduction in certain cases.**

(A) In general. No deduction shall be allowed for a contribution of an undivided portion of a taxpayer's entire interest in tangible personal property unless [1]*all interests in the property are* held immediately before such contribution by—

     (i) the taxpayer, or

     (ii) the taxpayer and the donee.

(B) Exceptions. The Secretary may, by regulation, provide for exceptions to subparagraph (A) in cases where all persons who hold an interest in the property make proportional contributions of an undivided portion of the entire interest held by such persons.

[2]**(2)**   **Recapture of deduction in certain cases; addition to tax.**

(A) In general. The Secretary shall provide for the recapture of an amount equal to any deduction allowed under this section (plus interest) with respect to any contribution of an undivided portion of a taxpayer's entire interest in tangible personal property—

     (i) in any case in which the donor does not contribute all of the remaining [3]*interests* in such property to the donee (or, if such donee is no longer in existence, to any person described in section 170(c)) [4]*on or before* the earlier of—

         (I) the date that is 10 years after the date of the initial fractional contribution, or

         (II) the date of the death of the donor, and

     (ii) in any case in which the donee has not, during the period beginning on the date of the initial fractional contribution and ending on the date described in clause (i)—

         (I) had substantial physical possession of the property, and

         (II) used the property in a use which is related to a purpose or function constituting the basis for the organizations' exemption under section 501.

(B) Addition to tax. The tax imposed under this chapter for any taxable year for which there is a recapture under subparagraph (A) shall be increased by 10 percent of the amount so recaptured.

[5]*(C) Initial fractional contribution. For purposes of this paragraph, the term "initial fractional contribution" means, with respect to any donor, the first gift of an undivided portion of the donor's entire interest in any tangible personal property for which a deduction is allowed under subsection (a) or (b).*

[6]*(4) Repealed.*

* * * * * * * * * * *

[For Analysis, see ¶ 601. For Committee Reports, see ¶ 5302.]

[Endnote Code Sec. 2522]

Matter in *italics* in Code Sec. 2522(e)(1)(A) was added by Sec. 11(a)(16)(A) of the Tax Technical Corrections Act of 2007, P.L. 110-172, 12/29/2007, which struck out:

1. "all interest in the property is"

Effective Date enacted 12/29/2007.

Matter in *italics* in Code Sec. 2522(e)(2) was added by Sec. 3(d)(2)(A) and (B), P.L. 110-172, 12/29/2007, which struck out:

2. "(2) Valuation of subsequent gifts. In the case of any additional contribution, the fair market value of such contribution shall be determined by using the lesser of—

"(A) the fair market value of the property at the time of the initial fractional contribution, or

"(B) the fair market value of the property at the time of the additional contribution.

"(3)"

Effective Date (Sec. 3(j), P.L. 110-172, 12/29/2007) effective for contributions, bequests, and gifts made after 8/17/2006.

Matter in *italics* in Code Sec. 2522(e)(2)(A)(i) was added by Sec. 11(a)(16)(B)(i)-(ii), P.L. 110-172, 12/29/2007, which struck out:

3. "interest"

4. "before"

Effective Date enacted 12/29/2007.

Matter in *italics* in Code Sec. 2522(e)(2)(C) and Code Sec. 2522(e)(4) was added by Sec. 3(d)(2)(A) and (C), P.L. 110-172, 12/29/2007, which struck out:

5. added subpara. (e)(2)(C)

6. "(4) Definitions. For purposes of this subsection—

"(A) Additional contribution. The term 'additional contribution' means any gift for which a deduction is allowed under subsection (a) or (b) of any interest in a property with respect to which the donor has previously made an initial fractional contribution.

"(B) Initial fractional contribution. The term 'initial fractional contribution' means, with respect to any donor, the first gift of an undivided portion of the donor's entire interest in any tangible personal property for which a deduction is allowed under subsection (a) or (b)."

Effective Date (Sec. 3(j), P.L. 110-172, 12/29/2007) effective for contributions, bequests, and gifts made after 8/17/2006.

[¶ 3068]   Code Sec. 3121.   Definitions.

* * * * * * * * * * * *

(v) Treatment of certain deferred compensation and salary reduction arrangements.

(1) Certain employer contributions treated as wages. Nothing in any paragraph of subsection (a) (other than paragraph (1)) shall exclude from the term "wages" —

(A) any employer contribution under a qualified cash or deferred arrangement (as defined in section 401(k)) to the extent not included in gross income by reason of section 402(e)(3) [1]*or consisting of designated Roth contributions (as defined in section 402A(c)),* or

(B) any amount treated as an employer contribution under section 414(h)(2) where the pickup referred to in such section is pursuant to a salary reduction agreement (whether evidenced by a written instrument or otherwise).

(2) Treatment of certain nonqualified deferred compensation plans.

(A) In general. Any amount deferred under a nonqualified deferred compensation plan shall be taken into account for purposes of this chapter as of the later of—

(i) when the services are performed, or

(ii) when there is no substantial risk of forfeiture of the rights to such amount.

The preceding sentence shall not apply to any excess parachute payment (as defined in section 280G(b)) or to any specified stock compensation (as defined in section 4985) on which tax is imposed by section 4985.

(B) Taxed only once. Any amount taken into account as wages by reason of subparagraph (A) (and the income attributable thereto) shall not thereafter be treated as wages for purposes of this chapter.

(C) Nonqualified deferred compensation plan. For purposes of this paragraph, the term "nonqualified deferred compensation plan" means any plan or other arrangement for deferral of compensation other than a plan described in subsection (a)(5).

(3) Exempt governmental deferred compensation plan. For purposes of subsection (a)(5), the term "exempt governmental deferred compensation plan" means any plan providing for deferral of compensation established and maintained for its employees by the

United States, by a State or political subdivision thereof, or by an agency or instrumentality of any of the foregoing. Such term shall not include—

(A) any plan to which section 83, 402(b), 403(c), 457(a), or 457(f)(1) applies,

(B) any annuity contract described in section 403(b), and

(C) the Thrift Savings Fund (within the meaning of subchapter III of chapter 84 of title 5, United States Code).

* * * * * * * * * * * *

[For Analysis, see ¶1202. For Committee Reports, see ¶5307.]

[Endnote Code Sec. 3121]
Matter in *italics* in Code Sec. 3121(v)(1)(A) was added by Sec. 8(a)(2) of the Tax Technical Corrections Act of 2007, P.L. 110-172, 12/29/2007.
1. added matter in subpara. (v)(1)(A)
Effective Date (Sec. 8(b), P.L. 110-172, 12/29/2007) effective for tax. yrs. begin. after 12/31/2005.

[¶3069]   Code Sec. 3301.   Rate of tax.
There is hereby imposed on every employer (as defined in section 3306(a)) for each calendar year an excise tax, with respect to having individuals in his employ, equal to—

(1) 6.2 percent in the case of calendar years 1988 through [1]*2008*; or

(2) 6.0 percent in the case of calendar year [2]*2009* and each calendar year thereafter;
of the total wages (as defined in section 3306(b)) paid by him during the calendar year with respect to employment (as defined in section 3306(c)).

[For Analysis, see ¶1201. For Committee Reports, see ¶5101.]

[Endnote Code Sec. 3301]
Matter in *italics* in Code Sec. 3301(1) and Code Sec. 3301(2) added by Secs. 1501(a)(1) and (2) of the Energy Independence and Security Act of 2007, P.L. 110-140, 12/19/2007, which struck out:
1. "2007"
2. "2008"
Effective Date (Sec. 1501(b), P.L. 110-140, 12/19/2007) effective for wages paid after 12/31/2007.

[¶3070]   Code Sec. 4041.   Imposition of tax.

* * * * * * * * * * * *

(d)   Additional taxes to fund Leaking Underground Storage Tank Trust Fund.

(1)   Tax on sales and uses subject to tax under subsection (a). In addition to the taxes imposed by subsection (a), there is hereby imposed a tax of 0.1 cent a gallon on the sale or use of any liquid (other than liquefied petroleum gas and other than liquefied natural gas) if tax is imposed by subsection (a)(1) or (2), on such sale or use. [1]*No tax shall be imposed under the preceding sentence on the sale or use of any liquid if tax was imposed with respect to such liquid under section 4081 at the Leaking Underground Storage Tank Trust Fund financing rate.*

(2)   Liquids used in aviation. In addition to the taxes imposed by subsection (c), there is hereby imposed a tax of 0.1 cent a gallon on any liquid (other than gasoline (as defined in section 4083))—

(A) sold by any person to an owner, lessee, or other operator of an aircraft for use as a fuel in such aircraft, or

(B) used by any person as a fuel in an aircraft unless there was a taxable sale of such liquid under subparagraph (A).
No tax shall be imposed by this paragraph on the sale or use of any liquid if there was a taxable sale of such liquid under section 4081.

(3) Diesel fuel used in trains. In the case of any sale for use or use after December 31, 2006, there is hereby imposed a tax of 0.1 cent per gallon on any liquid other than gasoline (as defined in section 4083)—

(A) sold by any person to an owner, lessee, or other operator of a diesel-powered train for use as a fuel in such train, or

(B) used by any person as a fuel in a diesel-powered train unless there was a taxable sale of such fuel under subparagraph (A).

No tax shall be imposed by this paragraph on the sale or use of any liquid if tax was imposed on such liquid under section 4081.

(4) Termination. The taxes imposed by this subsection shall not apply during any period during which the Leaking Underground Storage Tank Trust Fund financing rate under section 4081 does not apply.

(5) Nonapplication of exemptions other than for exports. For purposes of this section, the tax imposed under this subsection shall be determined without regard to subsections ^{2}*(b)(1)(A), (f), (g)*^{3}, *(h)*, and *(l)*. ^{4}*The preceding sentence shall not apply with respect to subsection (g)(3) and so much of subsection (g)(1) as relates to vessels (within the meaning of section 4221(d)(3)) employed in foreign trade or trade between the United States and any of its possessions.*

* * * * * * * * * * * *

[For Analysis, see ¶ 1002, ¶ 1003 and ¶ 1004. For Committee Reports, see ¶ 5305.]

[Endnote Code Sec. 4041]

Matter in *italics* in Code Sec. 4041(d)(1) was added by Sec. 6(d)(1)(A) of the Tax Technical Corrections Act of 2007, P.L. 110-172, 12/29/2007.

1. added matter in para. (d)(1)

Effective Date (Sec. 6(e)(1), P.L. 110-172, 12/29/2007) effective for fuel entered, removed, or sold after 9/30/2005.

Matter in *italics* in Code Sec. 4041(d)(5) was added by Sec. 6(d)(3), P.L. 110-172, 12/29/2007.

2. added matter in para. (d)(5)

Effective Date (Sec. 6(e)(2), P.L. 110-172, 12/29/2007) effective for fuel sold for use or used after 12/29/2007.

Matter in *italics* in Code Sec. 4041(d)(5) was added by Sec. 6(d)(2)(A)(i)-(ii), P.L. 110-172, 12/29/2007, which struck out:

3. "(other than with respect to any sale for export under paragraph (3) thereof)"

4. added matter in para. (d)(5)

Effective Date (Sec. 6(e)(1), P.L. 110-172, 12/29/2007) effective for fuel entered, removed, or sold after 9/30/2005.

[¶ 3071]   Code Sec. 4042.   Tax on fuel used in commercial transportation on inland waterways.

* * * * * * * * * * * *

(b) Amount of tax.

(1) In general. The rate of the tax imposed by subsection (a) is the sum of—

(A) the Inland Waterways Trust Fund financing rate,

(B) the Leaking Underground Storage Tank Trust Fund financing rate, and

(C) the deficit reduction rate.

(2) Rates. For purposes of paragraph (1)—

(A) The Inland Waterways Trust Fund financing rate is the rate determined in accordance with the following table:

If the use occurs:	The tax per gallon is:
Before 1990	10 cents
During 1990	11 cents
During 1991	13 cents
During 1992	15 cents
During 1993	17 cents

During 1994	19 cents
After 1994	20 cents

(B) The Leaking Underground Storage Tank Trust Fund financing rate is 0.1 cent per gallon.

(C) The deficit reduction rate is—

(i) 3.3 cents per gallon after December 31, 2004, and before July 1, 2005,

(ii) 2.3 cents per gallon after June 30, 2005, and before January 1, 2007, and

(iii) 0 after December 31, 2006.

¹*(3) Exception for fuel on which leaking underground storage tank trust fund financing rate separately imposed. The Leaking Underground Storage Tank Trust Fund financing rate under paragraph (2)(B) shall not apply to the use of any fuel if tax was imposed with respect to such fuel under section 4041(d) or 4081 at the Leaking Underground Storage Tank Trust Fund financing rate.*

(4) **Termination of leaking underground storage tank trust fund financing rate.** The Leaking Underground Storage Tank Trust Fund financing rate under paragraph (2)(B) shall not apply during any period during which the Leaking Underground Storage Tank Trust Fund financing rate under section 4081 does not apply.

* * * * * * * * * * * *

[For Analysis, see ¶ 1004. For Committee Reports, see ¶ 5305.]

[Endnote Code Sec. 4042]

Code Sec. 4042(b)(3), in *italics*, was added by Sec. 6(d)(1)(B) of the Tax Technical Corrections Act of 2007, P.L. 110-172, 12/29/2007, which struck out:

1. "(3) Exception for fuel taxed under section 4041(d). The Leaking Underground Storage Tank Trust Fund financing rate under paragraph (2)(B) shall not apply to the use of any fuel if tax under section 4041(d) was imposed on the sale of such fuel or is imposed on such use."

Effective Date (Sec. 6(e)(1), P.L. 110-172, 12/29/2007) Effective for fuel entered, removed, or sold after 9/30/2005. Sec. 6(d)(1)(C) of this Act, provides:

"(C) Notwithstanding section 6430 of the Internal Revenue Code of 1986, a refund, credit, or payment may be made under subchapter B of chapter 65 of such Code for taxes imposed with respect to any liquid after September 30, 2005, and before the date of the enactment of this Act under section 4041(d)(1) or 4042 of such Code at the Leaking Underground Storage Tank Trust Fund financing rate to the extent that tax was imposed with respect to such liquid under section 4081 at the Leaking Underground Storage Tank Trust Fund financing rate."

[¶ 3072]   Code Sec. 4081.   Imposition of tax.

* * * * * * * * * * * *

(d) Termination.

(1) In general. The rates of tax specified in clauses (i) and (iii) of subsection (a)(2)(A) shall be 4.3 cents per gallon after September 30, 2011.

(2) Aviation fuels. The rates of tax specified in subsections (a)(2)(A)(ii) and (a)(2)(C)(ii) shall be 4.3 cents per gallon—

(A) after December 31, 1996, and before the date which is 7 days after the date of the enactment [2/28/97] of the Airport and Airway Trust Fund Tax Reinstatement Act of 1997, and

(B) after ¹*February 29, 2008.*

(3) Leaking Underground Storage Tank Trust Fund financing rate. The Leaking Underground Storage Tank Trust Fund financing rate under subsection (a)(2) shall apply after September 30, 1997, and before October 1, 2011.

* * * * * * * * * * * *

[For Analysis, see ¶ 1001.]

[Endnote Code Sec. 4081]

Matter in *italics* in Code Sec. 4081(d)(2)(B) was added by Sec. 116(a) of Division K of the Consolidated Appropriations Act of 2008, P.L. 110-161, 12/26/2007, which struck out:

1. "September 30, 2007"

Effective Date (Sec. 116(d), Div. K, P.L. 110-161, 12/26/2007) effective 10/1/2007.

[¶ 3073]   Code Sec. 4082.   Exemptions for diesel fuel and kerosene.

(a) **In general.** The tax imposed by section 4081[1] shall not apply to diesel fuel and kerosene—

(1) which the Secretary determines is destined for a nontaxable use,

(2) which is indelibly dyed by mechanical injection in accordance with regulations which the Secretary shall prescribe, and

(3) which meets such marking requirements (if any) as may be prescribed by the Secretary in regulations.

Such regulations shall allow an individual choice of dye color approved by the Secretary or chosen from any list of approved dye colors that the Secretary may publish.

[2]*(b) Nontaxable use. For purposes of this section, the term "nontaxable use" means—*

(1) any use which is exempt from the tax imposed by section 4041(a)(1) other than by reason of a prior imposition of tax,

(2) any use in a train, and

(3) any use described in section 4041(a)(1)(C)(iii)(II).

The term "nontaxable use" does not include the use of kerosene in an aircraft and such term shall not include any use described in section 6421(e)(2)(C).

* * * * * * * * * * * *

(e) **Kerosene removed into an aircraft.** In the case of kerosene which is exempt from the tax imposed by section 4041(c) (other than by reason of a prior imposition of tax) and which is removed from any refinery or terminal directly into the fuel tank of [3]*an aircraft—*

(1) the rate of tax under section 4081(a)(2)(A)(iii) shall be zero, and

(2) if such aircraft is employed in foreign trade or trade between the United States and any of its possessions, the increase in such rate under section 4081(a)(2)(B) shall be zero.

[4]For purposes of this subsection, any removal described in section 4081(a)(3)(A) shall be treated as a removal from a terminal but only if such terminal is located within a secure area of an airport.

[5]*(f) Exception for leaking Underground Storage Tank Trust Fund financing rate.*

(1) In general. Subsection (a) shall not apply to the tax imposed under section 4081 at the Leaking Underground Storage Tank Trust Fund financing rate.

(2) Exception for export, etc. Paragraph (1) shall not apply with respect to any fuel if the Secretary determines that such fuel is destined for export or for use by the purchaser as supplies for vessels (within the meaning of section 4221(d)(3)) employed in foreign trade or trade between the United States and any of its possessions.

[6]*(g) Regulations.* The Secretary shall prescribe such regulations as may be necessary to carry out this section, including regulations requiring the conspicuous labeling of retail diesel fuel and kerosene pumps and other delivery facilities to assure that persons are aware of which fuel is available only for nontaxable uses.

[7]*(h) Cross reference.* For tax on train and certain bus uses of fuel purchased tax-free, see subsections (a)(1) and (d)(3) of section 4041.

[For Analysis, see ¶ 1002. For Committee Reports, see ¶ 5305.]

[Endnote Code Sec. 4082]

Matter in Code Sec. 4082(a) was deleted by Sec. 6(d)(2)(B)(i) of the Tax Technical Corrections Act of 2007, P.L. 110-172, 12/29/2007, which struck out:

1. "(other than such tax at the Leaking Underground Storage Tank Trust Fund financing rage imposed in all cases other than for export)"

Effective Date (Sec. 6(e)(1), P.L. 110-172, 12/29/2007) effective for fuel entered, removed, or sold after 9/30/2005.

Matter in *italics* in Code Sec. 4082(b) was added by Sec. 11(a)(28), P.L. 110-172, 12/29/2007, which struck out:

2. "(b) Nontaxable use. For purposes of this section, the term 'nontaxable use' means—

"(1) any use which is exempt from the tax imposed by section 4041(a)(1) other than by reason of a prior imposition of tax,

"(2) any use in a train, and

"(3) any use described in section 4041(a)(1)(C)(iii)(II).

The term 'nontaxable use' does not include the use of kerosene in an aircraft and such term shall not include any use described in section 6421(e)(2)(C)."

Effective Date enacted 12/29/2007.

Matter in *italics* in Code Sec. 4082(e), Code Sec. 4082(f), Code Sec. 4082(g) and Code Sec. 4082(h) was added by Sec. 6(d)(2)(B)(ii) and (d)(2)(C)(i)-(ii), P.L. 110-172, 12/29/2007, which struck out:

3. "an aircraft, the rate of tax under section 4081(a)(2)(A)(iii) shall be zero."

4. sentence subsec. (e) made flush

5. added subsec. (f)

6. "(f)"

7. "(g)"

Effective Date (Sec. 6(e)(1) and (3), P.L. 110-172, 12/29/2007) effective for fuel entered, removed, or sold after 9/30/2005. Sec. 6(e)(1), P.L. 110-172, 12/29/2007, reads as follows:

"(3) Amendment made by the SAFETEA-LU. The amendment made by subsection (d)(2)(C)(ii) shall take effect as if included in section 11161 of the SAFETEA-LU."

[¶ 3074]   Code Sec. 4101.   Registration and bond.

(a) **Registration.**

(1) **In general.** Every person required by the Secretary to register under this section with respect to the tax imposed by section 4041(a) or 4081 and every person producing or importing biodiesel (as defined in section 40A(d)(1)) or alcohol (as defined in section 6426(b)(4)(A)) shall register with the Secretary at such time, in such form and manner, and subject to such terms and conditions, as the Secretary may by regulations prescribe. A registration under this section may be used only in accordance with regulations prescribed under this section.

* * * * * * * * * * *

[1]*(5) **Reregistration in event of change in ownership.** Under regulations prescribed by the Secretary, a person (other than a corporation the stock of which is regularly traded on an established securities market) shall be required to reregister under this section if after a transaction (or series of related transactions) more than 50 percent of ownership interests in, or assets of, such person are held by persons other than persons (or persons related thereto) who held more than 50 percent of such interests or assets before the transaction (or series of related transactions).*

* * * * * * * * * * *

[Endnote Code Sec. 4101]

Code Sec. 4101(a)(5) in *italics*, was added by Sec. 11(a)(29), of the Tax Technical Corrections Act of 2007, P.L. 110-172, 12/29/2007.

1. redesignated para. (a)(4) as para. (a)(5)

Effective Date enacted 12/29/2007.

[¶ 3075]   Code Sec. 4261.   Imposition of tax.

* * * * * * * * * * *

(j) **Application of taxes.**

(1) **In general.** The taxes imposed by this section shall apply to—

(A) transportation beginning during the period—

(i) beginning on the 7th day after the date of the enactment of the Airport and Airway Trust Fund Tax Reinstatement Act of 1997, and

(ii) ending on [1]*February 29, 2008*, and

(B) amounts paid during such period for transportation beginning after such period.

(2) Refunds. If, as of the date any transportation begins, the taxes imposed by this section would not have applied to such transportation if paid for on such date, any tax paid under paragraph (1)(B) with respect to such transportation shall be treated as overpayment.

[For Analysis, see ¶ 1001. For Committee Reports, see ¶ 5305.]

[Endnote Code Sec. 4261]
Matter in *italics* in Code Sec. 4261(j)(1)(A)(ii) was added by Sec. 116(b)(1) of Division K of the Consolidated Appropriations Act of 2008, P.L. 110-161, 12/26/2007, which struck out:
1. "September 30, 2007"
Effective Date (Sec. 116(d), Div. K, P.L. 110-161, 12/26/2007) effective 10/1/2007.

[¶ 3076]   Code Sec. 4271.   Imposition of tax.

* * * * * * * * * * * *

(d) Application of tax.

(1) In general. The tax imposed by subsection (a) shall apply to—

(A) transportation beginning during the period—

(i) beginning on the 7th day after the date of the enactment [2/28/97] of the Airport and Airway Trust Fund Tax Reinstatement Act of 1997, and

(ii) ending on [1]*February 29, 2008*, and

(B) amounts paid during such period for transportation beginning after such period.

(2) Refunds. If, as of the date any transportation begins, the taxes imposed by this section would not have applied to such transportation if paid for on such date, any tax paid under paragraph (1)(B) with respect to such transportation shall be treated as an overpayment.

[For Analysis, see ¶ 1001.]

[Endnote Code Sec. 4271]
Matter in *italics* in Code Sec. 4271(d)(1)(A)(ii) was added by Sec. 116(b)(2) of Division K of the Consolidated Appropriations Act of 2008, P.L. 110-161, 12/26/2007, which struck out:
1. "September 30, 2007"
Effective Date (Sec. 116(d), Div. K, P.L. 110-161, 12/26/2007) effective 10/1/2007.

[¶ 3077]   Code Sec. 4940.   Excise tax based on investment income.

* * * * * * * * * * * *

(c) Net investment income defined.

(1) In general. For purposes of subsection (a), the net investment income is the amount by which (A) the sum of the gross investment income and the capital gain net income exceeds (B) the deductions allowed by paragraph (3). Except to the extent inconsistent with the provisions of this section, net investment income shall be determined under the principles of subtitle A.

(2) Gross investment income. For purposes of paragraph (1), the term "gross investment income" means the gross amount of income from interest, dividends, rents, payments with respect to securities loans (as defined in section 512(a)(5)), and royalties, but not including any such income to the extent included in computing the tax imposed by section 511. Such term shall also include income from sources similar to those in the preceding sentence.

(3) Deductions.

(A) In general. For purposes of paragraph (1), there shall be allowed as a deduction all the ordinary and necessary expenses paid or incurred for the production or collection of gross investment income or for the management, conservation, or maintenance of property held for the production of such income, determined with the modifications set forth in subparagraph (B).

(B) Modifications. For purposes of subparagraph (A)—

(i) The deduction provided by section 167 shall be allowed, but only on the basis of the straight line method of depreciation.

(ii) The deduction for depletion provided by section 611 shall be allowed, but such deduction shall be determined without regard to section 613 (relating to percentage depletion).

(4) Capital gains and losses. For purposes of paragraph (1) in determining capital gain net income—

[1]*(A) There shall not be taken into account any gain or loss from the sale or other disposition of property to the extent that such gain or loss is taken into account for purposes of computing the tax imposed by section 511.*

(B) The basis for determining gain in the case of property held by the private foundation on December 31, 1969, and continuously thereafter to the date of its disposition shall be deemed to be not less than the fair market value of such property on December 31, 1969.

(C) Losses from sales or other dispositions of property shall be allowed only to the extent of gains from such sales or other dispositions, and there shall be no capital loss carryovers or carrybacks.

(D) Except to the extent provided by regulation, under rules similar to the rules of section 1031 (including the exception under subsection (a)(2) thereof), no gain or loss shall be taken into account with respect to any portion of property used for a period of not less than 1 year for a purpose or function constituting the basis of the private foundation's exemption if the entire property is exchanged immediately following such period solely for property of like kind which is to be used primarily for a purpose or function constituting the basis for such foundation's exemption.

(5) Tax-exempt income. For purposes of this section, net investment income shall be determined by applying section 103 (relating to State and local bonds) and section 265 (relating to expenses and interest relating to tax-exempt income).

* * * * * * * * * * * *

[For Analysis, see ¶504. For Committee Reports, see ¶5302.]

[Endnote Code Sec. 4940]

Matter in *italics* in Code Sec. 4940(c)(4)(A) was added by Sec. 3(f) of the Tax Technical Corrections Act of 2007, P.L. 110-172, 12/29/2007, which struck out:

1. "(A) There shall be taken into account only gains and losses from the sale or other disposition of property used for the production of gross investment income (as defined in paragraph (2)), and property used for the production of income included in computing the tax imposed by section 511 (except to the extent gain or loss from the sale or other disposition of such property is taken into account for purposes of such tax)."

Effective Date (Sec. 3(j), P.L. 110-172, 12/29/2007) effective for tax. yrs. begin. after 8/17/2006.

[¶3078]   Code Sec. 4942.   Taxes on failure to distribute income.

* * * * * * * * * * * *

(i) Adjustment of distributable amount where distributions during prior years have exceeded income.

(1) In general. If, for the taxable years in the adjustment period for which an organization is a private foundation—

(A) the aggregate qualifying distributions treated (under subsection (h)) as made out of the undistributed income for such taxable year or as made out of corpus (except to the extent subsection (g)(3) with respect to the recipient private foundation or [1]*section 170(b)(1)(F)(ii)* [sic . 170(b)(1)(D)(ii)] applies) during such taxable years, exceed

(B) the distributable amounts for such taxable years (determined without regard to this subsection),

then, for purposes of this section (other than subsection (h)), the distributable amount for the taxable year shall be reduced by an amount equal to such excess.

(2) Taxable years in adjustment period. For purposes of paragraph (1), with respect to any taxable year of a private foundation the taxable years in the adjustment period are the taxable years (not exceeding 5) beginning after December 31, 1969, and immediately preceding the taxable year.

* * * * * * * * * * * *

[Endnote Code Sec. 4942]

Matter in *italics* in Code Sec. 4942(i)(1)(A) was added by Sec. 11(a)(14)(D), of the Tax Technical Corrections Act of 2007, P.L. 110-172, 12/29/2007, which struck out:

1. "section 170(b)(1)(E)(ii)"

Effective Date enacted 12/29/2007.

[¶ 3079]   Code Sec. 4958.   Taxes on excess benefit transactions.

* * * * * * * * * * * *

(c) Excess benefit transaction; excess benefit. For purposes of this section —

(1) Excess benefit transaction.

(A) In general. The term "excess benefit transaction" means any transaction in which an economic benefit is provided by an applicable tax-exempt organization directly or indirectly to or for the use of any disqualified person if the value of the economic benefit provided exceeds the value of the consideration (including the performance of services) received for providing such benefit. For purposes of the preceding sentence, an economic benefit shall not be treated as consideration for the performance of services unless such organization clearly indicated its intent to so treat such benefit.

(B) Excess benefit. The term "excess benefit" means the excess referred to in subparagraph (A).

(2) Special rules for donor advised funds. In the case of any donor advised fund (as defined in section 4966(d)(2)) —

(A) the term "excess benefit transaction" includes any grant, loan, compensation, or other similar payment from such fund to a person described in subsection (f)(7) with respect to such fund, and

(B) the term "excess benefit" includes, with respect to any transaction described in subparagraph (A), the amount of any such grant, loan, compensation, or other similar payment.

(3) Special rules for supporting organizations.

(A) In general. In the case of any organization described in section 509(a)(3) —

(i) the term "excess benefit transaction" includes —

(I) any grant, loan, compensation, or other similar payment provided by such organization to a person described in subparagraph (B), and

(II) any loan provided by such organization to a disqualified person (other than an organization described in [1]*subparagraph (C)(ii)*, and

(ii) the term "excess benefit" includes, with respect to any transaction described in clause (i), the amount of any such grant, loan, compensation, or other similar payment.

(B) Person described. A person is described in this subparagraph if such person is —

(i) a substantial contributor to such organization,

(ii) a member of the family (determined under section 4958(f)(4)) of an individual described in clause (i), or

(iii) a 35-percent controlled entity (as defined in section 4958(f)(3) by substituting "persons described in clause (i) or (ii) of section 4958(c)(3)(B)" for "persons described in subparagraph (A) or (B) of paragraph (1)" in subparagraph (A)(i) thereof).

(C) Substantial contributor. For purposes of this paragraph—

(i) In general. The term "substantial contributor" means any person who contributed or bequeathed an aggregate amount of more than $5,000 to the organization, if such amount is more than 2 percent of the total contributions and bequests received by the organization before the close of the taxable year of the organization in which the contribution or bequest is received by the organization from such person. In the case of a trust, such term also means the creator of the trust. Rules similar to the rules of subparagraphs (B) and (C) of section 507(d)(2) shall apply for purposes of this subparagraph.

2(ii) Exception. Such term shall not include

(I) any organization described in paragraph (1), (2), or (4) of section 509(a), and

(II) any organization which is treated as described in such paragraph (2) by reason of the last sentence of section 509(a) and which is a supported organization (as defined in section 509(f)(3)) of the organization to which subparagraph (A) applies.

(4) Authority to include certain other private inurement. To the extent provided in regulations prescribed by the Secretary, the term "excess benefit transaction" includes any transaction in which the amount of any economic benefit provided to or for the use of a disqualified person is determined in whole or in part by the revenues of 1 or more activities of the organization but only if such transaction results in inurement not permitted under paragraph (3) or (4) of section 501(c), as the case may be. In the case of any such transaction, the excess benefit shall be the amount of the inurement not so permitted.

* * * * * * * * * * * *

[For Analysis, see ¶ 505. For Committee Reports, see ¶ 5302.]

[Endnote Code Sec. 4958]

Matter in *italics* in Code Sec. 4958(c)(3)(A)(i)(II) and Code Sec. 4958(c)(3)(C)(ii) was added by Sec. 3(i)(1) and (2), of the Tax Technical Corrections Act of 2007, P.L. 110-172, 12/29/2007, which struck out:

1. "paragraph (1), (2), or (4) of section 509(a)"

2. "(ii) Exception. Such term shall not include any organization described in paragraph (1), (2), or (4) of section 509(a)."

Effective Date (Sec. 3(j), P.L. 110-172, 12/29/2007) effective for transactions occurring after 7/25/2006.

[¶ 3080]   Code Sec. 4962.   Abatement of first tier taxes in certain cases.

* * * * * * * * * * * *

(b) Qualified first tier tax. For purposes of this section, the term "qualified first tier tax" means any first tier tax imposed by subchapter A, C, *1D, or G* of this chapter, except that such term shall not include the tax imposed by section 4941(a) (relating to initial tax on self-dealing).

* * * * * * * * * * * *

[For Analysis, see ¶ 503. For Committee Reports, see ¶ 5302.]

[Endnote Code Sec. 4962]

Matter in *italics* in Code Sec. 4962(b) added by Sec. 3(h) of the Tax Technical Corrections Act of 2007, P.L. 110-172, 12/29/2007, which struck out:

1. "or D"

Effective Date (Sec. 3(j), P.L. 110-172, 12/29/2007) effective for tax. yrs. begin. after 8/17/2006.

[¶ 3081]　　Code Sec. 4965.　　Excise tax on certain tax-exempt entities entering into prohibited tax shelter transactions.

* * * * * * * * * * *

(c)　Tax-exempt entity. For purposes of this section, the term "tax-exempt entity" means an entity which is—

(1) described in section 501(c) or 501(d),

(2) described in section 170(c) (other than the United States),

(3) an Indian tribal government (within the meaning of section 7701(a)(40)),

(4) described in paragraph (1), (2), or (3) of section 4979(e),

(5) a program described in section 529,

(6) an eligible deferred compensation plan described in section 457(b) which is maintained by an employer described in *¹section 457(e)(1)(A)*, or

(7) an arrangement described in section 4973(a).

* * * * * * * * * * *

[Endnote Code Sec. 4965]

　Matter in *italics* in Code Sec. 4965(c)(6) was added by Sec. 11(a)(30) of the Tax Technical Corrections Act of 2007, P.L. 110-172, 12/29/2007, which struck out:

　1. "section 4457(e)(1)(A)"

Effective Date enacted 12/29/2007.

[¶ 3082]　　Code Sec. 5732.　　Payment of tax.

(a)　Condition precedent to carrying on business. No person shall be engaged in or carry on any trade or business subject to tax under this subchapter until he has paid the special tax therefor.

(b)　Computation. All special taxes under this subchapter shall be imposed as of on the first day of July in each year, or on commencing any trade or business on which such tax is imposed. In the former case the tax shall be reckoned for 1 year, and in the latter case it shall be reckoned proportionately, from the first day of the month in which the liability to a special tax commenced, to and including the 30th day of June following.

(c)　How paid.

(1)　Payment by return. The special taxes imposed by this subchapter shall be paid on the basis of a return under such regulations as the Secretary shall prescribe.

(2)　Stamp denoting payment of tax. After receiving a properly executed return and remittance of any special tax imposed by *¹this subchapter*, the Secretary shall issue to the taxpayer an appropriate stamp as a receipt denoting payment of the tax. This paragraph shall not apply in the case of a return covering liability for a past period.

[Endnote Code Sec. 5732]

　Matter in *italics* in Code Sec. 5732(c)(2) was added by Sec. 11(a)(32) of the Tax Technical Corrections Act of 2007, P.L. 110-172, 12/29/2007, which struck out:

　1. "this subpart"

Effective Date enacted 12/29/2007.

[¶ 3083]　　Code Sec. 6011.　　General requirement of return, statement, or list.

* * * * * * * * * * *

(c)　Returns, etc., of DISCs and former DISCs¹ and former FSC's.

(1)　Records and information. A DISC², *former DISC, or former FSC (as defined in section 922 as in effect before its repeal by the FSC Repeal and Extraterritorial Income Exclusion Act of 200)* all for the taxable year—

(A) furnish such information to persons who were shareholders at any time during such taxable year, and to the Secretary, and

(B) keep such records, as may be required by regulations prescribed by the Secretary.

(2) Returns. A DISC shall file for the taxable year such returns as may be prescribed by the Secretary by forms or regulations.

* * * * * * * * * * * *

[Endnote Code Sec. 6011]

Matter in *italics* in Code Sec. 6011(c) and Code Sec. 6011(c)(1) was added by Sec. 11(g)(19)(A) and (B) of the Tax Technical Corrections Act of 2007, P.L. 110-172, 12/29/2007, which struck out:

   1. "and FSC'S"

   2. "or former DISC or a FSC or former FSC"

Effective Date Enacted 12/29/2007.

[¶ 3084]   Code Sec. 6046.   Returns as to organization or reorganization of foreign corporations and as to acquisitions of their stock.

* * * * * * * * * * * *

(b) Form and contents of returns. The returns required by subsection (a) shall be in such form and shall set forth, in respect of the foreign corporation, such information as the Secretary prescribes by forms or regulations as necessary for carrying out the provisions of the income tax laws, except that in the case of persons described only in [1]*subsection (a)(1)(A)* the information required shall be limited to the names and addresses of persons described in [2]*subparagraph (B) or (C) of subsection (a)(1).*

* * * * * * * * * * * *

[Endnote Code Sec. 6046]

Matter in *italics* in Code Sec. 6046(b) was added by Sec. 11(a)(33)(A)-(B) of the Tax Technical Corrections Act of 2007, P.L. 110-172, 12/29/2007, which struck out:

   1. "subsection (a)(1)"

   2. "paragraph (2) or (3) of subsection (a)"

Effective Date enacted 12/29/2007.

[¶ 3085]   Code Sec. 6072.   Time for filing income tax returns.

* * * * * * * * * * * *

(c) Returns by certain nonresident alien individuals and foreign corporations. Returns made by nonresident alien individuals (other than those whose wages are subject to withholding under chapter 24) and foreign corporations (other than those having an office or place of business in the United States or [1]*a former FSC (as defined in section 922 as in effect before its repeal by the FSC Repeal and Extraterritorial Income Exclusion Act of 2000))* under section 6012 on the basis of a calendar year shall be filed on or before the 15th day of June following the close of the calendar year and such returns made on the basis of a fiscal year shall be filed on or before the 15th day of the 6th month following the close of the fiscal year.

* * * * * * * * * * * *

[Endnote Code Sec. 6072]

Matter in *italics* in Code Sec. 6072(c) was added by section 11(g)(20) of the Tax Technical Corrections Act of 2007, P.L. 110-172, 12/29/2007, which struck out:

   1. "a FSC or former FSC"

Effective Date enacted 12/29/2007.

[¶ 3086]   Code Sec. 6103.   Confidentiality and disclosure of returns and return information.

* * * * * * * * * * * *

(b) Definitions. For purposes of this section—

* * * * * * * * * * * *

(5) State.

(A) In general. The term "State" means—

(i) any of the 50 States, the District of Columbia, the Commonwealth of Puerto Rico, the Virgin Islands,[1] Guam, American Samoa, and the Commonwealth of the Northern Mariana Islands,

* * * * * * * * * * * *

(e) Disclosure to persons having material interest.

(1) In general. The return of a person shall, upon written request, be open to inspection by or disclosure to—

(A) in the case of the return of an individual—

(i) that individual,

(ii) the spouse of that individual if the individual and such spouse have signified their consent to consider a gift reported on such return as made one-half by him and one-half by the spouse pursuant to the provisions of section 2513; or

(iii) the child of that individual (or such child's legal representative) to the extent necessary to comply with the provisions of section 1(g);

(B) in the case of an income tax return filed jointly, either of the individuals with respect to whom the return is filed;

(C) in the case of the return of a partnership, any person who was a member of such partnership during any part of the period covered by the return;

(D) in the case of the return of a corporation or a subsidiary thereof—

(i) any person designated by resolution of its board of directors or other similar governing body,

(ii) any officer or employee of such corporation upon written request signed by any principal officer and attested to by the secretary or other officer,

(iii) any bona fide shareholder of record owning 1 percent or more of the outstanding stock of such corporation,

(iv) if the corporation was an S corporation, any person who was a shareholder during any part of the period covered by such return during which an election under section 1362(a) was in effect, or

(v) if the corporation has been dissolved, any person authorized by applicable State law to act for the corporation or any person who the Secretary finds to have a material interest which will be affected by information contained therein;

(E) in the case of the return of an estate—

(i) the administrator, executor, or trustee of such estate, and

(ii) any heir at law, next of kin, or beneficiary under the will, of the decedent, but only if the Secretary finds that such heir at law, next of kin, or beneficiary has a material interest which will be affected by information contained therein; and

(F) in the case of the return of a trust—

(i) the trustee or trustees, jointly or separately, and

(ii) any beneficiary of such trust, but only if the Secretary finds that such beneficiary has a material interest which will be affected by information contained therein.

* * * * * * * * * * * *

[2](10)   *Limitation on certain disclosures under this subsection.* In the case of an inspection or disclosure under this subsection relating to the return of a partnership, S corporation, trust, or an estate, the information inspected or disclosed shall not include any supporting schedule, attachment, or list which includes the taxpayer identity information of a person other than the entity making the return or the person conducting the inspection or to whom the disclosure is made.

* * * * * * * * * * *

[For Analysis, see ¶ 1102. For Committee Reports, see ¶ 5402.]

[Endnote Code Sec. 6103]
   In Code Sec. 6103(b)(5)(A)(i), Sec. 11(a)(34)(A) of the Tax Technical Corrections Act of 2007, P.L. 110-172, 12/29/2007, struck out:
   1. "the Canal Zone,"
Effective Date enacted 12/29/2007.

   Code Sec. 6103(e)(10) in *italics* was added by Sec. 8(c)(1) of the Mortgage Forgiveness Debt Relief Act of 2007, P.L. 110-142, 12/20/2007.
   2. added new para. (e)(10)
Effective Date (Sec. 8(c)(2), P.L. 110-142, 12/20/2007) effective 12/20/2007.

[¶ 3087]   Code Sec. 6104.   Publicity of information required from certain exempt organizations and certain trusts.

* * * * * * * * * * *

   (b)   Inspection of annual[1] returns. The information required to be furnished by sections 6033, 6034, and 6058, together with the names and addresses of such organizations and trusts, shall be made available to the public at such times and in such places as the Secretary may prescribe. Nothing in this subsection shall authorize the Secretary to disclose the name or address of any contributor to any organization or trust (other than a private foundation, as defined in section 509(a)) or a political organization exempt from taxation under section 527 which is required to furnish such information. In the case of an organization described in section 501(d), this subsection shall not apply to copies referred to in section 6031(b) with respect to such organization. In the case of a trust which is required to file a return under section 6034(a), this subsection shall not apply to information regarding beneficiaries which are not organizations described in section 170(c). [2]*Any annual return which is filed under section 6011 by an organization described in section 501(c)(3) and which relates to any tax imposed by section 511 (relating to imposition of tax on unrelated business income of charitable, etc., organizations) shall be treated for purposes of this subsection in the same manner as if furnished under section 6033.*

* * * * * * * * * * *

   (d)   Public inspection of certain annual returns, reports, applications for exemption, and notices of status.
   (1)   In general. In the case of an organization described in subsection (c) or (d) of section 501 and exempt from taxation under section 501(a) or an organization exempt from taxation under section 527(a)—
      (A) a copy of—
         (i) the annual return filed under section 6033 (relating to returns by exempt organizations) by such organization,
         [3]*(ii) any annual return which is filed under section 6011 by an organization described in section 501(c)(3) and which relates to any tax imposed by section 511 (relating to imposition of tax on unrelated business income of charitable, etc., organizations),*
         (iii) if the organization filed an application for recognition of exemption under section 501 or notice of status under section 527(i), the exempt status application materials or any notice materials of such organization, and

(iv) the reports filed under section 527(j) (relating to required disclosure of expenditures and contributions) by such organization,

shall be made available by such organization for inspection during regular business hours by any individual at the principal office of such organization and, if such organization regularly maintains 1 or more regional or district offices having 3 or more employees, at each such regional or district office, and

(B) upon request of an individual made at such principal office or such a regional or district office, a copy of such annual return, reports, and exempt status application materials or such notice materials shall be provided to such individual without charge other than a reasonable fee for any reproduction and mailing costs.

The request described in subparagraph (B) must be made in person or in writing. If such request is made in person, such copy shall be provided immediately and, if made in writing, shall be provided within 30 days.

(2) 3-year limitation on inspection of returns. Paragraph (1) shall apply to an annual return filed under [4]*section 6011 or 6033* only during the 3-year period beginning on the last day prescribed for filing such return (determined with regard to any extension of time for filing).

(3) Exceptions from disclosure requirement.

(A) Nondisclosure of contributors, etc. In the case of an organization which is not a private foundation (within the meaning of section 509(a)) or a political organization exempt from taxation under section 527, paragraph (1) shall not require the disclosure of the name or address of any contributor to the organization. In the case of an organization described in section 501(d), paragraph (1)shall not require the disclosure of the copies referred to in section 6031(b) with respect to such organization.

(B) Nondisclosure of certain other information. Paragraph (1) shall not require the disclosure of any information if the Secretary withheld such information from public inspection under subsection (a)(1)(D).

(4) Limitation on providing copies. Paragraph (1)(B) shall not apply to any request if, in accordance with regulations promulgated by the Secretary, the organization has made the requested documents widely available, or the Secretary determines, upon application by an organization, that such request is part of a harassment campaign and that compliance with such request is not in the public interest.

(5) Exempt status application materials. For purposes of paragraph (1), the term "exempt status applicable materials" means the application for recognition of exemption under section 501 and any papers submitted in support of such application and any letter or other document issued by the Internal Revenue Service with respect to such application.

(6) Notice materials. For purposes of paragraph (1), the term "notice materials" means the notice of status filed under section 527(i) and any papers submitted in support of such notice and any letter or other document issued by the Internal Revenue Service with respect to such notice.

(6 [sic (7)]) Disclosure of reports by Internal Revenue Service. Any report filed by an organization under section 527(j) (relating to required disclosure of expenditures and contributions) shall be made available to the public at such times and in such places as the Secretary may prescribe.

(6 [sic (8)]) Application to nonexempt charitable trusts and nonexempt private foundations. The organizations referred to in paragraphs (1) and (2) of section 6033(d) shall comply with the requirements of this subsection relating to annual returns filed under section 6033 in the same manner as the organizations referred to in paragraph (1).

[For Analysis, see ¶ 501 and ¶ 502. For Committee Reports, see ¶ 5302.]

[Endnote Code Sec. 6104]

Matter in *italics* in Code Sec. 6104(b), Code Sec. 6104(d)(1)(A)(ii) and Code Sec. 6104(d)(2) was added by Sec. 3(g)(1)-(3) of the Tax Technical Corrections Act of 2007, P.L. 110-172, 12/29/2007, which struck out:

1. "information"

2. added matter in subsec. (b)

3. "(ii) any annual return filed under section 6011 which relates to any tax imposed by section 511 (relating to impo-sition of tax on unrelated business income of charitable, etc., organizations) by such organization, but only if such or-ganization is described in section 501(c)(3),"

4. "section 6033"

Effective Date (Sec. 3(j), P.L. 110-172, 12/29/2007) effective for returns filed after 8/17/2006.

[¶ 3088]   Code Sec. 6110.   Public inspection of written determinations.

* * * * * * * * * * * *

(i) Special rules for disclosure of Chief Counsel advice.

(1) Chief Counsel Advice defined.

(A) In general. For purposes of this section, the term "Chief Counsel advice" means written advice or instruction, under whatever name or designation, prepared by any na-tional office component of the Office of Chief Counsel which—

(i) is issued to field or service center employees of the Service or regional or dis-trict employees of the Office of Chief Counsel; and

(ii) conveys—

(I) any legal interpretation of a revenue provision;

(II) any Internal Revenue Service or Office of Chief Counsel position or policy concerning a revenue provision; or

(III) any legal interpretation of State law, foreign law, or other Federal law relat-ing to the assessment or collection of any liability under a revenue provision.

(B) Revenue provision defined. For purposes of subparagraph (A), the term "revenue provision" means any existing or former internal revenue law, regulation, revenue rul-ing, revenue procedure, other published or unpublished guidance, or tax treaty, either in general or as applied to specific taxpayers or groups of specific taxpayers.

(2) Additional documents treated as Chief Counsel advice. The Secretary may by regulation provide that this section shall apply to any advice or instruction prepared and is-sued by the Office of Chief Counsel which is not described in paragraph (1).

(3) Deletions for Chief Counsel advice. In the case of Chief Counsel advice ¹*and re-lated background file documents* open to public inspection pursuant to this section—

(A) paragraphs (2) through (7) of subsection (c) shall not apply, but

(B) the Secretary may make deletions of material in accordance with subsections (b) and (c) of section 552 of title 5, United States Code, except that in applying subsection (b)(3) of such section, no statutory provision of this title shall be taken into account.

(4) Notice of intention to disclose.

(A) No taxpayer specific Chief Counsel advice. In the case of Chief Counsel advice which is written without reference to a specific taxpayer or group of specific taxpay-ers—

(i) subsection (f)(1) shall not apply; and

(ii) the Secretary shall, within 60 days after the issuance of the Chief Counsel ad-vice, complete any deletions described in subsection (c)(1) or paragraph (3) and make the Chief Counsel advice, as so edited, open for public inspection.

(B) Taxpayer-specific Chief Counsel advice. In the case of Chief Counsel advice which is written with respect to a specific taxpayer or group of specific taxpayers, the Secretary shall, within 60 days after the issuance of the Chief Counsel advice, mail the notice required by subsection (f)(1) to each such taxpayer. The notice shall include a copy of the Chief Counsel advice on which is indicated the information that the Secre-tary proposes to delete pursuant to subsection (c)(1). The Secretary may also delete from the copy of the text of the Chief Counsel advice any of the information described in par-agraph (3), and shall delete the names, addresses, and other identifying details of taxpay-ers other than the person to whom the advice pertains, except that the Secretary shall not delete from the copy of the Chief Counsel advice that is furnished to the taxpayer any information of which that taxpayer was the source.

387

* * * * * * * * * * * *

[For Analysis, see ¶ 1304. For Committee Reports, see ¶ 5309.]

[Endnote Code Sec. 6110]

Matter in *italics* in Code Sec. 6110(i)(3) was added by Sec. 10(a) of the Tax Technical Corrections Act of 2007, P.L. 110-172, 12/29/2007.

1. "and related background file documents"

Effective Date (Sec. 10(b), P.L. 110-172, 12/29/2007) effective for any Chief Counsel advice issued more than 90 days after 7/22/98. For special rules, see Sec. 3509(d)(2)-(4) of the Internal Revenue Service Restructuring and Reform Act of 1998, which reads as follows:

"(2) Transition rules. The amendments made by this section shall apply to any Chief Counsel advice issued after December 31, 1985, and before the 91st day after the date of the enactment of this Act by the offices of the associate chief counsel for domestic, employee benefits and exempt organizations, and international, except that any such Chief Counsel advice shall be treated as made available on a timely basis if such advice is made available for public inspection not later than the following dates:

"(A) One year after the date of the enactment of this Act, in the case of all litigation guideline memoranda, service center advice, tax litigation bulletins, criminal tax bulletins, and general litigation bulletins.

"(B) Eighteen months after such date of enactment, in the case of field service advice and technical assistance to the field issued on or after January 1, 1994.

"(C) Three years after such date of enactment, in the case of field service advice and technical assistance to the field issued on or after January 1, 1992, and before January 1, 1994.

"(D) Six years after such date of enactment, in the case of any other Chief Counsel advice issued after December 31, 1985.

"(3) Documents treated as Chief Counsel advice. If the Secretary of the Treasury by regulation provides pursuant to section 6110(i)(2) of the Internal Revenue Code of 1986, as added by this section, that any additional advice or instruction issued by the Office of Chief Counsel shall be treated as Chief Counsel advice, such additional advice or instruction shall be made available for public inspection pursuant to section 6110 of such Code, as amended by this section, only in accordance with the effective date set forth in such regulation.

"(4) Chief Counsel advice to be available electronically. The Internal Revenue Service shall make any Chief Counsel advice issued more than 90 days after the date of the enactment of this Act and made available for public inspection pursuant to section 6110 of such Code, as amended by this section, also available by computer telecommunications within 1 year after issuance."

[¶ 3089]   Code Sec. 6211.   Definition of a deficiency.

* * * * * * * * * * * *

(b)   Rules for application of subsection (a). For purposes of this section—

(1) The tax imposed by Subtitle A and the tax shown on the return shall both be determined without regard to payments on account of estimated tax, without regard to the credit under section 31, without regard to the credit under section 33, and without regard to any credits resulting from the collection of amounts assessed under section 6851 or 6852 (relating to termination assessments).

(2) The term "rebate" means so much of an abatement, credit, refund, or other repayment, as was made on the ground that the tax imposed by subtitle A or B or chapter 41, 42, 43, or 44 was less than the excess of the amount specified in subsection (a)(1) over the rebates previously made.

(3) The computation by the Secretary, pursuant to section 6014, of the tax imposed by chapter 1 shall be considered as having been made by the taxpayer and the tax so computed considered as shown by the taxpayer upon his return.

(4) For purposes of subsection (a)—

(A) any excess of the sum of the credits allowable under sections 24(d), 32, [1]*34, and* 35, and [2]*53(e), and 6428*over the tax imposed by subtitle A (determined without regard to such credits), and

(B) any excess of the sum of such credits as shown by the taxpayer on his return over the amount shown as the tax by the taxpayer on such return (determined without regard to such credits),

shall be taken into account as negative amounts of tax.

* * * * * * * * * * * *

[For Analysis, see ¶ 51. For Committee Reports, see ¶ 5501.]

[Endnote Code Sec. 6211]
Matter in *italics* in Code Sec. 6211(b)(4)(A) was added by Sec. 11(a)(35) of the Tax Technical Corrections Act of 2007, P.L. 110-172, 12/29/2007, which struck out:
1. "and 34 [sic 34]"
Effective Date enacted 12/29/2007.

———————

Matter in *italics* in Code Sec. 6211(d)(4)(A) [sic (b)(4)(A)] was added by Sec. 101(b)(1) of the Economic Stimulus Act of 2008, P.L. 110-185, 2/13/2008, which struck out:
2. "and 53(e)"
Effective Date Enacted 2/13/2008.

[¶ 3090]   Code Sec. 6213.   Restrictions applicable to deficiencies; petition to Tax Court.

* * * * * * * * * * * *

(g) Definitions. For purposes of this section—

(1) Return. The term "return" includes any return, statement, schedule, or list, and any amendment or supplement thereto, filed with respect to any tax imposed by subtitle A or B, or chapter 41, 42, 43, or 44.

(2) Mathematical or clerical error. The term "mathematical or clerical error" means—

(A) an error in addition, subtraction, multiplication, or division shown on any return,

(B) an incorrect use of any table provided by the Internal Revenue Service with respect to any return if such incorrect use is apparent from the existence of other information on the return,

(C) an entry on a return of an item which is inconsistent with another entry of the same or another item on such return,

(D) an omission of information which is required to be supplied on the return to substantiate an entry on the return,

(E) an entry on a return of a deduction or credit in an amount which exceeds a statutory limit imposed by subtitle A or B, or chapter 41, 42 43, or 44, if such limit is expressed—

(i) as a specified monetary amount, or

(ii) as a percentage, ratio, or fraction,

and if the items entering into the application of such limit appear on such return,

(F) an omission of a correct taxpayer identification number required under section 32 (relating to the earned income credit) to be included on a return,

(G) an entry on a return claiming the credit under section 32 with respect to net earnings from self-employment described in section 32(c)(2)(A) to the extent the tax imposed by section 1401 (relating to self-employment tax) on such net earnings has not been paid,

(H) an omission of a correct TIN required under section 21 (relating to expenses for household and dependent care services necessary for gainful employment) or section 151 (relating to allowance of deductions for personal exemptions),

(I) an omission of a correct TIN required under section 24(e) (relating to child tax credit) to be included on a return,

(J) an omission of a correct TIN required under section 25A(g)(1) (relating to higher education tuition and related expenses) to be included on a return,

(K) an omission of information required by section 32(k)(2) (relating to taxpayers making improper prior claims of earned income credit),

(L) the inclusion on a return of a TIN required to be included on the return under section 21, 24, *¹32, or 6428* if—

(i) such TIN is of an individual whose age affects the amount of the credit under such section, and

(ii) the computation of the credit on the return reflects the treatment of such individual as being of an age different from the individual's age based on such TIN, and

(M) the entry on the return claiming the credit under section 32 with respect to a child if, according to the Federal Case Registry of Child Support Orders established under section 453(h) of the Social Security Act, the taxpayer is a noncustodial parent of such child.

A taxpayer shall be treated as having omitted a correct TIN for purposes of the preceding sentence if information provided by the taxpayer on the return with respect to the individual whose TIN was provided differs from the information the Secretary obtains from the person issuing the TIN.

[For Analysis, see ¶ 51. For Committee Reports, see ¶ 5501.]

[Endnote Code Sec. 6213]

Matter in *italics* in Code Sec. 6213(g)(2)(L) was added by Sec. 101(b)(2) of the Economic Stimulus Act of 2008, P.L. 110-185, 2/13/2008, which struck out:

1. "or 32"

Effective Date Enacted 2/13/2008.

[¶ 3091]   Code Sec. 6230.   Additional administrative provisions.

(a)   Coordination with deficiency proceedings.

(1)   In general. Except as provided in paragraph (2) or (3), subchapter B of this chapter shall not apply to the assessment or collection of any computational adjustment.

(2)   Deficiency proceedings to apply in certain cases.

(A) Subchapter B shall apply to any deficiency attributable to—

(i) affected items which require partner level determinations (other than penalties, additions to tax, and additional amounts that relate to adjustments to partnership items), or

(ii) items which have become nonpartnership items (other than by reason of section 6231(b)(1)(C)) and are described in section 6231(e)(1)(B).

(B) Subchapter B shall be applied separately with respect to each deficiency described in subparagraph (A) attributable to each partnership.

(C) Notwithstanding any other law or rule of law, any notice or proceeding under subchapter B with respect to a deficiency described in this paragraph shall not preclude or be precluded by any other notice, proceeding, or determination with respect to a partner's tax liability for a taxable year.

(3)   Special rule in case of assertion by partner's spouse of innocent spouse relief.

(A) Notwithstanding section 6404(b), if the spouse of a partner asserts that ¹*section 6015* applies with respect to a liability that is attributable to any adjustment to a partnership item (including any liability for any penalties, additions to tax, or additional amounts relating to such adjustment), then such spouse may file with the Secretary within 60 days after the notice of computational adjustment is mailed to the spouse a request for abatement of the assessment specified in such notice. Upon receipt of such request, the Secretary shall abate the assessment. Any reassessment of the tax with respect to which an abatement is made under this subparagraph shall be subject to the deficiency procedures prescribed by subchapter B. The period for making any such reassessment shall not expire before the expiration of 60 days after the date of such abatement.

(B) If the spouse files a petition with the Tax Court pursuant to section 6213 with respect to the request for abatement described in subparagraph (A), the Tax Court shall only have jurisdiction pursuant to this section to determine whether the requirements of ²*section 6015* have been satisfied. For purposes of such determination, the treatment of partnership items (and the applicability of any penalties, additions to tax, or additional amounts) under the settlement, the final partnership administrative adjustment, or the decision of the court (whichever is appropriate) that gave rise to the liability in question shall be conclusive.

(C) Rules similar to the rules contained in subparagraphs (B) and (C) of paragraph (2) shall apply for purposes of this paragraph.

* * * * * * * * * * * *

[Endnote Code Sec. 6230]

Matter in *italics* in Code Sec. 6230(a)(3)(A) and Code Sec. 6230(a)(3)(B) was added by Sec. 11(a)(36) of the Tax Technical Corrections Act of 2007, P.L. 110-172, 12/29/2007, which struck out:

1. "section 6013(e)"
2. "section 6013(e)"

Effective Date (P.L. 110-172, 12/29/2007) enacted 12/29/2007.

[¶ 3092]   Code Sec. 6416.   Certain taxes on sales and services.

(a) Condition to allowance.

(1) General rule. No credit or refund of any overpayment of tax imposed by chapter 31 (relating to retail excise taxes), or chapter 32 (manufacturers taxes) shall be allowed or made unless the person who paid the tax establishes, under regulations prescribed by the Secretary, that he—

(A) has not included the tax in the price of the article with respect to which it was imposed and has not collected the amount of the tax from the person who purchased such article;

(B) has repaid the amount of the tax to the ultimate purchaser of the article;

(C) in the case of an overpayment under subsection (b)(2) of this section—

(i) has repaid or agreed to repay the amount of the tax to the ultimate vendor of the article, or

(ii) has obtained the written consent of such ultimate vendor to the allowance of the credit or the making of the refund; or

(D) has filed with the Secretary the written consent of the person referred to in subparagraph (B) to the allowance of the credit or the making of the refund.

(2) Exceptions. This subsection shall not apply to—

(A) the tax imposed by section 4041 (relating to tax on special fuels) on the use of any liquid, and

(B) an overpayment of tax under paragraph (1), (3)(A), (4), (5), or (6) of subsection (b) of this section.

(3) Special rule. For purposes of this subsection, in any case in which the Secretary determines that an article is not taxable, the term "ultimate purchaser" (when used in paragraph (1)(B) of this subsection) includes a wholesaler, jobber, distributor, or retailer who, on the 15th day after the date of such determination, holds such article for sale; but only if claim for credit or refund by reason of this paragraph is filed on or before the date for filing the return with respect to the taxes imposed under chapter 32 for the first period which begins more than 60 days after the date on such determination.

(4) Registered ultimate vendor or credit card issuer to administer credits and refunds of gasoline tax.

(A) In general. For purposes of this subsection, except as provided in subparagraph (B), if an ultimate vendor purchases any gasoline on which tax imposed by section 4081 has been paid and sells such gasoline to an ultimate purchaser described in subparagraph (C) or (D) of subsection (b)(2) (and such gasoline is for a use described in such subparagraph), such ultimate vendor shall be treated as the person (and the only person) who paid such tax, but only if such ultimate vendor is registered under section 4101.

(B) Credit card issuer. For purposes of this subsection, if the purchase of gasoline described in subparagraph (A) (determined without regard to the registration status of the ultimate vendor) is made by means of a credit card issued to the ultimate purchaser, paragraph (1) shall not apply and the person extending the credit to the ultimate purchaser shall be treated as the person (and the only person) who paid the tax, but only if such person—

(i) is registered under section 4101, and

(ii) has established, under regulations prescribed by the Secretary, that such person—

(I) has not collected the amount of the tax from the person who purchased such article, or

(II) has obtained the written consent from the ultimate purchaser to the allowance of the credit or refund, and

(iii) has so established that such person—

(I) has repaid or agreed to repay the amount of the tax to the ultimate vendor,

(II) has obtained the written consent of the ultimate vendor to the allowance of the credit or refund, or

(III) has otherwise made arrangements which directly or indirectly provides the ultimate vendor with reimbursement of such tax.

If clause (i), (ii), or (iii) is not met by such person extending the credit to the ultimate purchaser, then such person shall collect an amount equal to the tax from the ultimate purchaser and only such ultimate purchaser may claim such credit or payment.

(C) Timing of claims. The procedure and timing of any claim under subparagraph (A) or (B) shall be the same as for claims under section 6427(i)(4), except that the rules of section 6427(i)(3)(B) regarding electronic claims shall not apply unless the [1]*ultimate vendor or credit card issuer has certified* to the Secretary for the most recent quarter of the taxable year that [2]*all ultimate purchasers of the vendor or credit card issuer are certified* and entitled to a refund under subparagraph (C) or (D) of subsection (b)(2).

* * * * * * * * * * *

[For Analysis, see ¶ 1006.]

[Endnote Code Sec. 6416]

Matter in *italics* in Code Sec. 6416(a)(4)(C) was added by Sec. 11(d)(1)(A)-(B) of the Tax Technical Corrections Act of 2007, P.L. 110-172, 12/29/2007, which struck out:

1. "ultimate vendor" and all that follows through "has certified"

2. "all ultimate purchasers of the vendor" and all that follows through "are certified"

Effective Date (Sec. 11(d)(2), P.L. 110-172, 12/29/2007) effective for sales after 12/31/2005.

[¶ 3093]   Code Sec. 6426.   Credit for alcohol fuel, biodiesel and alternative fuel mixtures.

* * * * * * * * * * *

(d) Alternative fuel credit.

(1) In general. For purposes of this section, the alternative fuel credit is the product of 50 cents and the number of gallons of an alternative fuel or gasoline gallon equivalents of a nonliquid alternative fuel sold by the taxpayer for use as a fuel in a motor vehicle or motorboat, or so used by the taxpayer.

(2) Alternative fuel. For purposes of this section, the term "alternative fuel" means—

(A) liquefied petroleum gas,

(B) P Series Fuels (as defined by the Secretary of Energy under section 13211(2) of title 42, United States Code),

(C) compressed or liquefied natural gas,

(D) liquefied hydrogen,

(E) any liquid fuel derived from coal (including peat) through the Fischer-Tropsch process, and

(F) liquid [1]*fuel* derived from biomass (as defined in section 45K(c)(3)).

Such term does not include ethanol, methanol, or biodiesel.

(3) Gasoline gallon equivalent. For purposes of this subsection, the term "gasoline gallon equivalent" means, with respect to any nonliquid alternative fuel, the amount of such fuel having a Btu content of 124,800 (higher heating value).

(4) Termination. This subsection shall not apply to any sale or use for any period after September 30, 2009 (September 30, 2014, in the case of any sale or use involving liquefied hydrogen).

* * * * * * * * * * *

[2]*(h) Denial of double benefit. No credit shall be determined under subsection (d) or (e) with respect to any fuel with respect to which credit may be determined under subsection (b) or (c) or under section 40 or 40A.*

[For Analysis, see ¶ 1005. For Committee Reports, see ¶ 5304.]

[Endnote Code Sec. 6426]

Matter in *italics* in Code Sec. 6426(d)(2)(F) and Code Sec. 6426(h) was added by Sec. 5(a)(2)-(3) of the Tax Technical Corrections Act of 2007, P.L. 110-172, 12/29/2007, which struck out:

1. "hydrocarbons"
2. added subsec. (h)

Effective Date (Sec. 5(b), P.L. 110-172, 12/29/2007) effective for any sale or use for any period after 9/30/2006.

[¶ 3094]   Code Sec. 6427.   Fuels not used for taxable purposes.

* * * * * * * * * * *

(i) Time for filing claims; period covered.

(1) General rule. Except as otherwise provided in this subsection, not more than one claim may be filed under subsection (a), (b), (c), (d), (h), (l), (m), or (o) by any person with respect to fuel used (or a qualified diesel powered highway vehicle purchased) during his taxable year; and no claim shall be allowed under this paragraph with respect to fuel used during any taxable year unless filed by the purchaser not later than the time prescribed by law for filing a claim for credit or refund of overpayment of income tax for such taxable year. For purposes of this paragraph, a person's taxable year shall be his taxable year for purposes of subtitle A.

(2) Exceptions.

(A) In general. If, at the close of any quarter of the taxable year of any person, at least $750 is payable in the aggregate under subsections (a), (b), (d), (h), (l), (m), and (o) of this section and section 6421 to such person with respect to fuel used during—

(i) such quarter, or

(ii) any prior quarter (for which no other claim has been filed) during such taxable year,

a claim may be filed under this section with respect to such fuel.

(B) Time for filing claim. No claim filed under this paragraphshall be allowed unless filed during the 1st quarter following the last quarter included in the claim.

(C) Nonapplication of paragraph. This paragraph shall not apply to any fuel used solely in any off-highway business use described in section 6421(e)(2)(C).

(3) Special rule for [1]*mixture credits and the alternative fuel credit.*

(A) In general. A claim may be filed under subsection (e)(1) by any person with respect to a mixture described in section 6426 [2]*or under subsection (e)(2) by any person with respect to an alternative fuel (as defined in section 6426(d)(2))* for any period—

(i) for which $200 or more is payable under such subsection (e)(1) [3]*or (e)(2)*, and

(ii) which is not less than 1 week.

In the case of an electronic claim, this subparagraph shall be applied without regard to clause (i).

(B) Payment of claim. Notwithstanding subsection (e)(1) [4]*or (e)(2)*, if the Secretary has not paid pursuant to a claim filed under this section within 45 days of the date of the filing of such claim (20 days in the case of an electronic claim), the claim shall be paid with interest from such date determined by using the overpayment rate and method under section 6621.

(C) Time for filing claim. No claim filed under this paragraph shall be allowed unless filed on or before the last day of the first quarter the earliest quarter included in the claim.

(4) Special rule for vendor refunds.

(A) In general. A claim may be filed under subsections (b)(4) and paragraph (4)(C), or (5), of subsection (l) by any person with respect to fuel sold by such person for any period—

(i) for which $200 or more ($100 or more in the case of kerosene) is payable under paragraph (4)(C), or (5), of subsection (l), and

(ii) which is not less than 1 week.

Notwithstanding subsection (l)(1), paragraph (3)(B) shall apply to claims filed under subsections (b)(4), (l)(4)(C)(ii), and (l)(5).

(B) Time for filing claim. No claim filed under this paragraph shall be allowed unless filed on or before the last day of the first quarter following the earliest quarter included in the claim.

* * * * * * * * * * * *

(l) Nontaxable uses of diesel fuel, and kerosene.

(1) In general. Except as otherwise provided in this subsection and in subsection (k), if any diesel fuel or kerosene on which tax has been imposed by section 4041 or 4081 is used by any person in a nontaxable use, the Secretary shall pay (without interest) to the ultimate purchaser of such fuel an amount equal to the aggregate amount of tax imposed on such fuel under section 4041 or 4081, as the case may be, reduced by any payment made to the ultimate vendor under paragraph (4)(C)(i).

* * * * * * * * * * * *

(4) Refunds for kerosene used in aviation.

(A) Kerosene used in commercial aviation. In the case of kerosene used in commercial aviation (as defined in section 4083(b)) (other than supplies for vessels or aircraft within the meaning of section 4221(d)(3)), paragraph (1) shall not apply to so much of the tax imposed by section 4041 or 4081, as the case may be, as is attributable to—

(i) the Leaking Underground Storage Tank Trust Fund financing rate imposed by such section, and

(ii) so much of the rate of tax specified in section 4041(c) or [5]*section 4081(a)(2)(A)(iii)*, as the case may be, as does not exceed 4.3 cents per gallon.

(B) Kerosene used in noncommercial aviation. In the case of kerosene used in aviation that is not commercial aviation (as so defined) (other than any use which is exempt from the tax imposed by section 4041(c) other than by reason of a prior imposition of tax), paragraph (1) shall not apply to—

(i) any tax imposed by subsection (c) or (d)(2) of section 4041, and

(ii) so much of the tax imposed by section 4081 as is attributable to—

(I) the Leaking Underground Storage Tank Trust Fund financing rate imposed by such section, and

(II) so much of the rate of tax specified in section 4081(a)(2)(A)(iii) as does not exceed the rate specified in section 4081(a)(2)(C)(ii).

(C) Payments to ultimate, registered vendor.

(i) In general. With respect to any kerosene used in aviation (other than kerosene described in clause (ii) or kerosene to which paragraph (5) applies), if the ultimate purchaser of such kerosene waives (at such time and in such form and manner as the Secretary shall prescribe) the right to payment under paragraph (1) and assigns such right to the ultimate vendor, then the Secretary shall pay the amount which would be paid under paragraph (1) to such ultimate vendor, but only if such ultimate vendor—

(I) is registered under section 4101, and

(II) meets the requirements of subparagraph (A), (B), or (D) of section 6416(a)(1).

(ii) Payments for kerosene used in noncommercial aviation. The amount which would be paid under paragraph (1) with respect to any kerosene to which subparagraph (B) applies shall be paid only to the ultimate vendor of such kerosene. A payment shall be made to such vendor if such vendor—

(I) is registered under section 4101, and

(II) meets the requirements of subparagraph (A), (B), or (D) of section 6416(a)(1).

* * * * * * * * * * * *

⁶*(p)* **Cross references.**

(1) For civil penalty for excessive claims under this section, see section 6675.

(2) For fraud penalties, etc., see chapter 75 (section 7201 and following, relating to crimes, other offenses, and forfeitures).

(3) For treatment of an Indian tribal government as a State (and a subdivision of an Indian tribal government as a political subdivision of a State), see section 7871.

[For Analysis, see ¶ 1007 and ¶ 1008. For Committee Reports, see ¶ 5304.]

[Endnote Code Sec. 6427]

Matter in *italics* in Code Sec. 6427(i)(3) heading, Code Sec. 6427(i)(3)(A), Code Sec. 6427(i)(3)(A)(i) and Code Sec. 6427(i)(3)(B) was added by Sec. 5(a)(1)(A), (B) and (C) of the Tax Technical Corrections Act of 2007, P.L. 110-172, 12/29/2007, which struck out:

1. "alcohol fuel and biodiesel mixture credit"
2. added matter in subpara. (i)(3)(A)
3. added matter in clause (i)(3)(A)(i)
4. added matter in subpara. (i)(3)(B)

Effective Date (Sec. 5(b), P.L. 110-172, 12/29/2007) effective for any sale or use for any period after 9/30/2006.

Matter in *italics* in Code Sec. 6427(l)(4)(A)(ii) and Code Sec. 6427(p) was added by Sec. 11(a)(38) and (a)(39)(A)-(B), P.L. 110-172, 12/29/2007, which struck out:

5. "section 4081(a)(2)(iii)"
6. "(q)"

[¶ 3095]   *Code Sec.*¹ *6428.*   **2008 Recovery rebates for individuals**

(a) **In general.** *In the case of an eligible individual, there shall be allowed as a credit against the tax imposed by subtitle A for the first taxable year beginning in 2008 an amount equal to the lesser of—*

(1) net income tax liability, or

(2) $600 ($1,200 in the case of a joint return).

(b) **Special rules.**

(1) **In general.** *In the case of a taxpayer described in paragraph (2)—*

(A) the amount determined under subsection (a) shall not be less than $300 ($600 in the case of a joint return), and

(B) the amount determined under subsection (a) (after the application of subparagraph (A)) shall be increased by the product of $300 multiplied by the number of qualifying children (within the meaning of section 24(c)) of the taxpayer.

(2) **Taxpayer described.** *A taxpayer is described in this paragraph if the taxpayer—*

(A) has qualifying income of at least $3,000, or

(B) has—

(i) net income tax liability which is greater than zero, and

(ii) gross income which is greater than the sum of the basic standard deduction plus the exemption amount (twice the exemption amount in the case of a joint return).

(c) Treatment of credit. The credit allowed by subsection (a) shall be treated as allowed by subpart C of part IV of subchapter A of chapter 1.

(d) Limitation based on adjusted gross income. The amount of the credit allowed by subsection (a) (determined without regard to this subsection and subsection (f)) shall be reduced (but not below zero) by 5 percent of so much of the taxpayer's adjusted gross income as exceeds $75,000 ($150,000 in the case of a joint return).

(e) Definitions. For purposes of this section—

(1) Qualifying income. The term "qualifying income" means—

(A) earned income,

(B) social security benefits (within the meaning of section 86(d)), and

(C) any compensation or pension received under chapter 11, chapter 13, or chapter 15 of title 38, United States Code.

(2) Net income tax liability. The term "net income tax liability" means the excess of—

(A) the sum of the taxpayer's regular tax liability (within the meaning of section 26(b)) and the tax imposed by section 55 for the taxable year, over

(B) the credits allowed by part IV (other than section 24 and subpart C thereof) of subchapter A of chapter 1.

(3) Eligible individual. The term "eligible individual" means any individual other than—

(A) any nonresident alien individual,

(B) any individual with respect to whom a deduction under section 151 is allowable to another taxpayer for a taxable year beginning in the calendar year in which the individual's taxable year begins, and

(C) an estate or trust.

(4) Earned income. The term "earned income" has the meaning set forth in section 32(c)(2) except that—

(A) subclause (II) of subparagraph (B)(vi) thereof shall be applied by substituting "January 1, 2009" for "January 1, 2008", and

(B) such term shall not include net earnings from self-employment which are not taken into account in computing taxable income.

(5) Basic standard deduction; exemption amount. The terms "basic standard deduction" and "exemption amount" shall have the same respective meanings as when used in section 6012(a).

(f) Coordination with advance refunds of credit.

(1) In general. The amount of credit which would (but for this paragraph) be allowable under this section shall be reduced (but not below zero) by the aggregate refunds and credits made or allowed to the taxpayer under subsection (g). Any failure to so reduce the credit shall be treated as arising out of a mathematical or clerical error and assessed according to section 6213(b)(1).

(2) Joint returns. In the case of a refund or credit made or allowed under subsection (g) with respect to a joint return, half of such refund or credit shall be treated as having been made or allowed to each individual filing such return.

(g) Advance refunds and credits.

(1) In general. Each individual who was an eligible individual for such individual's first taxable year beginning in 2007 shall be treated as having made a payment against the tax imposed by chapter 1 for such first taxable year in an amount equal to the advance refund amount for such taxable year.

(2) Advance refund amount For purposes of paragraph (1), the advance refund amount is the amount that would have been allowed as a credit under this section for such first taxable year if this section (other than subsection (f) and this subsection) had applied to such taxable year.

(3) Timing of payments. The Secretary shall, subject to the provisions of this title, refund or credit any overpayment attributable to this section as rapidly as possible. No refund or credit shall be made or allowed under this subsection after December 31, 2008.

(4) No interest. No interest shall be allowed on any overpayment attributable to this section.

(h) Identification number requirement.

(1) In general. No credit shall be allowed under subsection (a) to an eligible individual who does not include on the return of tax for the taxable year—

(A) such individual's valid identification number,

(B) in the case of a joint return, the valid identification number of such individual's spouse, and

(C) in the case of any qualifying child taken into account under subsection (b)(l)(B), the valid identification number of such qualifying child.

(2) Valid identification number. For purposes of paragraph (1), the term "valid identification number" means a social security number issued to an individual by the Social Security Administration. Such term shall not include a TIN issued by the Internal Revenue Service.

[For Analysis, see ¶ 51. For Committee Reports, see ¶ 5501.]

[Endnote Code Sec. 6428]

Code Sec. 6428 in *italics* in was added Sec. 101(a) of the Economic Stimulus Act of 2008, P.L. 110-185, 2/13/2008 which struck out:

1. "Code Sec. 6428. Acceleration of 10 percent income tax rate bracket benefit for 2001.

"(a) In general. In the case of an eligible individual, there shall be allowed as a credit against the tax imposed by chapter 1 for the taxpayer's first taxable year beginning in 2001 an amount equal to 5 percent of so much of the taxpayer's taxable income as does not exceed the initial bracket amount (as defined in section 1(i)(1)(B)).

"(b) Credit treated as nonrefundable personal credit. For purposes of this title, the credit allowed under this section shall be treated as a credit allowable under subpart A of part IV of subchapter A of chapter 1.

"(c) Eligible individual. For purposes of this section, the term 'eligible individual' means any individual other than—

"(1) any estate or trust,

"(2) any nonresident alien individual, and

"(3) any individual with respect to whom a deduction under section 151 is allowable to another taxpayer for a taxable year beginning in the calendar year in which the individual's taxable year begins.

"(d) Coordination with advance refunds of credit.

"(1) In general. The amount of credit which would (but for this paragraph) be allowable under this section shall be reduced (but not below zero) by the aggregate refunds and credits made or allowed to the taxpayer under subsection (e) . Any failure to so reduce the credit shall be treated as arising out of a mathematical or clerical error and assessed according to section 6213(b)(1) .

"(2) Joint returns. In the case of a refund or credit made or allowed under subsection (e) with respect to a joint return, half of such refund or credit shall be treated as having been made or allowed to each individual filing such return.

"(e) Advance refunds of credit based on prior year data.

"(1) In general. Each individual who was an eligible individual for such individual's first taxable year beginning in 2000 shall be treated as having made a payment against the tax imposed by chapter 1 for such first taxable year in an amount equal to the advance refund amount for such taxable year.

"(2) Advance refund amount. For purposes of paragraph (1) , the advance refund amount is the amount that would have been allowed as a credit under this section for such first taxable year if—

"(A) this section (other than subsections (b) and (d) and this subsection) had applied to such taxable year, and

"(B) the credit for such taxable year were not allowed to exceed the excess (if any) of—

"(i) the sum of the regular tax liability (as defined in section 26(b)) plus the tax imposed by section 55, over

"(ii) the sum of the credits allowable under part IV of subchapter A of chapter 1 (other than the credits allowable under subpart C thereof, relating to refundable credits).

"(3) Timing of payments. In the case of any overpayment attributable to this subsection , the Secretary shall, subject to the provisions of this title, refund or credit such overpayment as rapidly as possible and, to the extent practicable, before October 1, 2001. No refund or credit shall be made or allowed under this subsection after December 31, 2001.

"(4) No interest. No interest shall be allowed on any overpayment attributable to this subsection."

Effective Date Enacted 2/13/2008.

Sec. 101(c)-(e), P.L. 110-185, 2/13/2008, provides:

"(c) Treatment of Possessions.

"(1) Payments to possessions.

"(A) Mirror code possession. The Secretary of the Treasury shall make a payment to each possession of the United States with a mirror code tax system in an amount equal to the loss to that possession by reason of the amendments made by this section. Such amount shall be determined by the Secretary of the Treasury based on information provided by the government of the respective possession.

"(B) Other possessions. The Secretary of the Treasury shall make a payment to each possession of the United States which does not have a mirror code tax system in an amount estimated by the Secretary of the Treasury as being equal to the aggregate benefits that would have been provided to residents of such possession by reason of the amendments made by this section if a mirror code tax system had been in effect in such possession. The preceding sentence shall not apply with respect to any possession of the United States unless such possession has a plan, which has been approved by the Secretary of the Treasury, under which such possession will promptly distribute such payment to the residents of such possession.

"(2) Coordination with credit allowed against united states income taxes. No credit shall be allowed against United States income taxes under section 6428 of the Internal Revenue Code of 1986 (as amended by this section) to any person—

"(A) to whom a credit is allowed against taxes imposed by the possession by reason of the amendments made by this section, or

"(B) who is eligible for a payment under a plan described in paragraph (1)(B).

"(3) Definitions and special rules.

"(A) Possession of the Untied States. For purposes of this subsection, the term 'Possession of the United States' includes the Commonwealth of Puerto Rico and the Commonwealth of the Northern Mariana Islands.

"(B) Mirror code tax system. For purposes of this subsection, the term 'mirror code tax system' means, with respect to any possession of the United States, the income tax system of such possession if the income tax liability of the residents of such possession under such system is determined by reference to the income tax laws of the United States as if such possession were the United States.

"(C) Treatment of payments. For purposes of section 1324(b)(2) of title 31, United States Code, the payments under this subsection shall be treated in the same manner as a refund due from the credit allowed under section 6428 of the Internal Revenue Code of 1986 (as amended by this section).

"(d) Refunds Disregarded in the Administration of Federal Programs and Federally Assisted Programs- Any credit or refund allowed or made to any individual by reason of section 6428 of the Internal Revenue Code of 1986 (as amended by this section) or by reason of subsection (c) of this section shall not be taken into account as income and shall not be taken into account as resources for the month of receipt and the following 2 months, for purposes of determining the eligibility of such individual or any other individual for benefits or assistance, or the amount or extent of benefits or assistance, under any Federal program or under any State or local program financed in whole or in part with Federal funds.

"(e) Appropriations To Carry Out Rebates.

"(1) In general. Immediately upon the enactment of this Act, the following sums are appropriated, out of any money in the Treasury not otherwise appropriated, for the fiscal year ending September 30, 2008:

"(A) Department of the Treasury.

"(i) For an additional amount for 'Department of the Treasury--Financial Management Service--Salaries and Expenses', $64,175,000, to remain available until September 30, 2009.

"(ii) For an additional amount for 'Department of the Treasury--Internal Revenue Service--Taxpayer Services', $50,720,000, to remain available until September 30, 2009.

"(iii) For an additional amount for 'Department of the Treasury--Internal Revenue Service--Operations Support', $151,415,000, to remain available until September 30, 2009.

"(B) Social Security Administration. For an additional amount for 'Social Security Administration--Limitation on Administrative Expenses', $31,000,000, to remain available until September 30, 2008.

"(2) Reports. No later than 15 days after enactment of this Act, the Secretary of the Treasury shall submit a plan to the Committees on Appropriations of the House of Representatives and the Senate detailing the expected use of the funds provided by paragraph (1)(A). Beginning 90 days after enactment of this Act, the Secretary of the Treasury shall submit a quarterly report to the Committees on Appropriations of the House of Representatives and the Senate detailing the actual expenditure of funds provided by paragraph (1)(A) and the expected expenditure of such funds in the subsequent quarter."

[¶ 3096]   Code Sec.¹ 6430.   Treatment of tax imposed at leaking underground storage tank trust fund financing rate.

No refunds, credits, or payments shall be made under this subchapter for any tax imposed at the Leaking Underground Storage Tank Trust Fund financing rate, except in the case of fuels—

(1) which are exempt from tax under section 4081(a) by reason of section 4082(f)(2),

(2) which are exempt from tax under section 4041(d) by reason of the last sentence of paragraph (5) thereof, or

(3) with respect to which the rate increase under section 4081(a)(2)(B) is zero by reason of section 4082(e)(2).

[For Analysis, see ¶ 1002. For Committee Reports, see ¶ 5305.]

[Endnote Code Sec. 6430]

Code Sec. 6430, in *italics*, was added by Sec. 6(d)(2)(D) of the Tax Technical Corrections Act of 2007, P.L. 110-172, 12/29/2007, which struck out:

1. "Sec. 6430. Treatment of tax imposed at Leaking Underground Storage Tank Trust Fund financing rate.

"No refunds, credits, or payments shall be made under this subchapter for any tax imposed at the Leaking Underground Storage Tank Trust Fund financing rate, except in the case of fuels destined for export."

Effective Date Effective for fuel entered, removed, or sold after 9/30/2005. Sec. 6(d)(1)(C) of this Act, provides:

"(C) Notwithstanding section 6430 of the Internal Revenue Code of 1986, a refund, credit, or payment may be made under subchapter B of chapter 65 of such Code for taxes imposed with respect to any liquid after September 30, 2005, and before the date of the enactment of this Act under section 4041(d)(1) or 4042 of such Code at the Leaking Underground Storage Tank Trust Fund financing rate to the extent that tax was imposed with respect to such liquid under section 4081 at the Leaking Underground Storage Tank Trust Fund financing rate."

[¶ 3097]   Code Sec. 6501.   Limitations on assessment and collection.

* * * * * * * * * * * *

(m) Deficiencies attributable to election of certain credits. The period for assessing a deficiency attributable to any election under section 30(d)(4), 30B(h)(9), 30C(e)(5), 40(f), 43, 45B, 45C(d)(4), ¹*45H(g)*, or 51(j) (or any revocation thereof) shall not expire before the date 1 year after the date on which the Secretary is notified of such election (or revocation).

* * * * * * * * * * * *

[For Analysis, see ¶ 401. For Committee Reports, see ¶ 5306.]

[Endnote Code Sec. 6501]

Matter in Code Sec. 6501(m) in *italics* was added by Sec. 7(a)(2)(B) of the Tax Technical Corrections Act of 2007, P.L. 110-172, 12/29/2007.

1. "45H(g),"

Effective Date (Sec. 7(e)(1), P.L. 110-172, 12/29/2007) effective for expenses paid or incurred after 12/31/2002, in tax. yrs. end. after such date.

[¶ 3098]   Code Sec. 6686.   Failure to file returns or supply information by DISC or ¹*former* FSC.

In addition to the penalty imposed by section 7203 (relating to willful failure to file return, supply information, or pay tax) any person required to supply information or to file a return under section 6011(c) who fails to supply such information or file such return at the time prescribed by the Secretary, or who files a return which does not show the information required, shall pay a penalty of $100 for each failure to supply information (but the total amount imposed on the delinquent person for all such failures during any calendar year shall not exceed $25,000) or a penalty of $1,000 for each failure to file a return, unless it is shown that such failure is due to reasonable cause.

[Endnote Code Sec. 6686]

Matter in *italics* in the heading of Code Sec. 6686 was added by Sec. 11(g)(21) of the Tax Technical Corrections Act of 2007, P.L. 110-172, 12/29/2007.

1. added matter in the heading

Effective Date enacted 12/29/2007.

[¶ 3099]　Code Sec. 6695A.　Substantial and gross valuation misstatements attributable to incorrect appraisals.

(a)　**Imposition of penalty.** If—

(1) a person prepares an appraisal of the value of property and such person knows, or reasonably should have known, that the appraisal would be used in connection with a return or a claim for refund, and

(2) the claimed value of the property on a return or claim for refund which is based on such appraisal results in a substantial valuation misstatement under chapter 1 (within the meaning of section 6662(e)), [1]*a substantial estate or gift tax valuation understatement (within the meaning of section 6662(g)),* or a gross valuation misstatement (within the meaning of section 6662(h)), with respect to such property,

[2]*then such person* shall pay a penalty in the amount determined under subsection (b).

* * * * * * * * * * * *

[For Analysis, see ¶ 1101. For Committee Reports, see ¶ 5302.]

[Endnote Code Sec. 6695A]

Matter in *italics* in Code Sec. 6695A(a)(2) was added by Sec. 3(e)(1), P.L. 110-172.

1. added material in para. (a)(2)

Effective Date (Sec. 3(j), P.L. 110-172, 12/29/2007) effective for appraisals prepared for returns or submissions filed after 8/17/2006, except as provided in Sec. 1219(e)(3) of P.L. 109-280, which reads as follows:

"(3) Special rule for certain easements. In the case of a contribution of a qualified real property interest which is a restriction with respect to the exterior of a building described in section 170(h)(4)(C)(ii) of the Internal Revenue Code of 1986, and an appraisal with respect to the contribution, the amendments made by subsections (a) and (b) shall apply to returns filed after July 25, 2006."

Matter in *italics* in Code Sec. 6695A(a)(2) was added by Sec. 11(a)(40) of the Tax Technical Corrections Act of 2007, P.L. 110-172, 12/29/2007, which struck out:

2. "then such person"

Effective Date enacted 12/29/2007.

[¶ 3100]　Code Sec. 6696.　Rules applicable with respect to sections 6694, 6695, and 6695A.

* * * * * * * * * * * *

(d)　**Periods of limitation.**

(1)　**Assessment.** The amount of any penalty under section 6694(a)[1], *section 6695, or 6695A* shall be assessed within 3 years after the return or claim for refund with respect to which the penalty is assessed was filed, and no proceeding in court without assessment for the collection of such tax shall be begun after the expiration of such period. In the case of any penalty under section 6694(b), the penalty may be assessed, or a proceeding in court for the collection of the penalty may be begun without assessment, at any time.

(2)　**Claim for refund.** Except as provided in section 6694(d), any claim for refund of an overpayment of any penalty assessed under section 6694, 6695, or 6695A shall be filed within 3 years from the time the penalty was paid.

* * * * * * * * * * * *

[For Analysis, see ¶ 1101. For Committee Reports, see ¶ 5302.]

[Endnote Code Sec. 6696]

Matter in *italics* in Code Sec. 6696(d)(1) was added by Sec. 3(e)(2) of the Tax Technical Corrections Act of 2007, P.L. 110-172, 12/29/2007, which struck out:

1. "or under section 6695"

Effective Date (Sec. 3(j), P.L. 110-172, 12/29/2007) effective for appraisals prepared for returns or submissions filed after the 8/17/2006, except as provided in Sec. 1219(e)(3) of P.L. 109-280, which reads as follows:

"(3) Special rule for certain easements. In the case of a contribution of a qualified real property interest which is a restriction with respect to the exterior of a building described in section 170(h)(4)(C)(ii) of the Internal Revenue Code of 1986, and an appraisal with respect to the contribution, the amendments made by subsections (a) and (b) shall apply to returns filed after July 25, 2006."

[¶3101]   Code Sec. 6698.   Failure to file partnership return.

(a) General rule. In addition to the penalty imposed by section 7203 (relating to willful failure to file return, supply information, or pay tax), if any partnership required to file a return under section 6031 for any taxable year—

(1) fails to file such return at the time prescribed therefor (determined with regard to any extension of time for filing), or

(2) files a return which fails to show the information required under section 6031,

such partnership shall be liable for a penalty determined under subsection (b) for each month (or fraction thereof) during which such failure continues (but not to exceed [1]*12 months*), unless it is shown that such failure is due to reasonable cause.

(b) Amount per month. For purposes of subsection (a), the amount determined under this subsection for any month is the product of—

(1) [2]*$85*, multiplied by

(2) the number of persons who were partners in the partnership during any part of the taxable year

* * * * * * * * * * * *

[For Analysis, see ¶1102. For Committee Reports, see ¶5402.]

[Endnote Code Sec. 6698]

Matter in *italics* in Code Sec. 6698(a) and Code Sec. 6698(b)(1) was added by Sec. 8(a) and (b) of the Mortgage Forgiveness Debt Relief Act of 2007, P.L. 110-142, 12/20/2007, which struck out:

    1. "5 months"

    2. "$50"

Effective Date (Sec. 8(d), P.L. 110-142, 12/20/2007) effective for returns required to be filed after 12/20/2007.

[¶3102]   *Code Sec.*[1] *6699.*   *Failure to file S corporation return.*

(a) *General rule.* *In addition to the penalty imposed by section 7203 (relating to willful failure to file return, supply information, or pay tax), if any S corporation required to file a return under section 6037 for any taxable year—*

(1) fails to file such return at the time prescribed therefor (determined with regard to any extension of time for filing), or

(2) files a return which fails to show the information required under section 6037,

such S corporation shall be liable for a penalty determined under subsection (b) for each month (or fraction thereof) during which such failure continues (but not to exceed 12 months), unless it is shown that such failure is due to reasonable cause.

(b) *Amount per month.* *For purposes of subsection (a), the amount determined under this subsection for any month is the product of—*

(1) $85, multiplied by

(2) the number of persons who were shareholders in the S corporation during any part of the taxable year.

(c) *Assessment of penalty.* *The penalty imposed by subsection (a) shall be assessed against the S corporation.*

(d) *Deficiency procedures not to apply.* *Subchapter B of chapter 63 (relating to deficiency procedures for income, estate, gift, and certain excise taxes) shall not apply in respect of the assessment or collection of any penalty imposed by subsection (a).*

[For Analysis, see ¶ 1103.]

[Endnote Code Sec. 6699]

Code Sec. 6699, in *italics*, was added by Sec. 9(a) of the Mortgage Forgiveness Debt Relief Act of 2007, P.L. 110-142, 12/20/2007.

1. added new Code Sec. 6699

Effective Date (Sec. 9(c), P.L. 110-142, 12/20/2007) effective for returns required to be filed after 12/20/2007.

[¶ 3103]   Code Sec. 6707A.   Penalty for failure to include reportable transaction information with return.

* * * * * * * * * * * *

(e) Penalty reported to SEC. In the case of a person—

(1) which is required to file periodic reports under section 13 or 15(d) of the Securities Exchange Act of 1934 or is required to be consolidated with another person for purposes of such reports, and

(2) which—

(A) is required to pay a penalty under this section with respect to a listed transaction,

(B) is required to pay a penalty under section 6662A with respect to any reportable transaction at a rate prescribed under section 6662A(c), or

(C) is required to pay a penalty under section 6662(h) with respect to any reportable transaction and would (but for ¹*section 6662A(e)(2)(B))* have been subject to penalty under section 6662A at a rate prescribed under section 6662A(c),

the requirement to pay such penalty shall be disclosed in such reports filed by such person for such periods as the Secretary shall specify. Failure to make a disclosure in accordance with the preceding sentence shall be treated as a failure to which the penalty under subsection (b)(2) applies.

* * * * * * * * * * * *

[Endnote Code Sec. 6707A]

Matter in *italics* in Code Sec. 6707A(e)(2)(C) was added by Sec. 11(a)(41) of the Tax Technical Corrections Act of 2007, P.L. 110-172, 12/29/2007, which struck out:

1. "section 6662A(e)(2)(C)",

Effective Date (P.L. 110-172, 12/29/2007) enacted 12/29/2007.

[¶ 3104]   Code Sec. 6724.   Waiver; definitions and special rules.

* * * * * * * * * * * *

(d) Definitions. For purposes of this part—

(1) Information return. The term "information return" means—

* * * * * * * * * * * *

(B) any return required by—

(i) section 6041A(a) or (b) (relating to returns of direct sellers),

(ii) section 6043A(a) (relating to returns relating to taxable mergers and acquisitions),

(iii) section 6045(a) or (d) (relating to returns of brokers),

(iv) section 6050H(a) ¹*or (h)(1)* (relating to mortgage interest received in trade or business from individuals),

(v) section 6050I(a) or (g)(1) (relating to cash received in trade or business, etc.),

(vi) section 6050J(a) (relating to foreclosures and abandonments of security),

(vii) section 6050K(a) (relating to exchanges of certain partnership interests),

(viii) section 6050L(a) (relating to returns relating to certain dispositions of donated property),

(ix) section 6050P (relating to returns relating to the cancellation of indebtedness by certain financial entities),

(x) section 6050Q (relating to certain long-term care benefits),

(xi) section 6050S (relating to returns relating to payments for qualified tuition and related expenses),

(xii) section 6050T (relating to returns relating to credit for health insurance costs of eligible individuals),

(xiii) section 6052(a) (relating to reporting payment of wages in the form of group [term] life insurance),

(xiv) section 6050V (relating to returns relating to applicable insurance contracts in which certain exempt organizations hold interests),

(xv) section 6053(c)(1) (relating to reporting with respect to certain tips),

(xvi) subsection (b) or (e) of section 1060 (relating to reporting requirements of transferors and transferees in certain asset acquisitions),

(xvii) section 4101(d) (relating to information reporting with respect to fuels taxes),

(xviii) subparagraph (C) of section 338(h)(10) (relating to information required to be furnished to the Secretary in case of elective recognition of gain or loss),

(xix) section 6039(a) (relating to returns required with respect to certain options), and

(xix [sic (xx)]) section 264(f)(5)(A)(iv) (relating to reporting with respect to certain life insurance and annuity contracts), or

(xx [sic (xxi)]) section 6050U (relating to charges or payments for qualified long-term care insurance contracts under combined arrangements), and

(C) any statement of the amount of payments to another person required to be made to the Secretary under—

(i) section 408(i)(relating to reports with respect to individual retirement accounts or annuities), or

(ii) section 6047(d) (relating to reports by employers, plan administrators, etc.).

Such term also includes any form, statement, or schedule required to be filed with the Secretary with respect to any amount from which tax was required to be deducted and withheld under chapter 3 (or from which tax would be required to be so deducted and withheld but for an exemption under this title or any treaty obligation of the United States).

(2) Payee statement. The term "payee statement" means any statement required to be furnished under—

(A) section 6031(b) or (c), 6034A, or 6037(b) (relating to statements furnished by certain pass-thru entities),

(B) section 6039(b) (relating to information required in connection with certain options),

(C) section 6041(d) (relating to information at source),

(D) section 6041A(e) (relating to returns regarding payments of remuneration for services and direct sales),

(E) section 6042(c) (relating to returns regarding payments of dividends and corporate earnings and profits),

(F) subsections (b) and (d) of section 6043A (relating to returns relating to taxable mergers and acquisitions).[,]

(G) section 6044(e) (relating to returns regarding payments of patronage dividends),

(H) section 6045(b) or (d) (relating to returns of brokers),

(I) section 6049(c) (relating to returns regarding payments of interest),

(J) section 6050A(b) (relating to reporting requirements of certain fishing boat operators),

(K) section 6050H(d) ²or (h)(2) (relating to returns relating to mortgage interest received in trade or business from individuals),

(L) section 6050I(e) or paragraph (4) or (5) of section 6050I(g) (relating to cash received in trade or business, etc.),

(M) section 6050J(e) (relating to returns relating to foreclosures and abandonments of security),

(N) section 6050K(b) (relating to returns relating to exchanges of certain partnership interests),

(O) section 6050L(c) (relating to returns relating to certain dispositions of donated property),

(P) section 6050N(b) (relating to returns regarding payments of royalties),

(Q) section 6050P(d) (relating to returns relating to the cancellation of indebtedness by certain financial entities),

(R) section 6050Q(b) (relating to certain long-term care benefits),

(S) section 6050R(c) (relating to returns relating to certain purchases of fish),

(T) section 6051 (relating to receipts for employees),

(U) section 6052(b) (relating to returns regarding payment of wages in the form of group-term life insurance),

(V) section 6053(b) or (c) (relating to reports of tips),

(W) section 6048(b)(1)(B) (relating to foreign trust reporting requirements),

(X) section 408(i)(relating to reports with respect to individual retirement plans) to any person other than the Secretary with respect to the amount of payments made to such person,

(Y) section 6047(d) (relating to reports by plan administrators) to any person other than the Secretary with respect to the amount of payments made to such person,

(Z) section 6050S (relating to returns relating to qualified tuition and related expenses),

(AA) section 264(f)(5)(A)(iv) relating to reporting with respect to certain life insurance and annuity contracts),

(BB) section 6050T (relating to returns relating to credit for health insurance costs of eligible individuals)

(CC) section 6050U (relating to charges or payments for qualified long-term care insurance contracts under combined arrangements).

Such term also includes any form, statement, or schedule required to be furnished to the recipient of any amount from which tax was required to be deducted and withheld under chapter 3 (or from which tax would be required to be so deducted and withheld but for an exemption under this title or any treaty obligation of the United States).

(3) Specified information reporting requirement. The term "specified information reporting requirement" means—

(A) the notice required by section 6050K(c)(1) (relating to requirement that transferor notify partnership of exchange),

(B) any requirement contained in the regulations prescribed under section 6109 that a person—

(i) include his TIN on any return, statement, or other document (other than an information return or payee statement),

(ii) furnish his TIN to another person, or

(iii) include on any return, statement, or other document (other than an information return or payee statement) made with respect to another person the TIN of such person,

(C) any requirement contained in the regulations prescribed under section 215 that a person—

(i) furnish his TIN to another person, or

(ii) include on his return the TIN of another person, and

(D) any requirement under section 6109(h) that—

(i) a person include on his return the name, address, and TIN of another person, or

(ii) a person furnish his TIN to another person.

(4) Required filing date. The term "required filing date" means the date prescribed for filing an information return with the Secretary (determined with regard to any extension of time for filing).

* * * * * * * * * * *

(e) Special rule for certain partnership returns. In any partnership return under section 6031(a) is required under section 6011(e) to be filed on magnetic media or in other machine-readable form, for purposes of this part, each schedule required to be included with such return with respect to each partner shall be treated as a separate information return.
[For Analysis, see ¶ 203.]

[Endnote Code Sec. 6724]
Matter in *italics* in Code Sec. 6724(d)(1)(B)(iv), Code Sec. 6724(d)(2)(K) was added by Sec. 11(b)(2)(A) and (B) of the Tax Technical Corrections Act of 2007, 12/29/2007, which struck out:
  1. added matter in clause (d)(1)(B)(iv)
  2. added matter in subpara. (d)(2)(K)
Effective Date (Sec. 11(b)(3), P.L. 110-172, 12/29/2007) effective for amounts paid or accrued after 12/31/2006.

[¶ 3105]   Code Sec. 7651.   Administration and collection of taxes in possessions.
Except as otherwise provided in this subchapter, and except as otherwise provided in section 28(a) of the Revised Organic Act of the Virgin Islands and section 30 of the Organic Act of Guam (relating to the covering of the proceeds of certain taxes into the treasuries of the Virgin Islands and Guam, respectively)—

* * * * * * * * * * *

[1]*(4)* **Virgin Islands.**

    (A) For purposes of this section, the reference in section 28(a) of the Revised Organic Act of the Virgin Islands to "any tax specified in section 3811 of the Internal Revenue Code" shall be deemed to refer to any tax imposed by chapter 2 or by chapter 21.

    (B) For purposes of this title, section 28(a) of the Revised Organic Act of the Virgin Islands shall be effective as if such section 28(a) had been enacted before the enactment of this title and such section 28(a) shall have no effect on the amount of income tax liability required to be paid by any person to the United States.

[Endnote Code Sec. 7651]
Matter in *italics* in Code Sec. 7651(4) and Code Sec. 7651(5) was added by section 11(a)(34)(B), of the Tax Technical Corrections Act of 2007, P.L. 110-172, 12/29/2007, which struck out:
  1. "(4) Canal Zone. For purposes of this section , the term 'possession of the United States' includes the Canal Zone."
  "(5)"
Effective Date (P.L. 110-172, 12/29/2007) enacted 12/29/2007.

[¶ 3106]   Code Sec. 9002.   Definitions.
For purposes of this chapter—

* * * * * * * * * * *

    (3) The term "Commission" means the Federal Election Commission established by [1]*section 306(a)(1)* of the Federal Election Campaign Act of 1971.

* * * * * * * * * * *

[Endnote Code Sec. 9002]
Matter in *italics* in Code Sec. 9002(3) was added by section 11(a)(42)(A) of the Tax Technical Corrections Act of 2007, P.L. 110-172, 12/29/2007, which struck out:
  1. "section 309(a)(1)"

Effective Date (P.L. 110-172, 12/29/2007) enacted 12/29/2007.

[¶ 3107]   **Code Sec. 9004.**   **Entitlement of eligible candidates to payments.**

(a)   **In general.** Subject to the provisions of this chapter—

(1) The eligible candidates of each major party in a presidential election shall be entitled to equal payments under section 9006 in an amount which, in the aggregate, shall not exceed the expenditure limitations applicable to such candidates under [1]*section 315(b)(1)(B)* of the Federal Election Campaign Act of 1971.

* * * * * * * * * * * *

[Endnote Code Sec. 9004]

Matter in *italics* in Code Sec. 9004(a)(1) was added by Sec. 11(a)(42)(B) of the Tax Technical Corrections Act of 2007, P.L. 110-172, 12/29/2007, which struck out:

    1. "section 320(b)(1)(B)"

Effective Date (P.L. 110-172, 12/29/2007) enacted 12/29/2007.

[¶ 3108]   **Code Sec. 9006.**   **Payments to eligible candidates.**

* * * * * * * * * * * *

(b)   **Payments from the fund.** Upon receipt of a certification from the [1]*Commission* under section 9005 for payment to the eligible candidates of a political party, the Secretary of the Treasury shall pay to such candidates out of the fund the amount certified by the [2]*Commission.* Amounts paid to any such candidates shall be under the control of such candidates.

* * * * * * * * * * * *

[Endnote Code Sec. 9006]

Matter in *italics* in Code Sec. 9006(b) was added by Sec. 11(a)(43) of the Tax Technical Corrections Act of 2007, P.L. 110-172, 12/29/2007, which struck out:

    1. "Comptroller General"

    2. "Comptroller General"

Effective Date enacted 12/29/2007.

[¶ 3109]   **Code Sec. 9032.**   **Definitions.**

For purposes of this chapter—

* * * * * * * * * * * *

(3) The term "Commission" means the Federal Election Commission established by [1]*section 306(a)(1)* of the Federal Election Campaign Act of 1971.

* * * * * * * * * * * *

[Endnote Code Sec. 9032]

Matter in *italics* in Code Sec. 9032(3) was added by Sec. 11(a)(42)(C) of the Tax Technical Corrections Act of 2007, P.L. 110-172, 12/29/2007, which struck out:

    1. "section 309(a)(1)"

Effective Date enacted 12/29/2007.

[¶3110]   Code Sec. 9034.   Entitlement of eligible candidates to payments.

* * * * * * * * * * * *

(b) Limitations. The total amount of payments to which a candidate is entitled under subsection (a) shall not exceed 50 percent of the expenditure limitation applicable under [1]*section 315(b)(1)(A)* of the Federal Election Campaign Act of 1971.

[Endnote Code Sec. 9034]

Matter in *italics* in Code Sec. 9034(b) was added by Sec. 11(a)(42)(D) of the Tax Technical Corrections Act of 2007, P.L. 110-172, 12/29/2007, which struck out:

1. "section 320(b)(1)(A)"

Effective Date (P.L. 110-172, 12/29/2007) enacted 12/29/2007.

[¶3111]   Code Sec. 9502.   Airport and Airway Trust Fund.

* * * * * * * * * * * *

(d) Expenditures from Airport and Airway Trust Fund.

(1) Airport and airway program. Amounts in the Airport and Airway Trust Fund shall be available, as provided by appropriation Acts, for making expenditures before [1]*March 1, 2008*, to meet those obligations of the United States—

(A) incurred under title I of the Airport and Airway Development Act of 1970 or of the Airport and Airway Development Act Amendments of 1976 or of the Aviation Safety and Noise Abatement Act of 1979 or under the Fiscal Year 1981 Airport Development Authorization Act or the provisions of the Airport and Airway Improvement Act of 1982 or the Airport and Airway Safety and Capacity Expansion Act of 1987 or the Federal Aviation Administration Research, Engineering, and Development Authorization Act of 1990 or the Aviation Safety and Capacity Expansion Act of 1990 or the Airport and Airway Safety, Capacity, Noise Improvement, and Intermodal Transportation Act of 1992 or the Airport Improvement Program Temporary Extension Act of 1994 or the Federal Aviation Administration Authorization Act of 1994 or the Federal Aviation Reauthorization Act of 1996 or the provisions of the Omnibus Consolidated and Emergency Supplemental Appropriations Act, 1999 providing for payments from the Airport and Airway Trust Fund or the Interim Federal Aviation Administration Authorization Act or section 6002 of the 1999 Emergency Supplemental Appropriations Act, Public Law 106-59, or the Wendell H. Ford Aviation Investment and Reform Act for the 21st Century or the Aviation and Transportation Security Act or the Vision 100—Century of Aviation Reauthorization Act [2]*or the Department of Transportation Appropriations Act, 2008*;

(B) heretofore or hereafter incurred under part A of subtitle VII of title 49, United States Code, which are attributable to planning, research and development, construction, or operation and maintenance of—

(i) air traffic control,

(ii) air navigation,

(iii) communications, or

(iv) supporting services,

for the airway system; or

(C) for those portions of the administrative expenses of the Department of Transportation which are attributable to activities described in subparagraph (A) or (B).

Any reference in subparagraph (A) to an Act shall be treated as a reference to such Act and the corresponding provisions (if any) of title 49, United States Code, as such Act and provisions were in effect on the date of the enactment of the last Act referred to in subparagraph (A).

* * * * * * * * * * * *

[3](e) Limitation on transfers to trust fund.

(1) In general. Except as provided in paragraph (2), no amount may be appropriated or credited to the Airport and Airway Trust Fund on and after the date of any expenditure from the Airport and Airway Trust Fund which is not permitted by this section. The determination of whether an expenditure is so permitted shall be made without regard to—

(A) any provision of law which is not contained or referenced in this title or in a revenue Act; and

(B) whether such provision of law is a subsequently enacted provision or directly or indirectly seeks to waive the application of this subsection.

(2) Exception for prior obligations. Paragraph (1) shall not apply to any expenditure to liquidate any contract entered into (or for any amount otherwise obligated) before [4]March 1, 2008, in accordance with the provisions of this section.

[Endnote Code Sec. 9502]

Matter in *italics* in Code Sec. 9502(d)(1) and Code Sec. 9502(d)(1)(A) was added by Sec. 116(c)(1)(A), (B) and (c)(2), Div. K, P.L. 110-161, 12/26/2007, which struck out:

  1. "October 1, 2007"

  2. "added matter at then end of subpara. (d)(1)(A)

Effective Date (Sec. 116(d), Div. K, P.L. 110-161, 12/26/2007) effective 10/1/2007.

Matter in *italics* in Code Sec. 9502(e) was added by Sec. 11(f)(1) of the Tax Technical Corrections Act of 2007, P.L. 110-172, 12/29/2007, which struck out:

  3. "(e) Certain taxes on alcohol mixtures to remain in general fund. For purposes of this section, the amounts which would (but for this subsection) be required to be appropriated under subparagraphs (A), (C), and (D) of subsection (b)(1) shall be reduced by—

  "(1) 0.6 cent per gallon in the case of taxes imposed on any mixture at least 10 percent of which is alcohol (as defined in section 4081(c)(3)) if any portion of such alcohol is ethanol; and

  "(2) 0.67 cent per gallon in the case of fuel used in producing a mixture described in paragraph (1)."

Effective Date (Sec. 11(f)(4), P.L. 110-172, 12/29/2007) effective for fuel sold or used after 12/31/2004.

[¶ 3112]   Code Sec. 9503.   Highway Trust Fund.

* * * * * * * * * * * *

(c) Expenditures from Highway Trust Fund.

* * * * * * * * * * * *

[1]**(6) Transfers from the trust fund for certain aviation fuel taxes.** The Secretary shall pay at least monthly from the Highway Trust Fund into the Airport and Airway Trust Fund amounts (as determined by the Secretary) equivalent to the taxes received on or after October 1, 2005, and before October 1, 2011, under section 4081 with respect to so much of the rate of tax as does not exceed—

(A) 4.3 cents per gallon of kerosene subject to section 6427(l)(4)(A) with respect to which a payment has been made by the Secretary under section 6427(l), and

(B) 21.8 cents per gallon of kerosene subject to section 6427(l)(4)(B) with respect to which a payment has been made by the Secretary under section 6427(l).

Transfers under the preceding sentence shall be made on the basis of estimates by the Secretary, and proper adjustments shall be made in the amounts subsequently transferred to the extent prior estimates were in excess of or less than the amounts required to be transferred. Any amount allowed as a credit under section 34 by reason of paragraph (4) of section 6427(l) shall be treated for purposes of subparagraphs (A) and (B) as a payment made by the Secretary under such paragraph.

* * * * * * * * * * * *

[Endnote Code Sec. 9503]

Matter in *italics* in Code Sec. 9503(c)(6) was added by Sec. 11(a)(44) of the Tax Technical Corrections Act of 2007, P.L. 110-172, 12/29/2007, which struck out:

  1. "(7)"

Effective Date enacted 12/29/2007.

Tax Increase Prevention Act of 2007
One Hundred Tenth Congress
1st Session
P.L. 110-166

Act sections of the Tax Increase Prevention Act of 2007, P.L. 110-166, 12/26/2007, or portions thereof, that do not amend specific Internal Revenue Code sections follow. Sections of the Internal Revenue Code as amended are reproduced at *Code as Amended.*

[¶ 4001] Sec. 1. Short title. This Act may be cited as the "Tax Increase Prevention Act of 2007"

[¶ 4002] Sec. 2. Extension of increased alternative minimum tax exemption amount.
* * * * * * * * * *

(b) Effective Date. The amendments made by this section shall apply to taxable years beginning after December 31, 2006.

[¶ 4003] Sec. 3. Extension of alternative minimum tax relief for nonrefundable personal credits.
* * * * * * * * * *

(b) Effective Date. The amendments made by this section shall apply to taxable years beginning after December 31, 2006.

Mortgage Forgiveness Debt Relief Act of 2007
One Hundred Tenth Congress
1st Session
P.L. 110-142

Act sections of the Mortgage Forgiveness Debt Relief Act of 2007, P.L. 110-142, 12/20/2007, or portions thereof, that do not amend specific Internal Revenue Code sections follow. Sections of the Internal Revenue Code as amended are reproduced at *Code as Amended.*

[¶ 4011] Sec. 1. Short title. This Act may be cited as the "Mortgage Forgiveness Debt Relief Act of 2007"

[¶ 4012] Sec. 2. Discharge of indebtedness on principal residence excluded from gross income.
　　* * * * * * * * * *

(b) Effective date. The amendments made by this section shall apply to discharges of indebtedness on or after January 1, 2007.

[¶ 4013] Sec. 3. Extension of treatment of mortgage insurance premiums as interest.
　　* * * * * * * * * *

(b) Effective date. The amendment made by this section shall apply to amounts paid or accrued after December 31, 2007.

[¶ 4014] Sec. 4. Alternative tests for qualifying as cooperative housing corporation.
　　* * * * * * * * * *

(b) Effective date. The amendment made by this section shall apply to taxable years ending after the date of the enactment of this Act.

[¶ 4015] Sec. 5. Exclusion from income for benefits provided to volunteer firefighters and emergency medical responders.
　　* * * * * * * * * *

(c) Effective date. The amendments made by this section shall apply to taxable years beginning after December 31, 2007.

[¶ 4016] Sec. 6. Clarification of student housing eligible for low-income housing credit.
　　* * * * * * * * * *

(b) (b) Effective date. The amendment made by this section shall apply to—
　　(1) housing credit amounts allocated before, on, or after the date of the enactment of this Act, and
　　(2) buildings placed in service before, on, or after such date to the extent paragraph (1) of section 42(h) of the Internal Revenue Code of 1986 does not apply to any building by reason of paragraph (4) thereof.

[¶ 4017] Sec. 7. Application of joint return limitation for capital gains exclusion to certain post-marriage sales of principal residences by surviving spouses.
　　* * * * * * * * * *

(b) Effective date. The amendment made by this section shall apply to sales or exchanges after December 31, 2007.

[¶ 4018] Sec. 8. Modification of penalty for failure to file partnership returns; limitation on disclosure.

* * * * * * * * * *

(c) Limitation on Disclosure of Taxpayer Returns to Partners, S Corporation Shareholders, Trust Beneficiaries, and Estate Beneficiaries.

* * * * * * * * * *

(2) Effective date. The amendment made by this subsection shall take effect on the date of the enactment of this Act.

(d) Effective date. The amendments made by subsections (a) and (b) shall apply to returns required to be filed after the date of the enactment of this Act.

[¶ 4019] Sec. 9. Penalty for failure to files S corporation returns.

* * * * * * * * * *

(c) Effective date. The amendments made by this section shall apply to returns required to be filed after the date of the enactment of this Act.

[¶ 4024] Sec. 10. Modification of required installment of corporate estimated taxes with respect to certain dates. The percentage under subparagraph (B) of section 401(1) of the Tax Increase Prevention and Reconciliation Act of 2005 in effect on the date of the enactment of this Act is increased by 1.50 percentage points.

Energy Independence and Security Act of 2007
One Hundred Tenth Congress
1st Session
P.L. 110-140

Act sections of the Energy Independence and Security Act of 2007, P.L. 110-140, or portions thereof, that do not amend specific Internal Revenue Code sections follow. Sections of the Internal Revenue Code as amended are reproduced at *Code as Amended*.

[¶ 4026] Sec. 1. Short title; Table of contents.

(c) Short Title. This Act may be cited as the "Energy Independence and Security Act of 2007".

* * * * * * * * * *

[¶ 4027] Sec. 1500. Amendment of 1986 Code. Except as otherwise expressly provided, whenever in this title an amendment or repeal is expressed in terms of an amendment to, or repeal of, a section or other provision, the reference shall be considered to be made to a section or other provision of the Internal Revenue Code of 1986.

[¶ 4028] Sec. 1501. Extension of additional 0.2 percent FUTA surtax.
* * * * * * * * * *

(b) Effective Date. The amendments made by this section shall apply to wages paid after December 31, 2007.

[¶ 4029] Sec. 1502. 7-year amortization of geological and geophysical expenditures for certain major integrated oil companies.
* * * * * * * * * *

(b) Effective date. The amendment made by this section shall apply to amounts paid or incurred after the date of the enactment of this Act.

505

Tax Technical Corrections Act of 2007
One Hundred Tenth Congress
1st Session
P.L. 110-172

Act sections of the Tax Technical Corrections Act of 2007, P.L. 110-172, or portions thereof, that do not amend specific Internal Revenue Code sections follow. Sections of the Internal Revenue Code as amended are reproduced at *Code as Amended*.

[¶ 4036] Sec. 1. Short title; amendment of 1986 Code; Table of contents.

(a) Short title. This Act may be cited as the "Tax Technical Corrections Act of 2007".

(b) Amendment of 1986 Code. Except as otherwise expressly provided, whenever in this Act an amendment or repeal is expressed in terms of an amendment to, or repeal of, a section or other provision, the reference shall be considered to be made to a section or other provision of the Internal Revenue Code of 1986.
　　* * * * * * * * * * * *

[¶ 4037] Sec. 2. Amendment related to the Tax Relief and Health Care Act of 2006.
　　* * * * * * * * * *

(b) Effective date. The amendment made by this section shall take effect as if included in the provision of the Tax Relief and Health Care Act of 2006 to which it relates.

[¶ 4038] Sec. 3. Amendments related to Title XII of the Pension Protection Act of 2006.
　　* * * * * * * * * *

(j) Effective date. The amendments made by this section shall take effect as if included in the provisions 15 of the Pension Protection Act of 2006 to which they relate.

[¶ 4039] Sec. 4. Amendments related to the Tax Increase Prevention and Reconciliation Act of 2005.
　　* * * * * * * * * *

(b) Amendments related to section 202 of the act.
　　* * * * * * * * * *
　　(3) The Internal Revenue Code of 1986 shall be applied and administered as if the amendments made by section 202 of the Tax Increase Prevention and Reconciliation Act of 2005 and by section 410 of division A of the Tax Relief and Health Care Act of 2006 had never been enacted.
　　* * * * * * * * * *

(d) Effective date.
　　(1) In general. Except as otherwise provided in this subsection, the amendments made by this section shall take effect as if included in the provisions of the Tax Increase Prevention and Reconciliation Act of 2005 to which they relate.
　　(2) Modification of active business definition under section 355.
　　　　(A) In general.
　　Except as otherwise provided in this paragraph, the amendments made by subsection (b) shall apply to distributions made after May 17, 2006.
　　　　(B) Transition rule. The amendments made by subsection (b) shall not apply to any distribution pursuant to a transaction which Is—

(i) made pursuant to an agreement which was binding on May 17, 2006, and at all times thereafter,

(ii) described in a ruling request submitted to the Internal Revenue Service on or before such date, or

(iii) described on or before such date in a public announcement or in a filing with the Securities and Exchange Commission.

(C) Election out of transition rule. Subparagraph (B) shall not apply if the distributing corporation elects not to have such subparagraph apply to distributions of such corporation. Any such election, once made, shall be irrevocable.

(D) Special rule for certain pre-enactment distributions. For purposes of determining the continued qualification under section 355(b)(2)(A) of the Internal Revenue Code of 1986 of distributions made on or before May 17, 2006, as a result of an acquisition, disposition, or other restructuring after such date, such distribution shall be treated as made on the date of such acquisition, disposition, or restructuring for purposes of applying subparagraphs (A) through (C) of this paragraph. The preceding sentence shall only apply with respect to the corporation that undertakes such acquisition, disposition, or other restructuring, and only if such application results in continued qualification under section 355(b)(2)(A) of such Code.

(3) **Amendment related to section 515 of the act.** The amendment made by subsection (c) shall apply to taxable years beginning after December 31, 2006.

[¶ 4040] Sec. 5. Amendments related to the Safe, Accountable, Flexible, Efficient Transportation Equity Act: a Legacy for Users.
* * * * * * * * * *

(b) **Effective date.** The amendments made by this section shall take effect as if included in the provisions of the SAFETEA-LU to which they relate.

[¶ 4041] Sec. 6. Amendments related to the Energy Policy Act of 2005.
* * * * * * * * * *

(e) **Effective date.**
(1) **In general.** Except as otherwise provided in this subsection, the amendments made by this section shall take effect as if included in the provisions of the Energy Policy Act of 2005 to which they relate.
(2) **Nonapplication of exemption for offhighway business use.** The amendment made by subsection (d)(3) shall apply to fuel sold for use or used after the date of the enactment of this Act.
(3) **Amendment made by the SAFETEA-LU.** The amendment made by subsection (d)(2)(C)(ii) shall take effect as if included in section 11161 of the SAFETEA-LU.

[¶ 4042] Sec. 7. Amendments related to the American Jobs Creation Act of 2004.
* * * * * * * * * *

(1) **Effective date.**
(1) **In general.** Except as otherwise provided in this subsection, the amendments made by this section shall take effect as if included in the provisions of the American Jobs Creation Act of 2004 to which they relate.
(2) **Identification requirement of amendment related to section 888 of the American Jobs Creation Act of 2004.** The amendment made by subsection (d)(2)(A) shall apply to straddles acquired after the date of the enactment of this Act.

[¶ 4043] Sec. 8. Amendments related to the Economic Growth and Tax Relief Reconciliation Act of 2001.

* * * * * * * * * *

(b) Effective date. The amendments made by this section shall take effect as if included in the provisions of the Economic Growth and Tax Relief Reconciliation Act of 2001 to which they relate.

[¶ 4044] Sec. 9. Amendments related to the Tax Relief Extension Act of 1999.
* * * * * * * * * *

(c) Effective date. The amendments made by this section shall take effect as if included in the provisions of the Tax Relief Extension Act of 1999 to which they relate.

[¶ 4045] Sec. 10. Amendment related to the Internal Revenue Service Restructuring and Reform Act of 1998.
* * * * * * * * * *

(b) Effective date. The amendment made by this section shall take effect as if included in the provision of the Internal Revenue Service Restructuring and Reform Act of 1998 to which it relates.

[¶ 4046] Sec. 11. Clerical corrections.
* * * * * * * * * *

(b) Clerical amendments related to the Tax Relief and Health Care Act of 2006.
* * * * * * * * * *
(3) Effective date. The amendments made by this subsection shall take effect as if included in the provision of the Tax Relief and Health Care Act of 2006 to which they relate.

(c) Clerical amendments related to the Gulf Opportunity Zone Act of 2005.
* * * * * * * * * *
(2) Effective date. The amendments made by this subsection shall take effect as if included in the provisions of the Gulf Opportunity Zone Act of 2005 to which they relate.

(d) Clerical amendments related to the Safe, Accountable, Flexible, Efficient Transportation Equity Act: a Legacy for Users.
* * * * * * * * * *
(2) Effective date. The amendments made by this subsection shall take effect as if included in the provisions of the Safe, Accountable, Flexible, Efficient Transportation Equity Act: A Legacy for Users to which they relate.

(e) Clerical amendments related to the Energy Policy Act of 2005.
* * * * * * * * * *
(3) Effective date. The amendments made by this subsection shall take effect as if included in the provisions of the Energy Policy Act of 2005 to which they relate.

(f) Clerical amendments related to the American Jobs Creation Act of 2004.
* * * * * * * * * *
(4) Effective date. The amendments made by this subsection shall take effect as if included in the provisions of the American Jobs Creation Act of 2004 to which they relate.

Exclusion from Income for Payments from the Hokie Spirit Memorial Fund

One Hundred Tenth Congress

1st Session

P.L. 110-141

Act sections of the Exclusion from Income for Payments from the Hokie Spirit Memorial Fund, P.L. 110-141, or portions thereof, that do not amend specific Internal Revenue Code sections follow. Sections of the Internal Revenue Code as amended are reproduced at *Code as Amended.*

[¶ 4051] Sec. 1. Exclusion from income for payments from the Hokie Spirit Memorial Fund. For purposes of the Internal Revenue Code of 1986, gross income shall not include any amount received from the Virginia Polytechnic Institute & State University, out of amounts transferred from the Hokie Spirit Memorial Fund established by the Virginia Tech Foundation, an organization organized and operated as described in section 501(c)(3) of the Internal Revenue Code of 1986, if such amount is paid on account of the tragic event on April 16, 2007, at such university.

[¶ 4052] Sec. 2. Modification of penalty for failure to file partnership returns. For any return of a partnership required to be filed under section 6031 of the Internal Revenue Code of 1986 for a taxable year beginning in 2008, the dollar amount in effect under section 6698(b)(1) of such Code shall be increased by $1.

Consolidated Appropriations Act, 2008
One Hundred Tenth Congress
1st Session
P.L. 110-161

Act sections of the Consolidated Appropriations Act, 2008, P.L. 110-161, or portions thereof, that do not amend specific Internal Revenue Code sections follow. Sections of the Internal Revenue Code as amended are reproduced at *Code as Amended.*

[¶ 4056] **Sec. 1. Short title.** This Act may be cited as the "Consolidated Appropriations Act, 2008".

* * * * * * * * * *

[¶ 4057] **Sec. 116. Extension of taxes and expenditure authority relating to Airport and Airway Trust Fund.**

(d) Effective date. The amendments made by this section shall take effect on October 1, 2007.

Economic Stimulus Act of 2008
One Hundred Tenth Congress
2nd Session
P.L. 110-185

Act sections of the Economic Stimulus Act of 2008, P.L. 110-185, or portions thereof, that do not amend specific Internal Revenue Code sections follow. Sections of the Internal Revenue Code as amended are reproduced at *Code as Amended.*

[¶ 4066] Sec. 1. Short title.

(a) Short Title. This Act may be cited as the "Economic Stimulus Act of 2008".

* * * * * * * * * * * *

[¶ 4067] Sec. 101. 2008 Recovery rebates for individuals.

* * * * * * * * * * * *

(c) Treatment of possessions.
  (a) Payments to possessions.
   (A) Mirror code possession. The Secretary of the Treasury shall make a payment to each possession of the United States with a mirror code tax system in an amount equal to the loss to that possession by reason of the amendments made by this section. Such amount shall be determined by the Secretary of the Treasury based on information provided by the government of the respective possession.

   (B) Other possessions. The Secretary of the Treasury shall make a payment to each possession of the United States which does not have a mirror code tax system in an amount estimated by the Secretary of the Treasury as being equal to the aggregate benefits that would have been provided to residents of such possession by reason of the amendments made by this section if a mirror code tax system had been in effect in such possession. The preceding sentence shall not apply with respect to any possession of the United States unless such possession has a plan, which has been approved by the Secretary of the Treasury, under which such possession will promptly distribute such payment to the residents of such possession.

  (2) Coordination with credit allowed against United States income taxes. No credit shall be allowed against United States income taxes under section 6428 of the Internal Revenue Code of 1986 (as amended by this section) to any person--
   (A) to whom a credit is allowed against taxes imposed by the possession by reason of the amendments made by this section, or
   (B) who is eligible for a payment under a plan described in paragraph (1)(B).

  (3) Definitions and special rules.
   (A) Possession of the United States. For purposes of this subsection, the term "possession of the United States" includes the Commonwealth of Puerto Rico and the Commonwealth of the Northern Mariana Islands.

   (B) Mirror code tax system. For purposes of this subsection, the term "mirror code tax system" means, with respect to any possession of the United States, the income tax system of such possession if the income tax liability of the residents of such possession under such system is determined by reference to the income tax laws of the United States as if such possession were the United States.

   (C) Treatment of payments. For purposes of section 1324(b)(2) of title 31, United States Code, the payments under this subsection shall be treated in the same manner as a refund due from the credit allowed under section 6428 of the Internal Revenue Code of 1986 (as amended by this section).

**(d) Refunds Disregarded in the Administration of Federal Programs and Federally As-
sisted Programs.** Any credit or refund allowed or made to any individual by reason of
section 6428 of the Internal Revenue Code of 1986 (as amended by this section) or by reason
of subsection (c) of this section shall not be taken into account as income and shall not be
taken into account as resources for the month of receipt and the following 2 months, for purposes of determining the eligibility of such individual or any other individual for benefits or
assistance, or the amount or extent of benefits or assistance, under any Federal program or
under any State or local program financed in whole or in part with Federal funds.

(e) Appropriations to carry out rebates.
(1) In general. Immediately upon the enactment of this Act, the following sums are appropriated, out of any money in the Treasury not otherwise appropriated, for the fiscal year
ending September 30, 2008:
(A) Department of the Treasury.
(i) For an additional amount for "Department of the Treasury--Financial Management
Service--Salaries and Expenses", $64,175,000, to remain available until September 30,
2009.
(ii) For an additional amount for "Department of the Treasury--Internal Revenue Ser-
vice--Taxpayer Services", $50,720,000, to remain available until September 30, 2009.
(iii) For an additional amount for "Department of the Treasury--Internal Revenue Ser-
vice--Operations Support", $151,415,000, to remain available until September 30,
2009.
(B) Social Security Administration. For an additional amount for "Social Security Ad-
ministration--Limitation on Administrative Expenses", $31,000,000, to remain available
until September 30, 2008.
(2) Reports. No later than 15 days after enactment of this Act, the Secretary of the Treasury shall submit a plan to the Committees on Appropriations of the House of Representatives and the Senate detailing the expected use of the funds provided by paragraph (1)(A).
Beginning 90 days after enactment of this Act, the Secretary of the Treasury shall submit a
quarterly report to the Committees on Appropriations of the House of Representatives and
the Senate detailing the actual expenditure of funds provided by paragraph (1)(A) and the
expected expenditure of such funds in the subsequent quarter.

**[¶ 4068] Sec. 102. Temporary increase in limitations on expensing of certain depreciable
business assets.**
* * * * * * * * * * * *

(b) Effective date. The amendment made by this section shall apply to taxable years beginning after December 31, 2007.

[¶ 4069] Sec. 103. Special allowance for certain property acquired during 2008.
* * * * * * * * * * * *

(d) Effective Date. The amendments made by this section shall apply to property placed in
service after December 31, 2007, in taxable years ending after such date.

[¶ 5000] Congressional Committee Reports Accompanying the Mortgage Forgiveness Debt Relief Act of 2007

This section, in ¶ 5001 through ¶ 5004, reproduces all relevant parts of the House Report (H. Rept. 110-356, 10/1/2007) accompanying H.R. 3648, the Mortgage Forgiveness Debt Relief Act of 2007 (P.L. 110-142, 12/20/2007). Also reproduced is a relevant provision from the Joint Committee on Taxation Description of the Chairman's Amendment in the Nature of a Substitute to H.R. 3997, the Heroes Earnings Assistance and Relief Tax Act of 2007 (JCX-107-07, 11/1/2007).

[¶ 5001]   Section 2.   Discharges of indebtedness on principal residence excluded from gross income.

(Code Sec. 108)

[House Report 110-356]

Present Law

Gross income includes income that is realized by a debtor from the discharge of indebtedness, subject to certain exceptions for debtors in Title 11 bankruptcy cases, insolvent debtors, certain student loans, certain farm indebtedness, and certain real property business indebtedness (secs. 61(a)(12) and 108).[1] In cases involving discharges of indebtedness that are excluded from gross income under the exceptions to the general rule, taxpayers generally reduce certain tax attributes, including basis in property, by the amount of the discharge of indebtedness.

The amount of discharge of indebtedness excluded from income by an insolvent debtor not in a Title 11 bankruptcy case cannot exceed the amount by which the debtor is insolvent. In the case of a discharge in bankruptcy or where the debtor is insolvent, any reduction in basis may not exceed the excess of the aggregate bases of properties held by the taxpayer immediately after the discharge over the aggregate of the liabilities immediately after the discharge (sec. 1017).

For all taxpayers, the amount of discharge of indebtedness generally is equal to the difference between the adjusted issue price of the debt being cancelled and the amount used to satisfy the debt. These rules generally apply to the exchange of an old obligation for a new obligation, including a modification of indebtedness that is treated as an exchange (a debt-for-debt exchange).

For example, assume a taxpayer who is not in bankruptcy and is not insolvent owns a principal residence subject to a $200,000 mortgage debt. If the creditor forecloses and the home is sold for $180,000 in satisfaction of the debt, the debtor has $20,000 income from the discharge of indebtedness which is includible in gross income. Likewise, if the creditor restructures the loan and reduces the principal amount to $180,000, the debtor has $20,000 includible in gross income.

Reasons for Change

The Committee believes that where taxpayers restructure their acquisition debt on a principal residence or lose their principal residence in a foreclosure, that it is inappropriate to treat discharges of acquisition indebtedness as income.

Explanation of Provision

The bill excludes from the gross income of a taxpayer any discharge of indebtedness income by reason of a discharge (in whole or in part) of qualified principal residence in-

---

1. A debt cancellation which constitutes a gift or bequest is not treated as income to the donee debtor (sec. 102).

debtedness. Qualified principal residence indebtedness means acquisition indebtedness (within the meaning of section 163(h)(3)(B) without regard to any dollar limitation) with respect to the taxpayer's principal residence. Acquisition indebtedness with respect to a principal residence generally means indebtedness which is incurred in the acquisition, construction, or substantial improvement of the principal residence of the individual and is secured by the residence. It also includes refinancing of such indebtedness to the extent the amount of the refinancing does not exceed the amount of the refinanced indebtedness. For these purposes the term "principal residence" has the same meaning as under section 121 of the Code.

If, immediately before the discharge, only a portion of a discharged indebtedness is qualified principal residence indebtedness, the exclusion applies only to so much of the amount discharged as exceeds the portion of the debt which is not qualified principal residence indebtedness. Thus, assume that a principal residence is secured by an indebtedness of $1 million, of which $800,000 is qualified principal residence indebtedness. If the residence is sold for $700,000 and $300,000 debt is discharged, then only $100,000 of the amount discharged may be excluded from gross income under this provision.

The basis of the individual's principal residence is reduced by the amount excluded from income under the bill.

Under the bill, the exclusion does not apply to a taxpayer in a Title 11 case; instead the present-law exclusion applies. In the case of an insolvent taxpayer not in a Title 11 case, the exclusion under the bill applies unless the taxpayer elects to have the present-law exclusion apply instead.

Under the bill, the exclusion does not apply to the discharge of a loan if the discharge is on account of services performed for the lender.

Effective Date

The provision is effective for discharges of indebtedness on or after January 1, 2007.

[¶ 5002]   Section 4.   Alternative tests for qualifying as cooperative housing corporation.

(Code Sec. 216)

[House Report 110-356]

Present Law

A tenant-stockholder in a cooperative housing corporation is entitled to deduct amounts paid or accrued to the cooperative to the extent those amounts represent the tenant-stockholder's proportionate share of (1) real estate taxes allowable as a deduction to the cooperative which are paid or incurred by the cooperative on the cooperative's land or buildings and (2) interest allowable as a deduction to the cooperative that is paid or incurred by the cooperative on its indebtedness contracted in the acquisition of the cooperative's land or in the acquisition, construction, alteration, rehabilitation, or maintenance of the cooperative's buildings.

A cooperative housing corporation generally is a corporation (1) that has one class of stock, (2) each of the stockholders of which is entitled, solely by reason of ownership of stock in the corporation, to occupy a dwelling owned or leased by the cooperative, (3) no stockholder of which is entitled to receive any distribution not out of earnings and profits of the cooperative, except on complete or partial liquidation of the cooperative, and (4) 80 percent or more of the gross income of which for the taxable year in which the taxes and interest are paid or incurred is derived from tenant-stockholders.

Reasons for Change

Under present law, tenant-stockholders of a cooperative housing corporation are allowed to deduct their proportionate shares of the cooperative's deductible real estate taxes and mortgage interest only if the cooperative's nonmember income is no more than 20 percent of its total gross income. To satisfy this rule, some cooperative housing corporations have made rentals to commercial tenants at below-market rates. The Committee believes that the tax rules should not create an incentive to charge below-market-rate rents. Accordingly, the Committee's bill provides two non-income-based alternatives to the 80-percent requirement of present law.

Explanation of Provision

The provision amends the fourth requirement listed above to provide that the requirement is satisfied if, for the taxable year in which the taxes and interest are paid or incurred, the corporation meets one of the following three requirements: (1) 80 percent or more of the corporation's gross income for that taxable year is derived from tenant-stockholders (the present law requirement); (2) at all times during that table year 80 percent or more of the total square footage of the corporation's property is used or available for use by the tenant-stockholders for residential purposes or purposes ancillary to such residential use; or (3) 90 percent or more of the expenditures of the corporation paid or incurred during that taxable year are paid or incurred for the acquisition, construction, management, maintenance, or care of the corporation's property for the benefit of tenant-stockholders.

Effective Date

The provision is effective for taxable years ending after the date of enactment.

[¶ 5003]   Section 5.   Exclusion from income for benefits provided to volunteer firefighters and emergency medical responders.

(Code Sec. 139B)

[Joint Committee on Taxation Report — JCX-107-07]

Certain tax reductions or tax rebates provided by a State or local government

The Internal Revenue Service has provided guidance[11] that reductions or rebates of taxes by State or local governments on account of services performed by members of qualified volunteer emergency response organizations are taxable income to the taxpayers receiving these reductions or rebates of taxes.

Deduction for certain State or local taxes

For purposes of determining regular tax liability, an itemized deduction is permitted for certain State and local taxes paid, including individual income taxes, real property taxes, and personal property taxes. The itemized deduction is not permitted for purposes of determining a taxpayer's alternative minimum taxable income. For taxable years beginning before January 1, 2008, at the election of the taxpayer, an itemized deduction may be taken for State and local general sales taxes in lieu of the itemized deduction provided under present law for State and local income taxes.

The otherwise allowable itemized deduction for these State or local taxes is not reduced by the amount of any reduction or rebate on account of services performed as a member of a qualified volunteer emergency response organization.

---

11. Chief Couns. Adv. 200302045 (Jan. 10, 2002)

Charitable deduction for certain expenses

In computing taxable income, a taxpayer who itemizes deductions generally is allowed to deduct the amount of cash and the fair market value of property contributed to an organization described in section 501(c)(3), to a Federal, State, or local governmental entity, or to certain other organizations.[12] The amount of the deduction allowable for a taxable year with respect to a charitable contribution of property may be reduced or limited depending on the type of property contributed, the type of charitable organization to which the property is contributed, and the income of the taxpayer. Within certain limitations, donors also are entitled to deduct their contributions to section 501(c)(3) organizations for Federal estate and gift tax purposes.

Description of Proposal

Certain tax reductions or tax rebates provided by a State or local government

The bill provides an exclusion from gross income to members of qualified volunteer emergency response organizations for: (1) any qualified State or local tax benefit; and (2) any qualified reimbursement payment. A qualified State or local tax benefit is any reduction or rebate of certain taxes provided by State or local governments on account of services performed by individuals as members of a qualified volunteer emergency response organization. These taxes are limited to State or local income taxes, State or local real property taxes, and State or local personal property taxes. A qualified reimbursement payment is a payment provided by a State or political subdivision thereof on account of reimbursement for expenses incurred in connection with the performance of services as a member of a qualified volunteer emergency response organization. The amount of such qualified reimbursement payments is limited to $30 for each month during which the taxpayer performs such services.

A qualified volunteer emergency response organization is any volunteer organization: (1) which is organized and operated to provide firefighting or emergency medical services for persons in the State or its political subdivision; and (2) which is required (by written agreement) by the State or political subdivision to furnish firefighting or emergency medical services in such State or political subdivision.

Denial of double benefits

The bill provides that the amount of State or local taxes taken into account in determining the deduction for taxes is reduced by the amount of any qualified State or local tax benefit.

Also, the bill provides that expenses paid or incurred by the taxpayer in connection with the performance of services as a member of a qualified volunteer emergency response organization are taken into account for purposes of the charitable deduction only to the extent such expenses exceed the amount of any qualified reimbursement payment excluded from income under the bill.

Effective Date

The provision is effective for taxable years beginning after the date of enactment.

---

12. Sec. 170(a), (c), and (e).

[¶ 5004]   Section 10.   Modification of required installment of corporate esti-mated taxes with respect to certain dates.

(Code Sec. None)

[House Report 110-356]

Present Law

In general, corporations are required to make quarterly estimated tax payments of their income tax liability. For a corporation whose taxable year is a calendar year, these estimated tax payments must be made by April 15, June 15, September 15, and December 15.

Reasons for Change

The Committee believes it is appropriate to adjust the corporate estimated tax payments.

Effective Date

The provision is effective on the date of enactment.

[¶ 5100] Joint Committee on Taxation Technical Explanation Accompanying the Energy Independence and Security Act of 2007

This section, in ¶ 5101 and ¶ 5102, reproduces all relevant parts of the Joint Committee on Taxation Technical Explanation (JCX-111-07, 12/12/2007) of the Revenue Provisions contained in Title XV of H.R. 6, the Energy Independence and Security Act of 2007 (P.L. 110-140, 12/19/2007).

[¶ 5101]   Section 1501.   Extension of additional 0.2 percent FUTA surtax.

(Code Sec. 3301)

[Joint Committee on Taxation Report — JCX-111-07]

Present Law

The Federal Unemployment Tax Act ("FUTA") imposes a 6.2 percent gross tax rate on the first $7,000 paid annually by covered employers to each employee. Employers in States with programs approved by the Federal Government and with no delinquent Federal loans may credit 5.4 percentage points against the 6.2 percent tax rate, making the minimum, net Federal unemployment tax rate 0.8 percent. Since all States have approved programs, 0.8 percent is the Federal tax rate that generally applies. This Federal revenue finances administration of the unemployment system, half of the Federal-State extended benefits program, and a Federal account for State loans. The States use the revenue turned back to them by the 5.4 percent credit to finance their regular State programs and half of the Federal-State extended benefits program.

In 1976, Congress passed a temporary surtax of 0.2 percent of taxable wages to be added to the permanent FUTA tax rate. Thus, the current 0.8 percent FUTA tax rate has two components: a permanent tax rate of 0.6 percent, and a temporary surtax rate of 0.2 percent. The temporary surtax subsequently has been extended through 2007.

Explanation of Provision

The provision extends the temporary surtax rate through December 31, 2008.

Effective Date

The provision is effective for labor performed on or after January 1, 2008.

[¶ 5102]   Section 1502.   7-year amortization of geological and geophysical expenditures for certain major integrated oil companies.

(Code Sec. 167)

[Joint Committee on Taxation Report — JCX-111-07]

Present Law

Geological and geophysical expenditures ("G&G costs") are costs incurred by a taxpayer for the purpose of obtaining and accumulating data that will serve as the basis for the acquisition and retention of mineral properties by taxpayers exploring for minerals. G&G costs incurred by independent producers and smaller integrated oil[158] companies in connection with oil and gas exploration in the United States may generally be amortized over two years.[159] Major integrated oil companies are required to amortize all

---

158. Generally, an integrated oil company is a producer of crude oil that engages in the refining or retail sale of petroleum products in excess of certain threshold amounts.
159. Sec. 167(h)(1).

G&G costs over five years.[160] For purposes of this proposal, a major integrated oil company, with respect to any taxable year, is a producer of crude oil which has an average daily worldwide production of crude oil of at least 500,000 barrels for the taxable year, had gross receipts in excess of one billion dollars for its last taxable year ending during the calendar year 2005, and generally has an ownership interest in a crude oil refiner of 15 percent or more.[161]

In the case of abandoned property, remaining basis may not be recovered in the year of abandonment of a property as all basis is recovered over the applicable amortization period.

Explanation of Provision

The provision extends from five years to seven years the amortization period for G&G costs for major integrated oil companies.

Effective Date

The provision is effective for amounts paid or incurred after the date of enactment.

---

160. Sec. 167(h)(5).
161. Id.

[¶ 5200] **Congressional Committee Reports Accompanying the Tax Increase Prevention Act of 2007**

This section, in ¶ 5201, reproduces all relevant parts of the House Report (H. Rept. No. 110-431, 11/6/2007) accompanying H.R. 3996, as amended by the Senate, the Tax Increase Prevention Act of 2007 (P.L. 110-166, 12/26/2007).

[¶ 5201]   **Section 2, 3.   Extension of increased alternative minimum tax exemption amount; Extension of alternative minimum tax relief for nonrefundable personal credits.**

(Code Sec. 55, 26)

[House Report 110-431]

Present Law

Present law imposes an alternative minimum tax on individuals. The alternative minimum tax is the amount by which the tentative minimum tax exceeds the regular income tax. An individual's tentative minimum tax is the sum of (1) 26 percent of so much of the taxable excess as does not exceed $175,000 ($87,500 in the case of a married individual filing a separate return) and (2) 28 percent of the remaining taxable excess. The taxable excess is so much of the alternative minimum taxable income ("AMTI") as exceeds the exemption amount. The maximum tax rates on net capital gain and dividends used in computing the regular tax are used in computing the tentative minimum tax. AMTI is the individual's taxable income adjusted to take account of specified preferences and adjustments.

The present exemption amount is: (1) $62,550 ($45,000 in taxable years beginning after 2006) in the case of married individuals filing a joint return and surviving spouses; (2) $42,500 ($33,750 in taxable years beginning after 2006) in the case of other unmarried individuals; (3) $31,275 ($22,500 in taxable years beginning after 2006) in the case of married individuals filing separate returns; and (4) $22,500 in the case of an estate or trust. The exemption amount is phased out by an amount equal to 25 percent of the amount by which the individual's AMTI exceeds (1) $150,000 in the case of married individuals filing a joint return and surviving spouses, (2) $112,500 in the case of other unmarried individuals, and (3) $75,000 in the case of married individuals filing separate returns or an estate or a trust. These amounts are not indexed for inflation.

Present law provides for certain nonrefundable personal tax credits (i.e., the dependent care credit, the credit for the elderly and disabled, the adoption credit, the child tax credit, the credit for interest on certain home mortgages, the HOPE Scholarship and Lifetime Learning credits, the credit for savers, the credit for certain nonbusiness energy property, the credit for residential energy efficient property, and the D.C. first-time homebuyer credit).

For taxable years beginning before 2007, the nonrefundable personal credits are allowed to the extent of the full amount of the individual's regular tax and alternative minimum tax.

For taxable years beginning after 2006, the nonrefundable personal credits (other than the adoption credit, child credit and saver's credit) are allowed only to the extent that the individual's regular income tax liability exceeds the individual's tentative minimum tax, determined without regard to the minimum tax foreign tax credit. The adoption credit, child credit, and saver's credit are allowed to the full extent of the individual's regular tax and alternative minimum tax.[1]

Reasons for Change

The Committee is concerned about the projected increase in the number of individuals who will be affected by the individual alternative minimum tax for 2007. The provision will reduce the number of individuals who would otherwise be affected be the minimum tax.

Explanation of Provision

The bill provides that the individual AMT exemption amount for taxable years beginning in 2007 is (1) $66,250, in the case of married individuals filing a joint return and surviving spouses; (2) $44,350 in the case of other unmarried individuals; and (3) $33,125 in the case of married individuals filing separate returns.

For taxable years beginning in 2007, the bill allows an individual to offset the entire regular tax liability and alternative minimum tax liability by the nonrefundable personal credits.

Effective Date

The provision is effective for taxable years beginning in 2007.

---

1. The rule applicable to the adoption credit and child credit is subject to the EGTRRA sunset.

[¶ 5300] Joint Committee on Taxation Description Accompanying the Tax Technical Corrections Act of 2007

This section, in ¶ 5301 through ¶ 5310, reproduces all relevant parts of the Joint Committee on Taxation Description (JCX-119-07, 12/18/2007) accompanying H.R. 4829, the Tax Technical Corrections Act of 2007 (P.L. 110-172, 12/29/2007).

[¶ 5301]   Section 2.   Amendment related to the Tax Relief and Health Care Act of 2006.

(Code Sec. 53)

[Joint Committee on Taxation Report — JCX-119-07]

Individuals with long-term unused credits under the alternative minimum tax (Act sec. 402 of Division A).

Under present law, an individual's minimum tax credit allowable for any taxable year beginning after December 20, 2006, and before January 1, 2013, is not less than the "AMT refundable credit amount." The AMT refundable credit amount is the greater of (1) the lesser of $5,000 or the long-term unused minimum tax credit, or (2) 20 percent of the long-term unused minimum tax credit. The long-term unused minimum tax credit for any taxable year means the portion of the minimum tax credit attributable to the adjusted net minimum tax for taxable years before the 3rd taxable year immediately preceding the taxable year (assuming the credits are used on a first-in, first-out basis). In the case of an individual whose adjusted gross income for a taxable year exceeds the threshold amount (within the meaning of section 151(d)(3)(C)), the AMT refundable credit amount is reduced by the applicable percentage (within the meaning of section 151(d)(3)(B)). The additional credit allowable by reason of this provision is refundable.

The provision amends the definition of the AMT refundable credit amount. The provision provides that the AMT refundable credit amount (before any reduction by reason of adjusted gross income) is an amount (not in excess of the long-term unused minimum tax credit) equal to the greater of (1) $5,000, (2) 20 percent of the long-term unused minimum tax credit, or (3) the AMT refundable credit amount (if any) for the prior taxable year (before any reduction by reason of adjusted gross income).

The provision may be illustrated by the following example: Assume an individual, whose adjusted gross income for all taxable years is less than the threshold amount, has a long-term unused minimum tax credit for 2007 of $100,000 and has no other minimum tax credits. The individual's AMT refundable credit amount under present law is $20,000 in 2007, $16,000 in 2008, $10,240 in 2009, $8,192 in 2010, $6,554 in 2011, and $5,243 in 2012. Under the provision, the individual's AMT refundable credit amount is $20,000 for 2007 (as under present law), and in each of the taxable years 2008 thru 2011 the AMT refundable credit amount is also $20,000. The minimum tax credit in 2012 is zero.

[¶ 5302]   Section 3.   Amendments related to title XII of the Pension Protection Act of 2006.

(Code Sec. 408, 1366, 170, 2055, 2522, 6695A, 6696, 4940, 6104, 4962, 4958)

[Joint Committee on Taxation Report — JCX-119-07]

Tax-free distributions from individual retirement plans for charitable purposes (Act sec. 1201).

Under the provision, when determining the portion of a distribution that would otherwise be includible in income, the otherwise includible amount is determined as if all amounts were distributed from all of the individual's IRAs.

Contributions of appreciated property by S corporations (Act sec. 1203).

Under present law (sec. 1366(d)), the amount of losses and deductions which a shareholder of an S corporation may take into account in any taxable year is limited to the shareholder's adjusted basis in his stock and indebtedness of the corporation. The provision provides that this basis limitation does not apply to a contribution of appreciated property to the extent the shareholder's pro rata share of the contribution exceeds the shareholder's pro rata share of the adjusted basis of the property. Thus, the basis limitation of section 1366(d) does not apply to the amount of deductible appreciation in the contributed property. The provision does not apply to contributions made in taxable years beginning after December 31, 2007.

For example, assume that in taxable year 2007, an S corporation with one shareholder makes a charitable contribution of a capital asset held more than one year with an adjusted basis of $200 and a fair market value of $500. Assume the shareholder's adjusted basis of the stock (as determined under section 1366(d)(1)(A)) is $300. For purposes of applying the limitation under section 1366(d) to the contribution, the limitation does not apply to the $300 of appreciation and since the $300 adjusted basis of the stock exceeds the $200 adjusted basis of the contributed property, the limitation does not apply at all to the contribution. Thus, the shareholder is treated as making a $500 charitable contribution. The shareholder reduces the basis of the S corporation stock by $200 to $100 (pursuant to section 1367(a)(2)).

Recapture of tax benefit for charitable contributions of exempt use property not used for an exempt use (Act sec. 1215).

The Act permits a charitable deduction in the amount of the fair market value (not the donor's basis) for tangible personal property if an officer of the donee organization certifies upon disposition of the donated property that the use of the property was related to the purpose or function constituting the basis of the donee's tax-exempt status. It was not intended that the donee's use, though so related, not also be substantial. The provision adds to the certification requirement that the officer certify that use of the property by the donee was substantial.

Contributions of fractional interests in tangible personal property (Act sec. 1218).

The Act added an income tax provision providing for treatment of contributions of fractional interests in tangible personal property. A special valuation rule is provided under this rule that creates unintended consequences under the estate and gift tax. The provision therefore strikes the special valuation rule for estate and gift tax purposes.

Time for assessment of penalty relating to substantial and gross valuation misstatements attributable to incorrect appraisals (Act section 1219).

Section 1219 of the Act added a penalty for substantial and gross valuation misstatements attributable to incorrect appraisals (Code sec. 6695A). First, the Act omitted to apply the penalty with respect to substantial valuation misstatements for estate and gift tax purposes, and the provision clarifies that the penalty applies for such purposes. Second, in the cross references for the penalty, the language of Code section 6696(d)(1), relating to the time period for assessment of the penalty, was not properly described. The provision adds a cross reference to section 6695A in section 6696(d).

Expansion of the base of tax on private foundation net investment income (Act sec. 1221).

The Act expands the base of the tax on net investment income of private foundations. The provision clarifies that capital gains from appreciation are included in this tax base. This clarification conforms the statutory language to the technical explanation.

Public disclosure of information relating to unrelated business income tax returns (Act sec. 1225).

The Act added a provision requiring that section 501(c)(3) organizations make publicly available their unrelated business income tax returns. However, as drafted, the requirement that, with respect to a Form 990, an organization make publicly available only the last three years of returns (sec. 6104(d)(2)) does not apply to disclosure of Form 990-T, because Form 990-T is required by section 6011, not by section 6033. The provision clarifies that the 3-year limitation on making returns publicly available applies to Form 990-T. The provision clarifies that the IRS is required to make Form 990-T publicly available, subject to redaction procedures applicable to Form 990 under section 6104(b).

Donor advised funds (Act [sic, sec.] 1231).

The Act imposed excise taxes in the event of certain taxable distributions (Code sec. 4966) and on the provision of certain prohibited benefits (sec. 4967), but does not cross refer to these provisions in the section 4962 definition of qualified first tier taxes for purposes of tax abatement (though a cross reference to them is included in section 4963). The provision adds a cross reference to them in Code section 4962 (relating to abatement).

Excess benefit transactions involving supporting organizations (Act sec. 1242).

New Code section 4958(c)(3) provides that certain transactions involving supporting organizations are treated as excess benefit transactions for purposes of the intermediate sanctions rules. Under the Code, certain organizations described in Code sections 501(c)(4), (5) or (6) are treated as supported organizations, although they are not public charities or safety organizations. The provision provides that the excess benefit transaction rules of the Act generally do not apply to transactions between a supporting organization and its supported organization that is described in section 501(c)(4), (5), or (6).

[¶ 5303]   Section 4.   Amendments related to the Tax Increase Prevention and Reconciliation Act of 2005.

(Code Sec. 954, 355, 911)

[Joint Committee on Taxation Report — JCX-119-07]

Look-through treatment and regulatory authority (Act sec. 103(b)).

Under the Act, for taxable years beginning after 2005 and before 2009, dividends, interest (including factoring income which is treated as equivalent to interest under sec. 954(c)(1)(E)), rents, and royalties received by one controlled foreign corporation ("CFC") from a related CFC are not treated as foreign personal holding company income to the extent attributable or properly allocable to non-subpart F income of the payor (the "TIPRA look-through rule").

The provision clarifies the treatment of deficits in earnings and profits. Under the provision, the TIPRA look-through rule does not apply to any interest, rent, or royalty to the extent that such interest, rent, or royalty creates (or increases) a deficit which under section 952(c) may reduce the subpart F income of the payor or another CFC. The provision parallels the rule applicable to interest, rents, or royalties that would otherwise qualify for exclusion from foreign personal holding company income under the "same country" exception (sec. 954(c)(3)(B)). Thus interest, rents, and royalties will be treated as subpart F income, notwithstanding the general TIPRA look-through rule, if the payment creates or increases a deficit of the payor corporation and that deficit is from an activity that could reduce the payor's subpart F income under the accumulated deficit rule (sec. 952(c)(1)(B)), or could reduce the income of a qualified chain member under the chain deficit rule (sec. 952(c)(1)(C)). For example, under the provision, items that do not qualify for the "same country" exception because they meet the terms of section 954(c)(3)(B) will also not qualify under the TIPRA look-through rule.

Modification of active business definition under section 355 (Act sec. 202).

The provision revises Code sections 355(b)(2)(A) and 355(b)(3) to reflect that the provision modifying the active business definition that was enacted by section 202 of the Act was made permanent by section 410 of the Tax Relief and Health Care Act of 2006. Conforming amendments are made as a result of this change.

The provision clarifies that if a corporation became a member of a separate affiliated group as a result of one or more transactions in which gain or loss was recognized in whole or in part, any trade or business conducted by such corporation (at the time that such corporation became such a member) is treated for purposes of section 355(b)(2) as acquired in a transaction in which gain or loss was recognized in whole or in part. Accordingly, such an acquisition is subject to the provisions of section 355(b)(2)(C), and may qualify as an expansion of an existing active trade or business conducted by the distributing corporation or the controlled corporation, as the case may be.

The provision clarifies that the Treasury Department shall prescribe regulations that provide for the proper application of sections 355(b)(2)(B), (C), and (D) in the case of any corporation that is tested for active business under the separate affiliated group rule, and that modify the application of section 355(a)(3)(B) in the case of such a corporation in a manner consistent with the purposes of the provision.

The provision further clarifies that the rule regarding the application of the new rules to determine the continued qualification under section 355 of a distribution that occurred before the effective date of the new rules, shall apply only if such application results in continued qualification and is not intended to require application of the new rules in a manner that would disqualify any distribution that satisfied the active business requirements of section 355 under prior law that was applicable to the distribution.

Computation of tax for individuals with income excluded under the foreign earned income exclusion (Act sec. 515).

The provision clarifies that in computing the tentative minimum tax on nonexcluded income, the computation of tax is made before reduction for the alternative minimum tax foreign tax credit. This conforms the computation of the tentative minimum tax to the computation of the regular tax, so that both computations are made before the application of the foreign tax credit.

The provision also corrects an error in present law in the case where a taxpayer has net capital gain in excess of taxable income. Under the provision, if a taxpayer's net capital gain (within the meaning of section 1(h)) exceeds taxable income, in computing the tax on the taxable income as increased by the excluded income, the amount of net capital gain which otherwise be taken into account is reduced by the amount of that excess. The excess first reduces the amount of net capital gain without regard to qualified dividend income, and then qualified dividend income. Also, in computing adjusted net capital gain, unrecaptured section 1250 gain, and 28-percent rate gain, the amount of the excess is treated in the same manner as an increase in the long-term capital loss carried to the taxable year.

Similar rules apply in computing the tentative minimum tax where a taxpayer's net capital gain exceeds the taxable excess.

The provision is effective for taxable years beginning after December 31, 2006.

The following examples illustrate the provision:

Example 1.—For taxable year 2007, an unmarried individual has $80,000 excluded from gross income under section 911(a), $30,000 gain from the sale of a capital asset held more than one year, and $20,000 deductions. The taxpayer's taxable income is $10,000. Under the provision, the regular tax is the excess of (i) the amount of tax computed under section 911(f)(1)(A)(i) on taxable income of $90,000 ($10,000 taxable income plus $80,000 excluded income), over (ii) the amount of tax computed under section 911(f)(1)(A)(ii) on taxable income of $80,000 (excluded income). In applying section 1(h) to determine the tax under section 911(f)(1)(A)(i), the net capital gain and the adjusted net capital gain are each $10,000. The regular tax is $1,500, which is equal to a tax at the rate of 15 percent on $10,000 of adjusted net capital gain.

Example 2.—For taxable year 2007, an unmarried individual has $90,000 excluded from gross income under section 911(a), $5,000 gain from the sale of a capital asset held more than one year, $25,000 unrecaptured section 1250 gain, and $20,000 deductions. The taxpayer's taxable income is $10,000. Under the provision, the regular tax is the excess of (i) the amount of tax computed under section 911(f)(1)(A)(i) on taxable income of $100,000 ($10,000 taxable income plus $90,000 excluded income), over (ii) the amount of tax computed under section 911(f)(1)(A)(ii) on taxable income of $90,000 (excluded income). In applying section 1(h) to determine the tax under section 911(f)(1)(A)(i), the net capital gain is $10,000. $5,000 is unrecaptured section 1250 gain ($25,000 less $20,000) and $5,000 is adjusted net capital gain. The regular tax is $2,000, which is equal to a tax at the rate of 15 percent on $5,000 of adjusted net capital gain and a tax at the rate of 25 percent on $5,000 of unrecaptured section 1250 gain.

[¶5304]   Section 5.   Amendments related to the Safe, Accountable, Flexible, Efficient Transportation Equity Act: A Legacy for Users.

(Code Sec. 6427, 6426)

[Joint Committee on Taxation Report — JCX-119-07]

Timing of claims for excess alternative fuel (not in a mixture) credit (Act sec. 11113).

Present law provides that the alternative fuel (not in a mixture) credit is refundable. Code section 6427(i)(3) permits claims to be filed on a weekly basis with respect to alcohol, biodiesel, and alternative fuel mixtures if certain requirements are met. This rule, however, does not refer to the alternative fuel credit (for alternative fuel not in a mixture). The provision clarifies that the same rules for filing claims with respect to fuel mixtures apply to the alternative fuel credit.

Definition of alternative fuel (Act sec. 11113).

Code section 6426(d)(2) defines alternative fuel to include "liquid hydrocarbons from biomass" for purposes of the alternative fuel excise tax credit and payment provisions under sections 6426 and 6427. The statute does not define liquid hydrocarbons, which has led to questions as to whether it is permissible for such a fuel to contain other elements, such as oxygen, or whether the fuel must consist exclusively of hydrogen and carbon. It was intended that biomass fuels such as fish oil, which is not exclusively made of hydrogen and carbon, qualify for the credit. The provision changes the reference in section 6426 from "liquid hydrocarbons" to "liquid fuel" for purposes of the alternative fuel excise tax credit and payment provisions.

[¶ 5305]   Section 6.   Amendments related to the Energy Policy Act of 2005.

(Code Sec. 45J, 30C, 41, 4041, 4042, 4221, 4082, 4081, 6430)

[Joint Committee on Taxation Report — JCX-119-07]

Credit for production from advanced nuclear power facilities (Act sec. 1306).

The provision clarifies that the national capacity limitation of 6,000 megawatts represents the total number of megawatts that the Secretary has authority to allocate under section 45J.

Clarify limitation on the credit of installing alternative fuel refueling property (Act sec. 1342).

The present-law credit for qualified alternative fuel vehicle refueling property for a taxable year is limited to $30,000 per property subject to depreciation, and $1,000 for other property (sec. 30C(b)). The provision clarifies that the $30,000 and $1,000 limitations apply to all alternative fuel vehicle refueling property placed in service by the taxpayer at a location. The provision is consistent with similar deduction limitations imposed under section 179A(b)(2)(A) (relating to the deduction for clean-fuel vehicles and certain refueling property).

In addition, Code section 30C(c)(1) provides that qualified alternative fuel vehicle refueling property has the meaning given to the term by section 179A(d). However, section 179A(d) defines a different term. The provision modifies the language of section 30C(c)(1) to refer to the correct term.

Clarify that research eligible for the energy research credit is qualified research (Act sec. 1351).

The energy research credit is available with respect to certain amounts paid or incurred to an energy research consortium. The provision clarifies that the credit is available with respect to such amounts paid or incurred to an energy research consortium provided they are used for energy research that is qualified research.

Double taxation of rail and inland waterway fuel resulting from the use of dyed fuel on which the Leaking Underground Storage Tank Trust Fund tax has already been imposed; off-highway business use (Act sec. 1362).

Section 4081(a)(2)(B) of the Code imposes tax at the Leaking Underground Storage Tank Trust Fund financing tax rate of 0.1 cent per gallon on diesel fuel at the time it is removed from a terminal. Section 4082(a) provides that none of the generally applicable exemptions other than the exemption for export apply to this removal even if the fuel is dyed. When dyed fuel is used or sold for use in a diesel powered highway vehicle or train (sec. 4041), or such fuel is subject to the inland waterway tax (sec. 4042), the Code inadvertently imposes the Leaking Underground Storage Tank Trust Fund tax a second time. Section 6430 prohibits the refund of taxes imposed at the Leaking Underground Storage Tank Trust Fund financing rate, except in the case of fuel destined for export. The provision eliminates the imposition of the 0.1 cent tax a second time if the Leaking Underground Storage Tank Trust Fund financing tax rate previously was imposed under section 4081. The provision permits a refund in the amount of the Leaking Underground Storage Tank Trust Fund financing rate if such tax was imposed a second time under 4041 or 4042 from October 1, 2005 through the date of enactment. The provision also clarifies that off-highway business use is not exempt from the Leaking Undergound Storage Tank Trust Fund Financing rate. For administrative reasons associated with collecting the tax, the off-highway business use clarification is effective for fuel sold for use or used after the date of enactment.

Exemption from the Leaking Underground Storage Tank Trust Fund financing rate for aircraft and vessels engaged in foreign trade (Act sec. 1362).

Fuel supplied in the United States for use in aircraft engaged in foreign trade is exempt from U.S. customs duties and internal revenue taxes, so long as, where the aircraft is registered in a foreign State, the State of registry provides substantially reciprocal privileges for U.S.-registered aircraft. However, the Energy Policy Act of 2005 imposed, without exemption, the Leaking Underground Storage Tank Trust Fund financing rate on all taxable fuels, except in the case of export. As a result, aviation fuel is no longer exempt from the Leaking Underground Storage Tank Trust Fund financing rate. According to the State Department, almost all of the United States' bilateral air services agreements contain provisions exempting from taxation all fuel supplied in the territory of one party for use in the aircraft of the other party. The United States has interpreted these provisions to prohibit the taxation, in any form, of aviation fuel supplied in the United States to the aircraft of airlines of the foreign countries that are parties to these air services agreements. The amendment provides that fuel for use in vessels (including civil aircraft) employed in foreign trade or trade between the United States and any of its possessions is exempt from the Leaking Underground Storage Tank Trust Fund financing rate.

[¶ 5306]   **Section 7.   Amendments related to the American Jobs Creation Act of 2004.**

(Code Sec. 45H, 280C, 1016, 6501, 179B, 45, 470, 1092)

[Joint Committee on Taxation Report — JCX-119-07]

Interaction of rules relating to credit for low sulfur diesel fuel (Act sec. 339).

Section 45H of the Code allows a credit at the rate of 5 cents per gallon for low sulfur diesel fuel produced at certain small business refineries. The aggregate credit with respect to any refinery is limited to 25 percent of the costs of the type deductible under section 179B of the Code. Section 179B allows a deduction for 75 percent of certain costs paid or incurred with respect to these refineries. The basis of the property is reduced by the amount of any credit determined with respect to any expenditure (sec. 45H(d)). Further, no deduction is allowed for the expenses otherwise allowable as a deduction in an amount equal to the amount of the credit under section 45H (sec. 280C(d)). The interaction of these provisions is unclear, and the basis reduction and deduction denial rules may have an unintentionally duplicative effect. Under the provision, deductions are denied in an amount equal to the amount of the credit under section 45H, and the provisions of present law reducing basis and denying a deduction are repealed.

Eliminate the open-loop biomass segregation requirement in section 45(c)(3)(A)(ii) (Act sec. 710).

For purposes of the credit for electricity produced from certain renewable resources, section 45(c)(3)(A)(ii) defines open-loop biomass to include any solid, nonhazardous, cellulosic waste material or any lignin material that is segregated from other waste materials, and that meets other requirements. The Act added municipal solid waste to the category of qualified energy resources giving rise to the credit. Thus, both open-loop biomass and municipal solid waste can be treated as qualified energy resources. The provision therefore strikes the requirement that open-loop biomass be segregated from other waste materials in order to be treated as qualified energy resources.

Clarification of proportionate limitation applicable to closed-loop biomass (Act sec. 710).

Section 45(d)(2)(B)(ii) provides that when closed-loop biomass is co-fired with other fuels, the credit is limited to the otherwise allowable credit multiplied by the ratio of the thermal content of the closed-loop biomass to the thermal content of all fuel used. This limitation duplicates a similar limitation in section 45(a), which provides that the credit is equal to 1.5 cents multiplied by the kilowatt hours of electricity produced by the taxpayer from qualified energy resources (and meeting other criteria). The present-law section 45(a) rule has the effect of limiting the credit (or duration of the credit) to the appropriate portion of the fuel that constitutes qualified energy resources, in the situations in which qualified energy resources are permitted to be co-fired with each other, or are permitted to be co-fired with other fuels. The provision clarifies that the limitation applies only once, not twice, to closed-loop biomass co-fired with other fuels, by striking the duplicate limitation in section 45(d)(2)(B)(ii).

Treatment of partnerships under the limitation on deductions allocable to property used by governments or other tax-exempt entities (Act sec. 848).

Code section 470 generally applies loss deferral rules in the case of property leased to tax-exempt entities. This rule applies with respect to tax-exempt use property, which for this purpose generally has the meaning given to the term by section 168(h) (with exceptions specified in section 470(c)(2)). The manner of application of section 470 in the case of property owned by a partnership in which a tax-exempt entity is a partner is unclear.

The provision provides that tax-exempt use property does not include any property that would be tax-exempt use property solely by reason of section 168(h)(6). The provision refers to section 7701(e) for circumstances in which a partnership is treated as a lease to which section 168(h) applies. Thus, if a partnership is recharacterized as a lease pursuant to section 7701(e), and a provision of section 168(h) (other than section 168(h)(6)) applies to cause the property characterized as leased to be treated as tax-exempt use property, then the loss deferral rules of section 470 apply.

Under section 7701(e)(2), a partnership may be treated as a lease, taking into account all relevant factors, including factors similar to those set forth in section 7701(e)(1) (relating to service contracts treated as leases). In the case of property of a partnership in which a tax-exempt entity is a partner, factors similar to those in section 7701(e)(1) (and in the legislative history of that section) that are relevant in determining whether a partnership is properly treated as a lease of property held by the partnership include (1) a tax-exempt partner maintains physical possession or control or holds the benefits and burdens of ownership with respect to such property, (2) there is insignificant equity investment by any taxable partner, (3) the transfer of such property to the partnership does not result in a change in use of such property, (4) such property is necessary for the provision of government services, (5) a disproportionately large portion of the deductions for depreciation with respect to such property are allocated to one or more taxable partners relative to such partner's risk of loss with respect to such property or to such partner's allocation of other partnership items, and (6) amounts payable on behalf of the tax-exempt partner relating to the property are defeased or funded by set-asides or expected set-asides. It is intended that Treasury regulations or guidance may provide additional factors that can be taken into account in determining whether a partnership with taxable and tax-exempt partners is an arrangement that resembles a lease of property under which section 470 defers the allowance of losses.

The provision is effective as if included in the provision of the American Jobs Creation Act of 2004 to which it relates. It is not intended that the provision supercede the rules set forth by the Treasury Department in Notice 2005-29, 2005-13 I.R.B. 796, Notice 2006-2, 2006-2 I.R.B. 1, and Notice 2007-4, 2007-1 I.R.B. 260, with respect to the application of section 470 in the case of partnerships for taxable years of partnerships beginning in 2004, 2005, and 2006. These notices state that the Internal Revenue Service will not apply section 470 to disallow losses associated with property that is treated as tax-exempt use property solely as a result of the application of section 168(h)(6), and that abusive transactions involving partnerships an other pass-through entities remain subject to challenge by the Internal Revenue Service under other provisions of the tax law. Accordingly, for partnership taxable years beginning in 2004, 2005, and 2006, the Internal Revenue Service may apply section 470 to a partnership that would be treated as a lease under section 7701(e)(2).

Treatment of losses on positions in identified straddles (Act sec. 888).

Under Code section 1092, the term "straddle" means offsetting positions in actively traded personal property. Generally, a loss on a position in a straddle may be recognized only to the extent the amount of the loss exceeds the unrecognized gain (if any) in offsetting positions in the straddle (sec. 1092(a)(1)(A)). Special rules for identified straddles provide a different treatment of losses and also provide that any position that is not part of an identified straddle is not treated as offsetting with respect to any position that is part of the identified straddle. A taxpayer is permitted to treat a straddle as an identified straddle only if, among other requirements, the straddle is not part of a larger straddle.

Before the enactment of the Act, the rules for treating a straddle as an identified straddle required that all the positions of the straddle were acquired on the same day and either that all of the positions were disposed of on the same day in a taxable year or that none of the positions were disposed of as of the close of the taxable year. A loss on a position in an identified straddle was not subject to the loss deferral rule described above but instead was taken into account when all the positions making up the straddle were disposed of.

The Act changed the rules for identified straddles by providing, among other things, that if there is a loss on a position in an identified straddle, the loss is applied to increase the basis of the offsetting positions in that identified straddle. Under section 1092(a)(2)(A)(ii), the basis of each offsetting position in an identified straddle is increased by an amount that equals the product of the amount of the loss multiplied by the ratio of the amount of unrecognized straddle period gain in that offsetting position to the aggregate amount of unrecognized straddle period gain in all offsetting positions. The Act also provided that any loss described in section 1092(a)(2)(A)(ii) is not otherwise taken into account for Federal tax purposes.

The Act left unclear the treatment of a loss on a position in an identified straddle in at least two circumstances: first, when there are no offsetting positions in the identified straddle with unrecognized straddle period gain, and, second, when an offsetting position in the identified straddle is or has been a liability to the taxpayer.

The provision addresses the treatment of losses in these two circumstances. In general, the provision reaffirms that a loss on a position in an identified straddle is not permitted to be recognized currently and also is not permanently disallowed.

The provision provides that if the application of section 1092(a)(2)(A)(ii) does not result in a basis increase in any offsetting position in the identified straddle (because there is no unrecognized straddle period gain in any offsetting position), the basis of each offsetting position in the identified straddle must be increased in a manner that (1) is reasonable, is consistent with the purposes of the identified straddle rules, and is consistently applied by the taxpayer, and (2) allocates to offsetting positions the full amount of the loss (but no more than the full amount of the loss). At the time a taxpayer adopts an allocation method under this rule, the taxpayer is expected to describe that method in its books and records.

Under the provision, unless the Secretary of the Treasury provides otherwise, similar rules apply for purposes of the identified straddle rules when there is a loss on a position in an identified straddle and an offsetting position in the identified straddle is or has been a liability or an obligation (including, for instance, a debt obligation issued by the taxpayer, a written option, or a notional principal contract entered into by the taxpayer). Under this rule, if a taxpayer, for example, receives $1 to enter into a five-year short forward contract and the next day $100 of loss is allocated to that position, the resulting basis of the contract is $99.

Under present law, a straddle is treated as an identified straddle only if, among other requirements, it is clearly identified on the taxpayer's records as an identified straddle before the earlier of (1) the close of the day on which the straddle is acquired, or (2) a time that the Secretary of the Treasury may prescribe by regulations. The provision clarifies that for purposes of this identification requirement, a straddle is clearly identified only if the identification includes an identification of the positions in the straddle that are offsetting with respect to other positions in the straddle. Consequently, taxpayers are required to identify not only the positions that make up an identified straddle but also which positions in that identified straddle are offsetting with respect to one another. The offsetting positions identification requirement added by the provision is effective for straddles acquired after the date of enactment.

The provision provides that regulations or other guidance prescribed by the Secretary for carrying out the purposes of the identified straddle rules may include the rules for the application of section 1092 to a position that is or has been a liability or an obligation. Regulations or other guidance also may include safe harbor basis allocation methods that satisfy the requirements that an allocation other than under section 1092(a)(2)(A)(ii) must be reasonable, consistent with the purposes of the identified straddle rules, and consistently applied by the taxpayer.

[¶ 5307]   Section 8.   Amendments related to the Economic Growth and Tax Relief Reconciliation Act of 2001.

(Code Sec. 402, 3121)

[Joint Committee on Taxation Report — JCX-119-07]

Application of special elective deferral limit to designated Roth contributions (Act sec. 617).

Code section 402(g)(7) provides a special rule allowing certain employees to make additional elective deferrals to a tax-sheltered annuity, subject to (1) an annual limit of $3,000, and (2) a cumulative limit of $15,000 minus the amount of additional elective deferrals made in previous years under the special rule. Present law provides a rule to coordinate the cumulative limit with the ability to make designated Roth contributions, but inadvertently reduces the $15,000 amount by all designated Roth contributions made in previous years. The provision clarifies that the $15,000 amount is reduced only by additional designated Roth contributions made under the special rule.

Application of FICA taxes to designated Roth contributions (Act sec. 617).

Under Code section 3121(v)(1)(A), elective deferrals are included in wages for purposes of social security and Medicare taxes. The provision clarifies that wage treatment applies also to elective deferrals that are designated as Roth contributions.

[¶5308]   Section 9.   Amendments related to the Tax Relief Extension Act of 1999.

(Code Sec. 45, 856)

[Joint Committee on Taxation Report — JCX-119-07]

Renewable electricity sold to utilities under certain contracts (Act sec. 507).

Code section 45(e)(7) provides that a wind energy facility placed in service by the taxpayer after June 30, 1999, does not qualify for the section 45 production tax credit if the electricity generated at the facility is sold to a utility pursuant to certain pre-1987 contracts. The provision clarifies that facilities placed in service prior to June 30, 1999, that sell electricity under applicable pre-1987 contracts are not denied the section 45 production tax credit solely by reason of a change in ownership after June 30, 1999.

Treatment of income and services provided by taxable REIT subsidiaries (Act sec. 542).

The provision clarifies that the transient basis language in the definition of a lodging facility applies only in determining whether an establishment other than a hotel or motel qualifies as a lodging facility.

[¶5309]   Section 10.   Amendment related to the Internal Revenue Service Restructuring and Reform Act of 1998.

(Code Sec. 6110)

[Joint Committee on Taxation Report — JCX-119-07]

Redactions for background documents related to Chief Counsel Advice documents (Act sec. 3509).

The Internal Revenue Service Restructuring and Reform Act of 1998 established a structured process by which the IRS makes certain work products, designated Chief Counsel advice ("CCA"), open to public inspection. To afford additional protection for certain governmental interests implicated by CCAs, section 6110(i)(3) governs redactions that may be made to CCAs, including the exemptions or exclusions available under the Freedom of Information Act, 5 U.S.C. § 552(b) and (c) (except that the provision for redaction under a Federal statute excludes Title 26), as well as the exemptions pertaining to taxpayer identity information described in section 6110(c)(1). Section 6110(i)(3) does not expressly address redactions to the "background file documents" related to a CCA. The provision clarifies that the CCA background file documents are governed by the same redactions as CCAs.

[¶5310]   Section 11.   Clerical corrections.

(Code Sec. 21, 25C, 26, 34, 35, 38, 45L, 48, 48A, 121, 125, 167, 170, 1400S, 4942, 2522, 852, 857, 856, 954, 1016, 1260, 1297, 1298, 1362, 1400O, 4082, 4101, 4965, 5432, 5121, 5732, 6046, 6103, 7651, 6211, 6230, 6427, 6695A, 6707A, 9002, 9004, 9032, 9034, 9006, 9503, 168, 6724, 24, 6416, 6427, 41, 9502, 1298, 904, 56, 54, 245, 275, 291, 441, 884, 901, 906, 936, 951, 952, 956, 992, 1248, 1297, 6011, 6072, 6686)

[Joint Committee on Taxation Report — JCX-119-07]

The bill includes a number of clerical and conforming amendments, including amendments correcting typographical errors.

[¶ 5400] Joint Committee on Taxation Technical Explanation Accompanying the Exclusion from Income for Payments from the Hokie Spirit Memorial Fund

This section, in ¶ 5401 and ¶ 5402, reproduces all relevant parts of the Joint Committee on Taxation Technical Explanation (JCX-110-07, 12/6/2007) accompanying H.R. 4118, a bill to exclude from gross income payments from the Hokie Spirit Memorial Fund to the victims of the tragic event at Virginia Polytechnic Institute & State University (P.L. 110-141, 12/19/2007).

[¶ 5401]   Section 1.   Exclusion from income for payments from the Hokie Spirit Memorial Fund.

(Code Sec. 61)

[Joint Committee on Taxation Report — JCX-110-07]

Present Law

Following the shooting event at Virginia Polytechnic Institute and State University ("Virginia Tech University") on April 16, 2007, a payment program for victims and survivors of the event was established. Under the program, survivors of the murder victims and surviving victims of the event are eligible to receive cash payments from the university. In lieu of receipt of a cash payment, claimants under the program may instead donate their payments to a section 501(c)(3) organization for the purpose of funding scholarships at the university.

Under section 61 of the Code, gross income includes all income from whatever source derived. The Code includes a number of exceptions from this rule. These include exceptions for amounts received by gift (section 102), amounts of any damages received on account of personal physical injuries (section 104(a)(2)), and amounts received as qualified disaster relief payments (section 139). There is no specific exclusion from gross income for amounts received pursuant to the Virginia Tech University program described above.

Explanation of Provision

The provision excludes from gross income specified amounts that an individual receives from Virginia Tech University under the program described above. Under the bill, the exclusion applies to any amount received from Virginia Tech University out of amounts transferred from the Hokie Spirit Memorial Fund established by the Virginia Tech Foundation, an organization organized and operated as described in section 501(c)(3), if such amount is paid on account of the tragic event on April 16, 2007, at such university.

Effective Date

The provision is effective on the date of enactment.

[¶ 5402]   Section 2.   Modification of penalty for failure to file partnership returns.

(Code Sec. 6698)

[Joint Committee on Taxation Report — JCX-110-07]

Present Law

A partnership generally is treated as a pass-through entity. Income earned by a partnership, whether distributed or not, is taxed to the partners. Distributions from the partnership generally are tax-free. The items of income, gain, loss, deduction or credit of a partnership generally are taken into account by a partner as allocated under the terms of the partnership agreement. If the agreement does not provide for an allocation, or the agreed allocation does not have substantial economic effect, then the items are to be allocated in accordance with the partners' interests in the partnership. To prevent double taxation of these items, a partner's basis in its interest is increased by its share of partnership income (including tax-exempt income), and is decreased by its share of any losses (including nondeductible losses).

Under present law, a partnership is required to file a tax return for each taxable year. The partnership's tax return is required to include the names and addresses of the individuals who would be entitled to share in the taxable income if distributed and the amount of the distributive share of each individual. In addition to applicable criminal penalties, present law imposes a civil penalty for the failure to timely file a partnership return. The penalty is $50 per partner for each month (or fraction of a month) that the failure continues, up to a maximum of five months.

Explanation of Provision

The provision increases the present-law failure to file penalty for partnership returns by $1 per month.

Effective Date

The provision is effective for partnership returns required to be filed for a taxable year beginning in 2008.

[¶ 5500] Joint Committee on Taxation Technical Explanation Accompanying the Economic Stimulus Act of 2008

This section, in ¶ 5501 through ¶ 5503, reproduces all relevant parts of the Joint Committee on Taxation's Technical Explanation of the Revenue Provisions (JCX-16-08, 2/8/2008), of P.L. 110-185, the Economic Stimulus Act of 2008 (2/13/2008).

[¶ 5501]   Section 101.   2008 recovery rebates for individuals.

(Code Sec. 6428, 6211)

[Joint Committee on Taxation Report — JCX-16-08]

Present Law

In general

Under the Federal individual income tax system, an individual who is a citizen or a resident of the United States generally is subject to tax on worldwide taxable income. Taxable income is total gross income less certain exclusions, exemptions, and deductions. An individual may claim either a standard deduction or itemized deductions.

An individual's income tax liability is determined by computing his or her regular income tax liability and, if applicable, alternative minimum tax liability.

Income tax liability

Regular income tax liability is determined by applying the regular income tax rate schedules (or tax tables) to the individual's taxable income (sec. 1). This tax liability is then reduced by any applicable tax credits. The regular income tax rate schedules are divided into several ranges of income, known as income brackets, and the marginal tax rate increases as the individual's income increases. The income bracket amounts are adjusted annually for inflation. Separate rate schedules apply based on filing status: single individuals (other than heads of households and surviving spouses), heads of households, married individuals filing joint returns (including surviving spouses), married individuals filing separate returns, and estates and trusts. Lower rates may apply to capital gains.

A taxpayer may also be subject to an alternative minimum tax.

Child tax credit

An individual may claim a tax credit of $1,000 for each qualifying child under the age of 17 (sec. 24). Generally, a qualifying child must have the same principal place of abode as the taxpayer for more than one-half the taxable year and satisfy a relationship test. To satisfy the relationship test, the child must be the taxpayer's son, daughter, stepson, stepdaughter, brother, sister, stepbrother, stepsister, or a descendant of any such individual. The credit is phased-out at higher-income levels. A child who is not a citizen, national, or resident of the United States may not be a qualifying child. No credit is allowed unless the individual includes the name and taxpayer identification number of each qualifying child on the income tax return.

Earned income credit

Low and moderate-income workers may be eligible for the refundable earned income credit (EIC). Eligibility for the EIC is based on earned income, adjusted gross income, investment income, filing status, and immigration and work status in the United States. The amount of the EIC is based on the presence and number of qualifying children in the worker's family, as well as on adjusted gross income and earned income. Earned income is defined as (1) wages, salaries, tips, and other employee compensation, but only if such amounts are includible in gross income, plus (2) the amount of the individual's net self-employment earnings.

Explanation of Provision

In general

The provision includes a recovery rebate credit for 2008 which is refundable. The credit mechanism (and the issuance of checks described below) is intended to deliver an expedited fiscal stimulus to the economy.

The credit is computed with two components in the following manner.

Basic credit

Eligible individuals receive a basic credit (for the first taxable year beginning) in 2008 equal to the greater of the following:

• Net income tax liability not to exceed $600 ($1,200 in the case of a joint return).

• $300 ($600 in the case of a joint return) if: (1) the eligible individual has qualifying income of at least $3,000; or (2) the eligible individual has a net income tax liability of at least $1 and gross income greater than the sum of the applicable basic standard deduction amount and one personal exemption (two personal exemptions for a joint return).

An eligible individual is any individual other than: (1) a nonresident alien; (2) an estate or trust; or (3) a dependent.

For these purposes, "net income tax liability" means the excess of the sum of the individual's regular tax liability and alternative minimum tax over the sum of all nonrefundable credits (other than the child credit). Net income tax liability as determined for these purposes is not reduced by the credit added by this provision or any credit which is refundable under present law.

Qualifying income is the sum of the eligible individual's: (a) earned income; (b) social security benefits (within the meaning of sec. 86(d)); and (c) veteran's payments (under Chapters 11, 13, or 15 of title 38 of the U. S. Code). The definition of earned income has the same meaning as used in the earned income credit except that it includes certain combat pay and does not include net earnings from self-employment which are not taken into account in computing taxable income.

Qualifying child credit

If an individual is eligible for any amount of the basic credit the individual also may be eligible for a qualifying child credit. The qualifying child credit equals $300 for each qualifying child of such individual. For these purposes, the child credit definition of qualifying child will apply.

Limitation based on adjusted gross income

The amount of the credit (including both the basic credit and the qualifying child credit) is phased out at a rate of five percent of adjusted gross income above certain income levels. The beginning point of this phase-out range is $75,000 of adjusted gross income ($150,000 in the case of joint returns).

Valid identification numbers

No credit is allowed to an individual who does not include a valid identification number on the individual's income tax return. In the case of a joint return which does not include valid identification numbers for both spouses, no credit is allowed. In addition, a child shall not be taken into account in determining the amount of the credit if a valid identification number for the child is not included on the return. For this purpose, a valid identification number means a social security number issued to an individual by the Social Security Administration. A taxpayer identification number issued by the Internal Revenue Service is not a valid identification number for purposes of this credit (e.g., an ITIN).

If an individual fails to provide a valid identification number, the omission is treated as a mathematical or clerical error. As under present law, the Internal Revenue Service (the "IRS") may summarily assess additional tax due as a result of a mathematical or clerical error without sending the taxpayer a notice of deficiency and giving the taxpayer an opportunity to petition the Tax Court. Where the IRS uses the summary assessment procedure for mathematical or clerical errors, the taxpayer must be given an explanation of the asserted error and given 60 days to request that the IRS abate its assessment.

Rebate checks

Most taxpayers will receive this credit in the form of a check issued by the Department of the Treasury.[2] The amount of the payment will be computed in the same manner as the credit, except that it will be done on the basis of tax returns filed for 2007 (instead of 2008). It is anticipated that the Department of the Treasury will make every effort to issue all payments as rapidly as possible to taxpayers who timely filed their 2007 tax returns. (Taxpayers who file late or pursuant to extensions will receive their payments later.)

Taxpayers will reconcile the amount of the credit with the payment they receive in the following manner. They will complete a worksheet calculating the amount of the credit based on their 2008 tax return. They will then subtract from the credit the amount of the payment they received in 2008. For many taxpayers, these two amounts would be the same. If, however, the result is a positive number (because, for example, the taxpayer paid no tax in 2007 but is paying tax in 2008), the taxpayer may claim that amount as a refundable credit against 2008 tax liability. If, however, the result is negative (because, for example, the taxpayer paid tax in 2007 but owes no tax for 2008), the taxpayer is not required to repay that amount to the Treasury. Otherwise, the checks have no effect on tax returns filed for 2008; the amount is not includible in gross income and it does not otherwise reduce the amount of withholding.

In no event may the Department of the Treasury issue checks after December 31, 2008. This is designed to prevent errors by taxpayers who might claim the full amount of the credit on their 2008 tax returns and file those returns early in 2009, at the same time the Treasury check might be mailed to them. Payment of the credit (or the check) is treated, for all purposes of the Code, as a payment of tax. Any resulting overpayment under this provision is subject to the refund offset provisions, such as those applicable to past-due child support under section 6402 of the Code.

Examples of rebate determination

The following examples show the rebate amounts as calculated from the taxpayer's 2007 tax return.

Example 1.–A single taxpayer has $14,000 in Social Security income, no qualifying children, and no net tax liability prior to the application of refundable credits and the child credit. The taxpayer will receive a rebate of $300 for meeting the qualifying income test.

Example 2.–A head of household taxpayer has $4,000 in earned income, one qualifying child, and no net tax liability prior to the application of refundable credits and the child credit. The taxpayer will receive a rebate of $600, comprising $300 for meeting the qualifying income test, and $300 per child.

---

2. To the extent practicable, the Department of the Treasury is expected to utilize individuals' current direct deposit information in its possession to expedite delivery of these amounts rather than the mailing of rebate checks.

Example 3.–A married taxpayer filing jointly has $4,000 in earned income, one qualifying child, and no net tax liability prior to the application of refundable credits and the child credit. The taxpayer will receive a rebate of $900, comprising $600 for meeting the qualifying income test, and $300 per child.

Example 4.–A married taxpayer filing jointly has $2,000 in earned income, one qualifying child, and $1,100 in net tax liability (resulting from other unearned income) prior to the application of refundable credits and the child credit (the taxpayer's actual liability after the child credit is $100). The qualifying income test is not met, but the taxpayer has net tax liability for purposes of determining the rebate of $1,100. The taxpayer will receive a rebate of $1,400, comprising $1,100 of net tax liability, and $300 per child.

Example 5.–A married taxpayer filing jointly has $40,000 in earned income, two qualifying children, and a net tax liability of $1,573 prior to the application of refundable credits and child credits (the taxpayer's actual tax liability after the child credit is - $427). The taxpayer meets the qualifying income test and the net tax liability test. The taxpayer will receive a rebate of $1,800, comprising $1,200 (greater of $600 or net tax liability not to exceed $1,200), and $300 per child.

Example 6.–A married taxpayer filing jointly has $175,000 in earned income, two qualifying children, and a net tax liability of $31,189 (the taxpayer's actual liability after the child credit also is $31,189 as the joint income is too high to qualify). The taxpayer meets the qualifying income test and the net tax liability test. The taxpayer will, in the absence of the rebate phase-out provision, receive a rebate of $1,800, comprising $1,200 (greater of $600 or net tax liability not to exceed $1,200), and $300 per child. The phase-out provision reduces the total rebate amount by five percent of the amount by which the taxpayer's adjusted gross income exceeds $150,000. Five percent of $25,000 ($175,000 minus $150,000) equals $1,250. The taxpayer's rebate is thus $1,800 minus $1,250, or $550.

Treatment of the U.S. possessions

Mirror-Code possessions[3]

The U.S. Treasury will make a payment to each mirror code possession in an amount equal to the aggregate amount of the credits allowable by reason of the provision to that possession's residents against its income tax. This amount will be determined by the Treasury Secretary based on information provided by the government of the respective possession. For purposes of this payment, a possession is a mirror code possession if the income tax liability of residents of the possession under that possession's income tax system is determined by reference to the U.S. income tax laws as if the possession were the United States.

Non mirror-Code possessions[4]

To each possession that does not have a mirror code tax system, the U.S. Treasury will make a payment in an amount estimated by the Secretary as being equal to the aggregate credits that would have been allowed to residents of that possession if a mirror code tax system had been in effect in that possession. Accordingly, the amount of each payment to a non-mirror Code possession will be an estimate of the aggregate amount of the credits that would be allowed to the possession's residents if the credit provided by the provision to U.S. residents were provided by the possession to its residents. This payment will not be made to any U.S. possession unless that possession has a plan that has been approved by the Secretary under which the possession will promptly distribute the payment to its residents.

---

3. Possessions with mirror code tax systems are the United States Virgin Islands, Guam, and the Commonwealth of the Northern Mariana Islands.
4. Possessions that do not have mirror code tax systems are Puerto Rico and American Samoa.

General rules

No credit against U.S. income taxes is permitted under the provision for any person to whom a credit is allowed against possession income taxes as a result of the provision (for example, under that possession's mirror income tax). Similarly, no credit against U.S. income taxes is permitted for any person who is eligible for a payment under a non-mirror code possession's plan for distributing to its residents the payment described above from the U.S. Treasury.

For purposes of the rebate credit payment, the Commonwealth of Puerto Rico and the Commonwealth of the Northern Mariana Islands are considered possessions of the United States.

For purposes of the rule permitting the Treasury Secretary to disburse appropriated amounts for refunds due from certain credit provisions of the Internal Revenue Code of 1986, the payments required to be made to possessions under the provision are treated in the same manner as a refund due from the recovery rebate credit.

Federal programs or Federally-assisted programs

Any credit or refund allowed or made to an individual under this provision (including to any resident of a U.S. possessions) is not taken into account as income and shall not be taken into account as resources for the month of receipt and the following two months for purposes of determining eligibility of such individual or any other individual for benefits or assistance, or the amount or extent of benefits or assistance, under any Federal program or under any State or local program financed in whole or in part with Federal funds.

Effective Date

The provision applies to taxable years beginning after December 31, 2007.

[¶ 5502]   Section 102.   Temporary increase in limitations on expensing of certain depreciable business assets.

(Code Sec. 179)

[Joint Committee on Taxation Report — JCX-16-08]

Present Law

A taxpayer that satisfies limitations on annual investment may elect under section 179 to deduct (or "expense") the cost of qualifying property, rather than to recover such costs through depreciation deductions.[5] For taxable years beginning in 2008, the maximum amount that a taxpayer may expense is $128,000 of the cost of qualifying property placed in service for the taxable year. The $128,000 amount is reduced (but not below zero) by the amount by which the cost of qualifying property placed in service during the taxable year exceeds $510,000.[6] In general, qualifying property is defined as depreciable tangible personal property that is purchased for use in the active conduct of a trade or business. Off-the-shelf computer software placed in service in taxable years beginning before 2011 is treated as qualifying property.

---

5. Additional section 179 incentives are provided with respect to qualified property meeting applicable requirements that is used by a business in an empowerment zone (sec. 1397A), a renewal community (sec. 1400J), or the Gulf Opportunity Zone (sec. 1400N(e)).

6. Amounts applicable for 2008 are set forth in Rev. Proc. 2007-66, 2007-45 I.R.B. 970. Present law provides that the maximum amount a taxpayer may expense, for taxable years beginning in 2007 through 2010, is $125,000 of the cost of qualifying property placed in service for the taxable year. The $125,000 amount is reduced (but not below zero) by the amount by which the cost of qualifying property placed in service during the taxable year exceeds $500,000. The $125,000 and $500,000 amounts are indexed for inflation in taxable years beginning after 2007 and before 2011.

The amount eligible to be expensed for a taxable year may not exceed the taxable income for a taxable year that is derived from the active conduct of a trade or business (determined without regard to this provision). Any amount that is not allowed as a deduction because of the taxable income limitation may be carried forward to succeeding taxable years (subject to similar limitations). No general business credit under section 38 is allowed with respect to any amount for which a deduction is allowed under section 179. An expensing election is made under rules prescribed by the Secretary.[7] For taxable years beginning in 2011 and thereafter, other rules apply.[8]

Explanation of Provision

The provision increases the $128,000 and $510,000 amounts under section 179 for taxable years beginning in 2008 to $250,000 and $800,000, respectively. The $250,000 and $800,000 amounts are not indexed for inflation.

Effective Date

The provision is effective for taxable years beginning after December 31, 2007.

[¶ 5503]   Section 103.   Special allowance for certain property acquired during 2008.

(Code Sec. 168)

[Joint Committee on Taxation Report — JCX-16-08]

Present Law

A taxpayer is allowed to recover through annual depreciation deductions the cost of certain property used in a trade or business or for the production of income. The amount of the depreciation deduction allowed with respect to tangible property for a taxable year is determined under the modified accelerated cost recovery system ("MACRS"). Under MACRS, different types of property generally are assigned applicable recovery periods and depreciation methods. The recovery periods applicable to most tangible personal property range from three to 25 years. The depreciation methods generally applicable to tangible personal property are the 200-percent and 150-percent declining balance methods, switching to the straight-line method for the taxable year in which the taxpayer's depreciation deduction would be maximized.

Section 280F limits the annual depreciation deductions with respect to passenger automobiles to specified dollar amounts, indexed for inflation.

Section 167(f)(1) provides that capitalized computer software costs, other than computer software to which section 197 applies, are recovered ratably over 36 months.

A taxpayer that satisfies limitations on annual investment may elect under section 179 to deduct (or "expense") the cost of qualifying property, rather than to recover such costs through depreciation deductions.[9] For taxable years beginning in 2008, the maximum amount that a taxpayer may expense is $128,000 of the cost of qualifying property placed in service for the taxable year. The $128,000 amount is reduced (but not below zero) by the amount by which the cost of qualifying property placed in service during

---

7. Sec. 179(c)(1).
8. Under the rules in effect for taxable years beginning in 2011 and thereafter, a taxpayer with a sufficiently small amount of annual investment may elect to deduct up to $25,000 of the cost of qualifying property placed in service for the taxable year. The $25,000 amount is reduced (but not below zero) by the amount by which the cost of qualifying property placed in service during the taxable year exceeds $200,000. The $25,000 and $200,000 amounts are not indexed. In general, qualifying property is defined as depreciable tangible personal property that is purchased for use in the active conduct of a trade or business (not including off-the-shelf computer software). An expensing election may be revoked only with consent of the Commissioner (sec. 179(c)(2)).
9. Additional section 179 incentives are provided with respect to qualified property meeting applicable requirements that is used by a business in an empowerment zone (sec. 1397A), a renewal community (sec. 1400J), or the Gulf Opportunity Zone (sec. 1400N(e)).

the taxable year exceeds $510,000.[10] In general, qualifying property is defined as depreciable tangible personal property that is purchased for use in the active conduct of a trade or business. Off-the-shelf computer software placed in service in taxable years beginning before 2011 is treated as qualifying property. For taxable years beginning in 2011 and thereafter, other rules apply.[11]

Explanation of Provision

The provision allows an additional first-year depreciation deduction equal to 50 percent of the adjusted basis of qualified property.[12] The additional first-year depreciation deduction is allowed for both regular tax and alternative minimum tax purposes for the taxable year in which the property is placed in service.[13] The basis of the property and the depreciation allowances in the year the property is placed in service and later years are appropriately adjusted to reflect the additional first-year depreciation deduction. In addition, there are no adjustments to the allowable amount of depreciation for purposes of computing a taxpayer's alternative minimum taxable income with respect to property to which the provision applies. The amount of the additional first-year depreciation deduction is not affected by a short taxable year. The taxpayer may elect out of additional first-year depreciation for any class of property for any taxable year.

The interaction of the additional first-year depreciation allowance with the otherwise applicable depreciation allowance may be illustrated as follows. Assume that in 2008, a taxpayer purchases new depreciable property and places it in service.[14] The property's cost is $1,000, and it is five-year property subject to the half-year convention. The amount of additional first-year depreciation allowed under the provision is $500. The remaining $500 of the cost of the property is deductible under the rules applicable to five-year property. Thus, 20 percent, or $100, is also allowed as a depreciation deduction in 2008. The total depreciation deduction with respect to the property for 2008 is $600. The remaining $400 cost of the property is recovered under otherwise applicable rules for computing depreciation.

In order for property to qualify for the additional first-year depreciation deduction it must meet all of the following requirements. First, the property must be (1) property to which MACRS applies with an applicable recovery period of 20 years or less, (2) water utility property (as defined in section 168(e)(5)), (3) computer software other than computer software covered by section 197, or (4) qualified leasehold improvement property (as defined in section 168(k)(3)).[15] Second, the original use[16] of the property must com-

---

10. Amounts applicable for 2008 are set forth in Rev. Proc. 2007-66, 2007-45 I.R.B. 970. Present law provides that the maximum amount a taxpayer may expense, for taxable years beginning in 2007 through 2010, is $125,000 of the cost of qualifying property placed in service for the taxable year. The $125,000 amount is reduced (but not below zero) by the amount by which the cost of qualifying property placed in service during the taxable year exceeds $500,000. The $125,000 and $500,000 amounts are indexed for inflation in taxable years beginning after 2007 and before 2011.
11. Under the rules in effect for taxable years beginning in 2011 and thereafter, a taxpayer with a sufficiently small amount of annual investment may elect to deduct up to $25,000 of the cost of qualifying property placed in service for the taxable year. The $25,000 amount is reduced (but not below zero) by the amount by which the cost of qualifying property placed in service during the taxable year exceeds $200,000. The $25,000 and $200,000 amounts are not indexed. In general, qualifying property is defined as depreciable tangible personal property that is purchased for use in the active conduct of a trade or business (not including off-the-shelf computer software). An expensing election may be revoked only with consent of the Commissioner (sec. 179(c)(2)).
12. The additional first-year depreciation deduction is subject to the general rules regarding whether an item is deductible under section 162 or instead is subject to capitalization under section 263 or section 263A.
13. However, the additional first-year depreciation deduction is not allowed for purposes of computing earnings and profits.
14. Assume that the cost of the property is not eligible for expensing under section 179.
15. A special rule precludes the additional first-year depreciation deduction for any property that is required to be depreciated under the alternative depreciation system of MACRS.
16. The term "original use" means the first use to which the property is put, whether or not such use corresponds to the use of such property by the taxpayer. If in the normal course of its business a taxpayer sells fractional interests in property to unrelated third parties, then the original use of such property begins with the first user of each fractional interest (i.e., each fractional owner is considered the original user of its proportionate share of the property).

mence with the taxpayer after December 31, 2007.[17] Third, the taxpayer must purchase the property within the applicable time period. Finally, the property must be placed in service after December 31, 2007, and before January 1, 2009. An extension of the placed in service date of one year (i.e., to January 1, 2010) is provided for certain property with a recovery period of ten years or longer and certain transportation property.[18] Transportation property is defined as tangible personal property used in the trade or business of transporting persons or property. Special rules, including an extension of the placed-in-service date of one year (i.e., to January 1, 2010) also apply to certain aircraft.

The applicable time period for acquired property is (1) after December 31, 2007, and before January 1, 2009, but only if no binding written contract for the acquisition is in effect before January 1, 2008, or (2) pursuant to a binding written contract which was entered into after December 31, 2007, and before January 1, 2009.[19] With respect to property that is manufactured, constructed, or produced by the taxpayer for use by the taxpayer, the taxpayer must begin the manufacture, construction, or production of the property after December 31, 2007, and before January 1, 2009. Property that is manufactured, constructed, or produced for the taxpayer by another person under a contract that is entered into prior to the manufacture, construction, or production of the property is considered to be manufactured, constructed, or produced by the taxpayer. For property eligible for the extended placed in service date, a special rule limits the amount of costs eligible for the additional first year depreciation. With respect to such property, only the portion of the basis that is properly attributable to the costs incurred before January 1, 2009 ("progress expenditures") is eligible for the additional first-year depreciation.[20]

Property does not qualify for the additional first-year depreciation deduction when the user of such property (or a related party) would not have been eligible for the additional first-year depreciation deduction if the user (or a related party) were treated as the owner. For example, if a taxpayer sells to a related party property that was under construction prior to January 1, 2008, the property does not qualify for the additional first-year depreciation deduction. Similarly, if a taxpayer sells to a related party property that was subject to a binding written contract prior to January 1, 2008, the property does not qualify for the additional first-year depreciation deduction. As a further example, if a taxpayer (the lessee) sells property in a sale-leaseback arrangement, and the property otherwise would not have qualified for the additional first-year depreciation deduction if it were owned by the taxpayer-lessee, then the lessor is not entitled to the additional first-year depreciation deduction.

The limitation on the amount of depreciation deductions allowed with respect to certain passenger automobiles (sec. 280F) is increased in the first year by $8,000 for automobiles that qualify (and do not elect out of the increased first year deduction). The $8,000 increase is not indexed for inflation.

Effective Date

The provision is effective for property placed in service after December 31, 2007.

---

17. A special rule applies in the case of certain leased property. In the case of any property that is originally placed in service by a person and that is sold to the taxpayer and leased back to such person by the taxpayer within three months after the date that the property was placed in service, the property would be treated as originally placed in service by the taxpayer not earlier than the date that the property is used under the leaseback.

    If property is originally placed in service by a lessor (including by operation of section 168(k)(2)(D)(i)), such property is sold within three months after the date that the property was placed in service, and the user of such property does not change, then the property is treated as originally placed in service by the taxpayer not earlier than the date of such sale.

18. In order for property to qualify for the extended placed in service date, the property is required to have an estimated production period exceeding one year and a cost exceeding $1 million.

19. Property does not fail to qualify for the additional first-year depreciation merely because a binding written contract to acquire a component of the property is in effect prior to January 1, 2008.

20. For purposes of determining the amount of eligible progress expenditures, it is intended that rules similar to sec. 46(d)(3) as in effect prior to the Tax Reform Act of 1986 shall apply.

¶ 6000. Act Section Cross Reference Table

Act § cites are to the 2008 Economic Stimulus Act unless otherwise indicated.
* denotes 2007 Tax Increase Prevention Act
† denotes 2007 Mortgage Relief Act
+ denotes 2007 Energy Act
** denotes 2007 Technical Corrections Act
‡ denotes 2007 Virginia Tech Victims Act
++ denotes 2008 Appropriations Act

Act §	Code §	Topic	Generally effective date	Analysis ¶	Com Rep ¶
1‡	61	Certain payments received by surviving victims and survivors of slain victims of the Virginia Tech shootings are excluded from gross income	Dec. 19, 2007	303	5401
2‡	6698(b)(1)	Monthly failure to file partnership return penalty is increased; inspection of returns by persons having a material interest is restricted	Returns required to be filed after Dec. 20, 2007	1102	5402
2(a)†	108(a)(1)(E)	Discharges of up to $2 million of acquisition debt on taxpayer's main home in 2007 through 2009 are excluded from income	Discharges of indebtedness after Dec. 31, 2006, and before Jan. 1, 2010	201	5001
2(a)**	53(e)(2)(A)	AMT refundable credit for individuals is revised to allow at least $5,000 a year for five years	Tax years beginning after Dec. 20, 2006 and before Jan. 1, 2013	103	5301
2(a)(1)*	55(d)(1)(A)	AMT exemption amounts for 2007 are increased to $44,350 for unmarrieds, to $66,250 for joint filers, and to $33,125 for marrieds filing separately	Tax years beginning in 2007	101	5201
2(a)(2)*	55(d)(1)(B)	AMT exemption amounts for 2007 are increased to $44,350 for unmarrieds, to $66,250 for joint filers, and to $33,125 for marrieds filing separately	Tax years beginning in 2007	101	5201

Act §	Code §	Topic	Generally effective date	Analysis ¶	Com Rep ¶
2(b) †	108(h)	Discharges of up to $2 million of acquisition debt on taxpayer's main home in 2007 through 2009 are excluded from income	Discharges of indebtedness after Dec. 31, 2006, and before Jan. 1, 2010	201	5001
2(c)(1) †	108(a)(2)(A)	Discharges of up to $2 million of acquisition debt on taxpayer's main home in 2007 through 2009 are excluded from income	Discharges of indebtedness after Dec. 31, 2006, and before Jan. 1, 2010	201	5001
2(c)(2) †	108(a)(2)(C)	Discharges of up to $2 million of acquisition debt on taxpayer's main home in 2007 through 2009 are excluded from income	Discharges of indebtedness after Dec. 31, 2006, and before Jan. 1, 2010	201	5001
3(a) †	163(h)(3)(E)(iv)(I)	Interest deduction for mortgage insurance premiums is extended to amounts paid or incurred after 2007 and before 2011	Amounts paid or accrued after Dec. 31, 2007	202	None
3(a) **	408(d)(8)(D)	Rule clarified for determining what portion of an IRA distribution that includes nondeductible contributions is tax-free under the IRA qualified charitable distribution rules	For IRA distributions made during 2006 and 2007	602	5302
3(a)(1) *	21	Nonrefundable personal credits may offset AMT through 2007 (instead of 2006)	Tax years beginning in 2007	102	5201
3(a)(1) *	22	Nonrefundable personal credits may offset AMT through 2007 (instead of 2006)	Tax years beginning in 2007	102	5201
3(a)(1) *	23	Nonrefundable personal credits may offset AMT through 2007 (instead of 2006)	Tax years beginning in 2007	102	5201
3(a)(1) *	24	Nonrefundable personal credits may offset AMT through 2007 (instead of 2006)	Tax years beginning in 2007	102	5201

Act §	Code §	Topic	Generally effective date	Analysis ¶	Com Rep ¶
3(a)(1)*	25	Nonrefundable personal credits may offset AMT through 2007 (instead of 2006)	Tax years beginning in 2007	102	5201
3(a)(1)*	25A	Nonrefundable personal credits may offset AMT through 2007 (instead of 2006)	Tax years beginning in 2007	102	5201
3(a)(1)*	25B	Nonrefundable personal credits may offset AMT through 2007 (instead of 2006)	Tax years beginning in 2007	102	5201
3(a)(1)*	25C	Nonrefundable personal credits may offset AMT through 2007 (instead of 2006)	Tax years beginning in 2007	102	5201
3(a)(1)*	25D	Nonrefundable personal credits may offset AMT through 2007 (instead of 2006)	Tax years beginning in 2007	102	5201
3(a)(1)*	26(a)(2)	Nonrefundable personal credits may offset AMT through 2007 (instead of 2006)	Tax years beginning in 2007	102	5201
3(a)(1)*	904(i)	Nonrefundable personal credits may offset AMT through 2007 (instead of 2006)	Tax years beginning in 2007	102	5201
3(a)(1)*	1400C	Nonrefundable personal credits may offset AMT through 2007 (instead of 2006)	Tax years beginning in 2007	102	5201
3(b)**	1366(d)(4)	Charitable deduction allowed where S corporation's charitable contribution of property reduces shareholder's basis only by contributed property's basis	Contributions made in tax years beginning after Dec. 31, 2005	603	5302
3(c)**	170(e)(7)(D)(i)(I)	Donee's use of donated "applicable property" for its exempt purpose or function must be substantial for taxpayer to avoid reduction or recapture of deduction for contribution	Contributions after Sept. 1, 2006	605	5302

Act §	Code §	Topic	Generally effective date	Analysis ¶	Com Rep ¶
3(d)(1)**	2055(g)	Limits on estate and gift tax charitable deductions for series of fractional contributions of tangible personal property are retroactively repealed	Bequests and gifts made after Aug. 17, 2006	601	5302
3(d)(2)**	2522(e)	Limits on estate and gift tax charitable deductions for series of fractional contributions of tangible personal property are retroactively repealed	Bequests and gifts made after Aug. 17, 2006	601	5302
3(e)(1)**	6695A(a)(2)	Penalty for valuation misstatements attributable to incorrect appraisals applies to substantial estate or gift tax valuation understatements and is subject to 3-year limitation period	Appraisals prepared for returns or submissions filed after Aug. 17, 2006	1101	5302
3(e)(2)**	6696(d)(1)	Penalty for valuation misstatements attributable to incorrect appraisals applies to substantial estate or gift tax valuation understatements and is subject to 3-year limitation period	Appraisals prepared for returns or submissions filed after Aug. 17, 2006	1101	5302
3(f)**	4940(c)(4)(A)	Excise tax on private foundation's net investment income applies to capital gains from appreciation, including gains on assets used for exempt purposes	Tax years beginning after Aug. 17, 2006	504	5302
3(g)(1)(B)**	6104(b)	IRS must allow public inspection of unrelated business income tax (UBIT) returns of tax-exempt organizations, such as Form 990-T, filed under Code Sec. 6011	Returns filed after Aug. 17, 2006	502	5302
3(g)(2)**	6104(d)(1)(A)(ii)	Code Sec. 501(c)(3) organizations must make available for public inspection copies of Form 990-T relating to UBIT for three years	Returns filed after Aug. 17, 2006	501	5302

Act §	Code §	Topic	Generally effective date	Analysis ¶	Com Rep ¶
3(g)(3)**	6104(d)(2)	Code Sec. 501(c)(3) organizations must make available for public inspection copies of Form 990-T relating to UBIT for three years	Returns filed after Aug. 17, 2006	501	5302
3(h)**	4962(b)	Donor advised fund excise taxes added to list of "qualified first tier taxes" for abatement purposes	Tax years beginning after Aug. 17, 2006	503	5302
3(i)(1)**	4958(c)(3)(A)(i)(II)	Excess benefit transactions rules don't apply to transactions between supporting organizations and Code Sec. 501(c)(4), Code Sec. 501(c)(5), or Code Sec. 501(c)(6) supported organizations	For transactions occurring after July 25, 2006.	505	5302
3(i)(2)**	4958(c)(3)(C)(ii)	Excess benefit transactions rules don't apply to transactions between supporting organizations and Code Sec. 501(c)(4), Code Sec. 501(c)(5), or Code Sec. 501(c)(6) supported organizations	For transactions occurring after July 25, 2006.	505	5302
4(a)†	216(b)(1)(D)	Cooperatives can use alternative tests based on square footage or expenditures in lieu of the 80/20 gross income test to qualify as a cooperative housing corporation	Tax years ending after Dec. 20, 2007	1302	5002
4(a)**	954(c)(6)(B)	TIPRA look-through rule doesn't apply to interest, rent or royalty payments between related CFCs that create or increase a deficit that reduces subpart F income	Tax years of foreign corporations beginning after Dec. 31, 2005 and before Jan. 1, 2009, and tax years of U.S. shareholders with or within which such tax years of foreign corporations end	702	5303

Act §	Code §	Topic	Generally effective date	Analysis ¶	Com Rep ¶
4(b)(1)**	355(b)(2)	Modification of active business definition under Code Sec. 355	Distributions made after May 17, 2006	1301	5303
4(b)(2)**	355(b)(3)(C)	Modification of active business definition under Code Sec. 355	Distributions made after May 17, 2006	1301	5303
4(b)(2)**	355(b)(3)(D)	Modification of active business definition under Code Sec. 355	Distributions made after May 17, 2006	1301	5303
4(c)**	911(f)	Computation of regular tax and AMT modified where foreign earned income or housing exclusion is claimed	Tax years beginning after Dec. 31, 2006	701	5303
5(a)†	139B	Tax relief and expense reimbursements provided by state and local governments to volunteer firefighters and emergency medical responders for services performed are tax-free for 2008 - 2010 tax years	Tax years beginning after Dec. 31, 2007 and before Jan. 1, 2011	302	5003
5(a)(1)(A)**	6427(i)(3)(A)	Expedited excise tax refund claims permitted for alternative fuels, for any sale or use for any period after Sept. 30, 2006	Sale or use for any period after Sept. 30, 2006	1008	5304
5(a)(1)(B)**	6427(i)(3)(A)(i)	Expedited excise tax refund claims permitted for alternative fuels, for any sale or use for any period after Sept. 30, 2006	Sale or use for any period after Sept. 30, 2006	1008	5304
5(a)(1)(B)**	6427(i)(3)(B)	Expedited excise tax refund claims permitted for alternative fuels, for any sale or use for any period after Sept. 30, 2006	Sale or use for any period after Sept. 30, 2006	1008	5304
5(a)(2)**	6426(d)(2)(F)	Fuel eligible for alternative fuel excise tax credit is expanded retroactively	Any sale or use for any period after Sept. 30, 2006	1005	5304
5(a)(3)**	6426(h)	Fuel eligible for alternative fuel excise tax credit is expanded retroactively	Any sale or use for any period after Sept. 30, 2006	1005	5304

Act §	Code §	Topic	Generally effective date	Analysis ¶	Com Rep ¶
6(a) †	42(i)(3)(D)(ii)(I)	Rule that prevents full-time students from disqualifying housing units from the low-income housing credit is clarified	Housing credit amounts, whenever allocated, and certain tax-exempt-financed buildings, whenever placed in service	902	None
6(a) **	45J(b)(2)	IRS cannot allocate more than the national capacity limitation of 6,000 megawatts for purposes of advanced nuclear power facilities credit computation	Production in tax years beginning after Aug. 8, 2005	409	5305
6(b)(1) **	30C(b)	Dollar limits on credit for alternative fuel vehicle refueling property apply to all property placed in service at a location	Property placed in service after Dec. 31, 2005 and before Jan. 1, 2010	402	5305
6(b)(2) **	30C(c)	Definition of "qualified alternative fuel vehicle refueling property" is clarified	Property placed in service after Dec. 31, 2005 and before Jan. 1, 2010	403	5305
6(c)(1) **	41(a)(3)	Research credit for research by an energy research consortium is clarified to require that the research be qualified energy research	Amounts paid or incurred after Aug. 8, 2005	405	5305
6(c)(2) **	41(f)(6)(E)	Research credit for research by an energy research consortium is clarified to require that the research be qualified energy research	Amounts paid or incurred after Aug. 8, 2005	405	5305

Act §	Code §	Topic	Generally effective date	Analysis ¶	Com Rep ¶
6(d)(1)(A)**	4041(d)(1)	Double LUST tax on certain dyed diesel fuel and kerosene and fuels used on inland waterways is eliminated retroactively, for fuel entered, removed, or sold after Sept. 30, 2005	Fuel entered, removed, or sold after Sept. 30, 2005	1004	5305
6(d)(1)(B)**	4042(b)(3)	Double LUST tax on certain dyed diesel fuel and kerosene and fuels used on inland waterways is eliminated retroactively, for fuel entered, removed, or sold after Sept. 30, 2005	Fuel entered, removed, or sold after Sept. 30, 2005	1004	5305
6(d)(2)(A)**	4041(d)(5)	Fuel used in vessels or aircraft in foreign trade or trade between U.S. and its possessions is exempted from the LUST tax retroactively, for fuel entered, removed, or sold after Sept. 30, 2005	Fuel entered, removed, or sold after Sept. 30, 2005	1002	5305
6(d)(2)(B)**	4082(f)	Fuel used in vessels or aircraft in foreign trade or trade between U.S. and its possessions is exempted from the LUST tax retroactively, for fuel entered, removed, or sold after Sept. 30, 2005	Fuel entered, removed, or sold after Sept. 30, 2005	1002	5305
6(d)(2)(C)**	4082(e)	Fuel used in vessels or aircraft in foreign trade or trade between U.S. and its possessions is exempted from the LUST tax retroactively, for fuel entered, removed, or sold after Sept. 30, 2005	Fuel entered, removed, or sold after Sept. 30, 2005	1002	5305
6(d)(2)(D)**	6430	Fuel used in vessels or aircraft in foreign trade or trade between U.S. and its possessions is exempted from the LUST tax retroactively, for fuel entered, removed, or sold after Sept. 30, 2005	Fuel entered, removed, or sold after Sept. 30, 2005	1002	5305

Act §	Code §	Topic	Generally effective date	Analysis ¶	Com Rep ¶
6(d)(3)**	4041(d)(5)	Fuel sold for use, or used, for an off-highway business use isn't excepted from the LUST tax rate imposed under the retail fuel tax rules	Fuel sold for use or used after Dec. 29, 2007	1003	5305
7(a)†	121(b)(4)	$500,000 exclusion applies to gain from certain sales or exchanges of a principal residence by a surviving spouse within two years of the death of the spouse	Sales or exchanges after Dec. 31, 2007	301	None
7(a)(1)(A)**	45H(d)	The low sulfur diesel fuel credit rules are amended retroactively to eliminate duplicate basis reduction and to permit election not to take credit	Expenses paid or incurred after Dec. 31, 2002	401	5306
7(a)(1)(B)**	280C(d)	The low sulfur diesel fuel credit rules are amended retroactively to eliminate duplicate basis reduction and to permit election not to take credit	Expenses paid or incurred after Dec. 31, 2002	401	5306
7(a)(1)(C)**	1016(a)(31)	The low sulfur diesel fuel credit rules are amended retroactively to eliminate duplicate basis reduction and to permit election not to take credit	Expenses paid or incurred after Dec. 31, 2002	401	5306
7(a)(2)(A)**	45H(g)	The low sulfur diesel fuel credit rules are amended retroactively to eliminate duplicate basis reduction and to permit election not to take credit	Expenses paid or incurred after Dec. 31, 2002	401	5306
7(a)(2)(B)**	6501(m)	The low sulfur diesel fuel credit rules are amended retroactively to eliminate duplicate basis reduction and to permit election not to take credit	Expenses paid or incurred after Dec. 31, 2002	401	5306
7(a)(3)(A)**	179B(a)	The low sulfur diesel fuel credit rules are amended retroactively to eliminate duplicate basis reduction and to permit election not to take credit	Expenses paid or incurred after Dec. 31, 2002	401	5306

Act §	Code §	Topic	Generally effective date	Analysis ¶	Com Rep ¶
7(a)(3)(A)**	45H(b)(1)(A)	The low sulfur diesel fuel credit rules are amended retroactively to eliminate duplicate basis reduction and to permit election not to take credit	Expenses paid or incurred after Dec. 31, 2002	401	5306
7(a)(3)(A)**	45H(c)(2)	The low sulfur diesel fuel credit rules are amended retroactively to eliminate duplicate basis reduction and to permit election not to take credit	Expenses paid or incurred after Dec. 31, 2002	401	5306
7(a)(3)(A)**	45H(e)	The low sulfur diesel fuel credit rules are amended retroactively to eliminate duplicate basis reduction and to permit election not to take credit	Expenses paid or incurred after Dec. 31, 2002	401	5306
7(a)(3)(C)**	179B(a)	The low sulfur diesel fuel credit rules are amended retroactively to eliminate duplicate basis reduction and to permit election not to take credit	Expenses paid or incurred after Dec. 31, 2002	401	5306
7(b)(1)**	45(c)(3)(A)(ii)	Open-loop biomass segregation from other waste materials requirement is retroactively eliminated for purposes of the Code Sec. 45 electricity production credit	Electricity produced and sold after Oct. 22, 2004	407	5306
7(b)(2)**	45(d)(2)(B)(ii)	Clarification of proportionate limitation applicable to closed-loop biomass for purposes of the credit for electricity produced from renewable resources applies retroactively to electricity produced and sold after Oct. 22, 2004	Electricity produced and sold after Oct. 22, 2004	406	5306
7(c)(1)**	470(c)(2)(B)	Ownership by certain pass-thru entities making nonqualified allocations is no longer a reason for property to be subject to the "tax-exempt use loss" rules	Property acquired after Mar. 12, 2004	803	5306

Act §	Code §	Topic	Generally effective date	Analysis ¶	Com Rep ¶
7(c)(1)**	470(c)(2)(C)	Rules treating partnerships as leases are made expressly applicable to the "tax-exempt use loss" rules	Leases entered into after Mar. 12, 2004	805	5306
7(c)(2)**	470(d)(1)(A)	The "limited-available-funds" requirement for excepting certain leases from the "tax-exempt use loss" rules must be satisfied for the full lease term	Leases entered into after Mar. 12, 2004	804	5306
7(d)(1)**	1092(a)(2)(A)(iii)	Loss in identified straddle where there is no offsetting gain position or where an offsetting position is a liability results in basis increase to offsetting positions under reasonable, consistent method	Positions established after Oct. 21, 2004	802	5306
7(d)(2)(A)**	1092(a)(2)(B)	Identification of offsetting positions in identified straddles is required	Straddles acquired after Dec. 29, 2007	801	5306
7(d)(2)(B)**	1092(a)(2)(A)	Loss in identified straddle where there is no offsetting gain position or where an offsetting position is a liability results in basis increase to offsetting positions under reasonable, consistent method	Positions established after Oct. 21, 2004	802	5306
7(d)(2)(C)**	1092(a)(3)(B)	Loss in identified straddle where there is no offsetting gain position or where an offsetting position is a liability results in basis increase to offsetting positions under reasonable, consistent method	Positions established after Oct. 21, 2004	802	5306
7(d)(3)**	1092(a)(2)(C)	Loss in identified straddle where there is no offsetting gain position or where an offsetting position is a liability results in basis increase to offsetting positions under reasonable, consistent method	Positions established after Oct. 21, 2004	802	5306

Act §	Code §	Topic	Generally effective date	Analysis ¶	Com Rep ¶
7(d)(4)**	1092(a)(2)(D)	Loss in identified straddle where there is no offsetting gain position or where an offsetting position is a liability results in basis increase to offsetting positions under reasonable, consistent method	Positions established after Oct. 21, 2004	802	5306
8(a)†	6698(a)	Monthly failure to file partnership return penalty is increased; inspection of returns by persons having a material interest is restricted	Returns required to be filed after Dec. 20, 2007	1102	5402
8(a)(1)**	402(g)(7)(A)(ii)(II)	Application of cumulative limit on designated Roth contributions corrected; elective deferrals designated as Roth contributions are FICA "wages"	Tax years beginning after Dec. 31, 2005	1202	5307
8(a)(2)**	3121(v)(1)(A)	Application of cumulative limit on designated Roth contributions corrected; elective deferrals designated as Roth contributions are FICA "wages"	Tax years beginning after Dec. 31, 2005	1202	5307
8(b)†	6698(b)(1)	Monthly failure to file partnership return penalty is increased; inspection of returns by persons having a material interest is restricted	Returns required to be filed after Dec. 20, 2007	1102	5402
8(c)†	6103(e)(10)	Monthly failure to file partnership return penalty is increased; inspection of returns by persons having a material interest is restricted	Returns required to be filed after Dec. 20, 2007	1102	5402
9(a)†	6699	Penalty imposed for failure to file timely S corporation return	Returns required to be filed after Dec. 20, 2007	1103	None

Act §	Code §	Topic	Generally effective date	Analysis ¶	Com Rep ¶
9(a) **	45(e)(7)(A)(i)	Credit for electricity produced at qualified wind facilities originally placed in service before July 1, '99 and sold to utilities under certain pre-'87 contracts is not disallowed due to a change in ownership	Dec. 17, '99	410	5308
9(b) **	856(d)(9)(D)(ii)	Hotels and motels are lodging facilities for qualified REIT subsidiaries purposes regardless of whether rentals are transient	For tax years beginning after Dec. 31, 2007	1303	5308
10 †	6655	Estimated tax payment amounts due from corporations with assets of $1 billion or more are increased for installments due in July, Aug., or Sept. of 2012	Dec. 20, 2007	1104	5004
10(a) **	6110(i)(3)	Permitted redactions to Chief Counsel Advice otherwise open to public inspection include redactions to background file documents related to Chief Counsel Advice issued after Oct. 20, '98	Chief Counsel Advice issued after Oct. 20, '98	1304	5309
11(a)(3) **	26(b)(2)(S)	List of taxes excluded from "regular tax liability" is expanded to include the 10% penalty taxes imposed for failures to maintain HDHP coverage or for recapture of charitable deduction claimed for a fractional interest contribution	Dec. 29, 2007	903	None
11(a)(3) **	26(b)(2)(T)	List of taxes excluded from "regular tax liability" is expanded to include the 10% penalty taxes imposed for failures to maintain HDHP coverage or for recapture of charitable deduction claimed for a fractional interest contribution	Dec. 29, 2007	903	None

Act §	Code §	Topic	Generally effective date	Analysis ¶	Com Rep ¶
11(a)(8) **	48(c)	Clarification that the definitions of qualified fuel cell property and qualified microturbine property apply for all purposes of the Code Sec. 48 energy credit	Dec. 29, 2007	411	None
11(a)(15) **	170(e)(1)(B)(i)	Definition of "applicable property" for purposes of reduced deduction for contribution is clarified	Dec. 29, 2007	604	None
11(a)(37) **	6427(e)(5)	Termination dates for excise tax refund/income tax credit rules for biodiesel mixtures, alternative fuel mixtures, and alternative fuels are corrected	Aug. 8, 2005	1007	None
11(b)(1) **	168(l)(3)	Bonus depreciation and AMT exemption rules for qualified cellulosic biomass ethanol plant property are retroactively corrected to permit non-enzymatic hydrolysis	Property purchased after Dec. 20, 2006 and placed in service before Jan. 1, 2013	408	None
11(b)(2)(A) **	6724(d)(1)(B)	Returns and statements relating to certain mortgage insurance premiums are subject to information return and payee statement penalties	Amounts paid or accrued after Dec. 31, 2006	203	None
11(b)(2)(B) **	6724(d)(2)(K)	Returns and statements relating to certain mortgage insurance premiums are subject to information return and payee statement penalties	Amounts paid or accrued after Dec. 31, 2006	203	None
11(c)(1)(A) **	24(d)(1)(B)	Errors in refundable child tax credit rules are corrected	Tax years beginning after Dec. 31, 2005	901	None
11(c)(1)(B) **	24(d)(1)(B)(ii)(II)	Errors in refundable child tax credit rules are corrected	Tax years beginning after Dec. 31, 2005	901	None

Act §	Code §	Topic	Generally effective date	Analysis ¶	Com Rep ¶
11(d)(1)**	6416(a)(4)(C)	Rules relating to registered credit card issuer's electronic excise tax refund claims for sales of gasoline to certain exempt entities, are clarified for sales after Dec. 31, 2005	Sales after Dec. 31, 2005	1006	None
11(e)(1)**	6427(e)(5)(B)	Termination dates for excise tax refund/income tax credit rules for biodiesel mixtures, alternative fuel mixtures, and alternative fuels are corrected	Aug. 8, 2005	1007	None
11(e)(2)**	41(f)(1)(A)(ii)	Energy research consortium amounts are included in allocation of the research credit among controlled group members and commonly controlled businesses	Amounts paid or incurred after Aug. 8, 2005	404	None
11(e)(2)**	41(f)(1)(B)(ii)	Energy research consortium amounts are included in allocation of the research credit among controlled group members and commonly controlled businesses	Amounts paid or incurred after Aug. 8, 2005	404	None
101(a)	6428	IRS will issue cash rebates in 2008 to eligible individuals to stimulate the economy	Tax years beginning after Dec. 31, 2007	51	5501
101(b)(1)	6211(b)(4)(A)	IRS will issue cash rebates in 2008 to eligible individuals to stimulate the economy	Tax years beginning after Dec. 31, 2007	51	5501
101(b)(2)	6213(g)(2)(L)	IRS will issue cash rebates in 2008 to eligible individuals to stimulate the economy	Tax years beginning after Dec. 31, 2007	51	5501
101(c)	6428	IRS will issue cash rebates in 2008 to eligible individuals to stimulate the economy	Tax years beginning after Dec. 31, 2007	51	5501
101(d)	6428	IRS will issue cash rebates in 2008 to eligible individuals to stimulate the economy	Tax years beginning after Dec. 31, 2007	51	5501

Act §	Code §	Topic	Generally effective date	Analysis ¶	Com Rep ¶
101(f)(2)	1(i)(1)	IRS will issue cash rebates in 2008 to eligible individuals to stimulate the economy	Tax years beginning after Dec. 31, 2007	51	5501
102(a)	179(b)(7)	Regular Code Sec. 179 expense deduction limit is increased to $250,000 and beginning of deduction phaseout is raised to $800,000 for tax years beginning in 2008	Tax years beginning in 2008	52	5502
103(a)	168(k)	50% bonus depreciation and AMT depreciation relief are revived for most new tangible personal property and software and certain leasehold improvements acquired during 2008	Property acquired and placed in service during calendar year 2008	53	5503
103(b)	168(k)(1)(A)	50% bonus depreciation and AMT depreciation relief are revived for most new tangible personal property and software and certain leasehold improvements acquired during 2008	Property acquired and placed in service during calendar year 2008	53	5503
103(c)(1)	168(k)(2)(B)(i)(I)	50% bonus depreciation and AMT depreciation relief are revived for most new tangible personal property and software and certain leasehold improvements acquired during 2008	Property acquired and placed in service during calendar year 2008	53	5503
103(c)(2)	168(k)(2)(B)(i)(IV)	50% bonus depreciation and AMT depreciation relief are revived for most new tangible personal property and software and certain leasehold improvements acquired during 2008	Property acquired and placed in service during calendar year 2008	53	5503
103(c)(3)	168(k)(2)(C)(i)	50% bonus depreciation and AMT depreciation relief are revived for most new tangible personal property and software and certain leasehold improvements acquired during 2008	Property acquired and placed in service during calendar year 2008	53	5503

Act §	Code §	Topic	Generally effective date	Analysis ¶	Com Rep ¶
103(c)(4)	168(k)(2)(F)(i)	First-year depreciation limit for passenger automobiles is increased by $8,000 if the passenger automobile is "qualified property"	Property acquired and placed in service during calendar year 2008	54	5503
103(c)(5)(A)	168(k)(4)	50% bonus depreciation and AMT depreciation relief are revived for most new tangible personal property and software and certain leasehold improvements acquired during 2008	Property acquired and placed in service during calendar year 2008	53	5503
103(c)(5)(B)	168(k)(2)(D)(iii)	50% bonus depreciation and AMT depreciation relief are revived for most new tangible personal property and software and certain leasehold improvements acquired during 2008	Property acquired and placed in service during calendar year 2008	53	5503
103(c)(6)	168(l)(4)(A)	50% bonus depreciation and AMT depreciation relief are revived for most new tangible personal property and software and certain leasehold improvements acquired during 2008	Property acquired and placed in service during calendar year 2008	53	5503
103(c)(10)	1400N(d)(6)(E)	50% bonus depreciation and AMT depreciation relief are revived for most new tangible personal property and software and certain leasehold improvements acquired during 2008	Property acquired and placed in service during calendar year 2008	53	5503
116(a)(Div. K, Title I)++	4081(d)(2)(B)	Airport and airway trust fund excise taxes are extended through Feb. 29, 2008	Oct. 1, 2007	1001	None
116(b)(1)(Div. K, Title I)++	4261(j)(1)(A)(ii)	Airport and airway trust fund excise taxes are extended through Feb. 29, 2008	Oct. 1, 2007	1001	None
116(b)(2)(Div. K, Title I)++	4271(d)(1)(A)(ii)	Airport and airway trust fund excise taxes are extended through Feb. 29, 2008	Oct. 1, 2007	1001	None

Act §	Code §	Topic	Generally effective date	Analysis ¶	Com Rep ¶
1501(a)+	3301	Additional 0.2% FUTA surtax is extended to apply through 2008	Wages paid in 2008	1201	5101
1502(a)+	167(h)(5)(A)	Amortization period of geological and geophysical (G&G) expenditures for certain major integrated oil companies is extended from 5 years to 7 years	Amounts paid or incurred after Dec. 19, 2007	412	5102

¶ 6001. Code Section Cross Reference Table

Act § cites are to the 2008 Economic Stimulus Act unless otherwise indicated.

* denotes 2007 Tax Increase Prevention Act

† denotes 2007 Mortgage Relief Act

+ denotes 2007 Energy Act

** denotes 2007 Technical Corrections Act

‡ denotes 2007 Virginia Tech Victims Act

++ denotes 2008 Appropriations Act

Code §	Act §	Topic	Generally effective date	Analysis ¶	Com Rep ¶
1(i)(1)	101(f)(2)	IRS will issue cash rebates in 2008 to eligible individuals to stimulate the economy	Tax years beginning after Dec. 31, 2007	51	5501
21	3(a)(1)*	Nonrefundable personal credits may offset AMT through 2007 (instead of 2006)	Tax years beginning in 2007	102	5201
22	3(a)(1)*	Nonrefundable personal credits may offset AMT through 2007 (instead of 2006)	Tax years beginning in 2007	102	5201
23	3(a)(1)*	Nonrefundable personal credits may offset AMT through 2007 (instead of 2006)	Tax years beginning in 2007	102	5201
24	3(a)(1)*	Nonrefundable personal credits may offset AMT through 2007 (instead of 2006)	Tax years beginning in 2007	102	5201
24(d)(1)(B)	11(c)(1)(A)**	Errors in refundable child tax credit rules are corrected	Tax years beginning after Dec. 31, 2005	901	None
24(d)(1)(B)(ii)(II)	11(c)(1)(B)**	Errors in refundable child tax credit rules are corrected	Tax years beginning after Dec. 31, 2005	901	None
25	3(a)(1)*	Nonrefundable personal credits may offset AMT through 2007 (instead of 2006)	Tax years beginning in 2007	102	5201
25A	3(a)(1)*	Nonrefundable personal credits may offset AMT through 2007 (instead of 2006)	Tax years beginning in 2007	102	5201

Code §	Act §	Topic	Generally effective date	Analysis ¶	Com Rep ¶
25B	3(a)(1)*	Nonrefundable personal credits may offset AMT through 2007 (instead of 2006)	Tax years beginning in 2007	102	5201
25C	3(a)(1)*	Nonrefundable personal credits may offset AMT through 2007 (instead of 2006)	Tax years beginning in 2007	102	5201
25D	3(a)(1)*	Nonrefundable personal credits may offset AMT through 2007 (instead of 2006)	Tax years beginning in 2007	102	5201
26(a)(2)	3(a)(1)*	Nonrefundable personal credits may offset AMT through 2007 (instead of 2006)	Tax years beginning in 2007	102	5201
26(b)(2)(S)	11(a)(3)**	List of taxes excluded from "regular tax liability" is expanded to include the 10% penalty taxes imposed for failures to maintain HDHP coverage or for recapture of charitable deduction claimed for a fractional interest contribution	Dec. 29, 2007	903	None
26(b)(2)(T)	11(a)(3)**	List of taxes excluded from "regular tax liability" is expanded to include the 10% penalty taxes imposed for failures to maintain HDHP coverage or for recapture of charitable deduction claimed for a fractional interest contribution	Dec. 29, 2007	903	None
30C(b)	6(b)(1)**	Dollar limits on credit for alternative fuel vehicle refueling property apply to all property placed in service at a location	Property placed in service after Dec. 31, 2005 and before Jan. 1, 2010	402	5305
30C(c)	6(b)(2)**	Definition of "qualified alternative fuel vehicle refueling property" is clarified	Property placed in service after Dec. 31, 2005 and before Jan. 1, 2010	403	5305

Code §	Act §	Topic	Generally effective date	Analysis ¶	Com Rep ¶
41(a)(3)	6(c)(1)**	Research credit for research by an energy research consortium is clarified to require that the research be qualified energy research	Amounts paid or incurred after Aug. 8, 2005	405	5305
41(f)(1)(A)(ii)	11(e)(2)**	Energy research consortium amounts are included in allocation of the research credit among controlled group members and commonly controlled businesses	Amounts paid or incurred after Aug. 8, 2005	404	None
41(f)(1)(B)(ii)	11(e)(2)**	Energy research consortium amounts are included in allocation of the research credit among controlled group members and commonly controlled businesses	Amounts paid or incurred after Aug. 8, 2005	404	None
41(f)(6)(E)	6(c)(2)**	Research credit for research by an energy research consortium is clarified to require that the research be qualified energy research	Amounts paid or incurred after Aug. 8, 2005	405	5305
42(i)(3)(D)(ii)(I)	6(a)†	Rule that prevents full-time students from disqualifying housing units from the low-income housing credit is clarified	Housing credit amounts, whenever allocated, and certain tax-exempt-financed buildings, whenever placed in service	902	None
45(c)(3)(A)(ii)	7(b)(1)**	Open-loop biomass segregation from other waste materials requirement is retroactively eliminated for purposes of the Code Sec. 45 electricity production credit	Electricity produced and sold after Oct. 22, 2004	407	5306

Code §	Act §	Topic	Generally effective date	Analysis ¶	Com Rep ¶
45(d)(2)(B)(ii)	7(b)(2) **	Clarification of proportionate limitation applicable to closed-loop biomass for purposes of the credit for electricity produced from renewable resources applies retroactively to electricity produced and sold after Oct. 22, 2004	Electricity produced and sold after Oct. 22, 2004	406	5306
45(e)(7)(A)(i)	9(a) **	Credit for electricity produced at qualified wind facilities originally placed in service before July 1, '99 and sold to utilities under certain pre-'87 contracts is not disallowed due to a change in ownership	Dec. 17, '99	410	5308
45H(b)(1)(A)	7(a)(3)(A) **	The low sulfur diesel fuel credit rules are amended retroactively to eliminate duplicate basis reduction and to permit election not to take credit	Expenses paid or incurred after Dec. 31, 2002	401	5306
45H(c)(2)	7(a)(3)(A) **	The low sulfur diesel fuel credit rules are amended retroactively to eliminate duplicate basis reduction and to permit election not to take credit	Expenses paid or incurred after Dec. 31, 2002	401	5306
45H(d)	7(a)(1)(A) **	The low sulfur diesel fuel credit rules are amended retroactively to eliminate duplicate basis reduction and to permit election not to take credit	Expenses paid or incurred after Dec. 31, 2002	401	5306
45H(e)	7(a)(3)(A) **	The low sulfur diesel fuel credit rules are amended retroactively to eliminate duplicate basis reduction and to permit election not to take credit	Expenses paid or incurred after Dec. 31, 2002	401	5306
45H(g)	7(a)(2)(A) **	The low sulfur diesel fuel credit rules are amended retroactively to eliminate duplicate basis reduction and to permit election not to take credit	Expenses paid or incurred after Dec. 31, 2002	401	5306

Code §	Act §	Topic	Generally effective date	Analysis ¶	Com Rep ¶
45J(b)(2)	6(a)**	IRS cannot allocate more than the national capacity limitation of 6,000 megawatts for purposes of advanced nuclear power facilities credit computation	Production in tax years beginning after Aug. 8, 2005	409	5305
48(c)	11(a)(8)**	Clarification that the definitions of qualified fuel cell property and qualified microturbine property apply for all purposes of the Code Sec. 48 energy credit	Dec. 29, 2007	411	None
53(e)(2)(A)	2(a)**	AMT refundable credit for individuals is revised to allow at least $5,000 a year for five years	Tax years beginning after Dec. 20, 2006 and before Jan. 1, 2013	103	5301
55(d)(1)(A)	2(a)(1)*	AMT exemption amounts for 2007 are increased to $44,350 for unmarrieds, to $66,250 for joint filers, and to $33,125 for marrieds filing separately	Tax years beginning in 2007	101	5201
55(d)(1)(B)	2(a)(2)*	AMT exemption amounts for 2007 are increased to $44,350 for unmarrieds, to $66,250 for joint filers, and to $33,125 for marrieds filing separately	Tax years beginning in 2007	101	5201
61	1‡	Certain payments received by surviving victims and survivors of slain victims of the Virginia Tech shootings are excluded from gross income	Dec. 19, 2007	303	5401
108(a)(1)(E)	2(a)†	Discharges of up to $2 million of acquisition debt on taxpayer's main home in 2007 through 2009 are excluded from income	Discharges of indebtedness after Dec. 31, 2006, and before Jan. 1, 2010	201	5001
108(a)(2)(A)	2(c)(1)†	Discharges of up to $2 million of acquisition debt on taxpayer's main home in 2007 through 2009 are excluded from income	Discharges of indebtedness after Dec. 31, 2006, and before Jan. 1, 2010	201	5001

Code §	Act §	Topic	Generally effective date	Analysis ¶	Com Rep ¶
108(a)(2)(C)	2(c)(2) †	Discharges of up to $2 million of acquisition debt on taxpayer's main home in 2007 through 2009 are excluded from income	Discharges of indebtedness after Dec. 31, 2006, and before Jan. 1, 2010	201	5001
108(h)	2(b) †	Discharges of up to $2 million of acquisition debt on taxpayer's main home in 2007 through 2009 are excluded from income	Discharges of indebtedness after Dec. 31, 2006, and before Jan. 1, 2010	201	5001
121(b)(4)	7(a) †	$500,000 exclusion applies to gain from certain sales or exchanges of a principal residence by a surviving spouse within two years of the death of the spouse	Sales or exchanges after Dec. 31, 2007	301	None
139B	5(a) †	Tax relief and expense reimbursements provided by state and local governments to volunteer firefighters and emergency medical responders for services performed are tax-free for 2008 - 2010 tax years	Tax years beginning after Dec. 31, 2007 and before Jan. 1, 2011	302	5003
163(h)(3)(E)(iv)(I)	3(a) †	Interest deduction for mortgage insurance premiums is extended to amounts paid or incurred after 2007 and before 2011	Amounts paid or accrued after Dec. 31, 2007	202	None
167(h)(5)(A)	1502(a) +	Amortization period of geological and geophysical (G&G) expenditures for certain major integrated oil companies is extended from 5 years to 7 years	Amounts paid or incurred after Dec. 19, 2007	412	5102
168(k)	103(a)	50% bonus depreciation and AMT depreciation relief are revived for most new tangible personal property and software and certain leasehold improvements acquired during 2008	Property acquired and placed in service during calendar year 2008	53	5003

Code §	Act §	Topic	Generally effective date	Analysis ¶	Com Rep ¶
168(k)(1)(A)	103(b)	50% bonus depreciation and AMT depreciation relief are revived for most new tangible personal property and software and certain leasehold improvements acquired during 2008	Property acquired and placed in service during calendar year 2008	53	5503
168(k)(2)(B)(i)(I)	103(c)(1)	50% bonus depreciation and AMT depreciation relief are revived for most new tangible personal property and software and certain leasehold improvements acquired during 2008	Property acquired and placed in service during calendar year 2008	53	5503
168(k)(2)(B)(i)(IV)	103(c)(2)	50% bonus depreciation and AMT depreciation relief are revived for most new tangible personal property and software and certain leasehold improvements acquired during 2008	Property acquired and placed in service during calendar year 2008	53	5503
168(k)(2)(C)(i)	103(c)(3)	50% bonus depreciation and AMT depreciation relief are revived for most new tangible personal property and software and certain leasehold improvements acquired during 2008	Property acquired and placed in service during calendar year 2008	53	5503
168(k)(2)(D)(iii)	103(c)(5)(B)	50% bonus depreciation and AMT depreciation relief are revived for most new tangible personal property and software and certain leasehold improvements acquired during 2008	Property acquired and placed in service during calendar year 2008	53	5503
168(k)(2)(F)(i)	103(c)(4)	First-year depreciation limit for passenger automobiles is increased by $8,000 if the passenger automobile is "qualified property"	Property acquired and placed in service during calendar year 2008	54	5503

Code §	Act §	Topic	Generally effective date	Analysis ¶	Com Rep ¶
168(k)(4)	103(c)(5)(A)	50% bonus depreciation and AMT depreciation relief are revived for most new tangible personal property and software and certain leasehold improvements acquired during 2008	Property acquired and placed in service during calendar year 2008	53	5503
168(l)(3)	11(b)(1)**	Bonus depreciation and AMT exemption rules for qualified cellulosic biomass ethanol plant property are retroactively corrected to permit non-enzymatic hydrolysis	Property purchased after Dec. 20, 2006 and placed in service before Jan. 1, 2013	408	None
168(l)(4)(A)	103(c)(6)	50% bonus depreciation and AMT depreciation relief are revived for most new tangible personal property and software and certain leasehold improvements acquired during 2008	Property acquired and placed in service during calendar year 2008	53	5503
170(e)(1)(B)(i)	11(a)(15)**	Definition of "applicable property" for purposes of reduced deduction for contribution is clarified	Dec. 29, 2007	604	None
170(e)(7)(D)(i)(I)	3(c)**	Donee's use of donated "applicable property" for its exempt purpose or function must be substantial for taxpayer to avoid reduction or recapture of deduction for contribution	Contributions after Sept. 1, 2006	605	5302
179(b)(7)	102(a)	Regular Code Sec. 179 expense deduction limit is increased to $250,000 and beginning of deduction phaseout is raised to $800,000 for tax years beginning in 2008	Tax years beginning in 2008	52	5502
179B(a)	7(a)(3)(A)**	The low sulfur diesel fuel credit rules are amended retroactively to eliminate duplicate basis reduction and to permit election not to take credit	Expenses paid or incurred after Dec. 31, 2002	401	5306

Code §	Act §	Topic	Generally effective date	Analysis ¶	Com Rep ¶
179B(a)	7(a)(3)(C) **	The low sulfur diesel fuel credit rules are amended retroactively to eliminate duplicate basis reduction and to permit election not to take credit	Expenses paid or incurred after Dec. 31, 2002	401	5306
216(b)(1)(D)	4(a) †	Cooperatives can use alternative tests based on square footage or expenditures in lieu of the 80/20 gross income test to qualify as a cooperative housing corporation	Tax years ending after Dec. 20, 2007	1302	5002
280C(d)	7(a)(1)(B) **	The low sulfur diesel fuel credit rules are amended retroactively to eliminate duplicate basis reduction and to permit election not to take credit	Expenses paid or incurred after Dec. 31, 2002	401	5306
355(b)(2)	4(b)(1) **	Modification of active business definition under Code Sec. 355	Distributions made after May 17, 2006	1301	5303
355(b)(3)(C)	4(b)(2) **	Modification of active business definition under Code Sec. 355	Distributions made after May 17, 2006	1301	5303
355(b)(3)(D)	4(b)(2) **	Modification of active business definition under Code Sec. 355	Distributions made after May 17, 2006	1301	5303
402(g)(7)(A)(ii)(II)	8(a)(1) **	Application of cumulative limit on designated Roth contributions corrected; elective deferrals designated as Roth contributions are FICA "wages"	Tax years beginning after Dec. 31, 2005	1202	5307
408(d)(8)(D)	3(a) **	Rule clarified for determining what portion of an IRA distribution that includes nondeductible contributions is tax-free under the IRA qualified charitable distribution rules	For IRA distributions made during 2006 and 2007	602	5302
470(c)(2)(B)	7(c)(1) **	Ownership by certain pass-thru entities making nonqualified allocations is no longer a reason for property to be subject to the "tax-exempt use loss" rules	Property acquired after Mar. 12, 2004	803	5306

Code §	Act §	Topic	Generally effective date	Analysis ¶	Com Rep ¶
470(c)(2)(C)	7(c)(1)**	Rules treating partnerships as leases are made expressly applicable to the "tax-exempt use loss" rules	Leases entered into after Mar. 12, 2004	805	5306
470(d)(1)(A)	7(c)(2)**	The "limited-available-funds" requirement for excepting certain leases from the "tax-exempt use loss" rules must be satisfied for the full lease term	Leases entered into after Mar. 12, 2004	804	5306
856(d)(9)(D)(ii)	9(b)**	Hotels and motels are lodging facilities for qualified REIT subsidiaries purposes regardless of whether rentals are transient	For tax years beginning after Dec. 31, 2007	1303	5308
904(i)	3(a)(1)*	Nonrefundable personal credits may offset AMT through 2007 (instead of 2006)	Tax years beginning in 2007	102	5201
911(f)	4(c)**	Computation of regular tax and AMT modified where foreign earned income or housing exclusion is claimed	Tax years beginning after Dec. 31, 2006	701	5303
954(c)(6)(B)	4(a)**	TIPRA look-through rule doesn't apply to interest, rent or royalty payments between related CFCs that create or increase a deficit that reduces subpart F income	Tax years of foreign corporations beginning after Dec. 31, 2005 and before Jan. 1, 2009, and tax years of U.S. shareholders with or within which such tax years of foreign corporations end	702	5303
1016(a)(31)	7(a)(1)(C)**	The low sulfur diesel fuel credit rules are amended retroactively to eliminate duplicate basis reduction and to permit election not to take credit	Expenses paid or incurred after Dec. 31, 2002	401	5306

Code §	Act §	Topic	Generally effective date	Analysis ¶	Com Rep ¶
1092(a)(2)(A)	7(d)(2)(B)**	Loss in identified straddle where there is no offsetting gain position or where an offsetting position is a liability results in basis increase to offsetting positions under reasonable, consistent method	Positions established after Oct. 21, 2004	802	5306
1092(a)(2)(A)(iii)	7(d)(1)**	Loss in identified straddle where there is no offsetting gain position or where an offsetting position is a liability results in basis increase to offsetting positions under reasonable, consistent method	Positions established after Oct. 21, 2004	802	5306
1092(a)(2)(B)	7(d)(2)(A)**	Identification of offsetting positions in identified straddles is required	Straddles acquired after Dec. 29, 2007	801	5306
1092(a)(2)(C)	7(d)(3)**	Loss in identified straddle where there is no offsetting gain position or where an offsetting position is a liability results in basis increase to offsetting positions under reasonable, consistent method	Positions established after Oct. 21, 2004	802	5306
1092(a)(2)(D)	7(d)(4)**	Loss in identified straddle where there is no offsetting gain position or where an offsetting position is a liability results in basis increase to offsetting positions under reasonable, consistent method	Positions established after Oct. 21, 2004	802	5306
1092(a)(3)(B)	7(d)(2)(C)**	Loss in identified straddle where there is no offsetting gain position or where an offsetting position is a liability results in basis increase to offsetting positions under reasonable, consistent method	Positions established after Oct. 21, 2004	802	5306

729

Code §	Act §	Topic	Generally effective date	Analysis ¶	Com Rep ¶
1366(d)(4)	3(b) **	Charitable deduction allowed where S corporation's charitable contribution of property reduces shareholder's basis only by contributed property's basis	Contributions made in tax years beginning after Dec. 31, 2005	603	5302
1400C	3(a)(1) *	Nonrefundable personal credits may offset AMT through 2007 (instead of 2006)	Tax years beginning in 2007	102	5201
1400N(d)(6)(E)	103(c)(10)	50% bonus depreciation and AMT depreciation relief are revived for most new tangible personal property and software and certain leasehold improvements acquired during 2008	Property acquired and placed in service during calendar year 2008	53	5503
2055(g)	3(d)(1) **	Limits on estate and gift tax charitable deductions for series of fractional contributions of tangible personal property are retroactively repealed	Bequests and gifts made after Aug. 17, 2006	601	5302
2522(e)	3(d)(2) **	Limits on estate and gift tax charitable deductions for series of fractional contributions of tangible personal property are retroactively repealed	Bequests and gifts made after Aug. 17, 2006	601	5302
3121(v)(1)(A)	8(a)(2) **	Application of cumulative limit on designated Roth contributions corrected; elective deferrals designated as Roth contributions are FICA "wages"	Tax years beginning after Dec. 31, 2005.	1202	5307
3301	1501(a)+	Additional 0.2% FUTA surtax is extended to apply through 2008	Wages paid in 2008	1201	5101
4041(d)(1)	6(d)(1)(A) **	Double LUST tax on certain dyed diesel fuel and kerosene and fuels used on inland waterways is eliminated retroactively, for fuel entered, removed, or sold after Sept. 30, 2005	Fuel entered, removed, or sold after Sept. 30, 2005	1004	5305

Code §	Act §	Topic	Generally effective date	Analysis ¶	Com Rep ¶
4041(d)(5)	6(d)(2)(A)**	Fuel used in vessels or aircraft in foreign trade or trade between U.S. and its possessions is exempted from the LUST tax retroactively, for fuel entered, removed, or sold after Sept. 30, 2005	Fuel entered, removed, or sold after Sept. 30, 2005	1002	5305
4041(d)(5)	6(d)(3)**	Fuel sold for use, or used, for an off-highway business use isn't excepted from the LUST tax rate imposed under the retail fuel tax rules	Fuel sold for use or used after Dec. 29, 2007	1003	5305
4042(b)(3)	6(d)(1)(B)**	Double LUST tax on certain dyed diesel fuel and kerosene and fuels used on inland waterways is eliminated retroactively, for fuel entered, removed, or sold after Sept. 30, 2005	Fuel entered, removed, or sold after Sept. 30, 2005	1004	5305
4081(d)(2)(B)	116(a)(Div. K, Title I)++	Airport and airway trust fund excise taxes are extended through Feb. 29, 2008	Oct. 1, 2007	1001	None
4082(e)	6(d)(2)(C)**	Fuel used in vessels or aircraft in foreign trade or trade between U.S. and its possessions is exempted from the LUST tax retroactively, for fuel entered, removed, or sold after Sept. 30, 2005	Fuel entered, removed, or sold after Sept. 30, 2005	1002	5305
4082(f)	6(d)(2)(B)**	Fuel used in vessels or aircraft in foreign trade or trade between U.S. and its possessions is exempted from the LUST tax retroactively, for fuel entered, removed, or sold after Sept. 30, 2005	Fuel entered, removed, or sold after Sept. 30, 2005	1002	5305
4261(j)(1)(A)(ii)	116(b)(1)(Div. K, Title I)++	Airport and airway trust fund excise taxes are extended through Feb. 29, 2008	Oct. 1, 2007	1001	None
4271(d)(1)(A)(ii)	116(b)(2)(Div. K, Title I)++	Airport and airway trust fund excise taxes are extended through Feb. 29, 2008	Oct. 1, 2007	1001	None

Code §	Act §	Topic	Generally effective date	Analysis ¶	Com Rep ¶
4940(c)(4)(A)	3(f) **	Excise tax on private foundation's net investment income applies to capital gains from appreciation, including gains on assets used for exempt purposes	Tax years beginning after Aug. 17, 2006	504	5302
4958(c)(3)(A)(i)(II)	3(i)(1) **	Excess benefit transactions rules don't apply to transactions between supporting organizations and Code Sec. 501(c)(4), Code Sec. 501(c)(5), or Code Sec. 501(c)(6) supported organizations	For transactions occurring after July 25, 2006.	505	5302
4958(c)(3)(C)(ii)	3(i)(2) **	Excess benefit transactions rules don't apply to transactions between supporting organizations and Code Sec. 501(c)(4), Code Sec. 501(c)(5), or Code Sec. 501(c)(6) supported organizations	For transactions occurring after July 25, 2006.	505	5302
4962(b)	3(h) **	Donor advised fund excise taxes added to list of "qualified first tier taxes" for abatement purposes	Tax years beginning after Aug. 17, 2006	503	5302
6103(e)(10)	8(c) †	Monthly failure to file partnership return penalty is increased; inspection of returns by persons having a material interest is restricted	Returns required to be filed after Dec. 20, 2007	1102	5402
6104(b)	3(g)(1)(B) **	IRS must allow public inspection of unrelated business income tax (UBIT) returns of tax-exempt organizations, such as Form 990-T, filed under Code Sec. 6011	Returns filed after Aug. 17, 2006	502	5302
6104(d)(1)(A)(ii)	3(g)(2) **	Code Sec. 501(c)(3) organizations must make available for public inspection copies of Form 990-T relating to UBIT for three years	Returns filed after Aug. 17, 2006	501	5302

Code §	Act §	Topic	Generally effective date	Analysis ¶	Com Rep ¶
6104(d)(2)	3(g)(3) **	Code Sec. 501(c)(3) organizations must make available for public inspection copies of Form 990-T relating to UBIT for three years	Returns filed after Aug. 17, 2006	501	5302
6110(i)(3)	10(a) **	Permitted redactions to Chief Counsel Advice otherwise open to public inspection include redactions to background file documents related to Chief Counsel Advice issued after Oct. 20, '98	Chief Counsel Advice issued after Oct. 20, '98	1304	5309
6211(b)(4)(A)	101(b)(1)	IRS will issue cash rebates in 2008 to eligible individuals to stimulate the economy	Tax years beginning after Dec. 31, 2007	51	5501
6213(g)(2)(L)	101(b)(2)	IRS will issue cash rebates in 2008 to eligible individuals to stimulate the economy	Tax years beginning after Dec. 31, 2007	51	5501
6416(a)(4)(C)	11(d)(1) **	Rules relating to registered credit card issuer's electronic excise tax refund claims for sales of gasoline to certain exempt entities, are clarified for sales after Dec. 31, 2005	Sales after Dec. 31, 2005	1006	None
6426(d)(2)(F)	5(a)(2) **	Fuel eligible for alternative fuel excise tax credit is expanded retroactively	Any sale or use for any period after Sept. 30, 2006	1005	5304
6426(h)	5(a)(3) **	Fuel eligible for alternative fuel excise tax credit is expanded retroactively	Any sale or use for any period after Sept. 30, 2006	1005	5304
6427(e)(5)	11(a)(37) **	Termination dates for excise tax refund/income tax credit rules for biodiesel mixtures, alternative fuel mixtures, and alternative fuels are corrected	Aug. 8, 2005	1007	None

Code §	Act §	Topic	Generally effective date	Analysis ¶	Com Rep ¶
6427(e)(5)(B)	11(e)(1)**	Termination dates for excise tax refund/income tax credit rules for biodiesel mixtures, alternative fuel mixtures, and alternative fuels are corrected	Aug. 8, 2005	1007	None
6427(i)(3)(A)	5(a)(1)(A)**	Expedited excise tax refund claims permitted for alternative fuels, for any sale or use for any period after Sept. 30, 2006	Sale or use for any period after Sept. 30, 2006	1008	5304
6427(i)(3)(A)(i)	5(a)(1)(B)**	Expedited excise tax refund claims permitted for alternative fuels, for any sale or use for any period after Sept. 30, 2006	Sale or use for any period after Sept. 30, 2006	1008	5304
6427(i)(3)(B)	5(a)(1)(B)**	Expedited excise tax refund claims permitted for alternative fuels, for any sale or use for any period after Sept. 30, 2006	Sale or use for any period after Sept. 30, 2006	1008	5304
6428	101(a)	IRS will issue cash rebates in 2008 to eligible individuals to stimulate the economy	Tax years beginning after Dec. 31, 2007	51	5501
6428	101(c)	IRS will issue cash rebates in 2008 to eligible individuals to stimulate the economy	Tax years beginning after Dec. 31, 2007	51	5501
6428	101(d)	IRS will issue cash rebates in 2008 to eligible individuals to stimulate the economy	Tax years beginning after Dec. 31, 2007	51	5501
6430	6(d)(2)(D)**	Fuel used in vessels or aircraft in foreign trade or trade between U.S. and its possessions is exempted from the LUST tax retroactively, for fuel entered, removed, or sold after Sept. 30, 2005	Fuel entered, removed, or sold after Sept. 30, 2005	1002	5305
6501(m)	7(a)(2)(B)**	The low sulfur diesel fuel credit rules are amended retroactively to eliminate duplicate basis reduction and to permit election not to take credit	Expenses paid or incurred after Dec. 31, 2002	401	5306

Code §	Act §	Topic	Generally effective date	Analysis ¶	Com Rep ¶
6655	10 †	Estimated tax payment amounts due from corporations with assets of $1 billion or more are increased for installments due in July, Aug., or Sept. of 2012	Dec. 20, 2007	1104	5004
6695A(a)(2)	3(e)(1) **	Penalty for valuation misstatements attributable to incorrect appraisals applies to substantial estate or gift tax valuation understatements and is subject to 3-year limitation period	Appraisals prepared for returns or submissions filed after Aug. 17, 2006	1101	5302
6696(d)(1)	3(e)(2) **	Penalty for valuation misstatements attributable to incorrect appraisals applies to substantial estate or gift tax valuation understatements and is subject to 3-year limitation period	Appraisals prepared for returns or submissions filed after Aug. 17, 2006	1101	5302
6698(a)	8(a) †	Monthly failure to file partnership return penalty is increased; inspection of returns by persons having a material interest is restricted	Returns required to be filed after Dec. 20, 2007	1102	5402
6698(b)(1)	2 ‡	Monthly failure to file partnership return penalty is increased; inspection of returns by persons having a material interest is restricted	Returns required to be filed after Dec. 20, 2007	1102	5402
6698(b)(1)	8(b) †	Monthly failure to file partnership return penalty is increased; inspection of returns by persons having a material interest is restricted	Returns required to be filed after Dec. 20, 2007	1102	5402
6699	9(a) †	Penalty imposed for failure to file timely S corporation return	Returns required to be filed after Dec. 20, 2007	1103	None

Code §	Act §	Topic	Generally effective date	Analysis ¶	Com Rep ¶
6724(d)(1)(B)	11(b)(2)(A)**	Returns and statements relating to certain mortgage insurance premiums are subject to information return and payee statement penalties	Amounts paid or accrued after Dec. 31, 2006	203	None
6724(d)(2)(K)	11(b)(2)(B)**	Returns and statements relating to certain mortgage insurance premiums are subject to information return and payee statement penalties	Amounts paid or accrued after Dec. 31, 2006	203	None

¶ 6002. Code Sections Amended by Acts

Act § cites are to the 2008 Economic Stimulus Act unless otherwise indicated.

* denotes 2007 Tax Increase Prevention Act

† denotes 2007 Mortgage Relief Act

+ denotes 2007 Energy Act

** denotes 2007 Technical Corrections Act

‡ denotes 2007 Virginia Tech Victims Act

++ denotes 2008 Appropriations Act

Code Sec.	Act Sec.	Code Sec.	Act Sec.
1(i)(1)(D)	101(f)(2)	45H(c)(2)	7(a)(3)(B)**
21	3(a)(1)*	45H(d)	7(a)(1)(A)**
21(e)(5)	11(a)(1)**	45H(e)	7(a)(1)(A)**
22	3(a)(1)*	45H(e)(1)	7(a)(3)(A)**
23	3(a)(1)*	45H(e)(2)	7(a)(3)(A)**
24	3(a)(1)*	45H(f)	7(a)(1)(A)**
24(d)(1)(B)	11(c)(1)(A)**	45H(g)	7(a)(1)(A)**
24(d)(1)(B)	11(c)(1)(B)**	45H(g)	7(a)(2)(A)**
25	3(a)(1)*	45J(b)(2)	6(a)**
25A	3(a)(1)*	45L(c)(2)	11(a)(7)**
25B	3(a)(1)*	45L(c)(3)	11(a)(7)**
25C	3(a)(1)*	48(c)	11(a)(8)**
25C(c)(3)	11(a)(2)**	48(c)(1)(B)	11(a)(9)**
25D	3(a)(1)*	48(c)(2)(B)	11(a)(9)**
26(a)(2)	3(a)(1)*	48A(d)(4)(B)(ii)	11(a)(10)**
26(a)(2)	3(a)(2)*	53(e)(2)(A)	2(a)**
26(b)(2)(S)	11(a)(3)**	54(g)(4)(C)(iv)	11(g)(2)**
26(b)(2)(T)	11(a)(3)**	55(d)(1)(A)	2(a)(1)*
26(b)(2)(U)	11(a)(3)**	55(d)(1)(B)	2(a)(2)*
26(b)(2)(V)	11(a)(3)**	56(g)(4)(C)(ii)(I)	11(g)(1)**
30C(b)	6(b)(1)**	61	1‡
30C(c)	6(b)(2)**	108(a)(1)(C)	2(a)†
34(a)(1)	11(a)(4)(A)**	108(a)(1)(D)	2(a)†
34(a)(2)	11(a)(4)(B)**	108(a)(1)(E)	2(a)†
34(a)(3)	11(a)(4)(C)**	108(a)(2)(A)	2(c)(1)†
35(d)(2)	11(a)(5)(A)**	108(a)(2)(C)	2(c)(2)†
35(d)(2)	11(a)(5)(B)**	108(h)	2(b)†
38(b)	11(a)(6)(A)**	121(b)(4)	7(a)†
38(b)	11(a)(6)(B)**	121(d)(9)	11(a)(11)(A)**
38(b)(30)	11(a)(6)(C)**	121(d)(9)	11(a)(11)(B)**
41(a)(3)	6(c)(1)**	125(b)(2)	11(a)(12)**
41(f)(1)(A)(ii)	11(e)(2)**	139B	5(a)†
41(f)(1)(B)(ii)	11(e)(2)**	163(h)(3)(E)(iv)(I)	3(a)†
41(f)(6)(E)	6(c)(2)**	167(g)(8)(C)(ii)(II)	11(a)(13)**
42(i)(3)(D)(ii)(I)	6(a)†	167(h)(5)(A)	1502(a)+
45(c)(3)(A)(ii)	7(b)(1)**	168(k)	103(a)(1)
45(d)(2)(B)(i)	7(b)(2)**	168(k)	103(a)(2)
45(d)(2)(B)(ii)	7(b)(2)**	168(k)	103(a)(3)
45(d)(2)(B)(iii)	7(b)(2)**	168(k)	103(a)(4)
45(e)(7)(A)(i)	9(a)**	168(k)	103(c)(11)(A)
45H(b)(1)(A)	7(a)(3)(A)**	168(k)	103(c)(11)(B)
45H(c)(2)	7(a)(3)(A)**	168(k)(1)(A)	103(b)

Code Sec.	Act Sec.	Code Sec.	Act Sec.
168(k)(2)(B)	103(c)(12)	904(d)(2)(B)(v)(II)	11(g)(10)(B) **
168(k)(2)(B)(i)(I)	103(c)(1)	904(d)(2)(B)(v)(III)	11(g)(10)(A) **
168(k)(2)(B)(i)(IV)	103(c)(2)	904(f)(3)(D)(iv)	11(f)(3) **
168(k)(2)(C)(i)	103(c)(3)	904(i)	3(a)(1) *
168(k)(2)(D)(iii)	103(c)(5)(B)	906(b)(5)	11(g)(11) **
168(k)(2)(F)(i)	103(c)(4)	906(b)(6)	11(g)(11) **
168(k)(4)	103(c)(5)(A)	906(b)(7)	11(g)(11) **
168(l)(3)	11(b)(1) **	911(f) ($515)	4(c) **
168(l)(4)(A)	103(c)(6)	936(f)(2)	11(g)(12) **
168(l)(4)(B)	103(c)(6)	951(c)	11(g)(13) **
168(l)(4)(C)	103(c)(6)	951(d)	11(g)(13) **
168(l)(4)(D)	103(c)(6)	952(b)	11(g)(14) **
168(l)(5)(A)	103(c)(7)(A)	954(c)(1)(F)	11(a)(19) **
168(l)(5)(B)	103(c)(7)(B)	954(c)(1)(H)	11(a)(20) **
170(b)(1)(A)(vii)	11(a)(14)(A) **	954(c)(1)(I)	11(a)(20) **
170(c)(1)(B)(i)(II)	11(a)(15) **	954(c)(2)(C)(ii)	11(g)(15)(B) **
170(e)(1)(B)(ii)	11(a)(14)(B) **	954(c)(6)(B)	4(a) **
170(e)(7)(D)(i)(I)	3(c) **	954(c)(6)(C)	4(a) **
170(o)(1)(A)	11(a)(16)(A) **	956(c)(2)	11(g)(15)(A)(ii) **
170(o)(3)(A)(i)	11(a)(16)(B)(i) **	956(c)(2)(I)	11(g)(15)(A)(i) **
170(o)(3)(A)(i)	11(a)(16)(B)(ii) **	956(c)(2)(J)	11(g)(15)(A)(i) **
179(b)(7)	102(a)	956(c)(2)(K)	11(g)(15)(A)(i) **
179B(a)	7(a)(3)(C) **	956(c)(2)(L)	11(g)(15)(A)(i) **
216(b)(1)(D)	4(a) †	956(c)(2)(M)	11(g)(15)(A)(i) **
245(c)(4)(C)	11(g)(3) **	992(a)(1)(C)	11(g)(16) **
245(c)(5)	11(g)(4) **	992(a)(1)(D)	11(g)(16) **
275(a)(4)	11(g)(5) **	992(a)(1)(E)	11(g)(16) **
280C(d)	7(a)(1)(B) **	1016(a)(31)	7(a)(1)(C) **
291(a)(4)	11(g)(6)(A) **	1016(a)(32)	7(a)(1)(C) **
291(a)(5)	11(g)(6)(A) **	1016(a)(33)	7(a)(1)(C) **
291(c)(1)	11(g)(6)(B) **	1016(a)(33)	11(a)(21) **
355(b)(2)(A)	4(b)(1) **	1016(a)(34)	7(a)(1)(C) **
355(b)(3)	4(b)(2) **	1016(a)(35)	7(a)(1)(C) **
355(b)(3)	4(b)(3) **	1016(a)(36)	7(a)(1)(C) **
355(b)(3)(A)	4(b)(3) **	1016(a)(36)	11(a)(22) **
355(b)(3)(D)	4(b)(3) **	1016(a)(37)	7(a)(1)(C) **
402(g)(7)(A)(ii)(II)	8(a)(1) **	1092(a)(2)(A)(i)	7(d)(2)(B)(i) **
408(d)(8)(D)	3(a) **	1092(a)(2)(A)(ii)	7(d)(1) **
441(b)(4)	11(g)(7)(A) **	1092(a)(2)(A)(ii)	7(d)(2)(B)(ii) **
441(h)	11(g)(7)(B)(i) **	1092(a)(2)(A)(ii)	7(d)(2)(B)(iii) **
441(h)	11(g)(7)(B)(ii) **	1092(a)(2)(A)(iii)	7(d)(1) **
470(c)(2)	7(c)(1) **	1092(a)(2)(A)(iv)	7(d)(1) **
470(d)(1)(A)	7(c)(2) **	1092(a)(2)(B)	7(d)(2)(A) **
501	1 ‡	1092(a)(2)(C)	7(d)(3) **
852(b)(4)(C)	11(a)(17)(A) **	1092(a)(2)(D)	7(d)(3) **
856(d)(9)(D)(ii)	9(b) **	1092(a)(2)(D)	7(d)(4) **
856(l)(2)	11(a)(18) **	1092(a)(3)(B)	7(d)(2)(C) **
857(b)(8)(B)	11(a)(17)(B) **	1248(d)(5)	11(g)(17)(A) **
884(d)(2)(B)	11(g)(8) **	1248(d)(5)	11(g)(17)(B) **
901(h)	11(g)(9) **	1260(c)(2)(G)	11(a)(23) **
904(d)(2)(B)(v)	11(g)(10)(C) **	1260(c)(2)(G)	11(a)(24)(B) **
904(d)(2)(B)(v)(I)	11(g)(10)(A) **	1297(b)(2)(D)	11(g)(18) **
904(d)(2)(B)(v)(II)	11(g)(10)(A) **	1297(d)	11(a)(24)(A) **

738

Code Sec.	Act Sec.	Code Sec.	Act Sec.
1297(e)	11(a)(24)(A)**	4965(c)(6)	11(a)(30)**
1297(f)	11(a)(24)(A)**	5121	11(a)(31)**
1298(a)(2)(B)	11(a)(24)(C)**	5432	11(a)(31)**
1298(b)(7)	11(f)(2)**	5732(c)	11(a)(32)**
1298(b)(8)	11(f)(2)**	6011(c)	11(g)(19)(B)**
1298(b)(9)	11(f)(2)**	6011(c)(1)	11(g)(19)(A)**
1362(f)(1)	11(a)(25)(A)**	6031	2‡
1362(f)(1)	11(a)(25)(B)**	6046(b)	11(a)(33)(A)**
1366(d)(4)	3(b)**	6046(b)	11(a)(33)(B)**
1400C	3(a)(1)*	6072(c)	11(g)(20)**
1400L(b)(2)(D)	103(c)(8)	6103(b)(5)(A)	11(a)(34)(A)**
1400N(d)(3)(A)	103(c)(9)(A)	6103(e)(10)	8(c)(1)†
1400N(d)(3)(B)	103(c)(9)(B)	6104(b)	3(g)(1)(A)**
1400N(d)(6)(E)	103(c)(10)	6104(b)	3(g)(1)(B)**
1400O(2)	11(a)(26)**	6104(d)(1)(A)(ii)	3(g)(2)**
1400S(a)(2)(A)(i)	11(a)(14)(C)**	6104(d)(2)	3(g)(3)**
2055(g)	3(d)(1)**	6110(i)(3)	10(a)**
2522(e)(1)(A)	11(a)(16)(A)**	6211(b)(4)(A)	11(a)(35)**
2522(e)(2)	3(d)(2)(A)**	6211(d)(4)(A)	101(b)(1)
2522(e)(2)(C)	3(d)(2)(C)**	6213(g)(2)(L)	101(b)(2)
2522(e)(3)	3(d)(2)(A)**	6230(a)(3)(A)	11(a)(36)**
2522(e)(3)(A)(i)	11(a)(16)(B)(i)**	6230(a)(3)(B)	11(a)(36)**
2522(e)(3)(A)(i)	11(a)(16)(B)(ii)**	6416(a)(4)(C)	11(d)(1)(A)**
2522(e)(4)	3(d)(2)(B)**	6416(a)(4)(C)	11(d)(1)(B)**
3121(v)(1)(A)	8(a)(2)**	6426(d)(2)(F)	5(a)(2)**
3301(1)	1501(a)(1)+	6426(h)	5(a)(3)**
3301(2)	1501(a)(2)+	6427(e)(3)	11(a)(37)**
4041	6(d)(1)(C)**	6427(e)(5)(B)	11(e)(1)**
4041(d)(1)	6(d)(1)(A)**	6427(i)(3)	5(a)(1)(C)**
4041(d)(5)	6(d)(2)(A)(i)**	6427(i)(3)(A)	5(a)(1)(A)**
4041(d)(5)	6(d)(2)(A)(ii)**	6427(i)(3)(A)(i)	5(a)(1)(B)**
4041(d)(5)	6(d)(3)**	6427(i)(3)(B)	5(a)(1)(B)**
4042	6(d)(1)(C)**	6427(l)(4)(A)(ii)	11(a)(38)**
4042(b)(3)	6(d)(1)(B)**	6427(p)	11(a)(39)(A)**
4081	6(d)(1)(C)**	6427(q)	11(a)(39)(B)**
4081(d)(2)(B)	116(a) Div K++	6428	101(a)
4082(a)	6(d)(2)(B)(i)**	6430	6(d)(1)(C)**
4082(b)	11(a)(28)**	6430	6(d)(2)(D)**
4082(e)	6(d)(2)(C)(i)**	6501(m)	7(a)(2)(B)**
4082(e)	6(d)(2)(C)(ii)**	6686	11(g)(21)**
4082(f)	6(d)(2)(B)(ii)**	6695A(a)(2)	3(e)(1)**
4082(f)	6(d)(2)(B)(ii)**	6695A(a)(2)	11(a)(40)**
4082(g)	6(d)(2)(B)(ii)**	6696(d)(1)	3(e)(2)**
4082(h)	6(d)(2)(B)(ii)**	6698	2‡
4101(a)(4)	11(a)(29)**	6698(a)	8(a)†
4101(a)(5)	11(a)(29)**	6698(b)(1)	8(b)†
4261(j)(1)(A)(ii)	116(b)(1) Div K++	6699	9(a)†
4271(d)(1)(A)(ii)	116(b)(2) Div K++	6707A(e)(2)(C)	11(a)(41)**
4940(c)(4)(A)	3(f)**	6724(d)(1)(B)(iv)	11(b)(2)(A)**
4942(i)(1)(A)	11(a)(14)(D)**	6724(d)(2)(K)	11(b)(2)(B)**
4958(c)(3)(A)(i)(II)	3(i)(1)**	7651(4)	11(a)(34)(B)**
4958(c)(3)(C)(ii)	3(i)(2)**	7651(5)	11(a)(34)(B)**
4962(b)	3(h)**	9002(3)	11(a)(42)(A)**

Code Sec.	Act Sec.	Code Sec.	Act Sec.
9004(a)(1)	11(a)(42)(B) **	9502(e)	11(f)(1) **
9006	11(a)(43) **	9502(f)	11(f)(1) **
9032(3)	11(a)(42)(C) **		
9034(b)	11(a)(42)(D) **	9502(f)(2)	116(c)(2) Div K++
9502(d)(1)	116(c)(1)(A) Div K++	9503(c)(6)	11(a)(44) **
9502(d)(1)(A)	116(c)(1)(B) Div K++	9503(c)(7)	11(a)(44) **
		9508	11(a)(46) **

¶ 6003. Act Sections Amending Code

Act § cites are to the 2008 Economic Stimulus Act unless otherwise indicated.

* denotes 2007 Tax Increase Prevention Act
† denotes 2007 Mortgage Relief Act
+ denotes 2007 Energy Act
** denotes 2007 Technical Corrections Act
‡ denotes 2007 Virginia Tech Victims Act
++ denotes 2008 Appropriations Act

Act Sec.	Code Sec.	Act Sec.	Code Sec.
1 ‡	61	3(d)(2)(A) **	2522(e)(2)
1 ‡	501	3(d)(2)(A) **	2522(e)(3)
2 ‡	6031	3(d)(2)(B) **	2522(e)(4)
2 ‡	6698	3(d)(2)(C) **	2522(e)(2)(C)
2(a)(1) *	55(d)(1)(A)	3(e)(1) **	6695A(a)(2)
2(a)(2) *	55(d)(1)(B)	3(e)(2) **	6696(d)(1)
3(a)(1) *	21	3(f) **	4940(c)(4)(A)
3(a)(1) *	22	3(g)(1)(A) **	6104(b)
3(a)(1) *	23	3(g)(1)(B) **	6104(b)
3(a)(1) *	24	3(g)(2) **	6104(d)(1)(A)(ii)
3(a)(1) *	25	3(g)(3) **	6104(d)(2)
3(a)(1) *	25A	3(h) **	4962(b)
3(a)(1) *	25B	3(i)(1) **	4958(c)(3)(A)(i)(II)
3(a)(1) *	25C	3(i)(2) **	4958(c)(3)(C)(ii)
3(a)(1) *	25D	4(a) **	954(c)(6)(B)
3(a)(1) *	26(a)(2)	4(a) **	954(c)(6)(C)
3(a)(1) *	904(i)	4(b)(1) **	355(b)(2)(A)
3(a)(1) *	1400C	4(b)(2) **	355(b)(3)
3(a)(2) *	26(a)(2)	4(b)(3) **	355(b)(3)(A)
2(a) †	108(a)(1)(C)	4(b)(3) **	355(b)(3)(D)
2(a) †	108(a)(1)(D)	4(b)(3) **	355(b)(3)
2(a) †	108(a)(1)(E)	4(c) **	911(f) ($515)
2(b) †	108(h)	5(a)(1)(A) **	6427(i)(3)(A)
2(c)(1) †	108(a)(2)(A)	5(a)(1)(B) **	6427(i)(3)(A)(i)
2(c)(2) †	108(a)(2)(C)	5(a)(1)(B) **	6427(i)(3)(B)
3(a) †	163(h)(3)(E)(iv)(I)	5(a)(1)(C) **	6427(i)(3)
4(a) †	216(b)(1)(D)	5(a)(2) **	6426(d)(2)(F)
5(a) †	139B	5(a)(3) **	6426(h)
6(a) †	42(i)(3)(D)(ii)(I)	6(a) **	45J(b)(2)
7(a) †	121(b)(4)	6(b)(1) **	30C(b)
8(a) †	6698(a)	6(b)(2) **	30C(c)
8(b) †	6698(b)(1)	6(c)(1) **	41(a)(3)
8(c)(1) †	6103(e)(10)	6(c)(2) **	41(f)(6)(E)
9(a) †	6699	6(d)(1)(A) **	4041(d)(1)
1501(a)(1)+	3301(1)	6(d)(1)(B) **	4042(b)(3)
1501(a)(2)+	3301(2)	6(d)(1)(C) **	6430
1502(a)+	167(h)(5)(A)	6(d)(1)(C) **	4041
2(a) **	53(e)(2)(A)	6(d)(1)(C) **	4042
3(a) **	408(d)(8)(D)	6(d)(1)(C) **	4081
3(b) **	1366(d)(4)	6(d)(2)(A)(i) **	4041(d)(5)
3(c) **	170(e)(7)(D)(i)(I)	6(d)(2)(A)(ii) **	4041(d)(5)
3(d)(1) **	2055(g)	6(d)(2)(B)(i) **	4082(a)

Act Sec.	Code Sec.	Act Sec.	Code Sec.
6(d)(2)(B)(ii)**	4082(f)	11(a)(3)**	26(b)(2)(T)
6(d)(2)(B)(ii)**	4082(g)	11(a)(3)**	26(b)(2)(U)
6(d)(2)(B)(ii)**	4082(h)	11(a)(3)**	26(b)(2)(V)
6(d)(2)(B)(ii)**	4082(f)	11(a)(4)(A)**	34(a)(1)
6(d)(2)(C)(i)**	4082(e)	11(a)(4)(B)**	34(a)(2)
6(d)(2)(C)(ii)**	4082(e)	11(a)(4)(C)**	34(a)(3)
6(d)(2)(D)**	6430	11(a)(5)(A)**	35(d)(2)
6(d)(3)**	4041(d)(5)	11(a)(5)(B)**	35(d)(2)
7(a)(1)(A)**	45H(d)	11(a)(6)(A)**	38(b)
7(a)(1)(A)**	45H(e)	11(a)(6)(B)**	38(b)
7(a)(1)(A)**	45H(f)	11(a)(6)(C)**	38(b)(30)
7(a)(1)(A)**	45H(g)	11(a)(7)**	45L(c)(2)
7(a)(1)(B)**	280C(d)	11(a)(7)**	45L(c)(3)
7(a)(1)(C)**	1016(a)(31)	11(a)(8)**	48(c)
7(a)(1)(C)**	1016(a)(32)	11(a)(9)**	48(c)(1)(B)
7(a)(1)(C)**	1016(a)(33)	11(a)(9)**	48(c)(2)(B)
7(a)(1)(C)**	1016(a)(34)	11(a)(10)**	48A(d)(4)(B)(ii)
7(a)(1)(C)**	1016(a)(35)	11(a)(11)(A)**	121(d)(9)
7(a)(1)(C)**	1016(a)(36)	11(a)(11)(B)**	121(d)(9)
7(a)(1)(C)**	1016(a)(37)	11(a)(12)**	125(b)(2)
7(a)(2)(A)**	45H(g)	11(a)(13)**	167(g)(8)(C)(ii)(II)
7(a)(2)(B)**	6501(m)	11(a)(14)(A)**	170(b)(1)(A)(vii)
7(a)(3)(A)**	45H(b)(1)(A)	11(a)(14)(B)**	170(e)(1)(B)(ii)
7(a)(3)(A)**	45H(c)(2)	11(a)(14)(C)**	1400S(a)(2)(A)(i)
7(a)(3)(A)**	45H(e)(1)	11(a)(14)(D)**	4942(i)(1)(A)
7(a)(3)(A)**	45H(e)(2)	11(a)(15)**	170(c)(1)(B)(i)(II)
7(a)(3)(B)**	45H(c)(2)	11(a)(16)**	170(o)(1)(A)
7(a)(3)(C)**	179B(a)	11(a)(16)(A)**	2522(e)(1)(A)
7(b)(1)**	45(c)(3)(A)(ii)	11(a)(16)(B)(i)**	170(o)(3)(A)(i)
7(b)(2)**	45(d)(2)(B)(i)	11(a)(16)(B)(i)**	2522(e)(3)(A)(i)
7(b)(2)**	45(d)(2)(B)(ii)	11(a)(16)(B)(ii)**	170(o)(3)(A)(i)
7(b)(2)**	45(d)(2)(B)(iii)	11(a)(16)(B)(ii)**	2522(e)(3)(A)(i)
7(c)(1)**	470(c)(2)	11(a)(17)(A)**	852(b)(4)(C)
7(c)(2)**	470(d)(1)(A)	11(a)(17)(B)**	857(b)(8)(B)
7(d)(1)**	1092(a)(2)(A)(ii)	11(a)(18)**	856(l)(2)
7(d)(1)**	1092(a)(2)(A)(iii)	11(a)(19)**	954(c)(1)(F)
7(d)(1)**	1092(a)(2)(A)(iv)	11(a)(20)**	954(c)(1)(I)
7(d)(2)(A)**	1092(a)(2)(B)	11(a)(20)**	954(c)(1)(H)
7(d)(2)(B)(i)**	1092(a)(2)(A)(i)	11(a)(21)**	1016(a)(33)
7(d)(2)(B)(ii)**	1092(a)(2)(A)(ii)	11(a)(22)**	1016(a)(36)
7(d)(2)(B)(iii)**	1092(a)(2)(A)(ii)	11(a)(23)**	1260(c)(2)(G)
7(d)(2)(C)**	1092(a)(3)(B)	11(a)(24)(A)**	1297(d)
7(d)(3)**	1092(a)(2)(C)	11(a)(24)(A)**	1297(e)
7(d)(3)**	1092(a)(2)(D)	11(a)(24)(A)**	1297(f)
7(d)(4)**	1092(a)(2)(D)	11(a)(24)(B)**	1260(c)(2)(G)
8(a)(1)**	402(g)(7)(A)(ii)(II)	11(a)(24)(C)**	1298(a)(2)(B)
8(a)(2)**	3121(v)(1)(A)	11(a)(25)(A)**	1362(f)(1)
9(a)**	45(e)(7)(A)(i)	11(a)(25)(B)**	1362(f)(1)
9(b)**	856(d)(9)(D)(ii)	11(a)(26)**	1400O(2)
10(a)**	6110(i)(3)	11(a)(28)**	4082(b)
11(a)(1)**	21(e)(5)	11(a)(29)**	4101(a)(4)
11(a)(2)**	25C(c)(3)	11(a)(29)**	4101(a)(5)
11(a)(3)**	26(b)(2)(S)	11(a)(30)**	4965(c)(6)

Act Sec.	Code Sec.	Act Sec.	Code Sec.
11(a)(31)**	5432	11(g)(9)**	901(h)
11(a)(31)**	5121	11(g)(10)(A)**	904(d)(2)(B)(v)(I)
11(a)(32)**	5732(c)	11(g)(10)(A)**	904(d)(2)(B)(v)(II)
11(a)(33)(A)**	6046(b)	11(g)(10)(A)**	904(d)(2)(B)(v)(III)
11(a)(33)(B)**	6046(b)	11(g)(10)(B)**	904(d)(2)(B)(v)(II)
11(a)(34)(A)**	6103(b)(5)(A)	11(g)(10)(C)**	904(d)(2)(B)(v)
11(a)(34)(B)**	7651(4)	11(g)(11)**	906(b)(5)
11(a)(34)(B)**	7651(5)	11(g)(11)**	906(b)(6)
11(a)(35)**	6211(b)(4)(A)	11(g)(11)**	906(b)(7)
11(a)(36)**	6230(a)(3)(A)	11(g)(12)**	936(f)(2)
11(a)(36)**	6230(a)(3)(B)	11(g)(13)**	951(c)
11(a)(37)**	6427(e)(3)	11(g)(13)**	951(d)
11(a)(38)**	6427(l)(4)(A)(ii)	11(g)(14)**	952(b)
11(a)(39)(A)**	6427(p)	11(g)(15)(A)(i)**	956(c)(2)(I)
11(a)(39)(B)**	6427(q)	11(g)(15)(A)(i)**	956(c)(2)(J)
11(a)(40)**	6695A(a)(2)	11(g)(15)(A)(i)**	956(c)(2)(K)
11(a)(41)**	6707A(e)(2)(C)	11(g)(15)(A)(i)**	956(c)(2)(L)
11(a)(42)(A)**	9002(3)	11(g)(15)(A)(i)**	956(c)(2)(M)
11(a)(42)(B)**	9004(a)(1)	11(g)(15)(A)(ii)**	956(c)(2)
11(a)(42)(C)**	9032(3)	11(g)(15)(B)**	954(c)(2)(C)(ii)
11(a)(42)(D)**	9034(b)	11(g)(16)**	992(a)(1)(E)
11(a)(43)**	9006	11(g)(16)**	992(a)(1)(C)
11(a)(44)**	9503(c)(6)	11(g)(16)**	992(a)(1)(D)
11(a)(44)**	9503(c)(7)	11(g)(17)(A)**	1248(d)(5)
11(a)(46)**	9508	11(g)(17)(B)**	1248(d)(5)
11(b)(1)**	168(l)(3)	11(g)(18)**	1297(b)(2)(D)
11(b)(2)(A)**	6724(d)(1)(B)(iv)	11(g)(19)(A)**	6011(c)(1)
11(b)(2)(B)**	6724(d)(2)(K)	11(g)(19)(B)**	6011(c)
11(c)(1)(A)**	24(d)(1)(B)	11(g)(20)**	6072(c)
11(c)(1)(B)**	24(d)(1)(B)	11(g)(21)**	6686
11(d)(1)(A)**	6416(a)(4)(C)	101(a)	6428
11(d)(1)(B)**	6416(a)(4)(C)	101(b)(1)	6211(d)(4)(A)
11(e)(1)**	6427(e)(5)(B)	101(b)(2)	6213(g)(2)(L)
11(e)(2)**	41(f)(1)(A)(ii)	101(f)(2)	1(i)(1)(D)
11(e)(2)**	41(f)(1)(B)(ii)	102(a)	179(b)(7)
11(f)(1)**	9502(e)	103(a)(1)	168(k)
11(f)(1)**	9502(f)	103(a)(2)	168(k)
11(f)(2)**	1298(b)(7)	103(a)(3)	168(k)
11(f)(2)**	1298(b)(8)	103(a)(4)	168(k)
11(f)(2)**	1298(b)(9)	103(b)	168(k)(1)(A)
11(f)(3)**	904(f)(3)(D)(iv)	103(c)(1)	168(k)(2)(B)(i)(I)
11(g)(1)**	56(g)(4)(C)(ii)(I)	103(c)(2)	168(k)(2)(B)(i)(IV)
11(g)(2)**	54(g)(4)(C)(iv)	103(c)(3)	168(k)(2)(C)(i)
11(g)(3)**	245(c)(4)(C)	103(c)(4)	168(k)(2)(F)(i)
11(g)(4)**	245(c)(5)	103(c)(5)(A)	168(k)(4)
11(g)(5)**	275(a)(4)	103(c)(5)(B)	168(k)(2)(D)(iii)
11(g)(6)(A)**	291(a)(4)	103(c)(6)	168(l)(4)(A)
11(g)(6)(A)**	291(a)(5)	103(c)(6)	168(l)(4)(B)
11(g)(6)(B)**	291(c)(1)	103(c)(6)	168(l)(4)(C)
11(g)(7)(A)**	441(b)(4)	103(c)(6)	168(l)(4)(D)
11(g)(7)(B)(i)**	441(h)	103(c)(7)(A)	168(l)(5)(A)
11(g)(7)(B)(ii)**	441(h)	103(c)(7)(B)	168(l)(5)(B)
11(g)(8)**	884(d)(2)(B)	103(c)(8)	1400L(b)(2)(D)

Act Sec.	Code Sec.	Act Sec.	Code Sec.
103(c)(9)(A)	1400N(d)(3)(A)	116(a) Div K++	4081(d)(2)(B)
103(c)(9)(B)	1400N(d)(3)(B)	116(b)(1) Div K++	4261(j)(1)(A)(ii)
103(c)(10)	1400N(d)(6)(E)	116(b)(2) Div K++	4271(d)(1)(A)(ii)
103(c)(11)(A)	168(k)	116(c)(1)(A) Div K++	9502(d)(1)
103(c)(11)(B)	168(k)	116(c)(1)(B) Div K++	9502(d)(1)(A)
103(c)(12)	168(k)(2)(B)	116(c)(2) Div K++	9502(f)(2)

¶ 6004. FTC 2nd ¶s Affected by Acts

FTC 2d ¶	Analysis ¶	FTC 2d ¶	Analysis ¶	FTC 2d ¶	Analysis ¶
A-4010	102	L-9312 et seq.	53	O-2447.6	702
A-4054	102	L-9314 et seq.	53	O-4401	102
A-4055	901	L-9315 et seq.	53	P-1710.01	401
A-4255	102	L-9315.2	53	P-1710.4	401
A-4405	102	L-9316 et seq.	53	P-1710.5	401
A-4455	102	L-9317	53	P-5021.1	802
A-4781	102	L-9318	53	Q-6002.2	601
A-8162	101	L-9321	53	R-5789.1	601
A-8163	101	L-9322 et seq.	53	S-2800 et seq.	502
A-8221	53	L-9324	53	S-5353	1104
A-8320	102	L-9325 et seq.	53	S-6305	1102
A-8809	103	L-9326 et seq.	53	S-6306	1102
D-1775	603	L-9326.2	53	S-6307	1102
D-6650	505	L-9327 et seq.	53	S-6308	1102
D-6654.1	505	L-9327 et seq.	53	S-6603	501
D-7211	505	L-9329	53	S-6644	501
D-7213.2	505	L-9337.8	53	T-4014.1	401
D-7509	504	L-9357	53, 408	T-4029	1101
D-8161	503	L-9907	52	T-10423	1304
D-8201	503	L-9907.1	52	V-1751	1103
E-1073; E-1074	1302	L-9952	52	V-1762	1102
E-6527.3	1303	L-10004.2	53, 54	V-1768	1103
F-4803	1301	L-10004.3	53, 54	V-1804	203
F-4803.5	1301	L-10032.1	53	V-1815	203
F-4828.1	1301	L-15317	404	V-2691	1101
F-10303	53	L-15425.4	405	W-1501	1001
H-1017.1	302	L-15811	902	W-1501.1	1001
H-4801	1201	L-16401	411	W-1515.2	1002
H-9157	1202	L-17552	401	W-1515.2C	1002, 1003,
H-12253.3	602	L-17553	401		1004
I-4559	301	L-17554	401	W-1519	1007
I-7526	802	L-17555	401	W-1519.1	1007, 1008
I-7527	801, 802	L-17557	401	W-1542	1002, 1004
J-1484	302	L-17558	401	W-1563	1006
J-7401	201	L-17696	409	W-1720	1002, 1003,
J-7404	201	L-17755	406		1004
K-3167.1	605	L-17764.1	410	W-1729	1002, 1003,
K-3167.2	604	L-17771	406		1004
K-3601	302	L-17771.1	407	W-1737.1	1005
K-4202	302	L-18041	401, 402	W-1737.2	1005, 1008
L-183	102	L-18043	403	W-2218	1002, 1003,
L-3164	401	L-18101	102		1004
L-3176	401	L-18103	903	W-3201	1004
L-6905	803, 805	N-3201	412	W-5101	1001
L-6907	804	O-1101.1	701	W-5103	1001
L-9311	53	O-2447.2 et seq.	702	W-5126	1001
L-9311 et seq.	53	O-2447.5	702	W-5201	1001

¶ 6005. USTR ¶s Affected by Acts

USTR ¶	Analysis ¶	USTR ¶	Analysis ¶	USTR ¶	Analysis ¶
25B4	102	1684.028	53	25,224	601
25D4	102	1684.0281	53, 54	35,014.07	1201
30C4	402	1684.0282	53	40,414	1002, 1003,
30C4.02	403	1684.029	53		1004
45H4	401	1684.0291	53	40,414.04	1002, 1003,
45J4	409	1684.0292	53		1004
179B4	401	1684.081	53, 408	40,424	1004
234	102	1704.37	302	40,814	1001
244	901	1704.42	604, 605	40,824	1002, 1003,
244.01	102	1794.01	52		1004
254.01	102	2164.02	1302	42,614.01	1001
264	102	3124.04	53	42,714	1001
264.01	903	3554.02	1301	49,404	504
280C4	401	3554.021	1301	49,584	505
414.03	404	402A4	1202	49,624	503
414.031	405	4084.03	602	60,334	502
424.60	902	4704	803, 805	61,034.08	1102
454.04	410	4704.01	804	61,044	501
454.09	406	5074	505	61,104.07	1304
454.10	407	8564.045	1303	64,164	1006
484	411	9044.01	102	64,264	1005
534	103	9114	701	64,274	1007
554.01	101	9544.02	702	64,274.01	1007, 1008
594	101	10,164	401	64,304	1002, 1004
614.006	302	10,924	801, 802	65,014.28	401
1084.01	201	13,664	603	66,514.01	1103
1084.02	201	14,00C4	102	66,554	1104
1214.10	301	14,00L4.15	52	66,95A4	1101
1674.126	412	14,00N4.021	53	66,964	1101
1684.025 *et seq.*	53	20,224	302	66,984	1102
1684.025	53	20,554	302	67,214	203
1684.026	53	20,554.21	601	67,224	203

¶ 6006. Tax Desk ¶s Affected by Acts

TaxDesk ¶	Analysis ¶	TaxDesk ¶	Analysis ¶	TaxDesk ¶	Analysis ¶
130,511.5	302	269,348	53	398,001	903
143,003.2	602	269,351	53	550,502	1201
188,011	201	269,351 *et seq.*	53	568,805	102
188,016	201	269,352 *et seq.*	53	569,104	102
191,001.1	701	269,354	53	569,105	901
198,208	302	269,355 *et seq.*	53	569,205	102
213,011.3	401	269,356 *et seq.*	53	569,505	102
216,029	802	269,356.2	53	569,551	102
225,739	301	269,357 *et seq.*	53	609,201	1104
228,415	802	269,359	53	614,716	603
228,416	801, 802	271,701	412	676,502.2	505
237,426.1	1301	307,103	401	676,505	505
261,205	803, 805	308,106	401	683,508	505
261,207	804	329,002	302	684,004	504
267,602.1	53, 54	331,613.1	605	685,516	503
267,602.2	53, 54	331,613.2	604	688,001	502
267,625.5	53	332,601	302	691,302	101
267,802	53, 408	380,502	102	691,303	101
268,411	52	381,602	411	691,509	103
268,413	52	382,302	401	696,514	53
268,502	52	382,303	401	733,002.1	601
268,602	52	382,304	401	777,002.1	601
269,332.1	53	382,305	401	838,027	1101
269,341	53	382,306	401	838,029	401
269,341 *et seq.*	53	382,307	401	861,001	1103
269,342 *et seq.*	53	383,007	902	861,002	1103
269,344 *et seq.*	53	384,014.1	405	861,035	203
269,345 *et seq.*	53	393,001	102	861,041	1102
269,345.2	53	397,201	401, 402	861,054	203
269,346 *et seq.*	53	397,203	403	867,201	1101
269,347	53	398,000	102		

¶ 6007. Pension Analysis ¶ s Affected by Acts

PCA ¶	Analysis ¶
28,408	1202
35,154.3	602

¶ 6008. Pension Explanations ¶ s Affected by Acts

PE ¶	Analysis ¶
402A-4	1202
408-4.03	602

¶ 6009. Estate Planning Analysis ¶ s Affected by Acts

EPTC/EPA ¶	Analysis ¶
44,390.1	601
48,304.2	601

INDEX

References are to paragraph numbers

U

V

W